Buried Treasures

Buried Treasures

Finding and Growing
the
World's Choicest Bulbs

Jānis Rukšāns

Timber Press
Portland • London

Published in 2007 by
Timber Press, Inc.
The Haseltine Building
133 S.W. Second Avenue, Suite 450
Portland, Oregon 97204-3527, U.S.A.
www.timberpress.com
For contact information regarding editorial, marketing, sales, and
distribution in the United Kingdom, see www.timberpress.co.uk.

Printed in China

Second printing 2008

Library of Congress Cataloging-in-Publication Data

Rukšāns, Jānis.
    Buried treasures : finding and growing the world's choicest bulbs / Jānis Rukšāns.
        p. cm.
    Includes bibliographical references and index.
    ISBN-13: 978-0-88192-818-1
    1. Bulbs. I. Title. II. Title: Finding and growing the world's choicest bulbs.
    SB425.R85 2007
    635.9'4—dc22
                                                        2006033040
A catalog record for this book is also available from the British Library.

To my family

Contents

Color plates follow pages 136 and 208

Foreword

JOURNALIST, author, nationalist politician, plantsman, plant breeder, plant explorer, and eminent nurseryman, Jānis Rukšāns is one of those rare individuals with the extraordinary ability to adapt to, and succeed in, a range of careers. It is very evident from this semi-autobiographical book that his success as a nurseryman and plant explorer is due to his abiding passion for bulbous plants and his determination to see them in their natural habitat, wherever possible, in addition to cultivating them at his home in Latvia.

Jānis's great enthusiasm and thirst for knowledge pervade the pages of this fascinating book, which describes both his travels and his experiences as a specialist nurseryman growing a huge range of bulbs in what many would consider a less than ideal climate, where winter temperatures may plunge to –48°C on rare occasions, alternating with warmer periods that are very unsettling for many bulbous plants—as well as the grower!

Buried Treasures is written in an informative and often amusing narrative style that exudes the author's excitement when discovering both new and well-known plants in the wild. It is a vast mine of information, describing not only the characteristics of the plants but also various ways to cultivate and propagate them successfully in spite of climatic and other setbacks, such as those the author himself has endured.

Jānis Rukšāns's overwhelming horticultural interests have been studying, growing, and distributing bulbous plants of the world, particularly (but by no means exclusively) those species occurring wild in many regions of the former USSR—the Caucasus, Crimea, Central Asia, central Siberia, and the Russian Far East—as well as the Czech Republic and Turkey, all very rich in their bulbous floras. While he has had a certain advantage as an erstwhile (and very reluctant) Soviet citizen who was able to travel, sometimes with likeminded colleagues, on his botanical forays to many countries once closed to the Western world, he was not immune to the vagaries of these regions and the suspicion that anyone wandering in the mountains and countryside must be up to no good.

Some of these incidents are recounted in entertaining descriptions of various expeditions in the wild, but the problems experienced by this innocent bulb enthusiast are perhaps best illustrated by a KGB investigation into an exchange of letters between Jānis and a horticultural friend over named cultivars of the Siberian dog's-tooth violet, *Erythronium sibiricum*. The cultivar names mentioned were thought by the agents monitoring his mail to be the names of rocket missiles! So the trials and tribulations of plantsmen in the former USSR did not only occur on expeditions.

Considerable benefits for gardens and gardeners have accrued as a result of Jānis Rukšāns's expeditions. Apart from introducing many bulbous plants previously unknown or extremely rare in cultivation, he has discovered a number of new species and has helped greatly to widen our knowledge of variations within populations, resulting in a better understanding of species limits. Additionally he has selected, bred, and introduced considerable numbers of attractive cultivars in many plant groups, including tulips, Juno irises, and crocuses like *Crocus korolkowii*.

The cultivation and propagation methods described by Jānis also provide insight into the way he has developed his extensive bulb collections into a fine commercial enterprise. He has done this by delving into botanical and horticultural literature, corresponding with and exchanging bulbs with kindred enthusiasts in many parts of the world, and carrying out his own experimental work. One of the innovative techniques he developed for more rapid propagation of the larger *Fritillaria* species like *F. imperialis*, which are very slow to increase from seed or offsets, has now been adapted by growers in Holland. As a result the price for such bulbs has been reduced considerably—a notable achievement in its own right!

There is much in this book to inform, entertain, and tantalize gardeners whether or not they have a specific interest in bulbs. Jānis's enthusiasm is infectious, and his joy in finding and growing bulbs shines throughout the text. Who after all could resist reading a section headed "Junos from the Minefield"? Does this refer to the goddess herself or to yet another beautiful plant among many other buried treasures? Read on and find out.

CHRIS BRICKELL, CBE, VMH
Former Director of the Wisley Garden and
Director General of the Royal Horticultural Society

Preface

THIS IS A BOOK about my life in the garden and the bulbs I love to grow. It would be a shame if everything I have learned should one day pass away with me, and it is for this reason that I have attempted to describe my experiences, mistakes, and pursuit of new methods. At the same time, I hope readers will benefit from what they find here.

I am a professional gardener, a nurseryman. I don't arrange decorative plantings or plant my bulbs in small pots to enjoy a nice collection. I propagate bulbs for distribution to other gardeners. However, I firmly believe that the knowledge I have obtained by growing bulbs in bulk is also suitable for collectors. We all work with the same thing, after all—a plant, a bulb—and the same attention is required regardless of the purpose for growing or the amount grown. At the same time, I am also a collector, since many of my plants are represented by only one or two specimens, though my total number of samples has reached several thousand.

During my forty years in the field I have gained a certain amount of experience. There have been many twinklings of enjoyment, as well as moments of despair when the only thought in my mind was to leave everything and devote myself full-time to my second profession, journalism. Yet the garden has always remained the most important thing for me. The single exception to this occurred over the couple of years in which I took an active role in helping restore Latvian independence. During that time the future of Latvia took center stage for me. For my efforts I was even honored to receive an award on behalf of the nation.

I have always made use of my journalism skills during plant expeditions by keeping a diary of each event. These diaries were a great help as I wrote this book, since they include details about the bulbs that were found, the environmental conditions, and the historical context of each trip. While traveling around the vast Soviet Empire, my colleagues and I faced all kinds of situations, and I tried to reflect these in my writing. Many of my adventures might seem incredible, even absurd, to people who have spent their lives in the free world, but all I can do is provide my own details of that bizarre period. Times have changed rapidly, and today's young people, even those here in Latvia, can hardly imagine what was everyday reality until the 1990s. Sometimes I even find myself regarding those days as ancient and unbelievable.

During my lifelong search for new bulbs I traveled around many countries, though I was mostly limited to the countries behind the so-called Iron Curtain. While I was kept inside these areas, gardeners from the free world were kept out. In fact, accessibility is rather restricted even now, since these territories are ruled by half-dictatorial regimes. For this reason I hope the descriptions of my adventures might be particularly interesting for plant collectors and wildlife lovers who have been unable to visit this part of the world.

I have written this book with the knowledge that it can never really be finished. Since adding the last full stop to the manuscript, I have taken part in two more expeditions. There will always be new plants in my collection and new adventures in my life, and I will never be able to span everything in one book. The more years of my life I bear on my shoulders, and the less time I have in front of me, the more I want to see and manage. It is a never-ending story. So I am going to work on this book for the rest of my life.

One final note: You'll find a description of new species (Descriptiones Plantarum Novarum) at the back of the book. As required by the *International Code of Botanical Nomenclature*, these new plants are described in Latin.

JĀNIS RUKŠĀNS
Bulb Nursery
Rozula
LV-4150
Cēsis District
Latvia

Acknowledgments

I MUST BEGIN by expressing my gratitude to Kristl Walek of the Canadian seedhouse Gardens North, who found me on the Internet one day to ask if I had any seeds she could include in her catalog. I always have extra seeds to share and so was happy to oblige. Kristl added information about my plants to her catalog and in doing so mentioned that I had been thinking of writing a book about bulbs and my experience with them. The message reached Tom Fischer, executive editor at Timber Press, and before I knew it Timber had offered to publish my book. It was as though I had already written it.

This changed my daily routine drastically. During the previous winter I had produced a page and a half, but now I started working twelve-hour days, including weekends. I began in January and put down the last full stop at the end of April. This, however, was when the real work began. Gunta Lebedoka and Mārtiņš Erminass spent uncountable hours translating my Latvian English into something more fluent. Gunta confessed later that it would have been easier for her if I had written the book in Latvian so that she could have translated it without having to change the word order all the time. Mārtiņš didn't comment on the issue, but somehow I doubt his fate was any easier.

I can't miss the opportunity to thank my teachers, many of whom have already passed away. All were true professionals in their field and generously passed their knowledge on to students such as myself. It would be too difficult to name them all, but I must at least mention Aivars Lasis, headmaster of the Bulduri Horticultural College during my time there. He prevented me from dropping out in the midst of my teenager's folly, and for me he has been, is still, and will always be *the* Headmaster and Teacher (both titles in capitals).

I can't leave out the numerous gardeners who supported my growth with their advice and assistance. Again I cannot thank everyone by name, but I must mention Aldonis Vēriņš (Latvia), who even in the darkest times of the Soviet regime managed to import the newest species from the free world through the Iron Curtain. Aldonis never held back his good advice, has given me numerous bulbs over the years, and in moments of despair has always showed me the way.

Among my most significant foreign friends and sponsors are Chris Brickell (Great Britain) and Michael Hoog (Netherlands). In addition to having sent me seeds and bulbs of the rarest species, both have offered priceless advice on how to grow many of these plants. Chris must also be thanked for my extensive botanical library. There is not a single book he would have refused to send me after my first request. His generosity and knowledge are admirable.

During Soviet times traveling was severely restricted and the only foreign countries I could visit were those of the Eastern Bloc. This determined my first gardening contacts from what was then Czechoslovakia, and the first rarities of my collection arrived there with the helping hand of Eva Petrová (Institute of Ornamental Gardening, Průhonice, Czech Republic) and her husband, Petr. Both guided me through many Czech and Slovak gardens and introduced me to numerous people, including outstanding gardeners and bulb collectors such as Václav Jošt. Both the Jošt and Petrová families welcomed me heartily and have even been my own guests on several occasions.

Brian Duncan from Northern Ireland invited me to visit him during the dark days of the Soviet era. After overcoming the obstacles of the Soviet bureaucracy and trials of the secret service (KGB), I felt entitled to watch the daffodils grow, arrange flowers for the London exhibitions, and meet some famous gardeners. It was a very unusual experience for me, and I was even interviewed on BBC television. My English was subtitled on the screen, an indication of how terrible it was then (despite my English friends repeatedly trying to tell me that my English was "perfect"). Brian gave me lots of wonderful flower varieties (and pollen), each a precious gift. These were very helpful in getting me to break loose from the stagnancy of Soviet times: I used them to create numerous beautiful, modern daffodil cultivars. Brian also introduced me to Jan Pennings of the Netherlands, whom I have probably visited more often than any other foreign gardener. Today it is Jan who is growing in bulk the bulbs that were bred by me. Since Latvia regained its independence, Jan is a regular springtime visitor in my nursery.

In London I met Kath Dryden and Norman Stevens. Both have generously donated their rarities to me without any kind of reward, despite the fact that bulb growing is their business. Whenever I expressed the slightest interest in any species or variety, Kath immediately supplied it to me even if there wasn't any in her collection. I received the same kindness and support from Jim and Jenny Archibald. Many of the plants in my collection originated from the seeds they generously donated me. Very special thanks must also go to Hendrik van Bogaert (Belgium), who annually presents me with rarities from his collections. On many occasions, just because of Hendrik's help, I have been able to restore valuable stock lost to poor weather or my own mistakes.

I have spent marvelous evenings dining at Peter Nijssen's (Netherlands) home, and I sincerely doubt anyone in the world can prepare a more delicious steak than Peter's dear wife, Annette. Peter once said to me, "Jānis, the day will come when young enthusiasts from around the world will want to practice growing flowers in your nursery in order to learn what you know about the subtleties of gardening." I deeply regret that he passed away prior to the publication of this book.

Henrik Zetterlund from the Gothenburg Botanical Garden in Sweden has always managed to raise funds for our expeditions, and I will remember our joint trips as the most pleasant and successful of my life. He has taught me many secrets about the cultivation of rare plants. Thanks to Henrik I have visited Gothenburg several times, and the staff there has always been extremely helpful to me, fulfilling my every request for plants.

I could go on endlessly but am limited by the size of this book, so I would ask all those not mentioned here to forgive the omission. I have not forgotten you. In fact I remember each of you whenever I look at my plants.

Although Arnis Seisums didn't take part directly in the preparation of this book, his encyclopedic knowledge of plants and the titanic amount of work he undertook in preparation for our expeditions made it possible for us to add so many rare plants to our collections. Without the plants there would be no point in taking up this work, and this is why I consider Arnis a kind of coauthor. The same can be said for Mart Veerus from Estonia, who dedicated many hours to spinning a long yarn about the so-called Baltic Expedition to eastern Siberia.

I'd also like to thank my editor, Mindy Fitch, for the enormous amount of work she did to edit my manuscript, checking countless geographical terms, fine-tuning my language for an American audience, and cutting away superfluous text. Cutting a book down to size is a very difficult job for an author, so I'm happy that Mindy was able to do this on my behalf (although I still haven't lost hope that the stories that didn't make it into this book will find their way into another!). We never met personally, but Mindy and I became friends through our frequent communication via the Internet, and I felt that something was missing on the days in which her name didn't appear in my e-mail inbox.

Finally, my biggest thanks must go to my family, who have long endured the heavy burden any obsession places on those closest to the obsessed. My loved ones have always waited patiently for my return from various expeditions and tolerated my innumerable hours in the garden. Without their understanding, support, and assistance, I would have no work, no success, and certainly no book. My wife, Guna, also served as the chief reviewer of this book, in addition to working tirelessly to assure that I was always fed and there was always coffee on my desk. It was Guna's idea in the first place that I should put my experience into a book, and it was she who spent uncountable hours alongside me in the garden, come rain or snow, helping me dig, clean, sort, pack—and, of course, replant my many bulbs.

Thank you, my dears!

Part I
Bulbs in the Garden

◈ 1
Beginnings

I'VE OFTEN ASKED MYSELF why I became a gardener. Where did my interest in gardening and bulb growing come from? I was born in Riga, in the very heart of the Latvian capital. Both my parents were journalists who had no real contact with soil. In fact, when I took the entrance exams for horticultural college, more than forty-five years ago, my parents were strongly against the idea. Moreover, the college examination committee didn't want to admit me because, in their experience, "city kids" rarely finished the program. They were convinced that this journalists' child would never be a gardener; only the high grades I scored on my entrance exams persuaded them to relent.

So why did I become a gardener? Maybe it's genetically determined, this deep love of the land that dwells in the heart of every Latvian. On weekends in spring and autumn, thousands of cars leave the city for the country—a temporary migration of city folk heading out to help their country-dwelling relatives with seasonal chores.

I never met my grandfathers. My mother's father, who ran a seed shop, died of cancer in 1943, three years before I was born. My father's father, a physician, was killed by the Stalinist regime in 1937. But both men were born in the country. My father had a medical education, too, but he saw so much blood during World War II, working in a field hospital, that he decided to change professions, and after the war he took a degree in philology. My mother trained at an English-language institute before the war, but the Communist regime often viewed such an education as a badge of disloyalty. Both my parents wound up working as journalists and editors. I think that must have contributed to my gene pool as well: for eighteen years I worked as an editor for the Latvian horticultural magazine *Dārzs un Drava* (*Gardening and Bee-keeping*), and wrote a myriad of articles and six books on gardening.

I grew up surrounded by books. The walls of our apartment in Riga were covered with bookshelves. There were many thousands of volumes, from novels to scientific works, and for as long as I can remember, books took up all my free time. I read constantly—while taking the tram, in school, at night under the blanket with a small flashlight so that my parents wouldn't find out. I soon exhausted the supply of books at home (even the ones I didn't understand, such as Karl Marx's *Das Kapital*), so I started going to the school library every week. When I finished with that, I started visiting the Riga young people's library. I soon discovered that books about nature interested me the most.

The library employees began to recognize me and set aside books they thought I'd like. At the time my interests were very wide-ranging: geology, medicine, botany, travel, adventure. One of my favorite novelists was Jules Verne. Books like *Twenty Thousand Leagues Under the Sea*, *The Children of Captain Grant*, and *The Mysterious Island* delighted me with their descriptions of exotic countries and plant and animal life. It was no surprise, therefore, that I decided to become a naturalist. But which branch to choose?

Ironically, a major influence on my choice of career came in the form of a book written by the notorious charlatan scientist Trofim Lysenko, who insisted that, through "saltatory evolution," one could plant potatoes but harvest tomatoes, or grow pine trees from the seed of a birch. Lysenko was one of Stalin's minions and had attained his position of power by making extravagant promises to revolutionize Soviet agriculture. During the years that he dominated Soviet biology, legitimate geneticists were accused of sabotage and espionage, and many wound up being killed in Soviet concentration camps.

The book I stumbled across was *The Handbook of a Young Naturalist*. It described "experiments" confirming Lysenko's "theories," which astonished me so much that I decided they must be true. While an eleven-year-old can be forgiven for such credulity, I was astounded, many years later, to discover that my professor of genetics at the Latvian Agricultural University still supported Lysenko's theories (in fact, he received his doctorate for an "experiment" confirming that one could obtain barley from the seeds of winter rye). We would debate this subject for hours.

The decisive turning point for me was the first exhibition of flowers, fruits, and vegetables to be held in Latvia after the war, in the autumn of 1957. After Stalin's death in 1953, a wave of moderate liberalization had allowed the surviving imprisoned scientists, farmers, and gardeners—whose only crime had been their outstanding professional achievement—to return from the gulags. Prewar professional associations were reestablished, among them the Latvian Society for Gardening and Beekeeping. One of the society's first activities was to mount its autumn show. Every day after school I went to the Museum of Natural History, where the show was held, and walked through the exhibition hall looking at fruits, conservatory plants, cacti, and other wonders. The show lasted a whole week, and every day there were lectures on gardening. Soon the exhibitors began to recognize me, and a few gave me cuttings of indoor plants. (At the time, my only "garden" was on a windowsill.) Coincidentally, it was here that I first met my future teacher of floriculture at the horticultural college. Noticing my interest in plants, she struck up a conversation and urged me to enroll in the horticultural college after I finished school. This was the first time I had ever heard of such a place. When she met me again five or six years later at the college, she exclaimed: "Oh, you're that boy from the flower show! You've made an excellent choice!"

Another important step in my becoming a gardener was my father's decision in 1958 to buy a small piece of land on which to build a summerhouse. Finally I could have a real garden! That first year I helped my father and his friends put up a small shed for overnight shelter. The next season we dug a patch where we planted strawberries and potatoes and sowed carrots, lettuce, and other "practical" things. The corner of the bed became my own private "garden," where I planted things I had found in the neighboring forests and meadows. Thus began my first plant hunting expeditions.

My family had to save every spare penny for our small summerhouse, so I went without pocket money. I was surrounded by beautiful wildflowers and started collecting and planting them in my garden. These included *Primula veris* and *P. officinalis*, *Hepatica nobilis*, various color forms of *Saponaria officinalis*, and some of my first bulbs: *Anemone nemorosa* and *A. ranunculoides*, *Gagea sylvatica*, and *Corydalis solida*. Few bulbous plants are native to Latvia, but I had almost all of them in my tiny corner garden. I suspect that my interest in the genus *Corydalis* can be traced back to that time. I was also eager to create a rockery, as these were very much in vogue at that time in Latvia. At its peak my rockery contained about two hundred varieties of plants, but many were merely dwarf or unusual forms of Latvian wildflowers I had found during my ramblings. My rockery exists to this day, despite the fact that no one has weeded or tended it for twenty years. Few of the original plants remain, but it still looks quite nice.

When school was in session, my parents would give me money for school lunches. Since I didn't get an allowance, I liked to skip lunch and spend what I had saved on plants, including my first gladioli, tulips, and other "cultivated" bulbs. Bit by bit, my collection grew, and I began conducting my first "experiments." They were naive, without any theoretical basis, but they served to intensify my interest in the plant world.

After finishing elementary school, I began my studies at the horticultural college. The college had been established at the very beginning of the twentieth century, and before the Communists came to power it had been one of the most famous horticultural schools in the Russian Empire. Even throughout the decades of the Communist regime, it managed to preserve its traditions and standards. The teachers were all highly qualified professionals, and graduates left the school well equipped for careers in horticulture. I finished college with top honors.

Gardening wasn't my only interest during this time. In my third year of college I fell in love with beekeeping. In fact, my diploma was in beekeeping, and my first job was as an assistant beekeeper at the college. The salary was so small, however, that after a year I took a job as curator of the rose garden at the University of Latvia botanical garden. At the same time my interest in bulbs was growing, and my garden at our family's summerhouse gradually expanded, with new beds devoted to tulips, daffodils, scillas, muscaris, and other bulbs. Later I worked for a number of years in the dendrological laboratory of the National Botanical Garden at the Latvian Academy of Sciences, and also helped with their seed exchange. During that time I was involved in preparing the *Dendroflora of the Baltics* and thus became acquainted with the basic principles of plant taxonomy. My summers were spent in field expeditions searching for trees and shrubs native to and introduced in the Baltic States, and I managed to find a variety of *Pseudotsuga* previously unknown in Latvia.

I continued my studies at the Agricultural University and was able to finish the program in two years because the courses I had taken at the horticultural college were at university level. My diploma work at the university was on wild tulips and their hybrids. Despite my general interest in garden cultivars, I've always preferred wild forms. My work surprised my professors; they even recommended that it qualify me for a doctoral degree. But this was during the gloomy years of the Communist regime, and each doctoral candidate had to pass an examination in Marxist-Leninist ideology. I didn't want to waste my time with such nonsense, so I waited until Latvia regained its independence to pursue my doctorate in biology. In 2003 I received my degree from the Latvian Academy of Sciences and became a member of the academy.

While working at the botanical garden I started to write my first articles about bulb growing. Quite soon I was invited to an interview at a publishing house and was offered a job as an editor of *Dārzs un Drava*. The salary they offered was much higher than what I had been making, and the working conditions were better, so after much deliberation (I liked my scientific work), I accepted their proposal. For the next eighteen years I worked at the journal, the first three years as an editor and then for fifteen years as editor in chief. During that time I wrote my first books: two on forcing flower bulbs, one on daffodils, and a monograph on crocuses. The monograph was nominated as a potential doctoral thesis, but again I declined because of the political requirements. I feel strongly that science must not be connected with politics. But that's how it was under the Soviet regime—nothing could happen without the approval of the Communist Party and its watchdog, the KGB.

My position at the magazine allowed me to take time off to go plant hunting in the mountains. To justify my time away, I'd write an article about my adventures. This marked the beginning of my plant hunting trips, and I still go to the mountains every year in search of new, unusual plants, collecting them and attempting to grow them back in Latvia. Each year brought new experiences. As I mentioned in the preface, one of the few "advantages" of being a Soviet citizen at the time was that we could travel to many places closed to foreigners; we also had very little competition when it came to plant collecting. At the same time, we were isolated from the outside world, and all our contacts with foreigners were under close surveillance by the KGB. But I have always been a bit of an anarchist, and I didn't like those unwritten rules. During one vacation, I went to Moscow, where I met the Dutch nurseryman Michael Hoog, who was eventually to become my great friend and teacher, as well as one of my first business partners. Many of the bulbs that I secretly gave Michael eventually made their way into Western gardens through his nursery. Among these were three different color forms of a new species of *Muscari* (at that time distributed as *M. pallens*), *Corydalis schanginii* subsp. *ainae* (a taxon I discovered in Central Asia, previously unknown to science), and many others. Our friendship lasted until his death. It was Michael who sent me my first English books about plants, such as E. A. Bowles's *Handbook of Crocus and Colchicum for Gardeners*, William T. Stearns's *Botanical Latin*, and the massive volumes of the *Flora Europaea*. Our letters were the length of a small book, some of them twenty or thirty pages long, written on both sides—a pure nightmare for KGB surveillance agents.

A funny thing happened shortly before one of Michael's visits to Moscow. I had sent a telegram to my Siberian friend Georgiy Skakunov, an *Erythronium sibiricum* breeder, with the request, "Please send me samples of 'Olga', 'Zoya', and 'White Fang' right away." Upon intercepting this, the KGB leapt to the conclusion that these were the secret code names of rocket missiles. I was interrogated by an agent, and it was only after I showed him all my correspondence with Mr. Skakunov, along with the articles I had written that mentioned 'White Fang', that I was cleared.

During my time at the magazine I met Aldonis Vēriņš, one of the foremost Latvian bulb growers and an expert on gladioli. Even during those difficult times—it was strictly forbidden for individuals to bring plant material or seeds into the Soviet Union—he found ways of surreptitiously importing the newest bulb varieties from the West. He, too, was frequently interrogated by the KGB. The KGB's thinking was very simple: if you had discovered a way of secretly importing bulbs, that meant you were also able to import anti-Soviet literature. Another friend of mine, a rose enthusiast, imported the newest varieties by concealing small grafts inside the spines of books. I myself relied mainly on old contacts from the seed-exchange group of the National Botanical Garden where I had worked.

In the spring of 1975 I accepted an invitation to visit Mr. Vēriņš. We sat in his garden drinking coffee with cognac and talking about some of the articles I had published in my magazine. I told him that I wanted to write a book about bulbs. At the time my main interest was tulips, but there were already two or three books about the subject in Latvian. Mr. Vēriņš said, "You should write a book about crocuses. I can help you with the plant material, but you'll need to do all the research yourself." This marked a turning point in my gardening life. I began writing letters to botanical gardens and to the Royal Horticultural Society asking for seeds of crocus species; as a result, I struck up a friendship with Chris Brickell, who at the time was the director of the RHS's garden at Wisley. Chris sent me seeds of the newest Turkish crocus species and supplied me with the latest botanical literature on bulbs during the gloomy years of the Communist regime. Eventually he became my biggest sponsor. It was Chris who, at our first private meeting in London in 1992 (he was by then the director general of the RHS), suggested that I publish an English version of my mail-order bulb catalog. He even suggested some people to whom I could send it. So that summer I prepared my first export catalog. It was four pages long and listed forty-eight bulb varieties. A recent catalog, by comparison, was seventy-two pages and listed 717 items. I have been in the bulb business for more than thirty years now. My collection numbers more than 3300 small bulbs and more than 1400 varieties of daffodil.

My debts to Aldonis Vēriņš are many. In addition to being the first to teach me about bulb growing, he instructed me in the difficult art of dealing with the secret police. It was he who first told me something that I repeat at all my lectures: "You can grow the same plants as your neighbor, you can watch him over the fence every day and do exactly what he does—water at the same time, fertilize in the same way—but you'll never get the same results. Only your own experience will show you how to raise beautiful plants. I can tell you only how *I* do it, but you'll have to choose your own path." I couldn't pick a better motto for this book.

◈ 2
Growing from Seed

GROWING BULBS FROM SEED is very important. On many occasions it has been just this that has saved me from losing my rarest varieties. It is interesting that in difficult seasons, when bulbs have perished, it was the large bulbs that suffered the most but the seedlings that survived—although sometimes the only seedlings that survived were those sown the previous autumn that had not yet started to germinate. I always force myself to collect seeds even from common plants, even from species already well represented in my collection. It is amazing, but at times I have thrown away kilos of bulbs of some particular species because I had so many, thinking that my garden was too small to accommodate all of them. Then, like clockwork, winter arrived and killed all the bulbs I had planted. Now I recommend that gardeners always collect seeds. Even if you will never actually sow them, you can always use them for a seed exchange.

Seed-raised progeny is usually free from viruses, the curse of every gardener who grows vegetatively propagated plants. In recent years every *Muscari* bulb I have received from a Dutch nursery or garden center has been virus-infected. The only way to rehabilitate such bulbs is to collect their seeds and rebuild a stock in isolation from the mother plants. It may even be necessary to grow two generations, since some viruses are very invasive and infect the seedlings before the mother stock is destroyed. I used this method to restore the cultivated stock of *Bellevalia pycnantha* before I collected healthy stock in the wild.

Propagating bulbs from seed has other advantages, too. Stock can be built up more quickly this way than by waiting for plants to reproduce vegetatively. And we always have to bear in mind that many bulbs are slow to reproduce vegetatively or do not do so at all. In nature vegetative reproduction is often a dead end more than an advantage. In a spot where one bulb grows, the next year there will be more bulbs; after some years there will be too little space and nutrients for all of them, and as a result the bulbs will become weak and die. In some cases plants escape overcrowding by forming stolons, but that trait is usually connected with an unfortunate trade-off: fewer flowers in exchange for vegetative reproduction. I saw examples of this in Central Asia—thousands of green-leaved plants without any flowers. There are populations of *Tulipa fosteriana* and *T. bifloriformis* that very rarely produce one or two flowers on a mat of green leaves some hundred square meters in size. The length of such stolons can even reach 40 cm. A similar habit is characteristic of some of the eastern American erythroniums. In Cincinnati I saw a large population of *Erythronium americanum* with only two or three blooms.

The additional advantage (or sometimes disadvantage) of growing bulbs from seed is the emergence of beautiful hybrids among the seedlings. Many of the varieties raised in my nursery originated as just such unintentional hybrids. In fact I never crossed any corydalis intentionally—the job was always done for me by bees. All I had to do was collect seeds and sow them in favorable conditions. What a myriad of beautiful colors appeared when the plants started to flower! Bees made such amazing crosses, even between different species, that among the seedlings emerged plants of absolutely new colors and color combinations. Not all bulbous plants make interspecific crosses as easily as *Corydalis*. Quite rarely I have found hybrids among *Allium* species, but many of them are very conservative, and even artificial hybridization does not yield seeds. The same is true with Juno irises.

But if you want to be certain that your seedlings will be true to name, you must isolate flowers and artificially pollinate them or plant the mother plants quite far from other species of the same genera. The distance depends on the species, the size of your garden, natural borders, and so forth. Once I planted half of my stock of *Corydalis solida* var. *transsylvanica* some 200 m away from other corydalis, and every seedling was absolutely identical with the mother plants: they flowered at the same time, the plants were the same size, and the color was identical. At the same time there were no identical plants among seedlings of the other half of the stock, which I had planted with the rest of the collection.

Growing from seed is the cheapest way to enlarge a collection. Seeds are usually not very expensive. I have never seen them sold for more than a dollar each, while a bulb of the same species may cost fifty to a hundred dollars. Growing from seed sometimes takes a lot of time, though. Brian Mathew (1998) reported that sixteen years passed before *Erythronium idahoense* he had grown from seed first flowered. Certainly this also depends on the conditions in which the seedlings are grown, but there are plants that even in the best conditions will not flower before they are seven or eight years old. Among these types is one of the most gorgeous fritillaries: *Fritillaria eduardii*. The earliest I ever saw it flower was in the seventh spring after germination. In such cases it is up to you to decide whether you want to pay a couple of dollars for a pinch of seeds and wait for years to see flowers, or leave the job to a professional nurseryman and pay twenty or thirty dollars for a flowering-sized bulb.

Many bulbs are rare and cultivated by only a few people, many of them only by amateurs or in botanical gardens. You will never find the names of these bulbs in catalogs, because they are generally too difficult and unprofitable for commercial growers. The only way to find such plants is to join gardening societies and use their seed exchange, and to start corresponding with botanical gardens, which usually edit an annual Index Seminum (seed list). There are usually very few seeds in a packet. Henrik Zetterlund from the Gothenburg Botanical Garden in Sweden told me that at Gothenburg there are usually four or five seeds in each packet; two of the seedlings can be expected to grow to flowering size, and then the gardener will be able to pollinate both plants and yield his or her own seeds. Many species are self-sterile, so you need at least two genetically different plants (not raised vegetatively from the same ancestor bulb) to get your own seed crop. This is of paramount importance when it comes to many *Corydalis* species—it can be very difficult to get any viable seed if you have only one tuber! If you want to build up your stock, especially in the case of species that do not increase vegetatively, you have to buy at least two tubers of the same species.

When it comes to wild plants, it is always best, for ecological reasons, to collect seeds rather than bulbs. Some companies specialize in collecting and offering wild-collected seed. By buying these seeds, you can build up a collection of plants from very distant countries. My quite impressive collection of American bulbs, for example, were built up from seeds I bought from American and Canadian seed companies run by professional botanists with extensive knowledge of their native flora.

It is very important to think about the best time for sowing seeds. My own experience has taught me that results are best if seeds are sown as soon as possible after they have been collected. Most bulbs need some cold period for the seeds to germinate and so should be sown in autumn for a good germination the next spring. Each species has its own optimal period of low temperatures for germination, but in general it is around one to two months, with an optimal temperature of 2°C–4°C. The temperature is essential, and the seeds must also be wet during this time. In the conditions of my own garden, sowing in September provides the right temperature regime and level of moisture.

Unfortunately, Latvian winters are very unstable. Cold periods take turns with shorter or longer periods of thawing, and consequently the seeds sometimes receive the necessary period of low temperatures before the winter ends. This can cause the seeds to germinate too early, and as frosts return the young seedlings can be killed. This kind of thing sometimes occurs with crocus or tulip seeds if they are sown outside. When I was young I often experimented with interspecific crosses of tulip species. Such crosses are not easy, and each seed is very valuable. At the time I kept my seeds until the middle of February in my living room—dry and warm. In the middle of February I mixed them with coarse, moist sand and placed the mixture in the refrigerator, where the temperature was around 2°C. In general, around mid-April, when the soil defrosted, my seeds started to germinate. I washed the sand away and with forceps placed each seed individually in shallow rows of an open garden bed. At first I tried to use sphagnum moss, but sometimes I noticed the start of germination too late and the shoots were 3–5 cm long. It is very difficult to take such seeds out of sphagnum without breaking the shoot. Sand is easy to wash away through a sieve.

The seeds of many plants cannot stay long out of soil without losing their capacity to germinate. Generally these are woodland plants. Woodland *Corydalis* species and many *Anemone, Trillium,* and *Erythronium* species have to be sown immediately after the seeds are harvested, otherwise they will lose their viability. They can be kept viable in humid, cool conditions, but it is best to just sow them right after harvesting. This does not mean they must be sown instantaneously; a week or ten days out of soil will not usually play any important role.

Surprisingly, even *Corydalis* species from arid growing conditions prefer immediate sowing. I initially sowed them in autumn, because in summer there is always too much work to be done, but the germination rate in the first spring was low, and some seeds germinated only in their second or even third year. Then I tried sowing them immediately, and the results were surprisingly good. The secret is that seeds of some plants are dispersed unripe and need a period of dormancy that takes place right in the soil as a result of moisture, soil chemistry, and microorganisms. Immediate sowing is very important for such genera as *Iris*, *Fritillaria*, and *Narcissus*. George Rodionenko, in his monograph about irises (1961), mentions that some seeds of *Iris* sown in spring germinate only after fifteen years, but the ones sown immediately after harvesting tend to germinate the very first spring. According to William Dykes (Rodionenko 1961), some seeds of Oncocyclus irises only germinated in the eighteenth year (!) after sowing. In my experience, Juno irises sown in autumn germinate gradually over the course of five years. I have found the same to be true with *Narcissus* and some other bulbs. Although early sowing always carries with it the risk that some of the seeds will come up in autumn, the potential losses are smaller than they would be if the seeds were sown late. If you visualize the processes that occur in nature, you will understand that all seeds naturally fall into the soil and break very soon after being dispersed. To grow bulbs successfully we have to follow the rules made by nature. The only exception in my nursery is with crocuses. I usually sow these seeds no sooner than the end of September. Otherwise they are too likely to begin germination in autumn and are then killed by frosts.

Early sowing doesn't always help with germination, especially when it comes to irises. Sometimes even after four or five years you will have perfect-looking seeds instead of bulbs or rhizomes. I once followed the recommendations made by George Rodionenko in his monograph. He explained how iris seeds he had harvested in 1949 were sown only in 1953 but did not show any signs of germination until 1955, although the boxes of seeds had been kept in continually favorable conditions. The seeds were washed free of soil and sterilized in alcohol (75%), and then with a sterile sharp knife he scratched their skin near the spot where the first shoot had to come out. The seeds were put on moist tissue paper in the dark at a temperature of about 8°C. After six days all the seeds had germinated. They were planted in a garden bed, where they brought forth perfect shoots. I repeated the experiment with seeds of *Iris kolpakowskiana*, but after scratching the seed skin I immediately sowed them in a box, beginning with a layer of soil, then a layer of clean, coarse sand, then the seeds, and then another layer of sand. Almost all of them soon produced beautiful shoots. This method requires time, patience, and sharp eyes, but it certainly pays off.

The seeds of some plants do not fall into dormancy, or the period of dormancy is very short and the seeds do not need any cold period. This is the case, for example, with the autumn-flowering *Cyclamen* species. Seeds sown immediately after the opening of the pods and kept moist during summer will germinate during the first autumn. Stored seed may germinate slowly and erratically, taking as long as four or even five years. In 1999 I received from Kees Sahin in the Netherlands one hundred seeds of the world's rarest cyclamen, *C. kuznetzovii*, known only from a single forest in the Crimean Peninsula that encompasses just a few acres. Immediately after returning from the Netherlands in October, I soaked the seeds for twenty-four hours in room-temperature water and sowed them, but the first leaves didn't appear until the spring of 2003, after I had lost all hope and kept them only out of spite. The germination continued in 2004 and 2005.

On the flip side are plants with delayed germination. These seeds need two periods of cold before they sprout out of the soil. This is characteristic of some *Lilium* species, all *Trillium* species, *Cardiocrinum* species, and some other plants. After the first period of cold, the seeds form small underground bulbs, but only after the second winter do they form the first leaf. In these cases it is also possible to dupe nature. Mix the seeds with moist vermiculite, put them in a freezer at 2°C–4°C for three months, then keep them for three months at 17°C, followed by another three months in the freezer at 2°C–4°C. At this point you can sow the seeds, which will germinate in two weeks. I have never tried this method personally, but it is reported to work quite well if you have a heated greenhouse in which you can keep the seedlings during the first growing season. There is another method, which I have used, that involves collecting the seeds before they are fully ripe (for *Trillium* species, they must still be white). If these unripe seeds are sown immediately after collecting, they will go through the first stage of germination and form underground bulbils in the first autumn, and green leaves will emerge in the first spring. I tried this method with wild *Paeonia* species and it worked perfectly. Conversely, if you wait until the *Paeonia* seedpods split, the seeds will germinate very slowly and irregularly for a number of years.

Sometimes even seeds collected very early can germinate. During my first visit to the Netherlands in August of 1988, Michael Hoog showed me an impressive bed of *Arisaema ciliatum* with newly developed seedpods. He offered me some pods and I took them, but I thought they were far too immature to ever germinate. At home the pods slowly turned red, and inside them I found small red berries with somewhat seed-like structures the size of poppy seeds. I was very surprised when leaves of *Arisaema* seedlings came up the following spring. Later I collected some very immature seedpods of *Bellevalia crassa* in Turkey, and again they contained small seeds that nevertheless germinated the following spring.

Each genus, even each species, has its own secrets for successful growing. Various species and forms of *Roscoea* are very nice and quite new in Latvian gardens. They can be grown outside here, though they don't belong to the hardiest genus. Planted some 25–30 cm deep, they overwinter well and come up nicely, flower, and usually set a good crop of seeds that germinate well and . . . disappear. The problem is that the seedlings lie very shallow in the soil and are killed by frost during the first winter. It is not possible to replant them any deeper, because they are still too small to reach the top of the soil. So in the first years they must be treated as tender plants; only when their tuberous rootstocks reach flowering size are they ready to be planted outside in a permanent place. I usually sow them in boxes kept in a frost-free cellar during the first two winters after germination, and then for a season I keep them in an unheated greenhouse, after which they are planted outside.

Seeds can be sown in pots, open beds, or boxes. Amateurs mostly use pots because the number of seeds sown is usually very small. If you use pots, clay pots are best, since plants in plastic pots are in more danger of becoming waterlogged (you have to be very careful with watering). I used pots when I first began growing bulbs. My first experience was with crocus seeds that Chris Brickell sent me during the Soviet era. I grew them in small clay pots and during winter covered the pots with glass. It worked quite well, but I soon found the biggest problem with using clay pots in my climate: despite the glass, the pots were broken or split by frost. When I switched to unbreakable plastic pots my seedlings often became waterlogged, especially in winter when the lower half of the soil in the pots remained frozen, thus preventing excess water from draining out.

This does not mean that I am absolutely against pots. It's true that I don't like growing bulbs in pots, but I do use them now and again. I use clay pots when growing very small numbers of seeds of plants that in the beginning develop very slowly and form tiny bulbs. Generally I sow *Colchicum* seeds only in pots. I grow seedlings without planting out for the first four years and then plant the young bulbs in beds. The greatest advantage of pots is that each stock is sown separately and you do not have to worry about mixing the stocks. For all other bulbs I prefer other ways of growing from seed.

It was only about a decade ago that I sowed all my seeds in open beds. Even if I had only a few seeds, I sowed them in the garden. The results depended on the species. Some species germinated well and provided plenty of seedlings after two to three years. Others produced plenty of shoots the first spring, but the following spring very few sprouted. There were also cases in which from hundreds of seeds sown, only a few or even none germinated. You can conduct such experiments if you have plenty of your own seeds. In those years I generally sowed only my own seeds; therefore, my financial losses were minor. Many *Allium* species germinated perfectly and survived, as did most *Crocus*, woodland *Corydalis*, some *Fritillaria*, some *Iris*, and many other plants. But the results were very unpredictable. I could never foresee what I might be harvesting after three years.

I still sow seeds on open beds, but now I do it only with a limited number of species. This includes certain woodland *Corydalis*, forms of *Erythronium sibiricum*, a few *Allium*, *Muscari*, *Ornithogalum*, and some other plants that dislike drying out during summer, or those that can easily survive rainy periods and of which I have plenty of seed. My seedling beds are 10 m long and 0.7 m wide, with passes 0.4 m wide between the beds. In these beds I sow seeds immediately after they have been collected (for *Corydalis* and *Erythronium*) or in the first ten days of October (for *Muscari* and *Allium*, among others). I make shallow (1–1.5 cm deep), parallel cross-rows that are 10 cm apart and strew seeds quite densely in the furrows, then slightly sprinkle soil on top of the seeds. After that the beds are covered with a thin (1–2 cm) layer of peat moss.

Mass germination usually begins the first spring, with some seeds germinating the second spring. Generally I dig up the seedlings after the third year of vegetation, at which point they are sufficiently big and easy to collect. Some of them even start to flower while in a seedling bed.

I now sow most seeds in standard Dutch plastic bulb boxes (40 × 60 × 23 cm). When filled with soil they are quite heavy, but some time ago I found a Latvian company that produced similar boxes of about half the size (40 × 30 × 23 cm). These are much easier to move about and are very comfortable to work with if the seed stocks are not big. Still, I prefer the larger ones, which have plenty of holes in the bottom and on the sides. To prevent the soil being washed out, I cover the sides with a thick polyethylene film and then fill the boxes with soil mix.

The question of what makes an optimal soil mix is a difficult one. It is nice to read in plant books that the best results can be achieved by mixing John Innes compost number 2 or the like with something else, but this advice will help very little if such compost is not available in your country. My friend and colleague Arnis Seisums uses a refined, neutralized peat moss with basic elements and microelements that is produced by a Latvian peat factory, but such a recommendation would be futile in any country outside my own. Gardeners usually use their own composts and soil mixes. My standard mix is made from equal parts peat moss, coarse sand, and loam. The loam is made from the turf on one of my meadows and composted for three to four years. I add dolomite lime and a complex low-nitrogen fertilizer with microelements. After mixing all of these components together, I check it with my fingers, often adding more sand to ensure better drainage. I use this soil mix in seed boxes and pots and for filling raised beds in my greenhouses. I usually bring samples of such mixes to a laboratory to check the pH and mineral content. The results may lead me to add some components, such as fertilizers, peat (if the pH is too high), or dolomite lime (if the pH is too low). In my opinion the best pH for a standard mix is around 6.5. If a mix is too acid or too alkaline, problems can arise with plant feeding, especially with the microelements.

When a box is filled with soil mix, I press it lightly and then sow the seeds. The air in the substrate is an essential ingredient, so it's important to avoid pressing too hard. Only on rare occasions do I have just the right amount of seeds to fill an entire box with one sample; I usually end up sowing seeds of more than one species in the same box. If there are many seeds, I scatter them evenly on top of the pressed soil, then leave a couple of centimeters of free space and sow the next species. If the amount of seed is small, I make shallow cross-rows with my finger and sow the seeds in one, two, or three rows, depending on the quantity. A question arises: how do you prevent mixing the various species when harvesting the seedlings? I solve this problem by placing genera with different-looking bulbs side by side. For example, in the same box there may be rows of *Allium*, *Fritillaria*, *Crocus*, and *Muscari*. Thus at seedling harvesting time I can immediately see which bulbs belong to which row. This makes it easy to avoid mixing stocks, which would inevitably occur if one box contained different species of the same genera. To facilitate the harvesting of the seedlings I use a special tool, an iron plate that I slide vertically into the soil between rows; this helps me when I'm separating the different stocks. I take the soil together with the young bulbs out of the box and shake it out through sieves of different sizes (Plate 3).

When the seeds are spaced, I cover them with a layer about 1 cm thick of coarse sand and again press down slightly. I put on top of this an extra 1 cm of mulch, which prevents the soil from drying out, keeps the sand from washing away during watering, and helps prevent soil compaction. In the beginning I used only peat moss. Unfortunately, when peat moss becomes dry (especially during winter) it forms a tight layer over the box. I have often seen this solid layer of peat pushed up by young seedling leaves trying to get through it. In such cases even immediate watering hasn't helped much. I later tried replacing the peat with vermiculite number 2, which is used successfully in the forestry industry to cover the seedling beds of birches in greenhouses. The difference, as it turned out, is that birch seeds need warm, damp air to germinate, so the greenhouse doors are always closed. Bulbs, on the other hand, need moist soil and dry air, so after the end of the frost season all the doors and windows of the greenhouse stay open. With the wind thus free to blow in and out, the light vermiculite is soon blown away. The solution ended up being a combination of both treatments: I now cover my boxes with a mix of equal parts peat moss and vermiculite. The vermiculite makes the peat more porous, while the peat keeps the vermiculite from blowing away. The results are marvelous.

Every season I sow thirty to fifty boxes. I grow seedlings in boxes for two to three (sometimes even four or five) years—it all depends how quickly the seeds germinate and how quickly the young seedlings develop. To keep track of how long ago the seeds were sown, I number all of my boxes. The first two digits denote the year, the next two denote the box number. Since seeds can be sown year-round, the year is important to include. This is not the year in which the seeds were actually sown but the year in which they normally send up the first shoots. A box containing seeds of *Corydalis* sown in May 2004 will be numbered 05–. Boxes containing seeds received from other companies and sown in January or the first half of February in 2005 will also be numbered 05–, but seeds sown later in the year will be numbered 06– because their germination in the first spring is quite doubtful. Every spring I note in my planting books which seeds have germinated; if a mass germination occurs, I jot down the year in which it took place. This helps determine when seedlings from a particular box must be harvested. It is not always so easy to make such a decision. One species in the box will germinate the first season, the other species in the second season. In such cases you must choose between leaving the box untouched for another year, risking losing some seedlings from overcrowding, or collecting the very young, small bulbs of delayed species, which can easily dry out. I usually leave such a box for an extra year.

Immediately after sowing, I place most of my seedling boxes in a greenhouse, where they stay until it is time to harvest the seedlings. During the entire frost-free season, and even during moderate frosts (up to –5°C), the doors and windows stay open. Adequate watering is very important. Some growers recommend soaking the seeds of certain genera (*Erythronium*, for example, especially if the seeds are not newly collected) in water before sowing. I find this quite difficult, because wet seeds tend to stick to fingers and are difficult to space evenly. I prefer to thoroughly water my boxes after sowing, so that the soil is uniformly damp rather than wet. It is important to combine plants with similar watering requirements in the same box. The results will be quite bad if you sow seeds of *Erythronium*, which likes summer moisture, together with *Allium* from the desert. During the summer months, boxes containing plants that dislike drying out (such as *Eranthis*, *Erythronium*, and some *Corydalis*) are placed outside in the shade of big trees; in late autumn I move them back into a greenhouse. Boxes of plants from arid areas stay in a greenhouse all summer long, where they get quite dry.

In the past I watered my seedling boxes with a garden sprinkler. This was a tricky process and made it quite difficult to provide the same quantity of water to every spot. The soil in the boxes that remained in the greenhouse during summer became dry and would not easily absorb water. During what would naturally be their rain season, I soaked these boxes by dipping them in a special basin filled with water. This was the heaviest labor in my nursery. Picture for a moment the size of these boxes, heavy even when filled with dry soil and much more so when soaked with water. It was enough of a nightmare to force me to look for another solution. I finally decided to install drip irrigation (Plate 4). This saved me a lot of work and provided a very even moisture level during the entire growing season. Now I water my boxes twice a week, the leaves of the seedlings are always dry, and the soil is evenly moist, so the young seedlings do not suffer from the stress caused by alternating periods of dryness and moisture. During the growing season I also spray the seedlings once a week with a weak solution of fertilizer.

Winters in Latvia are normally quite harsh. The lowest temperature I have recorded in my garden, –48°C, occurred shortly before Christmas of 1978. It was an exceptional winter, but temperatures around –30°C occurring over a couple of weeks are nothing extraordinary. For bulbs growing outside, these temperatures are not very dangerous, especially if the bulbs are covered with a good layer of snow. But my seedling boxes are placed in an unheated greenhouse covered by a double layer of long-lasting polyethylene. The polyethylene helps save young bulbs from extreme frost, but during the coldest nights, temperature in the greenhouse can drop to as low as –18°C. Seedling bulbs do not lie deep, and 1 cm of mulch is much too little covering to protect them from such low temperatures. The sides of my seedling boxes are well protected by a good layer of dry peat moss, but what protects the seedlings from frost that penetrates through the top? A layer of peat moss at least 10 cm thick would be needed for this, and putting it on during winter frosts and removing it in spring would be an enormous amount of work. It is also very easy to remove such covering too late; if the seedlings have started growing before the covering has been removed, the shoots will be weak and etiolated. I have found a very easy solution to this problem. After waiting a few days for the temperature in the greenhouse to drop to −8°C–10°C, I cover my boxes using sheets of rock wool 5 cm thick (Plate 5). Rock wool is very light in weight and provides excellent protection. Since the boxes are covered only after the soil has frozen, the rock wool also keeps the soil from defrosting during thaws. The bulbs that winter with leaves do not suffer from such covering. In addition, the rock wool sheets are 60 cm wide and fit my boxes perfectly; I can cover three boxes with one sheet.

◆ 3
Propagation by Division

IT IS NOT ALWAYS DESIRABLE, or even possible, to propagate bulbous plants from seed. If you wish to propagate hybrids, keep in mind that seed progeny usually vary to some degree. Many species are self-sterile, in which case you will need at least two plants from different origins to obtain seeds. In such cases vegetative propagation is useful. Many bulbs naturally increase by division quite quickly or make a lot of small, young bulbils at the base of the mother plant. At replanting time the clumps are divided and the bulbs separated. If nature is a bit lazy, you can use artificial methods for propagation.

Many bulbs naturally increase quite well. Normally each tuber of *Corydalis* from section *Solida*, whose species annually replace each old tuber with a new one, makes two shoots that in the next season form two new tubers. However, tuberous corydalis with perennial tubers only grow larger and larger without any natural splitting. Corms of crocuses have more than one bud, with a new corm forming at the base of each bud by the end of vegetation, but in many cases tiny cormlets are also produced. Bulbs of Reticulata irises form small, grain-like bulbils at their base that in two to three years grow into flowering-sized, mature bulbs. Very small grains are also formed at the base of many fritillary bulbs; these grains don't usually mature because the mother bulb suppresses them, but if the bulb is eaten by a pest, the grains replace it. The bulbs of many tulips, daffodils, and snowdrops split and in favorable conditions make large clumps in the garden. If the clumps aren't divided and replanted, they can become overcrowded and will stop flowering.

A gardener is never satisfied with the rate at which bulbs increase. Rare bulbs always increase too slowly, while more common plants such as the star of Bethlem, *Ornithogalum umbellatum*, increase too quickly and can become undesirable weeds. The latter happens much more rarely than the former. Gardeners, and especially nurserymen, are always looking for ways to boost the natural rate of increase for various genera and species.

The easiest method involves using the naturally produced cormlets, bulblets, or so-called grains that many species form at the base of the mother bulb or bulb-like structure. I try to collect the cormlets of all gladiolus and some crocuses, the bulblets of Reticulata irises, and the grains formed by fritillaries. For fritillaries such as *Fritillaria acmopetala* and *F. elwesii*, I do this to save my beds from new progeny, which can easily become a terrible weed if left uncollected at harvesting time. For others this helps me to build up my stock, because in my climate seeds are not formed very often, and during wet, rainy periods seedpods often start to rot, long before they can be harvested.

There is a great difference between *Fritillaria* species from Caucasian and Siberian woodlands and those from North America and Turkey. Grains the size of poppy seeds, sometimes a little larger, formed by some Caucasian and Siberian fritillaries are very susceptible to drying out. Therefore I collect them at harvesting time and immediately sow them in boxes. The grains of many Turkish species and American frits are much larger; these can be sown immediately or kept until autumn. If there are to be kept until autumn, I house them in cardboard boxes mixed with white sand. It is also possible to keep them mixed with sand in thin polyethylene bags, but this sometimes leads to problems with mold.

Grains develop only slightly faster than seeds, saving you about one year overall. Seeds are always preferable for their genetic diversity, while grains produce bulbs that are identical to the mother plant. This may be an advantage for a showman who wishes to exhibit a pot of identical plants flowering at the same time.

Not all fritillaries form grains or naturally split into two or more bulbs. Central Asian fritillaries are generally very slow to increase, as are some European and Middle Eastern species. For plants from a species group in which the bulbs are usually formed by two scales, such as *Fritillaria stenanthera*, *F. bucharica*, *F. olgae*, and *F. verticillata*, the simplest technique is to break the bulb into two parts, separating the scales. I do this soon after harvesting. I usually wash the bulbs free of soil, treat with fungicides, and after a week or so, when they are dry, break them in half, separating the scales, and leave them in a box until planting time. Sometimes I cover them with sand; for species from arid environments this is not essential, but it is best to cover woodland species to avoid desiccation. Keeping them in plastic bags is risky as it may lead to gray mold (*Botrytis*) or rot. After breaking the bulb you will see that the halves are not identical. Only one of them has a growing point at the base. The half with the growing point will flower perfectly the following spring and will replace a normal, full-sized bulb, sometimes also forming small additional bulbs. The other half will probably not flower the first spring but will form at least one flowering-sized bulb that will flower the following year; with luck, it will form smaller bulbs, too.

The most gorgeous frits are more difficult to increase, including such large-growing garden aristocrats as *Fritillaria eduardii*, *F. raddeana*, *F. persica*, and *F. imperialis*. Some forms of *F. imperialis* increase vegetatively quite well, but the same can't be said of close relatives *F. eduardii* and *F. raddeana*. I once had a bulb of *F. eduardii* the size of a child's head, but it didn't produce a single offset. The two or three scales of these fritillaries are joined by their sides and by wrapping one another inside the outer scale, so you can't break them apart and separate them. *Fritillaria persica* has the same type of bulb. In 1993 I received good stock of a white mutation of *F. persica* 'Adiyaman', which later received the Alpine Garden Society's Award of Merit under the name 'Ivory Bells'. The owner of the stock, Dutch nurseryman Jan Pennings, challenged me to find a way to increase the bulbs more quickly.

Having carte blanche, I tried everything. I sliced them up like an apple, made cross-cuttings to a third of the bulbs' height from the base, cut off grooves on the bulbs' sides, cut the scales into small pieces, and I don't know how this idea came into my head, but with some bulbs I cut horizontally at about a third to a half of the bulbs' height from the bottom. I did the same with bulbs of *Fritillaria eduardii* and *F. raddeana*. I cut them very soon after harvesting and kept pieces of the bulbs in the bulb shed in open boxes with the cut surface up until the first ten days of September, when they were all planted in open beds in my garden. The next summer at harvesting time I carefully counted and measured all the harvested bulbs, and the best results were achieved by my crazy horizontal cutting. The bottom half of the bulb flowered and produced a full-sized new bulb ready for cutting again. The top half made the greatest number of small young bulbs compared with other methods of cutting. I recorded the same tendency in all three species. The largest of them flowered in the third year, with the others following suit a year or two later. This method is much faster than propagating from seed, in which case seedlings usually begin to flower eight to nine years after sowing.

Jan Pennings now uses this method at his nursery, and it allows him to quickly build up his stock of *Fritillaria persica* 'Ivory Bells'. He keeps the bulbs, together with scooped-out hyacinths, in controlled climatic conditions at 23°C. The air is initially dry to encourage callusing. After a week, when the cut surface has dried, Jan raises the level of humidity. As a result of this practice, the price of 'Ivory Bells' has dropped dramatically. Now anyone can afford to buy this bulb without having to mortgage their house.

Various ways of cutting are used for other bulbs, too. The oldest methods involve cross-cutting and scooping out hyacinth bulbs, although these techniques can also be used for certain other small bulbs. I cross-cut the basal plate to quickly increase certain *Scilla* and *Muscari* species. To do this, use a sharp knife to cut the bottom of the bulb at a depth of 5–10 mm. Depending on the size of the bulb, you can make two, three, or even four cuts. It is essential throughout the process to make sure of the sterility of all equipment and bulbs. It is extremely easy to distribute various rots and viral infections via unsterile equipment or surroundings, and if you do so, you'll end up completely destroying the stock you wanted to increase. I once had a splendid *Muscari* hybrid found somewhere in Turkey by Czech friends. As a cross between different species, it was sterile and gave me no one seed. Unfortunately, it was also a very lazy increaser, so I had no choice but to build up my stock using artificial methods. I was lazy, too, however, and failed to sterilize the bulbs before I began cutting. As it turned out, the first bulb that I cut was infected with a bacterial rot, and as a result I lost every other bulb. The bulbs with cut bases must be kept upside down at 18°C–20°C until the normal planting season begins in September. During this time many small bulblets will be formed along the damaged basal plate. I plant those bulbs bottom up, and the next year they form many small new bulbs.

Chipping (slicing) and double-scaling are the most common techniques used to increase daffodil bulbs, but both are also widely used for snowdrops and have been used successfully for *Allium, Chionodoxa, Iris, Leucojum, Muscari, Ornithogalum, Scilla,*

and *Sternbergia*, among others. Tulips, on the other hand, do not multiply any more
quick[ly] ... techniques than they do in nature.

... You must start as early as possible; sometimes
bulb... ...uld normally be done. Begin by cleaning away
any... ...ose scales. With a sterilized knife, horizontally
cu... ...make downward cuts, dividing the bulb into
se... ...e. Depending on the species and the bulb's size,
th... ...ts. Each segment must be attached to some part
... ...u have prepared the chips. If you decide to try
... ...continued. Now you must carefully cut each chip
... ...the outer pair. Each pair consists of two scale frag-
... ...It is essential to keep at least two scales joined with
... ...don't form new bulbils, or do so only rarely, and only
... ...cut into single scales.
... ...he whole operation be kept as sterile as possible. All
... ...double-scaling must be carefully washed after harvest-
... ...ard fungicide mix. After quickly drying them, select

healthy-look... ... use formaldehyde to clean both bulbs and equipment,
but formaldehyde is not available or permitted in some countries and is quite poisonous, so I would recommend using 70% alcohol (industrial ethanol). Whatever you
use, make sure all tools and surfaces are clean. Carefully wash your hands, and wear
rubber gloves as you work.

After cutting each bulb, the prepared chips or scale pairs must be treated with
fungicide. I recommend using a solution twice the usual concentration. Place them in
a thin (120- to 150-gauge) polyethylene bag as you go along to keep them from drying
out while the rest of the bulbs of that variety or species are cut. When all bulbs have
been chipped or scaled, mix them with fresh, pure vermiculite and put them in a new,
clean polyethylene bag. Seal the bag, leaving as much air as possible under the tie, and
keep it in a dark space at a temperature of 18°C–20°C for three months. I usually use
a bookshelf in my bedroom or, to my wife's dismay, a shelf in the kitchen.

In my experience, the best incubation medium is vermiculite. The moisture level
is very important. It is usually recommended that each 500 ml of vermiculite be combined with 40 ml of cold boiled water. This must be done at least fifteen minutes
beforehand, because vermiculite initially warms up when put in contact with water.
Keep in mind, too, that too much vermiculite is better than too little.

All of these seemingly minor details—the thickness of the polyethylene, the proportion of scale pairs to vermiculite, the wetness of the vermiculite, the air space above
the scales—will affect the final outcome.

Some growers recommend mixing vermiculite with peat moss. During the Soviet
era vermiculite was not available and I used perlite, but it was too compact for incubation, so the addition of peat moss was essential. I have achieved my best results using
white sphagnum moss. Freshly collected sphagnum is sterile and contains natural

inhibitors of fungal and bacterial diseases. (During World War II it was even used in field hospitals of the Soviet Army in place of cotton and gauze bandages to cover wounds.) Sphagnum also has an excellent capacity to absorb excessive moisture. Its single fault is that it makes it more difficult to pick out the incubated young bulbs, especially if this is done too late when young shoots and roots have started to form. I squeeze the sphagnum in my hands to press out as much water as possible, making it perfect for the incubation of scales.

The bags of chips and scales must be checked regularly during incubation. Throw away any plant material that shows signs of mold. If necessary, wash the vermiculite off the chips and scales, repeat the fungicide treatment, and seal everything in a new bag with fresh vermiculite. When the young bulbs are incubated, take them out along with the scale remnants and plant them as units in a frost-free greenhouse during the first winter. My greenhouse isn't frost-free, so I use my seedling boxes and soil mix and cover everything with sheets of rock wool during winter spells.

The propagation of lilies is easier because their bulbs are composed of many separate scales joined only with the basal plate. At lifting time you can detach some outer scales and use them for propagation. If only a few scales have been removed, you can immediately replant the mother bulb and it will flower the next season without any trouble, but you can also use the whole bulb for propagation. The outermost scales are usually weak and somewhat sere, while the innermost are too fresh—neither are very useful for propagation. The presence of a basal plate is not essential for lilies. All other processes are the same as for double-scaling and chipping. I usually use this method to propagate Caucasian lilies. The incubation of their young bulbs is quite slow, with the entire process taking up to three years. I check the bags every month and take out the scales with young bulbs at their base, replacing the others. If a young bulb breaks off of the mother scale, the scale is replaced in the incubation bag and quite often produces additional bulbils. If any scales start to rot, I cut away the rotten tissue, treat again with fungicide, and put the scales back in the bag.

With Caucasian lilies, long scales can even be cut into two parts, and young bulbs can be incubated on each half scale. Again, the process is slow. If the soil isn't frozen, I immediately plant the young bulbils in boxes. If that isn't possible, young lily bulbils can be kept for two months in polyethylene bags in a refrigerator crisper and planted out at the first possibility.

The incubation of scales can save a bulb infected by *Fusarium*. Sometimes at digging time you will find that the base of a lily bulb is rotten and the scales freely fall away. Collect these scales, carefully cut off any damaged tissue, and treat them with fungicide before starting the incubation. The results are marvelous. You'll want to check the bags more often, however, for any infected scales that might have been overlooked.

Many tuberous plants can only be propagated vegetatively by breaking the tubers into parts. This is true for *Anemone*, *Eranthis*, and *Corydalis* species with perennial tubers, some tuberous *Geranium* species, and others. I prefer to break the tubers shortly before planting, when I can see growing points on top of the tubers. If the tuber is sufficiently large and mature, it usually has weak points, where it easily breaks. To prevent infection it is essential to treat the wounds with fungicide powder and allow the wounded surface to dry out. One particular "fungicide" used by Soviet gardeners during my youth works extremely well for this purpose and is both cheap and safe: powdered charcoal. When I was in school, to my mother's horror I used a coffee mill to prepare charcoal powder. I use it again now, these many years later, having found no modern fungicide more effective for treating wounds on tubers. When I plant perennial *Corydalis* tubers or *Geranium charlesii*, each wound or cut surface is powdered with charcoal, which not only dries the wound but also prevents infection. Nothing is better than well-forgotten wisdom.

❖ 4
Growing Bulbs in Greenhouses

THE PATCHES of warmer weather that often occur during winters in Latvia make bulb growing here somewhat dangerous. Our bulbs generally come from areas with long, stable winters. Most can withstand low temperatures during dormancy, and many come from places that provide a good covering of snow. Bulbs from the Central Asian mountains, for example, are covered with several meters of snow during winter; the climate is continental, with "winter" actually beginning in late autumn and ending in spring. In the Far East, monsoons bring enough snow to cover the soil until spring, so that the ground never becomes frozen. A lot of bulbs don't need a very long cooling period. The frost makes the soil "dry," and the bulbs only wait for the return of favorable conditions before growing. In Latvia, however, the soil sometimes begins to thaw in midwinter, and this is a signal to the bulbs to start growing.

The very few bulbs that can be considered native to Latvia are accustomed to such changes in weather. Some years ago, a hard frost arrived just after my beds of *Corydalis solida* and allied species had begun to flower. The frost completely killed all the foliage, and I thought I would have no crop at all. I was greatly surprised when a week later I noticed new shoots coming up. *Corydalis* species with annulate tubers have an underground scale leaf at the base of which is a dormant bud. In the case of my bulbs, this bud had awakened and made new foliage and flowers, and ultimately a healthy crop developed. A different situation occurred in the beds I had planted of *Corydalis* species with perennial tubers. These species don't have such a scale leaf, so no foliage replacement took place. Since the tubers were perennial, however, they didn't die but survived in a weakened state. Unfortunately, when the same weather conditions happened over the three following seasons, it was too much even for these tough bulbs, and I lost many nice species.

This forced me to build my greenhouses. My first greenhouse was 20 square meters and covered with glass. It had two raised beds along the sides and a path in the middle. It was basically a small toy for a large child, but it taught me many lessons as a nurseryman. On one side of the greenhouse I made a little rockery with small terraces and rocks from dolomite flagstone. I planted many different bulbs in this rockery, hoping they might flower for many years. On the opposite side were bulbs planted in pots plunged in coarse sand. The greenhouse had electric heat that I turned on whenever the temperature fell below zero. One very cold night (–20°C) the electricity disappeared. I covered the plants and beds with sheets of newspaper and lit five or six candles to warm the air. The plants managed to survive.

My first lesson came at the end of the first season at bulb harvesting time. I dug out some *Corydalis* tubers from my small rockery and the same species from a pot. The difference was shocking: the bulbs from the rockery were twice as large as those from the pots. From then on I quit growing bulbs in pots. (Never say never, however: later on I returned to pots in a few exceptional cases.)

My second lesson was much more painful and came a year later, although I only fully understood it after a few years. I built a glasshouse, and decided to use a heat-sterilized soil mix for the bulbs to be planted inside. During the first season these bulbs grew surprisingly well. I removed only a few and left the others for the next year. But many didn't come up again. They had suffered from various rots, and at that time I didn't understand the reason.

In my first polyethylene tunnel I made raised beds, too. Changing substrate is a heavy-duty job, so I decided to use soil sterilization and then crop rotation. The job was too big for my handmade sterilization equipment, which sterilized soil using heat, so I decided to use chemicals. I combined my soil mix with Basamid, watered it, and kept it covered with polyethylene film for a month. Basamid is a chemical that when combined with water exudes a poisonous gas that kills everything in the soil—weed seeds, pests, and diseases. After a month you can check the condition of the soil by sowing some lettuce seeds; if they germinate, the soil is free from gas and can be used to grow plants. As with my original glasshouse, the first year's crop was excellent. But since Basamid was expensive, and since using it posed health risks for both me and the environment, the next season I used only crop rotation. In the beds that had been used to grow irises I now planted fritillaries, in place of crocuses I now grew alliums, and so forth.

The next spring brought one of the greatest catastrophes of my gardening life. I lost an enormous number of bulbs, including those that had never suffered from any disease. The reasons for this are very simple to explain. In nature, plants and their pathogens coexist, and each pathogen has its own pathogens. This is the basis of biological plant protection: there is a natural balance between all forms of life. But a gardener doing this or that in search of a better crop breaks this balance. The soil in my greenhouses was sterile, but the bulbs planted in it had not been sterilized. Nothing can eliminate all spores and bacteria. Fungicides don't make bulbs healthy; they only stop the development of disease and prevent the spread of pathogens. If among the bulbs planted in sterile soil there is one bulb affected by some pathogen, there will be nothing in the soil to stop it from spreading. This was the lesson that I learned: if you start using sterile soil, you must do the same thing every year. Since this was very expensive and the use of chemicals was increasingly limited by environmental protection rules, I decided to return to the old methods of soil replacement and crop rotation. Yes, it was very hard to change the soil in my greenhouses, but I was able to get my problems under control.

I learned how comfortable it is to grow bulbs in large polyethylene tunnels on a visit to the Gothenburg Botanical Garden. Returning home I decided to build something similar in my nursery. I had already constructed a small polyethylene tunnel where I had grown tomatoes and cucumbers. (Homegrown vegetables are always more flavorful than those bought in the supermarket.) But as my nursery grew I had less and less time for other hobbies, and the plastic tunnel had stood empty for years. I decided to use it for bulbs, mostly varieties that suffered from strong spring frosts. Again I made raised beds inside it and planted acquisitions from my last expeditions, including some of the earliest Juno irises. But my results were poor. During the sunny days of March, the temperature inside the tunnel rose to 27°C–30°C regardless of the open ends, while at night the temperature quickly dropped to –10°C or even lower. In fact at nighttime there was no great difference between the temperature outside and inside the tunnel.

The secret was the polyethylene covering. One sheet of polyethylene film is only a thin barrier between the open air and the interior of the tunnel. It helps a little but can't protect the plants if there is no additional overnight heating. The tunnels that I use now have a double covering, two layers of polyethylene with 10 cm of air between both. This layer of air isolates the heat. During the day it prevents temperatures from increasing too quickly, and at night it protects plants from excessive cooling.

The second secret was the size of the greenhouse. My first and smallest tunnel is 7.5 m wide, 4.5 m high, and 20 m long. On a sunny day a great amount of air is warmed up within it, as is the soil, and at night this accumulated heat slows the cooling of the air. When a double covering of polyethylene film is used, the temperature inside the tunnel drops very steadily and rarely falls below –10°C even on the coldest nights. My last and largest tunnel is 10 m wide, 50 m long, and 7 m high.

The size of the greenhouse is very important. A friend of mine in Lithuania has a small (2.5 m tall and wide) polyethylene greenhouse for his rarest bulbs. Having learned of the advantages of double covering, he did the same on his small greenhouse, but the foliage of all the bulbs inside it was killed by the first serious frost. This was due to the amount of air enclosed within the greenhouse. Larger amounts of air heat up more slowly after sunrise and cool much more gradually at night.

Growing bulbs under covering has given me a lot of advantages. First, it allows me much more freedom from the waywardness of weather. When it is raining I can work in my tunnels, returning to the field when it is sufficiently dry. It also lengthens my working season. Bulbs in greenhouses ripen earlier and can be harvested when bulbs growing outside are still green. The growing season is also lengthened, and the covering helps protect plants from frost and excessive moisture.

One of the greatest advantages of growing bulbs in greenhouses is that it allows for a much more certain seed crop. Summers in Latvia are quite wet, and seeds often rot long before ripening if the bulbs are grown outside. When I was in college and experimenting with crosses between different tulip species, to ensure a seed crop I built a roof of polyethylene film over each bed of mother plants. I wouldn't have gotten a single seed without it. Now there is a beehive in each of my tunnels, and bees do most of the work of pollination for me. I only pollinate bulbs that flower at a time when even in the greenhouse it is too cold for bees. Sometimes hybrids emerge, but I like these kinds of surprises.

We must always learn from our mistakes, and sometimes the costs of those lessons are very high. I made one such mistake when looking for a place to build my third greenhouse. There was a spot in the garden where nothing wanted to grow. Although it was situated near the top of a slope, even in dry weather the soil was cold and wet. Certainly there must be some natural underground waterlines, I thought. I added drainage to this part of the garden, but even that didn't help. So I decided to use this spot for my greenhouse.

On top of the existing soil I made a sand basement (or "sand pillow") 0.5–1.5 m thick to level the area and ensure excellent drainage. But I forgot about one thing, something I had learned more than thirty years before at my horticultural college: the orientation of the greenhouse to the celestial poles. In my climatic zone, the greenhouse's longest dimension had to run north to south, so that the side slopes would be exposed east and west. However, the spot I had selected for the greenhouse was just the opposite. Early in the morning when the greenhouse would need some warming, only the short end would be turned toward the sun, while at midday when the air warmed naturally, the longest side would be exposed to full sun. The temperature in the greenhouse would rise enormously, even with fully opened ends and windows. During the first season, when I used this greenhouse to plant some *Corydalis*, *Fritillaria*, and *Tulipa* species, the flowers and leaves quickly burned.

Fortunately, the investment wasn't a complete loss. Now I use it to grow plants that need extra heat in the summer. Most of my *Allium* species, especially those from Central Asia and the American deserts, feel at home in this "hothouse." The same goes for *Eremurus* and many Oncocyclus and Regelia irises and their hybrids. In fact these plants never before flowered so abundantly for me, and I never had such excellent seed crops.

Of course, each stick has two ends. Although my hothouse is good for irises and many alliums, it isn't very comfortable to work inside. On sunny days I start to work in it at four or five o'clock in morning and must finish within three or four hours because of the heat.

When the weather becomes very wet and cool, as sometimes happens here in August, I sometimes keep other bulbs in this greenhouse, especially alliums and tulips. My bulb shed was built in the shade under great oak trees, and sometimes the air inside it becomes too wet. When this happens, the bulbs can be saved in the hothouse, which even on cloudy days is sufficiently warm and dry.

Other "Secrets"

Every winter I have the same problem: how best to save my greenhouse plants from night frosts? I still use fans and heaters, which results in astronomical electric bills. One recent year I decided to search for alternatives. I wanted to try using sheets of rock wool, as I do with my seedlings. To save the foliage of bulbs that form leaves in autumn, I needed to build special frames topped with wire netting to prevent direct contact between the leaves and the covering. As with the seedlings, I needed to allow some freezing of the soil, otherwise the plants would continue growing and weak foliage would develop in the darkness below the covering. Conditions would also be excellent for the development of *Fusarium nivale*, another great trouble in greenhouses during dark days with temperatures slightly above zero.

February is one of the most difficult months in Latvia. There are many snowstorms, temperatures can be very low, and the sky is usually covered by clouds. But in the garden there is normally nothing to do. March, on the other hand, is a much busier month. There still may be hard frosts, with temperatures down to –20°C, but the days are sunny. Every morning in March I have to open all the doors and windows in my greenhouses to keep the temperature from getting too high, and then in the afternoon I close everything again. Soil moisture must be checked very carefully so as to prevent excessive drying out in the bright sun.

March marks the beginning of abundant flowering for greenhouse plants. It is an extremely busy time. I must check plant names using various local floras and plant descriptions, and find names for samples still grown only under collection numbers. This is not easy because in many cases to correctly identify a plant I must see its flowers, bulbs, and seeds. On one trip to Turkey we found a nice *Scilla* species near the snow line in full flower, but to determine the species name we needed to know the seed color. Fortunately, on a well-exposed spot some 100 m lower, we found a specimen with nearly ripe seeds, so I was able to conclude without any doubt that it was *S. ingridae*. In the garden this is not possible, so I make careful notes in my planting books. I also take digital pictures of all my plants. These things allow me to find requested information later, when a final decision is made about the plant's name.

Digital photography has brought me many advantages. Before this technology was available, I frequently had to go into the city to get my film developed, and then only after receiving my prints was it possible to see the results. Sometimes there were mistakes, and I would want to take a replacement photo, but of course by then the flowers were gone and I would have to wait until the next year. Now, using my digital camera, I can simply go back to my office, join the camera with my computer, and carefully check each image. If a photograph doesn't satisfy me, I immediately return to the garden and try again. In the winter, as I work on my garden notes, these photos also often help me determine a correct species name.

◈ 5
Fertilizing

EBRUARY IS THE TIME to purchase fertilizers. In my nursery I use three basic types, buying any additional special fertilizer only on the rare occasion that an analysis of my soil shows an absence of some element. Soil analysis is very important because garden soil is always changing. You give the soil manure and fertilizers, microorganisms decompose the humus to release elements, and water from snow and rain washes the elements away. For these reasons you can never know what exactly is in your soil. Many years ago I grew a lot of tulip varieties. During crop rotation I planted them where I had earlier grown daffodils. The tulips grew well and flowered nicely, but at bulb harvesting time I was shocked to find not one large bulb, only bulbs of the smallest size. Searching for a reason, I checked my books and had my soil analyzed by a laboratory. It turned out that the pH of my tulip field was only 5.5. While such an acid soil is not dangerous to daffodils, it will cause tulips to form small bulbs. A few years earlier I had applied lime to all of my fields, but the following years were rainy, and calcium is one of those elements that is quickly washed out of soil.

One of the most important fertilizers I use is ammonium nitrate. This may shock many readers, since it is so often stated in plant books that nothing is more dangerous to bulbs than nitrogen. What the authors of such books are forgetting, however, is that nitrogen is one of the basic elements of organic life. Without nitrogen there can be no protein. Nitrogen fertilizers may not be so important in places where winters are very mild and temperatures rarely fall below zero, but the opposite is true in my region, with its generally cold winters, long rainy autumns, and many snow breaks. Plants can absorb nitrogen only in the form of nitrates (with the exception of papilionaceous plants, which in symbiosis with special bacteria can use nitrogen from the atmosphere), but nitrates are very easily washed away.

The nitrogen in soil is usually conserved in the form of humus, and soil microorganisms decompose the humus to release the nitrogen in the form of nitrates. Soil microorganisms are active only when soil temperatures rise above 8°C, but in regions such as mine, bulbs start to grow when soil surfaces are quite cool or even frozen. In Latvia the autumn rains wash away all the nitrogen in the soil that exists in a form usable by the plants, and so in early spring when the plants most need nitrogen for the development of new leaves and to build up new bulbs, corms, and so forth, they find supplies lacking. In the bulbs' native habitats, where summers are hot, the soil microorganisms are active and liberate a certain amount of nitrogen. The climate is generally dry, too, so the nitrates are not washed away during autumn and winter. In this way the bulbs have plenty of nutrients when they most need them. Soil analyses made in early spring in Latvia, on the other hand, show no trace of nitrates. Therefore I make it my mission as a gardener to help the plants along. After all, I have brought them here from very different conditions.

Immediately after the snow melts, when it is only just possible to walk on the field without sticking in the mud, I make my first application of ammonium nitrate, an easily soluble fertilizer with a high nitrogen content. The total dose is 50–70 grams per square meter. This may seem high, but since my beds are mulched with a good layer of peat moss, the peat absorbs the greatest part of the fertilizer, slowly releasing it into the soil when it rains.

The second basic fertilizer I use every year in my nursery is a slow-release complex fertilizer with all the basic elements plus microelements. My favorite is Hydrocomplex from Norway, with 12-11-18 NPK and microelements. I use it twice a year—first in spring, two or three weeks after applying ammonium nitrate, and then in autumn. The spring dose is 50–70 grams per square meter, which I disperse over the surface of the soil between the rows of bulbs. The autumn dose is 30–50 grams per square meter, which I apply as I prepare the soil for planting.

It is not possible to give concrete recommendations for everyone. Fertilizing is a very important, very difficult task, and the dose that is needed depends on many factors. Even different spots within a single garden may have different requirements. The best solution is to have your soil analyzed in a laboratory, but this is expensive and not always available.

For this reason I also use an easily soluble, usually crystalline-based, complex fertilizer with all the basic elements and microelements. This is what is called feeding plants through their leaves. Every week of the growing season I spray my plants, both in the greenhouses and on the open field, with a weak solution, making sure the leaves become wet. The concentration is 0.2%, which means that in 10 liters of water, 20 grams of fertilizer are dissolved. Such a concentration will not damage the leaves and provides the bulbs with all the minerals they need. Such fertilizers are not cheap, but the amount needed is so small that you end up saving money compared with feeding in the traditional way through the roots; when you feed the roots, you can't know if the bulbs will accept the fertilizer or if the fertilizer will be washed out of the soil. Feeding a plant through its leaves can compensate for any shortcomings in the soil mix. I have seen amazing results since I started feeding my bulbs this way. I usually spray on a dry day early in the morning so that the leaves quickly dry out. To avoid spreading diseases, I also add fungicide to the fertilizer solution.

◈ 6
Watering

To GROW WELL, plants need an adequate supply of water. In early spring the soil is usually wet, but it soon dries out, sometimes too early. In Latvia, May is usually the driest month, and during this time additional watering is very important. I have at times lost much of my crop just from a shortage of water during this period of active growth. Small bulbs that must be planted shallowly are especially sensitive. The upper level of the soil dries out much more quickly, especially on south-facing slopes. I never water daffodils, and even though my soils are clay-based, so that they hold water well, on south-facing slopes my bulb crops are always less prolific than those on east- and north-facing slopes. I am never able to grow bulbs as large as those grown by the Dutch nurseries, where the water level in the soil during active growth is artificially raised so that the root tips are in water. Watering is especially important in greenhouses, where plants are protected from rain.

The general principle on the open field is that watering once a week with a good amount of water is far better than spraying a small amount each day. During watering the soil must become wet thoroughly. At my nursery the weekly dose is about 40 liters of water per square meter. Although it seems paradoxical, it is better to water during cloudy, somewhat rainy days than in dry, sunny weather. Plants are living organisms that feel the conditions of their environment. When it is sunny and dry outside, a shower of cold water is as much shocking to a plant as it would be for a human.

Watering must be done in the morning hours before the dew has dried, especially if you are using sprinklers. This timing makes the watering almost as natural as rain, and the leaves soon dry with the rising sun, thus preventing the spread of diseases. It is best to water directly on the soil between bulb rows (or in pots) without wetting the foliage. If you are watering plants in a greenhouse, it is preferable to switch fans on after watering. The air movement not only dries the foliage and soil surface, it also stimulates the evaporation of water by the plants. It increases the flow of water and nutrients in the vascular tissues of each plant and as a result increases the rate of photosynthesis. Ultimately it increases the crop.

Drip irrigation is the most advanced method of watering. The installation isn't cheap, but it soon pays off. Before I installed drip irrigation in my nursery, one worker was always occupied exclusively with watering, and it was only possible to water the plants growing in tunnels once a week. Now the watering is done almost automatically. I only change the flow from one greenhouse to another, and all the watering takes only one day, so I can water my greenhouses twice a week with minor use of manpower. The same is true for the open field.

In the past I never watered my crocuses adequately, and my crop suffered each May. With drip irrigation, this is no longer a problem. I also once had a lot of problems with a crop of spring colchicums from Turkey that I grew in my greenhouse. These plants have very sensitive root systems. In the wild they grow in areas with very wet springs. In my region, where spring is hot and sunny, the temperature in the greenhouse rose too high and the soil quickly dried out, but my old watering system allowed me to water the colchicums no more than once a week. As a result, the bulb crop was terrible. With drip irrigation I saved not only the salary I had paid a worker but also saved my bulb crop. The investment paid for itself in just one season.

◈ 7
Controlling Plant Health

C HECKING THE HEALTH of your plants is another important job for spring. If a bulb planted in the ground has not yet begun to grow, dig up the soil around it and check the bulb for signs of infection or other problems. In my experience the vast majority of ailing bulbs do not recover and eventually rot. Leaving them in the soil only raises the risk of aggravating the problem. Any infection is likely to contaminate the soil and reach neighboring bulbs, for example. The best solution after noticing unhealthy bulbs is to immediately remove and destroy them. I burn all such infected material in a fireplace.

Only by visually checking can you find bulbs infected with viruses. Most people can easily recognize a virus-infected tulip or daffodil. The striped tulip flowers are so prominent that even someone who is color-blind can find them. More careful checking will be needed for viruses determined by lighter or darker stripes on the foliage. This symptom is common in daffodils and, with few exceptions, is the main symptom of infection. Symptoms in other plants may be less obvious. No plant is safe from viral infection, but not all plants suffer seriously; some are able to coexist with a virus without any depression of growth or change in flower color. It is important to note, though, that such plants serve as a source of infection for other bulbs.

In recent years almost all the stocks of *Muscari* that I have bought at garden centers have been virus-infected. Many beautiful species and varieties that have been grown for decades in the Netherlands catch an infection that is then distributed by bulb to gardens elsewhere in the world. Since the infected plants haven't suffered seriously or brought commercial losses to their growers, there is no great interest in controlling the virus or even in destroying the infected stock. The longer I grow bulbs, the more I see that no genus is safe from virus. *Galanthus*, *Scilla*, *Iris*, *Muscari*, *Crocus*, *Gladiolus*, *Arisaema*, and many others—all are vulnerable. Some viruses affect only certain plants, while the most dangerous infect a wide spectrum of plants. Some plants are very susceptible and quickly destroyed by virus.

Unfortunately, an infected plant never regains its health; there is no medicine to treat it, and the only solution is to destroy and burn it. A long time ago some Latvian gardeners told me they had found a way to defeat infection. They took infected tulip bulbs, planted them in excellent conditions with richly fertilized soil, and the next spring there were no symptoms of virus infection on the flowers. Unfortunately, though, the virus didn't disappear. The following season the bulbs were planted back in normal, traditional growing conditions and all the flowers immediately developed stripes again. The same effect can be seen among humans. A person infected with TB bacilli remains healthy because the immune system keeps the infection under control; when conditions change, however, and the person's immune system is weakened, he or she becomes ill.

Again, the only way to save your collection is by destroying all infected plants. Fortunately, most viruses are not transferred through seeds, so if infection destroys an exclusive stock, try to collect the seeds and replace your stock in that way.

One recent autumn I found plants with striped leaves among my stock of *Sternbergia sicula*, which I had bought some years before from a famous Dutch company. I also found plants with yellow- or white-striped leaves among my Reticulata irises. Many expensive snowdrops (*Galanthus*) that I had imported from Britain had to be destroyed the first spring because of their yellow-striped leaves, and my entire stock of *Gladiolus imbricatus* had to be completely burned after suddenly developing striped flowers. (Fortunately this last species is very easy to replace from seed, and seedlings started to flower in the third season.) On one occasion I failed to discover a virus infection until wintertime, as I was watching a slide show of images I had taken the previous spring. I had only two bulbs of *Iris reticulata* var. *bakeriana* (syn. *I. bakeriana*), and both had striped flowers. In spring after the soil thawed, I immediately visited the bed where they were located and destroyed both of them. Juno irises are very susceptible, some suffering seriously while others coexist for years. Infected *I. willmottiana* becomes sterile and dies within a few years. At the same time, almost all plants of the bicolored form of *I. bucharica* grown in large nurseries are infected and yet grow quite well, sometimes providing seeds but flowering less abundantly than healthy plants.

In my early years, when I mostly grew cultivated forms, I had a great collection of Dutch-raised crocuses. Crocuses are also susceptible to viruses, but it is quite easy to spot infected plants, which makes it easy to clean the stock. The flowers of a virus-infected crocus do not open even in full sunshine, the petals look somewhat crumpled, and the petals of dark-colored varieties develop darker or lighter segments. Looking more carefully at the leaves of large-flowering Dutch crocuses (*Crocus* ×*cultorum* or *C. vernus*), I found that they had short yellow stripes parallel to the venation. I immediately thought of virus infection, but they all grew perfectly and flowered nicely from year to year. All new imports from the Netherlands had the same leaves. Then I collected seeds from those cultivars and grew my own hybrids. The first flowering brought me a great surprise: the flowers of my seedlings were much larger and more abundant than I had ever seen before on Dutch varieties, and their leaves were without yellow stripes. This confirmed my suspicion about the infection of Dutch stocks. I didn't separate my seedlings by color, but now in my garden I grow only my own hybrids of *C. ×cultorum*. Many viruses don't damage the host plant seriously, and the two learn to coexist; these are called latent or symptomless viruses.

Viruses also exist in the wild. I have seen a virus-infected plant of *Tulipa greigii* during my travels in Central Asia, small population of virus-infected *Iris vicaria* on the heights of Sina, and a few plants of *Bellevalia pycnantha* in Turkey with distinctly yellow-striped leaves. In nature the distribution of viruses is slow. The plants rarely grow in close contact, so infections are not transferred as easily as they are in the garden. In the harsh growing conditions of the wild, infected plants soon die.

Two principal agents distribute viruses. The first are natural agents: insects, mostly aphids, and some nematodes living in the soil. After sipping sap from an infected plant, an insect moves on to healthy plants, thereby transferring the virus. The second agent is the gardener himself, especially when he cuts flowers with a knife or scissors. The blade of the knife becomes contaminated when an unhealthy plant is cut, and then the virus is transferred to healthy plants. For this reason I never cut flowers; I only break the stem or, in the case of small bulbs, pluck the stem out of the bulb. Only with lilies, which are extremely susceptible to virus infection, will I sometimes cut the flowers with a sharp knife, but in such cases I always sterilize the knife after each cut.

It is possible to keep viruses under control only by strictly following the rules of hygiene and carefully controlling insect pests. It is very important to spray with insecticide as soon as infestation is seen. Bulbs can even be damaged by aphids in a bulb store, and I have noted them rarely on shoots of *Arum* species in storage. Dipping them in insecticide eliminates the problem. Growers in the Netherlands use prophylactic sprays with mineral oil.

When I moved my collections to my own place, I began by looking for a good spot to start a nursery. I selected a field that was exposed to wind from every direction and carefully cut all the wild shrubs that were growing on both sides of it. This is just the sort of site on which Dutch nurseries grow their tulips and daffodils. The wind blows away the aphids and so is quite helpful in the endless battle with viruses. It certainly benefited my own nursery. The percentage of plants destroyed each year went way down. Now I find aphids very rarely on weeds and sometimes on seedpods. I have almost forgotten what it is like to spray with insecticides, because I only have to do it once every few years.

Although viruses are very dangerous to plants, they aren't the only problem. Many diseases and pests like bulbous plants. Plants damaged by fungal disease can't be cured. A gardener can only stop the expansion of the disease or, preferably, prevent the infection from occurring in the first place. There are many fungicides available on the market, but the best option is always prophylaxis. If you provide good growing conditions and introduce optimal plant rotation schemes, you will have few problems.

Never trust a person who tries to tell you that a particular plant is problem-free and invulnerable to disease. I often read about such new miracle plants in books. They may seem invincible during their first year, but they eventually succumb to the same pathogens that affect other bulbs. Suddenly you find that the plants that looked so happy last year are starting to wilt or are covered with unpleasant spots.

In my nursery I use fungicides very rarely. There are only two diseases I try to control in my fields through more or less regularly spraying. The first is gray mold, caused by *Botrytis*, which mostly damages tulips and lilies. Gray mold thrives in moist weather, and very rarely does a season pass when I don't need to use my sprayer to control it. In Latvia, tulips are usually sprayed twice each season—at flowering time and seven to ten days later. I start spraying when I see the first small brown spots on the tulip leaves. Wild tulips are the most susceptible to *Botrytis*. Tulips stop growing early, so it is usually sufficient to apply one more spray; rarely is a third spray needed. Lilies are more difficult to preserve. Those we spray all summer with intervals of ten days starting when the stems are 30 cm tall. But again, it all depends on the weather conditions. During a dry summer the plants might need one or two sprays, but during a rainy summer, with morning fogs, spraying must be more frequent. Ideally a different fungicide should be used each time to prevent development of resistant forms.

The second disease I control with spraying is rust, which often affects alliums, whose leaves develop bright orange pustules of spores. One spray of fungicide is usually sufficient if you catch the very beginning of this disease. I use the systemic fungicide Tilt, produced especially for use against rust on various crops, mostly used for grain.

Bulbs are also attacked by fungi from such genera as *Rhizoctonia*, *Phytium*, *Phytophtora*, *Fusarium*, and *Alternaria*. If you decide to use fungicides, remember that these fungi are a heterogeneous group. A chemical that controls *Botrytis* will have no effect on *Fusarium* or *Phytium*. Chemicals allowed for use in different countries also vary and change from time to time, and those allowed for professional use are not always allowed for use in the home garden. Therefore I'll avoid giving too many of my own recommendations, except to repeat that nothing is better than prophylaxis.

Only a few diseases that have become a problem over the last few years must be mentioned, although in most cases I can't recommend how to defeat them entirely, only how to minimize the damage.

The first is bacterial rot. This is nothing new in the plant world: a lot of vegetables suffer from bacterial rots. In my experience it is only a serious problem for aroids. It sometimes affects stock of *Scilla*, *Muscari*, or *Chionodoxa*, but cleaning the bulbs, exposing them to the sun, and providing good ventilation all help keep the problem under control. With aroids, bacterial rot attacks the tubers. If you forget to regularly check a box of tubers you have harvested, you can lose an entire stock within a few weeks to an infection that began with just one tuber. Fortunately the rot emits a fetid smell, so your nose should let you know you have a problem. To an outsider it might look funny, but I regularly walk along the boxes of aroid tubers in my bulb shed with my nose stuck out in an attempt to catch the first symptoms of bacterial rot. It is not difficult to stop this rot. The bacteria that cause it need acid conditions, so after harvesting all of my aroid tubers I keep them in boxes with a thin layer of lime on the bottom and then powder them with lime on top. I also try to space the tubers so that they are not touching each another. If you do sense the smell of disease, feel each tuber with your fingers; if a tuber is soft, burn it immediately, and wash your hands before continuing your inspection. If you catch an infection early enough it is possible to save the tuber. Aroid tubers are good survivors. After you have cut off all damaged tissue, try saving whatever portion remains healthy. If there is a bud with a small piece of tuber, all you have to do is powder it with lime and hope that it survives. I did this with a rare *Eminium* species and it helped me save a very valuable plant.

Another disease I want to mention is called "fat leaves" in Britain, but I call it the "plague of anemones" because it seems to spread as quickly as the plague in Europe during the Middle Ages. It is a fungal disease caused by *Dumontinia tuberosa* (syn. *Sclerotinia tuberosa*, *Whetzelinia tuberosa*; Plate 6), which forms small brown mushrooms and is parasitic to our native wild windflowers *Anemone nemorosa* and *A. ranunculoides*. In the wild it isn't very widespread or dangerous, but in the garden it attacks all types of anemones and can kill large collections in one or two seasons. In Britain the first symptom of infection is, as its common name suggests, the development of large, fat leaves. In my own country I haven't noted any changes in leaf shape, but growth ends earlier for infected plants, and at harvesting time the rhizomes or tubers look very fat and large. My first contact with *Dumontinia tuberosa* occurred when I imported cultivated forms of *A. nemorosa* from the Netherlands. I well remember how I enjoyed seeing such thick rhizomes of *A. nemorosa* 'Allenii'. I could never have imagined that I had imported death for my anemones. When they didn't come up the next season, I discovered soft rhizomes underground overlaid with a white, cottony coating, and the next spring small brown mushrooms appeared on top of the soil. Next I lost my stock of *A. caucasica*. Again the first symptom of infection was enlarged tubers, which were the size of peas instead of the normal 3–5 mm in diameter. I burned all infected rhizomes and mushrooms. Then I dug out all the soil in which the infected anemones had grown, going half a meter deep and out, and buried it in a deep hole far from my garden. Still, the problem comes back almost every year. I don't know whether it travels in from surrounding forests, which every spring are covered with white and yellow carpets of windflowers, or whether it still exists in some of my stocks, just waiting for favorable conditions to explode again. Many times each season I carefully check all my plantings of various anemones. When I note some spot where the leaves start to die earlier than others, I dig them all out, carefully check each one, and replant those that look healthy in a new place.

Keeping harvested rhizomes in a bulb shed requires special care, too. I never keep all my eggs in one basket. I divide even small stocks into at least two polyethylene sacks with peat moss that is very slightly moist (better a little too dry than too wet— slightly overdried rhizomes can be easily returned to living shape by soaking them for twenty-four hours in water just before planting). Once a week I open each bag and visually check each rhizome, destroying any that look suspicious. Then I change the bag, add fresh peat moss, and repeat the whole process until planting time. When dividing rhizomes I always check the broken surface. If it is solid white, there are no problems, but if there are small brown spots in the center, it is best to destroy it or at least cut it off piece by piece until a pure white surface appears.

The third problem I want to mention is quite new. I call it the black disease of corydalis. It has nothing in common with the ink disease of Reticulata irises, which is very dangerous but can be easily kept under control by dipping the bulbs in the benzimidazole fungicides Benlate or Topsin M. In 1997, Magnus Lidén and Henrik Zetterlund wrote in their monograph *Corydalis*, "The tuberous species are too ephemeral to host any serious disease." Newcomers in the garden usually seem to grow without special problems or diseases their first few years, but as they become more widely cultivated, problems suddenly appear as if from nowhere. Dutch bulb growers first noted these problems with corydalis. Plants on some part of a healthy-looking bed suddenly start to wilt, and the wilting quickly increases. The underground stem looks black and crumbled, and the tubers develop black spots and rot. Exactly what fungus causes this disease isn't yet clear, and there is no cure. I found it on my fields, too, but managed to escape from any serious losses by regularly replanting tubers on fresh soil and carefully controlling plants in the field. If I see the first sign of disease, I remove the suspected tubers along with the healthy ones growing in proximity and the soil where they grew. By my observations plants grown in full sunshine are more susceptible. Before replanting I dip my corydalis in the standard fungicide mix used by Dutch bulb growers, and during planting I destroy all suspicious-looking tubers.

Rodents are a nightmare pest for all gardeners, especially bulb growers, as they can destroy very large collections. I remember receiving a call from a friend in the 1960s: "Jānis, you are a specialist in crocuses. I will pay your expenses, but please come and tell me what has happened to my collection." The previous autumn he had planted crocuses over some 200 square meters, hoping to have plenty to sell the next season, but in the spring only eight shoots came up. When I dug up the soil, I saw nice lines of beautiful white roots and not one corm. It isn't so significant in such situations just who did it, whether mice, vole, or rat—all of them seem to have incredible appetites. In my collection they completely destroyed a beautiful form of *Crocus biflorus* subsp. *adamii* that I had collected near Tbilisi, Georgia, and carefully multiplied over the years from some corms to more than two hundred specimens. Not one survived an attack by rodents. They also nearly destroyed my stock of *C. tauricus* from Crimea, and sometimes they even damage such poisonous plants as *Colchicum*. No bulbous plant is safe from rodents. *Corydalis* species don't usually suffer from attacks, but I remember a year in which there seemed to be a mania among rodents, who could find nothing tastier than corydalis tubers.

There are a couple of more or less effective agents in the endless battle with rodents. The natural way is to keep a cat or two (I have five), but unfortunately cats seem to prefer birds over mice. Owls and foxes also prey on rodents. I place owl houses on the large trees around the nursery. Foxes lives in the nearest forest, and fox hunting is strictly forbidden on my property. I don't like using killing traps to catch rodents, since they sometimes catch a small bird or even a cat's leg, but various poisons can be very effective. In my bulb fields on each 100 square meters is a short tube in which I regularly place granules of rodent poison. I do the same in my greenhouses. The tubes prevent birds from eating the poison.

❖ 8
Performing the Work of the Bee

ANOTHER TASK FOR FLOWERS, which emerge by the hundreds every day in spring, is pollination. Bees help me immensely with this job. When the corydalis start to flower, the greenhouse is full of a sweet honey scent—nearly every plant has its own bee, and a buzz fills the air. In most cases I allow bees to do the pollination regardless of the chance that some hybrids will appear among the seedlings. For *Corydalis* and *Allium* this is sufficient to guarantee a good seed crop, but there are plants for which additional hand-pollination is essential. Some species, for example, flower very early when the air is still cold and the bees are still sleeping in their hives.

The most early-flowering crocuses, such as *Crocus alatavicus* and *C. michelsonii*, sometimes bloom long before spring starts and must be hand-pollinated to receive at least some seeds. I do the same with most Junos irises; in some seasons bees visit their flowers very well, but in others very few seedpods appear without additional pollination. Many fritillaries are hand-pollinated, too. I generally use soft, thin paintbrushes, the kind used for watercolors. I have a large bunch of brushes that I stick in the soil with the brush pointed up near the plants from which I need seeds. I do this before flowering starts. This way I won't have to look at my notes later on searching for the species that must be pollinated. I try to pollinate flowers before midday, when the stigma is still slightly wet and ready to accept pollen. I usually try to do it twice with each flower, in the first and third day of flowering. It is really only possible in the first few days, before too many flowers have opened. With the brush I touch the open anthers containing visible pollen, then bring the pollen to the flower's stigma on the other bulb. Each species has its own brush, and the brush is used only for flowers of that species. When the species finishes flowering, I sterilize the brush in 70% alcohol, after which it can be used for another species.

Tweezers or small forceps can also be used in place of a brush. I use these tools for pollinating tulips, daffodils, fritillaries, and some other bulbs. The transfer of pollen can be done by removing a complete anther from the pollen parent and then gently rubbing the anther across the selected stigma. The best results will be achieved if the stigma looks glossy and slightly wet, ready to accept pollen. Sometimes I use saliva to moisten the stigma to assist adhesion of pollen. Some people advocate applying a sugar solution. If you want to be 100% certain that cross-pollination with another species does not occur, the pollinated flower must be covered with a muslin bag. For tulips I use a small cylinder made from thin aluminum foil (chocolate foil) wrapped around a pencil of adequate diameter, placing this on a pollinated stigma (Plate 7). Thereafter, no bee will be able to make any corrections to my crossing plans.

Pollen can also be kept for some time in the freezer. Anthers are then placed in small gelatin capsules, such as can be found at a drugstore, and kept in an exsiccator at 2°C–4°C along with something moisture-absorbent. I do this only when I want to raise hybrids between species that don't flower at the same time. Mostly I have used this method when bringing daffodil pollen from the United Kingdom to Latvia, where daffodils flower a month later. In my experience the results have been very good. I have kept pollen without any problems for up to two months, but according to the literature it can even be kept until the next flowering season.

Don't forget to place a label near the seed parent plant when making an intentional hybridization. Never rely on your memory: a lot of things you may think are too elementary to forget are eventually forgotten. It is common when marking a label to begin with the name of the mother plant, followed by an × and the name of the pollen parent.

The appearance of natural hybrids very much depends on the genera. Some make hybrids easily, while for others spontaneous hybridization occurs only rarely between a few species. Hybridization between *Corydalis* species happens quite often if the species are flowering at the same time. You may only be able to guess at the pollen parent by looking for similarities with other species, and as a lot of corydalis are self-sowing, sometimes both parents remain a mystery. My friend Arnis Seisums selected just such an interspecific hybrid with uncertain ancestry. It is named 'Foundling', and one of its parents is most likely *C. solida*. The flowers, held in long, dense racemes, are very big and purple, with a sharply contrasting pale pink spur. The color combination is reminiscent of *C. popovii*, although the possibility of this species hybridizing with *C. solida* seems almost incredible.

Another hybrid, 'New Contender', was selected by Arnis among open-pollinated seedlings of *Corydalis ruksansii*. It was spotted in its first year of flowering due to its markedly bigger flowers and some other similarities to *C. schanginii* subsp. *schanginii*. It shares the abundant flowering of *C. ruksansii* but inherited the size of its light pink flowers from *C. schanginii*.

In his classic monograph *The Crocus*, Brian Mathew mentions only a few cases in which hybridization between *Crocus* species happens, but hybrids from time to time appear among seedlings and can also be made intentionally. I grow two beautiful *Crocus* species, both collected in the wild. One is the bright sky blue *C. reticulatus* subsp. *reticulatus* from Bessarabia and the Caucasus. It is so beautiful—far better than samples of the same species growing in the western part of its area—that I'm always short on corms of it. To build up my stock, I regularly collect its seeds. I had no problems when I grew only the cultivated form of *C. angustifolius* (syn. *C. susianus*), which is sterile. Seedlings of *C. reticulatus* nicely reproduced the form of their parents. When I introduced fertile wild forms of *C. angustifolius* from Crimea, the situation changed. Both species flower at the same time and in my garden are usually planted a short distance from each other. Now, among the blue seedlings, plants began to appear that were closer in color to *C. angustifolius* but with the shape of *C. reticulatus*.

Recently among seedlings of *Crocus korolkowii* in my garden, a beautiful plant appeared with white flowers and a deep purple throat. Since it came from open-pollinated seeds, I couldn't guess at the pollen parent with certainty. It looks like *C. michelsonii* because it has a bluish throat, but the parent could also be the white-flowered *C. alatavicus*. All three of these species are the only crocus that flower here so early, so no other species could be involved. In a similar situation, among seedlings of a white form of *C. cvijicii*, a hybrid suddenly appeared clearly showing features of both *C. cvijicii* and the purple *C. veluchensis*.

I found other beautiful hybrids in my first garden on a spot where *Crocus heuffelianus* grew for years. In terms of flower size and abundance of flowering they most closely resembled a large-flowered Dutch spring crocus (*C. ×cultorum*), but in color and corm shape looked more like *C. heuffelianus*. Three beautiful but different plants growing side by side were selected; all are natural crosses between *C. heuffelianus* and *C. ×cultorum*. I most enjoy 'National Park', with large, rounded, light purple flowers with a dark purple base, a longitudinal stripe and blotch on the upper part of the petals outside, and a white tip. 'Brian Duncan' and 'Wildlife' are both of equal beauty, although not so deeply colored. Another nice hybrid appeared among seedlings of *C. tommasinianus*. It is certainly a cross between *C. tommasinianus* and some large Dutch spring crocus variety, with silvery-shaded outer petals, beautifully contrasting purple inner petals, and a flower size intermediate between both parents. I named it 'Yalta', having received the seeds from the Nikitsky Botanical Garden in Yalta (Crimea).

Among open-pollinated seedlings of *Crocus chrysanthus* cultivars appeared one of my most exclusive seedlings—the first crocus with double flowers. It is clearly related to *C. chrysanthus* as evidenced by its color, which is a deep, bright yellow throughout. A great proportion of the flowers coming up from large corms have double or even triple the number of petals. Its only fault is that its corms must be a good size, otherwise the flowers will develop only the normal number of petals. I named it 'Goldmine', not only for its color but also for the financial return it gave me.

I also want to mention alliums, which have a reputation as plants that easily make hybrids between species. This is true, but they only do so when closely related species are involved. In such cases the hybrids are very similar to the parents, and very rarely does anything worth keeping appear. Hybrids do occasionally occur between species that are not close relatives, however, and some of these are real garden gems. One such excellent hybrid appeared at the breeding station of ornamental plants at Heřmanův Městec, Czech Republic. The breeders there mostly worked with lilies, tulips, gladiolus, and dahlias, but also grew other bulbous plants, including *Allium stipitatum* and *A. karataviense*. The first allium is a tall drumstick type with a flower stem more than 1 m high, while the other is a typical rockery plant with a dwarf habit. Both are quite lazy about reproducing vegetatively, so they were multiplied from seed. On one occasion a marvelous medium-sized allium appeared among the seedlings. It had a stem about 50 cm long, large umbels of light pinkish flowers, and reproduced well vegetatively. Named 'Globus', it is now one of the most popular varieties.

Impressive hybrids with great garden value are not common, but they appear from time to time in every collection where a great number of *Allium* species are grown together and where bees can fly freely. (Bees very much like the nectar from alliums, although it produces honey of a very dark, almost black color.) A nice hybrid between two Turkish species, *A. akaka* and *A. lycaonicum*, appeared in Arnis Seisums's garden. In foliage it is reminiscent of *A. akaka*, the umbel and flowers are somewhat intermediate, and from *A. lycaonicum* it inherited the delicate smell of carnations. It was named 'Turkish Delight'. A hybrid between the tall *A. stipitatum* and dwarf *A. nevskianum* appeared in my Lithuanian friend Augis Dambrauskas's garden, who named it *A. ×stipinewa*. My hybrid between *A. nevskianum* and *A. sarawschanicum* is similar. In another Lithuanian garden, Leonid Bondarenko selected a hybrid between *A. protensum* and *A. nevskianum*, named 'Gimli'. It has a huge umbel like *A. protensum* but is a good grower outdoors and increases well vegetatively.

Sometimes free crossing between species is a very undesirable feature. One of the most beautiful scillas is *Scilla rosenii*. Its flowers are light blue with reflexed petals, somewhat resembling the flowers of cyclamens. It does not increase very quickly by splitting the bulbs, so it is better to build up stock from seed. Seedlings start to flower in the third year, but unfortunately the species hybridizes easily with *S. siberica* and its allies. The hybrid I found was very beautiful, and I even gave it a name, *S. ×sibrose*, but it is no longer *S. rosenii*. So if you want to propagate your stock of *S. rosenii* from seed, it must be planted a good distance from other scillas.

The next level up is intentional hybridization. I will not touch here on crosses made between cultivars to make new varieties but will keep my attention on crosses between species. A hybrid of excellent beauty was raised in the Gothenburg Botanical Garden when Henrik Zetterlund crossed deep purple *Crocus pelistericus* with bright orange *C. scardicus*. This beautiful plant later received a special name: *C. ×gothenburgensis*. The flowers of first-generation (F_1) seedlings were rainbow-like in their color combinations, but more hybrids of incredible beauty appeared when those hybrids were intercrossed. My favorite, 'Henrik', named for its raiser, is blue at the base and top with a wide, white midzone.

Raising hybrids is one of the most intriguing undertakings in a gardener's life. You can never foresee the final results, which will come only after years. It is not easy to wait but is a worthwhile venture nonetheless, as E. A. Bowles wrote many years ago in *My Garden in Spring*:

> It has certainly the great disadvantage of a wait of at least three years for the first flowering, but years pass only too swiftly in a garden, and once that period is over every succeeding season brings fresh babes to flowering strength, and I know no garden joy equal to a visit on a sunny morning to the Crocus beds when seedlings are in full flowering.

◈ 9
The Seed Crop

THE FIRST CROP in every flower garden is, of course, flowers. The blooming period is a very busy and important time, during which all names must be checked and stocks must be cleaned of atypical, virus-infected, or misplaced plants. I prefer to dig out misplaced plants rather than marking them with a label or rope. Labels can always be lost, and at harvesting time you may suddenly be unable to determine exactly which bulb was marked with which stick (was it the one on the right side or the one on the left?), especially if the bulbs are planted densely. I usually destroy all bulbs dug out at flowering time, but if they are valuable it is possible to replant them in a separate bed, preferably in a shaded position. Replanting must be done without delay, and the bulbs must be dug with care to prevent root damage. In this way you can hope that losses will be minimal.

At flowering time I take hundreds of photos to preserve all of my beauties to enjoy with friends during winter. Photographs also provide important evidence that can be used to identify plants later on.

With few exceptions, I never liked cutting flowers, preferring instead to see them flowering on the field or in the greenhouse, so I personally can't name flowers as my first crop. For me the first crop is the seeds. Seed collecting starts in May and the first seeds in my nursery are usually from corydalis.

Collecting corydalis seeds is very tricky. In the morning you walk along your corydalis beds and all the seedpods are closed; a few hours later you walk along the same beds and find the seeds already dispersed. In addition, the seeds do not ripen at the same time even on the same spike. This is why I collect them when I see the lower capsules starting to split. With scissors I carefully cut off all the spikes (usually the upper flowers are only just starting to bloom) and put them in a box. I place this box in shade, where it stays for a week. Then I rub the dry stems between my palms and through a sieve separate the seeds from the remains of the stems. After that, they must be sown immediately.

Many years ago my corydalis beds seriously suffered from attacks by water rats. In the morning I enjoyed a nice clump of *Corydalis paczoskii* in full bloom, but by the afternoon the stems had dried away. When I checked to see what had happened, I found below the stems a large hole where all the tubers had been. I put the stems in a cardboard box, and after two weeks, very small, light brown, seed-like particles had developed. I sowed them without any hope, and to my great surprise the next spring they germinated. My stock of *C. paczoskii* was saved!

Erythronium seeds start to ripen at the same time or a little later than corydalis.

Erythronium seeds, at least those of the Eurasian species, dislike staying out of the soil too long. American *Erythronium* species can remain viable longer; I get seedlings from seeds said to have been collected a year or even two years earlier. I collect *Erythronium* seeds when the seedpods become yellow or start to split and keep them in small cardboard boxes mixed with slightly moist peat moss until all seeds of some species have been collected. Then I sow them immediately.

Seeds of corydalis, erythroniums, and some other bulbs are equipped with white, fleshy appendages known as elaiosomes. These appendages are rich in fat or protein and are highly esteemed by ants. Henrik Zetterlund once observed an ant carrying a seed of *Corydalis intermedia* some 20 m. Luckily, in my own nursery the ants haven't yet discovered this source of food.

Seeds of snowdrops ripen around the same time, and somewhat later those of *Leucojum*. After this point I have a short break from seed collecting, but then I spend the end of May and first half of June collecting *Crocus* seeds. The seedpods are hidden underground, and only at the end of vegetation do the scapes elongate and bring the seedpods out of the soil. It is best to pick them before they split. By gently pinching the seedpod you can determine when the seeds inside are hard enough to gather. Some of the seedpods remain underground and will only be found later on when you are harvesting the crocus corms. For a few species, such as *C. pelistericus* and *C. scardicus*, the scapes grow up to 20 cm high and the seeds ripen much later in the season (in Latvia not until the end of July or even later).

Tulip bulbs are ready for harvesting a month or more before the seeds ripen. This means that the plants with seed capsules must be left on the field long after the other bulbs have been harvested. Tulip seedpods are very susceptible to *Botrytis* infection, and in my climatic conditions they often rot before ripening. To guarantee a tulip seed crop, grow them in a greenhouse or covered with some kind of temporary roof to protect them from rain. It is much less work to plan next year's seed crop before planting any bulbs. Try planting all the mother bulbs together on a separate bed where they can be covered by a single roof.

Fritillaria seeds are less tricky than tulip seeds but are still very susceptible to rot; it is best to plant them in a greenhouse if you want to ensure a seed crop. Only our woodland *F. meleagris* and some other woodland species typically don't suffer from fungal infection. With fritillaries it all depends on whether the summer is dry or wet.

Allium, *Muscari*, and their allies give me only minimal trouble. You can collect flower heads containing *Allium* seeds before the seedpods split. They will open in boxes, and the seedpods can also open on the field; with a little attention you can collect them without any significant loss of seeds. *Muscari*, *Leopoldia*, and *Bellevalia* are similar to *Allium*, but their seeds fall more easily from dry, opened capsules so more care is needed.

Seeds of trilliums, aroids, and some other plants are the last in the garden to ripen. Trillium seeds are best collected before they are fully ripe, optimally just before they start to turn yellowish in the seedpod. If the seeds are sown immediately, you can hope for germination the first spring. I usually keep the seeds of *Symplocarpus* and *Lysichiton* in a small bowl of water for a week or two before sowing; this helps them germinate better.

Seeds of *Arum* and *Arisaema* are usually hidden within bright red berries that contain a germination inhibitor. For this reason the berry flesh must be cleaned off as soon as possible after harvesting to ensure a good germination rate the first season. You can clean them using your fingers, but the pulp may be very rich in calcium oxalate crystals. Unless gloves are worn while cleaning the seeds, the tingling sensation caused by the crystals can persist for a few days. (Not all species are as aggressive, but my wife, Guna, no longer wants to help me with this job.) The best way to avoid contact is by using a kitchen mixer. Put the berries in the mixer with a good amount of water, and blend. When the seeds are released from the berries, wash them underwater and dry them on tissue paper. Sometimes early autumn frost kills the foliage of *Arisaema* before the seeds are ripe. This isn't dangerous. Collect the green fruiting spikes and keep them in a cardboard box until they become orange or red. Then clean the seeds.

I keep the seeds that I have collected in my office. In the warm, dry air the seedpods dry, the seeds finish ripening, and I am able to clean the seeds from the seed capsules. With *Allium*, *Crocus*, and *Muscari*, I usually rub the seedpods between my palms and then clean the seeds using sieves. I then blow air over the box so that any rubbish left is lifted off the seeds. This won't work, of course, with lighter seeds that are naturally distributed by wind. I clean the seeds of *Fritillaria*, *Tulipa*, and *Lilium* carefully, opening each valve of the seedpod so that the seeds fall out by themselves.

Collecting the seeds of *Anemone* is more difficult. You must wait for the moment when the seed capsules open and then carefully collect the woolly seeds before they are blown away. The seedpods of *Alstroemeria* are very explosive and must be collected before they shoot their seeds. Every year in my greenhouse, *Alstroemeria pygmaea* plants appear on passes near the raised beds where they were growing the year before.

If you are collecting seeds in the wild, you must be careful not to inadvertently collect pests in the process. Once in Central Asia we filled a large paper bag with *Eremurus lactiflorus* seedpods. We immediately proceeded to clean them and found that in about 5 liters of seedpods only a few contained seeds, while all the others contained only a white worm. We made sure from then on to always check each seedpod's surface for a dark spot the size of a needle's head; this is the place where the eggs of the pest have been laid. When such a spot is found, there is almost always a small maggot inside.

Each genus, even each species, has its own special secrets when it comes to the seeds. It is not possible to explain all of these secrets here, though I have tried to describe the most common situations. Only personal experience can expose you to the great variability of seed dispersal, collection, and germination. For more information, see also "Growing from Seed."

◈ 10
The Bulb Crop

IT IS BEST TO REPLANT and divide bulbs during their period of summer dormancy. I can't understand how the idea developed that snowdrops are best replanted at flowering time. The concept even has a special name: "planting in the green." It is probably left over from the years in which millions of *Galanthus* bulbs were taken from the wild and exported to Europe. They arrived badly desiccated and did quite poorly in the garden. To compensate for the problem, gardeners carefully harvested their snowdrop bulbs at flowering time and immediately divided and replanted them in a new place—with far better results. Buying a plant that was in flower also allowed gardeners to check the plant's identity. I harvest snowdrops only after the leaves are completely desiccated, then immediately replant them in a new bed. Surplus bulbs are kept in polyethylene bags mixed with slightly moist peat moss.

Before harvesting your bulbs, begin by looking over your planting schemes and checking all the labels. Are the labels in place? Do they accurately reflect any taxonomical changes? Can you read what is written on them? All damaged or misplaced labels must be repaired before you begin harvesting your bulbs. In my practice I always use two labels for each stock. When I harvest bulbs, I put the first label at the bottom of the box beneath the bulbs. There the label will be safe; it is covered by the bulbs and cannot be removed. I put the second label inside the box on top of the bulbs. This label is easy to see when I'm looking for a plant and prevents me from having to rifle through all the bulbs. It isn't as safe, however. It can be blown away by a strong wind (I usually place it halfway between the bulbs for this reason) and is especially in danger from birds such as tits. As autumn approaches, flies looking for a place to overwinter often choose to hide in my bulb boxes. Tits in search of the flies throw out not only the bulbs but also the large labels lying on top. In recent years tits have done greater damage to my stocks than even rodents. Most of my stocks marked "unknown" are the result of their activity. Using a two-label system has helped solve the problem.

It is not easy to decide what type of label is best. Each gardener has his or her own preferences. I have tried everything from wooden sticks to aluminum and plastic labels. I stopped searching when I started using plastic labels. These are light, inexpensive, and easy to write on with a graphite pencil or special marker. Their greatest fault is their tendency to become brittle when exposed to sun, although when inserted in soil they can survive for many years. The durability depends on the manufacturer. The labels I use are some twenty years old, but some labels become brittle after one or two seasons. Aluminum or anodized steel labels are permanent but expensive, and as my collection regularly changes, I have found them uneconomical. Now instead of pencil or marker I use special plastic self-adhesive film on which I print text using my laser printer. This allows me to put a lot of information on a small space. I include not only the name of the plant but also its date of origin and other important information.

On the open field I use a combination of wooden sticks and plastic labels. I use the sticks to separate the stocks, which helps me visualize where the stocks change, and push the plastic labels in the soil right by the wooden stick, since they won't be visible otherwise. Inserting the plastic labels into the soil helps protect against birds—crows and jackdaws like bright objects and have often pushed the colored plastic labels out of my soil. Once, years ago, a jackdaw that fell out of a nest near our home was taken in by my children and lived in my garden for a time. One of its hobbies was to sit near me on a bulb bed and carefully watch what I was doing there. Unfortunately, its interest in gardening was limited to removing labels, in some cases even digging them out from deep within the soil using its beak.

In my nursery the first harvested bulbs are always the corms of crocuses. Normally we harvest them when the leaves become a definite yellow and die; at this stage the bulbs are mature and there will be less trouble keeping them in the bulb shed until the beginning of the planting season. I have at times harvested crocuses a little earlier, when the leaves were almost yellow but still a little green at the base. This made it easier to collect all the corms in the soil, but it also raised the risk of the corms drying out during their stay in the bulb shed. This is especially true for annulate crocuses; early harvesting raises the proportion of corms that calcify, becoming hard and broken, like a piece of chalk. Usually all crocuses here are harvested in June.

Crocuses can be divided into three groups. In the first group are the species from arid growing conditions, such as the Central Asian *Crocus alatavicus*, *C. michelsonii*, and *C. korolkowii*. These plants like hot, dry summers and if left in wet soil can suffer from the excessive moisture. I harvest these species every year if I grow them on the open field. In the second group are the species from places where summers are not so hot and where rain occasionally falls during the period of summer rest. This includes most of the annulate species, such as *C. chrysanthus*, *C. biflorus*, and many species from Greece. These species don't require annual lifting. They can stay in the soil for two or more years or be harvested every season, but they prefer cooler conditions in the bulb shed. To the third group belong the species that come from places where the soil never becomes very dry, such as forests and high alpine meadows. They dislike being out of the soil very long and either prefer growing without replanting or require that replanting take place as soon as possible. These species suffer from drying out when kept in the bulb shed, so their corms must be kept in polyethylene bags mixed with slightly moist peat moss. Good examples include *C. banaticus*, *C. heuffelianus*, and *C. vallicola*.

Nothing in nature is dogmatic, so we can never put sharp borders between such groups. *Crocus korolkowii* from the first group can remain on open beds without replanting and usually doesn't suffer from it. *Crocus heuffelianus* from the third group can be kept out of polyethylene bags, too.

There are more tricky species among crocuses. Some species are never really without roots because the young roots start to grow long before the old ones die. This is one of the reasons why *Crocus scharojanii* from the high mountain meadows of the Caucasus is so difficult in cultivation. There really is no optimal time for harvesting and replanting. It always has roots, and its orange-yellow late summer flowers start to come out before the leaves of the previous growing season die. This growth habit is also seen in two species from southern Serbia and Montenegro, and northern Greece: bright yellow *C. scardicus* and deep purple *C. pelistericus*. In nature they grow on the banks of mountain streams, and flowers often appear through the water. In cultivation they keep their foliage until autumn. I grow both species in large pots and during summer place them in shallow trays of water so that the soil is always wet. For some years I also grew *C. pelistericus* on open beds, but I can't say that it was happy. My *C. scardicus* died within two years. Hybrids between both are less susceptible.

There is another splendid crocus with the same habit that grows perfectly outside, even increasing well, although it rarely appears in bulb catalogs. It is *Crocus veluchensis* from Bulgaria, Albania, Serbia and Montenegro, and northern Greece. It is never without roots, and new roots start to form before the leaves have died. The corms are best harvested just before the new roots start to form, even though the leaves are still green. I cut the leaves and take out the seedpods; the seedpods are not yet fully ripe but will finish ripening quite well in a box. The divided corms are immediately placed in polyethylene bags with slightly moist peat moss. I dispatch the bulbs to my customers early, usually during the first half of August. At that time short new roots of *C. veluchensis* are formed in the polyethylene bag, but they don't suffer if the corms are immediately moved to another bag (for shipment to the customer) with a moist medium, and if the customer plants them immediately.

Some fritillaries have the same tricky habit. Central Asian *Fritillaria olgae* is the most difficult when it comes to replanting, and the different forms of true *F. verticillata* are similar, although less difficult. I always try to get seeds from these species, which normally grow in my area on outside beds, but if I wait until the seeds ripen on *F. olgae*, there will be long new roots formed in the soil. Fritillaries generally dislike having their new roots damaged and broken, so *F. olgae* is one of those bulbs that must be harvested before the leaves turn yellow. Only personal experience will show you the best time for digging out this species in your own climatic conditions. It is possible to induce early rooting by providing moist soil and temperatures that are cool compared with the plant's native habitat. Bulbs that are dug out at the optimal time can normally be kept dry in open boxes in the bulb shed until autumn; they must be replanted before roots start to develop or while the roots are still too short to be broken.

The optimal time for harvesting tulip bulbs is when their leaves are still half-green, but this is for a different reason. Flower initiation in tulip bulbs occurs during summer dormancy, when they need warm, dry conditions. Just such conditions can be provided in a bulb shed. Tulips generally increase well vegetatively, but they are also very susceptible to *Botrytis*. If they are left in the ground for another season, the next spring you will have three or four stems instead of one, and the plantings will be over-crowded and more susceptible to infection. Harvesting tulip bulbs before their leaves dry out completely provides nice bulbs with good, healthy brown skin. On bulbs that remain in the soil too long, the skin darkens, splits, and becomes brittle; the soft white surface of the outer bulb scale is susceptible to mechanical damage during the harvesting, cleaning, sorting, and packing of the bulbs, and the bulbs lose market value. So the tulip bulb harvesting season is very short and sharply defined.

I must especially mention alliums. Although most of the species grown in my collection come from arid conditions, most can be grown in an open field, but they are very susceptible to wet weather. Generally just the bulbs start to rot. I find that the bulbs must be harvested very early, optimally when the last flowers in the flower head start to wilt. The leaves of most *Allium* species start to desiccate before the plant begins to flower and are usually dry at the end of flowering or shortly thereafter. Early harvesting doesn't have a great influence on the bulb crop's weight, but losses from basal plate rot will be marginal. It will be a little bit early for the seeds, but they ripen well on cut umbels.

Almost all bulbs, excluding the few just mentioned, can be harvested at any time during their period of rest, when the old leaves have died. You must only check that new roots haven't yet started to grow, at which point it will be too late. Shade plants such as woodland *Corydalis* and *Erythronium* are more difficult. If the summer is wet, rooting can start very early, in which case it will be best not to wait too long before harvesting the bulbs. It is possible to replant them when the new roots are still short, but this must be done quickly to prevent them from drying out. Such bulbs are no more useful for dispatching; in any case, they do not make a more top-quality product. In cold summers they sometimes start to make roots in the plastic bags in the bulb shed before you have replanted them. This isn't very dangerous if you plant them without exposing them for long to the open air and especially the sun.

Generally all bulbs can be left in the ground without harvesting for two years, sometimes even longer. There are a few exceptions to this, including *Tulipa*, some *Arisaema*, which are not sufficiently hardy in my climate, most Juno and Reticulata irises, and other bulbous plants that need a dry summer rest. I find that fritillaries produce their best flowers and bulb crop after two growing seasons; if left for the third year the results are poor. Most of my crocuses make their best flowers the second spring after replanting, but this is because I usually replant them too late. Crocuses are generally very good increasers; in the third year the clumps get so overcrowded that the bulb crop includes only corms of small sizes.

Some bulbs grow so well in my region that they start self-sowing. *Crocus*, *Muscari*, *Puschkinia*, *Chionodoxa*, *Scilla*, *Corydalis*, and many others fit into this category. If you leave them in the soil for a longer period, you can never be sure whether the bulb you are harvesting was derived from the planted bulb or is self-sown. In the case of species this isn't a great problem, but for cultivated, vegetatively propagated stocks it raises the possibility of original stock mixing with different seedlings.

I like to compare the harvesting of seedlings from an open bed with archeological digs. I lie flat on the bed and slowly, lifting up one layer of soil after another with my finger, search for tiny bulbs. Usually there are no great problems when it comes to collecting seedlings of *Corydalis*, *Allium*, and *Fritillaria*. They are generally yellow or white, contrasting well with the dark soil, and are placed approximately where the seeds were sown, only slightly deeper. It is much more difficult to collect bulbs with dark skin and that form so-called starch roots (or, more correctly, contractile roots), which pull the new bulb not only deeper into the soil but also to the side of the original location. This is very characteristic of *Scilla*, *Chionodoxa*, and some *Muscari*. I find *Erythronium* seedlings the most difficult to harvest. The young bulbs are very thin, brittle, and as much as 7–8 cm long. One imprudent touch made in haste and the seedling will be broken. I open the seedling row from the side at a depth of about 15 cm, and then they open—long, white beauties reminiscent of icicles hanging off the edge of a roof. With the knife's end slightly touching the soil on the side of the bulb, I cut it free. It happily falls into my hands and is placed in a pot with peat moss.

This is a pleasant, joyful job if the seeds germinate well and the bulbs develop to good size. Although they are generally still too small for flowering the next spring, I enjoy their future flowers in my mind. It is tedious work, however, if the seeds don't germinate and you are left wondering what you may have done wrong. The seeds may have been bad, winter may have been too hard, or the species may do better in a box kept in a greenhouse over winter. You run the soil through a sieve over and over hoping to find at least one seedling. To minimize such a tedious job, in spring I usually note how many seedlings have come up—many, a moderate amount, or only a few. If only a few come up, I try to count precisely how many there are and then mark their location with small sticks or matches. This saves me from superfluous searching. Normally over the course of a day I can collect all the seedlings from a bed that is 10 m long by 0.7 m wide.

I usually replant large autumn-flowering colchicums after only two seasons. In the first autumn (in the year of planting) they never normally flower because it isn't possible to plant them at a good time; most of them start to form etiolated white flowers in their boxes and even start to flower there. Consequently you can't get a correct impression about the variety. Only in the second autumn do they make normal flowers during their typical flowering time, at which point you can make sure they are correctly named and that there isn't some misplaced plant in the stocks. However, by then it is much too late for harvesting. So only after two growing seasons, when you harvest the bulbs in the summer before their third flowering, is it possible to guarantee that the bulbs you are selling are in fact what you think they are.

The last bulbs to harvest in my nursery are arisaemas, which in recent years have become very popular with gardeners. In nature they grow in large areas and in various growing conditions. Many are hardy, some are half-hardy, and many more are tender. In some winters I have lost even species thought to be very hardy. It is not easy to decide what to do with them in autumn, whether to harvest and keep the bulbs in a cool cellar or frost-free garage or to leave them in the soil for the next season. The biggest problem is that you can't predict which species will survive the coming winter in the garden and which will not. I once lost my entire stock of *Arisaema amurense*, which has a reputation as a very hardy species, while during the same winter the more tender *A. fargesii* survived without any problems. Regardless, I prefer to leave them in the garden over winter covered with a good layer of peat moss or dry leaves.

Some species of *Arisaema* start to grow very early and flower early in spring. Despite this early vernalization, new roots are only formed in spring. It is best to leave these arisaemas in the soil because in spring it is very easy to delay the planting time. Many species start growing only very late in the season. You can dig these out after night frosts have killed the leaves in autumn, then clean and dry the tubers in a warm room and overwinter them in boxes. Wrapping each individually in newspaper will protect the plants from frost and from contact with other tubers in case any of them catch bacterial rot. In Latvia arisaemas can be planted in May. The most important thing is to avoid exposing the tubers to heat too early, otherwise they will start coming out before the last night frosts end. I usually leave them in the garden and let nature select which species is for me and which is not. I plant them very deep, at least 30 cm down, and cover them with a good layer of peat moss. They usually come out of the soil at the very end of June, sometimes the first week of July or even later. Almost every year in the second half of June I lose my patience and start digging up the soil in search of shoots, only to find the tubers still sleeping.

With very few exceptions, harvested bulbs can't be exposed to direct sunlight. Tulip bulbs can be baked by the sun in less than half an hour. Even bulbs growing in the wild in very hot conditions suffer from direct exposure. When I am harvesting bulbs on the field or in the greenhouse, I always shade the box of bulbs with an empty box before bringing it to the bulb shed. Daffodils are the exception, as well as some bulbs that can suffer from bacterial rots. Sometimes I deliberately expose hyacinth, scilla, and muscari bulbs to the sun, but I do this after the bulbs are dried in the traditional way in shade. The sun warms the bulbs and kills any bacteria, and the layers of dry scales save the inner scales from baking.

I prefer to clean bulbs from their old, dry, outermost scales, and remove any remnants of old bulbs, at harvesting time, except when it comes to crocuses. With crocuses I have found that taking the old corm away from the new corm's base leads to a much greater proportion of calcified bulbs at replanting time. I only clean crocus corms just before preparing to send them to customers and before replanting them. Removing the old scales before the bulbs have dried can be difficult, but it is an important task, since diseases sometimes hide between scales. Cleaning the bulbs allows me to find the first signs of any health problems.

Immediately after harvesting and an initial cleaning, I wash all my bulbs in flowing water. This removes all remnants of soil, which is essential for any bulbs bound for exportation. The bulbs remain clean, as the old scales are now gone, and quickly dry out in the boxes. If necessary, immediately after washing the bulbs I place them in trays with a netted bottom and treat them with fungicides. At one time I treated all bulbs with fungicides, but now I harvest so many stocks every season that I select only those likely to experience problems. After they are washed and treated, the bulbs are placed in boxes and dried under flowing air provided by fans.

During their rest, my bulbs are kept in three bulb sheds, although only two were built for keeping bulbs after harvesting. The first shed was built in the shade beneath large oak trees beside a large pool. It is perfect for bulbs in that it is never too hot, but in the autumn when nights become misty, the air inside becomes quite wet and bulbs such as tulips and alliums suffer from gray mold (*Botrytis*). For vulnerable bulbs I built another shed in a sunny spot. Now the bulbs are first dried in the warm shed, and then those that need to be kept cool—*Corydalis*, *Erythronium*, and *Narcissus*, for example—are moved to the cool shed. The difference in temperature between the sheds isn't large but is significant nonetheless. The walls of the sheds were designed to provide sufficient space for air circulation, so that wind is able to blow through. The third shed is a polyethylene greenhouse where I keep bulbs that need heat during their rest to initiate flowering; I store bulbs here before replanting them or when outdoor temperatures fall too low.

◈ 11
Planting Bulbs in Autumn

AGAIN I RETURN to an essential question: when does the new season start for a bulb grower? I would reply that it starts in autumn, when we begin replanting our bulbs. In autumn bulbs obtain a new home, start rooting, sometimes even hurry to show us their first flowers, then make it through winter for us to enjoy over the next calendar year.

Before planting begins, you must select a site and prepare the soil there. This is a very important decision, since the site often decides the end results. For many years I grew bulbs of an unknown *Lycoris* species; I couldn't even remember from whom I had received it. It grew for decades but without flowering. One year as I was moving things around in my garden I planted these bulbs in an area of grass about a meter from the south-facing solid stone wall of my house. Then I forgot about it. One season its leaves were accidentally cut by a lawnmower, and then suddenly one day in August out came its marvelous flowers. Now it flowers almost every season. I have planted some of the bulbs in my greenhouse, and they make the loveliest flowers in early autumn.

Selecting an ideal site is especially important when growing rare plants from far-away countries. Early-emerging *Arum* and *Arisaema* species often suffer from late frosts in my region. They do best in a spot shaded the first half of the day—the shade saves the frozen leaves from sunlight by allowing them to slowly defrost. Many plants reputed to be shade lovers in their homeland can be planted in full sun in Latvia. This is because full sun in our northern latitudes is sometimes shadier than the shade of other places, such as Central Asia. This is true of *Arum korolkowii*, for example, which in Central Asia always grows in shaded spots among large stones, at the bottom of gorges, or inside deep shrubs. Here it needs full sun.

Some of the so-called shade lovers don't actually require shade. In nature they may grow in shade simply because there is less competition there. When the seeds of such plants fall into a less shady spot, any seedlings are quickly choked out by more vigorous growers. In the garden, however, you regulate the growing conditions, keeping the soil free of weeds, watering the plants, and so forth. With the threat of over-crowding removed, these shade lovers grow perfectly in sunny spots. In a nursery, everything depends on the land that is available. In the home garden, it is up to you whether you want to do very little work and provide natural conditions or keep a regular eye on your treasures.

It's easy enough to say that daffodils do best in a good loam, that crocuses prefer a well-drained sandy soil, and that lysichitons need a very moist corner with peaty soil, but what if your garden soil is heavy clay or coarse sand? The garden in which I first started growing bulbs was located in a clearing of a pine forest on very sandy podzol soil. Every year I incorporated large quantities of peat moss, leaf mold, and loam, but it all disappeared like water dropped on a hot iron. Tulips, my first small bulbs, thrived there. I even had success with my most difficult and fanciful Juno irises. But my daffodils grew weak and suffered from bulb flies, and bulb flies killed almost all of my snowdrop collection. The garden was always short on water because the soil dried out within minutes, even after a heavy shower.

My second garden was situated in a valley on the bank of a small river and had clay soil. The river flowed over stones some 20 m from my front door. Unfortunately, though, the valley was on the north-facing bank, and soon I lost many of the treasures that had been carefully collected in Central Asia in previous years. I built raised terraces filled with gravel and managed to save many of the bulbs this way, but I also lost many of them. And yet I never before (or later) had such beautiful daffodils. Snowdrops also grew like weeds there. In fact many years later this garden, without having been given any attention, became a source of replacements for lost *Galanthus* species I had collected from the slopes of the North Caucasus.

By the time I decided to again move my garden, I had learned a few things and knew that no site was ideal. However, having learned from personal experience the importance of excellent drainage, I now had one main condition: the garden must be situated on slopes. Earlier I had seen a large tulip field with a small depression in the middle of it where in spring nothing came up. This was where the soil froze, often very deeply, in winter, so that water from melting snow could not drain down. The bulbs in this depression became waterlogged. Even a small slope would help water drain in these situations.

Nothing is perfect. My third and last garden was situated on quite heavy clay soil. Now, after more than twenty years here, I can see no recognizable trace of the soil on which I started. Clay-based soils are in fact easier to improve than sandy soils. This is because clay particles are much smaller than those of sand. When incorporated into a sandy soil, clay is soon washed away, its smaller particles sinking deeper and deeper with each watering, so that soon you are again left with only sand. On the other hand you can mix any amount of sand into a clay-based soil because the large grains of sand can't move between the small gaps formed by the clay particles. For either type of soil, adding good quantities of humus will steadily make the soil more or less comfortable for any kind of bulb.

Walking around my land one day, I found an area with sandier soil in the shade of some trees. It was here that I built a shade garden for *Galanthus*, *Arisaema*, and similar woodland plants. I selected the northern slopes for growing daffodils but left places with brick-hard clay for lawns. For bogland plants I dug a row about half a meter deep and a meter wide, lined it with strong plastic film, and filled it with a very peaty soil mix. In this bed *Symplocarpus*, *Lysichiton*, and a few marginal perennials are perfectly at home. Now, after decades of incorporating peat moss and sand to make my soil suitable for growing bulbs, I am generally satisfied.

Slopes and soil structure aren't the only elements that provide proper drainage for a bulb garden. All of my bulbs (daffodils being the only exception) are always planted in a so-called sand bed (Plate 8). I put a layer of coarse sand at the bottom of each row, place the bulbs on top of this, and then cover the bulbs with coarse sand. In this way my bulbs are always planted in pure sand, which has a lot of advantages. First, it provides additional drainage. Second, it prevents the bulbs from making direct contact with the soil. For me, though, the most important advantage is that the sand, which is usually very light in color, contrasts well with the surrounding dark soil and helps me find the bulbs at harvesting time (Plate 9). This is especially useful when I'm harvesting small, dark tubers, such as those of *Anemone blanda* and *Eranthis* species.

Many years ago I did only inland business, but this included the large Soviet Union. One day I received a letter from a Russian customer who had ordered *Eranthis hyemalis*. He wrote, "What have you sent me? I ordered flower bulbs, but you sent small, carbon-like pieces of some rubbish!" In dark soil, finding and harvesting such "small, carbon-like pieces" is almost impossible, but white or yellow sand makes it easy to find and collect even the smallest black tubers. Collecting bulbs only from sand also helps you avoid mixing the stocks.

For me, planting in sand makes harvesting a much quicker process. I simply brush away the dark surface soil until I see a light row of sand. I scoop up the sand along with the bulbs and put everything in a box with a sieve at the bottom. The sand easily falls through the sieve. This is especially useful when collecting smaller bulbs or seedlings that haven't yet started flowering. As a bulb exporter, I also appreciate an additional bonus: sand is much easier to wash from bulbs than soil, particularly clayey soil. My bulbs go into their boxes free of any soil precisely because they were never in direct contact with soil to begin with.

I have tried every possible way of planting during my nearly fifty years of bulb growing. At first I planted bulbs on traditional 1 m wide beds in parallel rows at a distance of 10 cm for smaller bulbs and 20–30 cm for tulips, daffodils, and garden giants such as drumstick *Allium* species and *Fritillaria imperialis*. Although such beds are quite economical in space, I found it difficult to reach individual plants situated in the middle of the bed. It is almost impossible to dig out some virus-infected tulip from the midzone of such a bed without touching or damaging its neighbors. Preparing a planting scheme was very difficult, too, because I grew so many small stocks. In each row I planted a few samples, some of them occupying all of one row and part of another. My planting scheme became a confusing piece of artwork, and it was very easy to misunderstand which side of the bed was right and which was left.

I soon rejected beds with transversally oriented rows in favor of beds with longitudinally oriented rows. This made it much easier to see and reach each individual plant, but for me the most important thing was that my planting schemes were less confusing. Varieties were listed on each planting scheme in sequence as I planted them from the beginning to the end of each row. This planting style was only one small step away from my present method. As I became older I decided that harvesting plants from the middle row was too hard on my back. Now I have two planting schemes. I plant large-growing "small" bulbs (*Allium*, some *Fritillaria*, autumn-flowering *Colchicum* varieties), tulips, and daffodils in ridges placed some 70 cm apart. These ridges are made by a tractor and furrower normally used by potato growers.

I plant daffodils at the bottom of the ridges and close the ridges using a rake or spade. Daffodils like moisture, so their bulbs can lie lower than the path between the ridges. For *Tulipa*, *Allium*, *Fritillaria*, and *Colchicum* I use a hand furrower, by which I make a row at the top of the ridge to provide excellent drainage. This part of the garden looks like a single line of raised beds with paths between the ridges lower than the planted bulbs.

Planting really small bulbs at such great distances is too much of a waste of land. While these are still planted on beds, there are only two rows running the length of each bed. The beds are 60–70 cm wide, the paths between them 30–40 cm wide, so each bed and path occupies a space 1 m wide. The traditional length of my beds is 10 m. After each 10 m, the beds are interrupted by a cross-path. The reason for this is very simple: if you grow many small stocks, it isn't easy to find a particular stock if the list of bulbs planted in one row is too long. Sometimes even 10 m seem much too long. Some rows may contain twenty to thirty stocks.

I try to plant similar or closely allied species and varieties side by side, since this makes it possible to compare them and note even minor differences. I always start with the largest bulbs in the stock and gradually end with the smallest ones. This helps me find problem plants. If some plant is shorter than its neighbors despite having identical or nearly identical bulbs, this may be the first sign of a virus or infection.

The planting scheme is of utmost importance. Even if you use double labeling you can never predict what will happen in your garden. My nursery is situated between forests, which means wild animals sometimes come to visit. To my great surprise, they have rarely damaged my plants (rodents being an exception). Sometimes in early spring, a bird plucks a crocus flower or nips at the damaged foliage of some bright form of *Fritillaria imperialis*, or a hare eats a few fresh crocus leaves, but the damage has never been serious. Sometimes wild boars even pass my beds looking for something to eat, but it seem that ornamental bulbs aren't to their taste—except for a recent summer when they seemed to find some of my geranium tubers quite delicious. Unfortunately, in such circumstances wooden sticks and labels that separate the stocks are broken and pushed aside. Garden plans that note where and what is planted will help restore some order. Similar damage is sometimes done by the trampling legs of elks and deer.

Not only marshland plants need specially created conditions. Many gardeners gripe about their *Fritillaria imperialis* growing well but rarely flowering. I have found that this large plant needs very rich soil. I dig out a pit half a meter deep, place some 20 cm of well-rotted manure at the bottom, cover that with 10 cm of good garden soil, then a few centimeters of coarse sand, and finally add the large bulbs. I again cover the bulbs with coarse sand and adjust the soil level using good garden soil. Given such conditions, my bulbs of *F. imperialis* flower without any problems. I replant them only when the clumps become too dense, causing the flowering to weaken. Surprisingly, the closely allied and superficially quite similar *F. eduardii* flowers perfectly every spring on ordinary nursery beds without any special preparation.

Every evening when I first return to my office from the field, I sit at my computer and list everything I have planted. At the end of the planting season I copy all of my planting schemes to CD, and I also keep all handwritten drafts made on the field until I have harvested my bulbs. In this way I am triply protected from losing this valuable information.

When replanting bulbs, I usually begin with the shade-loving plants that start rooting early, such as *Anemone*, *Corydalis*, and *Erythronium* species. After these I plant autumn-flowering bulbs, hoping they will flower the first autumn. Then I plant crocuses. In Latvia crocuses are best planted in August; when planted in September, they never develop well, their flowers often remaining underground in spring. Autumn-flowering colchicums are hopeless, so they are planted only after all the crocuses have been planted.

Planting is most difficult when it is snowing. When I worked in a publishing house and could only garden on the weekends, I sometimes planted bulbs in these conditions. Nothing is colder than snow melting on your fingers and legs, regardless what kind of boots or wool socks you might be wearing. With clenched teeth, my wife and I planted lilies in the first days of October, every half an hour rushing to the sauna to warm our fingers. By the evening everything was covered with 5 cm of snow, but the lilies had been planted.

The best time to plant tulips is at the end of September when the soil temperature drops below 9°C. Old Latvian gardeners recommend looking in the field where you grew tulips a year before and searching for some bulbs left in the soil—when they start rooting, this is the best time to plant your tulip bulbs. In exceptional cases tulips can be planted even in spring. This method is used by Russian gardeners in places where winters are hard and snow can be blown away. In such environments, tulip bulbs that have been planted in autumn are usually killed by frost. The gardeners keep the bulbs in a cool veranda and plant them as early as possible in spring. In the 1960s I left a hundred top-sized bulbs of the Darwin hybrid tulip 'Parade' in my father's unheated summerhouse for the winter. On the coldest days the temperature inside fell to –20°C. In early spring I planted the bulbs in a slightly shaded part of my garden and they all flowered, though they were some 10 cm shorter than bulbs normally planted in autumn.

The last bulbs I plant in the garden are alliums, *Muscari* and *Ornithogalum* species whose leaves appear in autumn, some arums, and Regelia and Regeliocyclus irises (Oncocyclus irises are not possible to grow outside here). I try to plant arums and irises when the soil starts to freeze. If they are planted earlier, their leaves usually develop in autumn and are killed by the frosts that soon follow. This growing method helped me hang on to many old Regeliocyclus iris hybrids until I started planting them in unheated greenhouse, where they now grow without any problems.

It is very important to follow planting with a good watering. My gardening years in Latvia have included a few very dry autumns. Some gardeners who didn't water their bulb beds on these occasions had serious losses from frost damage—one of my colleagues lost his entire daffodil collection. Moisture is essential for good root development, and perfectly rooted bulbs are much hardier. Watering also improves contact between bulb and soil, and rooting starts earlier.

I rarely dip bulbs in fungicide before planting them. This is a very common practice in the Netherlands, but the bulbs there are planted with machines so that workers never come in contact with any poison. I only dip bulbs in exceptional cases, perhaps if I have observed *Anemone nemorosa* rot or the black disease of corydalis, and then I make sure to plant them only while wearing rubber gloves. I hate gloves, though. I never use them in the garden, even when working with bees. Taking a bulb in my fingers, I can feel it as a living organism. I feel when it is ill or dead, even talk with it. I could never do this with gloves covering my hands.

It is a good idea to dip bulbs in water for several minutes before planting, since a moistened bulb starts rooting much more quickly than a dry one. I did this in earlier years when my collection was smaller. Planting wet bulbs does slow the process down a bit, however, and now I don't have the time. When time permits, I use a hand sprayer to wet the bulbs all at once before covering them with sand.

Winters in Latvia are very unstable. Freezes alternate with thaws, quite often producing ice, so the bulbs must be covered well for winter. In the Netherlands the most popular covering is straw. I don't like straw for the single reason that it is popular with mice, who are attracted to whatever grain is left in it. Some people use dry leaves, which is an excellent cover but quite difficult to remove at the right time in spring. Others use sawdust, which becomes quite solid during winter and sometimes isn't so good for the soil; also, the best sawdust comes from leaf trees, but you can never know for sure whether conifer sawdust has gotten mixed up with it. I prefer peat moss, which is light and free of weed seeds; it provides good thermal insulation and is a good source of humus for the soil. It also accumulates fertilizers and slowly releases them with rain and watering. The one downside to peat moss is the price. It's not cheap. Fortunately, there is a peat factory only 20 km from my nursery, so I save on the cost by buying directly from the factory. Every year I use some 250–300 cubic meters of dry peat moss to cover my beds for the winter and to add to soil mixes for the greenhouse.

On average I cover my beds with a layer of peat moss 10–15 cm thick, covering not only the top but also the sides of the bed. For more tender plants, such as *Fritillaria persica* and various *Arisaema* species, I might spread it up to 30 cm thick. Slightly moist peat moss works best: dry peat moss is very dusty and can be blown away by strong winds, while thoroughly wet peat moss is too heavy to work with and doesn't provide good thermal insulation.

I always begin by covering the beds that contain any bulbs that flower or form leaves in autumn. I cover these beds immediately after planting the bulbs, and only after that is done do I return to planting other bulbs. When all the planting is finished, I cover the rest of the beds, and as a last touch I cover the beds in my green-houses. Sometimes during winter I need to add additional covering. I'm especially careful to check autumn-flowering *Colchicum* varieties, which can start to grow leaves during winter thaws. This is very dangerous if frost returns when there is no snow. I once lost the greatest part of my *Colchicum* collection from just such a frost, even though the frost was not particularly heavy. I was short on peat moss and could cover only some of the *Colchicum* leaves that had started to appear. On the covered beds, not one bulb died. Since then I always make sure to have enough peat left for winter emergencies.

Every year I amend my clay soil with lots of sand and peat moss to make it more suitable for bulbs. Peat moss is usually acid, so after large amounts have been incorporated, the soil pH changes. Every third year I give my soil a good dose of dolomite lime to compensate for the rising acidity. Exactly how much lime is needed can only be determined by analyzing the soil. Peat moss is quite variable; some factories produce a very acid peat moss, while others produce peat with a pH that is almost optimal for bulb growing.

The best time to cover beds is when the soil starts to freeze. This helps protect planted treasures from mice, which can't dig through frozen soil, and keeps the soil frozen during moderate thawing. If you have only a few beds to cover, the process can be completed in a couple of hours. For me, it takes three to four weeks. One word of warning: Never cover bulbs over snow, especially with peat moss or anything similar. The covering will keep the snow from melting when spring begins and thereby increase the damage caused by plants becoming waterlogged. I did this once myself and the results were poor even on a daffodil field. Sometimes snow falls before bulb fields can be covered. The snow itself is like a protective blanket, shielding plantings from frost, but of course it will not work as mulch during the growing season. Many bulbs can be covered with mulch even in spring, but this can be done only with linear-leaved plants. Rosettes of tulip leaves open so early that it is almost impossible to cover the beds with mulch in spring without filling the leaf bases with peat moss; conversely, there are no problems with daffodils and similar plants. Keep this in mind when planning the sequence of jobs to be done.

Mulching not only saves bulbs from frost damage but also provides nourishment during the growing season. A good mulch accumulates fertilizers and slowly releases them during rain and watering, and it saves the soil from compacting. It is also much easier to remove weeds from the loose soil beneath mulch than from compacted soil on nude beds. Again, my preference is for peat moss.

Mulch does not always save plantings from frost, however. Sometimes the covering is too thin or winter is too hard and free of snow. On occasion my garden has looked quite shocking in spring. The worst was the spring of 1979, after a winter in which the temperature at snow level had fallen to $-48°C$. Although the garden had been covered with 5 cm of very powdery snow, this proved to be too little covering, and in spring almost nothing came up. Even the tulips were almost completely killed or damaged by frost. I dug up a few beds to plant new bulbs that I had received in autumn, but left the others untouched. In the spring of 1980 I was greatly surprised when on those untouched beds small, grass-like leaves appeared. These were crocuses, daffodils, and some other bulbs. What had happened? The old crocus corms and roots were killed, but the buds on top of the corms, from which new corms are formed, survived because they were covered by old, dry scales. With the daffodils, the same thing happened when the basal plate was killed.

Frost first kills the roots and basal plate, then the bottom part of the scales, and finally the tips of the scales. If the tips remain alive, they sometimes regenerate small new bulbils. I saw similar regeneration on my autumn-flowering *Colchicum* collection. After very serious damage by midwinter frost, spring brought not one leaf, but after three years I harvested some bulbs from almost every stock. Therefore this is my recommendation: if possible, avoid rushing to replace frost-damaged bulbs with new ones. If you leave them in the soil, some might regenerate. This may at least be worthwhile in the case of very valuable bulbs that would not be easy to replace. The exception is tulips. It is best to dig out tulip bulbs and leave them in boxes to dry. On one occasion late in summer in the center of my largest tulip bulbs I found some small replacement bulbs formed from surviving tissue. These had been moved to boxes. Those left in the soil had completely rotted.

Sometimes a special mulch is needed. I had great problems with narcissus fly (*Merodon equestris*) on my snowdrops when I grew them in my first garden on sandy soil. Michael Hoog recommended I cover my snowdrop beds with a few centimeters of dry pinewood needles. It worked surprisingly well. I don't know if the deciding factor was the color, smell, or something else, but the damage was significantly reduced.

◈ 12
Bulbs in the Garden

HERE ARE NUMEROUS BULB BOOKS, each recommending a variety of ways and places to plant bulbs. It would be pointless to repeat those recommendations here. I have planted very few bulbs among my ornamentals, and most of my best displays have been made accidentally, generally when I had too many bulbs to keep all of them in my nursery beds. Some of the most beautiful displays happen in spots where bulbs once grown for the nursery have been left to develop naturally. This kind of natural development, usually called naturalization, is the best thing you can provide for your garden. Naturalized bulbs need little attention and provide the best appearance.

Naturalization is very common in gardens. Many terrible weeds, for example, are imported from other countries, as are many pests and diseases. *Galinsoga parviflora* is a widespread weed in Latvian gardens that was imported here by Napoleon's army with forage for horses. In some cases botanists can't determine whether a plant is native or an escaped weed because it has naturalized so well. In Latvia this applies to some bulbs.

Tulipa sylvestris is a definite garden escapee, growing only near old castle parks, where it looks quite natural. The same can be said of *Ornithogalum umbellatum*, which I tend to think of as a weed. Only a few bulbs are undoubtedly native to Latvia: *Gladiolus imbricatus*, a true gem of flooded meadows in river valleys, three or four woodland *Corydalis* species, five or six *Allium* species, and four *Gagea* species, only one of which has sufficiently large flowers to be accepted as an ornamental plant.

When a bulb naturalizes in your garden it means that you are providing the optimal growing conditions. The greatest enemy of such a bulb may be the gardener himself, with some of the greatest damage taking place during autumn cleaning, when fallen leaves are collected for compost or even burned (oh, how foolish to produce a lot of dioxins by burning leaves instead of using them to make a perfect humus in a compost heap!). Old leaves make the best covering for winter, providing optimal wetness for seed germination while also improving the soil. Some gardeners will complain that wind blows the leaves around the garden and that this is undesirable for the lawn, but it is easy to secure leaves to one spot with a layer of peat moss or compost. The germination of bulb seedlings the next spring and a marvelous carpet of bright flowers a few years later will be excellent compensation.

It was Michael Hoog from the Netherlands who taught me the importance of letting fallen leaves and twigs form natural humus. During my first visit when he was running only a small nursery near his house, I noted how he picked up every small branch that fell on his beds from surrounding trees, broke it into small pieces, and put the pieces back on the bed where they had fallen. When I returned home I started consciously doing the same, and now it is something I find myself doing automatically anytime I walk through my garden.

There was once a garden near the center of Riga shaded by large trees. The owner of the garden, a famous artist during his lifetime, paid no attention to it. In spring a spectacular blue carpet of *Scilla siberica* appeared beneath the trees, later replaced by the white, pendulous bells of *Convallaria majalis* and *Polygonatum multiflorum*. The plants stayed green until autumn. After the artist died, the new owners of the property arranged for an annual cleaning, and within a few years all of the beautiful plants disappeared. Subsequent attempts to create a traditional lawn also failed, because the area was too shady and the tree roots kept it too dry in summer.

There are two different kinds of naturalization. The first kind occurs when you plant your bulbs so they will look as natural as possible. The second kind is the real thing, which will happen only if your bulbs start to reproduce by self-sowing.

I used the first kind of naturalization when I had too many bulbs of one kind to be planted in the nursery, even after distributing much of my surplus to friends, schools, and neighbors. To avoid having to burn them on the roadside, I planted them in the grass around my house. I removed the upper level of soil to a depth of 25–30 cm, planted the bulbs, and replaced the turf. This works perfectly with daffodils, autumn-flowering colchicums, and some other bulbs. Deep planting is essential. All bulbous plants have a common tendency: shallowly planted bulbs increase better but form smaller bulbs, while deeply planted bulbs increase slowly but make large bulbs. Deep plantings produce the most natural look. Some of my daffodils have grown and flowered brilliantly each spring for more than twelve years without any attention from my side.

Galanthus nivalis has also grown perfectly in my grass. Many years ago I placed a few bulbs in some spots near a group of *Thuja occidentalis* bordering the front lawn of my house. They are the first flowers greeting me each spring, even before the snow has melted. They always start flowering before the same bulbs planted on the nursery beds.

Many authors recommend growing crocuses in grass. In Latvian conditions this is nonsense. All of my attempts to plant various large-flowering crocuses, varieties of *Crocus chrysanthus*, have failed. The crocuses flowered nicely in one, two, or mostly three years, and then disappeared. The turf on my Latvian lawn was simply too dense for them. Only two species demonstrated a capacity to survive in battle with the roots of the grass, and only in somewhat shaded places where the lawn wasn't too dense. These were *C. heuffelianus* and *C. tommasinianus*.

To successfully grow bulbs in grass, it is important to leave the foliage alone for at least three to four weeks after flowering before using a mower. Plant the bulbs in the periphery of your lawn where the longer grass will look quite natural. You can mow over them when the leaves start to die. My lawn is surrounded by perennial beds, with bulbs planted not far from the perennials. The spots of uncut grass really don't disturb the overall appearance.

I left my father's garden about thirty years ago. Over the last fifteen years, nothing has been done in the garden. Now when I visit the place each spring I find beautiful carpets of *Crocus heuffelianus* in various shades of purple, with a few albinos growing among them in half shade between very large *Corylus avellana* 'Atropurpurea' and *Betula pendula* 'Youngii'.

Various bulbs grow in another spot in the old garden, under some large apple trees where I planted my first introductions. This is where I kept the bulbs brought back from my first expeditions or that I received from other bulb collectors, including plenty of *Crocus heuffelianus*, *Corydalis bracteata*, *Fritillaria camschatcensis*, and *Erythronium sibiricum*. All are self-sowing and in the shade of the trees experience little competition from native plants. Autumn leaves remain where they fall, too, so the bulbs feel very comfortable. Every spring I visit this garden and look for any seedlings that might arise through the gentle care of Mother Nature. I have even found plants here that I have lost from my collection. Such was the case with *Crocus gargaricus*, which slowly increased by stolons between the two apple trees over the years and eventually formed a large spot of bright yellow flowers. *Corydalis fumariifolia* was another beauty renewed to my collection. This corydalis appears so early in spring that its foliage is often killed by frost. Under the large apple trees, where it is more protected from night frosts, it has managed to survive and even start self-sowing.

Corydalis grow extremely well in Latvia in "natural" conditions, even too well, self-sowing almost as abundantly as a weed. All the woodland *Corydalis* species from the Far East and Siberia feel perfectly at home here. One of the real gems for naturalizing is *C. buschii*. It is a very strange species with rhizomes somewhat resembling those of *Anemone nemorosa*, only bright yellow and very thin. They are extremely brittle, so it is almost impossible to harvest all of them. One nice feature of this species is that it adjusts itself to the correct planting depth—if you plant it too deep or too shallow, it makes a new layer of rhizomes at the correct depth within one season. It soon becomes a weed in the garden but is a very pleasant addition and doesn't really affect its neighbors. In Latvia it comes up during the first week of May. Flowers appear in mid-May, and the leaves die at the end of the month. The beautiful reddish purple flowers nicely decorate the somewhat shaded parts of the garden before the leaves of larger plants cover the soil. I plant it under berry bushes. It dislikes open areas where its fine foliage will be burned by any intense sunshine.

On the riverbank where I had my second garden, I plowed up a narrow meadow. On one side were very large lime and maple trees, on the other side gray alders. On this site I grew different species of *Corydalis*, *Galanthus*, *Leucojum*, *Cyclamen*, and *Colchicum*. Now after twenty years there is again a meadow, but in early spring it is covered with thousands of yellow, white, pink, and purple flowers. Most of my snowdrops died when I replanted them one last time, not having yet found their favorite spot. A few years ago I visited my old garden and re-collected many of the *Galanthus* species.

At the base of an old lime tree in this garden I found marvelously flowering seedlings of *Cyclamen coum* subsp. *elegans*, which had been collected in the Talish Mountains during a 1987 expedition. The tubers that I moved to my last garden didn't survive, but seeds had been left behind in the original location, and after a few years there were again plenty of cyclamen blooms. Unfortunately, when I later returned to pick up the tubers, I found that someone had gotten there before me.

When I moved everything to my last garden, I planted all my shade-loving plants under ash and maple trees where there was humus-rich soil. Regrettably, this was near the ruins of an old stone cattle shed frequented by water rats. I didn't know this before spring, when instead of finding flowers of beautiful woodland fritillaries and crocuses, I was greeted with empty beds. In this same location I had planted *Leucojum vernum* var. *carpathicum* bulbs collected near the village of Podpolozje in the Eastern Carpathians. The rodents didn't like these bulbs, and the leucojums took well to the site. For many years I saw no signs of these earlier beds, but *L. vernum* occupied almost the entire spot; it is self-sowing and really flourished there. I no longer plant this species in my nursery beds—I dig all the bulbs I need for my customers from this one site.

Another plant that flourishes there is the common winter aconite, *Eranthis hyemalis*, which starts to flower as the snow melts. It is not possible to sell this bulb, however: finding its small black tubers in the humus-rich soil, full of small pieces of tree branches and half-decomposed leaves, would be a hopeless job. The ground beneath the lilacs is also a paradise for *Erythronium sibiricum*. In spring they look so natural that sometimes I forget I'm in Latvia and not beside a forest in the Kemerovo region of Siberia.

The greatest problem with planting bulbs in an ornamental garden is the short life of the leaves. When the leaves die away, they leave an empty spot. My wife grows perennials: peonies, phlox, asters, and others. She finds it best to plant spring bulbs between clumps of peonies and hostas. The bulbs flower when the perennials are still underground or are still very short, but by the time the bulb leaves die, the perennials are large enough to cover the bare spot. This is just one of the many ways you can place bulbs in the garden so that the garden will look nice year-round.

◈ 13
Winter Tasks

IT IS DECEMBER. The past week has brought moderate frosts that have hardened the surface of the beds. I sit at my computer, warm inside my house, while outside the snowflakes dance through the air. I hope the bulbs on my field and in my greenhouses are comfortable, too. The first snowdrop (*Galanthus reginae-olgae*) in the greenhouse has started to flower. I sit watching the fire in my fireplace, thinking about my life, my garden, and my next expedition.

In winter I go through my planting books from the last season and record all my notes on the computer. I list all of my plantings, leaving sufficient space between each plant name to record a few notes. I include observations such as when flowering began and ended, flower color, whether I noticed any special forms, and so on. I mark which plants have already been photographed and which still need their pictures taken. I also get my new planting books ready. In total there are almost three hundred pages. I check my stocks on paper and mark those that are available in large enough quantities to be included in the catalog. Less than a decade ago I thought I didn't need a computer—my children essentially pressured me into buying one. Now, of course, I can't imagine working without it. My catalog shelf still holds thousands of filing cards made in earlier years, waiting to be transferred to computer when I find the time. Winter always seems too short when it comes to finishing up paperwork and too long when it comes to waiting for bulbs to flower.

I spend all of December writing text and preparing pictures for my new catalog, which will be printed in early January. It is a pleasant but difficult job. Our winters are so unstable and there are so many problems that can attack my treasures that I can never anticipate what bulbs will be ready at shipping time. The inclusion of certain special plants is always risky. They usually grow very well before I list them in the catalog, but just when I decide it's safe to sell them, problems arise. I never know if I will have *Anemone nemorosa* cultivars, snowdrops, and many other rarities the next autumn. It is always a gamble. I never had to play cards at a casino or place any kind of bet—my excitement has always been reserved for bulbs.

I don't really like business. If I had a million dollars in my bank account, I would be nothing but a grower. I would grow bulbs for my own pleasure and for exchanging with other collectors, and I would visit every corner of the world where bulbs grow in the wild. Unfortunately, of course, this is only a dream: I must limit myself to just one expedition each year and use the rest of my time for commercial breeding. I would like very much to have more time for writing, but winter is so short. It seems that only yesterday I sent out my last catalog, but the manuscript for the new catalog now sits before me.

As I grow older I can see that not so many years remain before me. Who will continue my job? What will happen to my collections when I am gone? This is the number one problem of all Latvian gardeners and plant breeders. Our children learned from an early age how difficult and heavy the gardener's life can be. My daughters still remember asking me to go to the beach. "Okay," I would reply, "but first I must weed a garden bed." By the time I finished, it had started to rain. This is a problem all over the world. I look at the old catalogs of the Van Tubergen nursery, established in 1868 by the Hoog family. In 1914 E. A. Bowles wrote of some crocuses in *My Garden in Spring*: "They originated at Haarlem in that centre of creation of new plant forms, the Zwanenburg Nursery, where Mr. Van Tubergen and his two nephews, Mr. John and Mr. Thomas Hoog, always have some fresh revelation of beauty awaiting the visitor." The Van Tubergen nursery no longer exists as it once did. It was a great tragedy for my friend Michael Hoog when his family decided to sell their collections after finding that the introduction of new plants wasn't commercially profitable. He split with other family members to continue his job on a very small scale, a job that is continued by his son, Antoine, in France. Nowadays, pioneers in the introduction and distribution of new plants are just small nurseries and amateurs, as well as some botanical gardens. The world is changing. Not long ago my youngest daughter, Ilze, began her studies at the same horticultural college I attended more than forty years ago. Her motivation? "Someone has to look for your treasures, Dad."

I'm a nurseryman. All of my bulbs are grown in beds and kept for the best bulb crop. But all the basic principles applied in a professional bulb nursery are also valid in a small home garden. You must feed and water your plants, save them from unfavorable weather conditions, and regularly replant them to prevent overcrowding. All of this must be done the same way, only on a smaller scale. I hope my experience will help you better understand what bulbs need, and perhaps give you some new ideas to try in the conditions of your own garden.

Galanthus reginae-olgae is flowering in the greenhouse. A new gardening season has begun!

Part II

Bulbs in the Wild

❖ 14
Bulb Nomenclature

THE NAMING OF PLANTS is an extremely difficult issue. For each botanist in the world there seems to be a separate opinion about the correct names of plants. Sometimes plant names change so often that it is difficult to follow even general trends in plant taxonomy.

When I started my studies at the horticultural college in Latvia, there were only three principal families of bulbous plants: Amaryllidaceae, Liliaceae, and Iridaceae. All were monocotyledons, that is, plants with only one seed leaf in the embryo. The majority of flowering plants are dicotyledons, having two seed leaves in the embryo. Among the dicots are some families with bulb-like plants. The main bulbous families are Primulaceae (*Cyclamen*), Fumariaceae (*Corydalis*), Ranunculaceae (*Anemone*), Araceae (*Arum*), and Oxalidaceae (*Oxalis*).

The typical bulbous families have since been split. The way they are classified now looks more natural, as it joins much more closely allied plants into separate families. The following are considered to be monocot bulb families: Amaryllidaceae (*Galanthus, Leucojum, Narcissus, Ixiolirion, Sternbergia*), Asphodelaceae (*Eremurus*), Hyacinthaceae (*Hyacinthus, Muscari, Scilla, Ornithogalum*), Convallariaceae (*Convallaria* [I'm not including lily-of-the-valley among the bulbs, however, and mention it here only for completeness]), Liliaceae (*Erythronium, Lilium, Tulipa*), Alliaceae (*Allium, Bloomeria, Ipheion*), Iridaceae (*Crocus, Iris, Gladiolus*), Trilliaceae (*Trillium*), and Colchicaceae (*Colchicum*).

The names of genera and species change even more often than family names. The genus *Colchicum* is a good example. When I started studying plants, *Colchicum* was split into three separate genera, *Colchicum, Merendera*, and *Bulbocodium*, but now these plants are lumped together under the same hat (although this is not accepted by some). In general, botanists fall into one of two groups: there are the splitters, who tend to split plants into smaller groups and taxa (these are often the authors of local floras, guided by patriotism), and the lumpers, who tend to join different small taxa under one larger concept with more variability.

In general, gardeners are disappointed when plants grown under one name for a long time are suddenly given a new name. *Scilla hispanica*, for example, was first called *Endymion hispanica* and then *Hyacinthoides hispanica*. But just as we gardeners have our *International Code of Nomenclature of Cultivated Plants*, botanists have their own *International Code of Botanical Nomenclature*, which is *sine qua non* for them. Unfortunately, the rules of botanical nomenclature sometimes force us to use a name even if it is misleading. *Lilium pensylvanicum*, for example, has nothing to do with Pennsylvania in the United States. In reality it grows in eastern Siberia and northeastern China, and the name *L. dauricum*, a synonym, would be more appropriate. The same is true of *Scilla peruviana*, which doesn't grow in Peru at all. In only a few cases have some very popular names been preserved by the International Congress of Botanists regardless of the existence of another name that has the priority according to the *Code*.

There are difficult genera for which too little field material is available for studies; each local flora may treat these genera differently. My opinion has always been that field studies and laboratory research on a molecular level are not the only answers to the endless questions about plant taxonomy: observations made in the garden are also necessary. In fact, the gardeners growing and working with the living plants sometimes come to understand the facts better than the botanists working with herbaria.

Molecular research based on chromosomes and DNA sequences is now a part of plant taxonomy and has changed a lot of well-established opinions about the relationships between plants. However, to confirm the identity of plants in the field, gardeners need more visible, tangible evidence of the difference between plants. Sometimes it is very difficult just finding the simplest differences between two species. I still grow hundreds of plants known only by their collection numbers, still waiting for identification. In my records I try to follow the newest tendencies in plant taxonomy and frequently change the names according to the latest botanical publications.

Sometimes after just seeing a plant I feel that it is something new, and often these feelings are later confirmed by botanists. If someone were to ask me why this is, however, I wouldn't have a good answer. In addition to all the science involved in the naming of plants, perhaps there is an element of intuition.

❖ 15
The Ethics of Plant Collecting

WHAT IS THE ROLE of the plant hunter in the modern world? Is he a criminal destroying nature or an explorer working to expand our knowledge of nature?

Modern communication, the ease of travel, and business interests have all helped push many plants toward extinction, some of them having previously grown by the billions in their native habitats. Henrik Zetterlund told me of *Corydalis zetterlundii*, known only from its *locus classicus* (type locality) in Macedonia. The entire wild population of this species was collected by a commercial "gold digger" and directly offered in the trade. Most serious bulb growers are familiar with the beautiful picture of *Galanthus platyphyllus* on the Krestovy Pass, Georgian Military Highway, from Roger Phillips and Martyn Rix's superb book *Bulbs*. In the 1970s I was there too and even hid during a snowstorm behind the same stone pictured in the center of the photo. There were such a lot of *G. platyphyllus* flowers that it was difficult to distinguish the whiteness of the snow from the whiteness of the snowdrops. Sadly, there is nothing there now—all the bulbs of this snowdrop were dug out and sold to companies in western Europe. This kind of thing is hardly uncommon. Not long ago I read a report on the Web written by a so-called bulb collector from the Czech Republic: "During the whole day on *locus classicus* I found only fifty-eight plants. I damaged seven of them while collecting; twenty-five came up next spring." It isn't surprising that botanists are keeping the exact localities of new species top secret, especially when it comes to commercially popular plants like snowdrops.

But there is always a flip side. *Iris danfordiae*, which is grown by Dutch nurseries and sold every year by the billions to all corners of the world, is a classic example. No one would search for this bulb in the wild unless they were especially interested in samples from different populations for breeding purposes, as was the case with Alan McMurtrie from Canada. Using the "blood" of *I. danfordiae* he had collected in the mountains of Turkey, Alan raised many beautiful hybrids with color combinations never before seen in nature. Another iris, *I. winogradowii* from Georgia, was almost lost in the wild but was later reintroduced by George Rodionenko and his team. After building up the stock of this marvelous bulb at the Komarov Botanical Institute in Saint Petersburg, they replanted it on the slopes of the main Caucasus.

There are various opinions when it comes to the ethics of plant collecting. According to one philosophy, plants must grow and be investigated only in the wild. If a species disappears for natural reasons, it is fate and not something to interfere with. This is the opinion of green-policy hardliners, who tend to forget that all plants cultivated in farms and gardens and used as cut flowers or pot plants originated in the wild. Even these hardliners occasionally buy a bunch of tulips that were grown on thousands of hectares in the Netherlands. Needless to say, without the first plant hunters, there would be no tulips in cultivation. During one of our last expeditions to Turkey my colleagues and I spent half a day searching for a new *Bellevalia* species (*B. leucantha*) with white flowers. Ten years earlier it had been pictured on a mountain pass where it grew in abundance, and a couple of bulbs had been collected to confirm that it was in fact a new species. By the time we reached the plateau, there were no specimens of *Bellevalia*, only thousands of sheep, and the area seemed to have become a permanent base camp for local farmers. We found only a couple of *Ornithogalum* plants and *Colchicum*, all deep in the shrubs. It seems that this *Bellevalia* was lost before its publication.

It should be very clear when a modern plant hunter is serving progress and when he is simply destroying a wild population. One recent autumn, Trevor Jones of Britain sent me a photo of *Sternbergia lutea* with a splendid fully double flower. When I asked him for an offset of this beauty, Trevor replied that he had taken the picture during a green tour of Turkey, during which he had not been allowed to so much as touch a flower. This is complete nonsense. This plant will never survive in the wild nor produce any offspring; there is no stigma, no anthers, it will not produce seeds, and will not pollinate another plant. Sooner or later it will simply disappear, and Trevor's photo will be all that remains. If this bulb could be collected and then carefully reproduced vegetatively or by scaling, it would provide enjoyment to bulb enthusiasts in every corner of the world and live on for years and years. T. T. Mantel from Bovenkarspel, Netherlands, recently offered to sell the entire stock of the only double-flowering form of *Fritillaria imperialis* now in existence: 'Double Gold'. I don't know what price was paid for the stock, but I do hope that garden enthusiasts will be able to enjoy it for many years to come. This will never happen with the double *Sternbergia*.

I never studied botany in a professional way. The only botany I learned in college was the basic elements of plant morphology and some five hundred Latin names of the native plants of Latvia. At the National Botanical Garden I also learned the Latin names of trees and shrubs, both wild and cultivated. That was it. All the rest I learned on my own by reading plant books and articles, and mostly by working with plants. I smile when I think of the level of my knowledge in those early years. Although it won't paint a very flattering picture of me, I will tell you a story from my first excursion to Central Asia in 1975. At Chimgan, Uzbekistan, near melting snow I collected a yellow-flowering plant that I listed as "a strange *Corydalis*-like plant with horned tubers." A year later as I was heading to work by train, I noticed that the person beside me was flipping through an illustrated book about the mountains. There I glimpsed a photo of my strange *Corydalis*-like plant, clearly labeled *Gymnospermium albertii*. This shows you what a good botanist I was at that time.

In those early years I traveled to the mountains at flowering time, but now I generally go when the flowering season has ended and the seeds are starting to ripen. I no longer need to see the flower to recognize the plant. I always have the local flora with me and know what to look for, and I don't collect everything. Flowers are helpful when it comes to spotting a plant, but the bulb is still weak when in flower and won't make an ideal introduction. However, since the mountains have vertically arranged zones, it is not always possible to follow this rule. If in the foothills you find nothing more than the last remnants of foliage, in the midzone you will find mature bulbs with seeds, while at the snow line you will find everything in flower. For this reason, I still collect bulbs, though I no longer collect more than five to ten bulbs from a single population. Ten bulbs are collected only when I decide a bulb will be of interest to a botanical garden. When it comes to small populations, I only collect one or two bulbs. I visit many more places now on my expeditions, and collect many more different species, making sure all the while that no harm is done to nature.

I now trust my knowledge about growing bulbs and know perfectly well that plants that are able to grow will grow: no matter how many bulbs have been collected, they will set seed in my nursery and in a few years I will have a good stock. I much prefer collecting seeds these days. Seeds are light and allow me to start with a good stock of seedlings. In the wild only a small percentage of seeds find conditions favorable enough to germinate. Birds, insects, or animals eat the greatest part and the rest simply perish. When collecting seeds, I always try to loosen the soil surface near the mother plant and sow some of the seeds I have collected, thus providing them a greater chance of germinating and minimizing any damage I have caused.

There are so many beautiful bulbous plants still unknown to science and gardens. In my youth Michael Hoog told me that in Turkey you could find a new species in every valley. As it turns out, he was right. The mountain conditions of that region form isolated populations of unique species. When traveling in Central Asia, my colleagues and I almost always find plants that are different from anything we have seen before. During one of our last expeditions to Turkey, in which we were joined by scientists from the Gothenburg Botanical Garden, we joked that not a single day went by without discovering a new species. Even areas so densely visited by botanical expeditions as the Mediterranean, Middle East, and Central Asia still have plenty of "white spots" where unknown plants grow, including bulbs. Imagine the possibilities in the many countries left unexplored for centuries. Many countries remain inaccessible because of local wars or because areas of unexploded landmines would make any expedition too risky. It is possible that this lack of access will save some very decorative plants from extinction by overcollecting, but the same plants can be lost to overgrazing from rising local populations. Each stick has two ends.

In the golden age of plant exploration, it was a plant hunter's full-time job to travel the world discovering new plants and enriching our gardens with the many beauties that were found. The world has changed since then, but many enthusiastic plant hunters still travel to far regions in search of new plants. For them it isn't a business but a lifestyle. I belong to this group, too.

Bulb collecting is very hard work. In the Mediterranean and Middle East it is not so difficult—there are plenty of roads, you can rent a car, and sometimes you can find plants by just looking out the window as you drive along. Botanists have a special term for this kind of plant exploration: roadside botanizing. In Central Asia it is much more difficult. You have to carry all of your equipment and food on your back in a haversack and do most of your exploring on foot. Finding myself absolutely exhausted in the mountains, I have often said to myself, "What am I doing? Why am I here? This is the last time." It is a very expensive pleasure, too. If I didn't have my nursery I would never be able to go anywhere. Many of our expeditions have been partly financed by the Gothenburg Botanical Garden, which grows representatives of almost all the plants we have discovered. Without their support, many rare plants would remain hidden from the eyes of scientists.

When I return from the mountains the first thing I do is get the material I have collected in order. This mostly involves writing labels and checking field notes. The rest of "Bulbs in the Wild," in which I discuss my plant hunting trips to various parts of the world, is generally based on these field notes.

◈ 16
Bulbs in Latvia

ULBS GROW EVERYWHERE, even in such uncomfortable areas as Patagonia and northeastern Siberia. They grow in Latvia, too, and in fact were the targets of my first quests for plants. One species that I paid a lot of attention to was *Corydalis solida*, which is very widespread in my country. It also grows from Russia eastward to the Ural Mountains and to the south and west as far as northern Greece and even Spain. Not surprisingly, over this large area there is remarkable variability, but here in Latvia the plants are generally very uniform, all having dull grayish purple or blue flowers. Wandering around the mixed forests near my first garden, I could only find uniformly colored corydalis flowers. The only difference between plants was height, but even this variation disappeared when the tubers were moved to my home garden. In my garden the corydalis grew perfectly, soon finding a place for themselves near a fence.

During my excursions to the forest I always brought a small cotton bag and a knife. Along with *Corydalis solida* (syn. *C. halleri*) I collected a few *Gagea* species, but only one species, *G. lutea*, had flowers big enough to warrant growing in the garden. For some reason, though, *G. lutea* failed to impress me, and I eventually lost all interest in this genus, although I found some species growing by the zillions in alpine meadows, covering the ground like a yellow carpet. In the forest, beneath hazel bushes, oaks, and lime trees, I also found plenty of *Hepatica nobilis*. Its flowers were much more variable than those of *C. solida*, coming in different shades of blue and with various numbers of petals. On very rare occasions I even found plants with reddish flowers.

Many years passed. I found *Corydalis solida* growing almost everywhere in Latvia, but I no longer paid any attention to it, being almost certain of its lack of variability. Then one day in early spring, beneath gray alders and various shrubs on the bank of the Ogre River, I noticed something white among the bluish flowers of *C. solida*. I didn't think it was a corydalis but was curious to know what had interrupted the blue carpet. I was greatly surprised to find that it was in fact a white-flowered form of *C. solida*. It was the first differently colored corydalis I had ever seen. Promptly forgetting all about the friends who were with me, I lay down on the soil and slowly, piece by piece, removed all the old leaves, semi-rotten pieces of branches, and other humus until a small yellowish gray tuber appeared. The stem was joined to the tuber, and the white flower spike confirmed that this tuber was the correct one.

I carefully moved this one tuber to my garden. It flowered in its second spring, with two very dense spikes of milky white blooms. It was my first corydalis variety, and I never again saw anything quite like it. Not long ago my wife found another albino near Sigulda, but it was the traditional cold white shade quite common in other populations outside of Latvia. I named my corydalis 'Snowstorm' (Plate 11). It flowers earlier than other whites in my garden. The leaves are a glossy lettuce green.

The next *Corydalis solida* was found in the garden of my friend Aldonis Vēriņš. He grew *C. schanginii* subsp. *schanginii* from Central Asia in his collection, but our common muddy-colored *C. solida* was like a weed in his garden. One spring we found a pink-flowered form among all the plants of *C. solida*. It had a nice, soft, creamy pink color and very dense, compact spikes. It was so unusual that we immediately marked it, and later in the season it was replanted in a traditional bulb bed. From that plant came the second *Corydalis* variety raised in Latvia. We named it 'Blushing Girl' (Plate 12), though we still didn't know whether it was a mutation of the traditional *C. solida* or a natural hybrid with *C. schanginii*. Its seed color was strange, too—not glossy black, as is common for corydalis, but light brown. I collected seeds twice, but no seedlings appeared, which confirmed my suspicion about the plant's hybrid origin.

Around that time, two varieties widely grown in western Europe, both sent to me by Chris Brickell, appeared in my collection: the early-flowering *Corydalis solida* var. *transsylvanica* with light rosy red flowers, and the much more late-flowering, dark red 'George Baker'. There has been great confusion over both varieties in the market. With corydalis increasingly popular among gardeners, there has been an increase in requests for these forms, and many companies have started to offer various similarly colored seedlings under the same names. The legitimacy of names is a very confusing issue, because no one can really confirm that their plants are in fact the real thing. Each nurseryman announces that his stock is authentic. I do this myself. Both of my stocks were raised from a single tuber received very long ago from Chris, at a time when corydalis were still only the Cinderellas of the garden.

When I first began offering these forms to my customers in the Soviet Union, I received a letter from Vasilij Filakin from Kuzneck in the Penza region of Russia. He described a birch grove located not far from his home where *Corydalis solida* grew in various shades of white, blue, purple, and even deep reddish. He said that this was the only population with such variability—in other places the plants had traditional bluish lilac flowers. I expressed my interest and in 1982 received a parcel from which originated the ever-popular 'Penza Strain' (Plate 13). From the original tubers I selected some forty different color forms. Many were later named, while some are still grown under identification numbers and indexed by *P* for "Penza." Every year I collect seeds from these plants, and every year something new appears among the seedlings.

Later I received some named varieties from Willem van Eeden in the Netherlands, a legend among growers of small bulbs. Most interesting was that he named one of his seedlings with white, purple-rimmed flowers 'Kissproof', the same name I had given to one of my own seedlings, similar in color but more compact. As the corydalis increased in popularity, they were grown more and more. I received new forms from Henrik Zetterlund at Gothenburg, which holds the largest collection of these tiny beauties. (I suppose mine is the second largest.)

A real break in the color spectrum of *Corydalis solida* was made by Czech collectors Milan Prášil and Josef Kupec when in the Parâng Mountains, central Romania, they found an extremely variable population dominated by red-flowered plants. This stock received the name 'Prášil Strain' and was sold to Michael Hoog in Haarlem, Netherlands. In 1990 I visited Michael at his Zwanenburg House in the heart of Haarlem and brought him many new bulbs from my collection. As we sat on his terrace discussing plants, Michael's son, Antoine, appeared with a single tuber of *Corydalis*. "This offset is yours," Michael told me. "It is the most valuable bulb in my nursery."

When it flowered in my garden the next spring, I didn't trust my eyes. Never before had I seen anything so bright. It is the most dramatically colored corydalis in my collection, grabbing the attention of every visitor from a very far distance with its unusually luminous scarlet red flowers. It was later named 'Zwanenburg'.

This red acquisition led to new colors appearing among my seedlings (not immediately—the real color breakthroughs appeared in the second generation, and the first were marked in 1997). The most unusually colored newcomer was 'Falls of Nimrodel' (Plate 14), with a uniformly colored, slightly orange-toned, reddish pink spur and almost pure white lower and upper petals. It, too, is an advance in the color of corydalis, and there have been many others. The new reds are tinted with different colors, such as pinkish and other cooler shades. When naming the new hybrids I took inspiration from J. R. R. Tolkien's *Lord of the Rings*. The deepest purplish blue received the name 'Mordorland', the beautifully orange-red was named 'Rivendell', and so forth. For one seedling of exceptional beauty from the same progeny I used the diminutive form of my wife's name: 'Gunite' (Plate 16). In color type it is similar to 'Falls of Nimrodel', but the flowers are much more slender and are bright, light pink with white lower and upper petals.

I have never intentionally crossed corydalis. It would require a magnifying glass (or a clockmaker's lens, because your hands must be free), so tiny are the parts of the flower that must be opened to reach the pollens and stigma. For me the crossing is done by bumblebees and other types of bees. Unfortunately, though, instead of working for me the bumblebees often decide it is much easier to cut a hole in the spur to reach the nectar without having to open (and pollinate) the flower.

In addition to corydalis, two other bulb-like plants grow in our forests and flower early every spring: the early, white-flowered *Anemone nemorosa* and the slightly later, yellow-flowered *A. ranunculoides*. Sometimes they hybridize, forming intermediate forms such as *A.* ×*lipsiensis*, *A.* ×*pallida*, or *A.* ×*seemanii*, all with more or less creamy yellow flowers. There are only minor differences between the stocks offered under those names by several nurseries. In my many years in Latvia, I have only once found a population that seemed to be of hybrid origin. Although both species grow side by side, they have different flowering times, which limits the possibilities of intercrossing. There are so many *A. nemorosa* varieties of various colors and flower forms in the trade that it seems a very variable species. Sadly, in Latvia it is quite uniform. The only variations I have found are in the intensity of the pinkish shade on the petal exteriors in some groups, and in the size of the flowers.

One of the most pinkish forms was spotted by Arnis Seisums during our visit to the Gothenburg Botanical Garden. We were driving with Henrik Zetterlund through a forested area not far from Gothenburg and suddenly Arnis shouted, "Stop, stop!" On the roadside he had seen a very intensely toned dark pinkish form of *Anemone nemorosa*, which we later named 'Swedish Pink'. As is common for "pinks," the color only appears on the petal exteriors, but it is actually a very intense shade of purplish pink, and at the end of flowering the blooms become lilac-pink throughout.

An excellent form of *Anemone nemorosa* was found in Estonia by Mart Veerus during one of his walks through a forest not far from his house. This most unusual plant has comparatively smaller but uniformly deep blue flowers and markedly darker foliage. It also keeps its foliage much longer in summer—long after the leaves of any other form of *A. nemorosa* have grown desiccated, those of 'Mart's Blue' remain deep green. The foliage disappears only in August, so there are no empty spots in the garden.

Many cultivated forms of *Anemone nemorosa* are grown in gardens, but their susceptibility to disease makes them difficult to introduce. On many occasions I have tried to buy something new only to receive a reply that the plant can't be sold presently due to health problems. Still, I want to mention a few of these cultivars. First are the double-flowering forms. The most widespread and one of my favorites is 'Vestal', with beautiful doubling in the center of the bloom, forming the so-called buttonhole type of flower. It grows perfectly, flowers abundantly, and only rarely suffers from disease. Another double, received from Kath Dryden in Britain, is 'Blue Eyes', which has fully double flowers with deep blue centers. Unfortunately, the flowers are large and heavy, so as with any young, self-conscious lady, its blue eyes are mostly downturned.

Another group of *Anemone nemorosa* cultivars that I like very much are more or less curiosities. The flowers, or structures replacing the flowers, are strange enough to make each plant difficult to recognize, but they are always much admired by our visitors. The names of these cultivars were confused until recently. There are two varieties. The flowers of the first, 'Green Fingers', are very difficult to describe. They are white, with petals that are wider than normal for the species, and in the center of the bloom the anthers and styles are converted to a dense tuft of tiny, frond-like leaves. This cultivar makes smaller and noticeably more slender rhizomes than most other forms. It is sometimes also offered as 'Phyllodic Form'. The flowers of 'Viridescens' are even more strange. Each petal, anther, and style is converted to a small green leaf, resulting in an unbelievable mossy green tangle of a flower. This form is not fertile, so its flowers are very long-lasting, and it makes a fatter rhizome.

Anemone nemorosa has plenty of varieties, but its yellow-flowering ally *A. ranunculoides* has only one: 'Flore Plena'. It isn't fully double, having only an extra set or sets of petals, and the bloom is fertile. Despite the extra petals, the flowers are generally somewhat smaller than in the normal forms. Recently I received from Estonia several stunning forms of *A. ranunculoides* selected by teacher and amateur gardener Taavi Tuulik, who found them on Hiiumaa Island (Plate 18). They have quite variably colored petals and various types of doubling. There are monstrose forms, too, duplicating the best qualities of the species' white cousin. I have walked through fields of white and yellow anemones in Latvia but have never found anything similar to these wonders from the Estonian islands. As Taavi explained, these miraculous plants grow in an area resembling a narrow belt that crosses the islands like a straight line. They first appeared a few years after the Chernobyl nuclear catastrophe. This reminds me of the effects I observed in Latvia, which had supposedly escaped contamination. The spring following the disaster, all the tulips in Latvia, including my hybrids, flowered brightly and powerfully. I have never again seen such wonderful plants and blossoms. A small amount of radiation has the effect of stimulating plants, so this was evidence that Latvia had not gone unharmed by the calamity. However, Estonia was even more affected, and as a result we now have many gorgeous varieties of *A. ranunculoides*.

Anemone ranunculoides subsp. *wockeana* also has darker foliage and vivid yellow flowers. It is a smaller plant than the more widespread type subspecies, forming narrow, sharply toothed leaves. In the wild it grows in Como Province, Italy.

One of the greatest genera among bulbs is *Allium*. Some *Allium* species grow wild in Latvia, but I have only found one worth including in my collection. Like many other bulbous plants, *A. ursinum* is at its northeastern limit of distribution in Latvia; it is rare in the wild, growing mostly in the western part of the country, where the climate is milder. My plants come from the Salaca River valley, where they grow on moist meadows among shrubs, forming large groups in favorable conditions. It thrives where it is planted in my nursery beneath large maple trees, and it self-sows even though in summer the soil is dried out by the tree roots. Its nice white flowers are held on a stem some 30 cm tall, and it increases well vegetatively. It is a good plant for partial shade but can sometimes be invasive. The bulbs can be eaten, and the young leaves can be served fresh in salads in early spring.

The closely related *Allium victorialis* is similar, with cylindrical bulbs that are gathered around a short rhizome. It is very widespread from southern Europe through the Caucasus and Siberia to Japan and Korea. I grow only one of its variants, a plant collected in the Kemerovo region in Siberia that, according to the *Flora of the Soviet Union* (Komarov 1935), must be named *A. microdictyon*. It is taller, up to 50 cm high, with yellowish flowers, and I grow it along with *A. ursinum* where it self-sows in the shade of trees. I tried growing its Korean ally, *A. victorialis* subsp. *platyphyllum*, which has very beautiful, large, wide leaves, but never succeeded, although it seems quite comfortable in Gothenburg. I'm not sure why this is so. It's possible our winters are too hard, or I could have planted it in the wrong place, since it dislikes very dry soils. In any case I haven't yet lost hope of some day growing this very special, beautiful plant.

Latvia is the western border of distribution for the hardiest *Gladiolus* species. *Gladiolus imbricatus* (Plate 19) grows even in northern Finland at the polar circle. In Latvia it is a plant of moist meadows in river valleys. During Soviet times I never saw it in nature because all such meadows were harvested for hay before the plant had a chance to flower. After Latvia gained independence, there was a recession that affected farming, and with great surprise I began to see beautiful reddish purple flower spikes in the meadows where I had played during my childhood. *Gladiolus imbricatus* grows very well in the garden, too, although it can suffer from *Fusarium* and is very susceptible to virus infection. I always collect its seeds, and the seedlings start to flower in the third season. Compared with other hardy glads from the Middle East, it doesn't suffer from summer rains and is easily grown without any protection. It is much more floriferous in cultivation than in nature, with a spike up to 1 m high.

The last native bulb from Latvia I want to mention is the martagon lily, *Lilium martagon*. In nature it is distributed in a very wide area, from Portugal and the Pyrenees east through Asiatic Russia to northern Mongolia. It is variable in color, ranging from pure white (variety *album*) to almost blackish purple (variety *cattaniae*). On many occasions I have tried to introduce forms from Siberia, but none have established in my region, each in turn succumbing to *Botrytis* and dying. I still have a few bulbs, but none have flowered.

The question of whether the martagon lily is a Latvian native or a garden escapee has been discussed by botanists for a long time. The variant found wild in Latvia even has its own name, variety *daugavensis*, because it was mainly distributed on dolomite outcrops in the valley of the Daugava River near Koknese. All of those populations were destroyed by the great water reservoir of a hydropower station, and for some time popular opinion held that the plant had disappeared forever, along with some other plants recognized only from this valley. In more recent years, however, it has been found in a couple of nearby areas. The authors who prepared the last edition of the *Red Data Book of Latvia* (Andrusaitis 2003) didn't mention martagon lily at all among the rare and endangered plants, accepting it as a garden escapee not native to our flora.

The most important distinguishing feature of variety *daugavensis* is its capacity to germinate in the first spring rather than passing a year in the form of an underground bulbil, as is characteristic of the martagon lily. It's a shame that I never noticed this with my own plants; in fact, I never really saw seeds of *Lilium martagon*. The plants grow so well in my shaded, artificially made woodland soil that they self-sow perfectly, and I only collect small seedlings from around the mother plants. The flowers of variety *daugavensis* are darker or lighter purple and densely covered with small dark spots. Some are especially beautiful, and it would be worthwhile multiplying them by scales as clones, though I have never had time to try it.

Fritillaria meleagris is more likely to be a garden escapee. Like the martagon lily, it isn't included in the *Red Data Book of Latvia*, but the *Flora of Latvia* (Galenieks 1953) mentions it as an extremely rare plant found only in two small localities. Both localities are quite close to large cities, and this increases the doubt about the plant's origin. In the past, Latvian farmers lived in houses quite distant from their neighbors, and many of these houses were destroyed during the Russian occupation after World War II. The owners were either deported to Siberia or forced to relocate to villages where surveillance was easier to control. The remains of the houses and accompanying gardens were left unattended and soon disappeared, and now only a few ornamental trees and flowers are likely to mark a spot earlier inhabited by a family. I once found nice groups of *Galanthus nivalis*, *Leucojum vernum*, and even *Narcissus poeticus* grow-ing in deep grass near the stony remnants of a basement. I found a few plants of *Fritil-laria meleagris* over the course of that day, which was passed on the meadows near the Lielupe River. As it was seed time, I collected a few seed capsules, and from these I managed to build up my stock of this so-called native plant.

In my younger years I successfully grew *Tulipa sylvestris* in my garden, too, and I like it very much despite its peculiar habit of forming long stolons. In my first garden, where it grew in a corner without any attention, it increased perfectly, although there were more leaves than flowers. When I moved to a new garden I took some bulbs with me, but I planted them on a formal nursery bed among other tulips. Searching for the small bulbs at the ends of the long stolons took too much time, and the number of bulbs decreased from year to year until I finally lost this species altogether. I may try to reintroduce it at some point. Its small, bright yellow flowers with pointed petals lighten up the areas beneath shrubs at the garden's edge.

◈ 17
Eastern Carpathians

THE FURTHER SOUTH WE GO, the more bulbs we find growing in nature. A warmer climate and drier summers are more favorable for the development of bulb-like structures. The Carpathians are the first real mountains south of Latvia and are the nearest area in which many more native bulbs can be found. The regional climate is not very hot, and summer rains are infrequent, so most of the bulbs that grow there are quite easy to grow in my climate as well.

In the late 1970s I was working on *Crocuses*, a monograph published in 1981. The northern border for the distribution of genus *Crocus* is the Eastern Carpathian Mountains in western Ukraine (it's possible that some populations in Poland reach higher latitudes, but I haven't checked). The autumn-flowering *C. banaticus* and spring-flowering *C. heuffelianus* are recognized there. The Russian floras also mention *C. vernus* subsp. *albiflorus* (under the synonym *C. albiflorus*), but I suspect this is only the pure white form of *C. heuffelianus*. I have sometimes found such plants among ordinary purple ones, but I have never found a typical *C. vernus* subsp. *albiflorus*.

I don't agree that *Crocus heuffelianus* should be included in the *C. vernus* subsp. *vernus* complex. I have never seen a typical *C. vernus* subsp. *vernus* in the wild, and I grow only samples from other collectors, but they look so different in the garden that I prefer to regard them as a different species.

Crocus vernus is a very variable species with two subspecies. The small-flowering subspecies *albiflorus* has a style usually much shorter than the anthers. Subspecies *vernus* has larger flowers, with the style usually exceeding the anthers. All the forms of *C. vernus* subsp. *albiflorus* that I grow are raised from seed, mostly collected in the Alps (Italian, Swiss, and Bavarian), but some from Croatia and Romania. They are all very beautiful, with nice small flowers, and are very variable in color, although I have only white and blue forms. The whites are pure white or have a purple flower tube. I have never had any forms with striped flowers but often dream of acquiring some; I still look for wild-collected seeds, hoping that something striped will appear among the seedlings. Some forms from Slovenia have flowers with a dark tip at the end of the petals, and only their smallness and short stigma force me to place them under the name *C. vernus* subsp. *albiflorus*.

Flowers of *Crocus vernus* subsp. *vernus* have a similar range of variability. One of the best forms with purple flowers (collection number *Prášil-0273*) was found by Milan Prášil in Romania near Oradea. It blooms late and in great abundance, with variable dark purple blotches at the tips of its petals. I have lost the origin of another form, which has white flowers with a deep blue tube and forms very large corms, only slightly smaller than those of *C. ×cultorum*. A small-flowering form from Greece named *C. vernus* subsp. *vernus* var. *graecus* has long been in cultivation. It has small, deep blue flowers, but in my collection it blooms very rarely (when left for some years without replanting). I keep it only out of some kind of historical nostalgia.

Crocus heuffelianus and *C. scepusiensis* have the largest flowers of all the species in this complex, and you can separate them only by their throats: *C. heuffelianus* has a glabrous throat, *C. scepusiensis* a pubescent one. Otherwise both are very similar. I have some samples of *C. scepusiensis* grown from seed collected in Poland. The best one comes from the south of Poland (received from the Kraków Botanical Gardens) and is very vigorous and floriferous. It has large, bluish purple flowers with a dark blotch at the tips of the petals. Another batch of seedlings produced a large proportion of plants with a white stigma. Such a form was described by George Maw (1886) as variety *leucostigma* for *C. vernus*, so I used this name for my selection of *C. scepusiensis*, too. It reproduces well from seed but is a somewhat weaker grower than the form with an orange stigma.

My first encounter with *Crocus heuffelianus* took place at the Tallinn Botanical Garden in Estonia, where this species has naturalized perfectly and occupies the entire rockery. The chief of the bulb department, the late Aino Paivel, told me about her travels to the Eastern Carpathians and explained where I could look for this species. In the Uklin mountain pass she had even found forms with pinkish flowers. (Unfortunately, I wasn't to have the same luck.)

On 4 April 1978 I started one of my first mountain expeditions to the Eastern Carpathians, the nearest region with native crocuses. The departure of my flight was seriously delayed, so we landed three hours later than scheduled, and I only reached L'viv at one o'clock in the afternoon. I wanted to begin by visiting a lowland population of crocuses about 70 km north of L'viv, in the opposite direction from the mountains. It took me a little longer than an hour to get to the supposed population near the village of Velikiye Mosty. Despite it being quite late in the season, the lowland crocuses were still in full bloom. I hoped to find *Crocus scepusiensis* there, so I paid special attention to the throats of the flowers. Unfortunately, my hopes didn't come true—all the flowers I examined had nude throats. Later I found that there is a difference between these flower forms and the ones from the mountains. The difference is in the proportion of the anthers and filaments—in the mountain forms, they were generally equal in length, while in the lowland forms the anthers were one and a half to two times the length of the filaments. This character is even used in some botanical keys to identify the two forms. I later noted that the soil in which both populations grew was not the same at all. At Velikiye Mosty, *C. heuffelianus* grew on very sandy, loose soil, while in the mountains it grew on very sticky clay.

Overall it was a very successful first day. Over the course of three hours I caught a ride in four or five cars, covered 150 km, collected the plants I wanted, and returned to L'viv a quarter of an hour before the bus departed for Skole. Skole is the main city of the so-called pre-Carpathian region, although it is actually situated rather deep in

MAP 1: from Estonia to Bulgaria

the mountains in a narrow valley shortly before the highest mountain passes in the Eastern Carpathians. The main motorway from the Ukraine to the Czech Republic runs through the town. It was early spring, when snow melts in the mountain slopes. For the first time in my life I saw major flooding. Water covered the entire valley—only the roofs of the houses peaked out of the water.

I got to Skole at nine o'clock in the evening and headed straight for the town's only hotel. As expected, there were no vacancies. This trip took place during the darkest days of Communism, when there were two main powers in the Soviet Union: the Communist Party and the KGB. I was an editor of the Latvian horticultural magazine *Dārzs un Drava*, officially edited by the Latvian Society for Gardening and Beekeeping but actually controlled by the Communist Party, so my identification papers contained magic words that would open any door: "Central Committee of the Communist Party of Latvia." After the hotel receptionist saw my papers, an apartment suddenly opened up. It had been reserved for the local Communist Party Committee, a room with three twin beds and two television sets. Were the televisions for watching two programs at the same time, or were they meant to demonstrate the wealth of the town and how lavishly the hotel treated its VIP guests? I don't know. Needless to say, neither television worked.

Early the next morning I walked to the bus station and, boarding a bus, asked the driver the way to the mountain pass. He replied in Russian, in a very unfriendly tone, that he knew nothing. I had to name the point I wanted to get to and was only then finally allowed to enter. The bus was crowded. I came across as quite exotic to the rest of the passengers, with my different style of dress, large mountaineer's backpack, and strange accent. We started talking. As soon as they found out I was from Latvia, they asked me whether Latvians love Russians. I diplomatically replied, "Oh, yes, in the same way you do here." The whole bus exploded in laughter, and in a flash I became everyone's best friend. Like the Baltic States, the western Ukraine was occupied by Russians, and the last resistance movement had been squashed by the KGB in the mid-1950s. The attitude toward the Russian occupation was the same in the Ukraine as it was in Latvia. The bus driver announced that he would be happy to stop at any point I chose.

I left my bus at the Uklin mountain pass. At first look it didn't seem to be the paradise of crocuses I had heard about from Aino Paivel, but once I stepped away from the road I was greeted with millions of flowers. Since it was cloudy and a little rainy, the flower buds were closed and not easy to note. I turned to the right side of the motorway and, catching sight of something, stopped with my mouth wide open. I had never before seen such a wonderful flower—pure white, with a very dark purple blotch at the tips of the petals that continued as a narrow purple stripe down the axis of the petal, ending in a dark purple tube. In some ways it resembled a reversed *Crocus sieberi* 'Hubert Edelsten', whose flowers are purple with a white cross-band at the tips of the petals. I unearthed it very carefully with some soil around the corm and roots, then carefully packed it in a small clay pot. (I had brought a few such pots from Latvia for very special plants.) A painful blister soon appeared on my palm. I was still very inexperienced at this point. It wasn't until later that I found the most convenient tool for plant collecting to be the kind of ice pick used by mountain climbers.

This beautiful plant was a form of *Crocus heuffelianus*. Plants of this species are usually purple-flowered, although pure white specimens without any trace of purple on the petals are sporadically dispersed among the purple forms. At any rate, I never again found a crocus like this first wonder. Now it reproduces well in my nursery and I offer it in my catalog. It has been registered in the Netherlands and received the Alpine Garden Society's Award of Merit under the name 'Carpathian Wonder' (Plate 20). My trip to the Uklin mountain pass would have been worthwhile even if I had found nothing more than this one unique crocus. Surprisingly, only purple-flowering plants grew on the left side of the road, without any white forms among them. *Crocus heuffelianus* loves moisture in spring. This was the first time I saw bulbs with their flowers coming up through water. Melting snow made each small valley into a water-course, with bright lilac stars widely opening in the sunshine and blinking together with flecks of sunlight.

Driving up into the mountains I could see that there was still a lot of snow around. Spring had been delayed, but the weather was so warm and the snow was melting so rapidly that on our way back, the places that a few hours before had been blanketed with white now appeared dark and covered with thousands of crocus flower buds. On the way down my next stop was Lizja, a lower mountain pass. It was on an old road and I got there sitting in the narrow cabin of a tractor I had managed to hitch a ride on. Two forms of *Crocus heuffelianus* (Plate 21) dominate in Lizja, in approxi-mately equal proportions and without any intermediates: the very deep purple form and the white form with a very light purplish notch slightly below the tips of the pet-als. I grow both in my nursery and they reproduce very well.

The other bulb that grows here by the billions is *Leucojum vernum* var. *carpathi-cum* (Plates 23 and 24). It can be distinguished from other varieties by its wide petals, which have a bright yellow blotch at their tips, and by always having two flowers on a stem. In Latvian gardens only variety *vagneri* was grown earlier, with a green blotch at the tips of the somewhat angular petals. It has been very widespread in Latvian gardens since before World War II, although it is now rare in the West.

Leucojum vernum generally grows on meadows but can also be found by moun-tain slopes in forests. Near the village of Podpolozje in the Eastern Carpathians I came across a meadow of these plants, known as snowflakes, covering the ground like real snow. A river separated me from the meadow, so I had to cross it. I found a small island in the water and with a piece of wood some 2 m long built an extemporaneous bridge. I reached the island successfully, but the other part of the river was wider and my piece of wood was too short. I threw it in the water and tried to make a quick jump across. I soon found myself in the water. Even more, my backpack was so heavy and inertia so strong that I had to climb onto the riverbank on all fours.

Melting snow had washed thousands of *Leucojum* bulbs out of the soil in the meadow. Of all the samples of *L. vernum* var. *carpathicum*, this one turned out to be the most vigorous in Latvian conditions. It is now naturalized in my garden. I don't grow it on my beds; all the plants ordered from my catalog are simply dug out from under the large trees on my land, where they increase very well by self-sowing.

I soon found *Allium ursinum*, which grows everywhere in the Carpathians but is identical to plants from Latvia. Next, on the roadside on a very wet meadow, I noticed the large leaves of *Colchicum autumnale*. I collected one clump and was very surprised later when it flowered with pure white blooms. My entire stock of *C. autumnale* 'Alba' originated from this single clump, which was more vigorous than the Dutch garden form. Later by plant exchange I also received samples of the usual purple *C. autum-nale* that had been collected in the Carpathians, but they were weak growers and I soon lost them.

My attempt to introduce the blue and pink forms of *Scilla bifolia* that I had collected from near the city of Skole in the Carpathians was not at all successful. All of them were very weak growers and disappeared from my collection within a couple of years, while the samples from Crimea grew very well. The scilla from neighboring Czech Republic, *S. bifolia* subsp. *danubialis* (syn. *S. danubensis*), is also an excellent grower here, as is the form from Turkey collected at Bolu Pass and described by Franz Speta as *S. decidua*. This is quite characteristic of this species sensu lato—some populations dislike garden conditions, while other populations don't. There are some color forms in the trade, too. The most popular is the pink 'Rosea', but it is also very variable. I received the best sample from Chris Brickell, a deep pink form far better than the commercially distributed pale pink plants. I also received a pure white form from Antoine Hoog under the name *S. bifolia* 'Alba', although it turned out to be a beautiful white form of *Hyacinthoides italica*. Such misnaming isn't surprising, since both plants flower at the same time and are superficially quite similar.

Alternating between car and foot, I slowly made my way down from the mountains. Near the roadside, beneath majestic beech (*Fagus*) and hornbeam (*Carpinus*) trees, grew plenty of the usual purple *Crocus heuffelianus*, but none of them were white. Near the village of Jalovoje I collected a few white and purple forms of *Corydalis cava*. This species is native in my country, too, but is found there very rarely because Latvia is the northern limit of its distribution. The white form is registered only from a small island in a large lake, which is a strictly protected area. By contrast, in the Carpathians they grow everywhere by the billions. Since I started growing this plant in my garden, it has become a weed, self-sowing far more effectively than I would like it to.

The yellow-flowered *Corydalis marschalliana* is closely related to *C. cava*, differing in the shape of its leaves and its light yellow flowers. It is now considered to be a color form of *C. cava*, but I can't agree with such lumping. I have never seen them growing together, and all forms of *C. marschalliana* have distinctly different leaves with entire leaf lobes (versus the apically dentate leaves of *C. cava*) and smaller, more solid tubers. Even forms from the North Caucasus described as variety *purpureo-lilacina* have light yellow flowers, only at the top of the spike they are slightly purplish in shade. When I grew *C. marschalliana* and *C. cava* together in the garden, they never hybridized, and the seeds of *C. cava* produced only white and various purple-flowering plants, while those of *C. marschalliana* always produced yellow-flowered plants with or without lilac-shaded apical flowers.

In some parts of the mountains it still looked like deep winter, with a few meters of snow covering the ground, while only a hundred meters away you could see spots free of snow and covered in early spring flowers. In one such spot not far from the village of Kozeva I spotted something new: *Galanthus nivalis*. Although I already had this species at home, I collected a few as a sample. I was very surprised the next spring when they bloomed in my garden—the flowers were twice as large as those usually grown in Latvia. It was a good increaser, and after some years I offered it in my local catalog under the name 'Maxima'. Unfortunately, when I was later forced to move my garden, my collection of snowdrops disliked the new site, and within a few years I lost almost all of them, including this gigantic form of *G. nivalis*. Just a few years ago my friend Sulev Savisaar, a well-known plant collector from Tartu, Estonia, sent me a letter inquiring about the origin of this plant. It turned out he was still growing it, and it had increased marvelously in his garden. He sent me a hundred or so bulbs, and the snowdrops seem to like the spot I have made for them in my present garden. So once again I grow this wonder, but since the *International Code of Nomenclature of Cultivated Plants* doesn't allow for Latinized cultivar names, I now call it 'Carpathian Giant'.

The next day I had to catch an early bus to the mountain pass. I wanted to visit the western slopes of the ridge (Transcarpathian region) where *Erythronium dens-canis* was known to grow. This species is widely distributed from central Portugal to Central Europe, with the most eastern population growing in the Eastern Carpathians. It belongs to the Eurasian erythroniums, a group very different from its American counterparts. Four easily distinguished species are recognized, although not so long ago they were regarded as forms of *E. dens-canis*.

I watched the roadsides carefully, and just before the village of Lipcha I noticed my first erythroniums. They grew everywhere here in the shrubs and beneath trees near the plowed fields. The flowers were deep purple, their anthers blackish, the filaments of equal length—typical *E. dens-canis*.

I was greatly surprised in subsequent years to find that this was the most early-blooming form of *Erythronium dens-canis* in my collection. By the time the forms from Spain and Romania start flowering, the flowers of this form from Lipcha are long gone. Unfortunately, it doesn't increase vegetatively and I have never had any offsets of it. I harvest the seeds only infrequently and now, after nearly thirty years, have fewer bulbs than I started with.

Some 20–25 km south of Lipcha is a famous daffodil valley, the most northern wild population of *Narcissus poeticus* (or *N. angustifolius*, as it is named in the *Flora of the Soviet Union*). It grows in the border zone, where special permission is required for entrance. Not many years ago it was very widespread in the Transcarpathian region, but then all the meadows were plowed up for farming, and only a few acres were set aside as a nature reserve for this unique species. Russian botanists had told me earlier that it wasn't possible to find two identical plants there; they were all different in height, petal form, cup color, flowering time, and so forth. Nevertheless, it was much too early in the season for daffodils to be in flower, and I didn't want to risk sitting in jail for three days for illegally entering the border zone. I later received some bulbs of *N. poeticus* from the Tallinn Botanical Garden, and it turned out to be the most late-flowering narcissus in my collection. Unfortunately, however, it soon perished from *Fusarium* infection.

I had found everything I wanted. There were some plants I hadn't seen, but nothing I was particularly looking for. *Crocus banaticus* also grows in the Eastern Carpathians, but it would be impossible to find without its flowers, looking only for its small leaves, without knowing the exact locality. I have grown this beautiful autumn-flowering crocus from seed sent to me from Romania. I can't say that it is the easiest species, but it usually sets seed, reproduces vegetatively, and flowers beautifully every autumn. The most important thing is to keep the soil slightly wet and to water the beds during longer periods of drought. Between harvesting and planting, the corms must be kept in a plastic bag in slightly moist peat moss. *Crocus heuffelianus* can stay in even open boxes without any great problems, but in similar circumstances *C. banaticus* can die. There are some very beautiful white forms of it, too. I received my first sample from the Netherlands, but it turned out to be virus-infected. The next were sent to me by a Czech friend who found them in the wild in Romania. I later received another beautiful and very floriferous albino selection from Britain, 'Snowdrift' (Plate 25), which flowers later but more abundantly than other albino forms. There are bi-colored forms, too, in which the short inner petals are a much lighter shade than the larger outer ones.

The next morning I awoke at half past five. The morning greeted me with heavy rain. As the weather was warm, I used my warmest clothing to pad all the plant material in my backpack to keep it from getting damaged during transportation. The bus station was only about a hundred meters from the hotel, and I ran to it through the rain. The station was still closed, although it was supposed to be open an hour before any bus departure, but the bus was there and the driver let me on. It is quite common here for about a third of the passengers to pay directly into the driver's pocket; if tickets are checked at some stop along the way, part of this money moves into the pocket of the controller doing the checking.

Through the bus window I could still see some spots of purple-flowered *Crocus* and white-flowered *Leucojum*. The rain turned into light snow, then into a strong snowstorm, and soon everything around was covered in white. I fell asleep and didn't wake up until L'viv, then caught a taxi to the airport. The flight to Riga was delayed because of the snow, and when everyone finally boarded the plane, it flew first to Chişinău, Moldova, then back to Riga, without stopping again in L'viv. In Riga a real winter had returned; it was cold and snowing, but all my warm clothes were in my baggage. I ended up catching pneumonia, which even led to a minor heart attack, but I recovered perfectly in June when I visited the Kopet-Dag (Turkmenistan) to look for *Crocus michelsonii*.

Amazingly, it was just this sort of capricious weather that pushed me to go to Bessarabia, where more bulbs were known to grow. I had only been through here once, in my youth, after completing the entrance exams for my university. Some school-mates and I hitchhiked our way to the Black Sea, through Bessarabia and the foothills of the Eastern Carpathians, but I wasn't thinking then of looking for bulbs.

Most of the bulbous plants in my stock that grow in the wild in Bessarabia and are of interest to gardeners were received from Aino Paivel at the Tallinn Botanical Garden. I still grow the *Ornithogalum* species, but during a very hard winter the frost killed all my bulbs of *Colchicum fominii*, a beautiful, small-flowering relative of *C.*

umbrosum. This is one of the plants I would like to return to my collection. I would also like to have the true *Gymnospermium odessanum*, which is almost extinct in its wild habitat in Russia, though it is still possible to find in areas to the west and south. Plants received from the Gothenburg Botanical Garden under that name (the stock came from the Komarov Botanical Institute in Saint Petersburg) turned out to be identical with *G. altaicum* from Siberia.

There are two plants I would like to mention in particular, the first being *Crocus reticulatus* subsp. *reticulatus* (Plate 26). For years this crocus was dismissed by Western gardeners as a weak grower with almost translucent, inconspicuous flowers. However, the plants collected by Aino near a cultivated field in a sunny spot among deciduous trees are among the most beautiful spring-flowering crocuses, boasting very bright lilac-blue flowers with pointed petals. The petal exterior is pale with deep purple stripes; the throat is yellow. It is one of the brightest blue crocuses, flowering abundantly and increasing well both vegetatively and from seed. It must be planted some distance from the fertile wild forms of the Crimean *C. angustifolius*, with which it can easily hybridize; otherwise intermediate forms may appear among the seedlings. It is among my favorite crocuses.

Galanthus elwesii is another beauty that has come to my collection from Bessarabia through the kind hands of Aino. It is shorter than the Turkish forms, despite being called the giant snowdrop. In any case it is smaller than the plants from Turkey distributed by Dutch companies, but it keeps both basal and apical green marks on the inner petals. The outer petals are wide and nicely rounded. It is one of my loveliest snowdrops. *Galanthus elwesii* is easy to grow in cultivation and increases well by splitting the bulbs. The seedlings are somewhat variable. I grow it among other snowdrops in a partly shaded spot in slightly sandy soil. It receives some sun at midday but is shaded in the mornings and afternoons.

Another species grows in Moldova: *Leucojum aestivum*, the summer snowflake. It likes very wet spots but is less hardy than *L. vernum*. My stock of it came from Moldova, but I lost it during a hard winter, when all the forms of *L. vernum* survived without any problems. It demands an enormous amount of moisture. A large clump of *L. aestivum* once grew at the University of Latvia botanical garden at the side of a pond. It was positioned a meter above water level, and it never flowered. Later, when the pond's drainage system was damaged, the water level rose substantially and within a month the clump was underwater. We thought it had died, but the next spring it came up and flowered abundantly for the first time. I recently saw a clump growing out of some water in Turkey with seed capsules at the top of its flower stalks.

Although ornithogalums are classified by many gardeners as terrible weeds, this label is true for only a few species. When I started growing bulbs I was looking for everything new, and among the newcomers were *Ornithogalum umbellatum* and *O. nutans*, both species that leave so many bulbils in the ground that it's never possible to harvest them all. *Ornithogalum nutans* is less invasive but can become a weed. It took some years of regular spraying with Roundup to get rid of *O. umbellatum* after

I unintentionally introduced it among some other bulbous plants from the Netherlands. I once had the same battle with *O. nutans* after deciding that I didn't want to grow it anymore (since then I have acquired an excellent noninvasive form from Turkey). But I haven't found any other species of *Ornithogalum* to be as invasive as these two. *Ornithogalum refractum* has many bulbils at the base, too, but they never germinate here, so I increase my stock from seed.

My stock of *Ornithogalum flavescens* comes from Bessarabia. This species is now generally considered a synonym of *O. pyrenaicum*. Until my last trip to Turkey, when I saw forms of *O. pyrenaicum* intermediate between the plants of *O. flavescens* and *O. pyrenaicum* I had grown earlier, I thought both species were too different to include under the same name. Still, although both are very similar, I consider them sufficiently distinct to keep my stocks separated under different names. *Ornithogalum flavescens* isn't a very spectacular plant but has the most yellowish flowers of the Eurasian ornithogalums, though unfortunately they are placed very sparsely on a stem 1 m tall. Though easy to grow and often requested by gardeners, it is rarely offered in the trade.

Ornithogalum orthophyllum (Plate 27) is superficially similar to *O. umbellatum* but doesn't have those terrible bulbils at the base of the mother bulb. Its white flowers are held in a dense umbel among rosettes of narrow leaves. My stock was collected near the village of Sakharna in Bessarabia and most likely belongs to subspecies *kochii*, but classification of ornithogalums is very difficult due to the great variability of the taxa. The other species from this locality is *O. gussonei*, which is very similar to *O. orthophyllum*. The plants that I used to grow under this name have very fine white flowers in a dense umbel at ground level held well over a rosette of fine leaves. It is likely just a form of *O. orthophyllum*.

Before turning east I want to mention some other crocuses that are superficially comparable to *Crocus vernus*. One of them, *C. veluchensis* from the Balkans, is even regularly confused with *C. vernus*, although botanically they belong to different groups. I never saw *C. veluchensis* in the wild, and all my stocks of it are introduced in the form of seeds, but it is too beautiful to not mention. Because of their shape and bright purple coloring, the flowers resemble some of the large-flowering Dutch spring crocuses (*C. ×cultorum*), but otherwise, without dissection and careful checking of morphological details, it is not easy to decide whether this plant is *C. veluchensis* or some form of *C. vernus*. There is one special feature of *C. veluchensis*, however: it makes new roots before the leaves and old roots die. For this reason it is rarely offered by bulb nurseries, although it does not suffer much from replanting if planted immediately after the corms are obtained. The white form is very beautiful, too; its color can vary from the purest snow white to slightly bluish.

Crocus cvijicii is very similar to the best forms of *C. veluchensis* in almost all aspects, but color is a noticeable difference. Its flowers are usually bright orange, and it is even easier to grow than its lilac cousin because its roots are formed in the "normal" way. Nothing is perfect, however, and this species' biggest fault may be its unpronounceable name. In *A Handbook of Crocus and Colchicum for Gardeners* (1952), E. A.

Bowles pondered this very topic, wondering "whether it is better to imitate a sneeze" when attempting to pronounce the name, "or, as a witty friend of mine put it, 'to play it on the violin.'" There are also albino forms of *C. cvijicii*, but they are creamy in shade, or, according to nurseryman W. E. Th. Ingwersen, silvery lemon. Both *C. cvijicii* and *C. veluchensis* have similar chromosomes, so it isn't surprising that some hybridization can occur between both if they grow together. However, this seems to happen very rarely. After growing these species in my garden for more than ten years, I only recently found a clearly intermediate form among my seedlings of *C. cvijicii* var. *alba* (Plate 28). It has a yellowish throat and its petals are slightly creamy at the base with slight purple speckling over their exteriors. It is very floriferous. I predict a great future for it if it proves to be a good increaser, too.

Since I've already paused in my travels, I hope readers will allow me another side step—there are a few more very beautiful crocuses that I must mention. The first is the white-flowering *Crocus malyi*, which resembles the large Dutch spring crocuses because of the size and brightness of its flowers. It comes from the Velebit Mountains of western Croatia and is almost invariably the purest snow white, with slight variation in the color of the flower tube and style. It is a marvelous and very easy crocus for the garden and has made it through many bad winters on my property in Latvia.

Crocus versicolor (Plates 29 and 30) is very close to *C. malyi* botanically and in its growing capacity but has a very different area of distribution, growing in the Maritime Alps in southeastern France and extending into northwestern Italy. This species is largely forgotten by gardeners, and in my opinion, undeservedly so. In the nineteenth century almost twenty different varieties were described, but now only one is offered: *C. versicolor* 'Picturatus', also known as 'Cloth of Silver', which unfortunately is the poorest of all crocuses. In fact 'Picturatus' was once the top candidate for removal from my *Crocus* collection, but then I received a parcel of seeds Michael Hoog had collected in a mixed deciduous forest in the department of Var, France. The seeds germinated very well, and in the fourth spring I found myself standing at the seedling bed, camera in hand, unable to decide where to start taking pictures. The flowers were a great assortment of bright colors, sizes, and forms. They seemed to have nothing in common with the small, weak, pale 'Picturatus'. Dozens of these seedlings are clear candidates for cloning, and it is only because of my busy schedule that I haven't yet finished marking them. I grow some stocks marked "Not for sale! Plenty of beauties for sorting out." There are lighter and darker forms, with petals that are white and lilac at the base, some with deep, bright purple striping on the back of the outer petals.

❖ 18
Crimea

I HAVE VISITED the Crimean Peninsula many times, but only once, in 1983, did I travel there especially for bulbs. Now I must return to crocuses, because crocuses were my specific reason for the trip.

Mostly I was interested in *Crocus tauricus* (Plate 31). Taurus is an ancient name for Crimea and is sometimes confused with the Taurus Mountains of southern Turkey. When it comes to crocuses these names become even more confusing, because there are plants from both places in the same group: *C. biflorus* subsp. *taurii* comes from Turkey, whereas *C. tauricus* originated in Crimea. In *The Crocus* (1982), Brian Mathew includes *C. tauricus* as a synonym of *C. biflorus* subsp. *adamii*. I can't agree with him here, and not just because *C. tauricus* was described by the Latvian botanist N. Puring. The population of the Crimean crocus is quite isolated from other forms and subspecies of *C. biflorus*. It grows only on the Yaila Dag of the Crimean Peninsula (a yaila is a flat mountain meadow) and has a tunic with very hard, extremely long-toothed basal rings. During my studies of crocuses I often worked with herbarium sheets of native crocuses of the Soviet Union at the Komarov Botanical Institute in Saint Petersburg. On one occasion I covered the labels of all the annulate crocuses, mixed the sheets up, and then picked out *C. tauricus*. I made no mistakes! In addition to the basal rings, the bluish gray-green leaves are also very unique. As far as I know, the only other annulate crocus with such leaves is *C. biflorus* subsp. *weldenii*. I also can't agree with Brian Mathew that the character of the basal rings is of little taxonomical value; I have found that the basal rings are very different in various subspecies of *C. biflorus*.

I went to Crimea with my daughters and their rock climbing team, who were attending a training camp in the area. I joined the group to climb the mountains in search of plants, and one of my first targets was *C. tauricus*. It was early spring and there was still some snow on the yaila where *C. tauricus* grew. The plants had just started to flower, but the day was cloudy, and it was not easy to find the dark-colored flower buds. They were very variable in the amount of striping and shade of blue and purple on the petal exteriors.

Unfortunately, some time ago Antoine Hoog attached the name *Crocus tauricus* to stock of another crocus also collected in Crimea, *C. speciosus* (Plate 32), and this has at times caused confusion. I collected *C. speciosus* on the same yaila where I found *C. tauricus* but on a different occasion. My family and I were enjoying the beautiful weather of early autumn on the stony beach of the Black Sea. After parting with them I joined the botanists from the Nikitsky Botanical Garden in Yalta and headed up to the yaila to look for crocuses. It was a very dry season and *C. speciosus* was only beginning to flower. Later, when I grew it back in Latvia, it turned out to be the earliest autumn-flowering form of the species. Normally in my region *C. speciosus* starts to flower in September, but this form always flowered in the box before replanting in early August. Only *C. scharojanii* started somewhat earlier. It was very nicely striped and had a yellow throat, and Brian Mathew even compared it with subspecies *xantholaimos*, which grew only in a rather restricted area of Turkey. Unfortunately, this beauty was unable to survive an endless battle with an army of rodents.

On the yaila of Ai-Petri I collected a beautiful *Ornithogalum* species that was later identified as *O. fimbriatum* (Plate 33) by its very hairy leaves. Later, not far from our camp, I collected another ornithogalum. Although it looked very different, it was in fact the same species. The highland form has very narrow leaves, while the lowland form has much wider leaves. Both are extremely hairy. This dwarf species is at its most beautiful early in the morning, when on each hair tip sits a brilliant dewdrop. I named both forms after the places in which they were collected: narrow-leaved 'Ai-Petri' and wide-leaved 'Oreanda'. It is quite a variable species, growing in a very wide area all around the Black Sea. I now have many forms from Turkey, with flowers varying in size and number, and leaves varying in width and hairiness. But 'Ai-Petri' and 'Oreanda' remain my favorites.

Halfway down from the yaila, in a moist depression in the shade of large beech trees, I found a splendid large-flowering form of *Scilla bifolia* with bright blue flowers. Having had a bad experience with *S. bifolia* from the Eastern Carpathians, I was pleasantly surprised later to find that this population grew vigorously in my garden. The flowers are twice as large as those of traditional trade forms and much larger than those of its close relative *S. bifolia* subsp. *danubialis* from the Czech Republic. *Scilla bifolia* var. *taurica* (Plate 34), offered by Antoine Hoog, is another godsend; in my opinion it is much more worthy of its own species name than *S. bifolia* subsp. *danubialis* or *S. decidua*.

In a slightly lighter spot I collected a very large-flowering form of *Ficaria verna*, or *Ranunculus ficaria* as it is now named, which can also be classified as a bulbous plant. Many years later I brought home some color forms from Britain and also collected some in Turkey. They are not among my favorite plants, although they can lighten shaded and moist corners of the garden with their bright golden yellow flowers. Unfortunately, they sometimes get too comfortable and can become overly invasive.

I devoted the next day to the surroundings of our camp. It was based in a narrow valley, although it could have been called a gorge very close to sea level. Only a few spots between the sea and the yaila some 1000 m above it had never been touched by humans. These were mostly very steep or rocky places that couldn't be developed or walked upon. One such spot was located near a high rock that served as a training site for climbers. While walking around the area I found another *Crocus* species: *C. angustifolius* (syn. *C. susianus*). This species (sometimes called 'Cloth of Gold') had already long been in cultivation. It was an excellent grower with nice, golden yellow, starry flowers widely opening at soil level in bright sunshine. Deep purplish brown stripes marked the back of the outer petals. This cultivated form was sterile, however, so I now had an excellent opportunity to introduce a fertile sample of the species. At that moment I didn't understand how fruitful this finding would prove to be many years later.

The following spring I realized that I had actually collected two forms. I named one form 'Flavus' (an illegitimate name according to the *Code*, which doesn't allow Latinized forms for cultivars) because its petal exteriors were almost without stripes. The other form, 'Oreanda', was named for the nearest village. Both are taller and flower two to three days earlier than the commercial form of *Crocus angustifolius*, but vegetative reproduction is slower. The greatest advantage is that both are fertile and produce a good seed crop every year. In my nursery beds *C. angustifolius* is always planted side by side with *C. reticulatus*; in nature their areas overlap, and superficially they are quite similar, only one is yellow and the other is blue. I also regularly sow seeds of both species. This has resulted in plants with a yellow base color characteristic of *C. angustifolius*, though not as deep, and a habit like *C. reticulatus*.

The same happened in the garden of my Lithuanian friend Leonid Bondarenko, who received fertile stock of *Crocus angustifolius* from me. Being more diligent than I am, he selected many beautiful, vigorous forms, naming one such hybrid 'Jānis Rukšāns'. Its blooms are golden yellow throughout with wide, almost converged reddish brown stripes on the petal exteriors, and it flowers very early and abundantly, making eight to ten long-lasting flowers from a corm. Another selection, 'Nida', increases at a surprisingly high rate. It belongs to the most light-colored forms of this hybrid series, with a creamy yellow base color and very prominent reddish brown stripes on the petal exteriors. It reproduces even more productively than *C. angustifolius* and forms nice, large corms. 'Early Gold' is one of the most floriferous forms, producing up to thirteen blooms from one corm. The flowers are golden yellow throughout with purple stripes on the outer petals. All of these cultivars are sterile and very vigorous.

In the same part of Crimea I found a large group of *Galanthus plicatus* in a wet depression. In my opinion this species, rather than *G. elwesii*, deserves to be called the giant snowdrop. *Flora Taurica* (Wulff 1929) mentions plants with leaves 60 cm long and 4 cm wide. Only *G. platyphyllus* can compete with it in terms of size, but nothing is as vigorous. The form that I found grows at an altitude of 100 m in clearings among large deciduous trees on the east side of a gorge. It has glaucous leaves with a large green apical mark on the inner segments. I named it 'Oreanda'. It grows extremely well in the garden.

The mountains of Crimea seem to be the most extreme western tip of the Caucasus ridge. Looking at a map, the long line of the Caucasus ridge and small dot of Crimea are something like an exclamation point fallen flat on its face. The distribution areas of many plants overlap here. There are one or two populations of *Crocus tauricus* in the Caucasus Mountains (Krasnodar region) just near Crimea. Although *Galanthus plicatus* isn't known to grow there, I received a few bulbs of *Galanthus* species that were collected near the village of Enem in the Krasnodar region at the foothills of the Caucasus. When they flowered I noticed that the species was *G. plicatus*.

Although the collection site was outside the traditional distribution area, it was not far from Crimea. Unlike other stocks, this one has bright green leaves and a small green apical mark on the inner segments, so I decided to name it. Following my own tradition, I named it after the village nearest to where it had been collected: 'Enem'.

In a drier, sunnier spot somewhat higher in the same gorge, a nice group of *Corydalis paczoskii* was in full flower. The flowers of this species have a very delicate shape. They are light pinkish purple with a dark purple-brown nose and form quite loose but long spikes that give the plant a quiet charm. It is an easy plant in the garden, where it even self-sows, and can be grown in some shade as well as in full sun. Among my own seedlings of *C. solida* I quickly found a few with clear signs of having *C. paczoskii* blood in their ancestry. These have more compact and upright spikes with more densely placed flowers, retaining the admirable contrast between the very dark, almost blackish, inner petals and the light violet outer petals and spur.

The last plant I collected in this area was an *Arum* species with beautiful glossy leaves, which abundantly covered the shadiest spots at the very bottom of the gorge. The tubers lay deep in very peaty, loose soil. This was the first time I saw underground aphids, which covered the tubers like a silvery bluish gray frosting. Classifying this aroid was a very difficult task. I didn't take any field notes during this trip and later forgot some important details needed to determine the species. In addition, various local floras were very contradictory about the naming of aroids. Only after many years, when Peter Boyce's wonderful *Genus Arum* appeared, did classification become possible. There were two possibilities for my plant: *Arum orientale* or *A. elongatum* (Plate 35). Although both are superficially very similar, the leaf shape is different. The leaves of *A. orientale* are broadly hastate, while those of *A. elongatum* are sagittate-hastate. The leaf shape can't always be clearly determined, however. At the same time I was growing a very similar aroid from the surroundings of Enem, Krasnodar region. I felt that both aroids were different, but the question remained as to just what was what. My traditional style of growing bulbs—replanting them every season—didn't allow me to find the main difference between the species: the position of the tuber in the soil. When I moved all the shade lovers to my current shade garden, I left them in the soil for three years. During this time the tubers placed themselves in the positions characteristic of each species. When I went to collect some of the tubers, I found that those from Crimea were lying in the soil horizontally, as is typical for *A. elongatum*, and then I noticed that the leaf bases were hastate. The tubers from Enem turned themselves in a vertical position, so these were clearly *A. orientale*, with leaf bases that were sagittate-hastate.

Both species are quite hardy, so I was surprised when in the spring of 2003 they didn't come up, even though the frost during the previous December had been very hard (even the hardy arisaemas from the Far East had been killed). Luckily, I later had an opportunity to reintroduce these aroids into my collection, thanks to the friends with whom I regularly share plant material. Hearing that I had lost many of my aroids, my colleagues from Estonia (Sulev Savisaar) and Lithuania (Leonid Bondarenko, Augis Dambrauskas) immediately sent me a few tubers from the plants' original stocks, which they had received from me many years ago. Whenever I have more than three bulbs, I try to divide the extras among friends. Sharing in this way can help restore stocks in fatal situations.

For extra security, I suggest also planting bulbs in different parts of your own garden, even if you only have a few of each. This recommendation is especially important for crocuses. Just planting them in two different corners of the garden can save your stock from total extinction after an attack by rodents (presuming, of course, that both corners won't be attacked simultaneously).

The Crimean Peninsula is home to *Cyclamen kuznetzovii*, one of the rarest cyclamens in the world. It is closely related to *C. coum*—in fact, most botanists outside the former Soviet Union consider it a synonym. Many local variants of this species are described in local floras. They are regarded as subspecies by some authors, while others regard them as variants without taxonomic range. I haven't been able to decide which attitude is correct. I grow some of them under the names that were attached to them when they came to me from other growers.

Despite all this, the Crimean population of *Cyclamen kuznetzovii* is very isolated from the distribution area of *C. coum* sensu lato. It is not easy to tell whether this isolation occurred naturally or as the result of the destruction of forests and use of land for farming. Now this cyclamen grows only in a very small forest near Belogorsk in the southern part of the peninsula. The exact location is kept top secret to protect the small population from collectors.

I have never tried to introduce *Cyclamen kuznetzovii* in my collection regardless of the fact that it has been described as the hardiest wild cyclamen. To my surprise, however, I once saw it listed for an Alpine Garden Society seed exchange. I asked for seeds, but the demand was so great that I never received any. I recently learned that the donor of the seeds was Kees Sahin, owner of a famous Dutch seed company. We started corresponding with each other, and during one of my visits to the Netherlands I received an invitation from him. His company is famous for breeding cyclamens and for having raised the first cyclamen cultivar with yellowish flowers ('Winter Sun'). Kees is very hospitable and can tell endless stories about his travels to the most exotic corners of the planet. He told me one particularly amazing story about a visit to North Korea to meet with breeders of tuberous begonias. There he found hectares of nothing but bright red seedlings—since red was President Kim Il Sung's favorite color, all the others had been destroyed. I returned from the Netherlands with a hundred hand-pollinated seeds kindly presented to me by Kees's charming wife, Elizabeth. Now I have plenty of seedlings grown separately from all other forms of *C. coum* to be certain that the following generation will be true to its name.

Growing cyclamens is a very risky enterprise in Latvia. The various forms of *Cyclamen coum* (syn. *C. abchasicum*, *C. caucasicum*, *C. ibericum*) are generally rather hardy here, and the same can be said about the autumn-flowering *C. hederifolium*. However, you can never be certain whether these plants will survive the winter if planted outside. On one occasion I lost *C. hederifolium* even in an unheated greenhouse, while plants of the same origin survived without problems in a friend's garden under a large lime tree, even without any additional covering. I have found it best to prepare them for winter with a covering of dry leaves topped by a plastic sheet, which acts as a roof to protect the bulbs from moisture. The most complicated part of the process is the removal of the covering in spring. It has to be done very carefully so as not to damage the flower buds that sometimes poke up through the leaves. It should also be left for a cloudy day, since sunshine followed by night frost can burn the moist, sensitive leaves before they have adjusted to the open air.

During my trip to Crimea I was also looking for *Sternbergia colchiciflora* (Plate 36). This very tiny, beautiful sternbergia produces small, bright yellow flowers at soil level before the leaves come out, which happens only in spring. I now have many different stocks, which bloom beautifully for me each autumn, but all were collected in Turkey. I may have been in Crimea too early to find this species, since the autumn was very dry and tardy. But *S. colchiciflora* has a unique feature: in very dry seasons the flowers remain inside the bulbs instead of coming out of the soil. When this occurs, all the parts of the flower are left half-developed and pollination occurs inside the bulb, after which the seedpods begin to develop. I have never observed this myself because I normally water my plants in autumn and they flower nicely, but I have read of such cases in the journal of the Russian Botanical Society (1926).

I also collected some *Allium* species in Crimea, including *A. jajlae*, found near Simeiz in a soil pocket between large rocks. Although the species name refers to a yaila, or mountain meadow, this plant was actually growing on a slope halfway to the sea from any yaila. In my garden in Latvia it turned out to be a very nice, well-growing, midsummer-flowering species. Its beautiful, light purple or pinkish, upward-facing flowers are held in round, compact umbels on stems up to 40 cm tall. The petals of individual flowers are pointed and all of the same color. The bulbs split well, forming a few large replacement bulbs and a few small bulbils near the stem.

Some botanists consider *Allium jajlae* to be a smaller form of *A. rotundum*, but I don't agree. *Allium rotundum* is almost twice as tall. The petals of its blackish purple flowers are abrupt and more rounded, and the inner petals are lighter, almost white, so that the flowers look dichromatic. They are composed in very dense, spherical umbels on stems up to 70 cm tall. The bulb usually splits into only two small replacement bulbs, forming many small bulbils attached to the underground part of the flower stem (some of them even higher). I received this species from the surroundings of Enem in the Krasnodar region. The collector, local teacher Victor Korolev, warned me that it can become a terrible weed in the garden. During the first season I planted it in an isolated spot but found that the bulbils almost never germinated. Perhaps Latvian conditions are too harsh for them.

Another beauty from Crimea was introduced by Arnis Seisums. *Allium meliophilum* (Plate 37) is an endemic of the area. Its seeds were collected in a depression of the Yaila Dag near Tschornaya Gora (Black Mount). Some botanists place it in a separate genus, *Nectaroscordum*. Unfortunately, the least decorative species of this group—*A.*

siculum (very rarely found in Moldova, more widespread in southeastern Europe) and its variety *bulgaricum*—are the most widely distributed in gardens. The far more beautiful Crimean *A. meliophilum* and Armenian *A. tripedale* are unknown to many gardeners, though both have found their way to recognition through my nursery.

Allium meliophilum looks much like a smaller version of *A. tripedale*. Its flower stem never exceeds 50 cm tall, and its lilac flowers are held in a dense umbel. *Allium tripedale* is one of the most gorgeous species of the genus. Its flowers are large, each 1.5–2 cm in diameter, campanulate, bright pink, and more compactly arranged than those of *A. siculum*. It blooms much earlier, too, and the nice inflorescence is placed on a stem 100–130 cm tall. A true gem, it was collected by Arnis in Armenia. Unfortunately, both species make very few or no offsets, and since it takes at least six years for them to flower from seed, both are scarce and expensive. This is a shame, as they can be counted among the best ornamental alliums.

A few more plants from the Krasnodar region are also worth mentioning, starting with the most beautiful, *Anemone blanda* (Plate 38). Though it is very widespread in Turkey, in the North Caucasus it is replaced by the smaller *A. caucasica*. Far from its other areas of distribution, just at the western end of the Caucasus ridge, is a single location on the northern coast of the Black Sea where *A. blanda* can also be found growing. It has large, deep blue flowers and is very floriferous. Some growers consider it to be the best blue form of this variable species, but it originates from a very uniformly colored population. I named it 'Enem', after the nearest village to where it had been collected; it was found about 50 km from the village on some clay soil below rocky outcrops. The tubers are somewhat different from the Turkish plants, resembling long, black, thin pieces of a tree branch. If the tubers are not planted in light sand, it is not possible to collect them at harvesting time. In my opinion this plant is worthy of subspecies designation due to the unusual shape of its tubers and its long-distance isolation from Turkish populations.

Various snowdrops grow in the Krasnodar region and east from there. For many years there was much confusion over how to correctly classify them, and for many years I followed Z. T. Artjushenko's *Amaryllidaceae of the Soviet Union*. In more recent years, however, two marvelous books have been published that describe these plants in detail: *The Genus Galanthus* (Davis 1999), which covers the wild species of snowdrops, and *Snowdrops* (Bishop et al. 2002). Naturally, many of the plant names firmly established in my mind have now been changed, which I'm not happy about. Two of my most lovely snowdrops come from just the Krasnodar region: *Galanthus caucasicus*, with wide, glaucous leaves (renamed *G. alpinus* var. *alpinus*), and *G. woronowii*, which is similar but with shiny green leaves. The shape and size of the flowers, and shape and size of the leaves, are very similar for both species, and I call them "the twins from Krasnodar." In my garden I began by planting them under large oaks where the soil in summer becomes very dry from the roots of the trees. However, noticing how uncomfortable they seemed there, I moved them to my new shade garden, where they have more access to water. Now they grow and increase splendidly.

Some of the many ornithogalums that I grow in my garden came from the same area. The correct naming of ornithogalums is extremely difficult, since there is great variability within the species. To classify them correctly, details about the shape of the bulb and seed capsule are important, and the plant has to be examined not only at flowering time but also afterward. The dwarf ornithogalums usually flower in early spring, while the tall ones open in the first half of summer. Two of the dwarf species come from the Krasnodar region. First is *Ornithogalum refractum*, which in some conditions can become a garden weed, forming numerous bulbils at the base of the mother bulb that stay dormant for at least a year. I have never seen them coming up in my garden, however, and I multiply the stock of this beautiful species from seed. The numerous white flowers are held in a compact umbel between rosettes of glabrous leaves with a white stripe on the upper surface. *Ornithogalum oreoides* is somewhat similar to *O. refractum*, but its leaves are narrower and without the white stripe, and its flowers are somewhat smaller and more numerous. With this plant, there are only one or two bulbils attached to the mother bulb. The seedlings of both species start to flower in the third year.

The third ornithogalum from Krasnodar is the tall-growing *O. arcuatum*, an attractive species with large white flowers up to 2 cm in diameter that are spaced on a spike 60 cm tall. The plant itself grows to 1 m tall. At fruiting time the pedicels elongate and remain horizontal at the base, but they gradually become arcuate, spreading up. The southern European *O. narbonense* is similar, but the fruiting pedicels of its flowers are strictly erect, more or less adpressed to the stem, which is also somewhat shorter. An endemic species of the southern Ukraine, *O. melancholicum*, grows on the opposite side of the Sea of Azov and is distinguished from *O. arcuatum* only by the color of its leaves, which are dark green below and lighter green above.

I didn't collect any of these tall-growing species myself, with the exception of *Ornithogalum ponticum*. This is the best tall-growing ornithogalum in my collection and is good not only for the garden: its long, very dense, pyramidal racemes of large, pure white flowers also make perfect cuttings. In the late 1980s the Latvian Society for Gardening and Beekeeping sent me to one of the largest bulb nurseries in the former Soviet Union to discuss buying bulbs for the society's garden. My destination was Sochi, located in the Krasnodar region along the Black Sea. The director of the nursery was not there when I arrived, and I used the extra time to take a short walk through the forest surrounding the nursery. I collected a few bulbs there, including species of *Galanthus* and *Ornithogalum*. I later identified the latter as a form of *O. ponticum*, which I named 'Sochi' (Plate 39). My visit with the nursery wasn't successful—nothing was sold to our society regardless of all the promises I was given—but to me the journey was worthwhile just because of this one beautiful ornithogalum.

Ornithogalum pyramidale, by the way, is the Central European ally of these tall-growing ornithogalums. In general it is very similar to *O. ponticum* but has longer spikes not so densely covered with white flowers. The scape is up to 80 cm long. Botanically, both are distinguished by the shape of the style and by the green stripe on the petal exteriors.

◈ 19
North Caucasus

N THE 1970S my friend and teacher in the bulb world Aldonis Vēriņš received a consignment from a gardener living near Nalchik, Kabardino-Balkaria, in the North Caucasus. It contained wild-collected *Muscari* bulbs said to be *M. pallens*. When they began to flower, there were three clearly distinguishable color forms, all unlike any other previously known *Muscari* species. They were given names and were initially distributed as varieties of *M. pallens*. I brought two hundred bulbs of each to Michael Hoog during my first visit to the Netherlands, and in this way they found their way into the world. All have long, distinctly dichromatic spikes and form a nice rosette of leaves in spring. There are no similar forms in the trade. The most ordinary is 'Dark Eyes', which has deep blue flowers at the bottom of the spike and light blue flowers at the top. 'Sky Blue' has beautiful sky blue flowers at the bottom and white ones at the top. The most unusual form is 'White Rose Beauty'. Its flowers are white when they first open, but the bottom flowers turn light pinkish while the upper flowers remain white. The problem is that the pinkish shade is brighter when the bulb is planted on acid soil in a cold climate. In the Netherlands, where springs are warm and soil pH is close to neutral, the flowers don't always turn pink, so some distributors have renamed it 'White Beauty'.

My Lithuanian colleague and friend Augis Dambrauskas examined thousands of seedlings of this trio as he researched the inheritance of particular features. Among the seedlings of 'White Rose Beauty', two forms with more intensely pink-toned flowers came up. Both without any doubt can be characterized as pink muscaris. One flowers early and is named 'Pink Sunrise', while the other, which opens when the first has finished flowering, is called 'Pink Sunset'. As with 'White Rose Beauty', the intensity of the pink for both forms depends a lot on soil pH and temperature. For this reason, 'Pink Sunrise', which flowers earlier when the weather is usually cooler, is often a deeper pink than its sister.

It remains to be seen which species these varieties originated from. In any case it wasn't *Muscari pallens*. They are not hybrids, either, although they are listed this way in the *International Checklist for Hyacinths and Miscellaneous Bulbs* (Van Scheepen 1991). In the wild *M. pallens* grows side by side with *M. neglectum* (syn. *M. racemosum*), so it is possible that the two species sometimes interbreed. Most likely, these varieties belong to a new, yet-to-be-described *Muscari* species. Unfortunately, no one knows exactly where the original bulbs were found and collected. Mr. Vēriņš lost the name and address of the gardener from Nalchik, and the situation in the North Caucasus is now much too dangerous for visits, so it doesn't seem likely that the mystery will be solved in the near future.

'White Rose Beauty', 'Pink Sunrise', and 'Pink Sunset' aren't the only known pink muscaris, however. The pink *Muscari botryoides* 'Carneum', known since the sixteenth century, is listed in the *International Checklist*. I never found its name in any catalog or plant list, so I always supposed it had been lost from cultivation. Recently, though, I received a letter and some beautiful pictures from Sulev Savisaar, who informed me that this variety is still grown by a few Estonian amateurs who found it in an old garden. The foliage is typical of *M. botryoides*, and the flower color leaves no doubt that the plant is 'Carneum'.

Bob and Rannveig Wallis of Wales also found a very beautiful pink-flowering form of *Muscari armeniacum* (collection number *RRW-9050*; Plate 40) growing among a large colony of the usual blue form on the Cilician Taurus Mountains north of Akseki, Turkey. It turned out to be a very good find, as the plants came true from seed. However, as with Aldonis Vēriņš's varieties, the intensity of pink depends on the temperature. In my garden, flowers from bulbs grown outside have far better color than those from bulbs grown under covering where the temperature is always higher.

Confused about the classification of Mr. Vēriņš's varieties, in 1983 I decided to go to the North Caucasus to find the true *Muscari pallens* (Plates 41 and 42). I would focus on North Ossetia, since Konstantin Popov, a botanist at the nature reserve there, had promised to help with my search for various bulbs.

I arrived late in the afternoon. The office of the nature reserve was located in Alagir, and for me the most important thing was to get there early enough to find Konstantin. By half past nine he was welcoming me into his apartment. We enjoyed a light evening meal, marveled over the high rate of precipitation in Alagir, and retired for a nice sleep.

The morning greeted us with rain, as expected, which would continue until noon. We planned to search the nearest surroundings for *Galanthus lagodechianus*. This plant was very rare here. During his eight years with the reserve and despite almost daily visits to the forests, Konstantin had only found it growing in a few spots in small groups. All the forest edges were covered with marvelously flowering *Rhododendron luteum*—no green was visible through the golden carpet of its flowers. It was a mixed beech-oak forest with dense hazel groves in the clearings. Below the large trees grew an abundance of some *Arum* species. According to Konstantin it was *A. orientale*, but the tubers appeared to be long and rhizomatous. Only much later, while at home, did I find that its correct name was *A. italicum* subsp. *albispathum*. I still have plants of this accession, although before I started growing it under covering I lost almost the entire stock. It may have been too cold outside or too wet in the summer, but in an unheated greenhouse it grows very well. It doesn't experience any problems in my friend's garden near Vilnius, Lithuania, where the climate is a little more continental and not as cold as it is here in northern Latvia. Its large white spathes are very impressive, although they stay below the leaves. Like all arums it has bright red berries in autumn, too.

We reached a slope where we expected to find a spot as large as some hundred square meters abundant with *Galanthus lagodechianus*. Some areas were a jungle of hornbeam and hazelnut, but I soon found several snowdrop leaves, then a large population formed by vegetative reproduction. At the moment the snowdrops were very overcrowded and depressed. We dug some of them out, divided them, and replanted them on the original site. I collected a few from this population and, for genetic diversity, from other spots, too. This nice snowdrop has wide, glossy green leaves and is very different from the other stock that I grow under the name *Galanthus cabardensis*, now considered a synonym of *G. lagodechianus*. My stock of *G. cabardensis* was collected at the Mzinta River near Kazachy Brod by a Czech collector; its name came from the *Flora of the Northern Caucasus* (Galushko 1978). The leaves are distinctly narrower than those of *G. lagodechianus* collected in North Ossetia. As the two plants are so different, I still grow them under their original names.

The new morning greeted us with sunshine, and we went up into the mountains by bus to examine the meadows where *Anemone caucasica* was thought to grow. This species is a smaller relative of *A. blanda* with deep blue flowers only 1–1.5 cm in diameter. It mostly grows under shrubs but can also be found growing abundantly in a plowed field, the tubers some 20–25 cm deep in the soil. When we reached this field, it appeared to have been planted with potatoes, so all the anemones were underground. There was nothing to do but search for them in the dense shrubs. I noticed the first one growing beneath *Rhododendron luteum*, but it was surrounded by nettles and too painful to reach. Then I saw a nice group of anemones near a large hornbeam shrub. Lying down below the lowest branches, I slowly removed old leaves and small bits of branches, careful to avoid breaking the stem of the anemone, and finally found the tuber. They lay shallowly, only 5–7 cm deep, and were very small, only some 3–5 mm in diameter. They grew in pure peat, and since they grew beneath rhododendrons they seemed to favor somewhat acid soil, although the stones in the peat looked like limestone. In cultivation the tubers grow a bit larger, reaching the size of peas. I like this plant very much but lost my stock to disease. All my attempts to reintroduce it from other growers failed; the samples I received never produced shoots.

We caught a ride down to a spring where hydrogen sulfide water flows from the mountain. This was where *Galanthus angustifolius* could be found, but the summer vegetation period had already started and there was little chance of finding the small leaves of snowdrops hiding among the luxurious growth of summer herbs. Still, we managed to spot some yellow leaves in deeper shade beneath shrubs of *Carpinus*, *Corylus*, *Crataegus*, *Rosa*, and a few *Fagus*. The soil was black, very peaty, and full of limestone chips, evidence that this species needs good drainage. *Galanthus angustifolius* never reproduces vegetatively in the wild, so we only found individual plants. It is very rare in cultivation. When I moved to my new garden I thought I lost it, but when I visited my old garden eighteen years later, I found some groups of snowdrops that were extremely similar to *G. angustifolius* growing beneath an old hazelnut shrub. During those years of naturalization it had made quite large clumps more characteristic of *G. nivalis* var. *angustifolius*, but I never had the latter in my collection, so this stock seemed to be true to name.

The next day Konstantin and I left home at five o'clock in the morning and were lucky enough to catch the early bus to Tbilisi. The highway was extremely narrow, with only a few centimeters seeming to separate the bus from a rocky cliff on one side and a gorge on the other. Far below us was the crazy course of the Terek River. The road passed one side ridge after another, all the time winding higher and higher. This was 25 May, but the road was covered in snow in some areas, and only a narrow pass made by a bulldozer allowed us to continue our way up. Remnants of the broken and twisted steel supports of an old power line served as evidence of the powerful avalanches that plagued the area. We drove through many artificial concrete tunnels that had been built to protect the road.

Krestovy Pass opened before us. Despite the lengthy bus ride, we were only 2395 m above sea level. We stepped out of the bus, walked some hundred meters ahead, and were greeted by a large field covered in endless clumps of *Galanthus platyphyllus* in full flower (Plate 43). This is another competitor for the title of giant snowdrop. Its leaves, which somewhat resemble those of tulips, are up to 35 cm long and 4 cm wide (some have even been recorded at 6 cm wide). It grows in full sun in wet, sticky clay, and reproduces well vegetatively. Each clump contains ten to twenty bulbs, sometimes more. Sadly, after returning from the mountains I forgot about the difference in growing conditions for this particular snowdrop and planted it with the others in the deep shade of large oaks. The soil in this location dries out in summer, and within two years I lost almost all of my bulbs. Luckily, I managed to plant the last two bulbs in an open field, and the stock began to increase. It suffered from a hard black frost a few years ago, however, and I again have only a few small bulbs.

Snowdrops weren't the only bulbs flowering in the pass. Among their small white bells bloomed the large brown bells of *Fritillaria latifolia* (Plate 44). In Western gardens this species is generally represented by very dwarf forms from Turkey, known under the name *F. latifolia* subsp. *nobilis*. Some botanists even think it is worthwhile making them a separate species, *F. nobilis*. Both plants are very different, not just in the wild but also in cultivation. The plants from Krestovy Pass are some 20 cm tall and hold the large blooms at the top of the stems well; they are the same deep plum-purple, but the color is lusterless. The flowers of the Turkish plants are the same size but are very short-stemmed, lie on the ground, and are a shining plum-purple. Their bulbs lie some 10 cm deep in the soil and are abundantly covered with grains the size of poppy seeds. Both fritillaries grow very well in cultivation, whether in an open field or greenhouse. However, they don't like staying out of the soil for long, so it is best to replant both forms as soon as possible.

We set out early the next morning for a two-day walk. Our targets were *Muscari pallens* and *Fritillaria collina*. We began the trip in a car, which brought us to the first bridge over the Ardon River, then along a road leading up into the mountains along a narrow side gorge, but soon we had to continue along a narrow footpath. We stopped for dinner in a nice valley, and there, growing among the rocks, I found the beauty I was searching for—the true *Muscari pallens*. There was no doubt about the name: in North Ossetia only two *Muscari* species are recognized, *M. pallens* and *M. neglectum*. *Muscari pallens* grows in quite dry conditions in small cavities between rocks. Sometimes only a teaspoonful of soil is available in the spot where a bulb grows; from a small pinch of moss a tiny flower spike rises up along with three or four narrow leaves. Now the rocks were wet but in summer they would dry out. The flowers were quite uniform in their combination of white and pale blue, with some rarely slightly buff-toned. The stunning flowers of *Androsace villosa* grew alongside the muscari.

Muscari pallens vernalizes very late in the season; in fact it is the last muscari to emerge from the soil in my garden each spring. It slowly multiplies vegetatively but also sets seed perfectly, and the seedlings germinate very well, flowering from their third season. It is among my loveliest and bestselling *Muscari* species. Among some small shrubs in the valley we also found *M. neglectum*, with large, deep blue flower spikes. However, I haven't found any intermediate forms between the two species. They are so different that the appearance of such forms would seem incredible.

The weather changed again. Dark clouds rolled in from the south and from time to time raindrops fell. We stumbled across what would be a real paradise for any rock gardener: *Anemone speciosa* flowering abundantly in all shades of white and yellow, side by side with the deep violet-blue blooms of *Centaurea salicifolia* (only 10 cm tall but with flowers as much as 8 cm in diameter), creamy yellow *Pulsatilla albana*, and other gems.

Alders and bird cherries were soon replaced by dwarf birches arranged among a bright yellow carpet of *Primula ruprechtii* flowers. Unfortunately, it was too dark to use my camera, so all of these beauties were preserved only in my diary. As we moved along we found our first flowering *Fritillaria collina*, shining from beneath a birch shrub (Plate 45). Overall this species resembles *F. latifolia*, only the flower is somewhat smaller and different in color: light yellow with slightly brownish and grayish tessellation. Whereas *F. latifolia* is a plant of open meadows, *F. collina* only grows in the protection of shrubs. Another difference is the total absence of grains on the bulbs of *F. collina*. Some grains appear on cultivated plants but never so plentifully as on *F. latifolia*. Higher in the mountains *F. collina* can also grow in more open areas, but there is still a tendency to favor depressions and more protected spots. A few years ago I almost lost *F. collina* entirely and was left with only a few seedlings. It grew for me without any problems for more than twenty years, but now I can only pray that this beauty will recover.

The rain came down harder and harder, and as we made our way up we found masses of *Allium victorialis* among shrubs in various meadows. The local people collected these plants for eating and pickled their stems. I have never tried growing the Caucasian form in the garden, but there should be no major problems with it. It grows in somewhat shaded spots that never dry out too much.

Predictably, in the morning it was raining again. We took a road leading down to the neighboring valley of Fiagdon, where a river of the same name begins. *Anemone speciosa*, *A. narcissiflora*, and many other plants flowered fantastically here. I even found a late flower of *Scilla siberica* in some deep shade. On a drier slope we found *Colchicum trigynum* (or *Merendera trigyna*, as it is named in local floras; Plate 46), which turned out to be a beautiful white-flowered form of the usually lilac-flowered plant. Arnis Seisums found another white-flowering population of this beautiful spring colchicum on Bitschenag Pass in Nakhichevan, Azerbaijan. Its flowers are fairly small, but there are as many as twelve per bulb and they bloom in succession, providing a long-lasting floral display. It is easy in the garden and increases well vegetatively.

With that, my North Ossetian travel came to end. There were many more excellent bulbs higher in the mountains, but it was too early to go there, as the high mountain meadows were still covered in snow.

Two excellent autumn-flowering crocuses also grow in this region: the white *Crocus vallicola* (Plate 47) and bright yellow *C. scharojanii*. I grew both some years ago, but they were lost for different reasons. I received *C. vallicola* from the Tallinn Botanical Garden. Aino Paivel had collected it near Dombai, a high mountain recreation center somewhat west of North Ossetia in the Krasnodar region. *Crocus vallicola* is remarkable for its creamy white flowers, which have perianth segments with very long, wispy tips; it can be easily distinguished from other species just by this one feature. It grows in places where the soil never dries out in summer yet isn't damp, and prefers slightly drier grassland than its close relative *C. scharojanii*. It is quite easy in the garden. I lost my North Caucasian stock only after a very hard black frost.

The Turkish forms of *Crocus vallicola* are not of such refined beauty as those from Dombai. I grow them in Latvia without any problems, but having learned from experience, I always check the covering before winter and put down additional peat when flowering ends. I keep the bulbs in open boxes covered with silvery sand, but it is very important to start replanting early in my region, otherwise they start to form flowering shoots at the start of August. This means they can start flowering in the boxes if replanting is delayed. In any case, the less time the bulbs spend out of the soil, the better they grow in the garden. There are some unusual forms in Turkey, too. The most interesting one (collection number *MP-8812*) was found in Artvin Province by Erich Pasche; the upper edge of its perianth segments looks somewhat hairy or fringed.

Crocus kotschyanus subsp. *suworowianus*, which grows from South Ossetia to northeastern Turkey, is very similar to *C. vallicola* in color but is easy to distinguish by the shape of its perianth segments. It is a plant of even drier conditions than *C. vallicola* and a good grower in the garden. Its corm lies on its side in the soil. I have some plants with lilac flowers named variety *lilacina*, some with pure white flowers (from Cam pass, where they grew near melting snow at 2640 m), and a few white ones with violet veins.

Crocus scharojanii is the most difficult crocus in the garden, although I grew it for some years without any major problems, until water rats got to it one winter. Two rows of this crocus had been planted in a bed 10 m long, and not one corm was left afterward! I had forgotten to avoid putting all of my eggs in one basket (or in this case, planting all of my crocus corms in one spot). *Crocus scharojanii* is the only autumn-flowering crocus with yellow blooms, although it would be more appropriate to say that it flowers in late summer. In Latvia blooming usually starts around the last ten days of July and ends during the second half of August. My stock never made stolons, as has been reported for this species. It also almost always flowered before the old leaves died; at least the new roots grew long before the old ones desiccated, so there was no real optimal time for replanting it. It is a plant of wet, peaty turf near rivulets and in depressions, where the soil never gets dry.

My stock comes from Lithuania, though it was collected by someone in the Caucasus. Although I requested the exact location of its origin, I never received a reply. I don't even know whether it was grown in the garden for a period of time or collected in the wild. The origin wouldn't be so important if it weren't for the fact that lilac blooms appear among the otherwise uniform-looking corms in spring. Superficially they are similar to *Crocus kosanini*, which grows wild in faraway southern Serbia. If they were collected with *C. scharojanii*, it would mean that there are some not-yet-described new species of spring crocus in the main Caucasus ridge. However, it is possible that the lilac forms are nothing more than another species that got mixed in with the *C. scharojanii* in the previous owner's garden. Unfortunately, I lost all corms of this mysterious crocus during our last black frost, just before sending samples to Brian Mathew and Gothenburg. Its corms were almost identical to those of *C. scharojanii*, but it flowered in spring, and it was not identical to *C. kosanini*, either.

The last autumn-flowering crocus from this area is *Crocus autranii* (Plate 48), known only from Abkhazia. Its flower shape is somewhat intermediate between *C. vallicola* and *C. kotschyanus* subsp. *suworowianus*. The perianth segments are less sharply pointed than in *C. vallicola*, but the flower is a rich mid-violet with a large, creamy white throat. My only attempt to find it in the mountains in the early 1980s was interrupted by a sudden snowfall, which ultimately forced me to leave the area before I could manage to see any flowers. It was later found by a Czech collector, and from there found its way to gardens, although it remains extremely rare. My stock came from the Gothenburg Botanical Garden. Like *C. vallicola*, it is easy to grow in Latvia, only it seems to be more susceptible to winter frost. I grow it in a large pot (one of the few exceptions to my rule about not using pots) and it passes the winter in my cold greenhouse. As soon as the weather is sufficiently warm, I place the pot out in the garden, always checking carefully that the soil never dries out. When pollinated artificially, it sets seed quite well. I restored my stock from seedlings after the original bulbs were killed by black frost.

Two other bulbs in my collection come from near Dombai, and both were collected by Aino Paivel. The first is the North Caucasus form of *Colchicum speciosum*. This species is very widespread in the Caucasus Mountains and is well known in cultivation. The flowers are very large and bright violet with a white or lilac throat. The plants from Dombai generally have a darker throat than those from Ordu Province, Turkey, which were originally offered for trade by Michael Hoog. One of the most beautiful, white, autumn-flowering colchicums belongs to this species: *C. speciosum*

'Album'. Unfortunately, *C. speciosum* can't be listed among the hardiest species for my region. I lost all of my stocks at least twice, and 'Album' was always the first to go. The form from Dombai proved to be the hardiest, although I was forced to replace it from stocks raised by friends living in milder areas.

Corydalis kusnetzovii is the second very beautiful plant from this area. It grows in Teberda, somewhat lower than Dombai, and has slightly pinkish, almost white flowers. The name of this species changed many times in my collection, and the final classification only occurred after the publication of the monograph *Corydalis* (Lidén and Zetterlund 1997). Many local floras had misled me: I had first classified it as *C. teberdensis* (now considered a synonym) and later as *C. vittae*. This species is easy to grow and can hybridize in the garden, so if you want to multiply your stock from seed, the mother plants have to be planted in some isolation from other species. In the garden it needs peaty soil and light shade.

Corydalis vittae (Plate 49) is a close relative of *C. kuznetzovii* and grows on the opposite side of the main ridge (facing the Black Sea) but flowers much later. It is one of my favorites in the garden. The flowers are white to slightly creamy with a golden flush, greenish in bud, big, and arranged in dense racemes. It is among the most late- and long-flowering bulbous *Corydalis* species, is undoubtedly among the best when it comes to keeping a nice, compact habit in the garden, and is easy to distinguish from other species by its original color. The plant I once grew as *C. angustifolia* 'Touch of Gold' is really *C. vittae*.

The Caucasus is also home to some close relatives of *Corydalis kusnetzovii* and *C. vittae*. Two of them, the light lilac *C. caucasica* and pure white *C. malkensis*, have the largest flowers. The latter is often offered as *C. caucasica* 'Alba'. Both have very large flowers composed in a dense vertical spike. They flower and seed freely in the garden but can also hybridize with other species. A large lip size dominates in the seedlings. Henrik Zetterlund characterizes *C. malkensis* as one of the true aristocrats in this section. The true *C. caucasica* is less well known in gardens, and the name is often misapplied to certain hybrids. I recently received from Czech collectors *C. caucasica* subsp. *abantensis*, which differs from the type subspecies in the shape of its raceme (it isn't one-sided) and in the different shape of its lower petals. In general it is also a somewhat smaller plant. I still haven't tried growing it outside, but it grows very well in the greenhouse and also sets seed. In the wild it forms quite an isolated population at Lake Abant, Bolu Province, northern Turkey, far from the place where subspecies *caucasica* has been recorded.

It occurs to me that I haven't mentioned anything about the tulips of the Caucasus Mountains. One of my first most representative collections was an assortment of tulips, though I mostly grew cultivars. During my first expeditions to Central Asia I devoted a lot of my research to tulips, but they no longer play such an important role. I still collect wild tulips if I find them during my expeditions, but I never search for them specifically. Although the Caucasus Mountains are quite rich in tulip species, I grow very few of them in my garden.

Tulipa schrenkii was the first Caucasian tulip to find its way to my garden. I bought the bulbs from a Latvian gardener who had collected them in a nearby forest during his stay at a sanatorium in the North Caucasus. This was a long time ago, however, and I have lost any hints I may have had about the origin of the stock. There were two general types: one was larger and deep red with a narrow yellow edge and pointed petals, while the other was dull purplish with more rounded petals. Both were lazy to flower in my region, and only a few bulbs flowered each spring. They mostly formed nothing but leaves, even from quite large bulbs. I kept them for a very long time, but they eventually caught a virus and I had to destroy my stocks.

Another tulip of unknown exact origin is *Tulipa eichleri*, which I still grow for its large, very bright red, nicely shaped flowers held on strong stems some 30–40 cm tall. The leaves are widely spaced, somewhat crispate, and pubescent. Overall it is a very beautiful plant, growing well in both garden and greenhouse, and increases quite quickly vegetatively. It was grown from seed I received from a botanical garden (presumably in Tbilisi, Georgia, but I'm not certain) in my early years. It is somewhat variable, and like most tulips it requires annual transplanting.

The other species I still grow, *Tulipa karabachensis*, is a very local endemic of the borderland between Armenia and Azerbaijan. It was collected by Arnis Seisums on Mount Hustup in the Zangezur Mountain Range, where it grows on stony, south-facing slopes. It is still almost unknown in cultivation but is an easy-growing, extremely decorative, well-increasing species with primrose yellow flowers 5–6 cm long on a 30 cm stem.

◈ 20
Near Lake Cherepash'ye

N GENERAL all my trips to the Caucasus Mountains have been very short. Such was my visit to Tbilisi, Georgia. I traveled there with my daughter Ilze and friend Āris Krūmiņš, who had accompanied me earlier to Central Asia. It was the mid-1980s, and the economy of the Soviet Union had begun to fluctuate, a sign of the impending collapse. I didn't keep a diary during those few days, but I still remember the trip very well because of the beautiful plants I found just outside the city.

Our intention was to stay in Georgia for a week or even longer and to visit many spots in the mountains. My friends had given me the name and address of a contact in Tbilisi who could help with accommodations and other concerns. At the time it was only possible to buy a one-way ticket, but we took the risk and landed in Georgia in early May.

Our apartments were just at the city border in the very last newly built block of five-flat houses. We could see a forest and something like a mountain just a few hundred meters away. The situation in Tbilisi was worse than we had suspected. There was no way out of the city or into neighboring villages by public transportation, and private drivers asked enormous fees for their services. The biggest problem was obtaining our return tickets to fly home. They had been sold out more than a month before this, and now the only tickets left were sold on the black market with an enormous surcharge. Fortunately, the owners of our apartments were related to an important officer of the KGB; with his help we were able to acquire tickets home three days after coming to Tbilisi. Since we spent the first day hunting for tickets, we had only two days to search for bulbs. The economic situation in the city was dramatic. Shops were empty; the prices at the market were enormously high. Although we were welcomed warmly, we didn't feel comfortable. We could see that accepting us with traditional Georgian hospitality was a very cumbersome ordeal for our hosts.

Friends who had visited Tbilisi earlier had told me about a nice lake just at the border or even inside the city named Cherepash'ye. There were plenty of bulbs growing around it. It turned out to be a very well known recreation spot that we could get to by trolley bus. The trolley stopped on a wide boulevard near a ski lift (no longer working) and some wide stairs made of stone. We took the stairs but soon left them in favor of a footpath leading up into the mountains. With our first steps we noticed the leaves of a crocus—the autumn-flowering *Crocus speciosus*. It was an amazingly nice form, later named 'Lakeside Beauty'. It blooms with exceptional abundance, its very large flowers an especially light silvery blue, with slightly deeper blue veins. Every visitor to my nursery always points it out as the best among my *C. speciosus* clones.

Crocus speciosus grew everywhere around us. I could only imagine how beautiful the slopes would be in autumn with all the plants in full flower. Many beautiful forms could certainly be found there. From all the Dutch-raised varieties of *C. speciosus*, only two are among my favorites: 'Albus', with pure white flowers, and 'Oxonian', with deep purple flowers and flower tube. I prefer my own selection and a pair of crocuses raised in Lithuania by Leonid Bondarenko. One is named 'Blue Web' and has egg-shaped flowers densely netted with dark blue veins on very light blue petals. Another is 'Lithuanian Autumn', which is somewhat similar to 'Lakeside Beauty', but the initially creamy outer petals become milky white.

Small, round Lake Cherepash'ye was named for the turtles that were said to live there, although we didn't see any. Plenty of *Crocus biflorus* subsp. *adamii* was growing nearby, but it was out of flower, and it was difficult to find the grass-like leaves among the luxurious vegetation surrounding the lake. At home it proved to be a very miniature form, with variable, paler or darker lilac flowers and prominent deep purple stripes on the exterior petals. It really is very different from the other forms of *C. biflorus* subsp. *adamii* I have seen, and I wasn't surprised to learn that Russian botanists consider it a separate species, *C. geghartii*. Unfortunately, all of my stock eventually served as forage for rodents. Not a single corm survived (and just when I had enough stock to offer it in my catalog). This is one of the plants I'd like to look for again in Georgia when the situation there becomes more stable.

Another form grown under the name *Crocus biflorus* subsp. *adamii* that was collected more to the south by Arnis Seisums fared better. It was a very beautiful, large-flowering population, extremely variable in color, from Bitschenag Pass in Nakhichevan, Azerbaijan, near the Armenian border. It was the best population I had ever seen of this very variable subspecies. In any case Arnis's form is far better than the other forms offered under this name. The flowers are blue or violet, tinted or striped darker, and very large, quite different from those I had collected near Lake Cherepash'ye. This form really seems to be another species or at least a separate subspecies. An abundantly flowering clone named 'Bitschenag Tiger' was selected from this stock. It has big, sky blue flowers conspicuously striped violet-purple on the outside.

Iris reticulata was much easier to find than the crocuses because of its long leaves and tendency to grow beneath shrubs where other vegetation is weaker. It was out of flower, so only later at home did I see its deep reddish purple blooms. I still grow it as variety *caucasica*, and it increases perfectly in my garden. Similar reddish purple forms seem to be the most widespread among the wild populations of this very variable species. One of the rarest irises seems to be the pure white selection made by Canadian iris grower and breeder Alan McMurtrie, who named it 'White Caucasus'. I have seen it only in photographs because Alan sold all the stock to the Netherlands and it hasn't yet appeared in the trade. I hope it doesn't catch a virus during commercial growing, as has happened with many other stocks of *I. reticulata* and its relatives in the Netherlands. Now I grow a similar one recently collected for me in Armenia.

A very atypical and beautiful form of *Iris reticulata* was found in 1990 by British nurseryman Norman Stevens at Halkis-Dag in Batman Province, Turkey. It is very unusual in color: the standards and style branches are distinctly light sky blue, but the falls are deep purplish blue, almost black. The ridge is very narrow and yellow, surrounded with a white, slightly dark-spotted zone. It was named 'Halkis' after the mountains where it was originally found.

Another form (collection number *GLUZ-98-323*) was found in Iran between the villages of Aligardaz and Schoolabad by Arnis Seisums during a joint expedition with the Gothenburg Botanical Garden and Iranian Institute of Botany. Its flowers are tiny but incredibly beautiful in color, with white standards and blackish falls. It looks so different from all other Reticulata irises that I'm certain it deserves a species name. In any case, taxonomically it is much more different from the traditional concept of *Iris reticulata* than the plants from the Kopet-Dag described by Dmitriy Kurbanov (from George Rodionenko's team) as *Iridodyctium kopetdaghense* (Plate 50). The only real difference between the Kopet-Dag plants and the Georgian form is that during flowering the leaves of the former are shorter than the flower, while those of the Caucasian form soon overtop the flower. Both are very similar in color, however, and there is little difference in all other aspects. The plants that were collected alongside this "new species" (near Nokhur, south of Karakala, at 2000 m) are absolutely identical in color, but their leaves are arranged in the same style as the leaves of the Caucasian plants. Using the epithet *kopetdaghense* for this plant can cause a lot of confusion because there is a Juno iris called *Iris kopetdagensis*. It seems that now only Russian botanists split bulbous irises into three separate genera. What's more, in 1999 George Rodionenko split Central Asian Reticulata irises into a fourth genus: *Alatavia*.

The fourth plant we collected near Lake Cherepash'ye was *Colchicum laetum*. This is a very late-flowering autumn colchicum that is also known in cultivation. The form distributed by Dutch nurseries has flowers at least twice as large as those of plants from Tbilisi, although they are identical in color. It seems that the Dutch form is a very large-flowering selection of unknown origin or a polyploid form arising during the long cultivation in gardens. During their first two seasons, my plants bloomed so late that sometimes a few flowers appeared even in spring. This later changed, though, and they now flower normally in autumn, making a nice addition to those giants from the Dutch nurseries. Unfortunately, *C. laetum* isn't among the hardiest colchicums. My plants suffered seriously from black frost on two occasions, although the stock was not lost completely; I left the beds untouched, and during the next season some leaves appeared and the stock started growing again. The Dutch form seems to be somewhat hardier than the wild one.

The following day we decided to visit the areas surrounding our living quarters, beginning near the village of Gldan. The roadsides were full of beautiful primroses with large, creamy yellow flowers, but in the forest, which starts with a very deep, steep gorge, there were only a few bulbs, mostly *Crocus speciosus*, *Muscari neglectum*, and *Anemone caucasica*. For me the best find was *Corydalis angustifolia*, a new addition to my collection, which was growing in deep shade beneath shrubs and large beeches.

It is a very elegant species with deeply dissected leaves and pure white, long-petaled flowers. The spike holds just a few blossoms. Although in the wild it looks quite weak (Plate 51), in the garden, where it doesn't have to compete with surrounding plants, it is a beautiful plant with large, very dense flower spikes (Plate 52)—it makes a dramatic change, from Cinderella to the belle of the ball. I have a similar white form from Iran. I named the form collected near Tbilisi 'Georgian White' because I later collected a different pink form in southern Azerbaijan.

Unfortunately, we had no success with our plans to visit places where beauties such as *Iris winogradowii* (Plate 53) and *Erythronium caucasicum* (Plate 54) grew. Although I already had these in my collection, I wanted to see them growing in the wild. *Iris winogradowii* is now very rare and is known to grow in only two locations, near Borjomi and in Abchasia. It is a plant of wet mountain meadows and as such dislikes drying out during summer, preferring either to be replanted early or grown without replanting for many years. It needs peaty soil and doesn't suffer from some shade. Its very large flowers are similar in shape and size to *I. histrioides* from Turkey, but they are a beautiful primrose yellow with some green spots on the falls. In Latvia it sets seed perfectly and reproduces vegetatively by splitting and by grains formed at the basal plate. I have two clones of it—one lighter, the other deeper yellow. Another form, 'Alba', was selected by Czech collectors, but I don't know whether it is of wild or garden origin. Its flowers are almost pure white with a very light bluish tint, so it may be of hybrid origin.

Hybrids between *Iris winogradowii* and *I. histrioides* known under the names 'Katharine Hodgkin' and 'Frank Elder' are far more widely grown. The former has pale blue flowers slightly suffused with a yellow that is most prominent on the falls, while the latter is usually more blue in shade. Otherwise both are very similar. Another cultivar, 'Sheila Ann Germaney', is easy to distinguish, having a narrow, bright yellow ridge on its falls instead of the wide, yellow-shaded blotch so characteristic of the other two forms. From *I. winogradowii* these cultivars inherited a preference for early replanting and a tolerance for summer rain, but they are not so susceptible to drying out. All are very quick increasers, forming plenty of bulbils, and the large bulbs usually split into two or three every season. Replanting at least every third season is recommended, but this can be avoided if the bulbs are planted deep enough to seriously decrease the rate of reproduction. The greatest problem is that many stocks of these forms are infected by a virus, especially 'Katharine Hodgkin' (see Mathew 1999 for a photograph of a virus-infected plant). Planted areas must be carefully checked during flowering time, and all plants with dark blue stripes or spots on the standards or petaloid style branches must be discarded.

Erythronium caucasicum is more widespread in the Caucasus Mountains than *Iris winogradowii* and grows in the western part of Georgia (Abkhazia) and the Krasnodar region of Russia. It replaces the European *E. dens-canis* in the Caucasus and is easy to distinguish from its European ally by its white, rarely slightly pinkish flowers and yellow anthers (the anthers of *E. dens-canis* are blackish even in the white forms). It is not very difficult in cultivation if provided woodland conditions, but it never multi-plies vegetatively, so stock can only be built up from seed. For this reason it is still very rare in gardens. Although both *E. caucasicum* and *E. dens-canis* are grown side by side in my collection, no hybrids have ever appeared among the seedlings. *Erythronium caucasicum* is also easy to distinguish from the white forms of *E. sibiricum*, which also have yellow anthers, by its filaments, which are unequal in length and are not flat-tened shortly below the anthers.

Traveling is now quite difficult in many parts of the Caucasus. Some areas are even dangerous due to the endless fight for independence from Russia in Chechnya. There are also conflicts in Abkhazia and South Ossetia, and in Nagorno-Karabakh the Armenian and Azerbaijani conflict is a burning issue. In earlier years, however, Arnis Seisums explored the area searching for bulbs, and I grow many of the plants that he found. Before turning eastward I would like to mention some of my favorites, beginning with corydalis.

The Armenian *Corydalis seisumsiana* (Plate 55) was named for Arnis. It is a new name given by Magnus Lidén from Gothenburg for what was earlier called *C. persica*. It has perennial tubers and can be propagated only by seed. Arnis found the plant on dry rocky slopes on the Zangezur Mountain Range. It has purple-blotched, white petals that turn pinkish with time, and a long purple spur. It is easy in the garden, usually sets seed, and is even self-sowing. Sometimes plants that look like crosses with other relatives appear among the seedlings.

Corydalis nariniana (Plate 56) is also sometimes offered under the name *C. per-sica*. This species grows in the wild south from Yerevan, Armenia, to Nakhichevan, Azerbaijan, and Turkey. Although it was introduced in the 1980s by Czech collectors (as *C. persica*) and is still grown in gardens, I can't boast about any great success I have had growing it. I have very few of these plants but still hope to get a good seed crop. The flowers of this beautiful species combine white with blackish purple stripes and a rich, deep carmine spur. It is a gorgeous plant and worth a try.

In the Elburz Mountains of Iran, Arnis collected *Corydalis verticillaris*, another elegant species closely related to *C. seisumsiana*. It has deeply divided leaves with very small lobes and long, white to pale pinkish flowers with a dark purple-tipped keel and sometimes with a purple spur that turns reddish at the end of flowering. It is another species to which the epithet *persica* has sometimes been applied. It was first introduced in the 1930s and appeared in *Curtis's Botanical Magazine* in 1937 but was later lost from cultivation. The two tubers kindly presented to me by Arnis produced a very good seed crop, thus allowing me to quickly build up my stock. This beautiful plant is easy to recognize just by its nicely divided foliage.

On two occasions I tried growing *Corydalis emanuelii* var. *pallidiflora* from the surroundings of Mount Elbrus in the western Caucasus and Georgia. It grows marvel-ously in Gothenburg and is characterized as one of the most successful species of its section. Yet with each try I lost it during the very first winter, both on the open field and in an unheated greenhouse. Its seeds germinated but the seedlings disappeared within a few seasons. Nevertheless, it is so beautiful with its erect stems and bright yellow flowers that I haven't lost hope of discovering its secret. I think my mistake was planting the small tubers too deep and allowing conditions to remain too dry in summer. Collecting the seeds of this species isn't easy because they get shot far away with the slightest touch of the seedpod.

The next genus of Caucasian bulbs I want to discuss is *Allium*. I wrote about *A. tripedale* when describing bulbs from Crimea, but it isn't the only species from Armenia worth growing in gardens. One very widespread species in both Armenia and Turkey is the variable *A. woronowii*. Onions are usually associated with an unpleasant odor, but the form of *A. woronowii* from the mountain pass at Dzhadzhur, Armenia, near Spitak, smells strongly of carnations. Its big, star-shaped, pink flowers are held in a tight umbel on a stem 40–50 cm tall. Without a doubt, this is one of the showiest alliums. We named it 'Spitak'. 'Vardahovit' is a much dwarfer (only 15–20 cm high) cultivar and is closer to the type collection, which is extremely dwarf. Its flowers are tinted slightly bluish. Among my seedlings of *A. woronowii* a few almost identical plants suddenly appeared, with flowers that were typical in form but unique in color— pure white (Plate 57). There were no similar *Allium* species or cultivars with white flowers, so this seedling made a very good addition to my quite ample collection of alliums. I decided to name it 'White Beauty'. *Allium woronowii* is very easy in the garden and sets seed well, but I'm afraid it might hybridize easily with other species, because I have found plants somewhat similar to *A. woronowii* among the seedlings of other species.

One of the most widespread species in gardens is *Allium oreophilum* (syn. *A. ostrowskianum*), which in the wild grows on high mountain slopes. Its species name combines *oreo-* ("mountain") and *-philos* ("loving"). It is widely distributed from the Caucasus Mountains to as far as western Pakistan, growing at altitudes over 2500 m on rocky screes. All but one of my stocks of this species were collected in Central Asia. I would not even mention it here if a white-flowering population of these normally reddish purple plants hadn't been recorded somewhere in Azerbaijan. We saw them only on herbarium sheets, and none of my friends have seen them in the wild. Discovering and introducing this white *A. oreophilum* would cause a real sensation among bulb growers. I have only one form from the Caucasus Mountains. It was collected in the upper course of the Samur River in Dagestan, where it grows on rocky slopes. It increases and grows in an open field better than the rest of my stocks of this species, its flowers arranged in large, dense, purplish red umbels on stems 10–15 cm long. Unfortunately, its leaves grow higher than the flower stem holding the head, and it forms so many small bulbils that it can turn into a weed. Recently among my seedlings of *A. oreophilum* I found a few plants with soft pink blooms of incredible beauty (Plate 58).

Some of the most large-flowering spring colchicums come from Armenia. They all belong to Armenian forms of *Colchicum szovitsii* (Plate 59), which has much larger flowers than the forms from Turkey. To separate the Armenian forms from the Turkish samples, for some years I applied the name *C. armenum* to the Armenian plants. Botanically, though, this is only a synonym of *C. szovitsii*. *Colchicum* expert Karin Persson from Gothenburg keeps to the traditional point of view, finding both names synonymous for one quite variable species. From a gardener's standpoint, the various clones are distinct enough to give them separate cultivar names. *Colchicum szovitsii* 'Snowwhite' differs from the other stocks of this species by its cleaner white color. The flowers are slender and open one to two weeks later than the other stocks. 'Tivi' was collected near the village of Tivi in Nakhichevan, Azerbaijan. It differs from the others by having large, white, star-shaped (instead of more or less bowl-shaped) flowers. 'Vardahovit' is one of the best forms, with large, nicely rounded, pure snow white flowers that sometimes have a light pinkish tint at the start of flowering. In the spring of 1997 it survived several nights of –15°C in full flower without any protection. It continued to bloom for two weeks after such severe conditions and even produced a good seed crop. It was collected in Armenia near the village of Vardahovit. All the Turkish forms that I grow have much smaller flowers and are light lilac.

The only spring colchicum I know of that can compete in size and beauty with the Armenian forms of *Colchicum szovitsii* is *C. kurdicum* from eastern Turkey and Iran. Until recently this early spring-flowering species was an unachievable dream plant for colchicum fans. It has a wide-open, star-shaped flower that seems to almost lie on the ground. In addition, this wide-petaled star is some 6–7 cm in diameter. It usually has pink flowers variable in shade, as with the form I have from Karabel Pass in eastern Turkey. I also have a form with white flowers from the central part of the Elburz Mountains in Iran. I never tried planting them in the open garden, but both grow splendidly in the greenhouse.

Some of the most beautiful forms of *Puschkinia scilloides* (syn. *P. hyacinthoides*) were also found in Armenia. These plants are so variable in the wild, with some forms even surpassing what is grown by large nurseries, that it is easy to doubt whether they are even puschkinias at all. One such clone from Turkey (collection number *KPPZ-90-221*) was identified for years as a *Hyacinthus* species in the Gothenburg Botanical Garden, so magnificent were its spikes (Plate 60). Arnis Seisums collected a form near Mount Aragats, which he named 'Aragats Gem'. It is slender and has bigger flowers and a far better arrangement of the raceme than the usually cultivated stocks. It also multiplies well. Two forms have come from eastern Nakhichevan, Azerbaijan. One very vigorous form with many milky white flowers was named 'Snowdrift'. The other, 'Zangezur', has big flowers (twice as big as in the usual variety *libanotica* [syn. *P. libanotica*]) arranged in a large, dense raceme. After introducing these beauties, I discarded all my traditional garden stocks of this species.

The Caucasus Mountains and neighboring countries are home to some of the most outstanding forms of *Scilla*. Identifying scillas isn't always easy. Not only is the flowering plant needed but sometimes it is also necessary to know the color of the seeds. In the last decades of the twentieth century Franz Speta attempted to split the genus *Scilla* into many microspecies, but it wasn't accepted by other botanists.

The most common species of this genus is certainly *Scilla siberica*, which despite its name is a plant of the European part of Russia, although it is grown very widely and naturalizes easily. A few named cultivars are distributed, the most popular being the deep blue and somewhat more floriferous 'Spring Beauty'. Similar forms can be found in the wild, too. My favorite is 'Alba', with pure snow white blooms, which perfectly regenerates from seed. About ten years ago I received a nice parcel containing bulbs of *Scilla* collected in the wild from the Poltava region of the Ukraine. When they flowered they brought me many pleasant surprises. At first there were two species mixed together, *S. bifolia* and *S. siberica*. The first was nothing special, but the second turned out to be extremely variable, and in the end I selected four different forms of it. All the Poltava forms of *S. siberica* turned out to flower much earlier than the other stocks. The pure white form from Poltava is at the end of flowering by the time the scapes of a traditional cultivar emerge from the soil. The traditional deep blue form had the same early flowering habit, but there were also two forms of a different shade. One had very light blue blooms, while the other had flowers that were violet-purple in tone, quite different from the traditional concept of *S. siberica*. All the stocks were separated and are now being increased in my nursery.

Scilla rosenii is among my favorite scillas. Its beautiful flowers, with their reflexed petals, resemble cyclamens or erythroniums. I first encountered this species during my childhood, when I saw a single plant being sold in full bloom at a market in Riga. I was so impressed by its flower that I bought it, although I didn't know its name. Although it never came up in my garden, my dream of this plant remained alive. On two later occasions I received bulbs but was unable to succeed with this high mountain plant, which naturally grows on meadows that never completely dry out in summer. When I finally received a new clone, however, I never again had problems with this beauty. I'm not sure why this was—perhaps I altered its growing style, or perhaps the new clone was more compatible with Latvian conditions. This plant's main fault is how slowly it reproduces vegetatively. If you want to build up the stock you need to collect and sow the seeds. The seeds germinate well if sown immediately after collecting, with seedlings starting to flower in the third season. Unfortunately, *S. rosenii* frequently interbreeds with *S. siberica* if grown in close proximity.

In general I grow two forms of *Scilla rosenii*. One, named 'Bakuriani', comes from Bakuriani, Georgia, and has vivid blue flowers with a white center. The other, named 'Cloudy Sky', has very light blue, almost white blooms. Certainly nothing can surpass the pure snow white 'Alba', which I saw for the first time in the Gothenburg Botanical Garden. This form remains at the top of my list of desiderata. Although a few plants with pure white flowers and yellow anthers have appeared among my seedlings, I'm afraid they might be hybrids with *S. siberica* 'Alba'. Recently I received another bulb of the so-called white *S. rosenii* from Czech bulb collector Eduard Hanslik.

I named the hybrid form, arising from an unintentional cross with *Scilla siberica*, as *S. ×sibrose*. This seedling shows all the vigor of such hybrids. Its flowers share the deep color of *S. siberica* and the large size of *S. rosenii*. It is intermediate in form and blooms with exceptional abundance. It was very much admired by some of my Dutch visitors, who wanted to buy the entire stock for a large sum of money. I love it so dearly, though, that I was able to resist the temptation.

The flower of *Scilla gorganica* (Plate 61) from Iran is similar in shape to that of *S. rosenii*. When I first saw it exhibited at the Royal Botanic Gardens, Kew, I decided it was a plant I must have, and after a long search I finally acquired a single bulb. Fortunately, it turned out to be self-compatible and gave me a very good crop of seeds. The plant I saw at Kew was a dwarf-growing, compact, pure white beauty with strongly reflexed petals and deep blue anthers that contrasted splendidly with the petal color. I don't know the reason for the dwarf habit of the Kew plant, but my own *S. gorganica* forms up to five long, abundantly flowered spikes, each holding as many as eighteen flowers, and blooms for a very long time. Although I was somewhat disappointed with regards to its larger size, it remains among my favorite scillas.

In my region the earliest of all spring-flowering scillas is *Scilla mischtschenkoana* (syn. *S. tubergeniana*). It comes from the Zangezur Mountain Range in the South Caucasus but is also widely distributed in northern Iran. Some of the variants are described as separate species. I have never had wild stock of it, and there are only two forms of garden origin in my collection. The most early-flowering form, which has somewhat darker flowers, is usually distributed under the species name, while the form that flowers somewhat later, with almost white flowers and a very pale blue midrib, is known as 'Zwanenburg'. Until recently I grew both without any problems and they increased well in the garden, but several enormously hard and late spring frosts over the last few seasons have killed the flowers and sometimes even the foliage. Otherwise *S. mischtschenkoana* has been easy to grow, with no special treatment required.

The other scilla with light blue flowers is *Scilla winogradowii*, which grows wild in Georgia at the upper tree line side by side with *Iris winogradowii*, as well as in northeastern Turkey. My plants were collected in Turkey and have beautiful, very light blue, wide-open flowers, up to five on a stem. *Scilla leepii* from eastern Turkey is very similar but somewhat more compact, with narrower, somewhat glossier leaves. Both species belong to the *S. siberica* group and are good growers, but they never reproduce vegetatively, so seeds have to be collected every year.

I have many stocks of *Scilla armena* plants that were collected on both sides of the border between the previous Soviet Empire and Turkey. All are very uniform in shape and number of flowers, and all are a vivid deep blue. Each scape brings only one or rarely two flowers, but this is compensated for by a large number of scapes—as many as ten on cultivated plants (Plate 62). It is a very charming dwarf plant. Its petals are conduplicate at the base.

Scilla cilicica from southeastern Turkey is taller, with a lax raceme of up to eight flowers. My stock was collected near the village of Tepekoy at 1200 m, where it grows under deep shrubs in peat among limestone rocks. Its flowers are more side-oriented or even upward-facing and a lighter blue. I can't agree with Brian Mathew (1987) when he says this is a weak plant that forms long leaves in autumn. This may be the case in Britain, with its long autumns and warm winters, but at my nursery in Latvia *S. cilicica* has never formed leaves in autumn, even in a greenhouse. The leaves come up in spring before the flower scapes. It is a nice-looking plant and makes a good addition to my collection of scillas.

I recently collected another relative of *Scilla siberica* from southern Turkey: *S. ingridae*. This charmingly named plant has only three to five pale blue flowers in a lax raceme and is easy to distinguish from *S. siberica* by its seeds not having a fleshy appendage (aril). It was collected near the mountain pass of Gezbeli. At an altitude of 1930 m I found it in seed in very peaty soil under large *Juniperus* trees side by side with *Corydalis tauricola*, but higher up at 2100 m it was growing near melting snow and still in full flower. For me finding *S. ingridae* was quite an important discovery, because earlier I had grown another scilla of the same group under this name. I received it under the name *S. ingridae* from my Czech friend Václav Jošt, but sometimes very similar plants are in the trade under the name *S. siberica* var. *taurica*. It forms five to seven tall spikes densely covered with as many as twenty deep blue flowers on a scape and is the most floriferous scilla from the *S. siberica* group that I have ever seen. I named it *S. siberica* 'Václav' (Plate 63) because I don't know its origin, although I suppose it is some garden form that sets seed and perfectly regenerates from them.

There is one more mysterious *Scilla* from Turkey—a beautiful double-flowered form found by Norman Stevens. I grow it under the name *S.* aff. *bifolia* 'Double' (Plate 64). In reality it has only an additional set of petals, and many flowers have both anthers and a pistil. It is superficially very similar to *S. bifolia* but was found far from the area where *S. bifolia* and its relatives grow. For reasons of safety I'll refrain from mentioning the exact locality where it grows, however. This is not for the safety of my business—this scilla grows well and increases quickly in the garden, so there are no problems building up the stock—but to protect the wild population from dishonest commercial gold diggers.

I also used to grow another relative of *Scilla bifolia* collected at Bolu Pass in Turkey and described by Franz Speta as *S. decidua*. I don't know whether there are any significant botanical differences between this form and other stocks I grow. It is a very uniform sample with somewhat smaller flowers, pinkish lilac anthers, and a constant flowering time that falls somewhere between other stocks. I'm quite doubtful it deserves a separate species name. It is an easy and beautiful plant, growing nicely in an open field as well as in a cold greenhouse.

I must also mention some fritillaries here. They are very close relatives and superficially so similar that it is not always possible to identify them correctly at first glance. *Fritillaria armena* and *F. caucasica* (Plate 65) have deep plum-purple blooms. My first stock of *F. armena* was collected by Arnis Seisums in Armenia, though he named it *F. caucasica*. I later received many samples of *F. armena* collected in Turkey, too, but found no differences between the Armenian and Turkish plants. Both *F. armena* and *F. caucasica* are distinguished by their styles and filaments. In *F. caucasica* the style is entire and the filaments smooth or sparsely papillose, while in *F. armena* the style is trifid and the filaments densely papillose. The plants also differ in size. *Fritillaria armena* looks like a smaller variant of the much stouter, larger (even twice as large) *F. caucasica*, but I can't agree that it is less showy than *F. caucasica*. Both species are very easy and grow well in my region in an open field in full sun. Both form grains appropriate to the size of the plant: the grains of *F. armena* are very small, those of *F. caucasica* much larger. I can separate both at harvesting time just by the size of the grains. In Turkey *F. armena* grows on shaly slopes in well-exposed sites, usually around patches of late snow, while *F. caucasica* tends to prefer peaty soils and clearings in *Juniperus* forests.

Some forms of the Turkish *Fritillaria pinardii* look somewhat similar to *F. armena*, but all the purple-flowering plants I have ever seen have petals that are yellow-edged at the top outside and yellowish- or greenish-toned inside. It is an extremely variable species not only in terms of flower color, which can range from greenish and brownish yellow to almost gunmetal purple, but also in terms of the bulblets. The traditional grains can be larger or smaller or even stoloniferous in some forms. The stolons push the small bulblets almost to the soil surface some 5–7 cm from the mother bulb. The form collected in Turkey between Hadim and Ermenek pushes the new bulblets out of the soil, where they even form a leaf (Plate 66). The way in which a plant forms its grains or stolons is inherited and may differ from population to population. I have never seen plants of both types in the same population. In the wild *F. pinardii* grows on rocky hillsides. I have mostly seen it growing in the protection of shrubs, but in these cases the plants from more open spots may have simply been grazed by sheep.

The Iranian *Fritillaria zagrica* is similar to *F. armena*. It has the same flower shape and a similar deep purple color, but at the tips of the petals there is always a bright yellow spot. It is a dwarf plant and is very rarely cultivated in gardens, but it is not difficult to grow, even though it forms very few bulblets (or even none). I grow it side by side with *F. crassifolia*, one of the easiest fritillaries to grow in my region. My stock comes from the plants Arnis Seisums collected in the Bakhtīarī region of Iran.

Sometimes *Fritillaria minuta* (Plate 67) is compared with *F. armena*, but in terms of flower shape it is more similar to *F. pinardii*. My plants always have more conspicuously recurved petals and the flowers are not as cylindrical as in *F. armena*. The flowers are small and reddish brown or even orange-shaded and are held on a stem 10–25 cm long, but most different are the leaves, which are shiny green in *F. minuta* and grayish in *F. armena* and *F. pinardii*. *Fritillaria minuta* likes deep planting (10 cm) in humus-rich soil and doesn't require summer rest; it should be treated similar to *F. crassifolia*. My plants were originally collected south of Lake Van, Turkey. Like most species of this group, they form many bulbils at the base of the mother bulb. Although this species is regarded as a plant that rarely flowers, my stock blooms every year regardless of my annual replanting of the bulbs.

PLATE 1. The shaded section of my fields in autumn

PLATE 2. The same field in spring when *Corydalis solida* is in full bloom

PLATE 3. The soil and young bulbs are separated through sieves of different sizes

PLATE 4. Boxes of seedlings are watered using drip irrigation

PLATE 5. The seedlings are covered with sheets of rock wool to protect them from winter frost

PLATE 6. *Dumontinia tuberosa*, the plague of anemones

PLATE 7. A tulip stigma can be isolated from undesirable pollen using a cylinder made of aluminum foil

PLATE 8. Bulbs are planted in a "sand bed"

PLATE 9. Even the smallest bulbs are easy to find when planted in white sand

PLATE 10. Bulb beds are prepared for winter with a covering of peat moss. The outdoor beds also receive drip irrigation

PLATE 11. *Corydalis solida* 'Snowstorm'

PLATE 12. *Corydalis solida* 'Blushing Girl'

PLATE 13. *Corydalis solida* 'Penza Strain'

PLATE 14. *Corydalis solida* 'Falls of Nimrodel'

PLATE 15. *Corydalis solida* 'Frodo'

PLATE 16. *Corydalis solida* 'Gunite'

PLATE 17. *Corydalis solida* 'Louise-Elizabeth'

PLATE 18. Various forms of *Anemone ranunculoides* from the Estonian islands. Photo by Taavi Tuulik

PLATE 20. 'Carpathian Wonder' is among the most unusually colored forms of *Crocus heuffelianus*

PLATE 19. *Gladiolus imbricatus* is extremely hardy, growing wild even near the polar circle

PLATE 21. Deep purple and white forms of *Crocus heuffelianus* growing side by side on the Lizja mountain pass

PLATE 22. *Crocus* 'National Park', a natural cross between *C. heuffelianus* and *C. ×cultorum*

PLATE 23. *Leucojum vernum* var. *carpathicum* covers the fields near the village of Podpolozje

PLATE 25. *Crocus banaticus* 'Snowdrift' blooms so late in Latvia that it is best grown in a greenhouse

PLATE 24. *Leucojum vernum* var. *carpathicum* 'Podpolozje'

PLATE 26. The best forms of *Crocus reticulatus* subsp. *reticulatus* grow in Bessarabia

PLATE 27. The filaments of *Ornithogalum orthophyllum* resemble a second row of small petals

PLATE 28. A hybrid between *Crocus cvijicii* var. *alba* and *C. veluchensis*

PLATE 29. *Crocus versicolor* is among the most variable species in the wild

PLATE 30. Another form of *Crocus versicolor*

PLATE 31. *Crocus tauricus* from the yaila of the Crimean Peninsula

PLATE 32. *Crocus speciosus* starts blooming in September

PLATE 33. The leaf margin of *Ornithogalum fimbriatum* is intensely hairy

PLATE 34. The Crimean form (variety *taurica*) of *Scilla bifolia* has the largest blooms in its group

PLATE 35. The marvelous spathe of *Arum elongatum* is hidden under bright green leaves

PLATE 36. *Sternbergia colchiciflora* blooms with tiny bright yellow flowers in autumn, producing leaves only in spring

PLATE 37. *Allium meliophilum* is among the showiest tall-growing alliums

PLATE 38. *Anemone blanda* is known only from a single locality in the territory of the former Soviet Union

PLATE 39. *Ornithogalum ponticum* 'Sochi' blooms in summer and makes a beautiful cut flower

PLATE 40. Very few *Muscari* cultivars are pink. The pink form of *M. armeniacum* found by Bob and Rannveig Wallis is among the brightest of these forms

PLATE 41. In the wild *Muscari pallens* grows on rock crevices, where it forms very tiny plants

PLATE 42. *Muscari pallens* is larger in cultivation and belongs to the most late-flowering species

PLATE 43. *Galanthus platyphyllus* grows in open fields on Krestovy Pass, where it forms large clumps

PLATE 44. *Fritillaria latifolia* subsp. *latifolia* on Krestovy Pass held its flowers well above the ground

PLATE 46. *Colchicum trigynum* is very variable in color. The most beautiful example in my collection is the white form collected by Arnis Seisums on Bitschenag Pass in Nakhichevan, Azerbaijan

PLATE 45. *Fritillaria collina* from mountain meadows on the main Caucasus ridge

PLATE 47. *Crocus vallicola* is widespread in the Caucasus and easy to identify by the long, thread-like tips of its petals

PLATE 48. *Crocus autranii* is a very rare endemic known only from a single gorge in Abchasia, but it is not difficult to grow in the garden

PLATE 49. *Corydalis vittae* is one of the nicest and most late-blooming species for the garden

PLATE 50. This form of *Iris reticulata* was described as *Iridodyctium kopetdaghense*

PLATE 51. *Corydalis angustifolia* is a tiny, inconspicuous plant in the wild

PLATE 52. In the garden *Corydalis angustifolia* is much improved

PLATE 53. *Iris winogradowii* is very rare in the wild but is a good grower and increases well in the garden

PLATE 54. *Erythronium caucasicum* is easy to distinguish from other Eurasian dog's-tooth violets by its yellow anthers, which differ in length

PLATE 55. *Corydalis seisumsiana* was named in honor of Arnis Seisums

PLATE 56. *Corydalis nariniana* is one of the brightest species with a perennial tuber

PLATE 57. This white form of *Allium woronowii* appeared among my seedlings

PLATE 58. A beautiful soft pink seedling of *Allium oreophilum* appeared in the same way

PLATE 59. In the wild *Colchicum szovitsii* likes very moist conditions in spring meadows

PLATE 60. Some forms of *Puschkinia scilloides* produce such large blooms that it isn't easy to distinguish them from hyacinths

PLATE 61. *Scilla gorganica* from Iran is among my favorites

PLATE 62. *Scilla armena* has only one or two flowers on a scape, but it compensates for this in the garden by having a number of scapes

PLATE 63. *Scilla siberica* 'Václav' is among the most floriferous in this group

PLATE 64. *Scilla* aff. *bifolia* 'Double' was found in Turkey by Norman Stevens

PLATE 65. In Latvia *Fritillaria caucasica* can be grown outside as well as in a greenhouse

PLATE 66. The stolons of some forms of *Fritillaria pinardii* reach the surface of the soil and form aerial bulbils with leaves

PLATE 67. *Fritillaria minuta* likes deep, humus-rich soil

PLATE 68. This form of *Allium paradoxum* var. *normale* never forms bulbils among its flowers and likes shade in my region

PLATE 69. *Iris hyrcana* is the most early-flowering Reticulata iris in my collection

PLATE 70. With its brilliant white blooms, *Lilium ledebourii* is among the most gorgeous Caucasian lilies

PLATE 71. *Lilium monadelphum* is extremely floriferous in cultivation

PLATE 72. In the Talish Mountains *Iris pseudocaucasica* has blooms of all possible shades

PLATE 73. *Fritillaria crassifolia* subsp. *kurdica* is very variable in height and flower color

PLATE 74. *Allium scabriscapum* is a rhizomatous species that in Latvia blooms only in a greenhouse

PLATE 75. I went to the Kopet-Dag specifically to look for *Crocus michelsonii*

PLATE 77. *Gladiolus atroviolaceus* is completely hardy but can suffer from excessive moisture

PLATE 76. The yellowish green *Iris kopetdagensis* isn't easy in cultivation

PLATE 78. In the wild *Arum korolkowii* always grows in protected, shaded areas

PLATE 79. *Allium brachyscapum* forms globular flower heads between long, ribbon-like leaves

PLATE 80. *Allium bodeanum* looks like a smaller version of the better-known *A. christophii*

PLATE 81. *Fritillaria raddeana* has somewhat smaller flowers than *F. imperialis*

PLATE 82. *Fritillaria imperialis* 'Argenteovariegata', with its whitish variegated leaves, gives the garden a very artistic look

PLATE 83. *Fritillaria eduardii* is the most gorgeous fritillary

PLATE 84. Deep gorges at Mount Duschak

PLATE 85. The marvelous knolls of *Gypsophila aretioides* at Kopet-Dag can reach even 1.5 m in diameter

PLATE 86. *Hyacinthus transcaspicus* is a plant of higher altitudes and grows well in my region, even outside

PLATE 87. *Eremurus olgae* is a plant of lower altitudes and is very difficult to grow in my region

PLATE 88. *Corydalis glaucescens* was the first bulbous plant I collected in Central Asia

PLATE 89. *Eremurus cristatus* is very hardy and even self-sows

PLATE 90. *Iris orchioides* 'Kirghizian Gold'

PLATE 91. *Iris kuschakewiczii* isn't a very bright plant but is beautiful nonetheless

PLATE 92. *Tulipa regelii*, the most unique tulip in the world

PLATE 93. *Tulipa greigii* is at its most variable at Berkara Gorge in the Karatau Range

PLATE 95. The long stalk of *Allium karataviense* subsp. *henrikii* holds the flower head well over the rosette of shorter leaves

PLATE 94. *Allium karataviense* from the Kuramin Ridge is the largest, most deeply purplish red, most late-blooming form of this variable species

PLATE 96. A form of *Fritillaria sewerzowii* with almost golden yellow blooms

PLATE 97. *Iris willmottiana* is a contender for the title of best Juno iris

PLATE 98. I call this tulip *Tulipa berkariense* although the name has not yet been published. This dwarf relative of *T. kaufmanniana* grows in the Berkara Gorge, Karatau

PLATE 99. *Tulipa orthopoda* is the showiest relative of *T. turkestanica*, with a very dwarf, compact habit

PLATE 100. *Eremurus hilariae* is among the most beautiful, short-growing foxtail lilies

PLATE 101. My first new taxa, *Corydalis schanginii* subsp. *ainae*

PLATE 102. Chimgan is a paradise for bulb lovers. Here, for example, grow species of *Scilla, Iris, Tulipa, Eremurus,* and *Gagea*

PLATE 103. In the wild *Corydalis ledebouriana* is among the brightest and most beautiful species with a perennial tuber

PLATE 104. *Eminium lehmannii* has a velvety purplish brown spathe at ground level

PLATE 105. *Gymnospermium albertii* is among the most spectacular plants of the genus

PLATE 106. *Eranthis longistipitata* needs very dry conditions

PLATE 107. *Eranthis stellata*, which grows in eastern Siberia, is another extreme rarity

PLATE 108. *Iris pseudocapnoides* is a new species

PLATE 109. Additional roots, from left to right: *Iris capnoides*, *I. orchioides*, and *I. pseudocapnoides*

PLATE 110. *Scilla puschkinioides* is superficially similar to the trade form of *Puschkinia scilloides*

PLATE 111. *Crocus alatavicus* is the first flower to bloom after the snow melts

PLATE 112. *Colchicum luteum* is another early-flowering plant, sometimes blooming right through the snow

PLATE 113. Valley of the Great Chimgan

PLATE 114. *Colchicum kesselringii* easily crosses with *C. luteum*. This hybrid, *C.* 'Jānis', was selected by Arnis Seisums

PLATE 116. The variable *Tulipa dubia*

PLATE 115. Looking for a special form of *Tulipa dubia*

PLATE 117. More color forms of *Tulipa dubia*

PLATE 119. *Iris capnoides*, a smoky-flowered relative of *I. orchioides*

PLATE 118. Beldersai

PLATE 120. This form of *Iris kolpakow-skiana* sensu lato was found growing in Uzbekistan

PLATE 121. Although in *Iris tubergeniana* the haft of the blade is described as winged, it is almost invisible

PLATE 122. 'Rosea', an extremely rare pink form of *Geranium transversale*

PLATE 124. *Iris subdecolorata*

PLATE 123. *Eremurus regelii* growing in the mountains at Tovaksai

PLATE 125. *Iris inconspicua*

PLATE 126. The flower spikes of *Eremurus regelii* swing in the breeze like cobra heads

PLATE 127. The bicolored form of *Iris orchioides* sensu lato from the Kuramin Ridge forms large clumps in the wild

PLATE 128. An unidentified, tiny, bright red *Tulipa* species from the Kuramin Ridge at Oudzhasai

PLATE 129. *Fritillaria stenanthera* is one of the easiest fritillaries of section *Rhinopetalum* in the garden

PLATE 130. *Tulipa kaufmanniana* 'Ugam' was registered by Dutch nurseryman Jan Pennings under the name 'Icestick'

PLATE 131. *Eremurus lactiflorus* is a plant of high altitudes

PLATE 132. The steep slopes of Urungachsai

PLATE 133. *Allium barsczewskii* 'Snowcap'

PLATE 134. The true *Iris albomarginata*

PLATE 135. The dwarfest form of *Iris orchioides* sensu lato from Urungachsai

PLATE 136. Packed and ready to leave the second lake of Urungachsai

PLATE 137. The petals of *Allium kaufmannii* are up to 5 cm long

PLATE 138. *Iris pskemense*, a new Reticulata iris species from Central Asia

PLATE 139. *Corydalis glaucescens* aff. 'Ihnatchsai'.

PLATE 141. *Iris korolkowii* is less variable than other Regelia irises from Central Asia

PLATE 140. The mountains at Ihnachsai

PLATE 142. Arnis Seisums (seated) and I rest at our tent in Ihnachsai

◆ 21
Talish Mountains

THE TALISH MOUNTAINS really begin just south of the easternmost corner of the Caucasus Mountains in what was once the Soviet Union. The northern tip lies in modern-day Azerbaijan, while the larger southern portion belongs to Iran. These mountains are home to a very specific flora, but it was not easy to get there in Soviet times. As with any borderland, special permission was required.

Three of us took part in this expedition: Arnis Seisums, Aina Zobova from the National Botanical Garden (who was working with lilies at the time), and me. Aina had some friends in Baku, so we had a place to rest after the tiresome flight from Riga.

The next morning we took a bus to the mountains. The landscape we passed through was remarkably strange. I had never seen so many oil pumps in such a small area. Most of them were still, but some slowly swung up and down. They were everywhere around us: in the foothills, on the beach (could it still be called a beach?), and in the sea.

Along the way we had to stop a few times to have our papers checked. After registering in one place to cross through the border zone, we reached the defense zone and were told that we didn't have the right papers: entering the defense zone required special permission from the headquarters of the KGB in Moscow. How could a normal civilian understand all the nuances of the Soviet border guarding system, especially if they were kept top secret? Though all of this frustrated me at the time, the experience ultimately proved helpful on my later visit to the Kopet-Dag, which forms the border between Turkmenistan and Iran.

Lerik was to be the base station of our expedition. Aina had come here for *Lilium ledebourii*, Arnis and I for all other kinds of bulbs. We decided to use the first afternoon to investigate the upper part of a river valley in the area.

It was 23 April, but the weather and vegetation made it feel like the end of May in Latvia. We were immediately surrounded by bulbs. All the slopes were covered with the white stars of *Ornithogalum sintenisii*. Some spots even looked as though they were covered with snow. The bulbs were very shallow in the soil, only some 5–6 cm deep, and didn't have any bulbils at the base (in those years I had only a few ornithogalums in my collection, and this seemed very exceptional to me). Regrettably, *O. sintenisii* is never as beautiful in cultivation as it is in the wild. In Latvia the leaves often come up in autumn, and even when they come up in spring, they grow too long before the flowering starts. In the wild, however, the plants are almost leafless at flowering time. I later realized that many *Ornithogalum* species are more spectacular in nature than they are in the garden, where they tend to run riot.

All the shrubs in the area were full of an *Arum* species, their spathes held by the long stalks over the shrubs. According to A. A. Grossheim's *Flora Caucasica* (1940), two arums could be found here: *A. italicum* subsp. *albispathum* (what Grossheim called *A. albispathum*) and *A. rupicola* var. *virescens* (what he called *A. elongatum*). We later determined that the form we had found was *A. rupicola* var. *virescens*. This arum mostly grows in sunnier places on dry slopes in clay among stones, but the most luxurious plants grow among small shrubs that provide some small amount of shade. The tubers were covered with bluish gray underground aphids, like those I had seen on *A. elongatum* in Crimea. I cleaned them off with my fingers, which was sufficient for now, but I would need to dip them in insecticide solution after returning home. This species grows perfectly in my nursery, both outside and in the greenhouse, and multiplies vegetatively using small corms formed at the base of additional buds. It also sets seed well. Superficially it is quite similar to the Central Asian *A. korolkowii*, but the spathe limb is purplish in shade on its inner surface and the petiole is plain green.

The shrubs were full of the leaves of another bulbous plant, which turned out to be *Scilla caucasica*, another close relative of *S. siberica*, sometimes regarded as only a subspecies. It has twice as many flowers as *S. siberica*, and they are held on longer stalks. The flowers are usually darker blue with a very deep blue midrib.

In the same area grew an abundance of *Muscari neglectum* with especially dark blue flowers. This form from the Talish Mountains is now the only *M. neglectum* I still grow in my collection. In color it is somewhat similar to *M. leucostomum* from the Kopet-Dag.

Across the river, on the other side of the valley, we saw a rock formation that looked like a balcony with a green meadow growing on it. The river wasn't difficult to cross, and I was soon on top of this small, lustrous meadow. I was surprised to find it covered with the leaves of *Galanthus transcaucasicus*—so densely, in fact, that it seemed the bulbs had to be packed into the soil like sardines in a can. Lerik is the type locality from which *G. transcaucasicus* is described.

We stepped down to the river to cook up some lunch beside a waterfall, and here we made another joyful discovery, stumbling across a beautiful form of *Allium paradoxum* var. *normale*. This is a superb plant for shaded spots. Its large, pendant, bell-shaped, snow white flowers look marvelous on stems some 20 cm tall. Unfortunately, most forms in cultivation have bulbils instead of flowers on the stem. This Talish form was the best I had ever seen—not a single bulbil, only wonderful flowers (Plate 68). It grows in a shady corner of my nursery without any attention, flowering wonderfully each spring and then disappearing beneath overhanging plants until the next season. When I need bulbs, I simply visit this spot and dig them out with a shovel. It doesn't like growing in regular beds where there is too much sun.

We also found a Reticulata iris. At first I named it *Iris reticulata*, but it turned out to be the most early-flowering Reticulata iris in my collection, blooming outdoors along with winter aconites (*Eranthis hyemalis*) and the earliest crocuses, immediately after the snow melts or even right through the snow. In the wild it always forms small groups, and the flower color is sky blue, sometimes in a very light shade. I decided to follow the thinking of A. A. Grossheim and classify it as *I. hyrcana* (Plate 69), a species that was originally described as coming from the surroundings of Lerik and growing separately from *I. reticulata*, which usually grows as solitary plants with purplish flowers. This is one of those rare cases in which I don't want to follow the general trend among botanists and join both species together, mainly because of the very early flowering time of this Reticulata iris. All forms of *I. reticulata* start to flower only when my *I. hyrcana* ends.

In a drier area we collected another beautiful allium, which Arnis later identified as *Allium lenkoranicum*, a late summer-flowering species. Although its flowers are not remarkably bright, I have added it to my list of favorites because it blooms very late and impedes my usual schedule for bulb replanting. Before I started growing it in the greenhouse I had never seen it flowering in the field, because the bulbs were harvested before they could produce flowers. So I enjoyed them in the bulb shed, watching the stem with pendulous, grayish lilac, small, bell-shaped flowers on comparatively long, somewhat arched pedicels coming out of the bulb box. In the greenhouse it flowers at the end of July, its beauty enhanced by the pinkish lilac of the pedicels. It is an excellent plant for pots, too.

The next day we went looking for Aina's *Lilium ledebourii*. Personally I thought this was an absurd enterprise: Caucasian lilies can't be replanted in spring and seriously suffer if disturbed before flowering. This was the worst time to collect them. Nevertheless this lily was the single interest of our companion, so we would do our best to find it.

The first plant we came across on our way was a tall *Fritillaria* species that looked like *F. kotschyana*, although the flower was still hidden in a tight bud. We searched all around the area but couldn't find any other specimens. When we later asked a shepherd whether he knew where to find the plant, he told us we would find plenty of them in about three weeks. Our finding was just an accidental forerunner, possibly growing in a warmer, more protected spot. Unfortunately, the single bulb collected by Arnis never came up, so we couldn't confirm its identity. This is even more of a pity because *F. kotschyana* subsp. *grandiflora* is unknown outside the Talish Mountains. The quite variable type subspecies is grown in gardens, and I too have different clones. One clone from Gothenburg has almost uniformly colored large, green flowers, almost without any tessellation. Another form from Gonbad Province, Iran, has broadly campanulate flowers with dense brown tessellation and a green midrib on the outer petals. Both are easy to grow and produce plenty of bulblets at the base of the mother bulb.

Fritillaria olivieri is very similar to *F. kotschyana* and differs generally by its plain green or very slightly tessellated flowers and much narrower, green (not grayish) leaves. Its stem is also papillose at the base, while with *F. kotschyana* it is glabrous. Although it originates from Iran, I grow it outside without any problems because in the wild it grows on boggy meadows near streams.

Fritillaria hermonis is another close relative. Two color forms of subspecies *amana* are generally grown in the garden: a form with green flowers and more or less brown tessellation, and a form with "yellow" flowers. From the traditional green-flowering forms I have the one collected by E. K. Balls. Its outer petals are green with light brown netting, but the inner petals have a wide green midzone edged on both sides by brownish purple zones of the same width. My yellow form came from Wim de Goede in the Netherlands, and its petals are actually a greenish yellow gradually changing to yellow at the tips, with some brown spots on the inner petals, more noticeable at the base. The type subspecies is extremely rare. All the plants I have received under that name have just been wrongly labeled.

We met several local people who explained how we might find *Lilium ledebourii*. They seemed quite surprised that we were looking for plants not currently in flower. We started along a goat path that wound its way through terribly spiny shrubs. At one point we missed a right turn and nearly walked off the edge of an extremely steep slope. Goats may have been able to follow this path, but not us. We returned to our starting point to look for another way. Later, looking at the goat path from the opposite side of the gorge, we realized that continuing along it would have been suicide.

Soon the first bulbs appeared, beginning with the same *Galanthus transcaucasicus*. Here it grew in deep shade in the narrow cracks of the rock, where only a pinch of soil was visible. All the shrubs were full of *Cyclamen elegans*, now called *C. coum* subsp. *elegans*. Cyclamen tubers were scattered everywhere, often not even covered with soil, sometimes tossed out by cattle or washed out by a stream. In some places we couldn't even take a step without mashing one of them. Arnis still grows this subspecies, hand-pollinating it every season to keep it pure. He grows it in an unheated greenhouse because it is more tender than other subspecies of *C. coum*. I lost the plants that I tried to grow outside within a few years despite having carefully covered them in winter with dry oak leaves.

In the same area we also found *Arum italicum* subsp. *albispathum* (syn. *A. albispathum*) with fat, stoloniferous tubers. It grew only in deep shade at the bottom of the gorge and didn't have any nauseating aphids on its tubers. Like the stock from North Ossetia, this form turned out to be somewhat tender in the garden, so I now grow it only in the greenhouse, although I feel it would prefer a more shaded position. Contrary to what has been stated by Peter Boyce (1993), these plants never start vegetation in Latvian conditions in early autumn, as usually occurs with forms of *A. italicum* subsp. *italicum*.

The sides of the gorge became more gently sloping and a marvelous beech forest unfolded all around us. Then, suddenly, there it was, the highlight of the day: *Lilium ledebourii* (Plate 70). There were hundreds of plants, yet they were only some 30 cm tall and without any stem roots. Arnis and I tried to persuade Aina that it was the wrong time to collect these bulbs, but none of our arguments seemed to reach her ears. Fortunately, the weather took a turn for the worse, and this convinced Aina to end her vandalism. The tops of the mountains were enveloped in clouds and a dense fog was coming down, so we had to hurry back. Luckily we knew the way well and soon reached the last place to cross the river and get back to the village.

It wasn't difficult to understand why *Lilium ledebourii* was so high on Aina's list. With its pure snow white flowers, it is definitely among the most beautiful Caucasian lilies. Its nicely recurved petals are greenish-shaded at the base, with small, deep purple spots on the throat of the flowers. It is actually very different from the plant described under the same name in *Lilies*, the famous monograph by Patrick Millington Synge. I carefully checked all the Russian botanical literature available to me, and every author described the flowers as white or greenish white, never creamy yellow. In fact, it is very easy to separate from other Caucasian species just by its awesome flower color. It is not a very difficult species in the garden, although it can only reproduce by seed or scaling. The bulbils on the scales develop very slowly. I was only able to plant out the last ones in the third year after scaling.

Other Caucasian lilies have lighter or deeper yellow flowers. Sometimes it is difficult to separate them because plants in each population are quite variable and their features occasionally merge. Some authors even regard them as variants of a single but very variable species. I have grown almost all of them (*Lilium kesselringianum*, *L. monadelphum*, *L. szovitsianum*) for years but only acquired *L. armenum* in 2006. All my stocks have been easy to distinguish from one another, but this doesn't mean there haven't been any intermediates I didn't know about. The deepest yellow flowers are characteristic of *L. szovitsianum*, which grows in North Ossetia and South Ossetia at elevations up to 2200 m, as well as in northeastern Anatolia, Turkey. Its remarkably strong petals seem to be waxy. The flowers are more densely packed on the stem, which is up to 1.5 m tall, much taller than in related species. The closely related *L. armenum* is a smaller plant with much narrower, smaller petals.

The flowers of *Lilium monadelphum* (Plate 71) are somewhat lighter, golden to slightly greenish yellow in shade. This species is most easily identified by its filaments, which are joined at the base, a rare feature among other species. It is a smaller plant rarely exceeding 1 m tall even in cultivation and seems to be the most widely distributed lily in the Caucasus Mountains.

Lilium kesselringianum is distinguished by having the lightest yellow flowers. In some forms the flowers are even ivory white, though they are never the bright, cold shade of snow white found in *L. ledebourii*. The darkest forms of *L. kesselringianum* can be mistaken for the lightest *L. monadelphum*, though the petals of *L. kesselringianum* are obviously narrower. In my collection this is the least vigorous species of the group, but in the wild it can reach up to 2 m tall with up to twenty flowers on a stem. There are even records of wild bulbs, formed of more than a hundred scales, reaching 30 cm in diameter and weighing in at 2 kg. *Lilium kesselringianum* is distributed along the coast of the Black Sea from the Krasnodar region of the western Caucasus to Artvin Province, Turkey, and usually grows on high alpine meadows and among shrubs up to 2400 m above sea level.

All Caucasian lilies are reported to be calciphiles, but in my garden they do quite well on any type of soil. The greatest problem I have is with rodents. These merciless creatures completely destroyed much of my Caucasian lily stocks, and I am only slowly recovering these stocks due to the help of friends who long ago received bulbs from me.

Some years ago during a visit to the Netherlands, at the bulb shed of Hoog and Dix Export, I saw open boxes containing very large (about 15 cm in diameter) bulbs labeled as *Lilium monadelphum* recently imported from Turkey. Regardless of their high price, I was unable to withstand the temptation and bought some of them. When I returned home I found that the base of each bulb was black and rotten-looking. Without hope, I planted them outside, and nothing came up the following spring. The next autumn I asked for some compensation from Hoog and Dix Export and received twice as many bulbs of the same size, shape, and . . . quality, too. I planted them again with the same results: nothing came up the following spring. Fortunately, I left the bulbs from both consignments right where they had been planted and gave them no further attention. A few years later while visiting the corner of my garden where all my Caucasian lilies grow, I noticed some strange flowering plants that I soon realized were the Turkish bulbs from Hoog and Dix Export. They had survived, recovered, and begun to flower. The blooms were stunning, though smallish, with light creamy yellow tips, and large petals that were almost blackish brown in their lower half. The long, ciliated leaf margins helped me identify the plants, which turned out to be *L. ciliatum*. (The other very similar possibility was *L. ponticum*, but it has a smooth leaf margin.) The flower color reminded me of *L. nepalense*, which I grew outside for some years before losing it. Now I have introduced a new stock of *L. nepalense* from the famous lily breeder Peter Schenk (Netherlands), hoping these plants will have a better fate. *Lilium nepalense* starts into growth very late, and its shoots can appear quite far—even 50 cm—from where the bulbs are planted. I once thought my new stock was lost, when at the end of June a mass of strong shoots appeared.

Back in Lerik the fog had become so dense that it started to condense into some kind of rain. We asked everyone we met how long the fog was expected to last. All the local people shrugged their shoulders and replied the same way: perhaps three or four days. For us this could be catastrophic. We decided to move on to Gosmelyan.

We caught a bus the next morning, which somehow made its way through the same thick fog. The air finally cleared as we passed the mountains. After covering some 5–6 km in the valley, we reached the village of Gosmelyan. The surrounding mountains didn't look at all promising—nothing but gray, sunbaked stones for many kilometers. We walked and walked but couldn't find a single spot to set up our tent. Then we reached the dry delta of a mountain stream that came down by a wide, shallow valley. It was crossed by a manmade dike to collect the water for a small irrigation canal. We decided to stop there. It was not an ideal spot, especially if it started to rain in the mountains, but at least it offered more than endless stones, and we would have access to drinking water.

After lunch we started our first climb and soon made a wonderful discovery. It was *Iris pseudocaucasica* (Plate 72), a gorgeous dwarf Juno with two or three large flowers on the stem and a very widely winged haft. It was a very variable population. I have seen this species in Turkey many times, but it was never as variable as it was here in the Talish Mountains. In general the flowers were a smoky yellowish lilac, quite muddy in color, but some were a very beautiful lighter and darker yellow. Even some forms with almost white or violet flowers could be found among them. This isn't the easiest species for the garden, although I have grown it for a long time in an open field and lost bulbs only when my garden was situated on a north-facing site in deep clay. Arnis grew his stock on his own sandy soil, and now I grow my stocks from Iran and Turkey on a raised greenhouse bed where they have excellent drainage. This species reproduces very well vegetatively and often produces seeds with the help of bees. Arnis later introduced a nice grayish form from Iran (near Tochal in the Elburz Mountains).

Only a short distance away we found another beautiful newcomer: *Fritillaria crassifolia* subsp. *kurdica* (Plate 73). At this elevation it grew alongside *Iris pseudocaucasica* in a mixed population, but as we climbed higher we saw more fritillaries and fewer irises, and soon we found nothing but fritillaries. This Talish form was the first of this frit in my collection. It is a very uniform, dwarfish form. Its two or three broadly campanulate, yellowish green flowers have yellow tips and light reddish purple tessellation at the bottom of the petals. In color *F. crassifolia* subsp. *kurdica* slightly resembles *F. michailovskyi*, but it isn't as bright and contrasting. I grow many different forms of subspecies *kurdica*. Some were collected by Arnis in Armenia and named after nearby villages. 'Bitschenag' is a nice uniform clone with very shiny flowers that are bigger and more greenish brown than the Talish strain, on a 15 cm stem. It was collected in Nakhichevan, Azerbaijan, near the village of Bitschenag. 'Aragats' is a uniform clone with dark brown, fairly rounded flowers (in the latter feature resembling subspecies *crassifolia*). It is 20 cm tall and was selected from plants originating on Mount Aragats in Armenia. 'Sevan' has fairly long, only slightly tessellated green flowers, the biggest of the group, and comes from near Sevan Lake in Armenia. 'Turkish Glow', a clone of unknown origin I received from the Netherlands, is similar in size but has almost uniformly shining brown flowers. 'Ordubad' is a uniform clone of dull yellow flowers with green tessellation, selected from a population near Ordubad, a town in the Transcaucasus. Almost every 'Ordubad' produces two flowers.

Fritillaria crassifolia subsp. *crassifolia* appears to be fairly distinct from the more widely grown subspecies *kurdica*. It is mainly distinguished by its rounded flowers and unique leaves, which are broader than those of subspecies *kurdica* (the lowest leaf is no more than three times as long as broad, while in subspecies *kurdica* the lowest leaf is up to seven times as long as broad). The flowers are green and tessellated dark greenish brown, with brown-edged segments. My stock was originally collected in the mountains between Bayburt and Erzurum in Turkey.

All forms of *Fritillaria crassifolia* are very easy in the garden and survive even the harshest winters without any trouble. This species regularly sets seed, which ripens in the open field even in the wettest summers, and successfully reproduces vegetatively. The single exception to this rule is the form introduced by Arnis from Zardekuh in the Kasan region of Iran, under the collection number *GLUZ-98-121*. This form starts growing much earlier than all the other forms and has shining green leaves. It is similar to subspecies *hakkarensis*, which grows on wetter spots in southeastern Anatolia and northern Iraq, but Arnis's form was found and collected very far from those localities. When planted outside in my region it always suffers from night frosts, so I grow it only in the greenhouse, where it blooms splendidly every spring. Unfortunately, it doesn't increase on its own, so the bulbs must be split to build up the stock. Gothenburg recently sent me subspecies *polunini* from northern Iraq; it is the smallest form of all and very rare in cultivation.

After a freezing cold night in our cramped tent, we decided to walk up the other gorge. At first we saw nothing new, only some *Colchicum* species, *Iris hyrcana*, and *Bellevalia caucasica*. But then luck shone on Arnis, who found a single plant of the long-searched-for *Allium akaka*. The other plants in the area were irises and fritillaries, many of them quite lovely. What a pity I had forgotten my camera in the tent! When I came across a large group of exceptionally gorgeous irises, I scratched a strong line on the pass and made a small stone pyramid to mark the place, then headed back in the direction of our campsite. Aina followed me, and a bit lower down we met Arnis. His face was radiant with joy—on the other scree he had found two more bulbs of *A. akaka*.

When I returned to my pyramid, this time with camera in hand, I couldn't find a single iris. I was extremely puzzled until I noticed small holes here and there in the soil. Sheep had passed through here and had themselves a meal along the way. They had plucked all the irises so carefully that even the underground parts of the stems were pulled out up to the bulb necks.

The clouds soon became denser, so we decided to leave Gosmelyan and head back in the direction of Lerik. On our way we found a new plant growing in a depression on stony clay. It was a form of *Ornithogalum platyphyllum*, and to separate it from other stocks collected by Arnis in Armenia, it was later named 'Talish'. It is a lovely large-flowering variety with green-white flowers in a compact raceme and wide leaves. It reaches up to 20 cm tall. In nature it grows in places that are very wet in spring but that later dry out. For this reason I replant it annually in my nursery, although it grows outside perfectly here. The Armenian 'Vardahovit' is a little taller.

Arnis collected two other ornithogalums in Armenia. The first, *Ornithogalum schmalhausenii*, is an explicitly dwarf species with a sessile umbel of white-green flowers between rosettes of numerous narrow leaves. It is an adorable addition to the showiest species and an ideal plant for a rock garden or alpine house. It was collected on Mount Hustup in the Zangezur Mountain Range and is a typical plant of high mountain meadows, where it flowers next to melting snow up to 3000 m. The second species, *O. tenuifolium*, is a plant of lowlands that rarely reaches the middle zone of mountains. It has white-green flowers in a dense umbel among numerous very narrow leaves and reaches up to 10 cm tall. It was collected in the Spitak region, where it grows on grassy, dry slopes. It is a good, noninvasive garden plant and grows well outdoors in my region.

On our way back to Lerik we passed the village cemetery. A funeral was taking place, and as is traditional for Muslims, only men were participating. After we had walked another 5 km or so, a bus carrying the people from the funeral stopped to give us a ride back to town. As always, Arnis spent the time staring out the window to scan the roadside for plants. His eye caught an interesting *Bellevalia* species with white lower flowers and blue upper ones.

During our stay in the mountains the fog had disappeared, and the next morning greeted us with bright sun. Aina headed to the village, while Arnis and I caught a ride along the road leading back to Gosmelyan. At the place where the gorge starts, we found a narrow scree slope to walk up, but we managed to find nothing more than *Ornithogalum sintenisii* and *Arum rupicola* var. *virescens* in a shaded spot among rocks. Then I heard Arnis shouting, "Champagne!" He had found the first corydalis of our trip. It was growing inside very spiny, dwarf rose shrubs. It turned out to be *Corydalis angustifolia*, a pretty, very uniform, light pink form that I later named 'Talish Dawn' to separate from the stock collected near Tbilisi. It forms dense racemes and is very floriferous.

In the afternoon Arnis returned to the slopes where he had found the single bulb of *Fritillaria kotschyana*, but instead found a few rootstocks of *Paeonia tomentosa*. This species now grows perfectly in the rockery of the National Botanical Garden in Latvia, and even self-sown seedlings can be found under the large clump. I lost the plant I once had and now grow just a single seedling from the botanical garden.

The next day we traveled to the village of Buludul some 25–30 km from Lerik. The name of the village means "healthy water" and refers to a magnificent spring of naturally carbonized water there. People from far away lined up at the spring for the chance to cure their wounds or ease their stomachs. We set up our tent and had a quick meal of local cheese and bread. The spring water was delicious. The last days of continuous walking and bad-quality boots had caused large blisters to develop on my feet, and they were so painful that I decided to stay in the camp while Arnis with Aina made the first reconnaissance. They found nothing we hadn't seen in Lerik except for *Corydalis marschalliana*. The form growing here was variety *purpureo-lilacina* with flowers that were slightly lilac-shaded at the top of the spike, but in overall appearance the plants were very similar to forms from the western end of the Caucasus.

The next day my feet were better and I ventured out of the tent while Aina stayed behind to cook. In general I was only taking photographs, because there was nothing new to collect. The landscape was spectacular—untouched forest starting some distance from the village, with rocks and slopes that seemed to be too steep even for lumbermen. An abundance of *Lilium ledebourii*, with gigantic bulbs, grew in a deep layer of leaf mold formed by fallen oak and beech leaves. In more open spots *Iris hyrcana* was just as plentiful.

We soon reached a place where the path was blocked by a rocky cliff, and all around us were jungles of excessively spiny bramble bushes. Using a fallen tree as a bridge, we crossed the river, but the banks were steep, slippery, and covered with dry leaves. In front of us we could see a rock some 15 m high and two waterfalls tumbling into a large basin. It seemed that we could pass the wall if the rock was not too slippery and if there was something to grab hold of. I was the first to take a few steps. A bit higher up I saw a thick root; I tried to catch it with my ice pick, but it was rotten and fell down. The climbing became rather problematic. Flattening myself against the rock, I tried to reach a small "balcony" formed by the trunk of a broken tree. When I finally succeeded in my effort, Arnis started along the same way, but he is shorter than I am and was unable to take long enough steps. He became stranded at the most problematic point, and although I tried to pass my ice pick to him, he wasn't able to reach it. He finally jumped, caught my ice pick, and safely landed on the balcony beside me. Luckily, the rest of the climb proceeded without any problems. We soon found ourselves on a sunny woodside, where we lay on the ground for a short rest.

That was the final adventure of our expedition to the Talish Mountains. Back in Riga the photo laboratory damaged my film, so unfortunately I don't have even a single habitat shot of the many plants we found in this region. All in all, though, it was another successful trip.

◈ 22
Kopet-Dag

THE KOPET-DAG acts as a natural border between Turkmenistan and Iran, where Central Asia departs from Europe by way of the Caspian Sea. It is an extremely interesting ridge of not very high mountains edged in the north by the Kara-Kum and in the south by the Iranian Plateau, gradually changing into the Elburz Mountains, which run along the southern coast of the Caspian Sea. I have visited the Kopet-Dag only once, so all the plants that I grow from there are special. I have always regarded it as a separate district from Central Asia. Many Kopet-Dag plants grow in Iran, and we can clearly see lines going through Iran into Turkey and Iraq. An expedition to Iran remains one of my great dreams, although I already grow many Iranian plants that were collected by Arnis Seisums and other plant hunters and growers.

My travel to Turkmenistan was closely connected to a book I was writing about crocuses. The Kopet-Dag is home to the westernmost Central Asian crocus species: *Crocus michelsonii*. The winter before my trip, I wrote a letter to the Central Botanical Garden of the Turkmenistan Academy of Sciences asking for some corms of this beautiful crocus. I later received word that the Komarov Botanical Institute in Saint Petersburg was planning an expedition to the Kopet-Dag and that people from the Tallinn Botanical Garden would also be taking part. I received a kind offer to join them.

To receive the necessary permission, I had to write letters to the director of the botanical garden of Turkmenistan, the border guard headquarters of Turkmenistan, the main border guard headquarters of the Soviet Union in Moscow, and so forth. Everywhere I went, they asked to see the following papers: my petition, a reference from the chief of administration of the publishing house, a reference from the chief of my trade union group, and a reference from the chief of the local group of the Communist Party. It all ended with an official document from the KGB office in Moscow stating that I was allowed to work behind the "border protection engineering structures" (in other words, behind the barbed-wire fence surrounding the Soviet Union). Lastly I had to take all of these papers to the local police headquarters to receive my official documents.

I finally found myself sitting in an airplane bound for sunny Turkmenistan. The total weight of my haversack came to 38 kg, which included provisions for two weeks, a tent, a sleeping bag, and other equipment. I was the only explorer from Latvia, so all my equipment would be my own responsibility.

I landed in Ashgabat early in the morning. It was an interesting city. After the terrible earthquake of 1948, it had been rebuilt with impressively wide streets—even in the event of total destruction, sufficient space would be left in the middle of the street for the rescue brigades. I caught a taxi from the airport and was soon standing next to the closed gates of the botanical garden. It was Sunday and no one was there. Even the guard meant to stand at the front gate had disappeared. I sat near the gate for some hours until he came. Luckily he had been informed of my arrival and showed me to a small room with a bed where I could stay overnight. Soon the chief of the bulb department, Svetlana Abramova, showed up and invited me to her place for an evening meal. I soon received word that the people from Tallinn and Saint Petersburg would be unable to come because they hadn't received the necessary papers. So I would be the only "foreigner" taking part in the expedition.

After a nice meal, Dr. Abramova showed me around the botanical garden. It had recently shrunk in size from 25 hectares down to 17. It seemed the Communist Party of Turkmenistan had needed a place for two new buildings—headquarters and a hotel for VIPs—and decided that the best construction site was the large dendrology park of the botanical garden. There were only 400 square meters reserved for bulbs in the garden, and everything looked as it did in my own collection, each label close to another. Alliums were the most plentiful, followed by local tulips and others.

I slept very poorly in the enormous heat and spent a restless night examining a large heap of botanical literature on the floor of the neighboring room. These were pre-war and even pre-revolution editions, all simply tossed out of the library. There were unique books among them, very rare editions that had escaped total destruction during the Stalinist regime. Among these pearls I found the *Flora of Siberia and the Far East* (Bush 1913), including the *Corydalis* volume that would help me so much later in my research on Siberian bulbs. I also found the *Flora Taurica* (Wulff 1929), about the bulbs of Crimea, and the second volume of *Flora of Turkmenistan* (Fedchenko et al. 1932), all about bulbs. Now I had a book about the plants of Turkmenistan and could better prepare myself for the expedition. I had had no time for such studies before leaving Riga.

As it turned out, our expedition van was unavailable, and we spent the next couple of days waiting for transportation issues to work themselves out. On 1 June at two o'clock in the afternoon we finally received the go-ahead. After two hours we arrived in Baharden for the first check of our documents and registration. On the left side of the road we saw nothing but endless mountains, while on the right side we saw a large irrigation canal and behind that the Kara-Kum. The name of this desert area comes from *gara*, meaning "black," and *gum*, meaning "sand," and the landscape is in fact dark gray, almost black. After Baharden our road entered the mountains along a rather wide valley crossed by a very thin wire that would trigger an alarm if someone touched it. At the crossing point, our papers were again carefully checked. It was late in the evening. After finding the first nice spot, we left our van to pass the night under the open sky.

The morning greeted me with the first discovery: a gorgeous, yellow-flowering, rhizomatous *Allium scabriscapum* (Plate 74). Confirming its identity wasn't difficult—it is the only *Allium* species with yellow flowers growing in Turkmenistan. It is very widespread here, growing on stony slopes and forming clumps 30–40 cm tall, with nice, fairly lax umbels formed by pendant, bell-shaped, yellow flowers. It is a common plant from Uzbekistan to Armenia and southeastern Anatolia. Before I built my green-houses I grew it in the open field, where it survived but never produced flowers. Now I grow it under covering and it has started to flower. I recently collected another form in Turkey near the Çavuştepe Castle on a fine, gritty, clay slope at an altitude of 1830 m. This bulb is a bit fatter than the bulbs from the Kopet-Dag, but it hasn't bloomed in my garden yet.

Our road ran alongside the so-called border protection engineering structures. They consisted of dense barbed-wire fences 2 m high, with a space of 10 cm between each wire. It was an electric fence, and the slightest touch would set off an alarm at the nearest checkpoint. There was a plowed zone several meters wide on the other side of the fence that would fix the footprints of anyone trying to escape. Beyond this was a special net of very thin, strong wire, known as "spider web." Anyone stepping into it was bound to be trapped, and any attempt to escape would only tighten the grip.

Our destination was Arvaz ("cup of winds"), located in the valley of the Kopet-Dag. A very pleasant, refreshing wind blows there all the time, so we never felt the heat as it rose up to 40°C during the daytime. The chief of the border guard was very welcoming, showing us a nice place to camp and informing us about the area. We were allowed to walk freely everywhere except behind the barbed-wire fence, where we must be accompanied by two soldiers. This was because the border with Iran was only 1–2 km from this point.

Arvaz was a real paradise for a bulb lover. I couldn't so much as put my leg on the ground without stepping on *Crocus michelsonii* (Plate 75). Every place that looked like a lawn wasn't actually covered with grass but with the leaves of crocuses. *Crocus michelsonii* is the most difficult species from the Central Asian trio (which also includes *C. alatavicus* and *C. korolkowii*) but is also one of the most beautiful. It is quite slow to increase vegetatively, but if the weather is favorable it goes to seed perfectly. The seeds are very large, perhaps the largest of any crocus. The flowers can be very variable but are generally tinted a specific bluish violet; in some, the shading over the petal exteriors is only slight, while in others it is very dark. Common to all of them is a large, deep blue throat. I used to grow this species in sandy soil and had no problems with it outside, but moving *C. michelsonii* to colder, wetter clay proved fatal to my stocks. Fortunately I was able to rebuild my stocks from corms I had given to friends, and now I grow this plant only under covering. The greatest problem is its very early flowering. In recent years it has always started flowering for me in early January, after which the pollen is inevitably damaged by night frosts, so I receive very little seed despite my careful hand-pollination. Some well-increasing clones were named by Leonid Bondarenko. The outer petals of 'Odyssey' are blue with a creamy edge, while the inner petals are pure white. 'God's Look' has a significant contrast between the very dark flower tube and the much lighter perianth segments. 'Turkmenian Night' has the darkest violet-blue exterior petals, with some white feathering appearing only at the very edge. All of these were selected from material I originally collected in Arvaz.

I recently received word from Henrik Zetterlund that he had collected *Crocus michelsonii* on the Iranian side of the Kopet-Dag, but higher in the mountains at Bajgiran, as well as near Mashhad. In cultivation both forms start flowering later than the bulk of spring crocuses. These plants are a very valuable addition, because it is the extremely early flowering of this species that can sometimes interfere with its successful cultivation. In my experience, plants from higher altitudes usually start flowering later than plants of the same species from lower altitudes, not only in the wild but also in the garden.

Another bulb we found growing in abundance around Arvaz was *Iris fosteriana*, one of the most unusually colored Juno irises. This species forms a clump up to 25–30 cm tall, each stem holding one or rarely two bicolored flowers. The falls and style branches are yellow to greenish yellow, and the standards are quite large (for a Juno), sharply downturned, and deep purplish violet. We found clumps with as many as thirty bulbs each. The bulbs themselves are very slim and unusually grayish green, without any markedly swollen storage roots. *Iris fosteriana* has the reputation of being a difficult plant, but it grows amazingly well at Kew, both in pots and in a rockery. It never flowered in my nursery, however, and only one of a fairly large number of bulbs survived. This surviving bulb grew outside for almost twenty years before I moved it to the greenhouse. I still have it and hope that at some point it will be strong enough to flower here, too. When Henrik Zetterlund visited the Iranian side of the Kopet-Dag, he was equally surprised by the millions of *I. fosteriana* clumps covering the mountain slopes; as with *Crocus michelsonii*, the samples collected higher in the mountains flower later than those from lower altitudes.

Iris kopetdagensis (Plate 76) was growing in more protected spots, though not so abundantly. This Juno is about 30–35 cm tall with very swollen roots and up to nine yellowish green flowers with a yellow blotch on the falls. The standards are much reduced, even bristle-like; the haft of the falls is very narrow with upturned edges. The shape of the haft margins and somewhat smaller flowers are the only real features that distinguish it from *I. drepanophylla*. The latter grows more to the east, and the margins of the haft are folded downward. I never grew *I. drepanophylla* until recently, when I bought seeds that were collected in northwestern Afghanistan. I am looking forward with impatience to future development of these plants and hope to see them flowering in a few years. *Iris kopetdagensis* belongs to a small group of Juno irises with very special bulbs. With most Junos, the old stem dies down after flowering and a new bulb is formed from fleshy scales. But a few species form new bulbs in another way. What happens is the base of the old stem becomes swollen, forming a bulb-like structure, and later in autumn a new shoot reminiscent of a true bulb-like bud starts to form. This unusual feature led George Rodionenko to place *I. kopetdagensis*, *I. drepanophylla*, and species from the *I. rosenbachiana* group in section *Physocaulon*. *Iris kopetdagensis* is very rare in cultivation but I grew it without serious problems in sandy soil in an open garden. Unfortunately, I lost the stock when moving to another place. I haven't had the opportunity yet to replace these bulbs. Everything I've received from other growers has turned out to be something else, mostly *I. bucharica*.

Two very different *Gladiolus* species, both at the peak of flowering, grew side by side in the same area. One was *G. atroviolaceus* (Plate 77), which has deep bluish violet flowers. The other was *G. italicus* (syn. *G. segetum*), with purplish red or magenta flowers quite similar in color to the Latvian native *G. imbricatus*. *Gladiolus italicus* is generally a larger plant and grows somewhat lower in the mountains. Here they both grew together, but as I climbed higher I found only *G. atroviolaceus*. I didn't find any intermediate form between the two species, although according to the *Flora of Turkmenistan* they hybridize often and intermediate forms are common. Both species are completely hardy and grow well outside in my region, although in wet summers they can suffer from *Fusarium*. I grow both species together with Turkish gladiolus in the greenhouse, and so far there have been no problems. They are good increasers, forming plenty of cormlets at the base of the mother corm that reach flowering size in one or two years.

We found plenty of *Tulipa hoogiana* in full flower, too. This beautiful, large-flowered, bright red tulip somewhat resembles *T. greigii* in terms of flower shape but has plain green leaves and a sharply pointed, narrow, black basal blotch inside the petals. Although it reproduces vegetatively, like many large-flowering Central Asian tulips it doesn't grow well in the garden, nor does it produce seed without artificial pollination. I grew it for many years, but my stock shrunk from year to year until I finally lost it altogether. It is a very narrow endemic of the central Kopet-Dag. Unfortunately, the *Flora of Turkmenistan* describes and pictures some other tulip species under the name *T. hoogiana*, most likely *T. kuschkensis*. The latter is another very narrow endemic of the most southern corner of Turkmenistan and differs from the former by the smaller size of its flowers and by its basal blotch, which is somewhat wider and black with a light yellow rim. An amateur gardener living near Kuschka sent me a few bulbs of *T. kuschkensis*, the town's namesake, but it was even more stunted in Latvian growing conditions than *T. hoogiana*. The true *T. hoogiana* is described in the *Flora of Turkmenistan* under the name *T. ingens*, which also has a pure black basal blotch but grows far away from the Kopet-Dag.

Here and there on more open spots grew *Hyacinthus litwinowii*, a beautiful plant with large blue flowers in a loose spike between very wide leaves. The leaves make this species easy to distinguish from other wild hyacinths. It grows at altitudes up to 1500 m, and at higher altitudes is replaced by *H. transcaspicus*. It is a surprisingly good grower in the garden. I have had more success growing *H. litwinowii* than the large Dutch hyacinth varieties. As is typical for hyacinths, it doesn't reproduce vegetatively but sets seed under favorable conditions. The seedlings start flowering in the fifth year. I also observed this species reproducing vegetatively when there was some mechanical damage to the bottom of the bulb. On one occasion I tried cutting the basal plates on purpose and lost all the prepared bulbs due to some lack of cleanliness. The bulbs caught a bacterial rot and died; only the smaller ones that I didn't cut survived. I never again had the courage to repeat this kind of experiment, preferring instead to propagate from seed.

Below our camp was the valley, where the soil was more moist. A large group of *Arum korolkowii* (Plate 78), just now in full flower, was hiding deep inside a shrub. In the wild this arum always grows in shaded, more protected spots that are wet at least in spring. My attempt to plant it in similar conditions in Latvia failed—what is full sun in my country seems to be shade in Central Asia. Nonetheless, this is an excellent grower, reproducing well vegetatively and usually producing a good crop of seeds. I prefer planting it late, both in the garden and in the greenhouse, because tubers that are planted early sometimes produce shoots before winter starts. At planting time the shoots in boxes are usually up to 10 cm long. Even when I plant late I have to check the spot from time to time and add some peat moss if the tips of the shoots become visible. This arum can stay in the garden for another year, but it is best to replant it annually because the tubers are very susceptible to rot in wet soil. Seeds that are harvested when green ripen perfectly in boxes, too. The tuber of this species is oriented vertically. *Arum korolkowii* is very similar to *A. jacquemontii*, which grows further east in southern Tajikistan and up to China and India. It is easy to separate them by the petioles, which in *A. korolkowii* are pale green with diffuse brownish green stripes, while those of *A. jacquemontii* are not striped but stained with dull purple. In another superficially similar species, *A. rupicola*, the petiole is concolorous green. The spathe limb of *A. korolkowii* is usually green with very faint purple flushing along a third of the limb.

The next day I left my colleagues at the campsite and headed toward the surrounding mountaintops. Standing on one peak, I had an outstanding view of the Iranian side—vast plowed fields all around, with the next mountain range on the horizon. A line of striped sticks on the top of every hill marked the border between both countries. On the opposite side was a fantastic gorge with vertical stone slopes.

I passed through a small flat meadow where some tall-growing *Allium* hadn't yet started flowering. Later it was identified as *A. pseudoseravschanicum*. It is a nice species with a medium-tall stem and a compact umbel of light pinkish lilac flowers. In the Kopet-Dag it replaces the very similar *A. sarawschanicum*, which grows further east and is a larger plant in all aspects, with less compact flower heads and darker flowers. Unfortunately, both species can hybridize, so if a true stock is needed they have to be planted separately. *Allium pseudoseravschanicum* was my single discovery of the day.

That evening the chief officer of the border guard gave me permission to visit the forbidden zone the next day. I would be the only one from the expedition allowed in the area, and I would be accompanied by soldiers. It would prove to be the best day of the trip for me.

In reality it was a very tough and arduous route with extremely steep slopes. We walked up, then down, then up, through deep grass and between rocks and scree slopes. When we returned late in the afternoon, after eight hours away, the soldiers told us we had covered some 20 km in the burning sun. The environment here was wonderful, and everything seemed to grow with double energy. Some plants of *Iris kopetdagensis* even reached 40 cm tall here and developed seedpods. I could not find any *I. fosteriana*, however, which prefers drier, more open slopes, while *I. kopetdagensis* hides in the protection of large *Juniperus turcomanica* or near rocks.

And then came one of the best discoveries of the trip: *Allium brachyscapum* (Plate 79). According to the *Flora of Turkmenistan* this allium had been found only once, some 100 km from Arvaz, but there was such a good picture of it that I had no problem determining its identity. Much later I read in a book that in the 1960s it had also been found in a spot closer to Arvaz. This tiny beauty generally grows on bare south-facing slopes composed of small stone chips interspersed with clay. The bulbs lie only some 5 cm deep. When I found it, the surface of the soil was so hot that just lightly touching it with my hand was painful. I liken this allium to a miniature *A. karataviense* growing in much more severe conditions. I never imagined it would grow in my northern climate. If there hadn't been so much of it growing in the wild I would never have collected it at all, feeling sure that it wouldn't survive outside its homeland. In Latvia, however, it has proved to be one of the best growers in my garden and reproduces well vegetatively. Every year the large bulbs split into two. It keeps its dwarf habit, too, forming small, globular flower heads between two long, ribbon-like, slightly curved leaves. Strangely, I never got any seeds from it. The first seedpods only appeared in the comparatively cool summer of 2004, twenty years after I found it in the wild.

Allium bodeanum (Plate 80), which I also found near Arvaz, grows in less blistering conditions, generally in peaty pockets between stones and on shaly slopes without direct sun exposure. This species has proved to be much less vigorous in the garden than *A. brachyscapum*. When I found it I supposed it was just a smaller form of *A. christophii* that was growing at lower altitudes on softer soils. In those years I didn't have a greenhouse, and although I kept the bulbs in full sun in very sandy soil, they became smaller and smaller with each passing year until they finally disappeared. I now grow this species from seeds I received from the Gothenburg Botanical Garden. In general *A. bodeanum* looks like a smaller version of *A. christophii* with fewer leaves, a shorter stem, and a slightly smaller flower head. The grayish flowers are not very conspicuous, but after flowering the petals remain strong and spiny. The plant's beauty is in the shape of its umbel and its overall appearance. Some botanists join *A. bodeanum* and *A. christophii* as two local variants. In this case the name *A. bodeanum* has the priority. I collected *A. christophii* in the botanical garden in Turkmenistan, where it grew as a weed, self-sowing everywhere. Its flower color was very similar, an inconspicuous grayish pink, very different from the beautiful, shining, bright purple flowers of cultivated *A. christophii*. This is a case in which the cultivated stock is far better than the wild one. In contrary to wild *A. christophii*, the bulbs offered by Dutch nurseries are very good growers. Although they rarely split, they regularly set seed and reach flowering size in three to four years.

I want to mention another species that looks somewhat similar, although it grows very far away. If *Allium bodeanum* can be regarded as a smaller version of *A. christophii*, then *A. schubertii*, which grows from Israel to southern Turkey, can be regarded as the giant of the family. It has very large, loose umbels of starry flowers that are perfect for dried flower arrangements. The imported bulbs of *A. schubertii* that have been planted outside in Latvian conditions as a rule survive the first winter. They flower, set seed, and die during the summer or following winter. The seeds germinate very well, and again they don't come up the following spring. For some years I have had a few bulbs of this species in the greenhouse, but I wouldn't say they are very happy. I suppose that our summers are too cold for the bulbs to mature. I would not even mention this plant if its name hadn't been misapplied in Soviet floras to other *Allium* species, usually to *A. protensum*.

I collected another rhizomatous *Allium* species just near our camp. It was out of flower when I found it and never flowered for me before I planted it in a greenhouse. More than twenty years passed before Arnis Seisums identified it as *A. flavellum*, a species he had long been looking for but had never succeeded in finding, although it had been cultivated here so closely to his garden. This plant flowers in midsummer, with a starry inflorescence of almost white, slightly greenish yellow blooms. It survived many years in my garden growing outside in wet, cold clay. Its only protest against such negligence was a lack of flowering. I have quickly built up my stock and feel really lucky to have it in my collection.

Finally, under a large *Juniperus*, I noticed the plant I had been checking each roadside for the whole time we were driving in the mountains. It was *Fritillaria raddeana* (Plate 81), a close relative of the crown imperials (*F. imperialis*) so widely grown in gardens. The pale greenish yellow or straw-colored flowers of *F. raddeana* are somewhat smaller than those of *F. imperialis*, and the plant doesn't have that unpleasant foxy smell. *Fritillaria raddeana* can reach up to 70–90 cm tall. It has a reputation as a slow vegetative increaser, and this has been true of all the Iranian stocks I have received from the Netherlands. Although the bulbs from the Kopet-Dag sometimes split in two, this isn't as common as it is with the garden forms of *F. imperialis*. Near Arvaz we generally found *F. raddeana* growing in very loose, peaty soil in the shade of trees. There were hundreds of these plants under every large tree, and all were flowering, though I only found one seedpod. The bulbs were comparatively small, but in another population growing in a more open place in the shade of rocks and without competition from tree roots, the bulbs were significantly larger. Despite their size they were still without seeds. This species grows perfectly in the garden, too, but not so well in the greenhouse—under covering it gets too hot, and the flowers and even leaves sometimes burn. In recent years the leaves and flowers of my outdoor plants have often been damaged by hard night frosts, and the plants have produced a bad seed crop or none at all. Nonetheless the plants have survived. They usually start forming roots in the box before being planted out, so they must be planted very carefully to avoid damaging the roots. I replant this species every year to provide a dry rest period, and it flowers each spring, which can't be said of *F. imperialis*.

There are four closely related *Fritillaria* species in this group: *F. raddeana*, *F. imperialis*, *F. eduardii*, and *F. chitralensis*. Some botanists even put them in a distinct genus: *Petilium*.

Fritillaria imperialis is the most common in gardens, with large brownish red to orange or yellow flowers on stems 1 m long. Of the many cultivars, a few are among my favorites. 'Rubra Maxima' is a form I looked for over a long period of time before finding the real thing. Unfortunately, an assortment of red clones are offered under this name by nurseries and garden centers. True 'Rubra Maxima' is a tetraploid variety with almost all parts of the plant twice the normal size. It has gigantic, more darkly veined, flame orange flowers and very wide, shiny green leaves. The size of the foliage alone is the best distinguishing feature. I still haven't succeeded in finding the true 'Lutea Maxima'; all plants bought under that name have turned out to be the ordinary yellow form. There are other good varieties with variegated leaves. Although known in cultivation since the seventeenth century, these are still very rare and offered by just a few growers. Two well-flowering cultivars, 'Argenteovariegata' (Plate 82) with whitish variegated leaves and 'Aureomarginata' with yellowish-edged leaves and red flowers on 1 m stems, give any garden a very artistic appearance. Both varieties are quite similar. From plants of 'Aureomarginata' I selected a mutation in which the yellow zone has moved from the edge to the middle of the leaves. It is called 'Golden Midway'. Sometimes plants with plain green or yellow leaves appear among both varieties, and these must be discarded.

In the wild *Fritillaria imperialis* grows in a wide area from northern Iraq and eastern Turkey through Iran and Afghanistan to Pakistan. It is very variable, too. Henrik Zetterlund, while searching in Iran for a bicolored (half yellow, half red) form of *F. imperialis*, found an exceptionally beautiful, bright flaming red population (collection number *T4Z-182*). I am growing seedlings in my own collection, but they haven't yet started flowering. 'Ruduke' is a good selection from Lithuania with somewhat brownish flowers; it is more floriferous in Latvian conditions than the traditional Dutch varieties. Some successful crosses between *F. imperialis* and *F. raddeana* have been made in the Netherlands, resulting in interesting hybrids with red flowers that are the size and shape of *F. raddeana*.

In my opinion *Fritillaria eduardii* (Plate 83), which grows in Tajikistan, is the best species of this group. Because of its similarity to *F. imperialis*, most botanists long regarded the name *F. eduardii* as a synonym. Attitudes changed, though, as it was recognized that these two species are quite different. *Fritillaria eduardii* is the largest species, a true aristocrat among the other crown imperials. In the garden it opens much earlier than *F. imperialis*, at the same time as *F. raddeana*. Its flowers are larger, more open, and more side-oriented, not pendant. The greatest advantage is that it generally lacks the unpleasant odor so characteristic of *F. imperialis*. Some bulbs do excrete a slight smell, but you would never think of plugging your nose around a large group of *F. eduardii*, as you would with *F. imperialis* on a sunny day. *Fritillaria eduardii* is the most floriferous species, too, and flowers every spring if large enough bulbs are planted, which can't be said about *F. imperialis*. But nothing is perfect, of course, and *F. eduardii* doesn't increase vegetatively. It sets seed well, but you have to wait seven to eight years until the seedlings finally produce flowers. Although this plant's flowering ends when *F. imperialis* has just begun, some overlapping occurs and both can hybridize, so it is better to plant them some distance from each other if you plan to gather seeds. *Fritillaria eduardii* forms bulbs of incredible size, up to 20 cm in diameter, and is surprisingly resistant to night frosts. On many occasions I have seen the stems and flowers lying on the ground in the morning, only to find them rising up by midday as temperatures increase. *Fritillaria raddeana* is resistant in the same way.

I have never collected *Fritillaria eduardii* in the wild myself. All my stock has come from plants collected by Arnis Seisums in some side gorge of the large Varzob Valley. These plants come from a very variable population, with flowers ranging from almost yellow to orange-red. All my attempts to find them in the same locality have been in vain, as have been Arnis's subsequent visits. I once saw people descending the mountains with large bunches of *F. eduardii* that had been plucked out of the soil, but I have never seen a single plant in the wild.

Fritillaria chitralensis, once regarded as a variety of *F. imperialis*, is the Cinderella of high mountains. All plants in cultivation seem to have originated from a few bulbs collected in 1970 by Mr. and Mrs. Piers Lee Carter in the Bash Gal Valley of Nuristan, Afghanistan, between Baricot and Kamu, where it grows at 3000 m above sea level. It is only some 30 cm tall with two to four smaller, bright greenish yellow flowers at the top. The best stock I have ever seen is grown superbly in Gothenburg by Henrik Zetterlund. I lost almost all my bulbs by planting them in the open garden and expecting them to be as frost-resistant as their larger relatives. In my region it comes up so early that the shoots are always killed by frost; as a result, the few bulbs I had planted became smaller and smaller. Now I grow them in the greenhouse without any problems. They are slowly returning to flowering size, and I hope for a good seed crop one of these years.

Back in Arvaz, some kind of spring *Colchicum* was growing abundantly around a shaly landslide. By the shape of the bulb and narrow lower leaf, I recognized it as *C. jolantae* (syn. *Merendera jolantae*). In the garden its flowers are pure white and have a rather amazing shape formed by the very narrow petals. I now have some bulbs that were collected west of Arvaz, at Ai-Dere, by Lithuanian botanist Augis Dambrauskas. His stock has wider petals and may be another species altogether, although using the same *Flora of Turkmenistan* he classified it as *C. jolantae*. It is a good grower in the greenhouse, sets seed well, and also reproduces vegetatively.

Two species grew everywhere here: in the shade it was *Fritillaria raddeana*, on the open slopes *Allium brachyscapum*. I also occasionally saw a few *Iris kopetdagensis*, all magnificent in size.

We approached the border with Iran. My escorts showed me the secret hair-thin wire crossing the pass and joined with the post. We slid beneath it carefully and there they were: two wooden stakes 2 m apart with a small stick halfway between them. The stake on the Soviet side was red and green and carried the blazon of the Soviet Union; the stake on the Iranian side was red and white, with the Iranian blazon. The area between both stakes was the so-called neutral zone. I asked the soldiers about trespassers. These were usually local shepherds looking for better grass and firewood (on the Soviet side there was a nature reserve, so the forests were left mostly untouched by humans and cattle). Such "trespassers" were arrested and held for about three days, during which time diplomatic notes were exchanged, and then they were returned to the Iranian gendarmes, who would beat the daylights out of them. Real trespassers were rare. They were usually caught very soon, though sometimes they succeeded in getting quite far into Iranian territory. One man was seized some 5 km inside Iran, where he felt safe enough to lay down to sleep.

The next day my colleagues and I made our way to Baharden. After a leisurely morning, we again turned our attention to the mountains. What we saw around us was fantastic: deep canyons, high rocks. A dream place for tourists, only it was the borderland, where a special pass was required.

Sometimes the road went over a flat rock, sometimes along a dry riverbed, and I often had no idea how our driver managed to find his way. After climbing a very steep slope, steep enough that it looked as though we might start to slide backward, we found ourselves on an equally steep descent. Luckily the traffic was minimal; we saw no more than one or two other cars the whole day.

The valley of Germab lay between two ridges. A large, powerful river flowed out from the rock, but the valley seemed abandoned. Only large fruit orchards and boarded-up houses bore witness to the previous wealth of the village. Neither television nor radio signals reached Germab, and without any regular traffic connecting the village with the outside world, all the youth had finally left. Before World War II as many as three thousand people lived here, and the village was famous for its resistance against the Communist system. Now it was practically empty.

Two days before this, a powerful mudslide had filled the bottom of the side gorge, just where our road was heading. A great section of the barbed-wire fence had been destroyed and the alarm systems were out of whack, so the valley was full of soldiers making repairs and keeping an eye on everyone who entered. The riverbed had changed and now the road was crossed by streams in many places. Our car occasionally got stuck in some deep pit, but it was a six-wheel vehicle, so we were able to manage.

We were searching the area for *Iris ewbankiana*, an Oncocyclus iris now named *I. acutiloba* subsp. *lineolata*. According to Brian Mathew (1981) this species is one of the easiest for the garden, but Oncocyclus irises don't grow well outdoors in Latvia.

All the grass in the area was dry and yellow, with clumps of *Artemisia* species providing the only green. In just such a clump we found the iris we'd be looking for. Back in Latvia *Iris ewbankiana* survived no longer than two seasons, even though I planted it in the sunniest spot of my rockery on almost pure sand. I would like to reintroduce it, however, since I now grow Oncocyclus irises without any major problems in my greenhouse, enjoying their brilliant flowers every spring.

I also found two *Tulipa* species. The first was *T. micheliana*, which has large, bright red blooms, purplish-striped leaves, and a uniquely shaped basal blotch that makes it easy to distinguish from the very similar *T. greigii*. The flower of *T. micheliana* is more crimson, and the basal blotch on the petal interiors is conspicuously wedge-shaped, with a pale yellow or whitish margin. Bulbs of *T. micheliana* usually lie very deep in the soil; I have never found flowering-sized bulbs any shallower than 30–40 cm deep. This species doesn't reproduce vegetatively, either. Although it is very widespread in Central Asia, nowhere had I seen entire meadows filled with it, as sometimes happens with *T. greigii*. This was usually due to overgrazing and plowing having destroyed its natural habitat. It didn't live long in my garden, either, and none of the plants from other locations that I later grew survived longer than three or four years. I even lost two bulbs that were planted in the greenhouse. I tried crossing *T. micheliana* with *T. vvedenskyi*. All the seedlings inherited the typical shape of its basal blotch. Unfortunately, they also inherited an exaggerated tendency for bulbs to lie very deep in the soil.

Tulipa turcomanica also grew here. This species belongs to section *Eriostemones*, a group of small, generally white or yellow tulips with more than one flower on the stem. They are my favorite tulips. The Turkmen representative of this group usually has two starry, almost pure white flowers with a small, greenish yellow basal blotch on the petal interiors, and a pleasant aroma. It grew well in my nursery until some mice found the box containing the bulbs. Unfortunately, the bulbs of this section are favored not only by me but also by rodents, and as such they are the first to get eaten.

A profusion of *Allium scabriscapum* was in full flower, forming large splotches in spots where no other vegetation was growing. I had sufficient stock of this species and so only took a few pictures. Meanwhile one of my colleagues stuffed a huge sack with bulbs of *Iris ewbankiana*. When she finished it looked as though wild boars had dug up the field. Was she taking these home as proof of how thoroughly she had worked during the expedition? I couldn't understand how someone could have such an attitude about a plant that was listed as a rare and protected species of Turkmenistan. But perhaps it was considered normal here. During a rest I read a small book I had bought in Baharden, *Wild Ornamental Perennials of Turkmenistan* (Iscenko et al. 1972). In a chapter devoted to *Fritillaria raddeana*, the author states in black-and-white, "Since from seeds this species starts to flower only in the seventh year, propagation is more profitable by bulbs, which flower in the first year. The best time to collect them in nature is early summer." I had never imagined that collecting wild bulbs might be called "propagation."

Soon after this our car broke down and I decided to leave the expedition and take another car to Duschak. As we left the gorge a large mountain plateau opened before my eyes, with Mount Duschak at the front, some 2100 m high (Plate 84). *Tulipa micheliana* bloomed marvelously all around. I decided to stay at Duschak for a couple of days and send my baggage along to the botanical garden, keeping only the most necessary items with me. The village of Chuli, where the buses run, was some 18–20 km from here; without my heavy haversack, walking down to it from the mountains would feel like a nice promenade. I could spend the night at the meteorological station here.

I headed out early in the morning and was surprised by the superb view of stony, shallow meadows full of flowering *Tulipa micheliana*, *Colchicum jolantae*, and *Ixiolirion tataricum*. I collected a few samples of *Allium christophii*, since the ones I had collected earlier came from the botanical garden, where they had naturalized. But there was no difference in the results, and both stocks disappeared from my collection over the following years. I had the same experience attempting to introduce *Ixiolirion* species from the wild. *Ixiolirion* is a genus of uncertain taxonomic status that is very widespread in nature, allocated by some botanists to the family Ixioliriaceae. A few species have been described, but classifying them isn't easy. I tried growing specimens collected in all parts of Central Asia and Turkey but never succeeded with them. However, the cultivated stock offered by Dutch nurseries grows perfectly and produces an abundance of seeds, with the seedlings flowering in their third year. Sometimes it is even self-sowing and grows like a weed.

Everywhere around me I saw splendid knolls of *Gypsophila aretioides* (Plate 85), some even larger than a meter in diameter, looking like green pillows scattered on the shallow slopes. I came to the edge of an impressively deep, rocky gorge. As I made my way past some rocks, I found the second hyacinth of the Kopet-Dag, *Hyacinthus transcaspicus* (Plate 86), hiding in the protection of *Juniperus* and spiny *Astragalus* species. This blue-flowered species grows at altitudes up to 2800 m and has narrow leaves, but in all other respects is very similar to *H. litwinowii*. Luckily, both hyacinths survived when I moved my garden and their growing conditions changed. Both are propagated from seed.

I continued my climbing down into the gorge, and another beautiful discovery soon followed. It was *Tulipa wilsoniana*, a tiny, bright red tulip with an attractively shaped flower on a stem some 10 cm tall, and a rosette of nicely wavy leaves at the base. At the base of the petal interior is a tiny, shining black blotch with a slightly diffused edge. It is the only tulip species from the Kopet-Dag still grown in my collection. A good increaser, it forms blackish brown bulbs covered with very hard skin. A tuft of woolly hair appears from the bulb apex. The meteorologists at the station later told me that some 3 km from here was a population with yellow flowers, but without a guide directing me to the spot it would be a hopeless enterprise. *Tulipa linifolia*, which grows in the very south of Tajikistan, is very similar to *T. wilsoniana* in terms of the flower and bulb, but has very narrow leaves. It is easy to grow in the garden and reproduces vegetatively. I have lost the exact origin of my stock; I only know that it started from the seeds I received in the early 1970s from a botanical garden.

In the gorge I found the first *Muscari* species, too: *M. leucostomum*, with very dark, almost blackish blue flowers with narrow white lobes. It is usually considered a synonym of *M. neglectum*, but the taxonomy of *Muscari* and related species remains unclear, and I prefer keeping it as a separate species for its distinctively dark color. Even the skin of the bulb is uniquely dark, somewhat greenish black, and the bulbils look different from those of other *Muscari* species. Although it produces many bulbils at the base, this muscari is less invasive than its relatives from the Caucasus and Europe grown under the name *M. neglectum*. It seems that the bulbils won't germinate without special care.

The next day I walked to Chuli. The expedition car, now repaired, was on its way to Germab to pick up my colleagues from the botanical garden. I decided to wander down by the road until they returned to pick me up. I was no longer so high in the mountains, and for this reason the plants of *Iris kopetdagensis* I saw growing had completely dry leaves. Still, they were growing excellently and forming clumps of three or four bulbs. *Eremurus olgae* (Plate 87) flowered here with magnificent spikes more than 2 m high densely covered in light pink flowers. Sometimes white-flowered plants occurred among the pink-flowered ones. I later bought three plants of this species from a Russian gardener. I was very surprised by the two-year-old seedlings I received for such a high price. They died during a cold winter even though I kept them in a greenhouse.

A gigantic allium with very wide leaves grew here, too. It was *Allium giganteum*, a most majestic species with large umbels of purple flowers on a 1.5–2 m stem. Unfortunately, it's not possible to grow this species outside in my region, and it is somewhat problematic even in a greenhouse. In Latvia its vegetation period starts too early, usually during the first long snow break after the New Year, and its leaves are always killed by frost. I later introduced some bulbs from Holland that start growing somewhat later. This form does better in the greenhouse, though I can't list it among the best growers. The Dutch stocks are also often virus-infected; it took several tries to receive healthy stock from Peter Nijssen.

I had hoped to find one of my dream plants, *Allium regelii*, here, but unfortunately I had no such luck. It is a unique species forming up to five inflorescences overtopping one another on the same stem, with large, starry, bright lilac flowers. Its distribution area ranges from desert to foothills as high as 1400 m. It isn't rare in the wild, but I still never found it. I later received one small bulb from the Gothenburg Botanical Garden, and it grew up to flowering size and produced an excellent crop of seeds. I soon had more than fifty bulbs. But then all the bulbs were lost during a very severe winter, even though I had grown them under covering. This was the same winter in which I lost my eremurus. I lay the blame on a company that had supplied me with a so-called remedy meant to protect bulbs from various strains of *Fusarium* and other pathogens. I airily used this panacea on all my beds without testing it on even a small spot. Fortunately, the *A. regelii* seedlings I had sown that autumn in boxes survived, and it is my hope that this species will flower again one day.

I was also unable to find *Fritillaria karelinii* (or *F. gibbosa*, or *F. ariana*—it's unclear just which of these fritillaries of section *Rhinopetalum* grows in the Kopet-Dag). It was collected later by a Lithuanian gardener, and I grew it for a long time until it was lost during an unfavorable season. *Fritillaria karelinii* was the only species mentioned in the *Flora of Turkmenistan* as growing in the Kopet-Dag, but Svetlana Abramova later added *F. gibbosa* to the list. She described both as growing like weeds in the Central Botanical Garden of the Turkmenistan Academy of Sciences, although we couldn't find any during my visit there. All the fritillaries of section *Rhinopetalum* remain at the top of my dream list. I have sown many seeds received from various sources, but they have always germinated poorly, generally turning out to be *F. stenanthera* or *F. bucharica*.

Of course, there were many other bulbs growing in the Kopet-Dag that I never found. It is a region with a very rich flora, and during such a short trip it was not possible to see everything. I was a very happy man for having found as much as I did, however. With few exceptions I felt I had brought home the cream of the crop. What a pity that the trip took place in the years when growing ornamental plants was suspected as some kind of sabotage of the "food program" announced by the Communist Party. Greenhouses for flower growing were forbidden even in small private gardens. Perhaps more plants would have survived had things been different.

Arnis later sent me *Ornithogalum arianum*, the easternmost species of this genus, which grows at the east end of the Kopet-Dag. It has four to seven leaves up to 2 cm wide, and the raceme is some 15–20 cm long with up to thirty flowers. The inflorescence is initially pyramidal but becomes scutate as the stalks of lower flowers elongate. The flower color is typical for ornithogalums of the northern hemisphere: white with a green midrib. It is a beautiful plant, its large inflorescence tucked between wide rosettes of bright, dark green leaves.

Arnis also gave me some tubers of *Corydalis chionophila*, a nice species from section *Leonticoides*, which he had collected in the Kopet-Dag. It has perennial tubers, which is why it doesn't increase vegetatively. The flowers form a dense spike and are pale pink, darkening to a reddish shade at the end of flowering. Subspecies *firouzii* from the eastern Elburz Mountains in Iran is superior in beauty, with a more compact spike and creamy yellow flowers. I received this subspecies from the Gothenburg Botanical Garden; it is a seedling offspring from a collection made by Per Wendelbo on Kuh-e-Abr in 1978. Both forms now successfully grow in my greenhouse and multiply well from seed.

My visit to the Kopet-Dag was too late for *Corydalis* species. All the foliage had dried out and blown away long before I arrived. Collecting species with perennial tubers isn't easy even when the leaves are green. The shoots initially move horizontally under the soil surface and then come up some distance from the place where the tuber lies. Finding the tuber is always something of a game, and the tubers are often damaged by the shovel. In my experience, the best approach is to find a slope where they grow in abundance and then start loosening the soil until the tubers roll out from wherever they may be hiding. Very few of these tubers are collected deliberately; they are usually accidental findings made while collecting some other nearby bulbs.

◆ 23
Central Asia

I F I HAD WRITTEN this book in chronological sequence, Central Asia would have taken up the first chapter, because my first trip to the mountains was in this region. Later it proved to be the part of the Soviet Union I visited most. It would be difficult to estimate how many times I traveled there, since I didn't always keep a diary. During my adventures I came again and again to the same places and later guided other people to the gorges and plants with which I had become familiar. I was young then and my life seemed to stretch endlessly before me. Now that I'm older I have to consider whether it is worthwhile returning to places I have already visited. No one can visit every place in the world—life is simply too short.

In this chapter I try to keep some sense of chronology, but I never return to places that have already been described, not without a special reason. Sometimes I even combine adventures from several trips into one story.

My First Excursion

I searched through all my papers to find exactly when my first trip took place. Although I remembered well how the idea came to me, and how I made it happen, I had forgotten the dates. According to notes made in my oldest surviving planting book, my first expedition occurred in 1975, when I was only twenty-eight years old and in my third year as editor of the Latvian horticultural magazine *Dārzs un Drava*. In this planting book, under CA-75 (Central Asia 1975), I had written the following strange notes: "—bogey from Chu-Ili, —pretty corydalis from the Kyrgyz Alatau, —ugly corydalis from Chorgolo gorge." It is not possible to decode the exact name of the last plant mentioned; it was lost before I was able to identify it. With the others I at least know what species are hiding behind those notes.

It all began in 1973. I had recently started working for *Dārzs un Drava*, and one winter evening my friend Aldonis Vēriņš visited. He brought with him Vladimir Sudorzenko, a bulb enthusiast from Bishkek (or at that time, Frunze), Kyrgyzstan. We talked about bulbs. I told him that I was very interested in native tulips and other bulbs from Central Asia, and he offered to help me. In autumn a parcel arrived containing tulips and a letter inviting me to visit Mr. Sudorzenko for some excursions into the mountains in search of bulbs. It was a very nice offer, but I couldn't afford to make the trip.

Then in the spring of 1975 the Latvian branch of Aeroflot (the national airline of

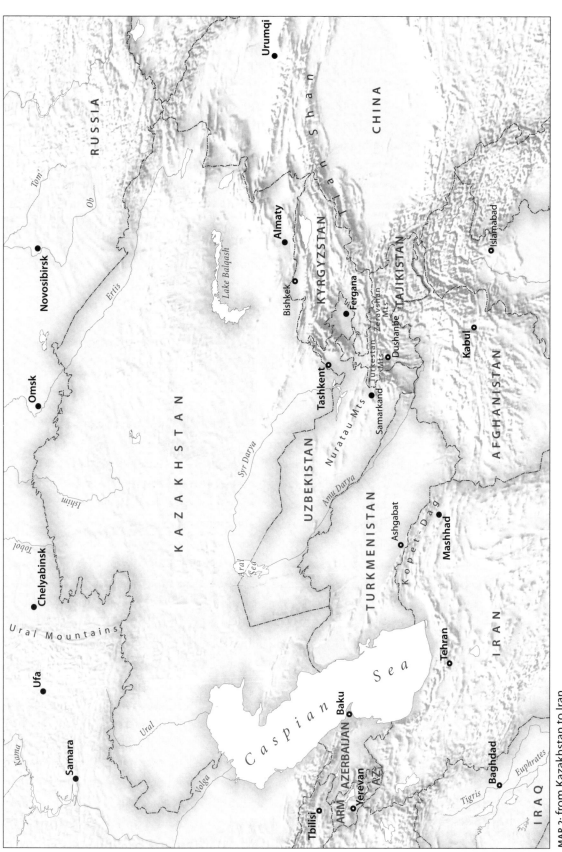

MAP 2: from Kazakhstan to Iran

the Soviet Union) started a new air route to Alma-Ata (now usually called Almaty), which was then the capital of Kazakhstan. Journalists from every newspaper and magazine in Latvia were offered a complimentary ticket for their first round-trip flight. I immediately accepted this proposal on the condition that I choose the return date myself. In this way the most difficult part of my travel—acquiring tickets to and from Central Asia—was arranged successfully. I immediately called Mr. Sudorzenko to announce that I would be in Alma-Ata and could fly from there to Bishkek.

I had never been to any mountains before and didn't know anything about them. Not having any idea what to wear, I arrived with little more than a handbag containing traditional presents for my friend and any other people I might meet along the way. I was wearing a suit (fortunately not my best one) and regular city shoes. Luckily there was space for a sweater and a small empty haversack in my bag. The flight was very pleasant. Half the plane was full of journalists enjoying the full service offered by Aeroflot for this special occasion. We were given free drinks and meals and even allowed to visit the pilots in their cabin.

When we landed in Alma-Ata, my mouth fell open—and didn't close for some time. The airport was built at the foot of monumental mountains, their steep slopes covered in snow. They were so magnificent, I fell in love with them immediately. Now I understood what mountain climbers meant when they said that only mountains could be more beautiful than mountains.

Alma-Ata enjoyed an excellent climate, with fresh winds from the mountains blowing away all the dust and cooling down the air. It would be a real paradise if it weren't for the mudslides that had destroyed half the city some years before. After that, the government decided to build a dam in the mountains to protect the area from both mudslides and avalanches. It was one of the largest dams ever built in the Soviet Union.

We were welcomed by local journalists, and as the youngest in the group I was appointed to the local youth newspaper. I told my interviewers that going to the mountains had always been my dream. The next day the limousine of the publishing house brought me deep into the mountains on an excellent motorway. The ascent was so steep that my ears started hurting. The first bulbs of the trip, *Corydalis glaucescens* (the "pretty corydalis from the Kyrgyz Alatau"), were in full bloom all around (Plate 88).

The trucks that I could see driving up the dam from the bottom of the mountains looked as small as ants. As my guides explained, half of the reservoir was filled with stones and mud, so the dam had to be erected higher and higher. On the sunny side of the valley, on some open ground near the roadside, I found more *Corydalis glaucescens* in full bloom. This was the origin of 'Medeo', one of the best and most brightly colored forms of this species, an excellent increaser with distinctly pinkish flowers. When Arnis Seisums visited this area later, he found another population southeast of Alma-Ata and not so high in the mountains. His finding was similar in color but flowered much earlier, and he named it 'Early Beauty'. It is one of the most early-blooming corydalis in the garden, producing an abundance of light pink flowers in very dense spikes.

Later in Bishkek I met up with my friend Vladimir Sudorzenko, who lived in an apartment just on the city border. Earlier he had lived in a house with a small garden, where he grew tulips and vegetables, but all the houses had been flattened to make space for blocks of apartments. He had tried planting his tulips near the apartment building, but all the bulbs were eaten by local children. I know this sounds strange, but it's quite true—early-spring tulip bulbs are in fact rather juicy and sweet. The local people even use them as a sweetener. They are only sweet at the very start of the season, however, before flowering; later on the biochemical process transforms the sugars into starch, and then they taste floury like uncooked potatoes. So for this reason you can't find any large tulips near the cities or villages of Kyrgyzstan. They all get eaten by children.

Vladimir was working as a photographer—an "art photographer," as he had named himself. Initially I didn't understand exactly what it was that he did. Later he explained how he would visit local villages and shepherds' camps and take black-and-white photos of the people there. At home he copied and enlarged the images, then colored them using aniline dyes, turning faces pinkish, lips red, eyes blue, hair brownish or blondish, and so forth. Finally he would frame the "improved" picture and return it to the owner. To me it seemed an incredible job, but his business was going very well. His wife taught Russian at the local school.

The foothills of the large Kyrgyz Alatau ridge started on just the other side of the street, and seeing my impatience, Vladimir offered to take a short walk with me in the faint hope of finding some tulips. On our promenade, we made our way through flowering stems of a wonderful foxtail lily with pretty, dense spikes of brownish white flowers. Vladimir called these plants *Eremurus regelii*, and I also used this name for a long time until I found out they were actually *E. cristatus* (Plate 89). Both are rather similar, but *E. regelii* is taller, with flower petals that are longer and narrower, and a spike that is not so dense; in general it can't win a beauty contest with *E. cristatus*. *Eremurus cristatus* is one of the easiest species in the garden when planted on sandy soil. When I planted it in my own garden it flowered every year, set seed, and increased well by splitting (sometimes even into three) and self-sowing. It has a nice, quite small rootstock and is one of the most early-flowering species in Latvia, usually blooming at the end of May. The flower spikes of other species start to show their noses between the rosettes of leaves only after *E. cristatus* has ended. It isn't a tall plant, usually no more than 1–1.2 m high in both the garden and the wild. On our way back I cut some spikes to give Vladimir's wife. Her eyes widened, and it seemed she was more offended than pleased by such a primitive gift. The next morning I saw the spikes in the rubbish bin.

At any rate, *Eremurus cristatus* doesn't belong to the showiest species. In the monograph *Eremurus* (1965), Russian botanist Andrey Hohrjakov divides this group of plants into four genera: *Ammolirion*, *Selonia*, *Eremurus*, and *Heningia*, thus following earlier botanists. The most beautiful species belong to *Heningia* and have large flowers with wide petals, the most common representative being *Eremurus robustus*. *Eremurus cristatus* belongs to the proper *Eremurus*, and plants in this group have smaller flowers. Many species are very decorative, too, although only a few are familiar to gardeners. The intriguingly named *E. spectabilis*, meaning "the beautiful eremurus," belongs to this group, but only a botanist unfamiliar with other species of *Eremurus* could give such a name to this Cinderella of the genus. (Although I suppose it could be called beautiful if it were compared with selonias or ammolirions.) As you might guess, plants belonging to *Ammolirion* and *Selonia* aren't worth growing in the garden, unless you want to build up a complete collection of foxtail lilies. From a gardener's point of view, Hohrjakov's revision of the genus can be useful, giving an immediate impression of the average look of the plants.

The next day we planned our first trip to the mountains. Vladimir showed me the tools he would bring. His heavy iron pickax resembled the ice picks used by mountaineers, but it weighed some 6–7 kg and was strong enough to split stones. He also brought binoculars for watching the slopes and searching for plants, and a collector's bag made of strong linen, which closed at the top with a rope that can be tied at the waist.

We awoke at four o'clock the next morning to catch an early bus, heading north toward the foothills of the Kyrgyz Alatau to the spot where the Chorgolo Valley begins. On our walk from the bus to the mountains I found a few *Allium* bulbs that turned out to be quite a common species, *A. caeruleum*. This species has bright sky blue flowers in a small but dense umbel held on a stem 1 m high. In Latvia it flowers late, during the second half of summer, and is an excellent increaser. In fact sometimes it can even become weedy, forming numerous small bulbils on the mother bulb and in the axils of the stem leaves, wrapping around the flower stem at the base. The single competing species in my collection is *A. obliquum* from the mountains of Altay in Siberia, which has light yellow flowers and elongated bulbs. *Allium obliquum* has a different shape of flower head, too, and would be a marvelous cut flower if not for the terribly strong smell of its leaves and bulbs. Although it reproduces well vegetatively, propagation from seed, which it sets in abundance, is far quicker. Seeds can be sown in an open field, and seedlings start to flower in the third season.

Only one Central Asian species can compete with *Allium caeruleum* in flower color and delicate overall appearance, and that is *A. litvinovii*, which was collected by Arnis Seisums at Sari-Chilek in the southeastern Chatkal Mountains of Uzbekistan. Its flowers are unusually bright blue, violet-veined, and held in tight umbels on stems only 40 cm tall. It is a very local endemic that is so far known only from its type locality. *Allium litvinovii* doesn't form any bulbils, but the bulbs usually split in two or even three every year, and it grows perfectly from seed. I have never found hybrids among its seedlings.

We began climbing a side ridge to reach the neighboring valley of Uzum-Bulak. The mountains seemed endless to me as I moved up slowly step by step. A while ago I had seen a large tree far in front of me and thought it was the point where the road turned down, but now the tree was far behind me and a new ridge opened—then another, and another. "Stupid Jānis," I thought. "Why the hell are you here? Why didn't you stay home?" And then I understood that this was punishment for all the bad things I'd done in my previous life, starting from childhood. There was nothing to do but continue walking up and up, with clenched teeth. If nothing else, the day was cloudy and cool.

We finally reached the pass to the neighboring valley, and our road turned down. Some of the plants that Vladimir had brought me here to see started to appear. The first was *Allium karataviense*, which I had seen before only in pictures. This was followed by the bright red *Tulipa greigii*. Far down in the valley was a village where Vladimir's relatives lived and where we would find lodging for the night. It was almost dark as we left the mountains, and well past midnight when we finally banged at the window of his brother-in-law's house. We had covered a total of 40 km, although that included some 10 km by car on our way up. Having had no previous training, I was absolutely exhausted and quickly fell into a deep sleep.

After a day of rest, we headed to an alpine camp in the Ala-Archa Gorge. My first discovery was hidden in a spiny shrub of some prostrate *Juniperus* species. It was a very small specimen of *Corydalis glaucescens* with only a couple of flowers on a spike. From this single plant came my 'White Beauty', a form with pure white flowers in strong, upright, dense racemes. Growing in a neighboring shrub was another color form with creamy yellowish flowers, a very unusual shade for this species, and from that one came 'Cream Beauty'. This stock was named by Henrik Zetterlund when he visited my garden in 1992. Its flower color is so uncommon, and its racemes so large and dense, that I even considered giving it a varietal rank.

People were coming down from the mountains with handfuls of a Juno iris. It was *Iris orchioides*, and a very unusual form of it: the flowers were pure yellow without any trace of white. (In following years I never again saw any populations with the same flower color, but then I never had the courage to go up alone to search for this beautiful plant.) Some days later, on visiting the Botanical Garden of the Kyrgis Academy of Sciences in Bishkek, I was presented with a few bulbs of this fabulous plant progeny, which I later named 'Kirghizian Gold' (Plate 90). It is the deepest yellow form of this very variable species, which should certainly be split into at least three or even four separate species. The various forms of *I. orchioides* differ distinctively not only in flower color but also in the shape of the additional roots of the bulb, hairiness of the falls, and so forth. The other Juno iris I received at the botanical garden was named *I. caerulea* (a synonym of *I. albomarginata*). The next spring at home I renamed it *I. zenaidae*, but I soon lost my only bulb. Introduction of the true *I. zenaidae*, which belongs to the most beautiful Central Asian Juno irises, was still many years away.

On our way back to Bishkek, Vladimir asked the bus driver to stop halfway, and we stepped out for a walk in the mountains. Here we found a place where *Corydalis schanginii* subsp. *schanginii* grows. It is a very widespread subspecies in the wild, possibly occupying the largest area of all Central Asian *Corydalis* species, but this was the only place I ever found it. It was to be the one locality from which all the bulbs in cultivation originated. Later Vladimir sent me hundreds of tubers, which I forwarded to Michael Hoog in the Netherlands. From Michael's nursery, they found their way to botanical gardens and plant collectors.

In the wild *Corydalis schanginii* subsp. *schanginii* grows on stony slopes among shrubs, but evidently in drier and less protected places than subspecies *ainae*, which I discovered a few years later on the Karatau Range in a gorge that Vladimir showed me. It has large spikes of long, light pink flowers and inner petals with very dark tips. It is one of the noblest and most large-flowering species in the section, and even more importantly, it is absolutely hardy and an excellent grower both outdoors and in a greenhouse. In the garden it forms tubers of astonishing size and reproduces well vegetatively. It has become quite a common plant in gardens.

The next day we headed in the opposite direction, to the low Chu-Ili Mountains separating two large rivers: Chu and Ili. Again we used the bus, which stopped for us somewhere along the road at a place known only to Vladimir. The hillocks around seemed low and bare, and didn't inspire my confidence. I followed Vladimir as we wandered into the mountains, although I had no idea how he knew where to go. It was sunny and hot, and I felt quite disappointed. Nothing was growing here. All I found was a single plant, which I stopped to collect only as an excuse for a little rest.

The plant I had stumbled across was the "bogey from Chu-Ili," but being still young and dimwitted, I didn't comprehend what I had collected. Years later I sent Michael Hoog a few strange tubers, and on 26 July 1981, he wrote me:

> I think your number 528 from Chu-Ili looks like a scorpion. The flowers resemble Geraniaceae, but the roots are quite different. I have never seen anything like it in my life. When you dig up the plants you will find that on top of the old scorpion-like root there is a complete new set of scorpion-like roots with claws in all directions and with growing tips on many ends. I think I shall call your plant the scorpion plant. It is so distinct! It is a plant of a different world, to my mind.

This "plant of a different world" was representative of so many overlooked tuberous geraniums. There are many books about geraniums, but nowhere will you find a complete, more or less satisfying description of all tuberous forms. All such geraniums may be somewhat similar when it comes to their flowers, but many can be separated and named only after seeing the tubers. Before our expeditions only one tuberous species, *Geranium tuberosum*, had really been grown in gardens. It is a very widespread plant in the wild from southeastern France to the Aegean region and Crimea, with knobby, globose tubers resembling small potatoes. All my plants are of Dutch origin, coming from Willem van Eeden, breeder and grower of Chrysanthus crocuses, erythroniums, and Reticulata irises.

My stock of *Geranium malviflorum* originated with Willem as well. Its tubers are very large, somewhat spindle-shaped, and covered with long leaf and stalk bases, resembling some ragged coiffure or a bundle of small claws. In the wild it grows in southern Spain, Morocco, and Algeria. Forms from Arabian countries reportedly produce leaves in autumn, while those from Spain produce leaves only in spring. In my garden the time of vernalization depends on the autumn: if it is long and mild, the leaves of Central Asian species come up in addition to those of *G. malviflorum*. Regardless of when the leaves come up, my plants of *G. malviflorum* are all completely hardy and have survived even the harshest winters in my open garden without any special treatment.

In the Talish Mountains I collected a tuberous geranium that more closely resembled the plant from Chu-Ili in terms of tuber shape. I classified it as *Geranium macrostylum*, which according to the *Flora Europaea* (Flora Europaea Editorial Committee 1980) grows in Greece and Albania. In *Hardy Geraniums* (2002), though, Peter F. Yeo extends its area to central and southwestern Turkey. The plants I collected in Talish are very similar to plants offered by Antoine Hoog as *G. macrostylum* from Uludağ, Turkey, and *G. macrostylum* 'Leonidas' from Greece. It is easy to differentiate them from the Central Asian plants just by the shape of the tubers.

From Chris Brickell I received another tuberous geranium under the name *Geranium macrostylum* with tubers like none I had ever seen. It was collected in Morocco by Peter Davis in the Atlas Mountains. The tubers are some 4–5 cm long, spindle-shaped, without branches, and covered with a thick, somewhat wool-like coat. This plant never flowered for me outside but grew and increased very well, and it began to flower after I moved it to a greenhouse. I can't imagine what its correct name might be, but it has geranium-like leaves and blooms.

The plant from Chu-Ili turned out to be *Geranium transversale* (syn. *G. linearilobum* subsp. *transversale*), which is quite variable in terms of shape and division of leaves but with tubers of a common scorpion-like shape. All forms of this species have more or less similar flowers; in some seasons they are more floriferous, in other seasons less so. When at their best they are completely covered with nice, purplish lilac flowers.

In the gorge at Bashkizilsai, not far from Tashkent, we found an unusual form of *Geranium transversale* with very narrow leaf lobes that look thin and spindly, giving the plant an airy, exotic appearance. We named it variety *laciniata*, although it had been given another name earlier and was described in a local botanical publication. It is a very local plant from Bashkizilsai and neighboring gorges. Unfortunately it is less floriferous than the typical form; it seems that the reduced area of leaf surface doesn't allow the plant to accumulate sufficient energy for abundant flowering. But in any case it is a very interesting and valuable plant, especially for those who like flower arrangements featuring exotic foliage.

Tuberous geraniums like *Geranium charlesii* from Uzbekistan and the somewhat similar *G. kotschyi* from the Kopet-Dag and Iran are not often mentioned in botanical literature. They have very special, upright, elongated, large tubers. While the earlier mentioned tuberous geraniums replace their tubers every year and reproduce well vegetatively, these two have perennial tubers that grow larger and larger, thus forming a new layer of tuber on top of the old one. These tubers persist for at least three to four years with some branching, but I have never observed them splitting naturally. To build up my stock I usually cut the large tubers into pieces, carefully checking that each piece has a growing point.

I collected my first tubers of *Geranium charlesii* in Uzbekistan on the Aman-Kutan mountain pass of the Zeravshan Mountains. In the wild the tubers were very small and very similar to those of *G. transversale*, only without claws. In the garden they increased in size and looked more obviously unique. My other stock, from Timur-lan Gate in the Nuratau Range, has less cut foliage. Both stocks bloom wonderfully each spring, with purplish violet flowers. All forms of this species are very floriferous, almost completely covering themselves with blooms, and in this aspect surpass all other tuberous geraniums. The habit of *G. charlesii* is smaller and more compact, too. It comes up perfectly from seeds, although the seeds are hard to collect because of their small size.

On the heights of Sina in the southwestern corner of Uzbekistan, we found an extremely beautiful form of *Geranium charlesii* with intensely purple-marked and -spotted leaves. We named it variety *punctata*. In cultivation the purple design is somewhat paler and disappears after flowering, but in any case it is a very beautiful plant. Recently we found a population of *G. macrostylum* from Turkey (near the Kizildağ pass, 51 km from Refahiye, at 1795 m) with similarly purple-spotted leaves.

Arnis Seisums collected *Geranium kotschyi* at Kuh-e-Bosphane, Iran, near Arak. It has hairy, very deeply divided leaves and is easy to distinguish from *G. charlesii*, although isn't so floriferous in my region.

We had been walking for more than an hour when a shallow valley opened before our eyes, covered in the brightest red tulips. These were *Tulipa greigii*, and now I saw why this species was often called the king of the tulips. They were all shades of red and orange-red with variously purple-marked leaves. The base of the petals was yellow, pure black, or rimmed with yellow, the shape of the flower that of a "double cup." The whole way here there had been nothing remarkable to see on the slopes, so this sudden beauty was a pleasant change. This kind of thing is common in Central Asia—you can walk for hours without seeing anything, and then in an instant the entire landscape changes. It is always good luck to find what you have been looking for. As the years go by you develop a feeling, some kind of sense that allows you to predict where bulbs will be found. Later, after working in the mountains with Arnis for so many years, he and I were often able to communicate without words. Sensing the presence of bulbs, we would exclaim simultaneously, "Stop here!"

Some kind of dwarf Juno iris was growing alongside the *Tulipa greigii*. It was *Iris kuschakewiczii* (Plate 91), not a very bright plant but a beautiful one, with pale bluish flowers very deeply blue-marked on the falls (a characteristic that makes this plant easy to distinguish from similar species). It grew surprisingly well for me in Latvia over a period of many years in an open field, when I didn't have a greenhouse, but was lost during a very unfavorable season, and all attempts to reintroduce it failed. All the plants I have bought from other nurseries have been very weak, not coming up at all or dying the following year. Now I grow seedlings, hoping they will be true to name. *Iris kuschakewiczii* is somewhat similar to *I. inconspicua*, with which it is easily confused, but the falls of the latter don't have the prominent dark spots or are a pale, dirty greenish. Both species can hybridize in nature in areas where they overlap.

At the bottom of the valley was a stream, but Vladimir kept me from fetching any water from it, explaining that the water came from uranium mines and was potentially very dangerous. We continued walking in a direction known only to Vladimir, but I now felt more optimistic. Soon something wonderful appeared before me: a bare, stony, south-facing slope covered with very dark bluish green, strangely shaped leaves lying flat on the ground. The leaves were longitudinally wavy with crests 1–2 mm high and grooves on the upper side. It was *Tulipa regelii* (Plate 92), the most unique tulip in the world, kept separate from other species in its own section, *Lophophyllon*. I grew this tulip in my garden for a few years, where it flowered with pinkish-tinged white blooms, but my plants were eventually lost during a harsh winter. I later received some more bulbs, which I sent to the Gothenburg Botanical Garden, where they are still grown under a special regime. The bulbs are kept at room temperature until New Year's Day and are only then planted to keep them from germinating too early in winter. Sometimes even some offshoots are formed.

While I was enjoying this tulip, the weather had started to change. The sun was replaced by a haze and strong wind. I soon understood why Vladimir had insisted we pack sweaters in our haversacks—in fact, I would have been happy to have packed an extra one. It was raining, a cold wind was blowing, and even snowflakes started dancing in the air. What a difference from the sunshine and warmth of the morning! Despite how fast I started walking, my extremities froze. I had learned another lesson that would serve me well in future trips: the weather in the mountains can change within a few minutes, so you always have to be ready for it. Fortunately, the bus soon arrived and after a few hours we were back in Bishkek.

Late that evening we started our trip to the Karatau Range by bus. (The name of this ridge has always fascinated me, since the well-known *Allium karataviense*, which is described as coming from here and is named after this particular place, is actually very widespread in Central Asia.) The way was long and we made it to Taraz (formerly Dzhambul) only early the next morning, changing buses going in the direction of the village of Karatau on the other end of the mountain range. After traveling some 70 km from Taraz we stopped at a bus station in the middle of a black stony steppe. From here we walked about 6 km through a mostly flat, though slightly uphill, sunbaked steppe, with a few spiny, low shrubs and some dry ephemeral grasses. We finally reached Berkara Gorge, destined to become a milestone in my career as a gardener: it was here just a few years later that I would find my first new species.

The word Karatau is from *kara* ("black") and *tau* ("mountains"), and Berkara is from *ber* ("stream") and, again, *kara* ("black"). So as might be expected, everything here was grayish black. The mountains were formed from grayish black shaly stone, the natural slate. The stream, though full of the purest water, was darkened by the black stones at the bottom; it came out of a narrow valley but disappeared very soon in the dry steppe. Vladimir had brought me here for *Tulipa greigii* (Plate 93), which in this gorge was mostly yellow but in very variable shades. Red forms were rare here, and just the yellow ones were the true kings of the tulips. In Berkara they ranged from very pale creamy yellow (possibly the legendary white *T. greigii*, which neither I nor my friends had ever seen in the wild) to the deepest golden yellow, through various shades of orange to almost brownish. Even the red ones in Berkara were very different from those seen at Chu-Ili, in tones from carmine to somewhat lilac with a metallic shine. A small number of forms naturally increased vegetatively and formed a group of two or three stems of identical blooms. I collected a few of them, and from one such clump came *T. greigii* 'Sunset', which has very large, bright yellow blooms with a large, fiery red triangle and spots in the middle of each segment inside and out. It reaches 20 cm tall, with flowers 12–15 cm across. It is usually dwarf, although I have seen it reach 45 cm high in some gardens where it has grown undisturbed for some years. Among tulips it is one of the best increasers in the garden; the large bulb can form five to seven replacement bulbs of varying sizes. A few other selections from Berkara Gorge are grown by my friend and previous assistant Mārtiņš Erminass, who now holds the largest collection of tulips in Latvia, with more than a thousand varieties.

I saw other marvelous bulbs at Berkara Gorge, too, including *Allium karataviense*, which grew on somewhat unstable scree slopes, as is typical of the species. This location was the origin of my stock named 'Kara Tau', with pale pinkish blooms on short stems in a rosette of short, broad leaves. My stock differs from the Dutch form in the purplish tinge of its seed capsules, making it beautiful even long after flowering. A beautiful form with pure white flowers and light greenish seed capsules was selected in the Netherlands and named 'Ivory Queen'.

For many years my plants from Karatau didn't increase vegetatively, and I multiplied them only from seed, but then something happened with my stock and many bulbs started to split in two. I have noticed such changes not only with *Allium karataviense*. Sometimes you grow stocks for years with limited success, and then suddenly something changes and the stock starts to develop. In such cases some natural adaptation to new conditions seems to take place. Genetically unsuitable plants are naturally eliminated, but those that are better suited to new conditions survive and multiply. This is another reason why growing from seed is so important: selection starts in the early stages of the plants' development, and nature eliminates genetic combinations that can't adapt to new conditions.

Allium karataviense is very variable in nature. I tend to associate it with somewhat pale, grayish or pinkish blooms. Although I have seen pictures with deep purplish flower heads, I have never encountered such specimens in the wild. The first plants with really superb, very large, deep purplish red flower balls and wide, bluish green leaves were brought to me by Arnis from the Kuramin Ridge at the valley of the Angren River (Plate 94). This form flowers very early, surpassing everything I saw before it, and I still think it is the best form of *A. karataviense*. I named it 'Red Giant'. In 2000, on a rocky roadside at Karanchitogai, Uzbekistan, we found another population, this one with deep reddish lilac flowers; it turned out to flower somewhat early in gardens, with darker but smaller flower heads than the plants from Kuramin. The darkest form comes from Chavlisai. The plants we found there were growing on very steep slopes, and their flowers were the same very deep, even blackish purple shade as the surrounding stones. In the garden this form is the last to flower.

We found the most unique form of *Allium karataviense* in 1996 just next to Tashkent in Tovaksai, the western end of the Karzhantau Range. We had a free day and decided to spend it on a nearby hill, called Camel Mount because of its strange shape. At that time my plants from Kuramin hadn't yet begun to flower, and the red balls on the mountainside and later on its slopes were the first red relative of *A. karataviense* I had seen. This form was extraordinary in other ways, too. It had an unusually long stalk, 20 cm or more, that held the inflorescence well over the rosette of basal leaves. When I sent some bulbs to the Netherlands the next spring, I was not surprised when they replied that this wasn't *A. karataviense*. Later we found out that it grew not only on scree slopes like its shorter relatives but also in the cracks of rocks covered by a thin layer of soil. In some areas it grew so abundantly that an entire slope seemed to be striped reddish purple. Generally the bulbs were not very deeply set, but they were arranged in strange straight lines. At first we called this peculiar form 'Red Globe', but I felt it was actually a subspecies of *A. karataviense*, and in honor of the longtime sponsor of our expeditions, Henrik Zetterlund, I decided to name it subspecies *henrikii* (Plate 95). In the garden it is the first to flower, and the seedlings are very uniform. I found no intermediates among them, although the flowering time somewhat overlaps with other early-blooming forms of typical *A. karataviense*.

In more protected places at Berkara, I found *Fritillaria sewerzowii* (Plate 96), which some botanists separate in its own monotypic genus and call *Korolkowia sewerzowii*. A hundred or so plants grew in the shade of a 2 m high rock in a space of just 5 square meters. This is a beautiful plant, the flowers scattered among the narrow leaves on stems that are usually up to 40 cm tall, forming a pyramidal inflorescence. The petals flare outward at the middle and are variable in color. Here at Berkara all the plants had greenish flowers, but later at Chimgan we saw mostly deep brownish purple ones. We found the greatest variability at Sangirsai in the Chatkal Mountains, with flowers ranging from plain green to deep purple, some of them bicolored. Some flowers had a nice, sharp design in the center of the blossom, although the design wasn't easily visible due to the downward-facing blooms.

Fritillaria sewerzowii doesn't usually increase vegetatively, but at Ihnachsai in the Pskem Valley we found a population in which each second plant formed a clump. The plants were of incredible size, too, with stems reaching up to a meter. The plants from this population reproduce vegetatively in the garden, too, the large bulbs usually splitting in two. The flowers are uniformly purplish brown.

One of the most beautiful forms of *Fritillaria sewerzowii* was collected by Arnis at Mount Spa in the Mogoltau Range, northern Tajikistan. Without any doubt this can be called a truly yellow form, unlike others that are reputed to be yellow but are in fact only green or yellowish green. Arnis found another beauty at the eastern end of the Alai Mountains in the Sari-Bulak Valley near Osh, Kyrgyzstan. Its flowers are almost twice the size of the usual forms. Unfortunately, only one bulb was collected—no one could imagine the plants would be so magnificent. Arnis and I both grow seedlings of it now, hoping that the size of the flowers will be inherited. It is called 'Gulliver'.

Higher in the mountains at Berkara on more open spots we found plenty of *Iris willmottiana* (Plate 97), a superb species that could compete for the title of best Juno iris. It is undoubtedly one of my favorites. The flowers are a very soft shade of light blue with a large white blotch on the falls. They are quite variable, and Arnis has selected a few clones. At Sajasu Valley, some distance from Berkara, an interesting form was collected with three to eight pretty, cobalt blue flowers, a nice white blotch on the falls, a short, stout stem about 20 cm tall, and quite densely packed foliage. 'Design Master', another form, is a dwarf plant with light blue flowers and falls with undulate margins. The plants from Berkara are the lightest blue. It is an easy species in the garden and also multiplies well in nature. I found clumps with up to five plants in each. I grew it in the garden for decades, but now to be safe I keep all of my stock in the greenhouse. Unfortunately, it is very susceptible to virus infection; infected plants become sterile and then perish in two to three years.

There is a beautiful Juno iris in cultivation under the name *Iris willmottiana* 'Alba', but it has nothing in common with the true *I. willmottiana*. In fact it is a garden hybrid with *I. vicaria* as one of the parents. The flowers are pure white with a yellow crest, and like most Juno hybrids it is sterile. It is very floriferous, can be grown outside, and is exceptionally impressive.

Tulipa greigii wasn't the only tulip species growing at Berkara. Near where we entered the gorge, beneath all the shrubs, we found plenty of tulip leaves and some flowers. It was one of those strange tulips that prefer to increase vegetatively by long stolons in the wild instead of flowering. Fortunately, in the garden it is much more floriferous, although it has the same habit of growing side-oriented stolons. Usually in the place where the flowering bulb used to grow no replacement bulbs are left, but all the energy is expended to form at least two long stolons with a nice, round bulb at the end of each one. The longest stolons I found in the garden were 37 cm long, but in the wild they are not much shorter. This tulip resembles a smaller *T. kaufmanniana* in terms of the flower and because the anthers open gradually. Because of the unique round shape of the bulbs, I consider it a new species. I call it *T. berkariense* (Plate 98) although this name is not yet officially published. The flowers are very starry, usually white with greenish exterior petals and a large, bright yellow basal blotch in the center. I gave the name 'Morning Star' to one clone. Another, 'Little Ilze', has very undulate, deep purple leaves with a few narrow green veins and white petals with brownish red backs. I have crossed both cultivars with *T. vvedenskyi*. Most of the resulting hybrids inherited the habit of growing long stolons, though only slightly side-oriented; other were good growers of "normal" habit with very beautiful blooms.

In an open spot on the clay ground, among the stones, I found one of the most beautiful tulips of section *Eriostemones*: *Tulipa orthopoda* (Plate 99). It is a close relative of the well-known *T. turkestanica* but of a very compact habit. The flower stem is short, and up to five white flowers with a very large yellow base form a beautiful, compact flower head. The inner petals are quite wide, almost twice as wide as the outer ones, giving the overall impression of a very round form with wide-open flowers. This unusual beauty is extremely rare in the wild and is so far almost unknown in gardens, although it grows well outdoors in my region.

Another plant greeted us where the mountains began. It was *Eremurus hilariae* (Plate 100), one of the most beautiful short-growing foxtail lilies. This species never exceeds 1 m tall, and its spikes are densely covered with large, creamy yellow flowers. I saw it only at Berkara, although it reportedly also grows on low hills northeast of Tashkent. I fell in love with this plant from the first moment I saw it, and it grew well for me, flowering every spring in my first garden before I replanted it in clay. It is very similar to *E. lactiflorus*, another favorite of mine. Both are nearly identical, but *E. lactiflorus* grows higher in the mountains and has milky white flowers and smooth green leaves (the leaves of *E. hilariae* are somewhat hairy and grayish green). Now I grow only *E. lactiflorus*, and it reproduces vegetatively and usually sets seed in the greenhouse. I suppose that it would grow well outside in a sunny spot with excellent drainage. In Russian literature it is described as a very frost-resistant species.

In more protected spots, generally between shrubs, we also found *Eremurus robustus*, the giant among foxtail lilies with its very wide leaves and inflorescence up to 4 m tall. This species flowers later. When we found it in Berkara we only saw the flower stem coming out of the rosette of basal leaves, with the dry old stalks from the previous season serving as evidence of how tall it could be. It was much too early to collect this form, but I grow some plants in my garden that were collected some years later at Chimgan. They grow well outside as well as in the greenhouse. The most difficult thing with this species is the replanting, because the thick roots can be as long as 1.5 m. In my experience it is best to use seedlings a year or two before they start to flower when replanting foxtail lilies. Then the roots can be dug out without threat of any serious damage, and the plants start growing easily in their new location. Old rootstocks are too large, tend to get broken, and often have problems with rot. The greatest enemies of *Eremurus* in the garden are moles. When these pests damage additional roots, the rot that develops at the wounds soon kills the plants.

As previously mentioned, I found my first new species some years later during my second visit to the Berkara Gorge. I was accompanied by two friends from Latvia who bred tulips. They had heard about the enormous variability of *Tulipa greigii* in this region and asked me to take them there. We camped in the area for two days, and on one of those days I stayed in the camp to guard our belongings. After updating my diary, I wandered somewhat higher in the mountains, and deep in a very spiny dwarf rose shrub I noticed the leaves of some *Corydalis* species. It was 26 April 1977. It was not easy to get to the tubers: the shrubs were extremely spiny, and the day before we had found scorpions hiding in the shade of such shrubs. Corydalis stems are also quite brittle, and in the wild the tubers are usually tiny, black, and almost invisible in the soil. I slowly opened the humus-like soil so as not to lose this treasure, the first *Corydalis* I had found here. I collected a few small tubers.

The next spring they bloomed in my garden, with incredibly beautiful tricolored flowers. The spur was a bright, light pink, the front half of the petals yellow, and the inner petals tipped a dark chocolate-purple, thus making a striking contrast. I attempted to classify the plant using all the floras available to me, but my efforts were in vain. It had to be a new species. I initially named it *Corydalis ainae*, but after Michael Hoog received some bulbs from me he suggested it would be better to keep it as a subspecies of *C. schanginii*. Magnus Lidén and Henrik Zetterlund later said of this plant, in the *Quarterly Bulletin of the Alpine Garden Society* (1988), "You can never forget it if you ever get a chance to see it."

I made my third visit to Berkara Gorge just to find this plant again. I wanted to know more precisely where it grew and what it needed in the garden. I made this trip with my travel partner of those years, Āris Krūmiņš. He was growing bulbs, too, but only commercial varieties, many of which he forced in winter with amazing skill. He was looking to the mountains for some rest after the busy winter season. We passed the second day searching for different plants, but I couldn't see my corydalis anywhere. As we slowly walked down late in the afternoon, I found a beautiful group of *Allium karataviense* and called Āris to come take some pictures. Suddenly, about halfway to me, he shouted, "How much will you pay me? Here is that yellow sparrow of yours!" (In Latvian, *Corydalis* is called *cīrulītis*, which means "small skylark." My friend liked to jokingly call it a sparrow.) My tiredness disappeared instantly, and I flew up by the scree slope. Yes! Here it was in full flower. I searched for other groups but found none.

It was becoming darker, so we had to hurry to the tent while the path was still visible. I took the shortest route back and during the last half hour found myself deep in a jungle of shrubs of *Crataegus*, *Amygdalus*, *Pyrus*, *Salix*, and *Rosa*. For some reason I moved toward a large shrub-like ash tree growing at the edge of a very steep slope covered by some larger trees. And then there it was: an entire slope covered with yellow-pink flowers of my long-searched-for beauty. Springs on the slope seemed to be keeping the peat very wet. All the plants we had found earlier were only marginal escapees of this main population. Here the tubers were much larger and many had formed clumps. The largest clump I found had eight tubers inside a common sheet formed from remnants of previous years. The slope was very steep—sometimes I had to hold tree branches to avoid sliding down. It was also eight o' clock in the evening, and the shade was already very deep. Only the river bubbling over the stones pointed me in the right direction. By the time I reached the tent it was almost completely dark. My legs felt like lead, but I was extremely happy.

Corydalis schanginii subsp. *ainae* (Plate 101) proved to be an excellent grower in my garden, forming very large tubers, even larger than those of subspecies *schanginii*. The tubers are a different color, too. While the tubers of subspecies *schanginii* are grayish, those of subspecies *ainae* are yellowish green. Subspecies *ainae* reproduces well in the garden and in the wild both vegetatively and from seed.

But now I must return to my first trip. Very late in the evening we returned to Taraz. There our routes split—Vladimir was on his way home, and I had to catch the bus to Tashkent. Plant lovers in Tashkent are usually directed toward Chimgan, the spot most often visited by foreign botanists and gardeners. I would not mention it here if it wasn't very important for all my future travels. At Chimgan I met my first true mountaineer, who taught me some things that would prove extremely useful for my future travels. I still have the map that he sent me, showing all the gorges around Chimgan.

When I arrived at Chimgan it was afternoon, and the tourist camp wasn't operating because the real season hadn't yet begun. Fortunately I was invited to overnight in a wagon normally used to house workers. It was quite a strange night. In the center of the wagon were bricks with some primitive, bare, red-hot electric cable wound around them. My host and I slept on both sides of this "oven." The side of my body facing the oven felt hot, while my other side was freezing, so I spent the whole night rolling from one side to the other. During the night it snowed.

There was nothing much to see in the morning, only some *Crocus alatavicus*, *Colchicum luteum*, and *Gymnospermium albertii* near the road. Everything else had been covered by an avalanche. A young man emerging from a tent nearby called to me, inviting me for a cup of coffee. I had been without coffee for some ten days already, since the local people drank only tea, and at home I normally drank coffee all day long. I could hardly turn down such an offer, so I soon found myself holding a huge cup of hot Nescafé.

It was the first time I felt faint from coffee. Mountain air, lower air pressure, and a week and a half without coffee all combined to dizzying effect—I felt as though I had drained a glass of vodka. I started talking with the young man. He turned out to be an instructor for mountaineers and was camped here waiting for a group that would arrive in a few days. He was extremely surprised by my clothes, shoes, and equipment and told me that only a lunatic would go into the mountains so badly prepared. He taught me about all the things I would need in the mountains if I was to return on my own feet rather than in a box. He gave me a lot of other useful advice, too, such as how to cross snow beds, where dangers can be hidden. So, although this first visit to Chimgan was poor in plants, it turned out to be very valuable for me in other ways. Later my friend sent me mountain boots and a framed haversack that was much more comfortable than the usual tourist backpacks available in Latvia at the time. He had come from Altay, a mountainous region in Siberia, where such things were common in shops. Only many years later would similar equipment finally appear in Latvian shops.

Such was the real beginning of my plant hunting.

Around Chimgan

When I look back, Chimgan is the place I visited most. Friends who joined me in the mountains always wanted to visit it. After Latvia regained its independence, when Arnis and I arranged our first trip to Central Asia, we both visited Chimgan. As I mentioned before, it is a well-known place widely visited by botanical tourists. It is situated quite high in the mountains—the tourist base is at 2000 m. The peak of the Great Chimgan is at 3309 m, but people interested in bulbs usually visit the valley of the Chimgan River not far from the main road and hotel. This is some 100 km northeast of Tashkent, near the point where the Ugam and Pskem mountain ranges start.

In the spring of 1996 Arnis and I went to Chimgan to take some beautiful pictures and collect some Juno irises, but as our car climbed the mountains, our optimism fell. It still looked like winter or very, very early spring. The snow had only just melted on the slopes, and we could see no flowers at all. The day was dull, too, and marked by occasional rain. We both quietly asked ourselves what we would do here, and felt grateful that we would be here for only two days. Everything around was very dirty—we felt as if we were in a city rubbish dump. In fact the landscape seemed to have changed dramatically since my last visit. Chimgan was now quite a popular skiing center, and since it was prone to experiencing avalanches, dynamite had been used to topple loose spots. The places where earlier I had seen plenty of *Corydalis darwasica* and *Fritillaria stenanthera* were no longer recognizable. There were now bare slopes covered with granite chips and funiculars.

Luckily, as we walked up along the stream of the river, things changed for the better. Yes, it was very early in the season, but the first bulbs were coming up already, and we were greeted with flowers of *Gymnospermium albertii*, *Crocus alatavicus*, *Scilla puschkinioides*, and *Eranthis longistipitata*. We found spectacular samples of *Corydalis ledebouriana* (Plate 103) that were generally very bright in color and quite variable. These Chimgan plants were far better than forms of this species I had found in other places.

Corydalis ledebouriana belongs to the species with perennial tubers. In the wild it is one of the brightest and most beautiful species from this group, forming dense spikes closely covered with deep purplish and very light pink or white blooms. In some places it grows by the millions together with a *Gagea* species, the splendid yellow color with the interspersed purple spots of *C. ledebouriana* resembling an Oriental rug. Unfortunately, in my garden *C. ledebouriana* has lost its natural beauty. It usually starts into growth too early and so as a rule is damaged by night frosts. The flowers are pale, too, and the spikes loose. Years later we introduced a highland form of this species from Sina that flowers in the garden much later; it is far better than its more early-flowering relatives. Among the traditionally purple and white plants of this species at Chimgan, we found individuals with some yellow- or cream-shaded blooms, which led us to believe some hybridization with plants of *C. darwasica* growing in the area had occurred.

Corydalis ledebouriana is a plant of richer soils, growing mostly on deep, sticky clay or leaf mold, although it is sometimes also found on more gravelly spots. Its close relative *C. darwasica* generally grows only on marble and granite screes. Typically a smaller plant, with deeply dissected leaves and beautiful creamy white blooms, it attracts less attention in the wild but is very beautiful in the garden, where it always flowers nicely. At Chimgan I usually found it on bare slopes on well-eroded granites. Both species belong to section *Leonticoides* and are self-incompatible, so at least two tubers are needed to obtain seeds.

We came to Chimgan with some particular plants in mind. My main target was *Eminium lehmannii* (Plate 104), a beautiful aroid with a large, velvety, purplish brown spathe at ground level, flowering in the wild before the leaves develop but somewhat later in the garden. In the garden I catch the start of its flowering just by the smell exuded by the opening blooms. As I pass through the beds, I get the idea some hare has died and lies rotting among my rows of plants. This, I can be sure, means that my eminiums have started to flower. Happily, the beauty of the flowers compensates for their odor. Both Central Asian *Eminium* species, *E. lehmannii* and *E. albertii*, are good growers in Latvia and have survived all the changes of my garden. They increase well vegetatively, too, and losses are always counterbalanced by new progeny. Growing these plants under covering is much safer, because their greatest enemy is summer moisture. In the greenhouse I even get seeds.

Eminium lehmannii is a plant of lower altitudes, with the most high-altitude population growing at Chimgan. At higher altitudes it is replaced by *E. albertii*, which is quite similar in flower but different in leaf shape. The leaves of *E. albertii* are distinctly trilobed, while those of *E. lehmannii* are lanceolate without basal lobes. Tubers of both species usually lie very deep in clay soil. At Chimgan, melting snow washed hundreds of tubers to the surface on some newly bulldozed slopes, so we collected some of these. I also collected *E. albertii* some years before this in Tajikistan at the Varzob Valley, where it grew on a flat meadow in strong clay. The growing requirements for both species are quite similar, although *E. albertii* reproduces better, forming more daughter tubers on top of the old one. These small tubers usually have very long contractile roots that push the young tubers very deep and slightly to the side of the old one. After harvesting them, I would recommend keeping the tubers hot (30°C and above) to prevent bacterial rot and help induce the next flowering.

Another plant I was looking for in Chimgan was *Gymnospermium albertii*, which I had seen on my first excursion and described as something "corydalis-like with horned tubers." From my earlier collections only two plants had survived, and even those had been re-collected as self-sown seedlings in my first garden. I needed to build up my stock more quickly. Gymnospermiums are very beautiful, tuberous plants that flower in early spring and can be propagated only from seed. Fortunately, they usually set seed quite well and have a good germination rate. My greatest failing during the early years of my career was keeping the harvested seedlings out of the soil. They all died from drying out. These plants survive better in soil, although they need excellent drainage. Now I keep new seedlings of *Gymnospermium* mixed with white sand in a thin polyethylene bag. They are quite good growers, and I have some tubers even 20 cm across that in spring produce up to fifty flowering stems. Not all of the harvested tubers survive, however, so every year I collect the seeds.

Gymnospermium albertii (Plate 105) is one of the most beautiful species for its bright maroon-red stems in early spring and nice, densely placed, bright yellow, pendant flowers with a bright coppery red midrib on the petal exterior. At flowering time the leaves are rolled lengthwise, but they later expand, and together with the stem they pale to a grayish green. *Gymnospermium altaicum* is a somewhat paler plant, lacking the red color of the stem, but this is compensated for by more abundant flowering and rounder flower shape. It grows more to the east, and its stock was collected by Arnis on the mountains of Altay in western Siberia some years earlier. It is very similar to *G. odessanum* but can be distinguished by its stamens, which are twice as long. I received seeds of *G. odessanum* from Gothenburg; the original stock came from the Komarov Botanical Institute in Saint Petersburg, but the seedlings were identical with *G. altaicum.*

There is one nice gymnospermium that I accidentally collected at the Varzob Gorge, Tajikistan. While looking for bulbs of *Iris vicaria* on a small, shady slope among trees, tubers of the *Gymnospermium* species simply started to roll out. At home this species proved to be different from *G. albertii.* Using an article by Martyn Rix published in *The Plantsman* in 1982, I identified it as *G. sylvaticum,* which had quite recently been discovered in northeastern Afghanistan. I grew it under that name until a visit to Gothenburg, which houses a very large collection of gymnospermiums, raised some doubt. True *G. sylvaticum* grows only in Afghanistan, and its leaflets are on long (1–6 cm) stalks. The correct name of my plant appears to be *G. darwasicum.* Its leaflets are on stalks that are at most 8 mm long.

On a grassy slope I also found *Eranthis longistipitata* (Plate 106), a common plant that is very widespread in Central Asia. I had collected it many times but had never been successful growing it—it would flower for some years and then disappear. It has been many years since I heard of any nursery offering this species. It sometimes appears on plant lists but soon disappears again. It looks quite similar to *E. cilicica* and *E. hyemalis* from Europe and Turkey, only its flowers are smaller and carried on a stalk rather than sessile. On the Iranian side of the Kopet-Dag, Henrik Zetterlund recently found another relative of *E. longistipitata* that looks like a new species. It has incredibly orange-toned flowers and uniquely shaped tubers.

Woodlander *Eranthis hyemalis* is very easy in the garden and usually naturalizes even in Latvia. I don't grow this species in my open beds, but it enjoys a spot in my old shade garden, where every spring its bright yellow flowers come up through melting snow at the end of March or first days of April. Turkish *E. cilicica* is not so easy to grow, as it requires somewhat drier conditions and more sun. Its leaves and bracts are a little tinged with bronze and are more dissected than those of *E. hyemalis.* Both species easily hybridize to form *E. ×tubergenii.* The best clone is *E. ×tubergenii* 'Guinea Gold', which has a large, bright golden yellow flower surrounded by a bronzy fringe.

There are many hybrids in the trade, and every nursery announces that their plant is the true one. Although 'Guinea Gold' is reputed to be sterile, this isn't true. It produces seeds, just not as abundantly as its parents. The best stock I have seen, and which I grow myself, comes from Gothenburg. Its incredibly large, globular flowers really are far better than all the other plants I have seen under the same name. 'Flore Plena' has somewhat greenish yellow, double flowers and a set of anthers and stigmas in the center. 'Aurantiaca' has different, slightly orange-shaded petals and anthers.

In eastern Siberia there are two species of *Eranthis*, *E. sibirica* and *E. stellata* (Plate 107), both incorrectly described in the *Flora of the Soviet Union* (Komarov 1935) as yellow-flowering plants. In reality both have white flowers—the herbarium samples that were used during the preparation of the flora had simply yellowed. Both species are distinguished by their pedicels: in *E. sibirica* they are glandular, but in *E. stellata*, which replaces *E. sibirica* to the east, they are white-hairy. All my post-war Russian botanical literature referred to *Eranthis* as a new genus, *Shibateranthis*, and when searching for *Eranthis* I was unable to find either species in library books about plants of Siberia and the Far East. When I finally discovered where the confusion was coming from, I realized that the mysterious white *Eranthis* species I had grown for years, from coastal forests surrounding the village of Olga some 200 km north of Vladivostok, was the long-searched-for *E. stellata*. It is a very beautiful plant with large, pure white flowers, white anthers, and yellow nectaries. I received my stock from Sulev Savisaar in Estonia. The trickiest thing with this plant is finding the best time for replanting. It seems that it is never without roots. Whenever I try to replant the tubers, they are surrounded by fresh white roots. *Eranthis pinnatifida* from Japan and Korea has blue anthers, yellow nectaries, and grayish green, dissected bracts. It is not so easy to grow in Latvia. After flowering nicely for a few years, my only tuber was lost over a harsh winter, and I haven't replaced it. The Korean *E. byunsanensis* has greenish yellow nectaries, lighter purplish anthers, and grayish, entire bract leaves. Sometimes it is distributed under the name *E. stellata*, which has soft green, apically dissected bracts.

Arnis was mostly looking for the plant I had collected at Chimgan many years ago during my first or second visit, which I later sent to Michael Hoog in the Netherlands and to the Royal Botanic Gardens, Kew. It is a Juno iris with very pale yellowish, almost white flowers. It is such a strange color that I never associate it with *Iris orchioides*. I made the mistake initially of naming it *I. capnoides*, a beautiful plant closely related to *I. orchioides* and growing not far from Chimgan. In reality this Juno iris from Chimgan was a new species, *I. pseudocapnoides* (Plates 108 and 109), well distinguished by the shape of its additional roots, which are thick and long, somewhat similar to those of *I. vicaria* and *I. magnifica*. The crest of the ridge on the falls is undulate but not hairy. In this aspect it approximates *I. capnoides*, but it is a plant of mountain meadows with purplish-toned blooms, and the additional roots are shorter, too. In all other variants of *I. orchioides* sensu lato the crest is distinctly more or less hairy. It is an excellent plant in the garden, growing up to 30 cm high with up to five large flowers in the leaf axils.

While I looked for *Eranthis longistipitata* and inspected a *Corydalis ledebouriana* plant with distinctly yellowish flowers, Arnis made his way to the snow where *C. darwasica* was just coming out. At around the same elevation, beneath a large archa (the local name for *Juniperus*), he found the sought-after *Iris* aff. *orchioides*. I decided to return to our camp by another steep scree slope and found, just 50 or 60 m from our tent, a very large group of the same Juno. Again it was generally growing beneath the archa, but here it was also on an open slope on a mix of granite chips and clay—beneath archa the soil contains more peat, while soils in open places are much heavier. They were just starting to grow and I was quite skeptical about collecting any of the bulbs, but to my surprise the bulbs we collected recovered perfectly and flowered after one season in my garden. It seems the food reserves had been transferred from the old bulb to the replacement bulb. When a bulb is collected at flowering time most of the food reserves are used to form the stem and flowers. When flowering ends, the reserves are slit in two—one part is used to form seeds, another part to form replacement bulbs. The priority is always given to the seeds. When I collect a plant with a seedpod, the bulb as a rule is small and weak; conversely, when I collect a bulb from a plant that hasn't yet flowered or in which pollination hasn't yet taken place, the bulb is usually large and strong.

Tulipa tschimganica was the only plant we were looking for but didn't find—it was much too early for it. This is a pity, because its taxonomic status remains uncertain: is it really a species or only a form of *T. kaufmanniana*? According to the Russian botanist A. I. Vvedenskyi (1971), it is a hybrid between *T. kaufmanniana* and *T. greigii*. I used to grow it many years ago, but I never found any indication of hybrid origin in the plants collected in the type locality. They looked exactly the same as those pictured in Z. P. Botschantzeva's marvelous *Tulips* and were very variable in color, ranging from almost pure yellow to bright red, some even bicolored. All had a characteristic brown ring on the yellow filaments, and the anthers opened gradually from the top, but didn't coil as in *T. kaufmanniana*. We wanted to collect it to see how it would respond to garden conditions. According to Botschantzeva, it must have brown-tipped yellow filaments and also flowers much later in the garden than *T. kaufmanniana*. I don't know whether *T. tschimganica* is sufficiently distinct to be considered an independent species. At any rate, my *T. berkariense* (nomen nudum) is more different from both *T. tschimganica* and *T. kaufmanniana* than these two plants are from each other.

As everywhere, we also collected various plants from the *Tulipa bifloriformis–T. turkestanica* complex. At Chimgan we had to find *T. bifloriformis*, whose anthers are mostly black. As it happens, we found plants with all variations of anther color: they were black, yellow, and yellow with a black tip. There were plenty of clones that never flower but increase only vegetatively by stolons. Different botanists use different criteria to separate these tulips. Some use anther color as the basic criterion, while others consider the hairiness of the inner surface of the tunics of the bulb. In each species there are strains with different chromosome numbers, too. In fact this group of tulips hasn't yet been investigated enough—using modern research based on chromosomes and DNA sequences could very well lead to some surprises.

Alongside our tent we found large clumps of *Ungernia sewerzowii*, a strange member of Amaryllidaceae that sends up leaves in spring but flowers in autumn long after the leaves have disappeared. As had happened earlier with eminiums, bulldozers had pushed some of these tubers to the surface, and we collected from these. *Ungernia sewerzowii* is not a good grower outdoors in my region. In those years I grew two or three bulbs that I had collected during my first trips, but I never saw them flower in the garden. On only one occasion, one of the bulbs flowered in the dark in the hot air of my attic. After I planted these bulbs in the greenhouse, a few years passed before the first flower scapes came out. The bulbs are very long and have thick, wire-like, perennial roots. If you decide it is worthwhile trying to grow them, you will need extra-long long tom pots—I'm afraid those used at Kew for Juno irises can be too short for *U. sewerzowii*. Other species are more floriferous and have smaller bulbs. In any case, ungernias are not commercial plants and are grown only as a novelty.

The night was very cold, and in the morning the roof of our tent was covered with ice. The day would be very sunny, though—not a single cloud in the sky. The leaves of the surrounding bulbous plants looked like they had been boiled, but they recovered surprisingly quickly.

Stunning clumps of *Scilla puschkinioides* (Plate 110) grew very close to our tent. This species is superficially very similar to the trade form of *Puschkinia scilloides*, so only checking the flower anatomy can clarify which plant is in front of you. Both plants grew in my first garden, where they were self-sowing in a mixed population, and only after many years did the more vigorous *Puschkinia* take over. *Scilla puschkinioides* is very beautiful in the mountains, but not so nice in the garden. Among the hardy scillas it is one of the most difficult to grow outside in my region, although it grows fine in the greenhouse. This plant serves as an excellent illustration of the importance of collecting a small sample from even very common plants when you encounter them in the wild. I have almost ten different samples of *S. puschkinioides*, and each one is different not in flower but in growing capacity. Some stocks never produce any offsets, and some form large bulbs with a few offsets. Some are weak growers, while the majority increase well and are great garden cultivars. In the case of *S. puschkinioides*, a very good stock was collected at Chimgan, but an even better one was found a year later on the heights of Sina, southeastern Uzbekistan.

The bright sun had opened the flowers of *Crocus alatavicus* (Plate 111), the first flower to bloom in this region. A field that had been covered with snow only a day before was now white with crocus flowers. I selected for my collection only the most ornamental forms with broad, rounded petals. *Crocus alatavicus* is a very good plant, although it shows all its beauty only when the sun is shining because the backsides of the petals are stippled and spotted ash gray or purplish gray (this is also why the closed flower buds are almost invisible). Although it is among the first spring crocuses to bloom in my garden, it is the laziest increaser. Sometimes some corms produce two or three replacement corms, but this doesn't happen regularly, so the clone selection is fruitless or very slow. I have been growing it with varying degrees of success. My stocks increase and set seed, then decline, leaving me back where I started. I recently passed such a period of depression, but my stock has again started to increase from the dozen or so corms that survived a harsh bout of black frost.

Somewhat higher on a more sun-exposed slope, where snow had recently melted, we also encountered a profusion of bright yellow *Colchicum luteum* (Plate 112). This is another plant that can sometimes flower right through snow. It is the only *Colchicum* species with yellow flowers. (Some forms of autumn-flowering *C. kotschyi* from Turkey have slightly creamy white or light straw-colored blooms, which could be called slightly yellowish, but these colors are nothing like the bright golden yellow of *C. luteum*.) The first form of this species known to Western gardeners came from Afghanistan and was large-flowering and a good increaser. It was grown with amazing skill by Dutch nurseryman Willem van Eeden, but one winter he lost all of his stock, and since then *C. luteum* has gone from being quite a common plant to a rarity.

The plants from previous Soviet republics of Central Asia are generally somewhat smaller, but the flower size increases in more southern populations, with the largest forms occurring around the border between Tajikistan and Afghanistan. The plants growing at Chimgan have the smallest flowers, but like everywhere else they are also quite variable. In the wild they mostly form one flower per bulb, but they sometimes form two, and I was looking for two-flowered plants. Most of the plants I selected have flowers with some brown tinting at least on the tube, sometimes reaching quite high on the back of the outer petals. 'Yellow Empress', nursed and propagated over the years by Arnis Seisums, has very large, elegant, elongated, very bright flowers (the brightest I have ever seen) without any brown speckle. Hendrik van Bogaert has also grown an orange-shaded form since 1992. The bulb shape is different in various populations of *Colchicum luteum*. Chimgan plants have slightly elongated but generally ovate bulbs.

At Tovilj-Dara, Tajikistan, another Central Asian spring-flowering colchicum, *Colchicum kesselringii*, grows alongside *C. luteum*. The base color of its petals is white, but the petal exteriors can vary widely from almost pure white to deepest purple with a narrow white rim. The flower color is so variable, in fact, that my customers have at times suspected I sent them the wrong plant. This very situation caused me to give cultivar names to samples from various populations of *C. kesselringii*. All were selected by Arnis. 'Modesty' has snow white flowers and a very narrow gray stripe, 'Boldness' has clean white flowers with a narrow but very bright purple-violet stripe, and 'Prosperity' has a wide, deep violet-purple stripe in the center of the petals that gradually fades to gray toward the margin, and only the narrow rim of the segments is white.

It is not surprising that *Colchicum kesselringii* and *C. luteum* sometimes hybridize if planted together. One such hybrid with beautiful creamy yellow flowers comes from the fields surrounding the airport at Tovilj-Dara. On my fiftieth birthday Arnis presented me with this bulb, which he had named 'Jānis' (Plate 114). Now Arnis grows three different clones of this hybrid. To my surprise, the hybrids are fertile and set seed, though the seedlings haven't flowered for me yet.

These Central Asian *Colchicum* species are further proof that even plants that seem common must be collected when visiting faraway, difficult-to-reach places. During our search for *Iris winkleri* at the heights of Kugart, we found a *Colchicum* species that I supposed was just ordinary *C. luteum* or *C. kesselringii*. I was greatly surprised when it flowered for me a few years later: its pure white blooms had petals that were absolutely unique in shape—wide and rounded at the tip. The flowers were so different from the general concept of *C. kesselringii* that I started to think that this must be a new species. Unfortunately, both my bulbs died before I got any seeds from them. If I had paid more attention to them, perhaps my stock would have been larger, and then there would have been seeds and a plant would be conserved in an herbarium for further research. All I can do now is regret my laziness, because I will never again go there.

At the end of the second day, despite the apprehension we had felt upon our arrival, we were very satisfied with the results of our outing to Chimgan. It had again proved worthwhile to explore this area, regardless of the fact that it is so often visited by tourists.

Beldersai

Tulipa dubia (Plates 116 and 117), another tulip species from the *T. kaufmanniana* group, grows in more exposed spots in Chimgan on granite rocks. I had seen it there during earlier visits, but this time its territory was covered with snow. I first collected it in 1977 on eroded hills at the upper course of the Beldersai River, where it grows only at the top of the ridge.

Beldersai (Plate 118) is situated some 10–15 km from Chimgan, and I went there with Āris Krūmiņš and Ludvigs Sidrēvics during my first real plant hunting trip to Central Asia. This was the first time I met Volodya Vinogradov, a real king of gerberas in Central Asia. His wife was born in Riga, so they often went there to visit her parents and meet with Latvian gardeners. I was present at one such meeting, and Volodya offered to let me use his house in Tashkent as the base camp for my trips to the mountains. When we journey to Central Asia, we usually try to visit three or four places, and Volodya's "camp" has proved extremely useful. Without his help we wouldn't have been able to complete one-tenth of our missions.

Volodya owned a car called a Volga, which was the ultimate status symbol in the Soviet Union. The most prestigious ones were black, such as those used by officials of the Communist Party in Moscow, so every businessman in Central Asia had to have a black Volga. Volodya's car was also black. Soviet cars had no air conditioning at the time, and a black car in the sun of Tashkent could heat up to the point where you couldn't even touch it. A white one would have been much more reasonable and comfortable, but a white car had no prestige. Although Volodya owned this car, he only ever used it inside the city. When I asked him why, his reply was very simple. "I don't want to feed those local policemen," he said. "They'll stop any car from another district and will only let you continue on your way after you give them some money."

We had a contact person in Brichmulla, a village farther than Chimgan, where the valley of the Chatkal River started. We wanted to go up by this valley to Kyrgyzstan (during Soviet times there were no real borders between Soviet republics) and needed some help with transportation. Unfortunately, we arrived in Brichmulla only to find that our contact person lived elsewhere during the summer, so as evening neared we had nowhere to sleep. Then a three-wheeler stopped next to us—a local policeman wanting to check our documents. Once again I presented the magic words "Central Committee of the Communist Party of Latvia." He spent a long time comparing my face with the photo on my documents, then asked to see my passport. My long hair fell down to my shoulders and I wore jeans covered with bright heart-shaped patches. I looked more like a hippie than a high-ranking functionary of the Party. In the end he offered us a spot on his three-wheeler. We again passed Chimgan, and after an hour or more of driving, during which our main concern was not allowing ourselves or our baggage to slide off the vehicle, we were left at a road sign to Beldersai. A pedestrian pass some 5 km long led to the mountains from here.

We found an excellent place for our tent somewhat higher than the Beldersai River and slept there like the dead. The new day greeted us with our first flowers: *Eminium lehmannii*. It was the first time I had seen this species in full flower. At Chimgan all the rock had been granite-based, but here everything was limestone. The water in the river was so calcareous that our soap didn't foam, and even our tea was muddy with lime. Despite all these great differences, though, the plants were generally the same as in Chimgan. After breakfast we began our trek into the mountains.

We soon reached a marvelous flat meadow covered with soft grass and just a few stones, in the middle of which was a beautiful spring. A few clumps of something similar to *Iris orchioides* grew there. Somewhat higher in the mountains these plants were still in flower and appeared to be the same whitish Juno we had seen in Chimgan (*I. pseudocapnoides*). We climbed higher and higher. The next meadow was golden yellow with *Gagea* flowers.

Then we saw the first tulips. They looked somewhat similar to *Tulipa kaufmanniana*, and this was initially what I thought they were, but the anthers opened gradually without any coiling and the flowers sat deeply in a rosette of nicely wavy leaves. Generally they were all light yellow with red petal exteriors, but sometimes among them were plants with deep red flowers or red flowers with a yellow-striped edge. Quite rarely there were also plants with very deep purple leaves, but then the leaf color was different from that of *T. greigii*. While *T. greigii* had generally green leaves marked by more or less densely spaced purple stripes and dots, this tulip had purple leaves with one or a few narrow green veins along their length. It looked identical to the plant pictured under the name *T. dubia* in Z. P. Botschantzeva's *Tulips*. The question was where the purple color on the leaves had come from. Was this a hybrid of *T.*

greigii? *Tulipa greigii* did grow here, though much lower in the mountains. As it turns out, this type of leaf coloration sometimes appears on plants growing high in the mountains as a kind of protection from the intensity of ultraviolet rays. I have encountered such plants in other genera, too. At Sina even the dandelions had deep purple leaves.

In the garden *Tulipa dubia* has much paler leaves and loses its nice compact habit. The flower stem also elongates, bringing the flower well out of the leaf rosette. The other problem with this otherwise beautiful species is that it forms long stolons, so harvesting the bulbs is always somewhat problematic. It grows well, though, reproduces well vegetatively, and sets seed. This species also grows at Chimgan, but in that location the leaves are erect rather than prostrate, as is more typical of true *T. dubia*. There is a tulip under this name grown by Dutch nurseries, but it has nothing in common with the true species, being whitish pink and of a different habit; most likely it is a garden hybrid of *T. kaufmanniana*. It has never set any seed for me.

As we continued our ascent, we soon saw no more tulips, having apparently exceeded their optimal elevation. All the time I looked for *Crocus alatavicus* with pure white petal exteriors; I had heard that such a form existed but had never encountered any during my travels. Soon we were on the ridge. The opposite slope was very steep. The small houses far below us in the valley looked like toys, and we could see the small white line of the river. On the opposite side, *Tulipa dubia* again appeared. If previously there were generally only yellow forms, here the flowers were mostly red, orange, or red with a narrow yellow edge. They were so beautiful that I put a rope around my waist and, supported by Āris, tried to make small steps on the slope with my ice pick. Still, I was unable to collect any of these beautiful specimens.

Bashkizilsai Valley

As I mentioned before, I initially thought the Juno iris we had collected at Chimgan was *Iris capnoides* (Plate 119). All I knew about *I. capnoides* was that it was described as coming from the Chatkal Nature Reserve, some 25–30 km from Chimgan. The only thing separating it from *I. orchioides* sensu lato was its flower color, which was described as "smoky." Since the flowers of all Juno irises included under the name *I. orchioides* are somewhat lilac-tinged by the end of flowering, it was very easy to make such a mistake. We only succeeded in collecting the true *I. capnoides* in 1996, from near its type locality, just at the border of the Chatkal Nature Reserve.

It was the third place we visited during our expedition. As a matter of fact the place we visited was called Sangirsai, but since it was a much smaller side valley of the main Bashkizilsai basin, we decided to use the main name. We were actually looking for another gorge, Iransai, the type locality of *Iris capnoides*, which had never been introduced in gardens. While we were searching for Iransai, some local people pointed us in the wrong direction, and we realized the mistake only after we'd walked more than an hour into the mountains. This mistake turned out to be one of our greatest fortunes. Iransai was located within the Chatkal Nature Reserve, where collecting plants even for an herbarium was strictly forbidden, so we would only be able to take pictures. Sangirsai, on the other hand, was just outside the reserve, and the flora had to be quite identical to the plants found within the reserve. The highest point was Mount Kizilkur (3267 m), just at the eastern end of the Chatkal Mountains. Further south was the Kuramin Ridge, another place where *I. capnoides* was known to grow, but Arnis hadn't found the iris on a trip he had taken there a year before with Victor Voronin, the tulip breeder from Alma-Ata (during which I was forced to stay home because of health problems).

Passing the small village of Sangirek, we walked into the mountains along a very narrow footpath. On the slopes grew *Eremurus* species and *Eminium lehmannii*, but all the other plants had been grazed by animals. I spotted the first Juno on my left: the seeds were just about to ripen, and I collected them. Soon the road widened. Our footpath turned into a road for tractors, and we soon came upon terraced mountain slopes used for village orchards.

After we set up our tent, I found a large group of *Iris kolpakowskiana* (Plate 120) growing nearby underneath a shrub. I had never found such a large quantity of this species. In fact, in my ten previous expeditions to the Central Asian mountains, I had never found more than two or three of these plants and had come to think of them as very rare indeed. *Iris kolpakowskiana* is not an easy garden plant, but I never lost hope of finding a good growing population. In the preceding winter we had discussed the possible splitting of this species in two with Arnis and Henrik Zetterlund, so I was interested in acquiring material from as many different localities as possible.

My first bulbs of *Iris kolpakowskiana* came from the surroundings of Alma-Ata and were sent to me by Victor Voronin. The standards of this plant are dark to light violet with a bluish tint, the falls are dark purple with a distinct dark yellow blotch, and the tube is greenish. The bulbs are a bright yellow. I later received some bulbs Arnis had collected at Matai in Kazakhstan, and they turned out to be very different from those I had grown earlier. The standards of the Matai plants are light violet and club-shaped; the falls are blackish purple with a white blotch in the throat, speckled and striped dark blue or purple without any touch of yellow; the tube is light violet; and the anthers are white. They flower much earlier than the plants from Alma-Ata, although both are collected in the foothills of mountains. The bulbs are also a much lighter yellow. Both forms looked so different that I immediately wondered if these were in fact two species listed under one name. Plants growing in the surroundings of Tashkent had a white blotch on the falls, too. I left it to Arnis to decide which one must be regarded as *I. kolpakowskiana* and which one needed a new name. We later found another new Reticulata iris in Central Asia that was very different from any other, so ultimately we doubled the number of these irises known in Central Asia. Although George Rodionenko (1999) separated Central Asian Reticulata irises into a new genus, *Alatavia*, based on leaf shape and other minor differences, this splitting was not accepted by other botanists.

Back at camp I lit our stove and went to look for Juno irises on the almost bare rocky slopes. I found a plant of medium height with long, quite thick, string-like additional roots. Arnis later found the same plant, this one with its last flower still attached, though a little damaged. It was pure yellow, and what is most important, the haft of the falls seemed to be without wings. Our first thought was that this might be a new species, but later we remembered that the haft of *Iris tubergeniana* (Plate 121) has very small wings that could easily go unnoticed on such a damaged flower. *Iris tubergeniana* is a splendid Juno with up to three golden yellow blooms on a stem that is initially short but later grows to 30 cm tall. The long additional roots seem to compensate for this plant's small, thin bulb. This feature changes in the garden, but the bulbs remain slimmer than those of other species.

Continuing my walk higher on a grassy field, I was suddenly stopped by a beautiful smoky blue-violet flower. It was the plant of our dreams, the goal of our trip—*Iris capnoides*, growing quite abundantly here in the grass. It would have been difficult to locate without its blooms, but we were lucky enough to arrive just at flowering time. It was easy to distinguish from the Junos we had collected earlier: its roots were shorter, thicker, and more swollen, somewhat resembling those of *I. rosenbachiana* or *I. kopetdagensis* but more slender. It replaced the yellow-flowering *I. tubergeniana* higher in the mountains. Although later we also found *I. capnoides* in quite rocky, open areas, it still seemed to prefer open meadows, while we found *I. tubergeniana* only on rocky openings and at lower elevations. There is no great variability in flower color, but nonetheless *I. capnoides* is a wonderful addition to any iris collection. It is now well established in my own garden and appears to be a good grower, reproducing well vegetatively and from seed. The only problem is with supply and demand: we're never able to build up quite enough stock to match the amount of requests we receive. *Iris capnoides* is a close relative of *I. orchioides* and is certainly in the same group, most similar to the plant from Chimgan in terms of its crinkled crest without any hair. They both also have thick additional roots. In any case the plants from Chimgan more closely resemble *I. capnoides* than *I. orchioides*, as was traditionally thought.

Arnis returned to the camp quite late and was very tired. Over the course of some hours he had walked to the highest peaks within reach of our camp, where he had found a number of plants. The area was incredibly rich. Like me, he had found *Iris capnoides*, and this was replaced at higher elevations by another species growing on more stony, shaded slopes—what Arnis thought must be *I. albomarginata*. In terms of its structure and environment it certainly seemed to be different from *I. tubergeniana* and especially from *I. capnoides*. Arnis had also found a plant near the snow line that he thought must be the same *I.* aff. *orchioides* we had seen at Chimgan. If this were true—and it seemed almost unbelievable—there would be four Juno irises in the same valley. As it turned out, it was the typical *I. orchioides* that grew everywhere here, so only three Junos were found. Nonetheless, in the garden this is a very robust form and probably the most floriferous one, producing as many as six bicolored (yellow and white) blooms per stem.

The next morning greeted us with clouds and mist. We packed the tent and walked with all our luggage higher in the mountains for an hour, where we found the last relatively flat place to leave our equipment. I took my camera and walked up the gorge to take some pictures of *Tulipa kaufmanniana*. It was very variable there, from pure yellow to dark red with all shades between, but not one flower had the brown ring on the filaments that is characteristic of so-called *T. tschimganica*. During our walk Arnis stopped to show me a beautiful form of *Geranium transversale* with very narrow, almost thread-like foliage. It was very attractive, an excellent addition to the tuberous geraniums.

We also found a nice form of a very common *Ixiolirion* species (its exact identity was unclear). It was growing everywhere in the lower mountains, where it had unusually curved, even spiraled leaves. At higher altitudes this plant was replaced by the usual form with "normal" straight or slightly curved leaves. Unfortunately, this curving of the leaves turned out to be caused by the environment, because the next spring in our gardens the plants reverted to the usual form. Also, like all the wild ixiolirions I had collected earlier, this one proved to be short-lived in the garden.

While walking up, Arnis checked each plant of *Fritillaria sewerzowii*. By the afternoon he had collected forms with very differently colored blooms, from almost black to yellow and even bicolored (greenish yellow with a dark brown center). As everywhere, we collected *Tulipa bifloriformis*, *Colchicum kesselringii*, *C. luteum*, and various *Allium*, including *A. tschimganicum*. This was the place from where *A. baschkizilsaicum* was described, but we didn't find it. We also collected *A. tashkenticum*, recently described by German botanist Reinhard Fritsch and Furkat O. Khassanov from Tashkent. It is a close relative of *A. sewerzowii*, which I collected in the Karatau Range, but has broader, nearly flat, glossy, yellowish green leaves and a more compact inflorescence.

Back in Tashkent we called the airport and found that our 2 May flight to Moscow had been cancelled. We would spend the extra day visiting nearby foothills. Camel Mount was visible from the main road. This and the Tovaksai Valley were our next destinations.

Tovaksai

All the slopes of Tovaksai had been grazed clean by cattle, and at first it seemed there would be nothing interesting to see here but the trampled remains of *Eremurus regelii*. Our only hope was Camel Mount, which had very steep slopes that might be too difficult for cows to reach. But Arnis stopped me just before we left the village. There was a group of *Allium suworowii* growing just at the side of the road. Although I had stock of this species in my collection that was gathered in Kuschk, Turkmenistan, by Arnis, this was the first time I had seen it in the wild. This allium is much rarer now than it used to be; in the past it was collected in the wild by the millions for cooking and pickling. It has narrow leaves and pinkish lilac flowers in dense, semi-globose to globose umbels on a stem 70–80 cm long. In cultivation it needs a sunny, well-drained spot and does far better in a greenhouse than in an open garden.

After passing through the village, we split. Arnis walked on the left side of the Tovaksai stream, I on the right. *Fritillaria stenanthera* and *Iris kolpakowskiana* grew just near the road on very steep slopes. The landscape remained the same: scree, a few small rocks, and very shortly cut grass from which only poisonous plants emerged, including *Eremurus regelii* and that strange, long-stalked, red form of *Allium karataviense*, subspecies *henrikii* (Plate 95). At the beginning of the path up to Camel Mount we finally found remnants of a Juno. Although there was almost no other vegetation besides the red allium, it was not easy to find the Juno, since cattle had worked over the area quite thoroughly. By the time we got to it there was almost nothing left, perhaps half a leaf or so.

We continued up a very steep and narrow path, climbing over large stones and scrambling up small cliffs. Within a short while we had found plenty of this Juno. It had achieved a magnificent size, up to 30 cm tall. The flowers were spent and the seeds would soon be ripe. It was a good time for collecting, and as we began it immediately became clear that this was the same *I. tubergeniana* we had collected only a day or two before. Its thickened roots were rope-like and long, hidden in the cracks of stones, while the proper bulb looked very thin and undeveloped. The contrast between the proper bulb and additional roots was even more distinctive than on the plants from Bashkizilsai.

On the flat, tabletop-like summit of Camel Mount, the vegetation was luxurious. There were bulbs of various kinds, including three tulip species: *Tulipa kaufmanniana*, *T. greigii*, and *T. bifloriformis*. Arnis even managed to find a large group of a vegetatively propagated natural hybrid between *T. greigii* and *T. kaufmanniana*. We found *Arum korolkowii* in full flower, *Fritillaria sewerzowii* in fruit, *Ungernia sewerzowii*, *Geranium transversale*, *Ixiolirion* species, and others. Again fortune smiled on Arnis, who found a beautiful mutation of *G. transversale* with clear, bright pink blossoms ('Rosea', Plate 122).

Unfortunately, time passed very quickly and we had to return. This place was not so rich in plants as our previous routes, but all the same we would never forget it. We had found two plants with very promising futures for garden use: *Allium* aff. *karataviense*, later named 'Red Globe' but raised by me as *A. karataviense* subsp. *henrikii*, and the marvelous *Geranium transversale* 'Rosea'. Very good results indeed for such a short trip made so near the city.

Searching for Uncommon Junos

We were looking for two groups of Juno iris in the areas surrounding Tashkent. One group included various forms of *Iris orchioides* sensu lato. The other group included species from the suburbs of Tashkent that were still unknown in gardens: *I. subdecolorata* (Plate 124), *I. inconspicua* (Plate 125), and the little-known *I. narbutii*.

Iris subdecolorata was found only once, long ago, in the eastern Tashkent suburb of Buz-Bazar. By now the area had been covered with rows of apartments, though we still hoped to find our iris somewhere within reach. The situation was similar with *I. inconspicua*. It was a great game. The foothills around Tashkent had either been grazed or plowed up, the city had grown enormously over the last decades, and many of the natural habitats of both species had been destroyed.

When planning our expeditions we always included a day trip into the mountains from Tashkent. As it turned out, we had a few free days, so we decided to use them this way. Our first trip was to Parkent, a small town some 30 km to the west. As everywhere, the slopes were totally grazed, with only *Eminium* and *Eremurus* species left untouched, but we saw one hill that looked more promising. It was quite far away, but the slopes in the area were terraced, with some tractor tracks even visible on the ground. It was on just such tracks that we had found our first Juno at Bashkizilsai, and Parkent was no exception. After a few steps, Arnis shouted, "Here it is! The first Juno!" But what species was it? The soil was dry clay, hard as a brick, and the bulb could only be seen after taking the soil away pinch by pinch. After half an hour of hard work, we finally had a clear view of the roots and were very disappointed to find that it was "only" *Iris tubergeniana*. How fastidious we had become! Most any gardener would be happy to find a species so rare in gardens, but we were not satisfied. Only the habitat was different from the specimens we had already found. At Bashkizilsai and Tovaksai, *I. tubergeniana* grew on stones, but here it was growing on meadows in very deep, hard clay.

Everywhere around us was *Tulipa greigii* in full bloom, though only the usual bright red forms. We also saw plenty of *Scilla puschkinioides*, *Eranthis longistipitata*, and *Crocus alatavicus*, all of which we paid no attention to. Our road was repeatedly crossed by deep cracks. On the left was a very high, sheer bank from which billions of cubic meters of earth slid down each spring in gigantic landslides. In a somewhat lower spot, we found *Iris tubergeniana* that had grown higher up on a meadow but had slid down and was now covered in layers of mud. We collected the exposed bulbs that nature had dug up for us.

In the lush grass Arnis also found *Iris kolpakowskiana*. How, I wondered, does he manage to spot the leaves of such plants among tall blades of grass? As I passed another spot where *I. kolpakowskiana* was growing, Arnis followed behind me, pointing it out again. We didn't find any *Iris subdecolorata*, but *I. tubergeniana* wasn't too bad, especially if it came from a different ecosystem.

The next spot we planned to visit was a village called Tut. We again found ourselves in the foothills quite close to the spot where *Iris capnoides* grows, but now in the opposite direction from Parkent. We passed old mines where long grass covered scattered pieces of limestone and where sheep were pastured by shepherds. Among the large rocks grew *Eremurus regelii* (Plate 126) in full flower, the slightly nodding tips of the flower spikes resembling cobras swinging their heads in the breeze. Although we saw cows and sheep everywhere, the area didn't seem overgrazed. Still, we found only *Eminium*, *Eremurus*, and *Crocus alatavicus*. We hadn't yet seen a single one of the Juno irises we were searching for. Since we didn't know exactly what they looked like, we were just looking for Junos in general. Soon we came across old rocky outcrops sandwiched between clay slopes—characteristic Juno habitat. We headed in the direction of the highest monticule. After walking a fair distance, I realized I hadn't seen Arnis for some time, so I turned back to search for him. He had found the first Juno and called out to me, but I hadn't heard him because of the strong wind.

Arnis's Juno looked very strange. It had additional rope-shaped roots, very similar to those of *Iris tubergeniana*, but the plant itself was very dwarf and compact, with short internodes. The leaves were pressed together in a rosette. It was in full seed, and we could see that the seedpods were different, too. While *I. tubergeniana* had long, slim seedpods, this iris had seedpods that were short, fat, and stumpy. The leaves were also different, dark green and more grayish in shade. Arnis thought it must be *I. inconspicua*, while I was more inclined to think it was *I. subdecolorata*. To know for sure, both flowers would be needed. We later named it *I. inconspicua*.

When I started writing this book, I looked through all my pictures of the plants grown in my nursery. When I opened the folder with pictures of *Iris inconspicua*, I was greatly surprised to see two different Juno species, both collected at Tut. This meant that Arnis and I had both been right: we had found both *I. inconspicua* and *I. subdecolorata*. Generally both species are distinguished by flower color. The flowers of *I. subdecolorata* are pale dirty greenish, almost translucent and decolorate. The flowers of *I. inconspicua* are light lilac, similar in color to *I. kuschakewiczii* but more violet and without the deep blue spots on the falls or with only very light and slightly greenish spots. The ridge of the crest in both species is very hairy, but in *I. subdecolorata* it is marked by deep green stripes, while in *I. inconspicua* the stripes are deep violet-blue. Are these differences sufficient to split them into two species? I don't think so, but only research on a molecular level can answer the question with certainty. Incidentally, the famous Russian botanist R. V. Kamelin (1988) was of the opinion that they represent a single species. If this turns out to be true, priority goes to the name *I. subdecolorata*.

Soon we reached the top. Everywhere around the stony outcrops grew Juno irises, all very compact. This couldn't be *Iris tubergeniana*, because although the *Flora of the Soviet Union* described the species as only 10 cm tall, we had never seen it shorter than 15–20 cm, and it was usually up to 30 cm. Finally we found one plant with the dry remnants of a flower, which seemed bluish. The flowers of *I. orchioides* turn lilac when drying, but this isn't characteristic of *I. tubergeniana*. We hoped we had found one of the rarities we'd been searching for.

In drier and more exposed spots, *Eremurus regelii* was replaced by another species that hadn't started to flower yet. It had narrower leaves, long pedicels, and a sparse spike very elegant in shape. Unfortunately, it didn't grow for me back in Latvia. We also encountered a few alliums. All of the most common species from the surroundings of Tashkent grew here, as well as *Tulipa korolkowii*. This beautiful, small, bright red tulip flowers very early but has proved difficult to grow in my region, even in a greenhouse. It is always among the first to start growing in the greenhouse and is always seriously damaged by frost. Perhaps in a frost-free greenhouse it would be more successful.

The Many Relatives of *Iris orchioides*

The next day we headed to the Kuramin Ridge by way of Oudzhasai, where according to our map the motorway would lead quite far inside the mountains. It was not a very comfortable spot to visit since just along the top of the ridge lay the border with Tajikistan. Soldiers with submachine guns stood at the point where the road turned into the mountains, but since our car was fitted with special government plates, our driver didn't stop.

Where the road ended, the real Oudzhasai River began. Here many smaller streams coming down from the mountains flowed together, and we followed along a glen as we made our ascent.

We had gone only about a hundred meters when the first Juno iris appeared before us. A bit deeper in the shade it was still in full flower. It was an excellent form of typical *Iris orchioides*, the plant for which I would like to keep this name. Its flowers are creamy white with a large, deep yellow blotch on the falls, and the tips of the style branches are light yellow, giving the whole plant a slightly yellowish appearance. Most characteristic, however, is the very hairy ridge throughout the falls. The additional roots of this group of *I. orchioides* sensu lato are much thinner than those of the plants from Chimgan, and both are easy to distinguish even by their bulbs. The closest to it is the deep yellow form from the Kyrgyz Alatau that we named 'Kirghizian Gold' (Plate 90). The population that grows at Oudzhasai also reproduces extremely well vegetatively (Plate 127). We found clumps in full flower with more than fifteen individuals in each. They generally grow up to 30 cm tall. What was left for us was again just picking up the plants washed out of the soil by the strong stream.

Next we were stopped by a beautiful, small, deep red tulip. At first glance it seemed similar to *Tulipa vvedenskyi*, but as we looked more closely we saw that it was very different. The design on the inner base of the petals was small and unique in shape, shining black, sharply lined, and the leaves were very undulate. Some of the plants increased vegetatively, too. It seemed to be a very well known species, but even after returning home and comparing it with descriptions in Z. P. Botschantzeva's *Tulips* we couldn't identify it. It seems similar to *T. rosea*, but the flowers are deep red with a metallic shine, not pink at all. It most closely resembles *T. nitida*, but this species is taller and doesn't grow in the same area. So our mysterious tulip is still grown only under its collection number, *ARJA-0066* (Plate 128).

While I stayed with our belongings, Arnis went off to check the higher parts of the mountains where there was still snow. After an hour he returned with his hands full of flowers. The mountaintop had been a real paradise—the snow was melting, and flowers of *Colchicum luteum*, *Crocus alatavicus*, and all the adjacent plants were opening. He had found a fantastic form of *Fritillaria sewerzowii* with bright green flowers.

He also found a clump of *Paeonia hybrida*, a beautiful species (not a hybrid, despite its name) that grows in western Siberia and the mountainous areas of Central Asia. Some botanists lump it together with *P. anomala*. Two forms have been described. *Paeonia hybrida* var. *typica* has narrowly dissected leaves, while in variety *intermedia* the leaf lobes are wider. Both have very bright purplish red flowers with a nice aroma. My attempts to introduce this species a few years ago from Ihnachsai in the Pskem Valley failed. Most likely I overdried the rootstocks, but they do need the same treatment after collecting as *Eremurus* and *Delphinium* rootstocks. I've had more success in recent years. I grow it outside now, although it rarely flowers there; in the greenhouse the air is usually too dry, and the flowers soon get burned. I received variety *intermedia* from Sulev Savisaar in Estonia. It has very different leaves, and the long, somewhat rhizomatous roots with tuber-like thickenings are different from those of variety *typica*.

On the way home we dropped into Karanchitogai, where we found a blackish red form of *Allium karataviense*. Then we again headed toward the vicinity of Tashkent, but now in the direction of Gazalkent, still searching for Junos. As we drove through Tashkent, on the right side of the road we saw the residence of the president, a very large estate enclosed by a high concrete fence and surrounded by armored policemen holding submachine guns. The local people used to joke, "What a pity that the president doesn't drive very far away from his residence, because the only well-paved roads are the ones used by him." When the president decided to visit some village, the road to it was immediately repaired and covered with new asphalt. His summer residence was situated high in the mountains at the top of the gorge. A single road led to it, and it was strictly forbidden to even come close to that road. There were many secret police—many more, in fact, than there had been in the time of the KGB—so people kept their mouths shut. There was no opposition, since criticizing the president was strictly forbidden. Still, most ordinary people seemed to like their president enough, preferring to blame lower-level ministers, local bosses, and so forth.

The people of Uzbekistan could now be divided into two distinct classes: the extremely rich and the incredibly poor. Our driver's salary was considered good, but when I tipped him a hundred dollars, tears came to his eyes. It was the equivalent of a nine-month salary.

Volodya showed us his gerberas. He grew them from seed, so there were different types with smaller and larger blooms. Only gigantic flowers were in demand, however, and this was what he sold. I asked why he didn't sell the smaller blossoms at lower prices. He explained that only very rich people bought flowers, and price wasn't important to them. It meant nothing to pay fifteen dollars for a single lily stem. In fact, they usually bought two or three hundred cut flowers and paid enormous amounts of money for them. Those who were not so rich didn't buy flowers at all. They were so poor they even switched off the freezers in their kitchens to save money on electricity. We felt as though we had been thrown back fifteen years to the Soviet regime.

In Gazalkent we easily found the road to the mountains, and it appeared to be in good condition for our limousine. We managed to get quite high in the mountains up to an *arik* (irrigation stream) crossing the road. From here we would have to continue on foot. To our left was the deep valley of Aksakatasai. Its banks were formed by vertical limestone rocks from which gigantic cliffs had split off and rolled down into the stream. Here the primary rocks consisted of carbonates, which were covered with thinner or thicker layers of clay soil with stone admixture. The layer of fertile soil was very thin. Everywhere we looked we saw vegetative forms of *Tulipa bifloriformis*, which produce long, non-blooming stolons. In the garden these clones only very occasionally produce a flower and some seed. We also encountered ubiquitous *Eremurus regelii*, *Eminium lehmannii*, *Scilla puschkinioides*, *Corydalis ledebouriana*, *Eranthis longistipitata*, *Anemone petiolulosa*, *Geranium transversale*, and *Crocus alatavicus*.

Then we found another plant, something that grew everywhere here but that for some reason we hadn't noticed earlier. It was the tiny *Fritillaria stenanthera* (Plate 129), an excellent plant that grows perfectly in Latvian conditions both outside and in the greenhouse. Its leaves are grayish green. The flowers are very variable in color, intermediate between soft pink and bluish shades, and somewhat bell-shaped, flaring outward at the mouth. It grows up to 15 cm tall, likes full sun, and needs to rest in a dry location in summer. It is easy to propagate by breaking the bulb in two and also reproduces well from seed. Some forms have beautiful, bright, light pink flowers, while the flowers of others are a dirty bluish. There is a large circle of purple around the nectaries, the whole being a dark-centered star. The most beautiful forms come from Tovaksai, the second most beautiful from Chimgan. In the wild I have never seen more than three to five flowers on a stem, but when well established in the garden, plants are very floriferous, forming up to twenty-five blooms in a beautiful pyramidal inflorescence. The white form, selected by Czech gardeners, has ivory flowers and slightly yellowish green leaves. In my garden *F. stenanthera* grows in abundance. One of the clumps we found outside Gazalkent had as many as twenty-seven bulbs.

Again Arnis was the first to find *Iris kolpakowskiana*. Here it generally grew in clumps. Below the old sheets of a larger bulb, plenty of tiny bulblets, forming only thin, thread-like leaves, were hiding.

The surrounding landscape was typical for carbonates, with plenty of holes in the land, many deepening where the native rock had been washed away. Some holes had even become small, shallow lakes, and the top was scored with glens some 10–20 m deep. At the bottom of one of these glens we took a rest. I put my bag between clumps of *Iris kolpakowskiana* without even noticing them.

The Juno irises started there, too. The first one I found was *Iris orchioides* in full bloom. It was the same type we had seen the day before—whitish yellow with a very hairy crest. Arnis found a cluster with nice, completely yellow flowers. After a closer inspection it seemed to be the same *I. orchioides*, but with narrower wings. Digging around another, slightly lower specimen not in flower, I instantly recognized the roots of *I. tubergeniana*. Now it was clear that the specimen with completely yellow blossoms was most likely a hybrid between these two species. A. I. Vvedenskyi (1971) also mentions such plants. Later at home, forcing a bud, we saw that the bloom was indeed something between these two species, with wings that were less prominent than *I. orchioides* but not as narrow as *I. tubergeniana*. Any remaining doubt was dispelled by a closer investigation: the anthers were sterile, so this really was a natural interspecific hybrid.

Soon after this we were confronted by a large, rather frightening snake, so we decided it was time to leave. The air was very sultry and we were sweating enormously, but the way down went quite fast because the slope wasn't steep. This time we chose the lower path, as opposed to the way we had come up, and used the cattle passes on the steep bank of the river. At first we saw nothing new growing here, but then Arnis suddenly jumped up, shouting, "Look!" At the same moment we had both noticed a beautiful group of deep reddish pink *Geranium transversale*. In recent years we have had two spring and two summer expeditions to Central Asia. The last plant found on the previous spring expedition was the light pink form of *G. transversale* at Camel Mount in Tovaksai. This new deep pink form, the last plant found on this spring expedition, was an even better, brighter color. An excellent ending for our trip!

Pskem Valley

Two expeditions took place in the valley of the Pskem River, which is bordered on the north by the Ugam Range and Kazakhstan and in the northeast by the Pskem Range and Kyrgyzstan. On a map the Pskem Valley looks like a narrow tongue, jutting out of Uzbekistan and sandwiched between two neighboring states. Despite these odd borders, the Pskem Valley is mostly inhabited by Kazakhs and Kyrgyz. There were few problems in the area during Soviet times, but now there are bouts of rebellion, intrusions from neighboring states, and so forth. The local governments use the situation effectively to excuse the enormous size of the army and secret police. All our later attempts to enter this valley failed just because of the military situation—checkpoints kept strict control over everyone passing in and out, and foreigners were not allowed. Fortunately, we had succeeded in making our main discoveries shortly before the door had been closed.

Urungachsai

Our first expedition to Urungachsai inside the Ugam Range took place in 1997. It was a much celebrated trip, during which we had found *Iris winkleri*, but we had been so exhausted by the trek through the heights of Kugart that we knew we would need an easier route this time around. Arnis had also been here two years ago, with Victor Voronin from Alma-Ata. Although Urungachsai is only 170 km from Tashkent, it took three and a half hours to get there, and we used 120 liters of petrol traveling by nineteen-year-old Russian military jeep. The car would be back to pick us up the next day at four o'clock.

In the Urungachsai Gorge are two lakes formed some million years ago by a gigantic earthquake that blocked the stream with stones and landslides. The first lake is about 3 km from the main road. The traditional plants of the district grew here, including plenty of *Allium karataviense*, which we found on the bottom of a large scree slope. Arnis collected it on an earlier trip and it turned out to be a very unimpressive form with pale, dirty grayish white flowers. All the other samples in our collections are much more decorative.

When we reached the first lake we made tea and ate lunch. My legs seemed to remember the previous climb to Kugart. During our rest I collected the seeds of *Tulipa*, *Allium*, and *Fritillaria* species, which were now, at the very end of June, ripe. There were two types of tulips here: a small *Tulipa bifloriformis*–*T. turkestanica* type and *T. kaufmanniana*. *Tulipa kaufmanniana* was very uniform there, the flowers always white with the outer petals bluish pink at the back. It was a very tall-growing form; even in the wild it reached 40–50 cm tall at seed time. In the northern conditions of Latvia it reaches the same height at flowering and is the first tulip that can be harvested from an open field as a cut flower. My *T. kaufmanniana* 'Ugam' (Plate 130), which can also be propagated very well vegetatively, came from this location. It has been registered by Dutch nurseryman Jan Pennings under the name 'Icestick'. It is not only the tallest but also the most early-blooming form of *T. kaufmanniana* in my collection, with large, somewhat pointed white blooms and a large, deep golden yellow base of petals. The flower truly resembles a water lily, and the species has been nicknamed the water lily tulip.

The water in the lake was crystal clear and a marvelous shade of bluish green. At the other end of the lake, a very steep, zigzagging pass began by a natural stone dike somewhere high in the sky. We walked up slowly but without stopping, and it seemed that our ascent would never end. When we finally reached the top, a wonderful lake opened before our eyes, comparable in beauty to the Shing lakes in Tajikistan where I had found *Corydalis ruksansii*.

Although the walking was easier now, the path continued to lead up and down along a very steep bank of the lake. The only possible place for a tent was at the other end of the lake. We saw plenty of *Eremurus lactiflorus* (Plate 131) with large, round seedpods, as well as another small-flowering *Eremurus* species. Plants of *Fritillaria sewerzowii* and *Tulipa kaufmanniana* had seeds, but *Ungernia sewerzowii* was just starting to show its flower stems. On the side of the path was a grotto with beautiful *Scrophularia* species in full flower on its roof.

A short distance away I came across the first *Ungernia* just beginning to flower. It was the first time I had seen it blooming, but since only the first bloom had opened and my camera wasn't handy, I decided to take a picture on the way back. Unfortunately, as usual, when we returned to the area I couldn't find the plant.

We finally reached the other end of the lake, but our path stopped at the water. It was too deep to cross with our haversacks on, and although there was a green meadow only 5 m ahead, we had to pass another high rock crossing our road. I still wonder how we managed to avoid slipping down the side, which was incredibly steep in some spots. If that had happened it would have been a fall of 50–60 m and there would've been no hope of surviving.

The only good spot for our tent was next to the lake where the bank had been formed by sandy silt. Every other spot was covered with sharp stones. Our campsite was wonderful, a small, sandy meadow and a little spring with cold, fresh, clean water to drink. We took a short rest, bathed, drank some tea, ate raisins and nuts, and then went up by the riverside in search of bulbs.

There was no path, only larger or smaller stones interspersed with *Rosa*, *Rubus*, *Crataegus*, and *Berberis*, the common feature between all of them being their terrible thorns. It was very difficult to walk because the stones were so unstable—even a large stone, touched by a foot, could suddenly shift or tumble down. We couldn't grasp the nearest branch, either, or we'd be spending a good deal of time removing splinters and thorns from our hands.

The day was very hot, and plentiful *Tanacetum* species and other plants filled the air with an intoxicating aroma. We started feeling uncomfortable somehow, and decided to return to our tent. Arnis told me that years ago he and our Estonian friend Mart Veerus had been forced to return from a similar valley, so toxic was the air.

At our campsite we took some medicine, and Arnis, feeling quite sick, decided to lie down for a rest. A local man and his son arrived on a horse. He informed us that there was no road up by the main stream—if we wanted to reach the alpine meadows and the mountain pass at the border with Kazakhstan, we would have to walk up along the side gorge. Since it was not yet late, I decided to check the road. There was at least some kind of path, although it was almost invisible on the scree slopes.

Eremurus lactiflorus grew plentifully along the path, and I started to collect the seeds. When my bag was full, I decided to open a few of the seedpods. Alas, inside each seedpod was nothing but a fat caterpillar. Almost all the seedpods I had found were in the same condition—no seeds, only caterpillars. Only a few (no more than 0.1%) were undamaged. As a result I collected some rootstocks of this wonderful foxtail lily, although they were heavy and large.

I also collected a couple of bulbs of *Allium pskemense*, which I found growing in abundance on a scree slope. I had this species at home, but my plants were of unknown origin, and now I had the opportunity to replace them. *Allium pskemense* is a protected plant because the local people use it extensively for food (the man we had talked to at our campsite had a large sack full of *A. pskemense* bulbs). It grows well outside in my region. I most enjoy it in spring when its thick, cylindrical leaves come out of the soil looking like large fingers. It flowers in the second half of summer, with dense, globular, white flower heads on stems 80 cm–1 m tall. Those who enjoy spicy dishes can add the foliage to salads. The bulbs are elongated and thick, and when cooked they become very sweet.

Higher up I came across a meadow full of *Tanacetum* and could smell its intoxicating aroma. I decided to turn back, and a few steps lower I found a nice form of *Allium barsczewskii* with white flowers. The color wasn't very pure, but since I had searched so long for a white form for my collection, I was very happy. *Allium barsczewskii* is very variable in terms of size and flower color. I collected one of the best forms in 1982 not far from here in the valley of the Akbulak River on the opposite side of the Pskem Range. It has upward-facing, bright reddish purple flowers that bloom in early summer on a 40 cm stem. It is one of the brightest forms of the species. It is not a difficult species, whether growing outside or in a greenhouse. It grows and reproduces well, forming several bulbs on a short rhizome. Division of the clumps must be done carefully, however, to avoid splitting them too much. I usually prefer to leave a couple of bulbs together.

At the camp we had nothing more than some tea with a slice of bread, then took some medicine and crept into our sleeping bags. Our legs still hurt from our trek through Kugart.

The next morning I woke up very early. We both felt much better than we had the previous evening. After breakfast we set out to find the form of *Iris orchioides* sensu lato that Arnis had collected here two years before. This is a wonderful dwarf form, keeping its habit even in Latvian conditions, with up to three big, light creamy blooms with a large, bright yellow blotch on the falls. Plants from this location have thin roots but are quite dwarf compared with forms from southeast of Chimgan. The crest on the falls is toothed, becoming hairy only on the haft in the throat.

In my opinion, all the forms of *Iris orchioides* sensu lato that I have grown can be divided into four types (including only plants from places I have visited myself). The first type includes plants from northeast of Chimgan (Urungachsai). These are dwarf irises with creamy flowers, a crest that is hairy only on the haft, and thin additional roots. (Plants from Aksakatasai are very similar but taller.) The second type, from south of Chimgan (Bashkizilsai, Oudzhasai, Rezaksai), includes tall plants with creamy flowers, a crest that is hairy throughout, and thin additional roots. The third type comes from the Kyrgyz Alatau and includes tall plants with bright yellow flowers, a crest that is hairy throughout, and thick additional roots. The fourth type represents a new species that I called *I. pseudocapnoides*. Its blooms are white or whitish with an entire crest. It is a tall plant and has thick and long additional roots. Its closest relative is *I. capnoides*, a tall plant with smoky bluish flowers, an entire crest, and thick but comparatively shorter additional roots.

At Urungachsai, *Iris orchioides* grows in the upper part of the right bank where the soil is rockier and drier and where the grass is not so dense. We decided to follow along a cattle path to pass all the side ravines. This tactic proved to be right—quite soon, not too tired, we would arrive at the place where two years ago Arnis had found this tiny Juno. To get there, however, we had to pass through large grassy fields covered in nettles (*Urtica urens*) more than 1.5 m high. An abundance of *Dictamnus* and *Prangos* species grew there, too, both of which can be quite dangerous if you touch the foliage. Arnis later developed a rash on his hands, probably from the *Prangos* species, but it was not very serious.

Soon the slope became steeper and we saw the first *Iris orchioides*. These plants were generally small, but some had ripe seeds, which we collected. We also noticed a group of very beautiful forms of *Allium barsczewskii* ranging in color from the purest snow white to a nice soft pink. The plants were taller than those I had seen the day before, and of a very clean shade. This would be the origin of 'Pink Cloud', with beautiful, clean, light pink flowers on a long stem, and 'Snowcap' (Plate 133), with pure snow white flowers—excellent additions to my large allium collection.

Ihnachsai

The last place in the vicinity of Chimgan that Arnis and I visited in 1998 was just on the opposite side of the Pskem Valley. It was a gorge and a river named Ihnachsai, starting somewhat higher than the village of Pskem and going deep into the Pskem Range, where there is a lake similar to the one in Urungachsai. Our target was another Juno species: *Iris albomarginata* (Plate 134), or *I. caerulea* as it is sometimes called. Plants under this name had already been offered in the trade for a long time, but these were very different from the true *I. albomarginata*—quite often they weren't *I. albomarginata* at all, but *I. zenaidae* or some similar hybrid. Our biggest problem was that *I. albomarginata* had been described as coming from a plant collected during Boris Fedchenko's expedition of August 1903 near a place named Sjemesas. Where exactly this Sjemesas was located we didn't know: we couldn't find the name even on our very detailed military maps. Arnis had to study herbaria of the Fedchenko expeditions thoroughly, paying a lot of attention to the dates, to even just roughly determine where this Sjemesas could be. He ultimately concluded it was somewhere around Ihnachsai and Lake Ihnachkul.

It was a very dramatic route, and we decided to begin with a day's rest. Unfortunately, during this time I became very ill. I was terribly exhausted and stricken by the most dreadful bout of diarrhea, accompanied by vomiting and a high fever. Only after a couple of days did I finally wake feeling more alive than dead. The trip would have to wait until I recovered.

Finally I was able to begin cleaning the seeds we had collected during the previous days. The seeds of *Iris magnifica* were the best; though the pods seemed not yet fully mature, the seeds inside them were ripe, and only one pod had been invaded by a caterpillar. By contrast, from the *I. warleyensis* we had collected in the same place, only two or three pods were undamaged. If we hadn't cleaned them now, later on at home we would have found only empty dry husks. The seeds of *I. vicaria* from Sina were comparatively good, but the *I. rosenbachiana* seeds had been very much nibbled by some other pest.

We talked over our route. We would try to drive as far as the village of Pskem (1400 m above sea level), traveling again by Russian military jeep. We hoped to cross the Pskem River and drive further into the mountains some 20–25 km, moving along the Ihnachsai River as far as Lake Ihnachkul, camp there, and then walk to the pass at Sarvaitugan (3594 m). According to the map the pass was open from July to September, and the road led up to the lake. (As usual, the map was wrong—an animal track was marked as a motorway.)

The jeep arrived at seven o'clock and off we went. Since I hadn't recovered yet, the brother of Volodya's daughter-in-law came along as a porter. The Pskem road had just been reconstructed following a downpour; if we had arrived several days earlier we wouldn't have been able to make it through. We had hardly crossed the bridge when our car stopped—the overheated brakes had gotten stuck. Fortunately, water and bottles were both close at hand. We poured water over the wheels, which hissed in response. When the brakes had cooled, we continued on our way.

We reached Urungachsai, where we had been a year ago, passed one more village, and finally arrived at Pskem. We successfully crossed the Pskem River but then came to another bridge that was in such bad shape that our jeep couldn't cross it. We would have to cover the rest of the road on foot. Soon a heavy rain started that turned the road into slippery clay mud. Walking became a torture.

At length we came to an apiary. I was dead beat, still recovering from diarrhea and fever, so when the beekeeper invited us for tea, I agreed instantly, although we usually tried to turn down invitations of that kind. We were treated to tea and last year's honey, and our host described the road conditions ahead. Arnis asked if he knew where Sjemesas was. It turned out we were basically there already. To the right was Kensai, to the left, Ihnachsai, and right in the middle was Sjemesas. This was superb news. It meant that Arnis had scored a direct hit.

The road continued to be difficult—covered in grass as tall as a man and paved with sloppy clay. There was no place to pitch a tent or even rest, so we slowly moved ahead. In the grass grew plenty of *Tulipa kaufmanniana*, half a meter tall, with big seed capsules, the bulk of which had rot damage because of the excessive moisture. *Fritillaria sewerzowii* also grew very tall here, with half-rotten seed bolls. *Eremurus regelii* and *Allium motor* grew everywhere, in full bloom.

We reached a steeper slope with grittier soil, so our feet stopped sliding back at each step, but there was still no place flat enough for camping. Eventually we found a more or less suitable spot along a small ridge, and pitched our tent there. While I went to look for some water for supper, tireless Arnis decided to run about along the slopes. Not far from here were some rather steep, bare rock outcrops. My path went through very long grass up to the snow bed, below which water flowed out. I wanted to take a shortcut, so I turned straight off the path. Surprisingly, the long grass had masked a short but very steep landslide, and I fell some 2 m into a damp bog—the source of a spring. Now I was completely wet. I was rewarded, though, when I found a peculiar *Allium* species growing here. It was *A. kaufmannii* (Plate 137), more than a meter tall, a species with big, somewhat grayish white flowers that later turn a bit pinkish. It is a close relative of *A. fedtschenkoanum*, which we had collected in Kugart, but is much more beautiful, with thinner leaves and unusually long (4–5 cm) petals. In a word it is fantastic. We didn't have any knowledge of this species' life cycle, however. It was the dampness of its origin that worried us the most—was it damp here year-round? And what happened in winter? Did snow pile up here? If so, the ground might not freeze at all and might remain very wet all the time. But what happened in the second half of summer when the rains stopped? Did the spring exist in summer, too? This species remains very rare in Central Asia because of its very specific ecology. There are not so many bogs.

On his own wandering, Arnis found a Reticulata iris. The bulb tunic was reticulate and the bulb was very light in color, almost white. We were rather high in the mountains, around 2800 m, so it couldn't be *Iris kolpakowskiana*, a typical foothill species. It also couldn't be *I. winkleri*, which we had found a year before, since that species has a longitudinally fibrous tunic (besides, it grew very far from here and was ecologically isolated). Was it possible we had found a new Central Asian Reticulata iris species? Even if it turned out to be *I. kolpakowskiana*, finding this species at such an altitude would be sensational enough. A foothill species growing as high as 3000 m! I would hardly believe it.

The species distinction in Central Asian Reticulata irises is much complicated by the great morphological similarity, especially in the flowers. However, when the iris from Ihnachsai bloomed the following spring, we could see that the shape and overall look of the flower were very special, and it could not be lumped together with other species. I decided to name it *I. pskemense* (Plate 138).

It may be helpful to describe the similarities and differences between *Iris kolpakowskiana* sensu lato, *I. winkleri*, and *I. pskemense*.

In *Iris kolpakowskiana* sensu lato, the bulb tunic is reticulate and the bulb is bright yellow, rarely somewhat lighter. The flowers are generally lilac-tinted and medium-sized. The standards are uniformly colored, lilac, and widely lanceolate; the falls are concolorous purple; and the ridge on the falls is yellow (Alma-Ata) or white (Tashkent). It grows in the foothills, up to 1000 m (Komarov 1935). In the wild it reproduces by small bulbils, which are often produced in large groups, sometimes singly.

In *Iris winkleri*, the bulb tunic is longitudinally fibrous and the bulb is white. The flowers are generally lilac-tinted and larger than in any of the other species. The standards are uniformly colored, lilac, and widely lanceolate; the falls are concolorous bluish purple to purple; and the ridge on the falls is yellow. This species grows in alpine meadows at 3000–4000 m (Komarov 1935). It rarely produces bulbils and sometimes splits, usually in two.

In *Iris pskemense*, the bulb tunic is reticulate and the bulb is cream to light yellow. Its flowers, which are generally bluish-tinted, are the smallest of all. The standards are bluish, sometimes darker veined or even white, narrowly lanceolate, and generally twisted. The falls are purple distinctly rimmed with white and the ridge on the falls is yellow. This iris grows on rocky slopes and in sparse grass among stones at 2500–3000 m. In the wild it reproduces by splitting and by producing bulbils, usually in small groups.

We originally planned on visiting another area not far from Ihnachsai but had to cancel this portion of the trip because of my illness. It would have taken us to the upper reaches of the Angren River, where *Iris winkleri* might possibly have been collected in the past. However, the herbarium specimen of this so-called *I. winkleri* was in bad condition and its identity in serious doubt. We could be almost certain that the plants from the Pskem Valley were identical to those from the neighboring upper reaches of the Angren. They didn't grow too far from each other, and the conditions in both places were rather similar. The supposed *I. winkleri* was surely identical to the iris we had collected at Ihnachsai (*I. pskemense*).

The next morning I headed down to the spring, where I found a corydalis blooming. It looked somewhat similar to *Corydalis glaucescens* but with very different foliage and flower color. All the samples of this species that I had collected earlier had very round leaf lobes, but here the leaf lobes were very long and lanceolate. The leaf division in *Corydalis* can vary a lot, but such extremes are more characteristic of species from the Russian Far East. Even more, the flowers were yellowish pink with a very prominent, long, dark crest on the upper petal, and these plants were growing outside the area where *C. glaucescens* was recognized. In my opinion, this form is at least a new subspecies of *C. glaucescens*, if not a new species. I offer it as *C. glaucescens* aff. 'Ihnatchsai' (Plate 139).

We walked up along a hardly visible path, naively hoping to spot Lake Ihnachkul from the ridge. Here and there *Tulipa greigii* leaves came into sight. Fortunately, the soil structure became more gravelly, so our feet did not slip so much. When we reached the ridge we realized we wouldn't be able to see the lake. *Eremurus lactiflorus* and a species of *Anemone* very similar to *A. narcissiflora* bloomed impressively all around. While I took pictures of a perfect specimen of *Paeonia hybrida*, Arnis found *Corydalis darwasica*. Now the path went downward, crossing semi-bare gravelly spots and stone outcrops, some covered in large junipers. Below the junipers were some Juno irises, but they had finished flowering long ago. In Arnis's opinion these were the same dwarf *I. orchioides* sensu lato from the opposite side of the Pskem Valley. I thought they looked too large, but classification was impossible without the flowers.

Arnis, who was walking a little ahead of me, soon stopped again, shouting triumphantly, "*Iris albomarginata*! In bloom!" Indeed, there it was—a charming specimen with its last flower in bloom, a flower that would fade within a day. I photographed it from all sides, and the camera lens provided an enlarged view, so I was able to study all the flower parts. The flower was light blue with a small, rather narrow white blotch with blue veining. The crest was conspicuously serrated and white with a narrow violet-blue rim. In this last respect the plant was similar to *I. zenaidae* from Kugart, yet the bloom and plant habit were different, and the crest was not hairy enough. Without a doubt, we had collected *I. albomarginata*. This was its type locality.

A snow bridge took us over the raging Ihnachsai River. A very steep but fortunately stony slant in front of us led to the top of the next ridge, where we found a more or less horizontal meadow covered in extremely long grass. We decided to camp here. At the side of the path we found fantastically tall (exceeding 1 m) specimens of *Fritillaria sewerzowii*. Moreover, we noticed that the species had reproduced vegetatively—we found several groups with three stems emerging from the same place. I had never seen anything like this in either the wild or the garden. In the garden we multiplied *F. sewerzowii* only by seed or cuttings. This form continued increasing well for me in Latvia, too; it is the only clone with this feature.

On the riverbank we found a lot of *Iris albomarginata* plants that were 2–3 m away from one another, most of them in flower. Arnis supposed they had been brought down by avalanches or scree from the upper heights. This was confirmed when we found among them a specimen of *Allium carolinianum*.

Iris albomarginata is quite variable here. The flowers are lighter and darker blue, but the most distinct feature is the intensity of the blue design on the falls. The darkest ones somewhat resemble the lightest *I. zenaidae* in color, but otherwise they are very different plants. The wings of *I. albomarginata* are less distinct and the leaves not as bright as in *I. zenaidae*. In general it is almost half as tall, although some plants produce up to five flowers even in the wild. Moreover, the shade of blue in *I. albomarginata* is somewhat pale or even dull in some forms, while *I. zenaidae* is a very bright, deep blue.

At half past five we returned to the tent and I began to make supper. We talked over the acquisitions of the day. They weren't many but were very valuable. In Arnis's opinion we had found the key plant of the expedition: *Iris albomarginata*.

I spent a very restless night. I awoke around four o'clock but didn't get up until it was light out, so as not to disturb Arnis. On the whole I still felt rather bad both mentally and physically. When I was finally able to crawl out of the tent, I went off to collect the gigantic *Fritillaria sewerzowii* at the side of the path.

Later in the day on our ascent—which was excruciating for me, as I was still worn out—we spotted a beautiful group of *Iris korolkowii* (Plate 141), an excellent species from the Regelia group. This iris is easily recognized by the shape of its flower and absence of beard on its standards, as well as by the way it forms thick, short-branched rhizomes. It is easy to grow in a frame or greenhouse. I grew it successfully outside for years, too, but it was not so floriferous. Like the other rhizomatous species from the Regelia and Oncocyclus groups, as well as their hybrids, *I. korolkowii* needs a good summer rest in a hot place. When I was growing it outside, after harvesting I usually kept the rhizomes in the greenhouse, where the temperature sometimes got up to 40°C during the day, and planted them very late, when the soil had started to freeze, to keep them from sprouting too early. In a well-drained hot spot, this iris can be grown even without replanting for two or three years, as I do in my greenhouses. The form from Ihnachsai has somewhat grayish white flowers with heavy brown-purple veining.

At the top of the ridge we decided to hide our bags and walk up the following ridge. We had walked only a short distance when *Iris albomarginata* suddenly appeared all over the place. They were outstanding specimens, and as we climbed higher we found even more of them, growing in great density only several centimeters from one another. Excellent forms of *Tulipa kaufmanniana*, mostly with bright red flowers, grew among them, creating a colorful carpet. Arnis found a pure golden yellow specimen of *T. kaufmanniana* without any red dots at the base and without any pinkish shading on the exterior petals. Nothing like it had ever been seen before. He also found a unique wild hybrid between *T. dasystemon* and *T. bifloriformis*, and I soon spotted a large group of *I. pskemense*. It had reproduced well vegetatively. The bulbs were light yellowish with conspicuously reticulate tunics. I collected the seedpods. A little further on, a wonderful *Fritillaria sewerzowii* was in full bloom; all were dark brown, with petals that were only occasionally somewhat greenish at the tip. To celebrate our luck, we decided to make a mountaineers' ice cream using condensed milk mixed with sugar and snow—a real delicacy.

We compared what we had collected to our findings from last year's expedition at Urungachsai, not far from here (in fact, we could see the entry into the Urungachsai Gorge from our camp only 10–15 km from here, on the other side of Pskem). We did not find any *Iris albomarginata* on that previous trip, and on this trip we had found no *I. orchioides*, which grew as densely at Urungachsai as *I. albomarginata* did here. Maybe at Urungachsai we simply had not climbed as high as *I. albomarginata* grows, and perhaps here we had searched too little at lower altitudes. *Tulipa kaufmanniana* plants found on either side of the Pskem were also different in color, though again I should mention that here we saw late-flowering highland forms; it may be that the plants below us with seed capsules were the same white-rose ones we saw at Urungachsai. Now I completely agreed with Arnis's opinion that those *I. albomarginata* specimens we had found the day before on the bed of a tributary of the Ihnachsai were most likely brought down by landslides and could not spread about very much because of the competing vegetation. Even in the most favorable places they grew apart from each other at a distance of 2–3 m, and the population on the whole was rather small. At the same time, on the top of the side ridge at about 2800–3000 m, where the competition was not so intense, *I. albomarginata* flourished. Moreover, they only grew on northern and western slopes. As we walked along the ridge, we saw *I. albomarginata* growing on the right (NNW and NW exposure) but not on the left (SE exposure), while tulips grew on either side of the ridge.

On our drive to Tashkent, Arnis spotted several withered stalks of Juno (*Iris* aff. *orchioides*) on a roadside wall. (How he ever notices such things remains a mystery to me.) We wondered how we could get to them. The slope was extremely steep, and the sunbaked gritty clay was hard as stone. Propping himself against a few stones, Arnis crept up some 6–7 m, while I tried to follow him. The first thing he passed me was an *Allium karataviense* umbel with half-scattered seeds. Its bulb had been eaten by caterpillars. As he worked, small stones came rattling down along the wall, and I marveled at how my colleague was able to hold onto this nearly vertical surface, all the while plucking out the Junos. The tuberous roots were especially long and fleshy, but almost every bulb had been damaged by caterpillars, although it seemed they would survive. I managed to creep my way to one plant and managed to gather its seeds. That was all I was able to do, because I soon lost my footing and quietly slid to the bottom. We felt content that we had saved these plants, which had clearly slid down here from higher areas. They would have soon been washed away by rain or buried by bulldozers. The plants we had collected turned out to be *I. pseudocapnoides*, which we had seen growing in Chimgan, but this form was slightly different in shade and had a slightly larger yellow blotch around the crest. (In both forms the blotch is very small.)

On the roadside I bought a liter of homemade *kumis*, a drink made from curdled mare's milk. It was the best thing I could do to rebuild the natural microflora in my digestive system after taking such strong medicine. It worked perfectly, and I returned home in good health.

Zeravshan Mountains

Iris magnifica Kingdom

The Zeravshan Mountain Range begins with the highest peaks of Pamir in northern Tajikistan, stretches west into the sands of the Kyzyl-Kum ("red sands" in Uzbek) and Kara-Kum ("black sands" in Turkmen) deserts, and in the northwest turns into the Nuratau Range of Uzbekistan.

The late Pastor Ludvigs Sidrēvics, a good friend of mine, joined me on my expedition to this area. When we first met, he was a well-known bulb grower and had started breeding and selecting new varieties of tulips. His main focus was *Tulipa fosteriana*, about which John M. C. Hoog wrote: "Is it not somewhat humiliating to consider, that we in Western Europe after more than three centuries of careful cultivation are not able to produce anything that can match this Bokhara tulip growing wild on the mountain slopes there?" (cited by J. F. Ch. Dix in the Royal Horticultural Society's *Daffodil and Tulip Year Book* of 1951–1952). To find his starting material, Ludvigs traveled to Central Asia, where he collected thousands of *Tulipa fosteriana* bulbs. From those he selected many nice varieties, which unfortunately seem to have been lost since his death. I once grew some of his best findings at my nursery, but when I was reducing my collection these were sold to other growers, and I don't know whether they are still grown.

When Ludvigs turned sixty he wanted to celebrate his birthday with a last trip to the mountains, thinking himself too old for many more such adventures. Having heard about my interest and previous excursion, he suggested we create a team that would include Āris Krūmiņš. Āris was the top bulb forcer in Latvia in those years. In the days before computers, he developed an automatic device with artificial lights that allowed him to force bulbs on multi-level racks in his house even when he was absent for several days. So with our team of three persons, we visited the Agalik Valley, where many years ago Ludvigs had started his *T. fosteriana* program.

Now when I read my diaries from those early years, I can only smile. I had so little knowledge, and even the simplest plants produced ecstasy in my heart. On one page I wrote, "Found a rootstock of the foxtail lilies with three stems. This means that *Eremurus* sp. also reproduces vegetatively in natural conditions." This and everything else was new to me then. What a pity I cannot decode exactly what species is hidden under those two letters, *sp.*, following the generic name.

We reached Agalik in the afternoon after a short flight to Samarkand. Everything had changed since Ludvigs's previous trips, and he could not find the house where he had lived then. But all our problems were solved by the traditional hospitality of the local people, who soon surrounded us—we seemed to look quite exotic here. We accepted an invitation to tea from a local teacher, who lived in a large house with a beautiful orchard, an arik (small irrigation canal) flowing through the garden, and a beautiful green lawn where a few sheep worked as lawnmowers. In the evening we all had tea and raisins. The patriarch of the family, a very old man with a long white beard and a chalma (cotton turban, traditional headgear for men), was reading the Qur'an in Arabic. It was the first time I had seen Arabic script and text running right to left.

We started at five o'clock in the morning. Just as we left, Āris drank a cup of water, and our host shook his head in disapproval—it is not a good thing to drink water in the morning. I learned this well during my first trip. If you start drinking water in the morning, you will feel thirsty all day long. You will drink and drink, and the result will be endless sweating. You will be tired in the evening, too, because your body will have lost a lot of salt. If, on the other hand, you can overcome your initial thirst, it will eventually disappear and the day will pass without any problems. This isn't a very easy rule to follow, but in my experience it always works.

We were accompanied by a group of villagers with four donkeys. The landscape was beautiful, with nice valleys and rounded knolls crossed by several streams. Each stream had its own name. One was called Obdorsai—from *obdor*, meaning "water," and *sai*, "stream." I encountered the first Juno irises in a meadow in the valley. The bulb lay very deep in the alluvial sand; it had clearly been washed down by spring waters from somewhere higher in the mountains. I later found that it was *Iris svetlaneae*, one of the most beautiful yellow-flowering Juno irises of Central Asia.

After walking for half an hour along a stream, we came to the Devshara (Devil's) Waterfall. It was about 10 m high, the main fall plunging into a large basin composed of hollowed-out granite. In some areas the water cascaded from a higher basin into the basin just below it, and then into the next one, and the next, some five times over. The water was crystal clear, and we could see large salmon trout in the basins. A profusion of *Tulipa fosteriana* (Plate 144) in full flower sprang from the cracks in the rocks, and lush clumps of magnificent *Arum korolkowii* grew lower down in the wet peaty clay.

PLATE 143. At Agalik our team was accompanied by several local people

PLATE 144. The local teacher who accompanied us stands amidst clumps of *Tulipa fosteriana*

PLATE 145. *Iris magnifica*, which my friends liked to call the "corn iris"

PLATE 146. *Allium oreophilum* 'Kusavli Curl' from the neighboring Turkestan Mountains

PLATE 147. At Agalik *Crocus korolkowii* is at its most variable. This form is called 'Yellow Tiger

PLATE 148. Posing with a "yellow belly"

PLATE 149. A clump of *Iris warleyensis* with a white mutation

PLATE 150. Did I find a white mutation of *Crocus korolkowii* or was this an unlikely combination of *C. korolkowii* and *C. alatavicus*?

PLATE 151. *Allium protensum* is often misidentified as *A. schubertii*

PLATE 152. *Corydalis maracandica*, a spectacular Central Asian species with perennial tubers

PLATE 153. *Tulipa butkovii*—was it worth the risk?

PLATE 154. Crossing the Akbulak River to reach *Tulipa butkovii*

PLATE 155. Mari Kits, myself, and Āris Krūmiņš at our camp at Shing

PLATE 156. The "bridge" leading to our camp at Shing

PLATE 157. *Iris svetlaneae* is among the most beautiful yellow-flowering Juno irises

PLATE 158. The color of the petal exterior is extremely variable in *Colchicum kesselringii*. Here is one of the darkest forms

PLATE 159. *Tulipa ingens* is very similar to *T. fosteriana* but can be distinguished by the glossy black base of its petals

PLATE 160. The second lake at Shing

PLATE 161. A dwarf form of *Iris warleyensis*

PLATE 162. *Corydalis ruksansii* as I found it at Shing

PLATE 163. *Corydalis ruksansii* is among the most floriferous species in the garden

PLATE 164. *Allium nevskianum* is a typical plant of scree slopes

PLATE 165. The spectacular *Allium sarawschanicum* 'Chinoro'

PLATE 166. *Iris vicaria* is one of the easiest Juno irises in the garden

PLATE 167. 'Tony' is a greenish yellow form of *Iris bucharica* from southern Tajikistan

PLATE 168. *Iris rosenbachiana* 'Varzob'

PLATE 169. A deep purple form of *Iris rosenbachiana* from Tovilj-Dara

PLATE 170. *Iris rosenbachiana* 'Harangon'

PLATE 171. The most early-blooming form of *Iris rosenbachiana* comes from Vahsh and has yellow anthers

PLATE 172. The wild form of *Tulipa praestans* usually has only one flower on its stem

PLATE 173. *Tulipa hissarica* is the most early-blooming tulip in my garden

PLATE 174. An excellent white form of *Iris hoogiana* from the Varzob Valley

PLATE 175. The mountains at Zaamin

PLATE 176. *Eremurus kaufmannii* is among the most beautiful and most difficult foxtail lilies

PLATE 177. *Allium alexejanum* grows on almost nude, sunbaked clay slopes

PLATE 178. An albino form of *Gentiana olivieri* grows among traditional deep blue forms

PLATE 179. *Iris tadshikorum* from Zaamin

PLATE 180. *Pseudosedum fedtschenkoanum* has tuber-like roots and can be grown like a bulb

PLATE 181. *Allium elburzense*

PLATE 182. *Allium haemanthoides*

PLATE 183. *Allium minutiflorum*

PLATE 184. *Allium shelkovnikovii*

PLATE 185. The best form of *Scilla puschkinioides* comes from Sina

PLATE 186. Flowers of *Iris stolonifera* at Sina, Uzbekistan, have the most fantastic colors

PLATE 187. The most beautiful form of *Geranium charlesii* has leaves streaked with reddish purple

PLATE 188. Sina is the type locality of *Iris parvula*

PLATE 189. The bright red *Tulipa carinata* from the heights of Sina grows well in my garden

PLATE 190. *Tulipa orithyioides* is easy to identify by its elongated style

PLATE 191. *Corydalis nudicaulis* is known as the coffee and cream corydalis

PLATE 192. *Corydalis ledebouriana* from Sina is the most late-blooming form in the garden

PLATE 193. *Eremurus aitchisonii* is similar to *E. robustus* but has glossy green leaves

PLATE 194. The fritillary of section *Rhinopetalum* that was found at Pulkhakim is so unique that I still can't decide whether it is *Fritillaria karelinii*, *F. bucharica*, or a new species

PLATE 195. The flower heads of *Allium baissunense* look like fireworks exploding in the sky

PLATE 197. True *Iris maracandica* from the Nuratau Range

PLATE 196. The creamy yellow *Delphinium semi-barbatum* isn't a bulb but has a strong rootstock and requires similar conditions

PLATE 198. We found this very unusual *Allium* species at Timurlan Gate

PLATE 199. *Iris narbutii* has trouble surviving in my region, where it usually blooms too early

PLATE 200. The light form of *Iris hippolytii*

PLATE 201. The dark form of *Iris hippolytii*

PLATE 202. The most beautiful forms of *Tulipa vvedenskyi* have undulate leaves

PLATE 203. Local boys selling *Tulipa vvedenskyi* blooms at the roadside

PLATE 204. The other form of *Iris hippolytii*

PLATE 205. *Allium oschaninii* grows in small pockets on an almost vertical rocky cliff

PLATE 206. Arnis Seisums at Kugart

PLATE 207. In gardens *Iris zenaidae* is usually grown under the name *I. albomarginata*

PLATE 208. One of the loveliest late-flowering alliums, *Allium carolinianum*

PLATE 209. *Tulipa dasystemon* is a valid species but the name is sometimes also applied to *T. tarda*

PLATE 210. After some hundred years, *Iris winkleri* has again found its way into gardens

PLATE 211. The heights of Kugart, where *Iris winkleri* grows

PLATE 212. *Allium gypsaceum* is a tiny allium with a very large flower head

PLATE 213. *Allium verticillatum* has very thin, grass-like leaves and a large inflorescence

PLATE 214. The best forms of *Iris warleyensis* grow in the Kugitang Mountains

PLATE 216. *Fritillaria olgae* reaches up to 60 cm tall and is a good grower in my region, even outside

PLATE 215. The Juno iris collected at the type locality of *Iris vvedenskyi* is very different from the original description of this species

PLATE 217. *Corydalis solida* subsp. *subremota* provides a link between the European *C. solida* and the Far Eastern *C. turtschaninovii*

PLATE 218. The spectacular *Corydalis bracteata* is an excellent grower

PLATE 219. *Erythronium sibiricum* is a Siberian representative of the Eurasian dog's-tooth violets

PLATE 220. I call this form *Erythronium sibiricum* subsp. *altaicum*

PLATE 221. *Erythronium sibiricum* subsp. *sulevii* is easy to distinguish by its black anthers

PLATE 222. *Erythronium japonicum* also has black anthers, but its filaments are of different lengths

PLATE 223. *Corydalis fumariifolia* has very bright blue flowers

PLATE 224. *Corydalis turtschaninovii* flowers later in Latvia than other blue species

PLATE 225. *Corydalis turtschaninovii* 'Eric the Red'

PLATE 226. The blue-flowered form of *Corydalis ornata* with very narrow, even somewhat thread-like leaf segments

PLATE 227. The white-flowered *Corydalis ornata* 'Blue Lip' resembles a Christmas tree covered in snow

PLATE 228. *Corydalis buschii* is the last of the spring-flowering corydalis to bloom in my garden

PLATE 229. *Corydalis gorinensis* is known from a single locality only half a square kilometer in size

PLATE 230. *Corydalis magadanica* is more widely distributed than *C. gorinensis* and much easier in the garden

PLATE 231. *Fritillaria verticillata* 'Kara-Sumbe' is very similar to the Chinese *F. yuminensis*

PLATE 232. Except for its color, *Fritillaria verticillata* from Urdzhar, Kazakhstan, has a different flower shape and resembles the Chinese *F. tortifolia*

PLATE 233. *Fritillaria walujewii* is more difficult in the garden and in the wild grows from northwestern China to Tajikistan and Uzbekistan

PLATE 234. To me the double form of *Fritillaria pallidiflora* 'Flore Plena' is more curious than beautiful

PLATE 235. *Fritillaria dagana* has only one rosette of leaves and forms underground stolons up to 10 cm long

PLATE 236. *Fritillaria maximowiczii* has petals that are toothed at the edge

PLATE 237. The flowers of *Fritillaria ussuriensis* are carried on a long, thin stem that in the wild is supported by surrounding shrubs

PLATE 238. *Fritillaria camschatcensis* grows in a very large area on both sides of the Pacific Ocean

PLATE 239. *Fritillaria camschatcensis* 'Lutea', a very rare yellow form

PLATE 240. *Fritillaria davidii* is one of the most unusual frits, forming flowers on a leafless stem

PLATE 241. *Fritillaria meleagroides* 'Giant' comes from the Penza region

PLATE 242. The form of *Fritillaria meleagroides* from the Ukraine is much smaller

PLATE 243. The flowers of *Fritillaria ruthenica* are superficially similar to those of *F. meleagroides* but feature winged capsules

PLATE 244. *Trillium camschatcense* is the most excellent white-blooming Asian trillium

PLATE 245. *Trillium kurabayashii* is the best-growing trillium in my collection

PLATE 246. The almost leafless blooms of *Symplocarpus foetidus* can be a surprise as they come out of the soil in early spring

PLATE 247. *Arisaema amurense* is among the hardiest early-blooming arisaemas in the garden

PLATE 248. What was once known as *Arisaema robustum* is now considered a synonym of *A. amurense*, although it has more robust foliage

PLATE 249. *Arisaema flavum* is self-sowing and grows like a weed in my garden

PLATE 250. *Arisaema fargesii* is surprisingly hardy but needs deep planting

PLATE 251. *Iris stenophylla* is among the most beautiful irises but requires greenhouse treatment

PLATE 252. "The goddess of Junos" from Turkey, a new species similar to *Iris stenophylla*

PLATE 253. *Iris pamphylica* is almost extinct in nature

PLATE 254. *Colchicum variegatum* has wide-open blooms even in bad weather

PLATE 255. A greenish white form of *Iris persica* found near Gaziantep (collection number *BATM-017*)

PLATE 256. An ash gray form of *Iris persica* from Ulukişla (collection number *RIGA-061*)

PLATE 257. A yellow population of *Iris galatica* from the roadside between Kayseri and Sivas (collection number *RUDA-067*)

PLATE 258. A reddish purple form of *Iris persica* growing near the village of Yavca (collection number *RUDA-135*)

PLATE 259. *Iris galatica* locality

PLATE 260. *Anemone blanda* at the Belpinar pass

PLATE 261. An ancient Roman tomb at Demircili resembles a small-scale version of the Leaning Tower of Pisa

PLATE 262. The flower spathe of *Arum dioscoridis* can vary from solidly deep purple to white-spotted

PLATE 263. *Iris caucasica* subsp. *turcica* is quite easy in cultivation

PLATE 264. The flower head of *Allium myrianthum* is composed of hundreds of small, pure white flowers

PLATE 266. A new locality for *Biarum eximium* or a new species?

PLATE 265. A Kurdish farmer shows Guna how to find food in the mountains

PLATE 267. An unusually colored form of *Iris paradoxa* f. *choschab*

PLATE 268. *Muscari polyanthum*

PLATE 269. *Bellevalia rixii* on the Czug pass

PLATE 270. The best forms of *Allium akaka* have bright pinkish or purplish blooms

PLATE 271. This form of *Iris reticulata* from Iran (collection number *GLUZ-98-323*) might belong to variety *kurdica*

PLATE 272. *Iris reticulata* var. *kurdica* has smaller flowers with a whitish haft

PLATE 273. *Iris iberica* subsp. *lycotis* near Yüksekova in eastern Turkey

PLATE 274. The last day for a population of *Iris barnumae* subsp. *barnumae* near Van. The next day these plants would be bulldozed to make way for a new road

PLATE 275. *Iris iberica* subsp. *elegantissima* collected from the foothills of Mount Ararat

PLATE 276. *Bellevalia forniculata* growing on a meadow covered by water

PLATE 277. The flowers of *Neotchihatchewia isatidea* have a very strong and long-lasting lilac-like aroma

PLATE 278. *Arum conophalloides* var. *caudatum*, one of the most magnificent arums

PLATE 279. *Muscari massayanum* in flower

PLATE 280. *Muscari massayanum* in fruit

PLATE 281. *Bellevalia crassa*, one of the rarest muscaris

PLATE 282. *Muscari* of a color never seen before (possibly a new species) in a very wet meadow near Erzincan

PLATE 283. *Muscari adilii* is known only from three localities and grows on pure white limestone

PLATE 284. Albino forms can be found in almost all *Muscari* species, as with this white *M. armeniacum*

PLATE 285. *Ornithogalum ulophyllum* growing near Uzumlu, just one of the many ornithogalums found in Turkey

PLATE 286. Henrik Zetterlund kneels beside a gigantic specimen of *Muscari comosum*. The bulbs of this plant were as large as those of *Fritillaria imperialis* and lay at a depth of half a meter

PLATE 287. A beautiful dwarf *Gladiolus* species at the top of Nemrut-Dag

PLATE 288. *Crocus biflorus* subsp. *isauricus*

PLATE 289. *Crocus biflorus* subsp. *nubigena*

PLATE 290. *Crocus biflorus* subsp. *atrospermus*

PLATE 291. The bright orange throat of *Crocus cyprius* compensates for the small size of the flowers

PLATE 292. A black stigma adds special beauty to *Crocus chrysanthus* 'Sunspot'

PLATE 293. *Crocus chrysanthus* 'Goldmine', the first *Crocus* variety with semi-double flowers

PLATE 294. *Crocus chrysanthus* with a deep purple flower tube from Gencek, Turkey

PLATE 295. My seedling of *Crocus chrysanthus* 'Snow Crystal'

PLATE 296. *Crocus gargaricus* grows much better for me when I ignore it

PLATE 297. The wild form of *Crocus fleischeri* is far more beautiful than the commercially grown one

PLATE 298. *Crocus adanensis* isn't very easy to grow in my region and needs some winter protection

PLATE 299. *Crocus baytopiorum* is one of the most unusually colored crocuses

PLATE 300. Of the blue, Turkish, non-annulate species, *Crocus abantensis* is the most growable

PLATE 301. Some of the most spectacular forms of *Crocus sieberi* belong to subspecies *sieberi* growing in Crete. This selection is called 'Cretan Snow'

PLATE 302. *Oxalis adenophylla* is very variable. I named the form with purple-centered leaves 'Purple Heart'

PLATE 303. *Alstroemeria pygmaea* is the dwarfest of all alstroemerias, generally growing to about 5 cm tall

PLATE 304. Returning from the mountains

The hills were very rounded—the granites had eroded and formed amazing shapes resembling animals, castles, and so forth. A stone at the edge of a hill had been named "turtle stone," and it really did look like some gigantic turtle ready to topple down into the valley. Small streams flowed out of each small depression, and everywhere around us grew the most outstanding Juno iris: *Iris magnifica* (syn. *I. amankutanica*; Plate 145). It reached up to 1 m tall here and in some places grew right out of the streams. This iris is sometimes compared with corn, and in shape and size the leaves do resemble miniature corn. The leaves are bright green without a white margin, and the flowers are various shades of blue—some brighter, some deeper, but always on the light side of the spectrum. Considering its natural habitat, I was not surprised to find that it is a good grower outside in Latvia, where it can remain in the ground for years without replanting, until the clump becomes too large. All that it needs is good drainage.

Iris cycloglossa is similar to *I. magnifica* in this aspect. It is one of the rare plants from Afghanistan that survived from the last botanical expeditions before the Russian invasion. In nature it grows in wet depressions, so it doesn't suffer from wet Latvian summers and is quite easy to obtain from various nurseries. It is a rather unique species with a branched stem (though I have never observed this in my nursery) and bright blue flowers of a very unusual shape, with incredibly wide, round falls and horizontal or only slightly upturned standards. All plants in cultivation came from an area southwest of Herat, where they were collected by Per Wendelbo.

The pass ended higher in the mountains and before us lay a spectacular vista. A round depression was surrounded by mountaintops, and we could see where all the waters of the Agalik River combined and flowed away from the valley through the Devshara Waterfall. Two plants grew everywhere around us: the bright red *Tulipa fosteriana* and the light bluish *Iris magnifica*. A superb iris with clean white blooms shone at the bottom of a spring; only a small yellow blotch on the falls spoiled its purity. My stock of *I. magnifica* 'Alba' (later renamed 'Virginity') came from this plant. 'Blue Dream' is another cultivar that originated with the Agalik form; its blooms are shaded violet-blue throughout, and only the falls are almost white. 'Margaret Mathew', which was selected at the Royal Botanic Gardens, Kew, is somewhat similar, only with more lilac flowers.

Another Juno iris grew on drier rocks. It was a dwarf plant, its leaves were edged in white, and according to local people it had bright yellow flowers. It turned out to be identical to a plant we had found far in the valley, confirming that the bulb had been washed there by spring waters. There was some doubt about its name—was it *Iris maracandica* or *I. svetlaneae*?—but the bright yellow flowers helped us identify it correctly as *I. svetlaneae*. Only many years later, when I had collected the true *I. maracandica*, did my doubt completely disappear.

In this same area we also encountered *Tulipa korolkowii* and a plant from the *T. bifloriformis–T. turkestanica* complex. Our guides explained that *T. micheliana* grew in the steppe some years ago, but all of its habitat had been plowed up and it was now a rare plant.

About four species of *Eremurus* grew here. The largest was *E. robustus*, with very wide leaves, which we found growing inside some very spiny rose and hawthorn shrubs. There was a gigantic *Allium*, too, with surprisingly hairy, wide leaves. The hairiness of the leaves later led me to misclassify this plant as *A. alaicum*, a much smaller species, but the correct name is *A. stipitatum*. It is a very widespread species in Central Asia but with a little variation between the populations. Another form of *Tulipa fosteriana* grew alongside the *A. stipitatum*. It had bright, shiny, lettuce green leaves and long stolons. There were a few cultivars with similarly colored leaves ('Cantata', 'Flaming Youth'), so I tried to collect some bulbs, but without any success. At that time I didn't know that there were forms of tulips in which the flowering was replaced by an extreme rate of vegetative multiplying by the very long stolons.

Fritillaria stenanthera was in bloom at the top of the mountain, its pale grayish bluish flowers looking quite unattractive. But I also found an unknown (at that time) *Allium* species that was only just showing the tips of its leaves out of the soil near some melting snow. If I had been more experienced at that time, I would have immediately recognized it as *A. oreophilum* by the characteristic shape of its leaves. This form turned out to be the tallest of the species and was later named 'Agalik's Giant'. The tall, strong flower stalk holding the large, bright purple inflorescence over the foliage is perfect for flower arrangements. In my opinion, though, the greatest advantage of this plant is that it flowers at the same time and reaches the same height as the bright golden yellow *A. moly* 'Jeannine'. Situating these plants side by side in the garden makes for a nice arrangement. 'Jeannine' was collected by Antoine and Michael Hoog in the Spanish Pyrenees at Valle del Roncal, Navarra Province, in June of 1978. It forms two flower stalks from a bulb and is in full flower when the usual commercial form of *A. moly* is only starting to stick its nose out of the ground. The flowers of the traditional form are greenish-tinted and have acute petals, while 'Jeannine' has soft yellow flowers with more rounded petals.

Allium oreophilum is an extremely variable species. On the Kuramin Ridge, Arnis found a very dwarf form that he later named 'Kuramin's Dwarf'. It seems to be among the smallest forms of this well-known species, with very dark purple flowers on a stem only 5–8 cm long. It looks very showy and excellent not only in a rockery but also when grown in a pot. From seedlings of 'Kuramin's Dwarf', Estonian plant collector Sulev Savisaar selected 'Sulev's Dark', an especially dark, even somewhat blackish red form with the same dwarf habit. Only one other *A. oreophilum* can compete with it in terms of beauty: a form from the heights of the Turkestan Mountains in Tajikistan, where it was collected at the upper course of the Kusavlisai at 3200 m. Named 'Kusavli Curl' (Plate 146), it has a very dwarf habit and unusually twisted leaves. It is a marvelous show winner in pots and a beautiful plant for a rockery. It is easy to grow in an open garden as well. All the Central Asian forms of *A. oreophilum* reproduce well vegetatively, but they never become weedy like the Caucasian form 'Samur' and the Dutch 'Zwanenburg'. A form found in Kugart is the laziest.

All the slopes were nearly covered with the leaves of *Crocus korolkowii*. The local people divided these plants, which they called "snowdrops," into two groups: the yellow-flowered plants of the mountains and the white-flowered plants of the foothills. According to their descriptions, I suspected that the latter group was *Colchicum kesselringii*, although this plant didn't grow in the foothills. I did not find any *C. kesselringii* bulbs, however, so I couldn't check to see what this "white snowdrop" really was. These plants were not differentiated by the locals—to them, a snowdrop was just a snowdrop. There were enormous quantities of the crocuses; in fact it was impossible to take a step without trampling them. They grew in the alluvial meadows, in the cracks of the rocks, and everywhere in between. Many of them had a surprisingly high rate of vegetative reproduction, with some clumps consisting of as many as twenty corms. I later found that this population had the most variable flower color of the species. Almost every plant was different. Most of my *Crocus korolkowii* varieties come from this locality. In other places that I visited later, the populations were more or less uniform in color, and nowhere else did I find such bright colors.

There are many good *Crocus korolkowii* cultivars, so it is not easy to list the best. The most early-flowering form is 'Lucky Number', which is now grown on several hectares in the Netherlands, having originated from a few handfuls I gave to Jan Pennings. 'Yellow Tiger' (Plate 147) is a very beautiful variety with large yellow flowers that are intensely speckled and striped with brown along the backside of the petals. It is now widespread in the Netherlands. 'Mountain Glory' is another very early form. It has bright yellow blooms with a wide brown stripe up to the middle on the petal exteriors. This is one of my favorites, especially when the flowers are half-opened. 'Kiss of Spring' has very large, rounded, pure deep yellow flowers. *Crocus korolkowii* was also among E. A. Bowles's favorites, and he selected various forms. Unfortunately, they were later lost in the gardens. I discovered one of them unexpectedly in the collection of an Estonian gardener who had found it in the castle garden of some pre-war landlord. 'Dytiscus' was reintroduced in Britain from that garden. It is a very small-flowering form that produces as many as twenty blooms from a corm, its deep purplish brown petal exteriors marked with a very narrow golden yellow rim. The abundant flowering of this form is quite characteristic of *C. korolkowii*. Many clones form fifteen to twenty blooms from a corm. They increase extremely well by forming very large corms vegetatively. It is easy to distinguish *C. korolkowii* from other Central Asian crocus species by the shape of the corms. Until the winter of 2002–2003, I thought *C. korolkowii* was indestructible in the garden, but a terrible black frost damaged my most vigorous forms, and only a few weak corms survived from many varieties.

The mountains here looked safe, without any steep rocks or deep gorges, so we decided to separate and come back together at two o'clock where the valley began. Everyone but Āris arrived at the meeting point shortly before two. Though I called out his name, I heard only an echo by way of reply, and after several more tries I decided to go look for him. Two hours of searching were in vain, however, so I started running back toward the meeting point with thoughts of forming a rescue team. In the midst of my panic, a snake suddenly flew like an arrow across the path in front of me. (I'll never fully comprehend the vigor of my jump, which sent me both up and backward.) Back at our camp the local people explained how the heights of Agalik had been called a "paradise for snakes." The snakes lay in the sun near the passes higher on the slopes, keeping an eye out for small animals. The snake I had encountered had surely been no less frightened of me than vice versa. I soon noticed a fat snake with a yellow abdomen near the path. This was a very widespread reptile here, with such a small mouth that it couldn't cause any injury to a human. The local people called these creatures "yellow bellies." I seized the chance to twist one around my neck and take a photo (Plate 148).

On returning to the camp I found that after bringing Ludvigs to the tent, our friends had gone back to search for Āris and had found him halfway to the campsite. Apparently he had simply thought the weather was too nice to return by the scheduled time. Hearing that I was searching for him, he decided to return to the mountaintops to look for me, but we had evidently missed each other. Meanwhile the villagers decided to return to the village with their large bunches of flowers, promising to send someone with a donkey the next day to help with our luggage. It soon grew dark, but Āris wasn't back yet, so we put some large logs on the fire to make a kind of beacon. Only when we were asleep did our "vagrant" finally appear. He had found the tent only because of the fire.

We went to the waterfall once more in the morning. Āris tanned himself in the sun despite my warning that the sunlight in the mountains can be very harsh and the outcome quite painful. As a result his back was burned, and over the following days he moaned whenever he put his haversack on or turned over in his sleeping bag.

When our donkey didn't show up, we picked up our bags ourselves—I put Ludwig's bag on my chest and was soon looking a bit like a donkey myself. Halfway down, though, we encountered a man on a donkey. All of our bags were loaded onto the donkey's back, with the owner sitting on top holding a portable radio. Our protests that this was too much weight for the poor animal, whose thin legs were swaying, were rejected with a single argument: it is a donkey, and such is a donkey's fate!

We again passed the night at Agalik and early in the morning took the first bus to Samarkand. From there we flew to Tashkent.

Aman-Kutan

On my next visit to the Zeravshan Mountains, Āris Krūmiņš was again my partner. We began in Samarkand with a plan to go to Pendzhikent, but it happened to be 1 May, a time of festivals, so there was no public transportation operating. We decided to forget Pendzhikent and head instead to the famous mountain pass of Aman-Kutan (or Tahta-Karacha, as it is now called). It was mentioned in many plant books, so we wanted to see what plants grew there.

It turned out to be a somewhat crazy trip. Only a week before I had been in bed suffering terribly from lumbago, unable to even put my shoes on without help. When

I had explained to my doctor that in one week I would be flying to Central Asia, his eyes opened wide. To climb mountains with a heavy haversack, to sleep on the ground—I needed a psychiatrist, not a physician! But he prescribed me strong medicine and physiotherapy, and in the end I was ready to leave, although I still felt terrible.

When we reached Samarkand, everything was closed. A private driver offered to take us to Aman-Kutan for thirty rubles, although he would go only as far as the checkpoint. The police were very strict and prosecuted private citizens earning money as taxi drivers; if they were caught they were charged fifty rubles, money that went straight into the pockets of the policemen.

The perfect asphalt road snaked its way through a narrow valley. The houses in the area had flat, grass-covered roofs, some even serving as small pastures for sheep or goats. The policeman at the checkpoint was blabbering with someone, so we were lucky enough to pass through more or less unnoticed. Now our driver would be able to drive us further, although we had to pay him ten more rubles. He brought us up to the pass and stopped along a dirt road going toward the mountaintops.

There was a strong wind, and rain occasionally fell in large drops, beating painfully into our faces. We needed a place to camp but found ourselves surrounded by nothing but steep slopes and stones, with no sign of water. We tried to walk up by the terraces crossing all the slopes. These were used to plant fruit trees. Sometimes the walking was rather easy, but the areas where the trees grew very well were not passable, so we switched to an even higher terrace. As we reached a stony meadow, I encountered something that made my jaw drop: never before had I seen such beautiful Juno irises. I immediately dropped my bag and grabbed my camera, and after taking numerous photos, I took out a pencil and started to write a detailed description of this plant for later classification. The falls of the flower were very dark purplish violet with a narrow white rim and a large, bright yellow blotch in the center. The style branches were very light violet. The plant was more than 30 cm tall and had five or six flowers on each stem. The most important thing was that it reproduced well vegetatively. There were clumps with five to fifteen plants in each. There was an echo in my head: "warley, warley." And it was true: when I checked the keys in the *Flora of the Soviet Union* (Komarov 1935), the plant turned out to be *Iris warleyensis* (Plate 149).

My mood immediately improved. When we reached the ridge, a spectacular meadow densely covered with flowering *Iris warleyensis* opened before us. It would have been worth coming all this way if only to see such beauty. We found a safe spot nearby to pitch our tent. Some 20 m away was a snow bed, at the bottom of which a small spring purled. We were in a real Garden of Eden. The water was somewhat muddy, but we built a small dike and a reservoir where the water could clear.

And then came the surprise: two crocus flowers at my feet, one yellow, the other white (Plate 150). It seemed incredible, *Crocus korolkowii* side by side with *C. alatavicus*. All botanical literature seems to indicate that although their areas can come into contact, these species never form mixed populations. I later sent a picture of this combination to Brian Mathew, who spread the information further in some articles about crocuses. In those years I could never imagine the occurrence of albinos in *C. korol-kowii*, and I didn't check the bulb, which looks different in both species. Later, some years before black frost killed it, I grew one of the rarest cultivars of *C. korolkowii*, 'Snow Leopard', with pure white flowers, slightly grayish on the back of the outer petals. The white crocus from Aman-Kutan looked different from 'Snow Leopard', the petal exteriors speckled grayish, the typical color of *C. alatavicus*. But as I looked at the more rounded shape of the flowers in the picture, some doubt rose in my mind: perhaps I had missed an opportunity to introduce a more frost-resistant white form of *C. korolkowii*.

While walking through the meadow among the purple clumps of *Iris warleyensis*, I suddenly noticed something white shining in the distance. It was a unique clump of *I. warleyensis*, half of it typically purple, the other half pure white. Many years before, when there had been only one seedling, some mutation had occurred. One of the daughter bulbs had kept its typical purple flowers, while the other turned white. The result was this beautiful, large, bicolored clump, with two parts that were identical in size but different in color. We later found another clump with similar coloring, though not so brightly white, with slightly visible blue shading near the rim of the falls.

Iris warleyensis isn't the best plant for growing on open ground, especially in clay soil. It is difficult to dig out because it has very long, thin additional roots that always get cut off. But I haven't yet lost the plants I collected in those early years. Now I grow them in the greenhouse in very light soil with controlled watering that leaves them almost dry at harvesting time. I dig out additional roots some 30–40 cm long. When I grew this iris outside, where conditions were too cool, it flowered only very rarely, but ever since I started growing it in the greenhouse it has flowered abundantly each season.

All around us at Aman-Kutan grew ample amounts of a nice allium with large flower heads. This was listed in the *Flora of the Soviet Union* as *Allium schubertii*, a species that actually grows very far from this location, in Asia Minor. The name was later changed to *A. bucharicum* by A. I. Vvedenskyi (1971), and I used this name for many years, but Per Wendelbo finally cast some light onto the mystery of these names when he described a new species, *A. protensum* (Plate 151), that is quite widespread in Central Asia and enters Iran. *Allium protensum*, it turned out, was the correct name of my allium from Aman-Kutan. The true *A. bucharicum* is a tiny plant with a large inflorescence growing in the foothills of southern Tajikistan; it is almost unknown in collections.

Allium protensum is a very good plant with a beautiful, large inflorescence similar in size to that of *A. christophii* but much denser. It is especially decorative for fresh flower arrangements and is also useful when dried. It can be grown outside in my climate, but the large bulbs are susceptible to rot, and it doesn't increase vegetatively, so the seeds have to be collected and sown regularly. Sometimes it forms a few aerial bulbils between pedicels inside the inflorescence. I like this allium very much. Recently a few interesting seedlings have appeared in my garden, apparently of hybrid origin.

Allium stipitatum grew in the same area of Aman-Kutan, and as in Agalik, it was usually seen among trees and shrubs. I found a group comprised of six vegetative bulbs. Until my visit to Hodji-Obi-Garm in Tajikistan I had never seen this species increase so well in the wild. We also found another allium that was very different from *A. stipitatum*. It was tall but with much narrower leaves, and later I found that an identical form had been collected in Agalik. Identification was not difficult because inside the flower between the filaments there were very characteristic small "teeth." It was clearly *A. sarawschanicum*, which has large, airy umbels of violet flowers on a stem 80 cm long and pedicels that differ in length. In this form, the center of the umbel is light green, and the leaves are wider than in other populations. I named it 'Agalik' after the place in which I had first found it. Another form found in the Chinoro Gorge of Tajikistan was named 'Chinoro'; the center of its umbel is dark purplish green, and it has narrower leaves. Both are excellent garden plants and are beautiful in flower arrangements whether fresh or dried. It is important to harvest their bulbs annually and early, soon after flowering ends, to keep them from rotting in extreme weather conditions. Both reproduce well vegetatively, too.

Around this time, Āris called to me, "Come, here are your sparrows!" On the steep, bare slope he had found yellow blooms of some *Corydalis* species, very different from those in Karatau. It turned out that it belonged to section *Leonticoides* and had perennial tubers. Determining the species was quite difficult. I couldn't find anything similar in the *Flora of the Soviet Union* and even stared to think it might be a new species. I even gave it the provisional name *C. mathewii* in honor of Brian Mathew, but soon found that in the same year this plant had been described by Russian botanist Marina Mikhailova and named *C. maracandica* (Plate 152). It is an excellent plant with beautiful creamy yellow flowers slightly suffused with pink at the top of the inflorescence. It looks like a yellow-flowering sister of *C. ledebouriana* and is superficially somewhat similar to it, but it has a different spur and nectary, and no intermediates are known in the wild. Both species can interbreed, creating beautiful and varied hybrids. *Corydalis maracandica* produces seed that ripens well, and it is easy in cultivation both outside and in the greenhouse. The first seedlings can flower in the third year, though they usually start in the fourth.

When Arnis Seisums and I later visited this spot, much later in the season when the seeds of the Junos were almost ripe, we found two beautiful forms of some other plants. One was *Allium barszczewskii* with very bright scarlet red flowers, a much shorter form than any I had grown earlier. Here it covered the small meadow like a bright red carpet. Growing beside it was a very unusual form of *Gentiana olivieri* whose blooms were light pink instead of the usual gentian blue.

The next morning at Aman-Kutan I awoke early. A strong wind was blowing, causing the tent to flutter, and when I stuck my head outside I saw that we were inside a cloud—deep fog had reduced visibility to only a few meters. It was extremely difficult to find our way back, and unfortunately I made the mistake of choosing the road down along the gorge, having had too little experience with how dangerous such gorges could be. Our boots didn't slide on the wet stones, but the wet clay slopes were more slippery than ice. We decided to take a risk and break into a cavity in the gorge. Fortunately it was only a meter deep, and we were rewarded when we found *Corydalis maracandica* and *Fritillaria bucharica* growing there in full flower. What a pity that I hadn't known about this spot the day before, when the sun was out and conditions were good for taking pictures.

I didn't notice exactly when we left the cloud, but I remember remarking about how the water had stopped streaming down our clothes and my hands had stopped freezing. The air was filled with a marvelous aroma. It was *Iris stolonifera* in full blossom, and very variable in color.

A large grotto appeared at the side of the gorge, with a magnificent stream flowing out of it. Now I understood why we had seen no water higher in the gorge—all the water flowed into the cavities in the rock and accumulated somewhere underground, finding its way out here.

When we reached the motorway our feet were covered in clay. We waded into the river to clean ourselves up. Two hours later we reached the checkpoint and the bus to Samarkand.

Beauties from Shing

The next spring we traveled to the central Zeravshan Mountains in the direction of Pendzhikent, and it turned out to be a very important expedition for me. We started as a four-person team. Aino Paivel from the Tallinn Botanical Garden and her assistant, Mari Kits, were to join me and Āris Krūmiņš. Aino had often helped me by providing plants and information about the Carpathian Mountains, so this was an opportunity to repay her. For Aino it turned out to be a very short trip. On our first route inside Akbulak Valley she suffered badly from contact with either *Dictamnus* or *Prangos*. She became so ill that she had to return home, where she was even hospitalized for a time. After our second route, Āris too returned home, with similar large ulcers covering his palms. Only Mari was with me until the end of the trip.

The trip to Akbulak was exhausting, particularly for Aino and Mari, who were unprepared for the weight of their haversacks. Āris and I were already carrying 25–30 kg on our backs, but wishing to be gentlemen, we took an additional bag of some 20 kg, which we carried in the front. Fortunately we were soon able stop a car, which brought us into the mountains, but the ladies were too tired by this point to follow us onto the ridge.

There I collected a beautiful form of *Allium barsczewskii* (later named 'Akbulak'), which for years was the only form of this species offered in my catalog, and on a small, bare slope I found *A. pskemense*, a very rare species in the wild. In the same area I also encountered a beautiful tulip that I identified only recently with the help of Z. P. Botschantzeva's *Tulips*. It was *Tulipa butkovii* (Plate 153), which has bright red flowers but is most interesting for its bright red filaments. I saw the flowers on a bare, stony slope on the opposite side of the Akbulak River, and from that distance I guessed that it was *T. vvedenskyi*. We found a wire rope tied tightly between two large trees across the river. A small wooden bench hung from it. Sitting on the bench and moving it forward with one's own hands, it was possible to cross some 15 m to reach the other side of the foaming, riffling stream (Plate 154). The first half of the distance was downhill and easy enough, but I had some difficulty with the second half, as the rope turned upward. Still, I managed to get there and back. There was a yellow form of *T. butkovii*, too. Was this single tulip species worth the risk I had taken? I think so, yes. I never again encountered this species during my expeditions, and I don't know anyone else growing it.

Later in Pendzhikent we took a taxi to Shing, an unimpressive-looking village surrounded by black, bare mountains and a muddy river. A few kilometers from town, a rope bridge led to a wonderful meadow over the river, just the right site for our camp (Plates 155 and 156).

The next morning Āris slept late while Mari and I headed out to explore. We stopped at the very first slope, an area that just yesterday had seemed so empty. The first Juno irises grew here, a very beautiful species with deep yellow flowers and narrow, white-edged, nicely wavy leaves. I later identified it as *Iris svetlaneae* (Plate 157). When I removed the first stone to uncover its roots, a large, greenish scorpion appeared beneath it, and so we were warned: be careful here! Somewhat higher *Colchicum kesselringii* (Plate 158) grew in abundance. This was the plant my Estonian colleagues were so interested in. The slope here was composed of stony, gravelly clay with plenty of lime chips, and nothing but irises and colchicums grew on it. I had never before encountered such a limey place, and I remembered how Michael Hoog had said that the best fertilizer for Juno irises is dolomite lime. After this point I started to powder the roots of my Juno irises with lime at planting time.

The slopes became too steep for us. I tried to make steps for Mari, but she couldn't make it up any further, so we decided to return. We slid down the scree slopes, a very fast but somewhat dangerous way to go, with Mari sometimes falling down and scraping her hands. At the camp I made tea and invited a man who had been working in a nearby field. He told me that the colchicums I had found had purple flowers, and later, when this form of *Colchicum kesselringii* bloomed for me in Latvia, I could see that the petals were very wide and had deep purple backs. The man also told us that the iris here at the camp had yellow flowers, but higher in the mountains we would find another species with bluish purple flowers.

In the afternoon we all walked to another narrow side valley. The slope was quite steep and on the small river one waterfall followed another. The *Berberis* shrubs, which were full of flowers, looked as though they had been dusted with gold. Somewhat higher on the slope was the first tulip, with large, bright red flowers, quite similar to *Tulipa fosteriana* but with petals that were pure shining black inside at the base. It was typical *T. ingens* (Plate 159), a close relative of *T. fosteriana* and really little more than a color variant of it, distinguished only by the design of the inner base. I grew *T. ingens* for many years, but it never produced any offsets, and I eventually lost it during an extremely hard winter.

We also found a nice form of *Allium komarowii* with bright violet-purple flowers in a dense, semi-globose umbel on a 40 cm stem. Its two elliptic, purplish-tinged, green leaves looked somewhat similar to those of *A. karataviense*. Back in Latvia this form proved to be a good grower in the greenhouse, as well as in the garden when good drainage is provided.

Somewhat higher up we encountered a flat spot densely covered with well-rotten sheep manure, and two different *Allium* species grew here. One had a few wide leaves and was easy to identify as the very common *A. stipitatum*. The other was somewhat shorter and had more numerous, narrower leaves and a larger but less dense inflorescence. Naming this plant was more difficult, since I was misguided by its ribbed flower stalk. Only after some five or six years did I realize, with the help of Arnis Seisums, that it was *A. jesdianum*, though a far better form than what I received in 1983 from the Main Botanical Garden in Moscow under the name *A. rosenbachianum*. The Moscow plant is the most late-flowering of all my samples of *A. jesdianum*, with dark purple flowers in a dense umbel on a 70 cm stem. I named it 'Purple King'. The form collected on the manure field, 'Shing', is the most unusual for its yellowish green leaves and yellowish bulbs (the others have grayish green leaves and white bulbs). It is the most early-flowering form, with a very dense, dark purple umbel on a 70 cm stem. The next day higher in the valley I found another form of *A. jesdianum* with a larger inflorescence. I later named it 'Pendzhikent'. It has bright purple flowers with white filaments on a 1.2 m stem. A form collected later on the opposite side of the Zeravshan Mountains in the Varzob Valley has the largest flower heads of all. Its inflorescence can reach even 15 cm in diameter, getting somewhat close to that of true *A. rosenbachianum*. It is a bit lighter in shade, early-flowering, and up to 1.2 m tall. I named it 'Michael Hoog' to honor the memory of my friend. All of these forms reproduce well vegetatively and grow perfectly outside, although sometimes they come up too early, in which case their leaves may be damaged by night frosts. They are all very popular and are grown in the Netherlands by many nurseries, as they are excellent plants for the garden. The fresh flowers and dry stems are beautiful in arrangements.

I later received another form of *Allium jesdianum* collected by Per Wendelbo on Shahtu Pass (2000 m) in Bamiyan Province, Afghanistan. It has wider leaves and very large umbels (up to 16 cm across) on a shorter stem (70–80 cm). The flowers are bright violet with a white style and filaments, and purple anthers. It forms larger bulbs but is much slower to reproduce vegetatively. It is more susceptible to summer rains, too. I named this stock 'Per Wendelbo' in honor of its collector. German botanist Reinhard Fritsch described it as subspecies *angustitepalum*.

The true *Allium rosenbachianum* has fewer and wider leaves, and grows further south in Tajikistan. Until recently *A. jesdianum*, *A. hollandicum*, and other alliums were grown under this name, while the true *A. rosenbachianum* was not even in cultivation. The typical subspecies *rosenbachianum* has a huge umbel, up to 15 cm in diameter, of nicely arranged, bright violet-purple flowers on a stem 70 cm long. Its leaves are shiny green, explicitly narrowing toward the base, and rather spreading. It is one of the most beautiful tall-growing species, but it reproduces slowly. Subspecies *rosenbachianum* was collected by Arnis Seisums at the southwestern end of the Darwas Mountains in southern Tajikistan. Subspecies *kwakense*, from the Rangon Range in Tajikistan, is similar but differs in its rather erectly held leaves, which taper only slightly at the base. The wine red flowers are held in large (16–18 cm), spherical umbels on a 1 m stem. Both forms are quite susceptible to excessive moisture in summer, so early harvesting is recommended, and the best way to build up the stock is from seed.

Among such seedlings of *Allium rosenbachianum*, my Lithuanian friend Leonid Bondarenko found an unintentional hybrid with *A. sarawschanicum* in which the best qualities from both parents had been joined. This new form has the marvelous shape and size of flower head of *A. rosenbachianum* and the excellent growth and rate of increase of *A. sarawschanicum*. The foliage is also resistant to late frost damage. Leonid named it 'Emir'.

The next day we were all up early because we wanted to walk up to the main Shing River. The tourist brochures informed us that the river flowed through a beautiful valley and that in many places it was blocked by natural dikes that had been formed in ancient times by a gigantic earthquake. These dikes had created a line of lakes of incredible beauty. The people in the area were Tajik and strictly followed Muslim traditions. The women, and even the young girls in modern dress, turned their faces away and covered up with a scarf as we came closer.

When we reached the first lake we were stunned by its beauty. It was so clean that even the smallest pebbles were visible at the bottom, and the water was all shades of blue and green, from deep ultramarine in the shadows and the brightest azure in the sun to a greenish color in shallow places. On an almost vertical slope a very strange plant with thick, deeply divided, metallic green foliage was growing. The rootstock was rope-like and long, and it seemed somewhat like an *Anemone* species, but it was difficult to say for sure.

A new serpentine road wound its way up as the next lake opened before our eyes (Plate 160). Here the water was deep blue and not as translucent. Bright red spots higher up on the slopes turned out to be *Tulipa ingens*. I immediately remembered our visit to the Tashkent Botanical Garden, during which the chief of the bulb department had told us that *T. ingens* didn't grow in this district.

We also saw *Fritillaria bucharica*, but it had been damaged by some disease—the leaves were marred by bright orange pustules of rust. This was the location from which *Allium jesdianum* 'Pendzhikent' originated. It was also home to a blue Juno iris that looked like a miniature version of *Iris warleyensis* (Plate 161). It was only 15–20 cm tall with up to two (rarely three) flowers on a stem. The blooms were much smaller, the falls were lighter and without the narrow white rim, and the blotches on the falls were whitish. Later I found a few plants with a creamy yellow blotch. It was a good grower, and I sent many bulbs to Michael Hoog, who then sent bulbs to different botanical gardens. I lost my stock when I moved my garden, but recently received similar plants. They were collected 50 km south of Pendzhikent at 1700 m in the surroundings of the village of Obiborik on marble limestone on steep scree slopes. They are of the same habit—dwarf, with late, very small flowers. This place is very close to Shing, so the plants must be identical.

At the third dike we found ourselves in a wide, brilliant green valley with a few large fruit trees that provided excellent shade. It was ideal, a place you'd want to stay in forever. After a rest we reached the fourth lake, which was the longest. There had to be three or four more lakes ahead, but they were too far for us. The road changed direction here. Earlier it had followed along the right bank of the lakes, but now it turned to the left onto the sunbaked, south-facing slope. Āris followed it there while Mari and I stayed on the shaded side. Here we found plenty of *Tulipa ingens* and the same *Allium jesdianum* form we had collected near the second lake. In addition we found *A. karataviense*, but I didn't collect it: in those years I couldn't imagine that it might be variable.

And then I made the discovery of my life. On a scree slope, between rocks, I glimpsed the tiny leaves of a *Corydalis* species. My heart trembled—it looked like a species from section *Corydalis*, so it had to be a good grower and reproduce vegetatively. The leaves looked somewhat different from any *Corydalis* I knew of at the time, and later at home I had trouble naming it. It looked somewhat similar to *C. glaucescens* but was more floriferous, its smaller flowers very densely placed on the stem. In the end I decided to call it *C. glaucescens* and give it a cultivar name honoring my great friend Chris Brickell, at that time the director general of the Royal Horticultural Society. It turned out to be an excellent grower and increaser, and some of its corms reached the Netherlands and Britain. Michael Hoog sent a few samples to Henrik Zetterlund in Gothenburg, who was working together with Magnus Lidén on a monograph about *Corydalis*. Henrik confirmed that this corydalis was in fact a new species, and nine years after the original tubers had been collected, it was named *C. ruksansii* (Plate 162).

The flowers of *Corydalis ruksansii* are white with a pinkish violet hue and contrasting dark-purple-tipped inner petals (Plate 163). The midvein of the upper petal forms a thin pinkish purple line. In an open garden it makes a very compact clump, each tuber usually forming a few inflorescences. In the greenhouse it sometimes grows too tall, thus losing its compact shape. It reproduces well vegetatively and usually also sets seed. It is very different from *C. nudicaulis*, with which it is sometimes compared.

A very strange plant appeared among the open-pollinated seedlings of *Corydalis ruksansii* in Arnis Seisums's garden. He spotted it right away in its first year of flowering due to its clearly bigger flowers and other similarities to *C. schanginii* subsp. *schanginii*. This hybrid features the abundant flowering of *C. ruksansii* but get its flower size from *C. schanginii*. The flowers are light pink, and it is a very good competitor for its more widely known parents. Arnis named it 'New Contender'.

From Shing we returned to Tashkent, where we were informed that Aino, who was by now very ill, had returned to Tallinn. Soon afterward Āris too had to return home, and Mari and I were left to complete the rest of the expedition.

That evening, while Mari and I drank tea at Volodya's house, the shelves in the kitchen began to swing. "What idiot is jostling the shelf?" I thought. "All the dishes are going to fall off!" But then I understood that it wasn't a person but an earthquake. Volodya shouted for everyone to leave the house, but everything soon calmed down. The next day we learned that the earthquake had been centered in the Chatkal Mountains, where we had been just a few days before, and the magnitude at the center had been seven points. The local people still remembered the great Tashkent earthquake, during which the greatest part of the city had been destroyed and many people had been killed. All the old houses where the native folks lived had toppled during the quake. Near Volodya's house was a high, long ridge that was made when bulldozers pushed aside the remnants of these houses, along with the remains of their inhabitants. In effect, it was an unofficial common grave. Local people did nothing there, and children never played in the area.

The next day we flew to Dushanbe, the capital of Tajikistan.

Varzob Valley

In Dushanbe, Mari and I were greeted with 27°C and ice cream. It was the first ice cream of the season for both of us. Again our arrival coincided with a festival, this time a celebration of Victory Day, so the city center was basically closed. With no public transport available, we decided to take a taxi. Then we found out, to our disappointment, that the road to Ziddi, our destination, was not open, so we had to change our plans and select a route along the Varzob Valley, which ended at Hodji-Obi-Garm.

We began our final trip by bus, looking out the window for a good spot to stop. The Varzob River was the largest, most powerful mountain stream I had ever seen. Here and there small bridges led to the opposite side of the river and the health resorts and camps situated there. We stopped at one such place. On the gate of the camp was a sign that read "Chinoro," the name of the gorge that started here. We were lucky enough to find a flat spot for our tent, a lovely site surrounded by streams and aromatic wild roses. For a moment I forgot all about plants and wanted only to rest here and listen to the murmuring water and singing birds.

We were not here for rest, however, so as soon as the tent was set up, we headed out to look for bulbs. We didn't have to search long: a beautiful group of alliums covered a long scree slope just 10 m from our tent. This species was somewhat similar to *Allium karataviense*, but its flowers formed a looser inflorescence and were bright violet-purple with narrower petals. Each plant had one leaf, rarely two, and the leaves were narrower. The stamens were also only half the length of the petal, while in *A. karataviense* they are at least equal to and more often longer than the petal. There was another important difference, too: this plant perfectly reproduced vegetatively. The largest clump I found contained eighteen bulbs. It seemed to grow in the same kind of environment as *A. karataviense*, however, and could be collected in the same way.

Classifying this allium was problematic. Based on the *Flora of Tajikistan* (Ovcinnikov 1963) I could classify it only as *Allium alexejanum*, but in many ways it didn't correspond to the description of this species. Only many years later did I find that the correct name was *A. nevskianum* (Plate 164). *Allium nevskianum* is an excellent grower in the garden as well as in pots. More importantly, it reproduces well vegetatively, although I regularly collect the seeds, too. In 1997 a nice hybrid with *A. sarawschanicum* appeared among my seedlings, with leaves like those of *A. nevskianum* but with a much taller flower stalk, up to 40 cm. The flower head is somewhat smaller than *A. nevskianum* but of the same color. This hybrid fits perfectly into the empty niche of medium-height alliums.

True *Allium alexejanum*, which I found much later with Arnis (who had collected it earlier, too, before we started traveling together), is lazy about reproducing and must be multiplied from seed. It is not such a good grower outside in the garden because in the wild it grows in quite arid conditions. That said, it is a more compact plant with pedicels that are more clearly unequal in length, so the inflorescence has a more artistic appearance, and it is an excellent pot plant for growing in the greenhouse. I have three different stocks, and each has something special. They were collected at Astara-Soru in Tajikistan, and at Sina and Zaamin in Uzbekistan, both of the latter very close to the Tajikistan border.

A tall *Allium* species that hadn't yet begun to flower grew here on a less stony, bare clay slope, somewhat protected by shrubs. The next season it was named *A. sarawschanicum*. (This was the location from which 'Chinoro' [Plate 165] came, with its purplish-centered umbel.) As everywhere, there were some *Eremurus* species and plenty of *Ixiolirion* species. Growing in the cracks of rocks, I found *Crocus korolkowii*, which mostly grew in clumps here, as it had in Agalik. Hoping to find a similar variability, I collected many groups from different places, but I was greatly surprised the next spring to find that they were all very uniform: bright yellow, large, rounded blooms with the petal exteriors shaded a grayish green. I named this form 'Varzob'. I find it less spectacular than the other clones, at least when the flowers are not open in the sun, but all the same it received the Alpine Garden Society's Award of Merit.

The next morning we started very early. Though we had come here mostly for *Iris rosenbachiana*, we still hadn't found it, and we expected a long search. Once again the first plant we encountered was *Allium nevskianum*. It grew only on scree slopes but in such abundance that there were some spots where the stones disappeared beneath the flower heads. The greatest clump contained thirty-eight vegetatively developed bulbs. When moving stones to inspect the bulbs, we encountered a few scorpions hiding themselves from the daylight.

Lower down by the stream we found *Iris vicaria* (Plate 166), the first Juno iris. Though normally a variable species, the form in Varzob (and much higher at Hodji-

Obi-Garm) was very uniform, with very pale blue, almost whitish flowers. The only difference between plants from this area was in the color of the stem base, which in some plants was pale green and in others was violet- or purplish-toned. I hoped that those with green bases might be *I. bucharica*, the yellow-flowering relative of *I. vicaria*, but at home they all turned out to be *I. vicaria*. I saw plenty of *I. vicaria* on top of a very large shelf of rock. It was not easy to climb, but I managed to do it, and was astonished by how some twenty-five to thirty large Juno irises could grow here on only a few scoops of earth. Both variants of the species grew side by side.

In general the form from Hodji-Obi-Garm looks like a smaller version of *Iris magnifica*. The main difference is the haft of the falls, which is winged in *I. magnifica* and straight in *I. vicaria*. Both species have long, thick additional roots, but in *I. vicaria* the roots are smaller and the bulb is larger. In *I. magnifica* it seems that most of the food reserves are accumulated in the additional roots, and the bulb, at least in flowering plants, is small; the bulbs are large, however, if they haven't yet begun to flower.

Again, *Iris vicaria* is generally a very variable plant, and its forms from Sina and Tupalang in the southeastern corner of Uzbekistan are reputed to be the best. They have violet-blue flowers and a large, light yellow blotch on the falls. The clone from Sangardak River valley in southern Uzbekistan is outstanding on account of its comparatively big blooms, bright color, and delicately violet-blue-rimmed falls. Its flowers are also pleasantly aromatic. 'Maihura', with light blue flowers, seems to be the dwarfest of all forms of *I. vicaria* and the most late-flowering of the known stocks. When other stocks are finishing their flowering, this cultivar has just begun. It was collected by Arnis Seisums in the valley of Maihura, Hissar Mountains, Tajikistan.

All forms of *Iris vicaria* are excellent growers both outdoors and in a greenhouse. They reproduce well vegetatively and usually set seed well, too. In Varzob, *I. vicaria* grew only on the east-facing slopes of the Varzob Valley, while *Allium nevskianum* grew only on the south-facing slopes. Despite this, these two species can be grown side by side in the garden.

I myself never collected *Iris bucharica*. My partner Āris Krūmiņš once collected it from somewhere near Dushanbe, but he didn't note the exact spot where it had been found. This form turned out to be a very good grower and is the origin of 'Dushanbe', which has pure yellow blooms with lighter style branches on a tall stem. It looks like a yellow twin of *I. vicaria* from Chinoro. Other forms are deep yellow throughout. One such form was collected by Arnis Seisums at Sanglok, Tajikistan, and has a large solid grayish brown blotch on the falls, while another from Baldjuan has an almost blackish blotch. Both are deep yellow, differing in their darker markings on both sides of a deeper yellow, crenate crest. My favorite form is the one from the Wasmin-Kuch Mountains of the Khasratischoch Range in the very south of Tajikistan, just near the Afghanistan border. It was collected at Obi-Pitau-Du Valley near the Jacksai River on river terraces and dry slopes at 1400 m. It is a dwarf plant, only 15 cm tall, with smaller blooms of a marvelous shade of light lemon yellow and with a slightly deeper yellow crest with coarse greenish markings on both sides of the ridge. I selected many forms with green markings, which are my favorites, and this one is the best. I haven't yet had the courage to try growing it outside, however, remembering the harsh conditions of the place from which it comes. I decided to name it 'Tony' (Plate 167) in honor of Tony Hall, keeper of the Juno collection at the Royal Botanic Gardens, Kew, and the best grower of Juno irises I have ever known. Certain forms of *I. bucharica* look so unique that some people have suspected that they must be more than one species.

In gardens the most commonly distributed form of *Iris bucharica* is bicolored, with white style branches and standards, and yellow falls. It is a very good grower and an excellent increaser. There are many variations between different stocks, some quite beautiful. I named one such selection 'Swan Wings' for the extremely long, nicely wavy, pure white lobes of the style branches. Its falls have a narrow, suffused white rim.

A very strange form of bicolored *Iris bucharica* with aborted style branches once appeared among my plants. When I first saw it I thought it was some kind of seasonal variation caused by abnormal temperatures, but when I saw that it had the same appearance the next year, I decided it was a genetic mutation. The falls are very large and deep yellow with a very prominent ridge, and the center of the open flower is pure white with erect white stamens in the middle. I have never found anything similar among Junos. Still, some doubt remains. This kind of abnormality is usually caused by a virus infection, although in this case I have found no mottling or striping on the leaves, and the plants are very vigorous. I named this form 'Monstrosa'.

The shallow slopes of Varzob changed to much steeper, rockier cliffs. The ascent wasn't easy. In some spots I had to construct small steps for us to walk on, but other places could only be passed by climbing up the rocks. I could say with certainty by this point that rock climbing wasn't my favorite pastime. If we fell here and slid far enough, our chances of surviving would be very slim. I mentioned as much to Mari, who joked, "No problem. You'll just be reincarnated and come back in some other shape." I would have nothing against being reincarnated as a short-lived housefly, I told her, since this might increase my chances of returning as a human sooner, but what if I were brought back as a tortoise, living until up to five hundred years?

Fortunately the rocks were not excessively high, and after we climbed them we found ourselves on a somewhat shallower slope. In the morning I had made the serious mistake of drinking coffee instead of tea, so now I was terribly thirsty. We had no water, however, having avoided bringing any specifically to avoid the temptation to drink it during the day. The leaf stalks of wild rhubarb helped slake our thirst instead. Rhubarb grew everywhere in Central Asia and was widely used by the local people. When the leaves were young and fresh, the stalks were juicy and sometimes even flavorful. Some were dry and flavorless, so we always checked a leaf—if it was good, we collected the stalks.

We reached the highland meadows. Mari was absolutely exhausted and decided to rest in the shade of a large archa (*Juniperus*) while I looked around. I soon found some Juno irises. Digging out a bit of earth to inspect a bulb, I excitedly uttered a victorious cry—"Yes! *Iris rosenbachiana*!" It had very typical, short, swollen, thick additional roots, and the bulbs lay very deep, much deeper than those of *I. vicaria* on the slopes. I noticed that someone had been here before us; the entire meadow was lined with deep grooves, a clear indication of wild boars. At first look it seemed that this species preferred sunnier spots in an open meadow, but I soon found that, as with *I. vicaria*, the most magnificent plants were growing somewhat lower on the shaded, east-facing slopes protected by shrubs.

In the garden *Iris rosenbachiana* increases very well vegetatively, though in the wild I have very rarely found plants with a daughter bulb. It is an excellent grower, too. While I was living at my father's house I had so many bulbs growing in the sandy soil of the garden that I even used them as pot plants for forcing in winter. After I moved to clay soil, my success was not so visible, but this species still belongs to those that can grow excellently outside. That said, in my region it is sometimes damaged by hard late frosts because it emerges early and blooms along with the first spring crocuses. Now I grow my stock in the greenhouse where it is safer, but despite this some stocks come out too early and the flowers are sometimes damaged by frost even in the greenhouse; as a result, there is no seed crop.

The greatest problem is with the classification of this Juno iris. George Rodionenko's monograph (1961) describes four closely related species generally distinguished by flower color: *Iris nicolai*, *I. rosenbachiana*, *I. baldschuanica*, and *I. popovii*. Later, two species from Afghanistan were also described: white-flowered *I. cabulica* and yellow-flowered *I. doabensis*. The last two were grown for a short time in Britain and then lost from cultivation. Since these plants are not available, it is impossible to check their taxonomic status, but at least *I. doabensis* seems to be a real species because of its unusual flower color. The description of *I. cabulica* resembles this species complex from Tajikistan, so it might be only a color variant. Alan McMurtrie thought that *I. nicolai* could be distinguished from *I. rosenbachiana* by the color of the anthers, which are yellow in *I. nicolai* and white in *I. rosenbachiana*. In truth the anther color is quite representative of the population, but it doesn't correlate with the flower color, which is the main mark for separating the species.

I prefer to recognize the plants from Tajikistan as nothing more than color variants, in which case the priority belongs to the name *Iris rosenbachiana*. I named the plants that Mari and I found at Chinoro Gorge 'Varzob' (Plate 168), although later I found that this wasn't the best choice for a name because differently colored populations of this iris grow in other gorges of the Varzob Valley. The population from Chinoro turned out to be truly unique, with very large, creamy or even light yellow flowers with velvety purple-black falls and yellow anthers. In flower color it is somewhat similar to the so-called *I. baldschuanica*. The Juno under the name *I. baldschuanica* was described as coming from the surroundings of the village Tovilj-Dara in northern Darwas, but Arnis Seisums collected another uniquely colored form with bright purple flowers there (Plate 169). Undoubtedly, it is the biggest deviation in terms of color for this species, which mostly corresponds with the typical color of *I. rosenbachiana*. Both forms grow well and reproduce vegetatively.

The best-growing form of *Iris rosenbachiana* is 'Harangon' (Plate 170) from the Gissar Range. Its flowers are very large, white, and violet-tinted, with purplish violet falls and white anthers. In flower color it closely resembles what is traditionally called *I. nicolai*. The plants from Harangon are quite variable; there are lighter forms with almost whitish flowers and others with light bluish or even very light violet flowers. It is the best increaser, best seed setter, and most prolific population in my collection. *Iris nicolai*, described as coming from the heights of Sina, is somewhat similar to 'Varzob' in color but is lighter and has style branches that are almost blackish at the back. Despite its nice color, it is a weaker grower than the other samples I have grown. The form from Vahsh (Plate 171) is very similar to 'Harangon' in terms of flower color, but it flowers very early—when 'Harangon' has only just started to bloom, this one has already finished. The anthers of the Vahsh form are yellow. We succeeded in collecting this form shortly before the entire population was destroyed by the great water reservoir of the Vahsh power station.

On the same meadow we found *Eminium albertii*, a close relative of *E. lehmannii* from Chimgan, but with leaves that are distinctly winged at the base. It grew extremely deep here, to 40–50 cm. For our return we selected an easier route, bypassing the rocks we had crossed on the way up. We soon heard the babbling of the stream. It gave us a second wind, and when we finally reached the spot where the spring came out from the rock, we drank and drank, and then washed ourselves. During this short rest I found more *Iris vicaria* and then stumbled upon *Gymnospermium darwasicum*, whose tubers had simply rolled out of the soil.

The next day we returned to the motorway and tried to catch a bus, but on account of Mari's charms, a limousine stopped for us. We drove as far as Hodji-Obi-Garm, a high mountain village and famous holiday resort. The slopes were very steep and lined with gravity-defying houses. There was a path going up, but even it was so steep that we had to stop every hundred steps to catch our breath. Next to the path we saw the first bulbs. They were different from those we had seen the day before. *Scilla*, *Anemone*, and *Allium* species were in bloom, whereas *Gymnospermium* had finished flowering. We encountered a villager holding a gigantic bunch of bright red tulips that turned out to be *Tulipa praestans* (Plate 172). I used the opportunity to ask about the availability of water higher up, and he told me there was water on both sides of the upper meadow.

At the top we found a campsite. *Crocus korolkowii* grew so densely here that we couldn't put up our tent without covering hundreds of them. The morning greeted us with clouds and rain, and everything was wet—very different from the previous hot days. The soil here was very hard reddish brown clay and the landscape generally flattish, with low hills and shallow depressions. The first plant we collected was *Scilla vvedenskyi*, a beautiful species with long, somewhat arched racemes of slightly pendulous, medium-sized, bright blue blooms. It was the only time I ever found it in the mountains. I still grow this scilla but rarely offer it in my catalog because it very seldom produces any offsets, mostly just when damage has been done to the basal plate (although in the wild I have found a few plants with two bulbs under common old scales). But it sets seed well, especially now that I grow it in the greenhouse. The bulbs generally lie deep in soil.

The next plant seemed to be the same Juno I had seen at the bottom of the Chinoro Gorge, and now all doubt disappeared—this was only *Iris vicaria*, despite the color of the stem base. A large clump with fifteen bulbs of vegetative origin grew on the bank where a new glen started (Plate 166). Here it grew in open places, too.

While looking for more Junos I found another *Tulipa* species. It was very dwarf and early-flowering, bearing large seed capsules. Its intensely curved leaves were beautiful, and most intriguingly, it had up to four flowers on a branched stem. I had no idea what it was. Only later in the garden, when it flowered along with the crocuses and I could see its bright yellow blooms, did I realize that it was *T. hissarica* (Plate 173), the most early-flowering tulip in Latvian conditions. In terms of flowering time, only tulips in the *T. bifloriformis–T. turkestanica* complex can sometimes compete with it, but they don't have such large, bright flowers. Unfortunately, in Latvia it never forms such nicely curved leaves and isn't as compact. I now have samples from different populations, but the form from Hodji-Obi-Garm is the best. It can be grown outside or in the greenhouse and reproduces vegetatively, although I sow the seeds to build up the stock more quickly.

Tulipa praestans, with its flame red petals and bright red filaments, was also in full flower. It had the typical look of this species, but no plant had more than one flower on the stem. Only after a long search did I find some with two blooms. What a great difference from the cultivated forms grown in the Netherlands, which can have four to six flowers compactly spaced at the top of the stem. Its bulbs lay extremely deep, as much as 30 cm down, and it generally dwelled inside very spiny dwarf shrubs of *Rosa* species. One bulb from this population has survived for more than twenty years, but neither it nor its "colleagues" have produced any offsets during those years, while the Dutch forms increase very well.

We encountered two *Anemone* species here: yellow-flowered *A. petiolulosa* and white-flowered *A. tschernjaewii*. *Anemone petiolulosa* grew by the millions, its rootstocks and blooms larger than forms from other places. Regrettably, I did not succeed in growing this form in Latvia, and now I have only two plants of *A. petiolulosa*, both collected in 1997—one from Urungachsai, the other from Zaamin. They both set seed, but I haven't gotten any seedlings. I am apparently doing something wrong, but I still hope to discover the secret to growing these plants before I lose the original samples.

Anemone tschernjaewii was not so widespread in the area, where it generally grew inside shrubs. Its tubers were smaller, too. As with *A. petiolulosa*, I didn't have any luck growing this form, nor the form collected near Tashkent. The blooms of one plant looked intermediate between *A. petiolulosa* and *A. tschernjaewii*. Overall it was similar to *A. eranthoides*, growing in the same area, but seemed to be a hybrid with large white blooms. I received the true *A. eranthoides* with yellow blooms from Antoine Hoog, and it grows well in my greenhouse.

The weather was quite good at the moment. There was no rain, but clouds had obscured the sun, so it wasn't so exasperatingly hot as it had been in previous days. The shrubs around us were full of *Fritillaria bucharica*, and I later found a group of the same species in an open spot. This fritillary is very variable in height; there are many-flowering giants and also small plants with two or three flowers on the stem. It seems that the height depends on the size of the bulb and the growing conditions. It is an excellent grower, even outside. I had some plants that reached 40 cm tall with up to fifty blooms on the stem. Proliferation is often observed when several flower stems grow together as one, and over the last few years in my garden this plant started to reproduce vegetatively without any special splitting of the bulb. Generally all the stocks are quite similar, differing somewhat in height but not in color and shape of flower or foliage.

A rhizomatous *Iris* species grew here, too. It seemed to be *I. hoogiana*, a beautiful, bright sky blue iris with a wonderful aroma. Although it is not a rarity, most of the cultivated stocks from the Netherlands have a virus infection, so this turned out to be a very important acquisition for me. In Latvia it grows well outside, but it rarely flowered for me until I planted it in a greenhouse, where it now flourishes. Among the plants I collected there are three color forms: bright blue with a yellow beard, light purple with a yellowish brown beard, and dark purple with a dark brownish beard on the falls. All reach some 60 cm tall with up to three large, magnificent flowers on the stem. The best form of *I. hoogiana* was found on the opposite side of the Varzob Valley by Arnis Seisums (Plate 174). It is a true gem, with pure snow white petals enhanced by a bright yellow beard on the falls. The old cultivated stocks were virus-infected, so this form disappeared from cultivation before we introduced it again from the wild.

Four *Allium* species grew here, but only two were later identified, and I still grow them. I had collected one of them, *A. stipitatum*, many times before, but here I found a group with twelve large bulbs growing together. From this group came a variety initially offered as 'Hodji-Obi-Garm' but later renamed 'Glory of Pamir'. In 1997 it received a Trial Garden Award from the Royal General Bulb Growers' Association in Holland. It has wide leaves with slightly hairy margins and a long, strong stem topped with a dense, globular, bright lilac flower head.

Allium stipitatum is very important in gardening. Many nice garden hybrids arise from its "blood," one of the most important being 'Globus', a hybrid with *A. karataviense*. Crosses with the purple *A. aflatunense* have resulted in 'Mars' and the pure white 'Mount Everest'. 'World Cup' is a cultivar I selected from the open-pollinated seedlings of *A. macleanii*. Judging by the flower it looks more like *A. macleanii*, but the bulb is closer to *A. stipitatum*. Its most unusual feature is its very decorative, large, wide leaves, which keep a decorative shape much longer than the other tall-growing species and hybrids. It is described in my notes as "fantastical." It makes huge bulbs and is an excellent increaser.

The other species from Hodji-Obi-Garm, *Allium darwasicum*, is much smaller, with the flower stem rarely exceeding 40 cm, but it has nice, upturned, pure white flowers. It is an excellent addition to any *Allium* collection; only a few Turkish species compare with it in terms of size and color, but there is nothing like it in terms of the shape of the blooms. A flower of the typical form is snow white throughout with a nice greenish midrib, but in the mountains of Tajikistan near Iol, Arnis Seisums found a tremendously rare form that has a deep yellow throat and creamy petals, so that the whole flower looks light yellow. It is an extreme rarity, and before this its occurrence had never before been recorded in botanical literature. Its seedlings are also yellow in shade, although they look somewhat lighter than the initial stock. It reproduces well vegetatively and grows perfectly outside, too. It has been named 'Darwas Wonder'.

A thunderstorm went on all afternoon, and as I inspected the last plant, some *Crocus korolkowii* just near our tent, a heavy shower started and we had to toss everything into the tent as quickly as possible. Later, as it started to darken, the rain stopped and I left for a last walk around the hills. The growing conditions here were very different. Our tent was on deep clay, in a short distance there were granite outcrops, then some shale, and after that there was a sandstone hill. On a very sandy slope grew copious amounts of *Gymnospermium darwasicum*. This was replaced at higher elevations by *Fritillaria bucharica*, whose flowers covered the slope like snow, and on the very top in eroded sandstone grew *Tulipa hissarica*. I reached the snow, where the crocuses and gymnospermiums were in full flower. The *C. korolkowii* blooms were uniformly yellow; the ones from Agalik and Aman-Kutan were far better.

The next day we took a bus to the airport. Halfway to Dushanbe a young man got on from a bus stop where another road turned toward Takob. He was holding a large bunch of wildflowers, including bright blue blooms of *Iris hoogiana*, red blooms of *Paeonia hybrida*, deep pink *Eremurus*, and about a dozen reddish and orange blooms of *Fritillaria eduardii*. I would have stopped here if our plane tickets weren't reserved for that afternoon. It wouldn't even have mattered that we had already eaten the last of our food. I supposed that it was here that Arnis had collected his stock of *F. eduardii*. I only have some bulbs of *I. rosenbachiana* from Takob that were collected by Czech plant collectors, but in color they more closely resemble the Harangon stock than the stock from Chinoro.

At the airport we found that all flights to Tashkent had been delayed until nine o'clock in the evening, but as it turned out, our flight didn't leave until the next morning. When we finally reached Tashkent, it was raining cats and dogs. Our flights home weren't scheduled until the next day, so we passed the time talking and dining with Volodya, who was kind enough to bring us several kilos of freshly gathered strawberries. Strawberries in May—this was something incredible for people of the Baltics during Soviet times. Despite our heavy luggage, Mari and I both bought 3 kilos to take home. The flight attendant, however, wouldn't allow us on the plane with them. There was a rule prohibiting fresh fruits and flowers from being transported by private persons. Needless to say, once our flight attendant had ten rubles in her pocket, everything was okay.

Zaamin

The Turkestan Mountains lie northeast of Pendzhikent. There are three parallel mountain ranges, all of which join in Tajikistan. The southernmost range is Hissar, which
we visited in Varzob; the middle range is Zeravshan, where at the Tajik end we visited
Shing; and the northernmost range is Turkestan, above which the border between
Uzbekistan and Tajikistan lies. I went there with Arnis Seisums, to Zaamin. *Allium
oreophilum* 'Kusavli Curl', a dwarf beauty with curled leaves, was known to grow on
the opposite side (the Tajik part).

During Soviet times most of my expeditions looked more like holidays, with minimal studies conducted beforehand about the plants growing in the area we were
traveling to. It was great luck that we found anything at all, much less so many valuable plants. My real scientific expeditions started after the Soviet era when I teamed
up with Arnis, whom I have now known a very long time. Arnis was a schoolboy when
he first received bulbs from me. He later studied at the University of Latvia, received
a doctorate from the Komarov Botanical Institute in Saint Petersburg, and began
his work at the National Botanical Garden of Latvia. His doctoral thesis was an examination of the taxonomy of alliums, but he is also very interested in bulbous irises
and many other bulbs and is working with Tony Hall (Kew) on a monograph about
Juno irises.

In the *Flora of Tajikistan* (Ovcinnikov 1963), A. I. Vvedenskyi mentioned unidentified Juno irises of the *Iris parvula* group found growing in the Turkestan Mountains
near Zaamin. Although he had never seen a live specimen, he said that the herbarium
specimens he had seen seemed very close to *I. tadshikorum*, which is described as coming from the northern slopes of the Darwas Mountains, very far to the south just at
the border with Afghanistan. *Iris parvula* was known from both sides of the Turkestan
Mountains, and *I. linifolia* was found not very far from Zaamin. We decided that we
needed to go to this area to try to find this mysterious Juno. There are four closely
related dwarf Juno irises known in Central Asia: *I. parvula*, *I. linifolia*, *I. tadshikorum*,
and *I. vvedenskyi*. Only *I. vvedenskyi* had been found in a place very far from Zaamin,
at the border with Turkmenistan (a location left for our last expedition to Uzbekistan), so the question was which iris grew at Zaamin.

We started at seven o'clock. Zaamin is quite far from Tashkent, and the trip to
the Supa mountain pass (2600 m) took five hours. It was a protected area, although
not strictly so, and the archa forests generally hadn't been destroyed. The foothills
greeted us with bright pink flowers of *Eremurus olgae* (again we made the usual mistake, agreeing to collect it on the way back, a promise that was never fulfilled), and
above 2000 m we encountered another very beautiful species, *E. kaufmannii* (Plate
176), with densely covered spikes of beautiful, large, creamy yellow flowers. This was
one of the most stunning eremurus I ever saw in the mountains, but sadly it also
turned out to be among the most difficult in cultivation. Its additional roots are thin

and deep-growing, not at all ideal for a gardener. In fact this species has a bad reputation among growers, even those living in Central Asia.

We stopped at the roadside, where water was trickling out of the rock just below us. There was no place to set up our tent, so we started our ascent by a beautiful but steep meadow where a lot of archa was growing. In the shade of some archa we had lunch and, after hiding our haversacks under a large tree, continued our quest for a campsite while simultaneously searching for plants. Here we found our first *Allium barsczewskii*. It was the usual form, light violet and not very spectacular, but later we found quite nice plants with very dark, almost blackish purple flowers. This species is among my favorites, so I was very satisfied. Unfortunately, though, the deep purple form didn't grow well for me back in Latvia, and I lost my stock within a few years.

We walked up a moderate slope. Zaamin was one of the most heavily forested parts of Central Asia I had ever been to. As the first open, exposed rocks came into view, we saw our first Juno irises. They looked very similar to *Iris parvula* but could also be *I. linifolia* or *I. tadshikorum*. Later at home we were able to identify them as *I. tadshikorum*. Fortunately, the seeds were perfectly ripe for collecting.

Juno irises differ a lot in how much they are able to regenerate a bulb from broken roots or form new roots from a bulb if the basal plate has been broken off. There is a method for increasing the rate of vegetative reproduction. Some growers recommend cutting off the fleshy roots together with a small part of the basal plate, so that they will then form a new bulb. Quite often some roots are broken off unintentionally, and at planting time you can sometimes (though not always) observe that at the top of this a new shoot has formed. I have never intentionally tried to break the roots, so I haven't checked the effectiveness of this method, and I don't know whether the roots that form a new growth really have a piece of the basal plate attached. I have found that all species from the *Iris parvula* group perfectly regenerate the bulb from additional roots, and the bulb makes new roots. In the case of *I. vicaria*, *I. orchioides*, and *I. magnifica*, the bulb very rarely survives without a basal plate. However, it does sometimes happen, and some roots can form new shoots, too. Experiments have to be carried out to find the conditions in which this works.

A *Tulipa* species from section *Eriostemones* was growing in the openings between large archas. It had fat seedpods. Identifying it would have to be done later at home, when it would flower in the garden. It turned out to be a poor grower, however, and we still don't know the name.

On top of this nice side ridge were wonderful meadows—excellent places to camp, except that there was no water in sight and everything around was absolutely dry. The nearest water source was the spring at the roadside. It wasn't very far, just down to the road again and about 2 km from there. The way down wasn't too difficult, although the temperature was around 30°C, but coming back up with our cans full of water was an arduous task. It took two to three hours out of each day because we needed water for tea and soup.

We decided to devote the first day to getting to know this area and the second day to exploring subalpine and alpine meadows. On a quite bare opening of stony ground some 10 m from our tent, we found a nice, very low, wide-leaved *Allium* species. The first name that came to mind was *A. nevskianum*, but it looked somewhat different from this species and the growing conditions weren't typical. Had we found *A. alexejanum* (Plate 177)? Our allium specialist, Arnis, was initially doubtful because the flowers had a purplish tint that was more characteristic of *A. nevskianum*, but a careful examination showed that the blooms were actually white, with purple tinting only at the midrib. The flower stalks were very thick, the pedicels generally uneven—more features used to distinguish between the two species. For me the growing conditions were the most important factor. I had only found samples of *A. nevskianum* on proper scree slopes, where the bulbs grew in peat washed down between stones, and it usually grew in groups—I had only rarely found individual plants. Here in Zaamin our allium was growing on flat or very slightly sloped, sunburned meadows with a thin layer of brick-hard clay soil covering the hard rock beneath it. It almost never made large groups, the bulbs were generally placed some distance from each other, and they didn't make line-shaped colonies as occurred with *A. nevskianum*. On the very rare occasions that we did find small groups of a few plants, they were still some distance apart. And this allium grew on the barest spots where there were no other plants.

Arnis felt that if he were the botanist who had discovered and described these two alliums, he would have hesitated to separate them into individual species, preferring to keep them as subspecies. But in any case, both are quite different. *Allium nevskianum* is an excellent grower in my nursery and reproduces well vegetatively. In my opinion it is far better than the usual commercial forms of *A. karataviense*. It can only be guessed how *A. alexejanum* will do in our gardens, but we collected enough stock to establish it in cultivation. Its natural growing conditions raise some doubt about how successfully it can be cultivated, but then I remember the few bulbs of *A. brachyscapum* I collected in the Kopet-Dag: though in the wild *A. brachyscapum* grows in much harsher, hotter, drier conditions, it has adapted surprisingly well to my Latvian climate and is an excellent grower. I still haven't risked planting *A. alexejanum* outside. I grow it only in the greenhouse, where it performs perfectly, but since it doesn't increase vegetatively I have to collect the seeds. It is a beautiful addition to my allium collection and is easy to distinguish in the garden from *A. nevskianum*.

We found an abundance of some *Anemone* species (possibly *A. petiolulosa*) and *Colchicum* species (possibly *C. luteum*), as well as some *Eranthis longistipitata*, but all had dry stems and seed capsules that had just started to open. It's a pity, but I didn't collect any of these, although later I collected seeds from a large-growing *Tulipa* species (possibly *T. affinis*). In the evening we walked down to fill our cans with water and have a wash.

At six o'clock the next morning we had some tea and started our way up to the mountain pass. We passed through a small valley, at the end of which was a tent. Out of the tent jumped a man dressed in sports clothes and whistling—a border guard. The border with Tajikistan cut right through the top of the Turkestan Mountains. The man checked our documents and asked for a special permit. Nothing helped—no amount of talking, no offering of money. He was very angry that we had woken him up so early in the morning. We would have to stay at our camp and spend the second day there without going up. If we had known this would happen, we would have gotten the necessary permit back in Tashkent with the help of our friends.

So we returned to our camp, where we took some photos and continued to explore the same ridge. We found a nice clump of a snow white mutation of *Gentiana olivieri* (Plate 178), and later found a very slightly bluish white one. We collected the latter form for Henrik Zetterlund. We also found *Ungernia oligostroma*, which was very different from all the other *Ungernia* species I had seen before. Its bulbs were comparatively small, round, and shallowly placed in the ground.

Since it seemed as though there wasn't anything to look for on the hill where we had camped, we decided to fetch water and then check the ridge on the opposite side of the road, which looked extremely dry, sunburned, and brown. It proved to be a good decision. We soon found another *Eremurus* species of subgenus *Heningia* with spikes of loose, light pink flowers still in bud.

The north side of the hill was much greener. In the meadows grew a great deal of *Allium stipitatum* plants and a few plants of *A. caesium*. The latter is a relative of *A. caeruleum* but is much smaller, only 30–40 cm high, and has tubular leaves. It turned out to be an excellent addition to my collection. The flowers are differently colored from the other samples I grow, bright blue with an even darker midvein. It has proved to be the best grower of all my acquisitions and reproduces well vegetatively, usually making three to six (sometimes as many as ten) large bulbils at the base, some at the stem. The bulbs rarely split. At Ihnachsai we found another excellently growing form, with more lax umbels and very light blue, slightly greenish-tinted blooms with a darker midvein. It resembles a blue summer sky with white clouds floating by. I named it 'Pskem's Beauty'. Unfortunately, it is a much slower increaser, and only a few bulblets are usually formed at the basal plate. Another form from Aravan in the Fergana Valley has pinkish violet blooms and flowers earlier than other forms. Its bulb doesn't form bulbils but usually splits in two or three. It is somewhat susceptible to rot, so the stock increases very slowly. Good drainage is necessary for *A. caesium* to grow successfully, but its beauty compensates for the effort required to grow it.

As we returned to our camp we passed a few *Allium alexejanum* and a small-growing *Tulipa* species of section *Eriostemones*. The seedpods of this tulip were different from those we had collected earlier from a larger tulip. In my collection the smaller form, *T. bifloriformis*, turned out to be the far better grower. It is dwarf in habit, half the size at flowering time, and hence much more attractive than the usual Dutch stock. Among my stocks of this species it is among the last to bloom, producing flowers after the others have already finished.

Getting back on the road, we again headed down to the spring for water, then decided to take the shortest way back up, which involved short zigzags up an extremely steep slope. On this slope grew a great deal of *Iris tadshikorum* (Plate 179),

Allium barsczewskii, *Tulipa* species of the *T. bifloriformis–T. turkestanica* type, and *Colchicum luteum*. There was a bit more shade here and the vegetation was richer. Surprisingly, when we got to the top we couldn't find our tent. In fact it looked as though someone had hidden our whole meadow away. It turned out we had come up the wrong way, so we had to return to our starting point and make a second weary trip up the mountain.

The next morning we decided to collect a few tubers of *Pseudosedum* species and look for *Tulipa affinis*. The previous evening Arnis had found *T. affinis* underneath some trees, but he had simultaneously encountered a wild boar protecting her piglets, so he fled. Now we could see that a lot of areas had been dug up, and all that remained of the tulips were a few shells. At least there was still plenty of *Pseudosedum*.

The rootstocks of some *Pseudosedum* species are very thick and tuber-like, which is why I include them in my collection as well as in this book. The leaves are succulent, resembling fat little sausages attached to the stem, like Latvia's native *Sedum acre* only with a much longer stem, on the top of which is a branched inflorescence. *Pseudosedum fedtschenkoanum* (Plate 180), which grew at Zaamin, has thin roots with round or egg-shaped, thickened parts. Its stems are up to 30 cm long and densely covered with small, cylindrical leaves, on top of which is a horizontally held, branched inflorescence of small pinkish blooms. Another species, *P. ferganense*, was collected in the Kugart Valley in Kyrgyzstan. In general it is quite similar to *P. fedtschenkoanum* but is very easily distinguished by its roots, which are very thick and tuber-like throughout. I grow both species only in the greenhouse, where they start forming leaves in late autumn. Neither is difficult to grow, but they can suffer from excessive moisture and are susceptible to *Fusarium nivale* in winter. For this reason it is necessary to regularly check for and detach any rotten stems. I have never lost any of these plants, since new stems appear in place of any dead ones, and the first sunny days usually put an end to *Fusarium*. *Fusarium nivale* thrives best in dark cloudy weather with temperatures only slightly above zero. It can be controlled with an excellent fungicide called Switch.

We saw a white car on the road far below us. Although it was only half past ten, our driver had come early and had already been waiting for us for more than an hour. In the mountains the temperature was 27°C, but as we drove lower the temperature rose. Soon it reached 38°C, then 41°C, and by the time we reached Tashkent it was 46°C. I had never before experienced such heat. Volodya's house was slightly cooler because it was shaded by grape leaves. He also kept the path in front of the house watered, so the evaporation cooled the air somewhat. In Tashkent the *chilya* had begun, a period without any rain and with daily temperatures above 40°C.

So now we had found *Iris tadshikorum*, but what should the true, typical *I. parvula* look like? The best way to check would be to look for it in the place from which it had been described. *Iris parvula* was described as coming from the heights of Sina Valley in the Chulbair Mountains in the southwestern corner of the Gissar Range, Uzbekistan. That would be our next destination.

Far Road to Sina

Sina is situated in southeastern Uzbekistan, and Arnis Seisums and I had to pass several mountains to reach it. We went there in 1998, which turned out to be one of the richest years for finding rare and new plants, even though I only took two trips, the first to Sina and the second to Ihnachsai.

Arnis had just returned from an expedition to Iran where he had worked with botanists from Gothenburg and the Iranian Institute of Botany. More than three hundred samples had been collected, and these were mostly plants that neither of us had previously grown. I most enjoyed *Geranium kotschyi* and a marvelous Reticulata iris found between the villages of Aligardaz and Schoolabad, but there were plenty of other beauties, too. Before moving on to Sina, I must mention a few of these plants that Arnis collected and that I now grow. At the top of the list is *Colchicum persicum*, which Arnis collected near Yazd. It is an extreme rarity and is especially important for bulb experts. The flowers are rich pink, comparatively big, and wide open, with a fairly thick (and therefore long-lasting) perianth, but the plant needs high summer temperatures to induce the flower buds. Proper drainage and as much sun as possible are also necessary. In northern latitudes, *C. persicum* is more appropriate for growing in a pot or frame. In the central Elburz Mountains, Arnis encountered another representative of Colchicaceae, *C. kurdicum* (described earlier in "Near Lake Cherepash'ye").

Many stunning alliums were also collected in Iran. All are of a type that I call "*Allium karataviense* compeers"—they have a large, globular inflorescence lying between two or more wider or narrower leaves at ground level. The question automatically arises: Why do we need these plants if we already have the well-tested, easy-growing *A. karataviense*? My reply is that each species has its own very special beauty. From these Iranian collections I still grow *A. elburzense* (Plate 181) from Tochal, *A. haemanthoides* (Plate 182) from Kuh-e-Pashmanu, *A. minutiflorum* (Plate 183) from Hunsan, *A. shelkovnikovii* (Plate 184) from Kuh-e-Bosphane, and some other acquisitions of those species. Superficially they are all somewhat similar, but if somebody asked me which one I liked best, I wouldn't be able to answer. I like them all. The differences are generally botanical—one of them has shorter petals (*A. minutiflorum*), another has yellow anthers (*A. shelkovnikovii*), the perianth of *A. elburzense* is star-shaped, that of *A. haemanthoides* is somewhat campanulate. The greatest advantage of all of them is their smaller size and relatively larger inflorescence compared with the foliage. None can be grown outside in my region; they need a good, dry summer rest, so I grow them only in the greenhouse, where they set seed perfectly. Collecting the seed is very important because none of these alliums has produced any offsets yet for me, but the seedlings grow perfectly, and I'll soon have a second generation of flowering size.

But now I return to Uzbekistan. The main goal of our expedition was to collect several bulbous iris species, namely a few Juno iris type specimens, which meant visiting the places from which these species had been described. In this way we would have a chance to find out exactly what plants the various species names had been applied to. We could also compare the type specimens with samples from other places and consequently discern whether species from different locations are just variations of the same thing or are in fact more than one species.

As had become quite common for all my expeditions, just before leaving home I came down with some health problems—perhaps my body's way of protesting my abandonment of home and garden. Anyway, a course of treatment and medication helped, and I received the final injection on my last day at home.

We flew from Riga to Tashkent by way of Moscow. The first morning in Tashkent we were up at six o'clock and reached the village of Sina at five o'clock in the afternoon. The river cut the road here, leaving large stones blocking the way, so we couldn't go any further by car. We parted from our driver. He would stay at a hotel in Denau for two days and then come back to pick us up.

The walking wasn't easy. Although we were going by the road and our haversacks weren't as heavy as they had been on past trips, our lack of training was obvious. After half an hour we stopped for a quick rest, then, feeling better, continued on until we reached a summer camp for schoolboys. The officials there checked our passports carefully, listing in their notebooks everything written in them, even all of our previous visas, and then allowed us to set up our tent at the upper end of the camp.

The territory of the camp was long and the upper end was almost a kilometer away from the entrance. However, for us this was a kind of bonus—the higher in the mountains we resided, the shorter the distance we would have to walk to reach the top. Our tent was situated under a large walnut tree. The Sina River flowed just beside it, and since there were no villages or houses this high in the mountains, the water was crystal-clear water and good for drinking. Arnis made the first discovery: just a few meters from our tent was a group of Juno irises, what appeared to be *Iris vicaria*. The seeds were almost ripe and later we collected many of them. We still needed to find *I. parvula* and *I. rosenbachiana*, both of which were described as coming from this location (the latter under the name *I. nicolai*).

The next morning we awoke early, at five o'clock. The first stage of the route was quite difficult for me as the ascent was rather steep. We went up along a short ridge, from where we could see the remains of a road. We later learned that higher up the mountain, at about 3000 m, some kind of ore had been found, after which a mine was opened up, lots of machines were brought together, and a 10 km road was built right up to the mine. But when all of this was finished the engineers realized they had forgotten to build an ore-processing factory, so the mine was filled up and the road abandoned. This had happened here only three years before, but the very same thing used to happen in the Soviet Union.

Although the road hadn't been kept in shape, it greatly facilitated climbing. It was not easy in the beginning. I was constantly out of breath, but I strained every nerve, clenched my teeth, and thought, "Ahead." The day before we had reached an altitude of 2000 m in a very short time and were not yet accustomed to the altitude.

An abundance of *Eremurus stenophyllus* grew on the hillside. It was still in bud and had very narrow, even thread-like leaves compared with other species. Higher up it was replaced by another *Eremurus* species that had shed its blossoms and had big round pods. Everywhere around us grew *Iris vicaria*, its leaves half-yellow and the seeds nearly ripe. It grew in stony, gravelly clay, both on scree by the roadside and on very steep slopes, generally exposed to the south, east, or west, where conditions were drier. The base of the stem was green or violet—just like in the Varzob Gorge in Tajikistan.

In many places the road had been washed away or covered by a landslide. In such places our only path was a slightly visible, sloping animal track. The main thing was to be courageous and move forward without looking down, and I soon realized that the swifter I crossed the landslide, the safer I would be. The road snaked around five big side gorges. The first two were dry but in the third there was a tiny spring of clean, clear water. I rinsed my hands and washed my face but did not drink. I filled my cap with water and put it on my head—very refreshing, although it dried quickly in the hot sun. Each new side gorge was deeper and steeper than the last, and here and there the path went along completely vertical cliffs. The springs flowing at the bottom of the gorges were now richer in water. As we climbed higher we approached the snow line and springtime—below us it was scorching summer, while up in the mountains it was still winter.

As the slope became less steep, *Iris rosenbachiana* started to appear. Again I noticed *I. vicaria* growing in a stonier habitat, whereas *I. rosenbachiana* tended to occupy more sheltered places facing northeast, north, and northwest, mountain meadows where the soil was more packed and clay-like, keeping its moisture longer. I never saw both species side by side. Here, as in the Chinoro Gorge of the Varzob Valley, one species ended and the other began. This seemed to be determined by soil conditions, because at higher altitudes *I. vicaria* reappeared.

Iris rosenbachiana, too, had shed its blooms long ago, and its seeds were almost ripe. The soil was also very moist from a downpour that had occurred a few days before. In general it had been a cool, very wet year in Central Asia. The bulbs were large and swollen, with mighty adventitious roots. In the wild both *I. rosenbachiana* and *I. vicaria* had gotten extra water during the growing period, and for this reason both grew fairly well in the conditions of my garden.

It was quite an easy walk; the road higher up had remained in good condition. There were some damaged places, but these could be easily walked around along an excellent animal track. Now and again we found some *Crocus korolkowii* plants as well as *Scilla puschkinioides* (Plate 185). The form of *S. puschkinioides* from Sina turned out to be the best grower and increaser in the garden, but *C. korolkowii* was of the same pale color as the form from Varzob.

As we came out of an archa thicket we entered a magnificently beautiful, relatively flat meadow with large groups of *Iris stolonifera* (Plate 186) flowering in the most fantastic colors. I took as many photos as I could while Arnis collected a sample of each for himself, me, and Henrik Zetterlund. This was the origin of my varieties of *I. stolonifera*. 'Sina Dark' has flowers of a strange purplish brown tint, not easy to describe. The midzone of the standards is distinctly light violet. 'Network' has intensely veined petals (thus the name) and very undulate standards. Brown, white, yellow, and light violet tints are beautifully joined in the flower. Other varieties are still grown only under numbers.

As magnificent as this meadow was, we didn't want to stay there for long. Arnis had to find type specimens of *Iris parvula* so that we could compare it with a sample collected last year in Zaamin. This would allow us to see whether they were in fact the same species. The road led further along the ridge of a side range. Our ascent became much easier because the slope was less steep, and we moved along at a fast pace.

All of a sudden I spotted a geranium. Judging by its leaves it must have been *Geranium charlesii* (Plate 187), though a unique dwarf form of it (a trait that could be well explained by the altitude). The color of the leaves was most striking—grayish green with very beautiful, bright reddish purple veining and stippling. The density of the dotting and streaking was variable but certainly gave the plant a special charm. While I was photographing this beauty, Arnis made his way higher up the cliff, and I soon heard his triumphant shout: "This is it! I've found *Iris parvula*!" A specimen from the type locality had been procured.

As we continued on we encountered more *Iris parvula* (Plate 188) and *Geranium charlesii* from time to time, and soon spotted our first tulips—some bright red ones grew some distance below us on the slope. These were rather tall tulips with petal bases that varied in color from yellow to black; the color of the filaments was also variable. Arnis thought they must be *Tulipa carinata* (Plate 189), which could grow here. In the same place we found some flowering plants of *I. parvula*. Here they were quite big, about 20 cm tall, compared with plants in Zaamin that were only 5–10 cm tall. *Iris parvula* is a beautiful species. Although its flowers are not big, they complement the fine foliage and slender stature. The plants from Zaamin are small, and in the garden their flowers are pale lilac, almost colorless. The plants from Sina, however, can be called very showy. I agree with Arnis that the Sina form is a different species from the form from Zaamin.

Interestingly, the higher we got, the more *Iris parvula* plants we found reproducing vegetatively. So we were faced with a dilemma—which ones should we collect? The higher forms would probably reproduce better, but the lower ones had more mature bulbs. On the other hand, the plants at lower altitudes grew in more extreme conditions, and since this species doesn't like too much heat, the plants there were more depressed. The plants at higher altitudes grew in more favorable conditions, which stimulated growing and increasing.

A little further along I noticed a very beautiful plant of *Iris vicaria*. The flowers were strongly blue with light yellow falls. I wondered what the flowers of the forms growing at considerably lower altitudes, which now had almost ripe seeds, would be like. I would have to wait until the next spring. I was most interested by the pattern we had found: first the most low-growing *I. vicaria*, then a belt of *I. rosenbachiana*, then *I. parvula* higher up, soon rejoined by *I. vicaria*, and at the very top only *I. parvula*. Later we also found *I. rosenbachiana* in the foothills.

And then—what's this? A cluster of *Iris vicaria* with yellow-striped leaves. Then another and another. They seemed to be badly virus-infected. The plants looked very weak, although they still had nice blooms. Unfortunately, virus infections aren't limited to gardens.

Now we had passed the ridge and our path again followed an old road into a neighboring gorge. At a beautiful spring with a waterfall we took some rest and had a short lunch of raisins and nuts. Here we found *Colchicum luteum* that had just finished flowering, unlike the forms growing along the snow beds that increasingly crossed our path, which were only just starting to bloom. We also noticed a very interesting tulip with flowers similar to those of *Tulipa bifloriformis* and rather broad, undulate leaves. It was the quite recently described *T. orithyioides* (Plate 190), well distinguished from other species by its elongated style. A year later I received a sample of a very similar tulip; in fact it was identical in terms of the shape of the plant, leaves, and flowers, and the flowering time, but had a less prominently extended style. It had been collected somewhere in Tajikistan by a Lithuanian grower. I classified it as *T. orithyioides*, too, despite the difference between the styles. The plant collected by the Lithuanian seems somewhat easier in the garden than the one from Sina.

Our road ended at a mine. It looked as though copper had been mined there because all the stones were greenish. There was no longer any path nor any reason to continue on, with only bare stones ahead, followed by a solid blanket of snow. We were quite happy and not at all weary even though we had managed to ascend more than 1500 m. Only a slight headache confirmed that we were now above 3000 m. We had covered about 10 km. On our way back we saw some very funny dandelions with purple-violet foliage, but I didn't collect them—we already had plenty of weeds at home. Afterward, though, I thought of how I would've liked to know whether they kept their leaf color at lower altitudes.

Then we found *Corydalis nudicaulis* (Plate 191). It was the first time I had seen it in the wild. All the stocks I grew in the garden had been collected by other plant hunters. *Corydalis nudicaulis* is a very special species, called the coffee and cream corydalis because of the two colors joined in its flowers: dark coffee brown with a creamy white spur. Compared with other stocks, this one is very late-flowering, so we keep it separately under the name 'Sina'. The stock from Varzob has comparatively smaller but abundant flowers in a lax raceme. Another one from Tovilj-Dara has narrower leaflets and longer pedicels. While inspecting *C. nudicaulis* I also encountered *C. ledebouriana* (Plate 192). It turned out to be a very late-flowering form—of my ten different stocks, this one flowers last. For this reason it is less susceptible to late spring frosts and much more valuable from a gardener's point of view.

On a similar bare slope we stopped to examine a dwarf *Allium* species. At first glance it seemed to be *A. nevskianum*, but there were no scree slopes, and in such places *A. alexejanum* was more common. After careful checking at home, it was identified as *A. alexejanum*, and in my opinion was the best sample yet.

By the time we passed the *Iris stolonifera* meadow, our legs had started to ache. Walking downhill can be even more difficult on the muscles than going up. It was seven o'clock when we returned to the campsite.

The next morning we parted. Arnis stayed in our camp to guard our belongings while I returned to the fields of *Iris rosenbachiana*. I began by descending a very steep slope to reach a huge *Eremurus aitchisonii* (Plate 193) plant. Next to it were plenty of small seedlings. *Eremurus aitchisonii* is as magnificent as *E. robustus* but is most impressive for its broad, bright green leaves. This feature allows it to be identified with certainty, for no other species has such leaves. Its additional roots are thick and short, so it is easy to replant in the garden. I also wanted to reach some purple-leaved dandelions, but a thunderstorm began, forcing me to return—if it started to rain, the path would get wet and the landslide areas would become very dangerous, or even impossible, to cross.

I still needed to collect the forms of *Iris vicaria* growing lower in the mountains. I soon noticed a large vegetative group of this iris on a very steep slope in a solid mixture of gravel and clay, and another large colony grew close to the road at the bottom of a stony cliff. There were many Junos with perfect seedpods, so I collected these and soon held a big paper bag full of seeds.

In the afternoon it was Arnis's turn to go up. On returning he made fun of my not spotting *Gymnospermium darwasicum*, which was growing next to *Iris rosenbachiana* beneath an archa. At once I remembered that I did notice the dry leaves but thought them to be *Corydalis ledebouriana*. I should have realized that *C. ledebouriana* never hides under trees and there is no use in trying to find it in such shade. What a pity indeed, because the last time I collected *G. darwasicum* was in the 1980s in Varzob and now I had only one or two tubers. Fresh "blood" would be useful to ensure a better seed crop. On the other side of the ridge grew *Eminium albertii*, another plant that I could use, but alas, I did not collect it. In some damper places Arnis saw *Allium jesdianum*, but it was surrounded by such steep slopes that it was impossible to reach. There were many plants of *A. stipitatum*, too, but we did not gather any; this species was very uniform everywhere, and we already had an excellent stock from Hodji-Obi-Garm.

From time to time a few raindrops fell, and when we looked up at the mountaintops we could see that they were covered in thick fog and that a heavy rain was starting to fall. It would be pointless to continue our work in this kind of weather. All those high mountain beauties would have to remain unknown to us.

The next day we headed back to the spot where our driver would pick us up. On the way Arnis's eye caught *Iris rosenbachiana* growing on an almost vertical roadside slope about 3 m high. It turned out to be identical to plants from higher altitudes. We also found a few plants of *Allium suworowii* growing near a cornfield. In this region it grows as a weed and is used by local people as both foodstuff and medicine. The bulbs taste much like garlic. It has narrow leaves and pinkish lilac blooms in dense, semi-globose to globose umbels on a stem 70–80 cm long. In the garden it needs a sunny, well-drained place.

What a pity that we had to leave this district after having come such a long way. An area just a few valleys closer to the Tajik border was the type locality for *Allium lipskyanum*, the pure white relative of the beautiful *A. winklerianum*. It grew high in the mountains here, but there was nothing we could do in these heavy rains. We could only hope that the rain wouldn't reach the valley, because we still wanted to stop there for some very special plants.

I wasn't in such great shape and felt exhausted by the time we met up with our driver. Each time I got out of the car or stood up from a table I could hardly bend my legs. Nevertheless I was glad to see that at my age I could more or less keep up with Arnis. We headed to Aman-Kutan, where we wanted to overnight.

We could see from the black clouds covering the mountains that trouble was brewing. How would we pass the road, which was already half-destroyed when we first came here? In some spots the asphalt was covered with a thick layer of mud and we had to push the car across. At other times I had to walk in front of the car showing the driver with my hands exactly where to go. We finally came to the bridge that would take us across the river, but it had been destroyed by floods and mudslides. There was a ford some distance away, so we waded out and removed some of the larger stones to make room for the car to drive across. This was our last major trial. There were still some spots ahead where only half the road remained, but it was nothing compared with what we had just gone through.

We drove along the Pulkhakim River valley. There were beautiful rock outcrops by the roadsides and we decided to stop and take some pictures of the landscape. Masses of the beautiful *Capparis herbacea* grew here, with very large white blooms and enormous thistles. The local people used the fruits to make a tasty jam. Arnis also pointed me in the direction of what seemed to be *Fritillaria karelinii*, which grew here in abundance. I ascended a little higher and spotted a lot of seedpods that had been beaten to the ground by rain. The showers had been so heavy that they washed away the stems, but there were more left on plants higher up the slope. I had never before seen so many fritillaries of section *Rhinopetalum* together; only *F. bucharica* in Hodji-Obi-Garm, Tajikistan, had come close, but the population there had been less dense. Then I spotted some exposed bulbs. The rains had washed away the soil, but the roots had kept the bulbs firmly in place. I walked along the slope searching for such specimens. Fortunately the weather hadn't been too hot and sunny, so the bulbs had not been burned. I also collected a lot of seeds. Although we thought this was *F. karelinii*, it turned out to be an exceptionally beautiful fritillary of section *Rhinopetalum* (Plate 194). I'm still very doubtful about its correct identity, though; the only thing I know for sure is that it isn't *F. stenanthera*. Checking various floras, we found the descriptions of *F. karelinii*, *F. ariana*, and *F. gibbosa* to be very contradictory. The flowers of our plant are white with more or less prominent green tessellation on the petal exteriors, the leaves are wide and gray-green, the basal leaves are intensely undulate, and the plant itself is up to 20 cm high. It somewhat resembles *F. bucharica* in terms of the flower, and some growers have classified it as such, but its foliage is absolutely different. I have never seen anything similar in the many acquisitions of *F. bucharica* I have grown. I am thinking seriously about a new species name for this beauty. It used to grow excellently for me and produced a good crop of seeds. I was sure that it was well established in my nursery, but I lost almost all of my plants to a mysterious pathogen.

A small-flowering tulip, possibly *Tulipa sogdiana*, was also growing here, and I gathered its seeds. Arnis came across two *Allium* species, too, and found a few Juno irises at the foot of a cliff. The latter turned out to be *Iris narbutii*. This is a very beautiful species but is not easy to grow even in a greenhouse—it tends to emerge in the first days of January, and as a result the leaves get seriously damaged by frost. The flowers are a bizarre combination of violet-blue and yellow; however, this plant's most striking feature is its very big standards. It is among the most unusual Juno irises. The form collected here was not as beautiful as the one pictured in the *Quarterly Bulletin of the Alpine Garden Society* in 1998, but it was better than the one we found later in the Nuratau Range.

One of the alliums we encountered at this stop, *Allium baissunense* (Plate 195), became one of my favorites. It is an extraordinary species with a huge (up to 35 cm in diameter) lax flower head of greenish white flowers on a 50 cm stem, resembling fireworks exploding in the sky. Having stiff, non-fading perianth segments, it remains beautiful for a long time. It was unknown to gardeners before we introduced it, and if I had to select only one *Allium* species for my own garden, this would be it. Good drainage is essential. I still grow it only in the greenhouse.

We also found *Delphinium semibarbatum* (Plate 196), one of the two perennial yellow-flowering *Delphinium* species growing in Central Asia. Though it isn't actually a bulb, it forms a black rootstock some 7–10 cm long that stays dry in the second half of summer and is similar in this way to true bulbs. Both *Delphinium* species are distinguished only by the absence or presence of small whitish hairs on the outer surface of their petals and pedicels and by the length of the spur. Their areas of distribution overlap. In my nursery I keep the rootstocks in dry sand until replanting, and they survive and flower fabulously in my greenhouse in the summer. This delphinium blooms very abundantly with beautiful, creamy yellow blossoms and is fully hardy, though it can be damaged by excessive moisture in winter. In the garden it forms an explicitly branched stem, reaching some 70 cm tall, and is much more floriferous than it is in the wild. It sets seed well, too, and the seeds germinate perfectly. It is possible to increase this species by breaking the rootstock into pieces, but growing from seed is the faster, easier way to go, since seedlings flower in two or three years. Another sample was collected during our last expedition to Uzbekistan at Kugitang; I recently determined that these plants are the closely related *D. biternatum*, which I had been searching for to complete my collection.

On the left side of the road we passed some rather high mountains notched by ravines and large caves in nearly vertical cliff walls. This was the Susitau Range, where Arnis had earlier collected *Fritillaria olgae*, another fritillary that grows comparatively well in the garden. Here *Iris vicaria*, which grows further south (closer to Dushanbe), was replaced by *I. warleyensis*, which grows further north (closer to Samarkand). Unfortunately the road leading through the mountains was closed, so our plans to make another stop there failed, and there was nothing left to do but drive along the western end of the Baisuntau Range. The next stop was not far from Shurab, where layers of white gypsum and red rock emerged by the roadside.

We wandered up into the mountains for a couple of hours. The gypsum outcrops were very peculiar. The top layers of rock were pure white and soft, easy to stab an ice pick into, but the layers underneath were hard. We soon spotted our first plants. I found a flower stalk without seeds and knew at once that it was *Bellevalia atroviolacea*, a nice small plant with very dark, almost black-violet flowers. Meanwhile Arnis found a wonderful onion, *Allium gypsaceum* (Plate 212), which in accordance with its name was growing on the gypsum outcrops. I was very happy with this discovery—now my collection could be replenished with a most outstanding acquisition. I collected another form of this species in Kugitang, where it grew on limestone, and both stocks turned out to be quite different in leaf color. The leaves of the plants from Shurab are soft green, while those from Kugitang are bluish gray-green. It is a unique species— nothing compares with it in all the world of alliums. The dense flower umbels are produced in early summer on stalks about 20 cm tall. They are packed with comparatively big, narrowly cup-shaped, brownish straw-colored flowers, prominently veined bright purple both on the midveins and on the margins of the segments. I don't know of any similarly colored flower. It needs good drainage and prolonged dry summer dormancy, so it can be grown only in a greenhouse. Its seeds must be collected too, as it doesn't increase vegetatively. But it is a very good pot plant and would certainly be a show winner if it were more widely grown.

Arnis, who had wandered rather far away, shouted to me that he had found *Allium protensum*, one of the species with huge umbels. Indeed, I soon found it on my own. I later also found *A. oschaninii*, one of the progenitors of edible onions and a plant still consumed by local people. It seemed to reproduce rather well vegetatively. It is true that *A. oschaninii* isn't among the most easy-growing *Allium* species, but it has grown in my garden on the open ground for more than twenty years, where it blooms splendidly each August. Its dense umbels of white flowers are held on long stems.

Iris svetlaneae was also growing here, but as Arnis continued searching for more Juno irises, I turned back in the direction of the car. This was when I chanced to notice another beauty in the grass: *Allium verticillatum* (Plate 213). Two years ago we had fumbled about on a field in the Nuratau Range trying to find its narrow, thin, grass-like leaves, but here it was in flower. It forms a large (up to 7 cm in diameter), globular, but not dense inflorescence on a 20 cm stem. These proportions alone make it extremely beautiful. It was later also collected in Kugitang, and again both stocks look somewhat different. I keep a dry inflorescence of this beauty on my table in a small glass perfume vial bought in Egypt. Its light, delicate appearance is perfect for just such a container. Like *A. gypsaceum*, this species would certainly be a show winner if it were widely cultivated. Its growing requirements are very similar to those of *A. gypsaceum* and it also must be grown from seed, but it is a more difficult species.

Around six o'clock in the evening we finally reached Aman-Kutan. After walking for half an hour we found a nice place for our tent among huge granite blocks that had been sculpted over time by wind, rain, and frost. This was among the most fantastic sites we saw during our expedition. Nearly every block was as interesting and unique as a modern sculpture.

An unusually bright form of *Allium barsczewskii* bloomed wonderfully all around, and here and there *Eremurus robustus* raised its mighty spikes. It was freezing cold, and as I started to make tea, Arnis returned from a walk. He had come across a very beautiful form of *Gentiana olivieri* with pink flowers, a nice companion to the white form we had found the year before at Zaamin. He had also seen many plants of *Geranium charlesii* and *Allium protensum* and had even encountered *Iris magnifica*, which I had failed to find here seventeen years before. It grew on rocks here as it had in the Agalik Valley and had the same range of color.

This was the first night of the trip in which I didn't take off my sweater. A strong wind blew all night long, and raindrops fell from time to time—we couldn't believe this was the middle of June in Central Asia. It took a very long time to fall asleep.

The next morning we headed up to look for the seeds of *Iris warleyensis*. We reached a small ravine made of weathered granite, and there we spotted the first tulips of the *Tulipa bifloriformis–T. turkestanica* complex. We also encountered *Geranium charlesii* and a very beautiful cluster of *Allium barsczewskii*. Hardly had we stepped on a shepherd's pass when we spotted the first plants of *I. warleyensis*. They were up to 40 cm tall, larger than any forms we had ever seen, and reproduced well vegetatively. In other places this species was usually much smaller and practically never increased vegetatively. I recalled how the plants of *I. warleyensis* that we found in Shing were always single, short-stemmed plants. I would not agree to recognize it as *I. warleyensis* because I had formed a very different notion of the species at Aman-Kutan. Frankly, I had thought that the form from Shing was a new species; but now, having discussed the matter with Arnis, I came to the conclusion that it was the population from Aman-Kutan that was atypical. There were too few seedpods. The wet, cold spring had obviously hindered the pollination. Moreover, most of the pods were damaged by pests—worms had eaten up the seeds. We had to carefully inspect each pod to avoid collecting any that had been nibbled.

On the declivity we came across *Allium aroides*, though it was not very ornamental, and Arnis inspected some plants of *Corydalis maracandica*. As for me, all I could do was sit and watch—I was completely exhausted. In fact I had never before felt so weak, and later in Tashkent I became terribly ill with diarrhea.

At eleven o'clock we were back at the pass, where our car was already waiting for us. A little local fellow was trying to sell a bunch of tulips. How unbelievable that on 12 June *Tulipa fosteriana* should be in bloom! They had lettuce green leaves and bright red flowers with a clear yellow base on long stems. The man must have found them growing at a very high altitude, because here on the pass they had long ago lost their blooms. The last time I was there they bloomed on 1 May.

Nuratau Range

The Nuratau Range lies northwest of the Zeravshan Mountains. When you travel from Tashkent to Samarkand you cross the eastern end of the Nuratau Range at Timurlan Gate, which is situated approximately 200 km from Tashkent on the Tashkent-Samarkand Road, two-thirds of the way to Samarkand. It is the narrowest place at the eastern end of the Nuratau Range, named the Koytash Mountains, which further to the southeast change into the Malguzar Mountains, then the Turkestan Mountains. Passing Samarkand you can drive south over the Zeravshan Mountains, but continuing west you will enter the Kyzyl-Kum, where the Nuratau Range ends with some hills in the desert.

Timurlan Gate is situated approximately 15 km from the town of Jizzakh in the direction of Samarkand at an altitude of 600–700 m. It is an area of foothills, where the snow melts early. When we arrived here, the weather was distinctly summery, regardless of the generally late spring. It was quite a dry place and the only place in which we had real problems finding water, since there were no springs.

The soil was rocky clay, which made it relatively hard to inspect any bulbs, and the flatlands had been plowed. *Tulipa micheliana* grew here but its bulbs were extremely deep. On the hilltop, a relative of *T. turkestanica* swung heavily in the strong wind. This was a place where typical *T. turkestanica* was known to grow, so there was no doubt about its true name. This species is very floriferous in the garden and a strong grower. A lot of work still has to be done to find the real differences between the quite similar, small, white, multi-flowered species of the *T. bifloriformis–T. turkestanica* complex. The color of the anthers doesn't appear to be as significant as I had once thought.

In this same area we also found *Tulipa korolkowii*, a delightful, small, bright red tulip growing on almost bare rocks in small crevices between stones. It grew in mixed populations with *T. turkestanica*, and the only thing distinguishing it from this species when the flowers were not present was its more undulate leaves. It is a species generally suitable only for growing in the greenhouse. Plants that Arnis had previously tried growing on an open field were soon lost, so he now took the bulbs to his greenhouse. When I built my own greenhouse, Arnis gave me some of these bulbs, but I lost them even then. *Tulipa korolkowii* is really quite difficult in cultivation. I still grow a few plants that we collected at the other end of the Nuratau Range, but I can't say they exactly flourish with me.

The next plant was *Corydalis sewerzowii*, one of the most beautiful yellow-flowering Central Asian species with perennial tubers. It was out of flower, but no other *Corydalis* species could grow here at such a low altitude. It generally grew beneath rose shrubs and so was extremely difficult to get to, but then we found remnants of a shrub that had been used as a fireplace by local shepherds. There were only a few charred branches left of the shrub, and the ashes had made the soil very fertile, so there were hundreds of *C. sewerzowii* plants growing around it.

We were most interested in Juno irises and two species were known to grow here: *Iris maracandica* (Plate 197) and *I. narbutii*. On a stony, slightly grassy slope we found copious amounts of a dwarf Juno iris. It wasn't easy to identify without flowers, but it looked most like *I. maracandica*. Later on in my garden I was able to confirm that this was the case, and then I realized that all the other stocks I had grown earlier under the name *I. maracandica* were actually *I. svetlaneae*. The main difference between the two species is flower color, which in *I. maracandica* is pale yellow and in *I. svetlaneae* yellow. But where do you draw the line between pale yellow and yellow? Without seeing both competitors side by side, it isn't easy to tell. Just the presence of plants from Timurlan Gate helped me identify the acquisitions I had been growing as *I. maracandica*. In both species the haft is winged, but the wings are wider in *I. svetlaneae*. *Iris maracandica* is 10–15 cm tall, rarely up to 20 cm, with two to four creamy yellow flowers. Dwarf forms of *I. orchioides* and sometimes *I. svetlaneae* have been offered under this name in various catalogs. True *I. svetlaneae* is a dwarfer, more compact plant and in my opinion is far more beautiful in both color and overall appearance.

Another surprise greeted us between the vertical stony cliffs of a side gorge: a very beautiful, medium-sized *Allium* species (Plate 198) with a large inflorescence of bright pinkish lilac flowers on a stem approximately 50 cm long and two wide, bluish green leaves. The soil was quite wet—some underground water came close to the surface here. The bulbs were not too deep in the soil, and many plants had reproduced vegetatively (I found a group of ten bulbs). Classifying it proved difficult even for such a great *Allium* specialist as Arnis. We initially thought it was *A. victoris*, but Arnis later decided it was probably a new species, something between *A. cupuliferum* and *A. victoris*. To me it looked very similar to *A. nuratense*, but the flowering times of these plants differ substantially. Later some new species and subspecies from this district were described by Reinhard Fritsch, but I'm still unsure whether our plant really was a new species or was something described by Fritsch. We found it only in this one very rocky side gorge in quite deep shade. Though we carefully searched similar gorges, we couldn't find anything more than this single population of about a hundred bulbs.

We found *Bongardia chrysogonum*, a member of the Berberidaceae, growing in various open, stony places. For me this was something new. Although it was nothing special and was offered quite cheaply by many nurseries from time to time, I had never visited the foothills where it grew. I wouldn't call it a spectacular bloomer; its beauty lies in its leaves, with the deep purple zigzagging line crossing each leaf blade. The tubers don't increase vegetatively, and it is a plant for a frame or greenhouse only. I have not been successful in growing it, however, and have never gotten any seeds.

By late afternoon the sky was covered with heavy clouds and flashes of intense lightning, though there was very little rain. The wind was so strong that it sometimes seemed our tent would blow away altogether, with both of us inside it, so we rolled our bodies to the sides of the tent to press it close to the ground. There was some rain overnight, and at the bottom of the gorge a small stream of muddy water appeared. We were not prepared for such a dry place and hadn't brought enough bottled water. The water here was very muddy but still usable for cooking. The soup we made with it was acceptable, but the tea was really awful, leaving us with sand between our teeth.

My watch had stopped, so we made use of the sunrise the next morning to estimate the time, and for this reason walked out of the mountains and reached the road two hours earlier than planned. Arnis took advantage of the extra time to visit some wooded roadside areas. He was looking for alliums but instead found a marvelous group of *Geranium charlesii* growing in the grass on the opposite west-facing slope. In my opinion this species is the best tuberous geranium. The form that Arnis found turned out to have different foliage from the stock collected at Aman-Kutan.

While waiting for the car I noticed some other plants from the *Tulipa biflorifor-mis–T. turkestanica* complex growing in the crevices of a rock, where there was almost no soil. The wind was extremely fierce so I had to press my body against the rock to keep from being blown off of it. Despite these conditions, however, I managed to obtain a representative sample of this tiny but very beautiful tulip.

Our car finally arrived. We were dehydrated after two days of working with very little water, so we stopped in the nearest roadside village to buy some large bottles of Coca-Cola.

This was the first route of my first post-Soviet trip to Central Asia. It was a strange time—the local dictatorship had only started to strengthen, there were still very few visitors from abroad, and it was easy to get almost anywhere if you could find transportation. On our last night I hardly slept at all, feeling too nervous about crossing the border. There were no institutions in place that could deal properly with the materials we had collected. In general everything was based on a mix of old Soviet and new post-Soviet regulations. We were foreigners but at the same time were not accepted here as true foreigners. So despite all assurances that everything would run smoothly, I felt worried.

At the airport we were accompanied by two sinewy men. Volodya whispered in my ear that the tallest one was the chief of the president's team of bodyguards. Upon seeing these men, the passport controllers became extremely nervous and opened our passports with trembling hands and downturned faces. We couldn't stop laughing afterward. During subsequent trips here, everything was different. The VIP hall was opened to us, and the airport staff was very kind and attentive—a call from the president's secretary always preceded our arrival.

Kokcha

We named the expedition of 2000 the Millennium Expedition, thus following the trend of the year. It was dedicated to the real foothills, so we started very early on 20 April.

As usual the trip involved a change in Moscow. Our flight to Tashkent was at midnight, but the only flight from Riga landed in the morning, so we had to pass the day at the airport. We bought ourselves some newspapers and beer and settled into a couple of chairs. A few moments later the waiting hall was surrounded by special forces with submachine guns. This was passport control, a very selective process. People with Caucasian features were singled out and often treated quite brutally. Seeing that Arnis and I were drinking beer, they asked us only one question: "Vodka?" "No," we replied with a smile, "just beer." They left us alone.

In Tashkent we received word that foreigners were now required to register with the police, and after much time and frantic effort we finally managed to do so. From there we returned to Volodya's house. Our car would arrive at seven o'clock the next morning.

We hoped to find four Juno species. The first, *Iris hippolytii*, was a typical semi-desert species that had never before been grown in cultivation and that as far as we knew had been collected only once. It grew in an extreme environment on the very edge of the Kyzyl-Kum. The next was *I. narynensis*, which had been described as coming from Naryn. Many years ago Arnis and Mart Veerus from Estonia had worked for two days and found only one cluster of this species, and all the cultivated plants had come from this single cluster. The other two species were *I. inconspicua* and *I. subdecolorata*.

Iris hippolytii was described as coming from Kokcha Mountain. It was a long way to drive—300 km to Samarkand and then 200 km more, first in the direction of Bukhara up to Nawoiy, then north into the desert in the direction of Uchquduq, where the road ended. This "mountain" was only about a hundred meters high and was situated practically by the roadside. It was essentially a short ridge rising up unexpectedly in the surrounding plane. You could easily walk around it in one day.

We hadn't yet started our ascent when Arnis noticed the first Juno irises. Judging by their roots they could be *Iris hippolytii*, but without a bloom it was hard to say for certain. They could also be *I. narbutii*, though we were far from this species' basic population and the leaves seemed different. The determining factors would be flower color and shape. *Iris hippolytii* has blue flowers and a winged haft. The flowers of *I. narbutii* (Plate 199) are violet and yellow and have a haft without wings.

The car took us to the base of Kokcha Mountain, where a small village of modern townhouses had been built just near the ridge. We could understand why the houses were situated this way—the ridge protected them from the desert wind. But we couldn't understand why such a village had been built here in the first place. There were no factories or mines that we could see, and the village seemed too large for a collective farm. There might have been some military base here, but everything seemed too peaceful. We didn't feel comfortable here, so we continued along to the other side of the mountain, where the desert started.

A very strong wind was blowing from the desert, but since the temperature was 36°C, we only found it refreshing. We reached a splintery slope and there found some Juno irises. These had long, thick tuberous roots, unlike the roots of *Iris maracandica*, which are usually thick and stumpy. We noticed a specimen with a dry bloom that seemed to have been blue. This could be *I. hippolytii*, but *I. narbutii* was also a possibility. Later on we found two more dry blooms—Arnis tried to unroll the petals, and it seemed to us that they were winged. Was it possible we had already achieved our goal? We could only answer this with certainty when the iris finally bloomed in our gardens. It was true: the first plant we encountered on this trip was *I. hippolytii*, the very one we had set out to find. It is a very dwarf species, reaching only 5–8 cm tall, the stem bearing one or two (or, when in cultivation, even three) gray-lilac blooms. The leaves are rather long and markedly arched. A robust interspecific hybrid of garden origin was cultivated for years under this name. The flower color can be quite variable: some of the plants in our collections have almost pure white, only slightly greenish flowers with a small, pale yellow blotch on the falls (Plate 200), while others have quite intensely violet-blue flowers with a white crest and a deep lemon yellow blotch on both sides (Plate 201).

Arnis soon found *Leontice incerta*, a beautiful low-growing species, and somewhat later I found a couple of them, too. This species has never flowered for me in Latvia, though—I only saw the first blooms of it in the Gothenburg Botanical Garden, where we sent samples of all the plants. There are years when it doesn't come up at all for me, although the tubers look strong and healthy. Perhaps it is too cool here for flowering to begin during the summer rest. After all, these plants originated in a desert.

The wind grew stronger and communication was possible only within a few meters—all other sounds were simply carried away. Arnis pointed to a tangle of white fog far off in the desert. It was in fact not fog but a dry salt lake. The wind was blowing tiny particles of salt up and ahead, creating the impression of white fog. Needless to say, the conditions in this area are normally very hard. In winter the temperature drops to –30°C and there is snow (as evidenced by a ski lift on the mountainside), but this is all the water that reaches the area, and the winters are followed by very hot summers. Springs are marked on maps of the area with notes about how many liters of water each one produces in an hour, and large water reservoirs have been built to collect water from the melting snow.

We found some species of *Tulipa*, *Colchicum* (possibly *C. jolantae*), and *Allium*, and then it was time to return. On the way back we saw that the southern slope was the real place for Junos. Here, where they were protected from desert winds, they grew in great numbers and were bigger and stronger, but despite all of this we were still unable to find more than one seedpod.

We decided to drive back toward Nawoiy and then turn again to the north, in the direction of the Nuratau Range, where the road crosses another Karatau Range—a side branch of the Nuratau Range. At Karakarga Pass we made up our minds to stay overnight. Our driver would return to the city to sleep in a hotel.

The night was very hot and we both slept almost nude. I woke up at five o'clock and started preparing breakfast while Arnis set out on a short run around the nearby hills. We secretly hoped that here, too, we might find *Iris hippolytii*, but it wasn't to be. Although we were very close to Kokcha Mountain (Kokcha is the end point of the Karatau Range, like the dot under an exclamation point), the vegetation here was completely different and on the whole did not differ what we saw some years ago in the vicinity of Timurlan Gate, though the latter is situated at least six times farther from Karakarga Pass than Kokcha. Arnis returned with a specimen of typical *I. maracandica* and an *Allium* species that seemed similar to *A. iliense* (later at home we realized that it was *A. nuratense*, a beautiful addition to our collections). He had also seen *Corydalis sewerzowii* and *Geranium charlesii*.

It was a holiday and this was a popular holiday resort for the people of Nawoiy, so the mountains soon filled with people. Bus after bus drove up to the pass, unloading hundreds of passengers. This was not a place where a tent could be left unattended, so we took all our belongings and headed down the slope toward a nice path snaking into the mountains. As we walked upward along a dry riverbed, we at once found our first plants: stately, simply outstanding specimens of *Iris maracandica*. We continued our way up. It was hot, around 30°C, but bearable. Soon we noticed something very good—*I. narbutii*, a Juno we had looked for in many places but had been lucky enough to find only a few times. The leaves clearly showed that it was not *I. maracandica*, which grew at lower elevations. This form had much narrower leaves, placed sparsely on the stem, with intensely undulate edges. Although it was not a new species in my collection and was rather widely distributed, until this point I had only grown two specimens from Pulkhakim, where I had found just three plants, one of which had withered away and another one of which only recently bloomed for the first time.

This was the first place where I could see this species in large quantities. The dry petals were clearly blue, dispersing any remaining doubts about the plant's identity. Now we were convinced that the Kokcha plant was *Iris hippolytii*, for there were differences in the leaves, habit, and tuberous roots. Only three Juno species could be found in this terrain: *I. maracandica*, *I. narbutii*, and *I. hippolytii*. Here we had found such an abundance of Juno irises that we were looking only for specimens that had reproduced vegetatively. The largest clump we found was a cluster of nine plants. It seemed that *I. narbutii* tended to grow in clayey soil, while *I. maracandica* grew in considerably rockier places.

But then we reached a slope that completely confused us. First we noted that *Iris maracandica* was replaced here by *I. narbutii*, or so it seemed when we compared leaves and habit, but now and then we came across plants whose leaves were similar but not identical to those of *I. narbutii*. The remains of the flowers made us think that *I. mara-*

candica also grew here, but then we found specimens with leaves and stature like *I. maracandica* but with dry petals that were undoubtedly blue. Was it possible that hybrids of the two species grew here? A. I. Vvedenskyi (1971) mentioned something of the kind. Though such interspecific hybrids are usually sterile, here they had ripe seeds. I was unable to grow any of these plants back in Latvia, so I cannot say for certain what they really were.

We again came to a place in which all that grew was typical *Iris narbutii* specimens with heavily undulate leaves. Here we collected seeds and gathered some outstanding plant groups. Now and then we collected seeds of *Tulipa korolkowii* and a tulip similar to *T. bifloriformis*. We also found *T. micheliana*, which I have since lost in my garden.

In this same location I collected seeds of *Leontice ewersmanii*, which I hope to reintroduce. I grew it a very long time ago when I worked on sandy soil, but I lost it after moving to my present location where the soil is more clayey. When it is in full seed it looks quite imposing. The tall branched stems are covered with white seedpods in a heart-like shape—an excellent plant for Valentine's Day if it sets seed in winter. In fact I later used some pictures of it for Valentine's Day cards.

It was a pity we hadn't collected *Geranium charlesii* that morning. I would have liked to have some seeds from here, too, but we couldn't find it growing on this side of the valley.

We returned to the main road and rejoined our driver, then decided to return by the other side of the Nuratau Range, since our map showed a good road there. The black asphalt band led us through the desert, where I saw my first saksaul trees. They were very big. The villages here were sparse but large, and there was a lot of development going on. Our driver explained that the land didn't cost anything, and the building material, marble, came from the mountains and was also free of charge. Each family in a given village had at least twelve children, and when the children grew up they each needed their own place to live, so the village continually expanded. The greatest problem here was with water, but the people used very little of it, only for cooking. We came across some herds of sheep on the roadsides, and I wondered what they could find in this bare desert. We would apparently need to visit the area in early March to see any plants.

As we left Nawoiy the quality of the road changed substantially. The first 100 km of roads in the Jizzakh region were full of holes, so we had to drive more slowly. At a roadside shop we bought some Coca-Cola (at home I never drink the stuff, but in Central Asia it is the only drink you can find on the roadside) and enjoyed the labels, which were plastered with the names and photos of various celebrities. The same images covered hundreds of products here. Whatever happened to copyright laws? I wondered if Arnold Schwarzenegger knew where his face was turning up.

The driver recommended we stop at the bridge over the Syr-Dar'ya, one of the largest rivers of Central Asia, and that we taste the sazan fished from its waters. We did so, but I was not very impressed by the meal. To me, fish is fish—most edible when dressed with a very spicy tomato sauce and pepper, and tastiest when accompanied by a bottle of beer.

Fergana Valley

We rested for just one day before again hitting the road, this time headed for the Fergana Valley in search of *Iris narynensis*. This iris was described as coming from Naryn, but this covered a very wide region of Kyrgyzstan and Uzbekistan, and the same name was also used for a part of the Syr-Dar'ya. The type locality, therefore, was not definable. To the south of Andijan were small hills with the highest peak at 858 m; to the northeast was another low ridge, southern Alamishik, which climbed to 919 m. We could look for our iris in both of these places, but the most promising site seemed to be an unnamed mountain range shown on our maps, with the highest peak at 1330 m, located on the border with Kyrgyzstan close to the city of Aravan. We weren't comfortable with its proximity to the border, but during Soviet times, when such borders didn't exist, Arnis and Mart had found their only specimen of *I. narynensis* in this very location.

We drove up by the Angren ravine. The old road leading directly to the Fergana Valley through Tajikistan had been closed for political reasons, and a new one was being built through the Camchik Pass at an altitude of 2267 m. It was an enormous construction project that had been going on for three years already, but there was still a lot to be done—long parts of the road were still very bumpy and hadn't yet been covered with asphalt. Before long something went wrong with our car and the driver had to stop at the roadside. It wasn't anything serious, but he would need to return to Tashkent to make repairs. We used the occasion to do a little climbing in the Chatkal Mountains. The ascent was very steep and rocky, but we were soon rewarded with wonderful red-purple *Allium karataviense*. Well, maybe they weren't as showy and compact as the ones growing on the opposite bank of the Angren River, but nevertheless they were excellent.

We were also rewarded with *Tulipa vvedenskyi* (Plate 202), the species I had used most frequently for cross-pollination. The forms growing here were pure yellow at the base of the flower and varied a little in the amount of red tinting and intensity of the coloring on the petal exteriors. I already grew various forms of this species with red petals that were blackish brown, sometimes edged with yellow, at the base, and Arnis mentioned that he had once found a yellow *T. vvedenskyi*, though his sample perished. The Chatkal plants also varied in terms of leaf form: plants with undulate leaf margins dominated and were overall the most beautiful, but there were also straight-leaved specimens. These plants grew on rocks and stones. On our way back we found an orange-flowered specimen and one whose petals were grayish white on the back.

As it turned out we had stopped just at the point where local people came down from the mountains with bunches of tulips for sale. Each collector brought many hundreds of flowers that had been pulled out of the ground up to the bulb. The long white bases of the stems showed that higher on the meadows *Tulipa vvedenskyi* grew quite deep in the soil. I saw only one stem that was still attached to a bulb, and the boy I purchased it from was very surprised when I asked for just the bulb.

It was interesting to observe how this business was conducted. One or two boys stood at the roadside holding up nice bunches of flowers as cars passed by (Plate 203). Hidden away in a side gorge in the shade of a large tree, a small dike had been built to collect the water from a spring. Here the flowers were sorted and kept fresh in the water. When one of the boys sold a bunch, he would run back to the water and return to the roadside with new flowers. A bunch of fifty flowers would be sold for roughly the price of a bottle of Coca-Cola. As flowers were sold, collectors continually brought new bunches down from the mountains, where they were growing some 5 km away. Every day many thousands of flowers were sold here for their small, brief pleasure—in the hot, dry air of the valleys they were very short-lived and usually thrown away in the evening. As you might expect, the population of tulips growing in the mountains moved further and further away each year.

After the pass we stopped at Rezaksai for lunch. A meal consisting of *shurpo* (a local soup made with vegetables and lamb), salad, and shish kebab had become traditional for us. Our driver, Rustam, recommended we try the local curdled milk, and it was excellent—prepared right in the glass and topped with a thick layer of cream. Arnis was unable to withstand the opportunity to make a short run into the mountains. He returned promptly after finding what seemed to be *Iris orchioides*.

It was seven o'clock in the evening when we reached Andijan. We wanted to sleep in a hotel, but the hotel couldn't accept our money without some sort of verification from the bank, and the banks had closed at five o'clock. We had no choice but to drive into the mountains, which were visible from town, and look for a place for our tent. The closer we got to the mountains, the more troubled we felt. There was a terrible smell coming from them. It was the dumpsite of the town and was full of vagrants, not the right place for us. After we crossed the hill and reached a deeply shaded area, I noted a small orchard where we could hide our tent. In complete darkness we pitched the tent and left our driver to return to the hotel. Rustam was a local, so he could pay without verification.

When Rustam returned for us the next morning, we decided to head to the border hills. The roads in this area were perfect, the land tilled to the utmost, and the roadsides were lined with houses. The Fergana Valley was the richest place in all of Uzbekistan, with the most productive soil and plenty of precipitation. We selected a village on the map that seemed closest to the slopes and drove there. There was some doubt about the straight blue line at the bottom of the hills, but it turned out to be a very wide canal with a good bridge over it.

I noticed a straight path between the houses of the village that led directly to the mountains. We turned there and were really very lucky—the road ended just at the bottom of the hills where the slope started. At the end of the road was a small hut inhabited by an old man, the overseer of the vineyards. We drank tea and listened to the man and some vineyard workers as they spoke to each other in Uzbek. Our chauffeur interpreted for us from time to time. The man was saying something about the road leading into the mountains and that there were steps there. Other people soon arrived, and a dish of rice and a small slice of meat were put on the table. The elder man cut the meat into microscopic pieces and offered some to us. We didn't want to accept his offer, since this seemed to be an entire day's worth of food for him, but we had to take a small piece so as not to seem to be rejecting his hospitality. We tried to compensate for what we ate with some cans of fish and chocolate; the only other thing we had was pork, which Muslims don't eat.

We climbed up along the slope, which was covered with spurs. I took the beginning too fast and had to slow down in order to reach the top. Absolutely everything had been nibbled by animals—there was nothing worthwhile. All we came across was a tiny specimen of some *Allium* species and, of course, eremurus, which grew everywhere. Arnis wandered off our path to peer over the nearly vertical cliffs; they were so steep and unpleasant that I found myself frightened, even though Arnis was the one standing beside them. There was a stench in the air. Was it coming from plants? Probably not. It seemed most likely to be coming from the cattle that grazed here.

As we climbed higher we found ourselves in a large, flat meadow the size of a football field. It was used as a cattle camp and almost nothing grew here but *Allium stipitatum*, which can be found almost anywhere that is well manured. On the right side was a high, almost vertical stone cliff. A smaller path climbing between the rocks made the ascent quite comfortable though it was very steep.

On the cliff Arnis found *Allium alaicum*, a species distinctive for its particularly fluffy leaves. Although it is not a very ornamental species, I had long wanted to find it. The true *A. alaicum* has only two narrow, highly fluffy leaves, a stem just 30–40 cm tall, and a small umbel. Although the plants that Arnis found were not yet in bloom, he reasoned (based on herbarium specimens he had seen) that this population would have considerably brighter, more beautiful flowers than the plants he already had in his collection. Here and there we also saw specimens of *Tulipa ferganica* growing in rock fissures, but there were no Juno irises here—in fact this was not a place in which they could grow. Beneath a shrub I noticed a cluster of a very beautiful form of *Allium caesium* with pinkish violet flowers—a new shade for my collection.

We reached the ridge. To the left in the valley we could see a big city. It was Aravan, in the territory of Kyrgyzstan. We were standing right on the border. To the right was a fantastic view of a spacious, gently sloping, circular depression, with quite poor vegetation and frequent stone outcrops. It looked like a perfect place for Juno irises; in fact it was probably our only bet—if we couldn't find our sought-after *Iris narynensis* there, we weren't destined to find it at all.

Then I heard one more victorious shout from Arnis: "Yes! Here it is, here it is!" As I took a couple of steps in his direction, I too saw a Juno right in front of me. The bulbs lay shallow in the ground. As soon as we had scraped away enough dirt to see the tuberous roots, we knew for certain we had found *Iris narynensis* (Plate 204). The tuberous roots of this species are short, stumpy, and thick. They resemble the roots of *I. kopetdagensis* and *I. rosenbachiana*, but the bulb is considerably smaller, and the bulb develops a cluster, so it reproduces vegetatively. The spring here had been very dry, but the bulbs were well ripened and large. We started to check the slope. Although we regularly came across irises, we found only two specimens with seedpods.

In total, *Iris narynensis* occupied some hundred square meters. It had no rival plants here, and this location provided the right amount of sunlight and good drainage. Some plants grew deep in the crevices of stones, but the stones were weathered and loose. So now we had found the second very rare Juno, another species practically unknown in gardens. We checked the time—we had been away four hours already, and we had promised to be back after five.

Returning along the same route would be easy but wouldn't show us anything new, so we decided to descend into the ravine and walk along the riverbed. The landscape was simply fabulous. On either side of the riverbed were nearly vertical cliffs fantastically notched with caves and grottos. *Rosa kokanica* flowered with vividly yellow blooms, *Lonicera* species with pink blooms, *Amygdalus nana* with purple-rose blossoms. On the rocks grew unusually huge clusters of *Fritillaria sewerzowii*, *Pseudosedum* species, and other plants. Arnis pointed to a big group of *Allium oschaninii* (Plate 205) growing in a rock cleft, with giant tops and last year's swollen stalks—an indescribably beautiful composition. Later on in my garden this form of *A. oschaninii* turned out to be the best grower.

The natural environment here was practically pristine, and with each turn a tremendous new sight opened before us. My only experience comparable to this had been in Kopet-Dag, the most beautiful place I ever saw during my mountain expeditions. The riverbed snaked here and there, all the time getting narrower and narrower. The cliffs beside us were vertical; without any mountain climbing equipment, one wouldn't be able to ascend them.

The path grew even narrower, and then . . . stop! What we had feared most we now saw before us: a waterfall about 10 m high. Our limbs went numb. This meant we would have to walk back all the distance we had come—at least another five hours of walking. But then I noticed an iron spike driven into a corner of the rock. A steel cable was attached to it, holding a 2 cm pipe. Suddenly I remembered the steps we had heard the old man mention back in the hut. Was this pipe part of these so-called steps? I climbed to the edge and looked down. Perhaps once upon a time these had been steps, but now there was only a pipe with some joints melded to it. If these had indeed been steps, stones rolled along by the water had long ago torn away all the rungs.

Arnis announced that we would have to go back. I didn't agree—I left Arnis my ice pick and plants, threw the camera bag on my back, and with trembling legs and pounding heart, started climbing down. I began with my face toward the cliff, holding onto the cable, then put my foot on something that looked like the remnants of a rung at the top end of the pipe. I clutched the pipe with my hands. As soon as I passed the ridge at the top, I was flipped over so that my back was now flat against the cliff wall. Rapidly moving one hand over another, I made my way down. The pipe was polished and smooth, even glittering, but my grip was sufficiently tight, and before long I made it to the bottom. At first I was overwhelmed with joy, but then quickly found myself seized by fear—what if another waterfall lay ahead? We would be trapped here. It would be impossible to clamber up this pipe.

Arnis threw down the ice picks and the bags of plants, then repeated my way down as I told him where to put his hands and feet. (Unfortunately I was so excited that I forgot to capture this historical climb on film.) Now at the bottom, Arnis congratulated me on my courage but explained that if he had been on his own he would have returned the way we had come. On our way down we encountered a few more waterfalls, but they were no higher than 2 m, somewhat sloping, and so polished by the water that we were able to slip down them like a swimming pool slide.

Our return was two hours later than planned and our driver had even started to think about sending a rescue brigade, but the greatest adventure of all our mountain expeditions was now behind us. Later on in the village we learned that at the same spot three locals had earlier fallen to their deaths. It only then occurred to me that before my descent I hadn't checked to see how firmly the pipe was fastened to the cable and the cliff.

The way back was without adventure. We stopped at a very wide turning place on the side of a newly built road. The slope there was extremely steep and only clumps of grass and small shrubs allowed us to fix our feet on it. *Tulipa vvedenskyi* was in full flower somewhat higher up, and among the thousands of red-flowered plants we found a single orange-flowered specimen. We also found a bright green (possibly even yellowish green) *Fritillaria sewerzowii*.

By three o'clock in the afternoon we were back in Tashkent.

In Search of *Iris winkleri*

This could have been called the *Iris winkleri* expedition, for this plant was the main reason we headed to Central Asia so late in the season. The selection of time and place resulted from Arnis's research at the herbarium of the Komarov Botanical Institute in Saint Petersburg, where he found a sheet of *I. winkleri* collected in Kugart, Fergana Mountains, Kyrgyzstan, at the end of June in an alpine meadow. It had been sent to Saint Petersburg from the botanical institute in Tashkent after having been collected in the 1960s. The correct location of Kugart was a problem. We didn't have any good maps to begin with, and then we learned that six places carried the name Kugart: a valley, a village, a collective farm, two rivers, and a mountain pass. We also didn't have good contacts in Kyrgyzstan, and with the establishment of independent states, the formalities of border crossing and the necessity of visas made this problem even more difficult. Fortunately, at that time there was still an agreement between these Central Asian independent states that allowed people from one state to enter the other state for a period of three days. We hoped to use this policy to enter Kyrgyzstan with Uzbek visas. The Fergana Mountains are much easier to reach from the Uzbekistan side, since they are not far from the Fergana Valley, but they are a long distance from Bishkek, with several high mountain ranges in between.

Iris winkleri was discovered by A. Regel in 1883 and mentioned in cultivation for the first and last time (as far as we know) by Olga Fedchenko in 1899, who wrote that this wonderful iris had survived two winters in her garden near Mozhaysk in Russia. It was collected a few times after this in various herbaria but was never again introduced into gardens. It is a close relative of *I. kolpakowskiana*, which is widespread in the foothills of northern and western Tian Shan, differing from the latter in the sheets covering its bulbs: in *I. kolpakowskiana* the sheets are clearly reticulate, while in *I. winkleri* the sheets of the current year are thin and papery, becoming somewhat split only during the following seasons. Most importantly, *I. winkleri* is a subalpine plant. Although I grow *I. kolpakowskiana* quite successfully in my nursery, it is generally rather difficult in the garden; *I. winkleri* should be much easier to grow because of the considerably wetter, cooler conditions of its natural environment. According to Fedchenko's description, the flower of *I. winkleri* must be of the same beauty as *I. kolpakowskiana*—a combination of purple, cherry red, and white.

Special expeditions were arranged in recent decades to find *Iris winkleri*, especially by the great authority in the genus *Iris*, George Rodionenko, but they weren't successful. As a result this species received a somewhat mysterious status in the world of gardeners. Everyone spoke about it, everyone wanted it and asked for it, but no one actually believed that it existed. What's more, many bulb specialists began to think that it was not a separate species at all and that the herbarium specimens were just poorly dried and pressed specimens of *I. kolpakowskiana*.

Arnis and I first attempted to visit the Fergana Mountains in 1995, but it wasn't possible to rent a car then and without it the expedition would be impossible. The same thing happened in 1996—though we received good support from our Tashkent friends, transport was provided only for use inside Uzbekistan. Then came 1997. The *Conspectus Florae Asiae Mediae* (Vvedenskyi 1971, 1974) lists a few places in which *Iris winkleri* has been collected. One location, considered doubtful, is in the upper reaches of the Angren River, Uzbekistan, so we considered this place an alternative destination in case we again encountered problems with driving out of Uzbekistan.

When we came to Tashkent we were welcomed with excellent news. First we were given a good map of the area we were most interested in exploring, and then we were told that our friends had arranged for a private car to bring us as far as possible into the mountains. According to the map there should be a good road leading right to the mountain pass. However, the reality turned out to be quite different from what was shown on the map, which was more than thirty years old.

Tashkent greeted us with terrible heat. Since that spring and early summer had been exceptionally cold in Latvia, the heat didn't seem so bad at first, but when daytime temperatures exceeded 40°C our thoughts changed. Early in the morning we set off to Fergana where another car, a Russian jeep, would be waiting for us.

Our first driver worked for the Ministry of Foreign Affairs and for this reason we made our way very quickly—the police allowed us to travel without delay, and by noon we reached the city of Fergana, where the air seemed even hotter than in Tashkent. Our hosts treated us to a good dinner and after a short while our next driver arrived. He would come with us to the mountains, stay with us at our camp, and drive us back to Fergana, where a car from the Ministry of Foreign Affairs would again be waiting for us.

We decided to set out on the road at night when temperatures were cooler. Our driver, Erik, prepared an evening meal for us and could not understand why we didn't want any vodka afterward. After we finally agreed to some wine, he brought us two bottles of a terrible, sweet, fortified Uzbek variety.

It was 24 June, Jānis' Day, my name day. Jānis' Day is a great festival that has been celebrated in Latvia since pre-Christian times, having survived not only the Inquisition but also the long years of the Soviet occupation. There was a period during the Communist regime when many names of things that incorporated the word Jānis were changed. This happened with certain plant names, for example—even the red currants that Latvians called Jānis-berries were renamed red black currants. Anyway, this was the first (though not the last) time I had been away from home on this holiday. Normally I would have spent the day drinking beer and eating soft homemade caraway cheese, singing folk songs that night around a fireplace until the first rays of sun appeared to greet all the "children of Jānis." This was the night when a young man would take a nice girl for a walk in the forest to look for the flower of a certain fern that according to legend bloomed only on midsummer's night, Jānis' Night.

We started at three o'clock in the afternoon and reached the border with Kyrgyzstan by early the next morning. Erik had to pay an unofficial "tax" to cross the border, but everything else was quite easy, and after being asked a few questions we found ourselves in the lower Kugart Valley.

It was immediately apparent that the people of Kyrgyzstan were much poorer than the Uzbeks, but you could buy petrol here on every corner. The price was double what it cost in Uzbekistan, but there were no queues and no limits on how much you could buy. The quality of the petrol was better, too. We bought 20 liters for Erik.

The thoroughfare that was marked on our map as a highway suddenly turned into a gravel road, though it was still of perfect quality. A long course of twists and turns guided us down to the Kugart River, which we crossed over on an excellent bridge. As we continued up a similar road flanked by brownish, sunbaked foothills, the wild Kugart flowed far below us. The first bulbous plant appeared: *Eremurus olgae*. The elegant long spikes, densely covered with very light pink blossoms, beautifully ornamented the foothills.

At the village of Kalmakirchin the normal road ended (on our map this was still marked as a highway) and a terrible serpentine road began, ending in an even more terrible bridge. Erik asked whether we thought the bridge was actually meant for cars, and we bravely assured him that it was a highway. So, hearts trembling, we crossed it. On the other side the road became narrower and shoddier with each kilometer. There were traces of mudslides and stone avalanches and whole areas had been washed away by landslides. After 10 km we reached the village of Kugart where the highway on our map ended and an "improved road" began. Needless to say there was no great improvement. In some places where the road had been washed away, someone had actually tried to fashion a new road out of stones and tree branches! (We could only wonder how it all stayed together.) Erik became increasingly nervous, and we had to employ our most extravagant words of encouragement to get him to go on. Finally we stopped at a recurrent side gorge where a river had cut the road. Large stones at the bottom of the river made it impossible to cross by car. We were 7 km from the end of the village of Kugart, and according to our map it was still 15 km in a straight line to Kugart Pass. We later found out that even if we had crossed the river we wouldn't have gotten much farther—after less than a kilometer the road ended. It seemed that thirty years ago there really had been a road here, with proper ditches and even paved with stone chips, but it had never been a highway, at least not as we understand the term. It had undoubtedly been built for military purposes.

By eleven o'clock we were ready to make ourselves familiar with the place. As for the next day, we planned to go up to the alpine meadows and the mountain pass. It was extremely hot and not easy to walk. At first we decided to walk a little further and then up to a side ridge, but our path led us deeper and deeper inside the mountains. There we spotted our first bulbous plants. On a small roadside rock Arnis found Juno irises with dry foliage and seedpods that were just starting to open. We collected the seeds. It could be one of two Juno species: the so-called *Iris orchioides* sensu lato or *I. zenaidae*, a poorly known and never cultivated relative of *I. magnifica* that had been described from this district. *Pseudosedum ferganense* with very thick, tuber-like roots grew alongside the Junos.

Our path climbed up and up, crossing a lot of side streams. *Eremurus robustus* was blooming magnificently and there were some other less ornamental species of subgenus *Eremurus* with small greenish yellow flowers. We decided to walk as far as the last confluence of two streams, where according to our map a serpentine road began winding its way up to the mountain passes. We later found that this "easy" bit of road took four hours to walk up and three hours to walk down. When a new side ridge appeared before us we thought it surely had to be the last, but then another would appear, and another.

Our path was brought to a halt when a river again cut into it, making a nearly vertical slope. The river was so swollen and crazy that it seemed impossible to cross, so we looked for a road up. On a slope nearby grew a wonderful pure white *Allium* species with a globular umbel. It was *A. backhousianum*. Arnis climbed up to it. I tried to follow but the large stone on which I had decided to balance suddenly fell and I plummeted some 6 m, injuring my left hand and right shoulder. Not a good start for the expedition.

The slope was so steep that we wondered how sheep could walk on it. We found it especially difficult to cross a certain small but very deep side ravine. We both decided that if one of us fell the other wouldn't waste time trying to find out what had happened, for there would be no chance of surviving. We used the same approach we had used in Sina. Seeing a few scuff marks on the opposite side of the ravine made by goats or sheep, we jumped across, slightly touching the almost vertical slope on the opposite side, and with the next step landed on a small balcony from where the pass continued.

There were plenty of alliums here, several large ornamental species growing along with *Allium backhousianum* and *A. aflatunense*. *Allium aflatunense* is a tall plant that is easy to grow in the garden. Its bright violet flowers are held in a dense umbel on a strong, thick stem 1.2 m tall. The true species is very different from the one usually grown under this name in the Netherlands. Its bulbs are large and ovoid with a pointed tip, so it is easy to distinguish from the somewhat similar *A. stipitatum* and *A. macleanii*. The bulb usually splits in two, sometimes even in three. All it needs is good drainage and a sunny spot. Many species can be offered under this name, and this would not be a big deal if instead of *A. aflatunense* a gardener received *A. stipitatum* or *A. macleanii*, which are similar in size; however, the plants distributed under this name are usually much smaller, and this can lead to some discrepancies in the garden design.

Most often the species hiding under the name *Allium aflatunense* is actually *A. hollandicum*, described by Reinhard Fritsch, who thought it was a garden hybrid from the Netherlands. Unfortunately, all *A. hollandicum* has in common with the Netherlands is its name. It actually comes from Iran—another one of those unfortunate cases in which we have to follow the rules of botanical nomenclature although the name of the plant does not correspond with its origin. It has large, light violet flowers arranged in a globe-shaped, moderately sized, somewhat loose umbel on a stem that is approximately 1 m long and thin but strong. The bulbs are medium-sized and round. 'Alba' is a form with slightly bluish-toned white petals and light purple anthers that enhance the generally pinkish or bluish impression of the flowers. 'Purple Sensation' and 'Purple Surprise' are very similar. Both have very bright, deep purple-violet flowers in large umbels. It seems that 'Purple Sensation' was used by Reinhard Fritsch, who described it as *A. ×hollandicum*. It is certainly not a hybrid, however, because it is fertile and reproduces from seed with little variation of color in following generations. 'Purple Surprise' flowers later and is somewhat brighter, larger, and taller than 'Purple Sensation'; it is undoubtedly a showier plant but also reproduces more slowly. The stem is up to 1 m long, whereas in 'Purple Sensation' the stem is only 70 cm long.

We had crossed the dangerous place and were at our destination of the day: the confluence of two large streams, with Koldama Pass (3062 m) on the left and Kugart Pass (3200 m) on the right. We could see the remnants of an old serpentine road going up the steep slope between both passes and then turning left to Koldama, but in many places the road had been washed away or was obstructed by scree or ravines. At least we knew where we had to go.

We finally turned up by a very steep side ridge that was covered with thick grass and small shrubs. We wanted to get up to at least the height of the archa (*Juniperus*). We still saw only alliums, followed by a *Tulipa* species (possibly *T. ferganica*) with dry leaves and another *Tulipa* species from section *Eriostemones*. Then we finally found a Juno iris. It looked quite unusual, the roots much thicker than is typical for *Iris orchioides*, but in this aspect it was not uniform—there were plants with thinner roots, too. Was it *I. zenaidae*? Without flowers it was difficult to decide. The seeds were almost ripe, and later at home after cleaning the seeds and comparing them with those of *I. orchioides*, they looked quite different. Further studies confirmed that the river Aubek, a side stream of the Kugart in its upper course, was the type locality of *I. zenaidae*. This meant that Kugart had given us two wonderful irises, although at that moment we were too tired to fully enjoy having found *I. zenaidae*. We could be sure about one thing, however: coming to Kugart had been successful, even if we didn't find *I. winkleri*.

Iris zenaidae (Plate 207) is among the most beautiful Juno irises, with very deep, bright blue flowers, and is an excellent grower both indoors and in the open garden. It reproduces vegetatively, though not particularly quickly, and sets seed well. Though the name is new to some gardeners, the plant itself is not new to gardens: it was simply offered earlier under the name *I. albomarginata*. In fact the plant I received from the Botanical Garden of the Kyrgis Academy of Sciences, Bishkek, came to me under that name. *Iris zenaidae* is very variable in terms of flower color, and there are some beautiful selections. In general the flowers are large, deep cobalt blue, and widely winged, with a white, blue-striped blade. In some forms the falls are uniformly blue. Actually it would be better to characterize the falls as blue with more or less large white spots around the crest, which in some forms merge into one uniform white spot with a narrow bluish edge. It is the distinct blue rim of the crest that led some botanists to mistake *I. zenaidae* for *I. albomarginata*, whose rim is similar but less prominent. *Iris zenaidae* is also twice as large as *I. albomarginata*.

At home I found I had another plant that was identical in flower color and shape to a very beautiful form of *Iris zenaidae*. It came from Potterton and Martin in Britain under the name *I. graeberiana* 'Dark Form'. It originated in the Czech Republic, where it was raised by a gardener before World War II, and is apparently still grown there although its parentage has been lost. Careful examination showed 'Dark Form' to be sterile, thus confirming its hybrid origin. I discarded the stock that was in my collection so as not to confuse it with *I. zenaidae*.

The slope became so steep that we started looking for trees below us that could stop our fall should our boots lose contact with the ground. After collecting the seeds of some Junos, we decided to slowly move down to a scree slope at the bottom of a side stream. There was still plenty of snow here, which provided us some refreshment. Then we started our way to the camp. When I saw a beautiful violet clump of some allium, I called to Arnis, saying, "Come and look! It seems I have found some 'poppies' for Henrik." This was followed by the joyful sound of Arnis's voice. He had found *Allium winklerianum*, possibly even a new subspecies similar to what he had collected in other localities.

Allium winklerianum is one of my longtime favorites for the garden and can be grown in the greenhouse as well. It is up to 50 cm tall with large, narrowly cup-shaped, purplish violet flowers. It is similar to *A. cupuliferum*, but the umbel is more compact and they differ in terms of leaf shape. Mari Kits and I collected *A. cupuliferum* in the Varzob Valley on the southern slopes of the Gissar Range. It has large, narrowly cup-shaped, upward-facing, purplish flowers. In the beginning the umbel is dense but it later becomes lax due to the elongation of the pedicels, which grow to be unequal in length. A most attractive allium, it is extremely beautiful in dried flower arrangements and is much loved by florists.

On our way back we discussed the next morning's route. Should we walk up along one of the side ridges and then head up from there as far as the mountain pass, or should we return the way we had come, following the remnants of the old road? From a distance the slopes looked quite suitable, but as we approached them they became very steep. The other side looked somewhat more promising, but trying to cross the Varzob River would be suicide. In the end we decided to go along the old road.

While we were away our driver had moved to a better spot for camping. It was flatter and less stony, though quite wet. We decided to rise at three o'clock the next morning and leave at four with the first light when the weather would be cooler. I applied some Finalgon unguent to my shoulder, which still felt sore from my fall, and quickly fell asleep. We awoke an hour later than planned, heading out at five o'clock after some tea and breakfast. We took with us some jumpers, clean socks, a camera and film, a few handfuls of raisins and nuts, and some chocolate. As we left our camp we warned the driver that it was very possible we wouldn't be back in the evening and would spend the night in the mountains.

Along the way we continued discussing where *Iris winkleri* could be found. On the opposite side of the ridge where the other Kugart River flowed the climatic conditions were different, so the flora there must also be different. The only possibility of finding *I. winkleri* was here on the high mountain meadows somewhere near the pass at 3200 m. It had been described from a few places on this side of the ridge along the upper courses of some rivers, but there were no roads even on our map. These places were some 50–100 km from the nearest villages, and without horses and a large, well-equipped expedition we would not be able to reach them.

We soon reached our dangerous slope again, but this time we were able to cross the river, which was not so swollen. (In the end we crossed the Kugart and its tributaries five times, and with each new crossing the water level was lower.) On the other side we met a man. "Shalom aleichem" and a few words in poor Russian followed. He had come from the other side of the Fergana Mountains and spent the night on Kugart Pass. He was kind enough to show us the best way up, and as we followed him he told us his story. He was sixty years old and didn't know how many years he had left, but he had never been to a city and wanted to see one before Allah asked for him. It did not matter that there was still a distance of more than 50 km ahead of him: he would go and see the city and then quietly return to his *aula* (a small village in Central Asia, sometimes comprised of just a few houses or families).

More than four hours had passed since we started our way up and it was quite doubtful we would find any water, so we stopped for a drink at a spring and ate some raisins and nuts. Then our Golgotha began.

We carefully confirmed all the plant associations and ecotypes as we ascended, more or less following the old destroyed serpentine road. We were surprised by how often they changed, corresponding to minor changes in the soil, moisture, sun exposure, and so forth. *Colchicum* species grew everywhere. Most looked to be *C. luteum* but some may have been *C. kesselringii*. They looked quite variable here—some plants had very narrow leaves, while others had wide leaves. The seeds were ripe and the capsules had just started to split. We collected only a few. Some years later at home I was very disappointed about having made such a small collection. The plants from Kugart bloomed with very different petal shapes, and I supposed they were a new species. I later lost all of them during a very hard winter.

We were on the sunny side and took many short rests because the path was so steep. We were still too low for subalpine or alpine plants, and in general the soil seemed too dry or too rich for *Iris winkleri*. All our hopes were bound with some dark green spots we could see much higher up. Up to this point I had been carrying our common haversack. It wasn't heavy, only about 5 kg, but since I didn't have much faith in my chances of reaching the top (I was already fifty-one at this point) I carried it to save Arnis's energy. One of us had to reach the top.

Everywhere around us a small *Tulipa* species was growing. It appeared to be the same species we had collected the day before much lower down. The seeds of yesterday's plants were ripe, but these capsules were still green, and we hoped to see some flowers higher in the mountains.

It was extremely hot. We had broken the golden rule of the mountains by drinking some water on our way up. Our mouths were now so dry that we could think of nothing but finding clean spring water, but the only water we found was muddy and undrinkable. When we were about a third of the way to the top, quite far to the left we saw a waterfall and turned in its direction. As I jumped across a small but deep ravine, my right leg was seized by intense cramps. All my hopes of reaching the mountain pass seemed lost, but after a thorough massage, some Finalgon unguent, and a few Pentalgin pills, I was able to continue. After this incident I took Pentalgin (a strong pain killer) every day to keep me going. My doctor later explained that if I had stopped then, my leg would not have recovered—it was the continuous walking that forced the blood to circulate and allowed the muscle to recover.

We reached the bright orange spots that we had noted from far below—marvelous groups of *Trollius asiaticus* with masses of bright orange blooms—and found a beautiful *Aquilegia* species with very light blue flowers. The blossoms of a medium-sized *Myosotis* species were extremely bright blue, much brighter than those of our common *M. arvensis*. In drier places *Colchicum*, *Gagea*, and some *Allium* species were also growing. A specimen of *Allium schoenoprasoides* was lovely (though by flower it looked quite similar to the common *A. schoenoprasum*, it had a true bulb). Its flowers were pink with only a slightly visible midvein on the petals, and it reached up to 40 cm tall. There was plenty of *A. carolinianum* (Plate 208), too, and as we moved higher the clumps grew richer though not as tall. This allium is rarely offered in catalogs but is a very beautiful species with large, elongated bulbs attached to a vertical rootstock, and it reproduces well vegetatively. The stem is up to 60 cm tall, with up to half its length enveloped by the leaf bases. Dense umbels hold whitish flowers with petals edged in a beautiful pink. The very prominent filaments are much longer than the petals, giving the whole plant a somewhat airy appearance. I'm really surprised that it is offered so rarely, as it sets seed well, too. This summer-flowering allium is one of my favorites.

Our zigzags became much wider. We carefully checked every plant association when the first subalpine plants appeared, but nothing caught our attention. Then we were stopped by the first nice specimens of *Allium oreophilum*. Some seemed to have increased vegetatively. There were at least two forms: one with straight leaves and another with curled, rolled, very decorative leaves. I immediately named the latter form 'Kugart's Curl', and from that moment I collected only plants with such unique foliage. Later on in the garden they all turned out to look very similar; all the curling of the leaves disappeared, and they were the slowest increasers among all my stocks and forms of *A. oreophilum*. What a great difference from the plants from Kusavlisai, Tajikistan, which kept the beautiful shape of their leaves in the garden.

After every 10–20 m increase in altitude we had to lie down to normalize our breathing. The mountain pass was still far ahead. It seemed as though we were continuously at the same altitude, but when we looked back we could see a meadow we had passed some time before very far below us. The horses in the meadow resembled small lapdogs. The vegetation was getting dwarfer and the first true alpines appeared. Our mouths were still dry, so we looked for wild *Rheum* species to help quench our thirst. The leaf stalks here were short, only 5–10 cm long, but the higher we moved the softer they became. Some plants had a nice, slightly sour taste, others were sweet, and still others were bitter or completely flavorless.

The vegetation was quite variable. Some *Carex*-like grasses made dense clumps. The dark green spots we had seen far in the distance near melting snow turned out to be *Allium fedtschenkoanum*, a very unusual species with yellowish flowers. It was so dominant here that there was no space left for other plants, especially not *Iris winkleri*. *Allium fedtschenkoanum* is very closely related to *A. kaufmannii*, which we found later at Ihnachsai, but is less spectacular, although it grows in identical extremely wet spots.

Our ascent became increasingly difficult and we decided to leave our haversack near an easily recognizable rock. Even our cameras seemed too heavy, so we left these as well. We lay down for just a few minutes, but I didn't want to get up at all. I felt as though I could rest quietly here forever. An old song played in my head:

> Why wait for more wonders
> They'd never come back
> To sleep here forever
> Without waking up . . .

When we had climbed another 100 m we encountered the first plants in bloom. How useful our cameras would have been! But to return for them . . . no, it was beyond our strength. We had reached the height of the Koldama Pass. The path was rocky but no longer so steep, and we soon reached Kugart Pass. The landscape on both sides was wonderful, but most beautiful was the pass itself. It was composed of two small parallel ridges that joined the neighboring tops, forming a nice valley between them with a small lake of ice-cold water. We saw *Tulipa* aff. *dasystemon* (Plate 209), *Cortusa turkestanica*, *Ranunculus* species, two *Myosotis* species, and *Gagea* species in full flower. However, *Allium fedtschenkoanum* brought the greatest surprise: its foliage started to grow still underwater at a depth of approximately 1 m. It was two o'clock in the afternoon, which meant that the climb had taken nine hours—four hours to reach the last slope and five hours from the slope to the mountain pass.

Everything looked wonderful but there was no *Iris winkleri*. We took a short rest to drink some water and nibble a few nuts and raisins, then started heading back, remarking to each other how incredible it would be if every expedition could be a success. Nothing doing this time—the secret of *I. winkleri* would have to wait for the twenty-first century. But at least we had found an excellent Juno species, and to some degree this would compensate for our efforts. After finding our haversack and taking another short rest, we chose a different way down.

Arnis wandered some 10 m to my left, and at about half past three I heard a loud shout from his direction. "Jānis!" he cried. "Here it is, I found it! I'm not joking! *Iris winkleri*!" All my exhaustion disappeared instantly. Arnis lay on the ground kissing the seed capsule. He had found a marginal plant of this population. If he had walked just a meter more to my side we would have missed it entirely. But the question remained: was this really *I. winkleri*? The seedpod was certainly that of a Reticulata iris, but we had to see the bulb. I took a knife and like a jeweler scratched away the soil very slowly. Luckily the bulb wasn't lying very deep. The bulb scales were not reticulate as they are in *I. kolpakowskiana* but were clearly longitudinally fibrous, and the bulb was white rather than bright yellow. Most importantly, we noted that *I. kolpakowskiana* is a foothill plant and *I. winkleri* a true subalpine plant, although the meadow here was not as wet as the habitat described in botanical literature. The flowering time differed—it was the end of June and our plants had nearly ripe seeds, while the literature described the flowering taking place at this time. But this would depend on the amount of seasonal snow. According to the local people, winter usually brought about 3 m of snow to the valley, but this winter there had been only 1 m of snow, which of course melted earlier and more quickly, thus allowing the iris to flower earlier.

We started creeping around in the short grass looking for seed capsules. The grass-like foliage of *Iris winkleri* was barely discernible. The plant density was not high—on average we found one capsule per 3 m. In places where the grass was shorter the density was slightly higher, but the entire population covered less than an acre.

At five o'clock we decided to finish up and try to return here the next day to continue searching the side ridges at approximately the same altitude. We very nearly ran down the mountain on our way back. At seven o'clock, having crossed the river, which was now twice as high, we arrived at the same terribly steep slope. This time we had to cross it because the swollen river had made the roundabout way too dangerous. As a thunderstorm started in the mountaintops, I felt a terrible pain in my right leg. It was clear that Arnis could get to our camp more quickly without me, and I wanted him to get enough rest for the next day, so he agreed to hurry off.

It soon became very dark. Fortunately the path was white and quite visible in the darkness, and the lightening flashed frequently enough to illuminate the road. I made mental notes of various landmarks. Soon a heavy rain started coming down and I became instantly wet. It was beginning to feel as though the mountains were angry with us for discovering the secret they had kept for so long. By the time I reached the camp, my right calf was twice as big as my left calf. We decided that the next day Arnis would go alone. I would try my best to follow him, but if the pain was too sharp I would stay here and examine the hillsides near our camp.

Again we awoke shortly after four o'clock. I made some soup and at six o'clock we began. We agreed to meet back at our camp by five o'clock in the evening in order to get out of the Kugart Valley before dark—out of this "hole," as our driver, Erik, had called it. If there was another thunderstorm with heavy rain, the road would be soaked and undrivable.

It was a day of suffering. I was tortured by the terrible pain in my leg. Walking to the mountain pass was just not a possibility, so while Arnis left the camp I stayed behind to prepare our things and slowly limp to the Juno irises we had seen when we first came here. As I passed some yurts I clenched my teeth and tried to imitate normal walking. Step by step, I finally reached the first Juno irises. I slowly climbed up to collect the seeds. While inspecting the bulbs I noticed other plants, such as *Pseudosedum* species, *Gymnospermium albertii*, a *Corydalis* species of section *Corydalis* (at this altitude I thought it could only be *C. ruksansii*, but it turned out to be *C. nudicaulis*) and one of section *Leonticoides* (probably *C. ledebouriana*), *Scilla puschkinioides*, and a few other plants whose leaves had long ago withered. My thirst and the pain in my leg became unbearable, so I limped to the nearest stream, where I drank some water and soaked my leg, then climbed back to our camp.

Our driver became nervous. Another thunderstorm had started, this one earlier than the last. I collected our things, packed our bags, and made dinner, and at half past four Arnis returned, absolutely exhausted. He had been to the *Iris winkleri* place again and had checked all the side ridges, sometimes crossing snow beds. He had found a fantastical plant kingdom: large, rich grasses up to a meter high, an abundance of *Aquilegia* species with purplish brown flowers, *Trollius asiaticus*, *Allium backhousianum*, *A. aflatunense*, and *A. carolinianum*. The soil was generally quite moist, even wet. In some places he had seen *Iris zenaidae* but found no more *I. winkleri*. After dinner we started on our way back. We drove just ahead of the rain, which followed us step by step, sometimes sending its regards in the form of small showers. At first we wanted to stop and collect two *Eremurus* species by the roadside, but the clouds looked so threatening that we decided against it. The goal of our expedition had been attained: we had found *I. winkleri* (Plate 210). We had even found *I. zenaidae*, another gem for gardens.

We crossed the border with Uzbekistan and arrived very late in Fergana. At noon the next day we were at the municipality again, where we were welcomed with a luxurious bowl of *shurpo*, the national meal. This was followed by five hours of terrible heat as we traveled through the Fergana Valley and over a mountain pass to Tashkent. The temperature rose continuously, beginning the *chilya*. That night we sorted our plants, had a luxurious meal with a great watermelon for dessert, and prepared our haversacks for the next trip, which would start early the next morning.

When I think about this expedition I still wonder how I managed to do it. Walking 50 km in one day isn't easy even on a perfect road, but at Kugart we covered this distance on mountain slopes, without a road, sometimes using cattle passes, often crossing streams, and all the while looking for plants. For trained mountaineers this might seem like nothing special, but we were gardeners who only left our homes once a year. Somehow we had managed to do it and in the process had found *Iris winkleri*.

Junos from the Minefield

Our last travel to Central Asia took place in 2001. The regime in Uzbekistan had become increasingly rigid and foreigners were faced with more and more restrictions. The same business with registration of passports continued, only now it was officially required in each district, with each registration leading to another three days of waiting. Without Volodya's help it would have been impossible for us to get anywhere at all.

We left Tashkent on 22 June at five o'clock in the morning. Our first route would take place over six days in Uzbekistan, beginning in the southernmost western corner at the border with Turkmenistan and from there heading to the southeastern corner at the border with Tajikistan. Both stops would be very close to the border with Afghanistan, which was at that time still ruled by the Taliban. Through the window of the car we had a very gloomy view of a hot, dry, sunburned landscape. The last time we had been here, at the end of June, local boys at Aman-Kutan had offered us bunches of *Tulipa fosteriana*. Now everything around was gray and only occasionally just near a pass could we see the large spikes of some eremurus (probably *Eremurus robustus*) covered in light pink blooms. Near Shurab, where on our last trip we had found *Allium gypsaceum* and *A. verticillatum* and everything had been gray, brown, pinkish, and in some places even white, the overwhelming color now was not of the plants but of the nude, baked soil. At times we felt as though we were on another planet. To top it off, on this trip our driver was a crazy young man, driving at speeds up to 145 km per hour, even on serpentine mountain roads.

We headed in the direction of the Kugitang Mountains. The first side road (25 km according to the map) led to the mountain range, on the opposite side of which was Hodja-Fil-Ata. *Iris vvedenskyi*, the last of the *I. parvula* group we wanted to find, had been described from this area. We passed three villages situated beside the road. The landscape resembled desert and the riverbed was absolutely dry. Surprisingly, a decent asphalt road led up to the last village on our map. The entrance to this village was somewhat strange. There was a gate and a sign written in Uzbek, but our driver (Uzbek by nationality) opened the gate and drove in regardless of the guard's shouting. His father was some high Tashkent official and apparently no rules existed for him. Only late the next day did we discover that we had entered a nature reserve.

At the end of this village we found a camping area with cottages that could be rented for the equivalent of four dollars. The director decided that if we had passed the gate it meant that we had very "strong papers," so he didn't ask us any questions. We took the "best" cottage, which he said had two beds and even electricity. As it turned out, the electric wires in the room had been torn, the lamps had been broken, and the beds were without mattresses—but at least we had light on the open veranda.

We left our bags in the cottage with our driver and went on a short trip into the mountains. Nearby grew the first Juno irises—scattered plants with broken, dry stems and seedpods still holding a few seeds. Soon some eremurus appeared, their leaves equally yellow and dry. It looked as though there were at least two species. One of them could be *Eremurus olgae*, but since it was very short I tended to identify it as *E. stenophyllus*. Arnis suggested that the shortness might have been caused by the enormously dry spring, and I conceded that he was probably right. After all, Kugitang is quite far from the area where *E. stenophyllus* is known to grow. The other eremurus seemed to be a large-blooming species with loose spikes. In general it resembled the species we had seen earlier in Zaamin and Tut. We collected seeds from both plants.

We started off on an old road but it soon ended. Where should we go? We decided to take the low-grade slopes that were about halfway to the ridge. We passed through a medium-dense archa forest, and in a clearing Arnis found a specimen of the small, late-flowering, very beautiful *Allium gypsaceum* (Plate 212). When we reached the meadows we found another *Allium*, this time *A. verticillatum* (Plate 213). This is a short plant with a comparatively large, globose flower head, but the most striking feature is its foliage: the leaves are narrow, thread-like, and almost indistinguishable from the surrounding grass.

We found *Gentiana olivieri* as well, an almost ubiquitous species in Central Asia. This was the first time we had seen it with desiccated, yellow leaves, one more confirmation that the season had been extremely early and dry.

We were surprised to find almost no cattle in the mountains. The meadows seemed to have been cultivated fields that someone was attempting to return to a natural state. They were terraced, and on the terraces grew two kinds of grass that had been planted sequentially, the same kinds of grass that grew naturally in the surrounding areas. In the corner of one meadow there were a lot of dry *Allium stipitatum* flower stems. As usual they were growing in very manure-rich soil, where a cattle stall had once been.

On the way back we discussed our route for the next day. Making a decision wasn't easy. In some spots the slope was crossed by steep rocks, while other areas were obstructed by dense shrubs or archa forests. Such forests were sometimes even more difficult to pass than cliffs. Finally we decided to begin by going along the dry watercourse (*sai*) and then along the scree slope, which seemed to be crossed by an only slightly visible zigzagging footpath.

As we talked we stumbled across a few Juno irises. They seemed to be *Iris warleyensis* (Plate 214), although I thought the bulbs were too fat and the additional roots too thick compared with what I had seen before. Arnis explained to me that this was quite normal for plants in southern Kugitang, where he had been many years before. When the plants flowered for me the next spring I saw that they really were *I. warleyensis*, and the most beautiful form of the species I had ever seen, with very dark, velvety blackish purple falls, bright bluish violet standards, and a bright orange crest. The special beauty of this plant is not only in the harmony of its bright flower color but also in its fairly dwarf overall appearance.

While we were in the mountains our driver had found vodka somewhere and was now fully drunk. Ignoring him, we made tea, ate supper, and went to sleep. We needed to wake up early the next morning, since the day would again be enormously hot and we wanted to take advantage of the morning coolness to reach the ridge. Just at the start of our walk we met an elderly man and I asked him about the way up. He confirmed that the only route was by the *sai* and after that by the footpath. He also warned us to be extremely careful here, explaining that the border guards had placed landmines along the ridge to thwart Muslim fundamentalist intruders. (The border between Uzbekistan and Turkmenistan ran through the mountain range somewhere south of the pass.) After a short discussion Arnis and I decided that this couldn't be true—why would they lay mines here, so far from Afghanistan? The border guards must have just told this story to locals to prevent them from allowing their cattle to wander the mountain meadows of neighboring Turkmenistan.

The walk was easy—we could still feel the early morning coolness. Again we found *Allium gypsaceum*, and after some distance we stumbled into another Juno iris. It seemed to be *Iris svetlaneae*, though we wouldn't know for sure until we saw it flowering the next spring. This species is among the most beautiful yellow-flowering Juno irises. It is a compact plant with large, bright flowers, and most importantly it grows well in the conditions of my northern garden.

Our footpath cut through medium-dense shrubs of *Rosa*, *Lonicera*, *Crataegus*, *Prunus*, and *Acer* species, following a narrow stream. We could see that higher up the mountain the stream disappeared between stones, so we used this last opportunity to refresh our faces, wash our hands, and fill our flasks with fresh water. It looked as though cattle had not been here for a long time. We repeatedly lost the path.

At half past eight we stopped to inspect a tulip, possibly *Tulipa lanata*. This nice species grows to some 30–40 cm tall and has bright red, somewhat bluish-shaded flowers similar in shape to those of *T. greigii*. The design on the inner base of the flower somewhat resembles that of *T. micheliana*, but the leaves are plain green and narrower. It is almost unknown in cultivation.

There were a lot of plants here but finding them wasn't easy. The nearly snowless winter had been followed by an extremely dry spring, and now everything was very dry and seed crops were minimal. We were mostly collecting seeds from the many stems that had broken off and blown away. So far our best findings were *Iris svetlaneae*, *I. warleyensis*, and both dwarf alliums, which turned out to be different forms of those we had collected in previous years.

Now we were on a bare, stony, south-facing slope. The sun was baking us mercilessly, though a light wind brought some small refreshment. Our mouths were dry so we stopped to rinse them with water—not to drink, only to rinse. A small tulip appeared, something that seemed to belong to the *Tulipa bifloriformis–T. turkestanica* complex, and then we saw a very tiny Juno iris. We carefully dusted away the soil to see the roots of the iris. It was a typical species from the *Iris parvula* group, and although we couldn't see the flowers we knew it was from a place close to the village from which *I. vvedenskyi* had been described.

Meanwhile at the top, where our path crossed the mountain range, an unpleasant surprise awaited us. We reached a high stone fence beside which lay a board with something written in Uzbek. We couldn't read the board but immediately remembered the early morning's talk with the elderly man. He had told us that the pass would be closed, and now this had turned out to be true. So what about the landmines? What would we do? Up to now we had found only two weak plants, but the Juno irises we were looking for didn't usually grow on south-facing slopes. They would be more typically found on the opposite slope that lay on the other side of the fence, where they would be more protected from the sun. And it was *Iris vvedenskyi* that was described as coming from this vicinity. After a short discussion we decided to cross the fence by climbing over some nearby rocks. We would be very cautious and avoid walking along the footpath, carefully looking where we put our feet, trying to jump from one large stone to another.

It was twenty past noon when we crossed the ridge by the rocks on the side of the fence. Now we could see that it really was the only way to the other side of the ridge—the rest of the pass was surrounded by impassable cliffs. On the opposite side we saw a good wide path coming down from the mountains into the middle of a very nice meadow. It looked too good to be true—no, we would avoid it. We kept ourselves close to the cliffs, although we really felt there could be no mines in such a peaceful landscape. Then, as we turned into a narrow, very steep rift in the rocks ending with a vertical cliff, we found it: *Iris vvedenskyi* (Plate 215). It grew here by the thousands, protected from the midday sun and from grazing cattle beneath dense shrubs of dwarf *Rosa* and *Prunus*.

We also noticed some large *Fritillaria* species growing on a small stone balcony a couple of meters above us. It seemed incredible, but this was *F. olgae* (Plate 216). There were plenty of seeds; we sowed half of them right there and took the other half with us. Despite careful searching we found no other fritillaries here, but *F. olgae* was enough. This beautiful species has pale green blooms suffused with pink on a 50–60 cm stem. It requires early replanting. In my collection it is the first species to make new roots (long before the old foliage dies or the seeds ripen).

At the side of the meadow we saw two *Eremurus* species. The one with very hairy leaves immediately reminded me of *E. kaufmannii* from Zaamin. At Zaamin the plants had only recently started flowering, and my attempts to introduce the species with rootstocks had failed. Now it was possible to collect the nearly ripe seeds. Unfortunately, even with the seeds I failed again—they germinated, but the plants disappeared over the following two or three years. The other eremurus seemed to be a small-flowering species with plicate seedpods. We collected some of its seeds as well, although it didn't seem to be a decorative species. The meadow was full of *Iris vvedenskyi*. As with *I. tadshikorum* from Zaamin, the additional roots of this species are very brittle and easily broken off the bulb. Fortunately, however, this is not a fatal injury for either the bulbs or the roots, both of which regenerate very well. The difference between the bulbs and roots when they become separated is that the bulb can produce flowers while the roots can only produce leaves.

Four closely allied and superficially quite similar Juno species, all in the *Iris parvula* group, grow in Central Asia. In 1998 we visited the highlands of Sina Valley in southern Uzbekistan, where *I. parvula* had been described, and so we were certain that we had a correctly named typical plant of this species for comparison. In 1997 at Zaamin (Turkestan Mountains) we found another species of this group. At first we thought it was a new species, but we later came to the conclusion that it must be *I. tadshikorum*, although the place where we found it was very far from its type locality (near Tovilj-Dara, Darwas Mountains). In the *Flora of Tajikistan* (Ovcinnikov 1963), A. I. Vvedenskyi had mentioned that another Juno very similar to *I. tadshikorum* but with smaller flowers grew on the Turkestan Mountains. Comparing our plants with the description of *I. tadshikorum*, we found no significant differences, so we supposed that despite the distance between both localities this was the same species. Unfortunately, it isn't possible now to visit Tajikistan in order to collect plants from the type locality of this species, so we can't confirm or deny whether the plants we found are the same species. The third Juno is *I. linifolia*. The sample of this species that I grow was received from the Gothenburg Botanical Garden; its exact origin is unknown, but the species is quite widespread in Central Asia. *Iris linifolia* is easy to distinguish from both *I. parvula* and *I. tadshikorum* by its flowers, which are whitish yellow with a yellow blotch on the falls and have a crenate, rarely slightly dissected crest; its leaves are glaucous and have a white margin. The flowers of *I. parvula* are greenish yellow with a hairy crest; its leaves are bright green. *Iris tadshikorum* has lilac-tinted flowers with a hairy crest; its leaves are also glaucous with a white margin. So far so good. Problems only arose when we started to search for the fourth species of this group: *I. vvedenskyi*. It had been collected only once, in the northern Kugitang Mountains, the natural border between Uzbekistan and Turkmenistan. In its original description it is said to have flowers that are more yellow than those of *I. linifolia*, with an orange blotch on the falls and a toothed crest. But when plants collected just near the type locality of *I. vvedenskyi* started to flower in the garden, they clearly had nothing in common with *I. linifolia*. The flowers looked much more like those of *I. tadshikorum*—lilac-tinted with an extremely hairy crest—but the leaves were bright green. So the question remains: was there an error in the original description of *I. vvedenskyi* or did we find a new species?

I later came across a Juno iris offered under the name *Iris vvedenskyi* by a mysterious "private botanical garden" in the Czech Republic without any real address other than a Web site (checks had to be sent to an address in Poland). The picture on the Web site was too bad to make a proper decision about the identity of the plant. There was a yellow fall with an orange-shaded blotch on it, but by its overall shape the plant looked too similar to *I. drepanophylla* or *I. kopetdagensis*, which must be greenish yellow. Despite repeated requests I received no seeds or plants from them.

There were a few *Allium* species, too. Just near the rock outcrops grew *A. protensum*, but on the meadow among irises there was a nice small species with bright reddish purple blooms. Overall it looked like a miniature *A. barszczewskii*. Arnis later identified it as *A. tenuicaule*, a good addition to pot-grown alliums or small rockeries where *A. barszczewskii* is too tall. Now having found all we had come here for, we decided to turn back.

As we approached our cottage we saw that a couple of men in uniform were waiting for us. I joked with Arnis that our welcoming committee had arrived, but in reality we both felt somewhat nervous—we had walked very close to the border, so who could predict what these men had in store for us? The questioning started immediately: who were we, what were we doing here, and who allowed us to walk here? They told us that we were in a nature reserve, which we hadn't known until this point. Why hadn't we registered? Why hadn't we paid to enter? We would have to pay a penalty, and since we were foreigners we would have to pay at a special rate. After all, we had walked without permission and were not accompanied by a guide. After a short discussion about the total sum of our penalty, both sides agreed that thirty dollars per person would be sufficient, and since we didn't ask for a receipt, we suddenly became the best of friends. (Thirty dollars was half a year's salary for each of them.)

They told us that the nature reserve had been established only five years ago (our maps, by contrast, were ten years old) and explained that the information we had seen written on the board by the stone fence was a warning about landmines. Both guards had been most afraid that we would blow ourselves up and that they would be blamed and spend the rest of their lives in prison. Walking without a guide was not allowed here specifically because of the mines. It certainly seemed the Lord had been with us this time. We finally understood why the mountains had not been grazed and why there were so few cows on the meadows.

Early the next morning we left the Kugitang Mountains and headed toward Tupalang, the last large valley before the Tajik border. There we wanted to find some nice alliums, possibly some that would be new to us, or another population of *Iris rosenbachiana*. Some very beautiful forms of *I. vicaria* had also been reported from Tupalang. It was a long way to go, but at three o'clock in the afternoon we reached the valley. The road was perfect, taking us higher and higher. We had passed more than half of what we intended, but then the road was blocked by the army. The soldiers explained that even if they were to allow us to pass we would soon be stopped and sent back because the situation in the mountains had become so dangerous. It was possible we could encounter Muslim fundamentalists. Large army maneuvers had recently started, and the army, police, and militia forces were all involved. The roadblock was surrounded by artillery and missile equipment. There was nothing for us to do but turn around.

On the roadside we saw some dry stems of *Iris vicaria*, and when we reached a side gorge that looked promising we asked our driver to stop so we could take a short trip to the mountains. It was enormously hot and we were soon out of breath. The sides of the gorge were extremely steep and dry. We saw remnants of vegetation, including some irises, only on the steepest spots where even sheep couldn't walk. Finally we found a slope with some small shrubs growing on it that we were able to use to secure our boots. There we found what turned out to be *Iris vicaria*, a nice species that is not difficult in the garden. If the plants from Tupalang really were as beautiful as they had been characterized by the botanists who were there during Soviet times, this would be a nice addition to our collections. In fact they turned out to be very similar to those from Sina, some valleys west of Tupalang.

Since we hadn't succeeded in Tupalang, we would go somewhat back from the border and try the previous gorge, Sangardak. The road there was not so good though still passable. A unique feature, the springs of Sharimazar, was marked on the map. It was a very large rock from which a lot of streams flowed out making wonderful waterfalls of very clean, refreshing water. Some 15 m away the temperature was more than 40°C, but here the air was moist, cool, even misty. It was an absolutely different world of plants, too, mainly composed of mosses, ferns, and algae. On account of our earlier experience, we asked some local people whether this was a protected area and whether we were allowed to walk in the mountains. We were told there should be no problems.

There was a nice meadow just before the village of Sangardak where a beekeeper kept his hives. We asked for his permission to camp there and he kindly allowed us. There were two possibilities for the next day's route: to cross the river in front of our camp and then walk up as far as possible, or to pass through the village and then try to reach the highest peak in the surrounding area. According to our map the Hursantag peak (4117 m) was 20 km away. At such an altitude we might find some beautiful alliums, so we decided to take the second route.

We began at dawn. We were almost past the village when someone called to us. It was a man dressed in civilian attire, and he immediately started asking question after question: who were we, where were we going, why didn't we register at the local police station? In the end he explained that we had to walk back to the other end of the village to register. This meant we would lose at least an hour. At the local municipality the man took us into a room on the door of which was written "Headquarters of Defense." We were given some paper on which we were to write who we were, where we had come from, and where we wanted to go. At the same time the man wrote something in Uzbek on another sheet of paper (before beginning he had asked us for a pen). At that moment we couldn't imagine that he was reporting to the District Headquarters of Defense about two very suspicious men who had entered the village through the mountains from the side of Tajikistan, inquiring about the religion and political sympathies of the local people. In his estimation he had disrupted the activity of "Tajik Muslim fundamentalist soldiers of fortune from the Baltic States." We were arrested, our passports were confiscated, and a local policeman transported us in our own car back to Tupalang, where the District Headquarters were located.

There a unique questioning began. On the Tajik side of the border lay almost impassable mountains, so where was our rock climbing equipment? Where were our maps, compass, cameras, video recorders? Where and of what had we taken photos? It was difficult to decide what we should tell them. The problem was that in the local slang *botanist* meant "drug collector." We decided it was better to tell them we were journalists; in any case it would not be a lie, since I still wrote for the Latvian newspapers. We failed to imagine how in such a totalitarian country a foreign journalist might be the second greatest enemy after Muslim fundamentalists. The questioning only intensified. Who allowed us to come here? How did we pass the checkpoints on the roads? They refused to believe that no one had asked for our documents on our way here. We were nervous about what they would think of our maps; they were military maps from the former Soviet Union, still "top secret" in Uzbekistan though freely obtainable in Latvian bookshops. Luckily they were afraid to search our equipment— we were foreign journalists, and if they found nothing it could raise diplomatic problems. So after several hours of questioning we were "free." Relatively free, anyway. We could walk almost anywhere inside the fence surrounding headquarters while a soldier with an automatic gun stood at the gate.

We were told we would have to wait here. First we must wait for the colonel to return, then we must wait until the colonel managed to contact the home office in Tashkent. We were invited to the colonel's table for the evening meal. He had a personal cook and the meal was delicious. We were even supplied with Heineken beer. "You Baltic people like beer," explained the colonel. Then he launched into a nice bit of brainwashing—a full Moscow assortment about all the bad Latvians who had forgotten the generous aid they received from their "great brother—helpful Russia."

We were invited to spend the night in the private apartments of the colonel (still inside the fence).

In the morning we were informed that we were being sent back to Tashkent to the Ministry of Home Affairs because the secretary of state, a general, wanted to meet us personally. Two soldiers would be sent with us. "Don't misunderstand the situation," the colonel explained. "This isn't a convoy, it is only for your safety." But we weren't allowed to stop anywhere on our way back. In the end since our car was so small only one soldier was sent to guard us. Before heading to Tashkent we would have to cross the whole of southern Uzbekistan again and drive to Termez to get our papers stamped at the Main Headquarters of Defense of the South District. Without this stamp our papers would be invalid.

When we reached Termez at noon, everything was closed. It was too hot to work and everyone was taking their midday rest, so we couldn't get our papers stamped. We passed the time in a city park in the shade of the trees, drinking the local beer (which, incidentally, was quite good). Later that afternoon we finally received our stamp and were able to continue on our way. Now it was certain we wouldn't reach Tashkent before night and would need to overnight in Samarkand. The hotel was quite good— nicely renovated apartments in a private house. We had a good sleep. Everything here had been reserved for us by Volodya, who was informed about our troubles by his friends "at the top."

In the morning as we headed to Tashkent we again ran into something unexpected. Farmers who had not received their wages for half a year were rebelling and had blocked the highway with their tractors. A limousine trying to pass through was pelted with stones, and all the windows were broken. Being foreigners, and therefore good targets should anyone want to take hostages, we knew we needed to leave this place as quickly as possible. Our new route took much longer and involved stopping at a checkpoint. The police there were waiting for special forces, something called "alpha group." We were asked what we had seen on the highway. When we asked what would happen to the farmers, we were given a short reply: "Seven to ten years in prison for any who are still alive after the attack." In Uzbekistan conditions this was equivalent to a death sentence—it would be better to be killed on the spot.

We didn't reach Tashkent until the afternoon. The Ministry of Home Affairs of Uzbekistan occupied several large buildings that took up a gigantic block. Which was larger, we joked, the Pentagon or this complex? After many hours of waiting outdoors, first in the heat of the direct sun and then in a shady park across the street that served as a "waiting room," we were guided from one parlor to another. We wrote out our story again, listing all of our contact people in Uzbekistan. Among our contacts was the chief of the president's bodyguards, and the faces of the officials changed upon seeing his name. We were immediately served tea and sweets, and our papers were taken away.

After an hour or so the door suddenly swung open and a man said in an angry voice, "Stop lying. Who are you?" A bit frightened, I answered, "Arnis is a biologist.

I'm a plant breeder, biologist, and journalist." Again the angry voice: "Why didn't you tell us from the beginning that you were biologists instead of giving us the impression that you were journalists?" Only at this moment did I fully understand that for the local regime, journalists—especially independent or Western journalists—were great enemies. In our naiveté we had hoped that the status of journalists would actually help us.

Now everything changed. We became friends, exchanged addresses, received promises for help in the future. But when we asked about the possibility of returning to the mountains, they strongly recommended we stay in Tashkent. "Tashkent is such a beautiful city," they explained. "So many nice buildings and monuments." This kind of recommendation amounted to an order, so there was nothing to do but return to our friend's house and look for the first flight home. We hadn't really lost much. We were here too late in the season anyway, and the most important plant, *Iris vvedenskyi*, had already been found. Besides, I had developed an aversion to heat. When I arrived back at home I couldn't set foot in a sauna for months, feeling that I would burn. This wasn't surprising after my experience in Central Asia, where even at night the temperature hadn't fallen below 30°C, with daytime temperatures in the valleys consistently above 45°C.

This was our last expedition to Central Asia. Since then the situation there has become more and more difficult for traveling, and although I would like to return, all the places that most interest me are no longer reachable. Tajikistan is still a possibility, but it isn't a very peaceful place, and since I don't have any good contacts among the local officials, there is nothing for me to do. Meanwhile Kyrgyzstan remains in the midst of a strange revolution, and no one can predict how things will go in the future.

In post-Soviet times almost all of our expeditions were dedicated to Juno irises, and any other acquisition was just a beautiful and pleasant bonus. When I check the list of Juno iris species grown in the territory of the previous Soviet Empire, I see now that we found most of them. *Iris leptorhiza* is a plant of the foothills of southern Tajikistan, which again is very dangerous to enter, and it flowers so early that very few other plants would be likely to bloom at the same time. I have bought some seeds of it, however. Meanwhile the taxonomic status of *I. popovii* and *I. baldschuanica* remains doubtful; I tend to include them as color forms of *I. rosenbachiana* and therefore cross them off my list of plants to search for. *Iris zaprjagajewii* of the same group is grown by Arnis and at Gothenburg, and some seedlings are also growing in my collection. It has beautiful, somewhat greenish-veined, white blooms with a slightly yellowish crest. Like the other species of this group, it must be a good grower. I did not look for nor find *I. drepanophylla*, a close relative of *I. kopetdagensis*, in Turkmenistan. Both species are so similar that for some time I even thought they were identical. Lastly, such names as *I. almaatensis*, *I. atropatana*, *I. issica*, and *I. schischkinii*, listed by Sergey Czerepanov in his enumeration of plants growing in the Soviet Union, are considered by other botanists to be only synonyms of other Juno irises.

❖ 24
Further East

HAVE NEVER BEEN east of Alma-Ata, the old capital of Kazakhstan. There was an occasion to take part in the so-called Baltic Expedition to Siberia for bulbous *Corydalis* species, financed by the Gothenburg Botanical Garden when Magnus Lidén and Henrik Zetterlund were working on the monograph *Corydalis*. But my legs were in bad shape, and the pain was so strong that I decided to stay home. Only Arnis Seisums from Latvia and Mart Veerus from Tallinn, Estonia, took part in this trip. This turned out to be a good decision, though, because there were times when only two seats were available on the plane or when it was possible to take only two people on a boat down the crazy rapids of the Gorin River during a search for *C. gorinensis*.

Central Siberia

The best Siberian bulbs and bulb-like plants are woodlanders. They grow in forests and on forest edges in places where the sun can reach them. From a gardener's point of view they have one thing in common: they can't stay out of the soil for long and must be replanted as soon as possible. In the bulb shed they generally must be kept (with very few exceptions) in thin polyethylene bags mixed with very slightly moistened peat moss. They usually transpire a sufficient amount of water to keep the peat moist. That's why the peat shouldn't be too wet to begin with. Only in the case of a very small stock of just a few bulbs should the peat be slightly wet, but then the risk of earlier rooting is increased. The bulbs that have started forming roots must be replanted immediately, taking them out of the bag for as short a time as possible. They will grow well even if some of the roots of neighboring bulbs are so tightly entangled that it is necessary to break some of them to separate the bulbs.

The first Siberian corydalis I want to discuss is *Corydalis solida* subsp. *subremota* (syn. *C. subremota*; Plate 217), which makes a link between Europe and Asia. It is just one of four subspecies of *C. solida*. The other three grow in Europe, reaching the Ural Mountains, with the exception of the Iberian Peninsula, British Isles, and Scandinavia. Subspecies *incisa* replaces the type subspecies in the Balkans and can be easily distinguished by its dissected bracts and generally thicker leaves. The white form of this subspecies, named 'Vermion Snow' and introduced by Brian Mathew from Mount Vermion in northern Greece, is among the best white forms of *C. solida*. It has up to twenty flowers in a large, dense, straight raceme; they are the purest snow white, with red pedicels and olive-green foliage. The collected material was not very uniform, and

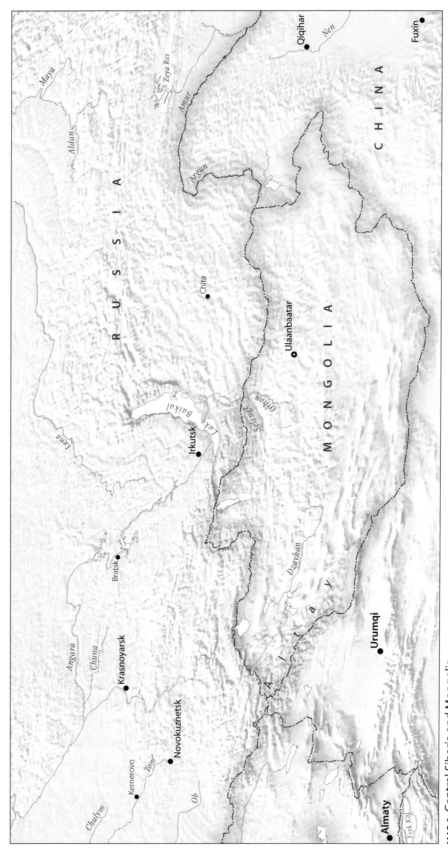

MAP 3: Central Siberia and Mongolia

I selected a smaller form with more finely divided, lighter green leaves and the same pure white blooms: 'Snow in Spring'. 'Cyrrus' from Mount Taygetos has dove gray flowers and especially finely dissected leaves that are thicker in texture. It is one of the most unusual forms in my collection. Subspecies *longicarpa* grows at the very southern tip of Greece, but I never had it in my collection. I wrote about subspecies *solida* when describing my first studies in the forests of Latvia, and now I grow more than 150 different selections of it.

Subspecies *subremota* was introduced into gardens as a result of the Baltic Expedition to Siberia. In nature it grows along the lower parts of dry slopes near small rivers. It resembles *Corydalis turtschaninovii* (syn. *C. remota*) in terms of its more distinct bluish flower color and was even compared with this species by M. Popov in the *Flora of the Soviet Union* (Komarov 1937). *Corydalis turtschaninovii* and *C. solida* both grow equally far from subspecies *subremota* but in opposite directions. On a map the distribution area of subspecies *subremota* looks like a blotch in the middle of Siberia in the Krasnoyarsk region, right between its two relatives. The climatic conditions there are very continental, with dry, quite hot summers and very snowy, severe winters. In the garden this corydalis grows brilliantly, reproduces well, and sets seed, so it is a good newcomer.

One close neighbor of subspecies *subremota* is *Corydalis gracilis*, another rarity introduced by the Baltic Expedition. In nature it is a much more common plant than subspecies *subremota*, although it grows in identical conditions. *Corydalis gracilis* is very similar to *C. bracteata*. Its blooms are the same color (lemon yellow) and size as those of *C. bracteata*, but it is a smaller plant that rarely reaches 15 cm tall, so it looks something like the younger sister of the famous beauty queen. Most interesting is its habit of forming an additional tuber at the base of the underground scale leaf, making it a quicker increaser despite its generally smaller tubers. Since the leaf stem sometimes grows somewhat obliquely, the additional tuber is formed a short distance from the mother plant, giving the impression of stolons; when left untouched for a number of years, a group of *C. gracilis* will slowly increase in size. However, the original tubers split, too. Although *C. gracilis* is very similar in flower to *C. bracteata*, the distribution areas of the two species do not overlap, and the seeds of *C. gracilis* have very distinct elaiosomes.

Corydalis bracteata (Plate 218), the first Siberian corydalis I ever grew, can be put at the top of all Siberian species. Well known in cultivation since the early nineteenth century, it is still quite rare in gardens and is always highly requested. It appears now and again in plant lists but then disappears again for some time. It does well in most gardens and has even been described by some as a beautiful weed. Since it comes from areas with very cold winters, it may not do as well where winters are sometimes too warm. Henrik Zetterlund once described *C. bracteata* to me this way: "When the herbage is about to become too dense, we are saved by the voles, which have a feast every fourth or fifth year, after which the remaining plants have to build themselves up once again." On three different occasions I have almost completely lost all my stocks of *C. bracteata* to rodents, and as with the Gothenburg plants they recovered from self-sown seedlings.

In my nursery I always collect the seeds of *Corydalis bracteata* and sow them on the open garden beds, where they start flowering in the third year. Requests for this species seem endless. The natural populations are very uniform—the large, bright lemon yellow flowers arranged in big spikes, their overall height near 25 cm. I received my first tubers from Georgiy Skakunov from the Kemerovo region in central Siberia east of Baikal. Mr. Skakunov worked as a teacher of biology and usually took a trip to the forest each spring with his students to teach them about the native plants of their district. During one such excursion a student named Marina found a plant of *C. bracteata*. It had a unique, almost white flower color. In twenty years Mr. Skakunov had never found anything like it in the wild, nor had I ever heard other collectors mention such a thing. The result was *C. bracteata* 'Marina'. Its flowers are initially lemon yellow but pale to an almost pure white within a few days. Surprisingly, a great proportion of 'Marina' seedlings have the same pale color, and when both yellow and white forms are grown together, white seedlings frequently appear among those of the yellow form.

Corydalis bracteata sometimes hybridizes with *C. solida* and this hybrid is named *C. ×allenii*. It is sterile, intermediate between its parents, and comparatively late-flowering. The flowers are large, yellowish, and flushed with purple or pinkish on the lip. It is a very vigorous grower that needs frequent replanting. Various forms of this natural hybrid can appear in any collection where both species are grown together. One such hybrid was found by my Estonian friend Enno Zupping from Tartu. He sent it to me and in his honor I named it 'Enno'. It has very large, creamy pink flowers, and the bract is slightly divided only at the top. The best form of *C. ×allenii*, 'Gilded Beauty', was found in the garden of Arnis Seisums. Its flowers are almost the size of those of *C. bracteata*, though it is generally a more compact plant. Its beauty lies in its deep purple flowers, the upper and lower petals of which have a narrow but impressive golden rim.

Erythronium sibiricum (Plate 219), another plant favored by Mr. Skakunov, is one of the most beautiful erythroniums, especially among the Eurasian species that form a group of close relatives very distinct from the American *Erythronium* species. The most common of these species is the European *E. dens-canis*, which grows in the wild from Spain to the Eastern Carpathians. In the Caucasus Mountains it is replaced by *E. caucasicum*, and this is followed by a great gap as far as the mountains of Altay. This is where *E. sibiricum* grows; its main distribution area is in Russia but it also enters eastern Kazakhstan and northern Xinjiang Province in China. Finally, after another large gap, *E. japonicum* can be found in Japan, Korea, and eastern China. This last species is a very typical woodland plant that grows well at forest edges and inside shrubs in moist places where competition from grasses is minimal.

For a long time *Erythronium sibiricum* was not accepted by most botanists as a separate species and was generally regarded as a variety of *E. dens-canis*, although both are very easy to distinguish by the morphology of their flower parts. The first forms of *E. sibiricum* to reach Latvia came from the Kemerovo region, where Mr. Skakunov spent a lot of time studying the variability of this species in the wild and selecting many splendid forms. Unfortunately, after the collapse of the Soviet system he became the victim of a dishonest businessman, who offered him mounds of gold for all his stocks and then disappeared with both the bulbs and the money. Now only a few bulbs remain in some private collections where he had sent them earlier.

The most typical form of *Erythronium sibiricum* has bright purple blooms and is easily distinguished from its European and Japanese relatives by its yellow anthers. *Erythronium caucasicum* also has yellow anthers, but these species have very different filaments and anthers. The filaments of all *E. sibiricum* subspecies are unique in shape, with a flattened, significantly wider part approximately at the middle or a third of the way below the anthers, which are all equal in length. In *E. caucasicum* three of the anthers are twice as long as the other three and the filaments are tapering. The leaves of *E. sibiricum* are usually intensely mottled; they may even look purplish, with round or elliptic green dots. Some forms reproduce quite well vegetatively, but *E. sibiricum* sets seed very well in Latvia, and the seeds germinate without any problems if sown on open beds soon after collecting.

On most occasions the flowers of *Erythronium sibiricum* are bright purplish pink, but some of the selections made by Georgiy Skakunov are a beautiful, pure, soft pink without any shade of purple. 'Zoya' and 'Olya' are the best examples of this coloring. There is a superb white variety, too, that Mr. Skakunov named 'Beliy Klik' and that later with his kind permission I renamed 'White Fang' (the same name, only translated from Russian into English). This extreme form has pure white flowers and narrower segments, without any marking in the center. It sends up its plain light green leaves when all the other forms of *E. sibiricum* have finished flowering. In all other aspects 'White Fang' is identical to typical *E. sibiricum*. 'Gornaya Shoria' flowers as late as 'White Fang' but has purple flowers.

In southern Altay near the border between Kazakhstan and Russia, Arnis Seisums collected a nearly uniform strain of *Erythronium sibiricum* with purplish pink blooms. It flowered earlier than the stocks usually offered in the trade and had rather narrow perianth segments. He named it 'Early Wonder'. I have many acquisitions of *E. sibiricum* collected by different people from all over its area of distribution, and in general they all share the same type of flower and growing capacity. There are no significant differences from Chinese plants, either.

Shortly before all our contacts with gardeners in Russia were cut off due to the disintegration of the Soviet Empire, when different customs regulations and other rules stopped the exchange of plant material, I received a consignment of very large bulbs from Altay under the name *Erythronium sibiricum*. They had been collected at the upper course of the river Ka-hem in the republic of Tuva at an altitude of 2300–2500 m, where they were reportedly growing on alpine meadows. They surprised me the first spring that they flowered by coming up very early in my garden, before all the other erythroniums had even poked their noses out of the soil. As it turned out, all other forms of *E. sibiricum* start flowering when this one is finished or nearly finished. The Altay form is a very large plant, at least one and a half times taller than the usual *E. sibiricum*, with unusually large, pure white blooms. Some of the flowers acquire a very light purplish tint as they fade. In the garden this form is a marvelous grower, reproducing well vegetatively and from seed. Its bulbs are larger and longer than the usual bulbs of *E. sibiricum*, nearly as large as those of *E. japonicum*. The foliage is plain green suffused with brown.

Intrigued by the unusual character of this newcomer, I tried to cross it with traditional forms of *Erythronium sibiricum* but failed—I couldn't manage to get a single seed no matter which forms I used as seed parents. At the same time artificially pollinated and isolated plants inside the group produced normal seeds that germinated very well. This experiment has led me to believe that the Altay plant is actually another species or at least subspecies of Eurasian erythroniums. Another factor backing up this theory is the flowering time of this plant. In the garden plants from higher altitudes usually flower significantly later than plants of the same species from lower altitudes. In the case of *E. sibiricum*, however, the opposite turned out to be true: the form from higher altitudes is the first to flower. For many years I offered this plant in my catalog as *E. sibiricum* 'Altai Snow', but I have since decided that it is a different, still undescribed subspecies and would like to name it *E. sibiricum* subsp. *altaicum* (Plate 220).

Although *Erythronium sibiricum* grows very well in Latvia, where it flowers beautifully each year, it does not do so well in the Netherlands or southern Britain. When I sent the first bulbs to Michael Hoog they didn't come up the first spring, although they looked perfect when he dug some of them out. They came up only the following season and turned out to be quite lazy about flowering. We later found out that *E. sibiricum* flowers well only after a cold winter, when the soil has been frozen for at least a short period of time. In this aspect subspecies *altaicum* is much more valuable because it blooms even in areas with mild winters.

Some confusion arose when I received some bulbs under the name *Erythronium sibiricum* from Sulev Savisaar in Estonia. He had acquired them from a correspondent living near the village of Altayskiy in the Altay region who had collected the plants at the forest edge near the border with the Altay Republic. This form was identical to subspecies *sibiricum* in everything but the color of the anthers, which were black. Its filaments where the same shape as those of typical *E. sibiricum*. I tried crossing this form with the typical forms, but my experiments failed, as had similar experiments with subspecies *altaicum*. I didn't try to cross it with subspecies *altaicum* because I had only a few bulbs, and unfortunately I later lost my black-anthered plants altogether. More recently, however, I received a few new bulbs from Sulev and decided to name this form subspecies *sulevii* (Plate 221) in his honor.

There was still the question of *Erythronium japonicum*, the fourth member of the Eurasian species. All my attempts to introduce it from Western nurseries failed. Each time I received bulbs they were of terrible quality and either didn't come up at all or turned out to be *E. sibiricum*. I had pretty much lost all hope of finding this species when I came across its name one day on a list of plants offered by a company in China. Over the years I had spent thousands of dollars on plants from this particular company, and none had ever grown well for me. Still, I couldn't resist the temptation, and in the autumn of 2003 I ordered a few dozen of both Eastern species of dog's-tooth violets (*E. sibiricum* and *E. japonicum*). Predictably the bulbs arrived in terrible shape. They had been packed too wet, more than two-thirds of them were broken, and many were half-rotten. I carefully cleaned off all the rotten tissue, treated the bulbs with fungicides, and carefully planted them in my new shade garden, though I did not expect them to germinate the following spring. They did germinate, however, and in great numbers. (In contrast, almost none of the frits I had received came up the following spring despite having looked far better at planting time.)

When plants of both species started to flower I was very surprised by the beauty of *Erythronium japonicum* (Plate 222). Its flowers are a more bluish shade of purple, but the most intriguing feature is the basal design on the petals, which is bordered with a dark violet, narrow, variously three-toothed line. Even more surprising, its anthers are placed at two levels; three of the filaments are only half as long as the other three. As with this plant's European relative, the anthers are black.

My experience in growing *Erythronium japonicum* has been very limited, so I can't predict how it will perform in Latvia, but if it is much like *E. sibiricum* it should grow well. I didn't harvest any bulbs after the first season, but I couldn't withstand the temptation to check on them the following autumn. They looked very nice—large and strong with healthy root systems. So I hope for a good future for this "Japanese" plant from China.

For the sake of clarity it might be useful to compare the features by which various forms of the versatile Eurasian dog's-tooth violets can be distinguished. *Erythronium caucasicum*, for the record, is a small plant with anthers that are yellow and unequal in length, and filaments that are tapering. It flowers early and its leaves are strongly mottled. *Erythronium dens-canis*, also a small plant, has black anthers and tapering filaments. Flowering occurs midseason and the leaves are strongly mottled. *Erythronium japonicum* is a medium-sized to large plant with black anthers and filaments that are tapering and unequal in length. It flowers midseason and has leaves that are mottled and plain. *Erythronium sibiricum* subsp. *sibiricum* is medium-sized and has yellow anthers and filaments that are flattened near the middle. Flowering occurs late and the leaves are generally mottled. *Erythronium sibiricum* subsp. *altaicum* is a large plant, and like the type subspecies it has yellow anthers and filaments that are flattened near the middle. It flowers early and its leaves are generally suffused. *Erythronium sibiricum* subsp. *sulevii* is medium-sized with black anthers and filaments that are flattened near the middle. Flowering occurs late and its leaves are generally mottled.

From a bit more to the east come three nice, tiny *Anemone* species that somewhat resemble our European windflowers. *Anemone altaica* generally looks very similar to our *A. nemorosa* and is sometimes merged with this species but is in fact fairly distinct.

It has pure white flowers, appearing much in advance of those of *A. nemorosa*, and distinctive light green foliage. The rhizomes are thick and yellowish (brown in *A. nemorosa*). In the wild it is very widespread and grows from forests on riverbanks to high alpine meadows, where it flowers immediately after the snow melts. My stock was originally collected in southern Altay.

Anemone jenisseensis appears in Siberian forests. It is related to and somewhat resembles the yellow windflower, *A. ranunculoides*, but is a much more delicate plant with short rhizomes. The flowers are smaller and often numerous on each stem. The rhizomes are so tiny that it is sometimes quite difficult to find them in their plastic bags among the peat moss. In my garden I always plant it in white sand to facilitate finding the rhizomes during harvesting. This species is much less distributed in the wild, growing from the Krasnoyarsk region up to Baikal. My stock was collected just near Krasnoyarsk in southern Siberia where it grows in moist forest clearings and among shrubs, sometimes just at the edge of bogs.

The third Siberian windflower is the blue-flowering *Anemone coerulea*. Its rhizomes are the same size as those of *A. jenisseensis*, but its small flowers are of a variable shade of light blue. The leaves are very finely dissected. It comes from southern Altay, too, and is easy to grow in the same conditions required for *A. nemorosa*. As with *A. jenisseensis* it is best planted in a thin layer of white sand.

These species are good additions to the more common windflowers. All three are easy to grow when given a somewhat shaded position in the garden. They self-sow and also spread by rhizomes.

Russian Far East

Far eastern Russia, including the Kuril Islands, Sakhalin, and Kamchatka, is much richer in bulbous plants than central Siberia, with more plant families that join the "club of bulbs." I will mention only the aroids and wood lilies (*Trillium*), but more genera from traditional bulbous families also grow in this region. These plants require growing conditions similar to those needed for plants from central Siberia, and the bulbs should be stored and cared for in the same way.

I will start with *Corydalis*. The first plant reached me from Sakhalin Island, where my longtime correspondent Jury Uspensky lived in the city of Tomari. Due to his kind care I received many of the rarest bulbs, and at the top of this list was one of the brightest blue species of *Corydalis*. I received it under the name *C. ambigua* and grew it under that name for many years until I read in the monograph by Magnus Lidén and Henrik Zetterlund (1997) that the correct name of this beauty is *C. fumariifolia* (Plate 223). Both species are very similar, differing only in minor details such as the glaucous leaf surface, rather small leaves, and fruit shape of true *C. ambigua*. It seems that the true *C. ambigua* was never cultivated and that most of the material distributed under this name has been *C. fumariifolia*. The true *C. ambigua* grows only in

Kamchatka. The Baltic Expedition didn't go there, but now there are frequent visits from the American side so it is very possible that some day this beauty might appear in Western gardens.

Corydalis fumariifolia is one of the most early-flowering species in the garden, and this is the greatest problem it poses in my nursery. Night frosts, which usually occur later and more intensely in northern Latvia than in other parts of the country, often lead to damage. I still grow it but would lose it for good if I didn't regularly look for seeds. In Arnis's garden it grows perfectly in the shade of a large apple tree. I recently collected some self-sown seedlings from where I had first located this plant in my garden; they had survived under a similarly large apple tree. The tubers of *C. fumariifolia* are unique in color, somewhat grayish or whitish, making this plant easy to distinguish from other woodland *Corydalis* species from the Russian Far East, which have distinctly yellowish tubers. This species reproduces well vegetatively.

In the wild *Corydalis fumariifolia* is much more widely distributed than *C. ambigua*, growing southward from the lower Amur to Vladivostok and entering northeastern North Korea, eastern Manchuria, and Sakhalin. It is very variable with regard to leaf shape and degree of foliage dissection. Many forms were described by earlier botanists, but they all grow in mixed populations and don't regenerate from seed. Some growers still separate *C. fumariifolia* var. *lineariloba*, which has very narrow, long leaf lobes. I have a few bulbs of this variety myself. The best specimens have bright blue flowers, though the flowers may also be lilac or light purplish in tone. On one occasion I received a white-flowering tuber, but it was eaten by a rodent shortly after flowering. Two subspecies are recognized: subspecies *fumariifolia* from the continental part of the distribution area, with more deeply dissected, narrower leaf lobes, and subspecies *azurea* from Sakhalin and northern Japan, with rounded leaf lobes. Both are of equal beauty.

Another species of Siberian *Corydalis* came to my collection from the continental part of the Far East, mostly from the so-called Primorsky region and neighboring Amur region in the west and the Khabarovsk region in the north. It is a region where there are no roads and no villages for thousands of kilometers, where it is possible to meet no one but trappers, gold diggers, and perhaps a few representatives of native tribes. There are remnants of the concentration and death camps of the Stalinist regime, where thousands of inhabitants of the Baltic States were sent to die after the occupation. Mart Veerus from Estonia and his parents were sent there, too, so his knowledge of local conditions played an important role in the success of the Baltic Expedition.

When I first developed an interest in *Corydalis* I sent letters to all the gardeners I knew from these places, asking them to send the plants that most fascinated me. I received many *Corydalis* tubers in reply, and when they started to flower in my garden I could see that I mostly had two different species, both with blue or slightly lilac-shaded blooms, but easily distinguished by flowering time. One bloomed early, the other blooming only after the first had finished flowering. The leaf shape was also different, but I was well acquainted with the variability of *Corydalis* foliage and knew that this characteristic was less important for classification. In some batches they were both mixed.

Using the literature available to me, I classified one species as *Corydalis remota*. The only alternative for the other was *C. repens*, although there were some differences between my plant and its description in local floras. Under those names both plants were sent to Michael Hoog, who distributed them across Europe. When they reached the Gothenburg Botanical Garden they were both identified as a single species: *C. turtschaninovii* (Plate 224).

As it turns out, *Corydalis turtschaninovii* has extremely variable foliage. *Flora of Siberia and the Far East* (Bush 1913) describes five different forms, noting that there are populations in which all of these forms grow together. The same flora compares this species with *C. solida* (under the synonym *C. halleri*), and on the distribution map it is clear that *C. turtschaninovii* is still not separated from *C. solida* subsp. *subremota*, although between them is a large gap from where no herbaria of bulbous *Corydalis* exist. Actually, there may be many still-unknown species in the Siberian taiga just waiting for some hard-working and daring explorer to find them.

Corydalis turtschaninovii is a late-flowering species. The flowers are generally bright blue, sometimes violet-shaded, on a 15–20 cm stem. I have never found any forms with white flowers. I grow this corydalis outside in fertile, humus-rich soil somewhat shaded by large trees. It can also be grown in full sun, although this will shorten the flowering time. It sets seed perfectly and reproduces well vegetatively, and as with *C. gracilis* it often forms an additional tuber at the base of an underground scale leaf. These tubers have an unusual, ragged, plicate form, and when I first noticed them I thought they had some kind of disease, if they were *Corydalis* tubers at all. However, they produced perfect flowering-sized tubers the following growing season.

During the Baltic Expedition, Arnis Seisums found a very beautiful form of *Corydalis turtschaninovii* with bright sky blue flowers near Vladivostok. It is among the most late-blooming varieties and has a large spike of flowers but is overall very compact in appearance. He named it 'Blue Gem'. Another form, 'Kedrovaya Padj', was found during the same expedition at the Kedrovaya Padj nature reserve and has bright blue flowers with a lilac tint. Its leaves are very light green and finely dissected like those of variety *lineariloba*, and it is more early-flowering. 'Amur' is a deep, bright blue form with very dark-colored and even more heavily dissected leaves (they are very thread-like, giving the plant a somewhat airy appearance). 'Vladivostok', another form found near Kedrovaya Padj, was so unusual even for this very variable species that I kept a question mark beside its name for a very long time. Its flowers are bright sky blue and held in large spikes, but its most unusual feature is the foliage, which is almost un-divided and spade-like, only shallowly dentate at the top of the lobes. It most closely resembles the form described as variety *pectinata*.

During one of Henrik Zetterlund's visits to my garden, as we checked the shaded beds of corydalis, he spotted a very unusual plant growing outside the beds deep inside a lilac shrub. It resembled *Corydalis turtschaninovii* but had uncharacteristically deep purple foliage. I had never before had anything like it in my collection, so it was clearly a spontaneous mutation occurring between my stocks of this species. The seeds had apparently been distributed far away from the formal beds, probably by ants or some other creature. I carefully dug it out and planted it in a bed, and in honor of my Swedish friend I decided to name it 'Eric the Red' (Plate 225) after the famous Swedish Viking. It turned out to be a very good grower and an excellent increaser in the garden. Unfortunately, though, the purple color of the leaves starts to diminish a little as the flowers fade.

I had many long discussions with Henrik and Magnus about the identity of another blue *Corydalis* that I had erroneously named *C. repens*. They both supposed it was only an early-flowering form of *C. turtschaninovii*, but I didn't agree. The early-flowering plant had rounder leaves with less divided lobes, never formed underground stem tubers, and was overall more compact in appearance. Finally one evening there came a telephone call from Gothenburg: "Jānis, where did you find this beautiful plant? It really is a new species. We're going to call it *C. ornata*."

The Latin name *ornata* means "ornate" and can be applied to this beauty without any doubt. It is very variable in color, with forms ranging from the purest white to the brightest blue and light violet. I even found some pinkish forms among my seedlings. I received my first plants in 1985 from Galina Kirsanova, who found this new species in a forest near the city of Arsenyev in the Primorsky region. Later I received tubers from other people living in the same region. Only Mrs. Kirsanova sorted them separately by color, and they were the first tubers I received from the Russian Far East, registered under the collection numbers *85-001* ("Albus"), *85-002* ("Caeruleus"), and *85-003* ("Lilacinus").

A few selections of *Corydalis ornata* (Plate 226) have been made, but I generally grow this species as a mixed color population because in my opinion this is the secret of its beauty—all the color forms flowering at the same time make a beautiful blue carpet resembling the sea, with white foam above blue and lilac waves. Still, one selection must be mentioned. 'Blue Lip' (Plate 227) is a pure white form with a crenulate lip thinly lined with blue. According to Henrik, who named it, "it is the most fabulous variant and one of the most beautiful plants in existence." I tend to associate it with Christmas trees, so conical and perfect is the appearance of the individual plant.

The true *Corydalis repens* is a very small plant even in cultivation. Each spike holds just a few pale blue or pale lilac (rarely whitish or pinkish) flowers, and there are few seeds in each capsule. It is most easily characterized by the small white spots on the surface of its leaves.

Among my *Corydalis* samples from the Russian Far East are a few unidentified plants that look intermediate between *C. turtschaninovii* and *C. ornata*. I believe they are another yet-to-be-described new species. I recently sent a sample to Gothenburg and am waiting for an opinion from both great specialists there.

Corydalis ussuriensis is another tiny species that was collected during the Baltic

Expedition. Mart and Arnis found it growing in its type locality side by side with *C. fumariifolia* and *C. turtschaninovii*. Only a few plants were found and all were growing beneath maple trees in deciduous woods alongside *Caltha silvestris*. Mart and Arnis were very lucky to have been there just at the right time—it is impossible to find these plants after flowering has finished and they have become concealed by long grass. *Corydalis ussuriensis* is a very beautiful species and seems to have the largest flowers of all blue corydalis from the Russian Far East. A few plants were sent to Gothenburg, where they are still grown, and a couple were left for Arnis. I have never had this species in my collection.

Plant hunting is a difficult task in the native tundra of Siberia, where plenty of enemies lie in wait for inexperienced, unprepared travelers. It's hardly worth mentioning bears and snakes, which can be quite dangerous in spring but usually try to avoid contact with humans. Mosquitoes are another unpleasant pest, though they aren't usually present in large numbers until summer. The greatest danger comes from the billions of ticks in the region disseminating tick-borne encephalitis. The ticks wait for their victims on shrub branches and in the grass near passes, jumping onto any animals or humans passing by. Travelers have to wear special garments that completely cover all the exposed parts of the body and that include special wings under which ticks can hide. Every half hour travel partners check over each other and collect the ticks from their clothing. According to Mart, during their expedition they sometimes found close to a hundred ticks on their clothing. Since tick-borne encephalitis is now quite widespread in Latvia, a national vaccination program is in place to allow everyone to be vaccinated, but this was not the case when Arnis and Mart traveled to Siberia.

For a long time I searched for another *Corydalis* species known to grow in this area: *C. buschii* (Plate 228). I was intrigued by its portrayal in the *Flora of the Soviet Union* (Komarov 1935), where it was described in a section of its own and characterized as having a tuber on a long, creeping rhizome. I also read that it was grown in the Main Botanical Garden in Moscow but had never set seed there. I paid a special visit to this garden and offered many of my rarest plants in exchange for a sample, but I received nothing more than promises to "think it over." I wrote many letters to contacts in the Russian Far East, too, but no one was familiar with this plant, although they promised to look for it. Then in 1987 I received a parcel from Vladivostok containing some peat-like substance labeled *C. buschii*; it had been collected on Popov Island, in the gulf near Vladivostok. Imagine my disappointment when instead of this long-searched-for plant I found some overdried peat with not even the slightest sign of tubers. In spite of this I made a few rows on a garden bed and sowed this humus-like dust there. The following spring I was extremely surprised when in just a few spots I saw something coming up. That something had very tiny, light green, corydalis-like leaves. One year later nice foliage came up, and beautiful deep reddish purple flower spikes appeared long after all the other species had finished flowering.

When I decided to replant *Corydalis buschii* I found that my plants had developed very strange, bright yellow, branched, rhizome-like structures with some knots at the branching points, nothing like what had been described in the *Flora of the Soviet Union*. *Corydalis buschii* turned out to be a beautiful, very ephemeral "weed" in my garden. It is practically impossible to collect all of its rhizomes at harvesting time, even if they have been planted in white sand. It moves itself to the correct growing depth by forming a new layer of rhizomes where it feels most comfortable. For this reason at harvesting time the rhizomes are everywhere—where you first planted them as well as a distance away, some even at the very surface of the soil. Yet in my garden it is a very nice weed. Its tiny foliage appears at the beginning of May, the flowers bloom a couple of weeks later, and by the end of the month there are no longer any signs on the soil surface that it ever existed. I find that this corydalis is best situated among deciduous shrubs, where it decorates the soil before the leaves of the shrubs open. This species definitely needs a shaded place. Unlike all the other Siberian woodlanders, which can be grown in full sun without great problems, *C. buschii* suffers from strong sunlight; its leaves can be scorched, and the flowers can wilt in one or two days. In shade it is long-flowering and abundantly covers the soil with small reddish purple spikes. In my region it also sets seed well, but it is such a good increaser that I have never collected the seeds. To protect the harvested tuber-rhizomes from desiccation, I immediately mix them with slightly wet peat moss and keep them in plastic bags.

One of the rarest *Corydalis* species in Siberia is *C. gorinensis* (Plate 229). It is known only from one location half a square kilometer in size at the second "bik" of the Gorin River. This bik is a hill sparsely covered with *Juniperus sibirica* and other shrubs, and surrounded by the raging Gorin River and endless bogs with completely different vegetation. *Corydalis gorinensis* grows on the hill in pockets of peat. Above this are boggy, peaty forests where *C. gorinensis* does not grow, but other plants are plentiful there, including *Fritillaria maximowiczii*, *Paeonia obovata*, *Clintonia udensis*, and a bluish purple form of *Corydalis turtschaninovii*.

There were two attempts to reach the Gorin River, a tributary of the Amur. When Arnis and Mart first landed in Komsomolsk-na-Amure some 70 km from the desired spot, they were too early—everything was still covered in snow. They flew back to Krasnoyarsk where spring had started earlier, and there they collected *C. gracilis* and *C. solida* subsp. *subremota*. Afterward they returned to Komsomolsk-na-Amure.

I still wonder how they had the courage to get there. Their only option for transport turned out to be a small motorboat steered by two drunk fishermen who would accept nothing but a bottle of pure ethanol as payment. The boat was extremely overloaded and my friends felt sure the next sizeable wave would put an end to more than just their travel. The boatmen left them on the bare riverbank at the bottom of the bik, promising to come back the next day and warning them about a bear living nearby. In addition to the bear, which did in fact visit them that night, leaving clear footprints a few meters from their tent, they also encountered plenty of snakes. They were pleasantly surprised when both fishermen actually showed up the next day to pick them up. There was no way to cross the virgin forest by the riverbank on foot.

Corydalis gorinensis, *C. magadanica*, and *C. gorodkovii* form a small group of species with somewhat strange tubers that seem to be branched. The most unique thing about *C. gorinensis*, however, is its foliage, which is thick, finely divided, and very different in shape and structure from other species of the Russian Far East. Its beautiful flowers are deep golden yellow, much more yellow than those of *C. bracteata*, though smaller. The greatest problem with this species is how early it emerges in the garden. Each spring its leaves are damaged or even killed by late frosts. In my own experience my plants became increasingly weak from year to year; I finally sent my last specimen to a grower in Canada hoping he would have better luck with it than I did. Arnis was more successful with it in his city garden, where the effects of night frost are minimized by the surrounding buildings, but even he can't boast of having had great success, and the same is true with plants grown at Gothenburg. Unfortunately, conditions in the greenhouse are too hot and too dry for this riverside beauty.

Corydalis magadanica (Plate 230) is distributed along the Sea of Okhotsk at 3–20 m above sea level, north from the city of Magadan in the direction of Ola. It is very similar to *C. gorinensis* in everything but its blooms and growing capacity. It has the same shape of leaves and tubers but the flowers are a beautiful soft white, slightly greenish in bud. Even in the wild *C. gorinensis* looks like a depressed, somewhat weak plant and never forms groups. *Corydalis magadanica*, however, grows on soft sandstone structures in much richer soils and only on open spots among *Betula ermanii*. It forms groups in the grass, often consisting of large vegetative clumps. In the garden it grows far better than *C. gorinensis*, coming up slightly later, although I haven't been very successful with it. Both species must take advantage of the very short summer in their homeland, so the rooting starts early, usually soon after the leaves die down. Sometimes the first tips of new roots are even visible at harvesting time.

Corydalis gorodkovii was introduced by Canadian bulb growers. In the wild it is distributed on the mountain ranges further north from Magadan and a bit more inside the continent. It is reported that in nature it keeps growing until August due to the very short, late-starting summer. I received tubers from Canada on two occasions. The first tubers were absolutely dry, so nothing came up in spring. The replacements were in slightly better condition, and two tubers showed weak leaves in the spring, but everything died by autumn.

Many bulbous *Corydalis* species are described from Japan, Korea, and especially China, but I have never had the opportunity to try any of them in my garden. All the intriguingly named plants I ordered from China always turned out to be non-bulbous species that can't be grown outside in my climate. The few that came up died the following winter.

For a short time I grew *Corydalis cashmeriana*, a Himalayan species. This bright blue beauty has a strange scaly bulb that somewhat resembles a miniature lily bulb. When I first saw it pictured I was so fascinated by it that I asked for Chris Brickell's help in acquiring some bulbs. This was during the dark days of the Soviet era, so the only way I could get anything was through friends at the seed exchange group of the National Botanical Garden. Chris sent the parcel using a courier service and it reached Riga two months later. (I used to joke that the courier had to walk all the way from London to Riga.) Naturally the bulbs died during such a long period of time, especially after so many inspections by the KGB (what, no microfilms hidden between the bulb scales?). When Chris and I finally met in person later in London, he gave me another couple of bulbs. They grew well for me in quite peaty soil in my shade garden and increased wonderfully, making good clumps that I divided every third year. I had built up a stock of several dozen plants when they all suddenly disappeared. I never found out what happened. Was it some natural factor, perhaps an overly harsh winter or some disease? Or had some rodents simply found them particularly scrumptious? I haven't yet tried growing them again. Oh, but I will!

Fritillaries from Siberia and China

Before I start with the easternmost fritillaries I must return momentarily to Central Asia, where two very beautiful frits originate. These bulbs come from the very eastern corner, where Kazakhstan meets China and where the mountains of southern Altay enter Kazakhstan, so they are really more connected to the plants of western Siberia than they are to those of Central Asia.

Arnis Seisums found two exceptionally beautiful forms of *Fritillaria verticillata* in this region. Both have very different flower shapes and grow perfectly in my garden in Latvia. The first form comes from the Kara-Sumbe Valley and has white, greenish-veined, somewhat stumpy blooms on a 50–60 cm stem (Plate 231). The flowers have beautiful green shoulders at the base of the petals, open much more widely than those of the second form, and are smaller. The second form comes from Urdzhar in the northern Tarbagatai Mountains in the same part of southern Kazakhstan and has much larger, longer, more closed, straightly bell-shaped flowers on a stem of the same height (Plate 232). Both forms are so different that it is difficult to accept that they represent the same species. They are easy to grow, generally don't suffer from summer rains, and flower abundantly every season. They don't increase vegetatively but are easily propagated by breaking the bulbs into two parts, and they usually set seed and germinate well. Like the more western *F. olgae* (which looks quite similar in everything but color) both forms of *F. verticillata* start rooting early, although not quite as early as *F. olgae*. It is important to remember this when replanting either of these forms so as not to miss the right time. In my experience these bulbs do not do well in polyethylene bags after harvesting. They fare much better when left free in open boxes or covered with white sand. Both belong to the drier side of moisture-resistant fritillaries.

Both of these forms, 'Kara-Sumbe' and 'Urdzhar', are very different from the plants offered under the name *Fritillaria verticillata* by Dutch nurseries, which are very lazy about flowering in my region and have much smaller blooms. Dutch *F. verticillata* more closely resembles another Chinese species, *F. thunbergii*, which grows around Shanghai on the opposite side of China, although the clone of *F. thunbergii* I received from China is much more floriferous than the one grown in Europe and usually blooms every year.

There has been much confusion about the naming of Chinese fritillaries, and this hasn't been helped by the often perplexing accounts found in various reference books. In addition to this, fritillaries imported from China are often very difficult to identify. Plants labeled with many different names may actually come from the same box and turn out to be identical in flower. Every conceivable synonym will have been used to increase the number of species for sale, so that the same species sometimes appears under five different names. Missouri Botanical Garden's English translation of the twenty-fourth volume of the *Flora of China* (Zhengyi and Raven 2000), which describes all the principal bulbous monocots, has been very helpful in clarifying these names. But a lot of things are still unclear, and finding the correct name isn't easy.

The famous British nurserywoman Kath Dryden wrote to me a few years ago: "Your *Fritillaria verticillata* 'Kara-Sumbe' looks exactly like *F. yuminensis* that we have from China under dozens of different names, but 'Urdzhar' looks like *F. tortifolia* [another Chinese species]." Both my stocks of *F. verticillata* were collected by Arnis in Central Asia (in the former Soviet Union) right beside the distribution areas for *F. tortifolia* and *F. yuminensis*. In fact the only difference between these species is flower color. *Fritillaria tortifolia* from China is identical to *F. verticillata* 'Urdzhar' in everything but its distinctly pinkish- or even purplish-dotted petals, which give the whole flower a slightly pinkish appearance. Chinese *F. yuminensis* is identical to *F. verticillata* 'Kara-Sumbe' except for its light pinkish flowers. Both my stocks of *F. verticillata* are pure white with a greenish shade. I didn't notice the differences in stigma or foliage that according to the *Flora of China* are used to separate these species.

I submit that the distribution area of *Fritillaria verticillata* is much larger than is supposed and that it is a very variable species, but for now I will follow the classification provided by the local floras. In all likelihood both forms of *F. verticillata* must be classified as different species or as subspecies, including under that name both *F. tortifolia* and *F. yuminensis*. In any case the name *F. verticillata* has priority according to the *Code*. As for deciding which flower form is really *F. verticillata*, I'll leave that to the botanists.

Two other fritillaries grow in the same area, both distributed in southern Kazakhstan and China. The first, *Fritillaria walujewii* (Plate 233), is very rare in gardens. China is the easternmost point of its distribution, but in the west it reaches as far as Tajikistan and Uzbekistan. It has as many as three distinctly pinkish brown flowers, with slightly greenish tessellation, on a 50 cm stem. The petals are wide and have very rounded tips. This species is not very difficult in the garden. Based on the conditions it requires, it is more similar to *F. verticillata* than *F. olgae* and likewise starts rooting early. Like both other species it must be propagated from seed or by breaking the bulb into halves. My stock was originally collected in Uzbekistan at Schachi-Mahlan by Mart Veerus and Arnis.

The second fritillary, *Fritillaria pallidiflora*, is a very well known species and seems to be the most widely grown in gardens. It is quite uniform in color, with large, green-ish or yellowish, more darkly veined blooms that are sometimes slightly purplish at the bottom of the petals. The best form, which now also seems to be the most distrib-uted form, originated from the Tallinn Botanical Garden where it was raised from seed collected in southeastern Kazakhstan somewhere near the border with China. It is far more vigorous than the paler clone grown earlier in Europe. Through the nurs-ery of Michael Hoog it soon overtook its competitor in European nurseries. I grew it from the seeds received from Tallinn and it has grown perfectly for me, having only one rare problem: rodents. In the beginning I propagated it from seed, but in more recent years I found that this species reproduces vegetatively as well. The large bulbs split in two and produce smaller offsets. The most commonly grown form reaches up to 50 cm tall with five to seven large, bell-shaped blooms. Plants from China have slightly more spectacular, more yellow-toned flowers but don't seem as vigorous as the Kazakhstan stock.

Fritillaria pallidiflora 'Flore Plena' (Plate 234) is a selection with double flowers that was introduced from the Czech Republic. It is quite difficult to judge its beauty—is it especially lovely or just a curiosity? I would compare it with *Helleborus* flowers, which face downward in the same way; their beautiful design and color can only be observed by cutting them off and placing them face up in a shallow dish. The high price of 'Flore Plena' is based on the extreme rarity of the plant—there are still only a hundred or so bulbs altogether. I break my bulbs in half each year to build up my stock, and this just covers the requests I receive for this curiosity.

Turning east again, in the heart of Altay we find the very unusual, tiny *Fritillaria dagana* (Plate 235). It grows on both sides of Lake Baikal, with its main area just to the south of it. A few populations also grow on both the western and eastern ends of the Sajan Mountains as far as the Yenisey River in the west and the upper course of the Amur River in the east. It mostly grows on high alpine meadows and in thin forests where they start to change into meadows. *Fritillaria dagana* makes only a single whorl of four to seven leaves and one large leafy bract at the base of the pedicel, with a single yellowish or greenish brown, more or less tessellated, nodding flower at the top of a stem up to 25 cm tall. Its small bulb is formed of several scales, but the most interest-ing feature is the long, thin, scaly stolon, which reaches some 10–15 cm in length, at the end of which another bulb is formed. This plant has to be harvested very carefully to avoid breaking the stolon. Otherwise it isn't a difficult species, just so long as it is not allowed to dry out.

Starting with *Fritillaria dagana*, all other Siberian and Chinese frits are best kept in peat moss after harvesting and in thin polyethylene bags that must be carefully checked from time to time for signs of mold. If mold appears, immediately transfer the bulbs to drier peat and repack them in a new bag. The sooner they are replanted the better.

The next species to the east is *Fritillaria maximowiczii* (Plate 236). It first appears in the Chita region somewhat east of Lake Baikal at the upper course of the Amur

River, then reappears near the Amur but at the very eastern end in the Primorsky and Khabarovsk regions, entering China as far as Beijing (although the plants I have received from China under the name *F. maximowiczii* have usually been *F. ussuriensis*). Arnis and Mart encountered the true species at the very top of the second bik of the Gorin River, where they were searching for *Corydalis gorinensis*. It is a medium-tall plant, reaching some 50 cm in height, with only one or rarely two whorls of leaves and one or two smaller leaves higher on the stem below the flower. The flower is nodding, campanulate, purplish brown with a greenish yellow midrib, and tessellated. The petals are papillose at the margin, giving the impression that they are edged with diminutive teeth. This feature makes the species easy to distinguish from other species growing in the Russian Far East. The bulb is multi-scaled and is so similar to that of *Lilium maximowiczii* that both species were collected together. I grew them both mixed together for a few years before they started blooming. Those without flowers looked absolutely identical in terms of their leaves and bulbs. Very careful checking of the bulb scales, however, shows that those of *L. maximowiczii* are more elongated and slightly waisted at the middle, while those of *Fritillaria* are of the same size but slightly rounder in appearance and without a waist. It is possible to separate the stocks by their bulbs, but this requires good eyesight and patience.

Fritillaria ussuriensis (Plate 237) is found further to the east. It grows in moist forests, thickets, and meadows from sea level to some 500 m and in Russia can be found at the very southeastern corner around Vladivostok. Its main distribution area is in northeastern China and North Korea. According to observations made by Mart and Arnis, it is a very widespread and common plant. It is tall, reaching up to 70–90 cm in height, but its stem is very thin. In the wild it relies on the support of neighbor plants to which it attaches itself using the tendrils on its leaf tips. This can sometimes be a problem in the garden, and if only a few plants are grown in an open place, strong winds can break the stems. The flowers are deep purple, with more or less yellow-green tessellation, and distinctly campanulate, with somewhat flared petals. *Fritillaria ussuriensis* forms many grains at the basal plate that can be used for propagation. In China it is widely used in folk medicine. Unfortunately, mice seem to like it, too: by the end of one winter only a few grains were left of the more than two hundred bulbs I planted in my garden. My stock is still slowly recovering.

One of the most widely distributed fritillaries from the Far East is *Fritillaria camschatcensis* (Plate 238), which grows on both sides of the Pacific, from Japan up to Magadan and further north, and in Alaska, northwestern Canada, and more southern parts of the United States. It is like a stranger among other frits, having at times been joined with lilies or even placed in its own genus, *Sarana*. In reference to the dark color of its flowers, *F. camschatcensis* is often called black sarana or black lily. The native people who use the bulbs as food call it sarana. In taste they resemble chestnuts and are used boiled. The bulbs are like grains of rice and often form thick, scaly stolons up to 5–10 cm long. In the wild this species grows on wet meadows and in forests on sandy soils. It does very well in the garden, too, although it is liked by mice. Having such a wide distribution area, it is not surprising that it is quite variable. The forms from Japan have a reputation as weak growers in the garden. I have never had the opportunity to grow any forms from the American side of the Pacific, although this is one of my dreams for the future.

I have many forms of *Fritillaria camschatcensis* that were collected in Russia and others that I received from Czech gardeners. They vary slightly by height and flower color, but most of them have up to eight more or less blackish maroon or dark purple-brown, slightly pendant, large, widely bell-shaped blooms on a 10–70 cm stem. In the garden they all need similar conditions. They should be kept in a bulb shed covered by peat moss in a plastic bag, and replanting should take place as quickly as possible. They can be grown in either half shade or full sun.

I received my first bulbs of this species from Sakhalin Island, where they were collected on a boggy meadow not far from the city of Tomari. It is the tallest form in my collection, 60–70 cm in height, with almost black blooms. It forms large bulbs but they consist of very small grains and are quite brittle, so this can't be listed among the best commercial forms. Another form was collected in the Primorsky region near the village of Ilyichevka and named 'Amur'. It is somewhat shorter and more late-flowering. It doesn't usually exceed 40–50 cm tall but has the same number of flowers on the stem: up to eight. Its bulbs are formed from much larger grains, which are firmly fixed at the base, making them easier to harvest and ship. Near Magadan, Arnis and Mart collected a very dwarf form of this fairly variable species with stems barely exceeding 10 cm tall and with two or three brownish black blooms.

In 1995 Potterton and Martin in Britain offered a "green-flowering" form of *Fritillaria camschatcensis*. Being very interested in this fritillary, I bought a few bulbs of what turned out to be a very dwarf form of the species, as well as a weaker grower. They arrived in terrible shape, broken and overdried, but I planted them nonetheless. The first spring nothing came up, so I crossed this form off my list, but the following year a few tiny leaves appeared. The first flowering took place in 2001. This form grows to some 15 cm tall with up to five blooms on the stem, but only the midrib of the brownish black petals is green. The bulbs are small-grained and very brittle.

From Czech growers I introduced *Fritillaria camschatcensis* 'Lutea' (Plate 239), a rare yellow-flowering form. The origin of this plant is unknown, but such frits are mentioned in Russian literature as very rarely occurring in nature. It has up to eight blooms on a stem some 50 cm tall. The flowers are greenish yellow with small purple-brown stripes and dots inside the petals. From Belgium I received 'Flore Plena', a deep blackish brown form with double flowers. It was grown in Hendrik van Bogaert's collection. It turned out to be the most floriferous form, producing up to nine flowers on a stem. Unlike the double form of *F. pallidiflora*, the blooms of *F. camschatcensis* are obliquely upturned and therefore easy to see without handling.

China is home to *Fritillaria davidii* (Plate 240), a very unusual species whose bulb somewhat resembles the miniature bulb of *F. camschatcensis*. It has only recently been introduced in gardens and is grown with amazing skill by Bob and Rannveig Wallis in Wales, the only place where I have seen it in full flower. In the wild it grows in the monsoon areas of western Sichuan where it is distributed on loose, peaty soils beneath *Betula alnoides*, on moist meadows, and in rocky places along streams. It is a very unique species, forming a mat-like cluster of partly cross-veined leaves that appear very early in autumn. Solitary leaves come out of the soil some distance from where the bulb was planted. This plant seems to need very little, if any, dry rest. I received my first few bulbs from the Chen Yi nursery in China. At that time I knew nothing about *F. davidii* and was very surprised by the leaves emerging in late autumn. I'm not sure why, but I dug them out when the leaves died and then kept the bulbs dry. They all died. When I later received a few bulbs from the Wallis's, I planted them in forest soil with plenty of humus, and now I grow them in a pot, which I take out of the greenhouse when night frosts are no longer a problem. They grow alongside a seedling of *Anemone nemorosa* that entered the pot together with the soil. All summer long these plants join pots of *Crocus pelistericus* and *C. scardicus* in a slightly shaded place in my nursery, where they are regularly watered. Although winter temperatures in my greenhouse sometimes drop below –12°C or even –15°C, the leaves of *F. davidii* have never been damaged. It grows very well in its pot, the surface of which is now covered in leaves. During a recent spring I was rewarded for my patience with its large, bell-shaped, yellow-brown speckled blooms. The petals are yellow-tipped, and as in *F. maximowiczii* the petal edge is minutely toothed or papillose.

According to the *Flora of China*, twenty-four species of *Fritillaria* are native to China. One of the names listed in the flora, *F. meleagroides* (Plate 241), is very well known to me. I grew it for many years and could never have imagined how widely distributed it is, growing from European Russia and the Ukraine to western Siberia and northwestern China.

I include this species here and not in the discussion of Europe, where my stocks of *Fritillaria meleagroides* originated, to illustrate this link between Europe and Asia. I received my first bulbs from the Penza region as *F. ruthenica*, and I grew *F. meleagroides* for many years under this name before accidentally noting that its seed capsules were without the wings so characteristic of *F. ruthenica*. The Penza form is so vigorous and so much larger than the other forms I have grown that I named it 'Giant'. It seems to be polyploid, although it is absolutely fertile. My eyes were only opened when I received from Gothenburg a sample collected near Novokhopersk somewhat west of Penza. It was very similar to 'Giant' in terms of flower size but had stems only half as long and with one or two blooms. I finally recognized that this giant was *F. meleagroides*, despite contradictions with the original description.

The plants of *Fritillaria meleagroides* that I received from the Ukraine also arrived under the name *F. ruthenica* (Plate 242). Regardless of their thinner structure, they are good growers. The stock collected near the village of Krugloye Ozero showed great variability. I selected the plants with pale greenish yellow and white blooms. These are smaller than in other samples and are carried on a 40–45 cm stem. They are usually placed singly on top of the stem, as is more characteristic of this species.

Despite the confusion over the names, these plants are easy to distinguish from *Fritillaria ruthenica* (Plate 243), which has distinctly winged capsules and a whorl of tendrils at the top of the stem. There are usually two to three flowers in *F. ruthenica*, but I have seen plants with as many as seven blooms. The stem is 40–50 cm tall and the blooms are campanulate, slightly flared at the mouth, and dark brown, with some lighter tessellation. In the wild *F. meleagroides* and *F. ruthenica* often grow in similar conditions among shrubs and on meadows and are quite tolerant of somewhat drier conditions. However, *F. meleagroides* sometimes grows knee-deep in water on wet meadows, while *F. ruthenica* tends to prefer drier spots in pine forests. I can't recommend keeping the bulbs in plastic bags, where they can easily fall victim to mold. It is best to replant them as soon as possible.

Many years ago when the borders between Russia and Latvia were closed, some twenty or thirty bulbs of *Fritillaria meleagroides* and tubers of *Corydalis solida* were sent from Penza to a friend of mine in Moscow. They waited there for a month or two before there was an occasion to forward them on to me via some visitor to Latvia. I couldn't imagine that a gardener in Moscow would keep these bulbs in a hot room beside a furnace. When they arrived they were absolutely dry and dead-looking. I put them all in water for twenty-four hours before planting them. To my great surprise, almost all the bulbs of *F. meleagroides* came up the next spring. (Less surprisingly, only some 10% of the bulbs of *Corydalis solida* survived.)

"Strangers" from the Far East

When I think of the Far East the first countries that come to mind are India, China, and Japan, all known for the uniqueness of their cultures, arts, and religions. Even the plants there are special. I wrote earlier about *Fritillaria davidii*, but it isn't the only "stranger" from this part of the world. World War II resulted in certain border revisions, and some of the territories of Japan became part of Russia, as did the plants growing there.

I will begin with *Cardiocrinum*, which is so closely related to lilies that some botanists lump it together with the genus *Lilium*. *Cardiocrinum giganteum* grows wild in China, Nepal, and India. It can reach a height of 3 m, with many gigantic, trumpet-like, white flowers on the stem. Unfortunately it isn't hardy enough to grow in my region. Even at Gothenburg, where it is grown outside during winter, it is covered with half a meter of straw to protect it from the frost. On Sakhalin Island it is replaced by a much hardier species, *C. glehnii*, sometimes regarded as *C. cordatum* var. *glehnii*. This is a smaller plant, rarely reaching a meter in height. It has up to ten large white flowers on a stem coming from a rosette of wide, roundish basal leaves and smaller, lanceolate stem leaves.

The greatest problem with cardiocrinums is that they are monocarpic, flowering only once during their life and then dying. It is not easy to grow them from seed, either, because they have delayed germination—after the first winter they form a small underground bulb, and only after the second cold period do the first leaves appear. In the wild cardiocrinums grow on wet, peaty soils in grass and among shrubs, and during winter they get covered by such a thick layer of snow that the soil rarely freezes. They set seed perfectly, but in the conditions of my region the young seedlings usually die during the second cold period. Fortunately, daughter bulbs are sometimes formed at the sides of the dying bulb after flowering has finished. The formation of such daughter bulbs can be greatly stimulated if the stem is cut off just after flowering, thus preventing seeds from being set. This ensures that all the energy is directed toward the daughter bulbs, which eventually grow large and can flower again after two or three years. So if you have a small group of these plants, they will flower every year, but you mustn't forget to cut off the stems immediately after the last flower starts to wilt. The earlier you do this the larger the replacement bulbs will get. In a nursery, where flowers are less important, it may be best to cut the stem just before the first flower opens.

When cardiocrinums grow in the wild the necks of the bulbs reach the soil surface, but in my nursery I planted them somewhat deeper. During winter I covered them with dry leaves, then with dry peat moss, and tried to remove this covering as early as possible in spring. I had no problems with them until one winter in which an army of rodents visited my shade garden. This happened after Latvia had separated from Russia, so I no longer had sources for rebuilding my stock. I recently received some specially treated seeds from Kristl Walek of the Canadian seedhouse Gardens North. They germinated perfectly in the first spring, and I am hopeful that by paying attention to overwintering and keeping my box of seedlings in a cold but frost-free cellar, I can restore my stock of these beautiful plants. They are well worth the effort.

I don't grow orchids in my collection on principle. I have a few plants that were sent to me as presents from friends, without any request on my part, but I can't boast of any great success in growing them. They simply need too much attention and I am too short on time. *Cremastra variabilis* has been the one exception to this rule. This terrestrial orchid from Sakhalin produces a thick, leathery leaf at soil level and a spike some 40 cm long of bright purplish blooms. It was sent for me to experiment with in my shade garden, and it actually grew very well there until the same winter in which I lost all my cardiocrinums. This orchid reproduces well vegetatively but forms its leaves in autumn, so great care must be taken to save them from frost. When there were frosts in my garden, I usually covered the bed where this orchid was planted with an upturned wooden box, then covered this with a layer of dry oak leaves. The most difficult thing is knowing how to correctly uncover it. This must be done on a cloudy day when no night frosts are expected so that the leaves can adjust to the drier conditions and light. Otherwise it is an easy plant.

The Far East is the only area where wood lilies (*Trillium*) can be found in the territory of the former Soviet Union. In Russia, two species are generally recognized. The most spectacular is *T. camschatcense* (Plate 244), which is described as coming from

Kamchatka, the southern end of which is the northernmost point where this species grows. In the wild it is distributed from the Kuril Islands and Sakhalin Island to the northern part of Japan, and on continental Asia from China to North Korea along the coast of the Sea of Japan. I have two stocks, one from Sakhalin and one from China, though the stock from China hasn't flowered yet. It is an easy species for the garden with large, upturned, pure white blooms. It sets seed well and also reproduces vegetatively, although not very quickly. In the wild it grows in boggy places, so it needs acid soil. I encountered some problems when I replanted my stocks in alkaline spots—the plants immediately developed chlorosis and only slowly recovered from it. It is possible to increase the rate of vegetative reproduction using a method described in *Trilliums* (Case and Case 1997), but I have never tried to do so myself. The most outstanding clump of *T. camschatcense* I ever grew was situated in my father's garden. After growing there for some ten years in peaty, sandy soil without any special attention, it formed a clump of twelve flowering stems with very large, pure white blooms and a dark purple eye between the petals.

The other species from the same district is the much more widely distributed *Trillium tschonoskii*, growing wild from southern Sakhalin and the Primorsky region in Russia through China up to the Himalaya. During the Baltic Expedition, Arnis Seisums and Mart Veerus found it only in the most shaded places under trees on very peaty soil. It has smaller blooms than *T. camschatcense*. I received it only recently from the Chen Yi nursery in China.

The best-growing trillium in my collection is *Trillium kurabayashii* (Plate 245), which is distributed on the West Coast of the United States in Oregon and California. I received the original plants from the University of Latvia botanical garden in Riga, where they were grown for years as *T. sessile*, the name usually misapplied for this species in Europe, without any knowledge of their origin. It is the best vegetative increaser, and its additional buds on the rootstock start development without any artificial interference. Usually two or three of them start to grow every year, but sometimes there are even more, so frequent replanting is suggested. In my own garden I cut off the new shoots, treat the wound with charcoal powder, and immediately replant them. Requests for this beauty have been so high that I have at times been left with nothing but a few mother plants, and at such times it has taken some years to build up my stock again. This species also sets seed perfectly and the seeds germinate well. In my region it never suffers from night frosts and belongs to the most beautiful plants in the shade garden. It is less moody than *T. camschatcense* when it comes to soil pH and doesn't suffer from chlorosis in the same way.

In recent years I have introduced the white-flowering *Trillium albidum*, which comes from the same part of the United States where *T. kurabayashii* grows in the wild. It appears to be a good grower but not such a quick increaser. Its leaves are more spectacular than those of *T. camschatcense*, mottled with darker spots, but *T. camschatcense* wins in terms of overall appearance—at least in my garden, where it is always a larger and more magnificent plant. The tiny and very beautiful *T. rivale* (also from the

West Coast of the United States) has grown in my garden for just a few years since I received a pot of it from Joy Bishop in Britain. I grow it on an outside bed and it has flowered nicely every season, although I haven't gotten any seeds. It reportedly forms heavy clumps in cultivation, and I hope this is true for my collection.

I have very few plants from other species of *Trillium* and can't draw any conclusions about their suitability for Latvian conditions. They grew up, then for some reason disappeared almost to nothing, and finally started slow recovering. I only once saw the beautiful *T. grandiflorum* 'Flore Plena' flowering in my garden. I still grow it, but it has never again flowered, and of my original three plants only two remain.

Now I come to aroids, those real strangers of the plant world. These are among my favorite plants. I can't boast of great success with them, but in some cases my results haven't been too bad. I will begin with plants from two genera that share a common name: skunk cabbage.

The first skunk cabbage is *Symplocarpus foetidus* (Plate 246), whose name translates from Latin to "fetid single fruiter." For many years I couldn't understand why this plant was called "fetid"—it didn't have the terrible smell so characteristic of some aroids at flowering time. When I wanted to replant some very large and well-established plants, I finally understood that the epithet applied to the rootstocks, which excrete the smell of garlic when wounded. I later noted that the blooms have the same aroma. The smell of garlic may seem fetid to some people, but it doesn't strike me that way. (More recently, however, I read that the American kin of this species does indeed have a very foul smell.) In nature it grows on wet meadows, riverbanks, and bogs, sometimes even directly in water, but it develops best in sparse, shrubby woods of *Alnus japonica* where its leaves can reach even 1 m in length, forming gigantic rosettes. It has never reached such proportions for me in Latvia, but leaves 0.5 m in length are typical here. Author Deni Bown (2000) describes *S. foetidus* as coming from eastern North America, where it grows around the Great Lakes, adding that it is replaced by *S. renifolius* in Siberia and Korea and by *S. nipponicus* in northern Japan. My plants were collected on Sakhalin Island, but they do not have the kidney-shaped leaves described for *S. renifolius*, nor do their fruits ripen only in the following spring, as should be the case with *S. nipponicus*. In fact when compared with the description of the American plants, those from Sakhalin look identical. What's more, Russian botanical literature describes *Symplocarpus* as a monotypic genus. I have never had an opportunity to try plants from America, Japan, or Korea, so I'm keeping the name *S. foetidus* for my plants from Sakhalin.

I have grown *Symplocarpus foetidus* in very different conditions. For many years it grew perfectly in grass in a shaded spot in my father's garden; it was lost there only after the leaves were cut off with a lawnmower when I moved out of the house. In my new garden I constructed a special artificial bog for it. I dug a hole about half a meter deep, added a layer of thick plastic film, filled the hole with equal parts peat moss and forest peat, and finally planted my treasures there, always making sure there was some water for them at the bottom. After three or four years I decided to move my skunk cabbages to a new spot. By the time I had dug out half of them, two spades had been broken by the strong, wiry roots. I left the second half to grow where they were, although the plastic film didn't help much with moisture retention. In both spots, old and new, the plants continued growing with the same capacity, making beautiful deep purple spathes at soil level soon after the snow melted and before the leaves appeared. Some rootstocks even formed several flowers. The leaf development of this species starts at the end of flowering, and the leaves are very large, somewhat lanceolate, and light green. I assume *S. foetidus* is so rarely offered just because of the size of the rootstock and the heavy-duty roots.

Symplocarpus foetidus sets seed perfectly in Latvia. The best way to get it to germinate is to collect the seeds just when the fruits start to break apart and then keep them in water until they're ready to be sown. I found this out accidentally. I once collected the seeds in a plastic box and then forgot it on the field. During the rains that followed, the box became filled with water, and since it was a rainy autumn the seeds never dried out. When I found the box I thought the seeds had been drowned, but I sowed them anyway. To my amazement these seeds germinated better than ever. In the years that followed I went back to my normal routine and found that almost no seeds germinated. Then I remembered my "mistake" and decided to repeat it. The results surpassed all my hopes. The flesh of *S. foetidus* fruits is reportedly sweet and aromatic, and the rootstocks can be used as food after boiling, but since some authors list this species among poisonous plants I would not suggest sampling it in the kitchen.

There are two more skunk cabbages belonging to a different genus, *Lysichiton*, and growing on both sides of the Pacific. *Lysichiton americanum* grows on the West Coast of the United States from Alaska to California. It is a larger plant with yellow flowers and leaves that can apparently reach up to 2 m long. It seems to like wetter places more than its white-flowering relative from the other side of the ocean, *L. camtschatcensis*.

I have never succeeded with *Lysichiton americanum*. I saw marvelously flowering specimens in Gothenburg where they grow just near water under large trees at the bottom of a rockery. I also saw plants growing up out of pools in the garden of the Průhonice Castle near Prague. I tried growing this species myself several times but always lost it in the first winter. I'm not sure why this was—perhaps our winters were too harsh or my peat bed was too dry. I may try growing it again if I find it at a reasonable price.

The smaller, white-flowering *Lysichiton camtschatcensis* is another story. I introduced it from Sakhalin, where it grows well in bogs, though not directly in the water, and less well in moist meadows. In my region it flowers almost every spring, but it isn't as vigorous as *Symplocarpus foetidus* and in recent years I haven't gotten any seeds from it. Where both *Lysichiton* species grow together, a beautiful cream-colored hybrid sometimes appears that is intermediate in size and color. I saw such plants in the Gothenburg Botanical Garden but never succeeded in growing them myself.

My wife, Guna, often asks me why we spend so much time pursuing foreign plants when so much of our native flora is just as beautiful. When it comes to arums she may be right, because a nice white-flowering species, *Calla palustris*, grows in the marshlands and boggy lakesides of Latvia. When planted alongside water this arum will bloom year after year without any problems, delighting you each summer with its beautiful, large, white spathes.

Cobra Lilies for Northern Gardens

Arisaemas, or cobra lilies, have become very popular in recent years. Guy and Liliane Gusman have written a superbly researched monograph, *The Genus Arisaema*, and it looks as though nothing more can be added, so I will write only about the species I have grown myself. Latvian conditions are really only favorable for a few species, unless you don't mind digging out your tubers every autumn and keeping them until spring in a room that is frost-free but not too warm, since too much warmth can cause the tubers to awaken prematurely.

From a practical gardening standpoint, I would like to divide *Arisaema* into some basic groups. Firstly I would separate those that come up and flower early in spring (including all species from the Russian Far East) from those that flower only in summer, in my region mostly at the end of June. Secondly I would divide those with inflorescences that are well hidden under the leaves from those with flowers that are held over the leaves or somewhere at the leaf level. The latter are more spectacular for observers, while the former receive more attention for their attractive summer foliage and autumn fruits.

My first *Arisaema* was *A. japonica*, now considered a synonym of *A. serratum*. My plants came from Kunashir Island, the southernmost island in the Kuril chain and one of the islands claimed by Japan. This species belongs to the early-emerging group, and its inflorescence is held well over the leaves. The flower spathe is nicely striped green-white or brownish white and held on a stalk some 70–80 cm tall. Unfortunately it is not very hardy in my garden, although it grows well in both Lithuania and Estonia. I had no problems with it on sandy soil; planted some 20–25 cm deep, it performed very well and flowered every spring. I'm afraid that in my new garden, however, the soil is a bit too heavy. I tried planting it at the top of the most sandy (though still quite clayey) hill in my property at the edge of a forest of pines and birches, but it suffered from excessive moisture during our harsh winters.

Arisaema robustum, now considered a synonym of *A. amurense*, and the highly variable *A. amurense* both represent the opposite group, having inflorescences that are hidden under the leaves, although both are quite distinct from a gardener's standpoint. They grow on southern Sakhalin Island and continental Russia near Vladivostok. Up until our last black frost I listed them among my hardiest, most unproblematic bulbs. But a full month of temperatures as low as −18°C without any snow proved too hard for them and none survived. Curiously, some of my more tender plants survived, so for me that particular winter will always represent a great mystery of plant hardiness. Fortunately, my friends in Lithuania had a lot of tubers, so it wasn't difficult to rebuild my stocks.

My stock of *Arisaema amurense* (Plate 247), which I have named subspecies *amurense*, was collected near Vladivostok. It is an easy-growing, shade-loving, beautiful *Arisaema* with a green, white-striped spathe in spring and bright red berries in autumn. The foliage can reach up to 35 cm high, with leaf lobes up to 10 cm long. A very beautiful form named 'Waves of the Amur' was selected by Leonid Bondarenko from Lithuania. The leaves are five-lobed, the edges of the leaflets intensely wavy. The flower spathe is elongated and similarly white-striped.

From southern Sakhalin comes the arisaema that I now list as *Arisaema amurense* subsp. *robustum* (Plate 248). It is much more robust than subspecies *amurense*, with leaves up to 55 cm long and leaf lobes up to 20 cm long. The spathe of most plants is, again, green and white-striped. A smaller form named 'Sakhalin' grows to no more than 30 cm tall and has more rounded, five-lobed leaves and a spathe that is intensely purple inside and white-striped outside. Its leaf lobes are somewhat oval. I list it under subspecies *robustum* only because of its origin on Sakhalin, where only this subspecies is noted in the Russian botanical literature I have seen. 'Ussuri', named for the taiga where it was collected, comes from the very south of the Primorsky region, where only subspecies *amurense* is listed. This particularly robust form grows to 60 cm tall and has seven-lobed leaves. The leaf lobes are rhomboid and the spathe is green with white stripes. Just the presence of the dwarf 'Sakhalin' among subspecies *robustum* and the gigantic 'Ussuri' among subspecies *amurense* confirms that this division is quite doubtful. But again, from a gardener's point of view this would seem acceptable if the name *amurense* was applied to smaller plants and *robustum* to larger ones.

Subspecies *amurense* and subspecies *robustum* are both quite tolerant of sun, but because they begin growing so early, when hard night frosts occur, it is important to plant them where the morning sun can't reach their frozen leaves. There are a few mornings almost every spring in which the leaves of these early-emerging arisaemas look like they have been boiled. When planted in shade where the temperature rises slowly and direct sun only reaches the foliage in the afternoon, they usually recover perfectly (this didn't happen for my plants in the spring of 2004, however, after a particularly severe frost). I once planted these arisaemas on an open field and the first sunbeams killed their frozen leaves. Both subspecies form plenty of small tuber buds on the surface of the old tuber, and the new tubers reach flowering size in two or three years, but they also set seed well. I plant them at a depth of 15–20 cm so as to delay their emergence in spring. They can also be dug out in autumn and kept in a frost-free room, because they start forming their roots only in spring.

Another group to which many beautiful species belong starts into growth very late in the season. When I first tried growing *Arisaema candidissimum* and *A. flavum* I thought they had died when nothing had come out of the soil by the last week of June. When I dug out some tubers I saw that they were healthy but without roots. After this I learned that they needed to be left without any attention and would emerge just fine when the appropriate time came. In the very cold summer of 2004 the first shoots appeared only in the middle of July.

Looking back, I have only had long-term success with a few species of this group of arisaemas. *Arisaema flavum* (Plate 249) has the longest history in my garden, having originated from seeds I received through a seed exchange when I still worked for the botanical garden. On the label I wrote "China," but I don't remember whether this was meant to indicate that the seeds had been collected in China or just that China was the homeland of the species. In truth my plants belong to subspecies *abbreviatum*, which doesn't grow in China, but the origin may be less important than the vigor with which this stock grows. Some years ago Antoine Hoog wrote me about this, saying, "Your stock is excellent, twice as vigorous as that grown in Holland!" These plants reach a height of 40 cm, with a deep yellow, slightly purple-striped flower spathe just over the foliage and attractive orange-red fruits in autumn. They are absolutely hardy in my region, can grow in full sun, and are able to withstand long periods of dry weather without being watered. *Arisaema flavum* increases well vegetatively and is an excellent seed producer, even self-sowing. I grow it in my woodland garden where the sun reaches it for only a few hours in the afternoon. The only problem is occasional loss to bacterial rot, the greatest enemy of all arisaemas. For this reason I regularly collect the seeds despite this plant's ability to increase vegetatively.

Arisaema ciliatum is an even more spectacular plant for its magnificent height, large spathe that is striped purplish brown and white, and long appendix. It was first offered by Michael Hoog and initially appeared in the trade under the name *A. consanguineum* (collection number *CT-369*). It was later found that this stock actually belongs to subspecies *liubaense*. It is among the most vigorous arisaemas for the garden. In my opinion its greatest fault is its stoloniferous habit because it sends its daughter tubers quite far from the spot where the mother plant is located. Though good for the ornamental garden, it is quite trying in nursery beds, sometimes encroaching upon plants of other species and thus making it difficult to keep stocks from mixing. I grow it in its own bed at a distance from other arisaemas and destroy any escapees that appear on the path. As with *A. flavum* its only trouble is with bacterial rot.

Bacterial rot is especially fond of aroids, and *Arisaema* is no exception. It can reach bulbs as they sit in the soil, rest in a bulb shed, or even overwinter in a frost-free room. The best way to escape this problem is to replant your stocks on fresh, well-drained soil that is more sandy than peaty. One of the reasons why I moved my entire shade garden was to evade the bacterial rot affecting my arisaemas (though I was also hoping to prevent attacks by water rats). I cleared the small trees and shrubs from the top of the sandiest hill on my property, leaving on one side a mixture of mature birch and pine trees and on the other side a stand of young oaks (at the time they were some 3 m tall, but by ten years later they had reached 7 m tall). This had been farming land until the late 1950s. My plants adapted well to this new place, though they were not protected from massive attacks by water rats the first winter despite the fact that this was the driest spot within some hundred meters of a small marsh. Now it seems that the rats have forgotten about this cache, and the only other pests there have been moles and mice.

I also have some tubers of the true *Arisaema consanguineum*. I like this species even more than *A. ciliatum* because of its very beautiful leaves with their long-tipped leaflets, although my plants are somewhat shorter than *A. ciliatum* and don't reproduce vegetatively. Another species, *A. taiwanense*, survived in my garden even when I left the bulbs in the ground over a few winters. I finally lost it, however, and have lost many other species from my quite large collection. The greatest surprise has been *A. fargesii* (Plate 250), which has survived for more than fifteen years without any problems. I received my first tubers from Jiří Obdržálek in Průhonice, Czech Republic, who warned that they must be planted at a depth of at least 30 cm. I always followed this recommendation and my plants of *A. fargesii* never suffered from frost. Despite only emerging in the first ten days of July, they form outstanding three-lobed leaves with very wide leaflets. Alas, the leaves completely hide the inflorescence, which in this species is at ground level, but this is of no great consequence since the leaves are this species' most beautiful feature. It increases vegetatively, too, but summers in Latvia are too short for producing a seed crop. Since *A. fargesii* has done so well for me, I've always been afraid to touch it—I left it growing as a little island in my old shade garden when I moved everything else to the new location.

I can't say that I've had any great success in growing *Arisaema candidissimum*. I still grow it but always wonder whether it will actually emerge from the soil, having frequently bought and lost tubers of this species. The clump in my first garden had the longest history. It grew there for more than fifteen years on very sandy soil under an old apple tree, greeting me with its beautiful pink and white-striped spathes every summer, but I never had any long-term success with it in my new garden. It's possible the soil is too heavy for it here, although a few plants still manage to come up every spring. Not long ago I invested quite a lot of money in arisaemas from the Chen Yi nursery. The tubers I received looked healthy and surprisingly large. I hope to find the white form of *A. candidissimum* among them (in any case the name *A. candidissimum* was written on the bag, although I could tell just by glancing at the tubers that a few were incorrectly named). As is usual with bulbs from China, they arrived during a hard frost, so I wrapped them individually in sheets of newspaper (a method used by Augis Dambrauskas, who has the largest collection of arisaemas in the Baltic States) and waited until mid-May to plant them outside.

I have lost all the stocks of American and Canadian *Arisaema triphyllum* that were kindly sent to me by Kath Dryden in Britain. They included various color forms of subspecies *triphyllum* and the stoloniferous subspecies *stewardsonii*. Both subspecies are from the northern United States and Canada and should be hardy in Latvia, but perhaps the black frost was too harsh for them or simply lasted too long.

The species of genus *Pinellia*, also known as the little green dragons, are one last group of aroids that I love very much, although many of the visitors to my garden can't see their subtle beauty. Some six species grow in eastern Asia. The best-known species is *P. ternata*, which forms small bulbils at the base of almost every leaf stalk. *Pinellia cordata* has a similar habit. *Pinellia* species are quite easy to distinguish by the shape of their leaves. What they all have in common is a very long, slim, green spathe. I have had no problems so far overwintering them in the garden; only a few plants have been killed by black frost. Augis Dambrauskas harvests them annually in his garden in Lithuania and keeps the tubers in a frost-free room until the arrival of spring. They are easily propagated by seed and in some species by the small bulbils formed at the leaf bases, while others form offsets on the mother tuber. If night frosts kill the foliage before the seeds ripen, the fruits can be collected so that the seeds can ripen in boxes.

◈ 25
Turkey

To me Turkey is the second most important place after Central Asia when it comes to bulbs. I first began to think of it more deeply when Central Asia started to become almost unreachable. Many of my plants had been collected there by other bulb enthusiasts, and in most cases they had proved to be quite good growers in my region. Meanwhile Arnis Seisums needed authentic plant material for his investigation into the taxonomy of Juno irises, so we decided to point ourselves in this direction.

We both had many friends who regularly visited Turkey, so we had a source of information about the conditions there. Despite this abundance of information, however, we prepared for our first trip as we always had for Central Asia. We could not imagine that almost everywhere we would find hotels and even good restaurants, so in addition to packing clothing, maps, an herbarium press, cameras, and paper bags for collecting seeds, we also packed tents, sleeping bags, and food.

When my wife, Guna, and Arnis's wife, Indra, heard about our plans to travel to Turkey, they asked to come along. They knew that Turkey was a popular holiday destination and wanted to see it for themselves. It would be the first time they accompanied us on an expedition.

Turkey greeted us with horrible heat and a long queue for visas at the airport. Much to our surprise, visas were issued right there and cost only ten dollars per person for a full month. What a great difference from Uzbekistan! The roads in Turkey were generally good, most of them asphalted, and we were never forced to stop or change our plans because of the absence of a road marked on our maps. The exchange rate worked in our favor, too, and everything was surprisingly cheap. The most expensive double-bed hotel room was only twenty-four dollars, and one restaurant deep in the mountains served freshly baked salmon trout with vegetables for only a dollar.

The biggest problem we encountered was thieves. Our jeep-style rental car had a canvas roof that closed with a zipper, so every evening we took our bags to our hotel rooms. One night we left our ice picks under the back seat, thinking that such a tool could be of interest to no one. By morning one of them had disappeared, and the other one remained only because it had become stuck under a bench. On a few other occasions we found that the zippers had been opened during the night.

There was another problem. There are two main groups of people in Turkey: Turks and Kurds. Eastern Turkey is mostly inhabited by Kurds, but in accordance with the government's policy of suppressing any attempts to gain autonomy, all the local names had been changed from Kurdish to Turkish. The notes we brought from friends who had traveled in the region used Kurdish names, and these were the names used on our older maps. So it was not always easy to find our way.

For half a century we Latvians had lived under the Russian occupation, so we well understood the attempts made by the Kurdish minority to preserve their national language, traditions, and culture. It was even forbidden to use the Kurdish language in schools. The same situation had existed in Latvia during the Czar's regime in the pre-Communist Russian Empire. A pupil caught speaking Latvian would be forced to hang a sign around his neck that read "I spoke Latvian." It is the Kurds I think of when I stand in support of Turkey entering into the European Union.

This was the first time I had driven along mountain roads. The road we chose was extremely narrow in some places, a strip just wide enough for our car, with a very steep slope on either side, one going downward and the other one upward. I did not see much of the slopes, however, because my eyes were focused only on the road, both to keep our car on top of it and to look for any car driving in our direction. Remembering how I had felt as a passenger during a drive through the Talish Mountains, I could imagine what our ladies and Arnis might be thinking and was not surprised by Guna's reaction. "I will forget all your past, present, and future faults," she said, "and I will forgive you your sins until the end of your life, only bring me back out of these terrible rocks to the seaside, where I will wait for you in a hotel until it is time to fly home. If you are so mad, go where you want, but don't involve me in it."

Fortunately, a day of rest in a city near the spectacular monuments of ancient Greece and the Roman Empire changed her mind, and both Guna and Indra accompanied us until the end of the trip. All the same, no future invitations to trips through the mountains were accepted.

Junos from Turkey

In Turkey I well understood the meaning of "roadside botanizing." Bulbs were everywhere. We even joked that we should drink more water so that we would have to stop more often. The main focus of our first expedition was Juno irises.

Not many Juno iris species are described from Turkey—or, more precisely, not many species are listed in the *Flora of Turkey and the East Aegean Islands* (Davis 1984, Güner et al. 2000); plenty are described, but many of the names used are now considered synonyms. I faced a dilemma while writing this book as I tried to figure out how much to say about the exact localities where we found plants. Turkey is not like Central Asia, where the mountain passes and other remote places where bulbs grow are extremely difficult to reach. Anyone can go to Turkey, rent a car, find some bulbs, and start digging. Our approach was very strict—we collected very few bulbs, only enough for a sample and for Arnis's studies. If the plant turned out to be suitable for cultivation, we would build up the stock from seed. Unfortunately, not everyone follows the same principles, and I well understood Norman Stevens, a very keen bulb grower from

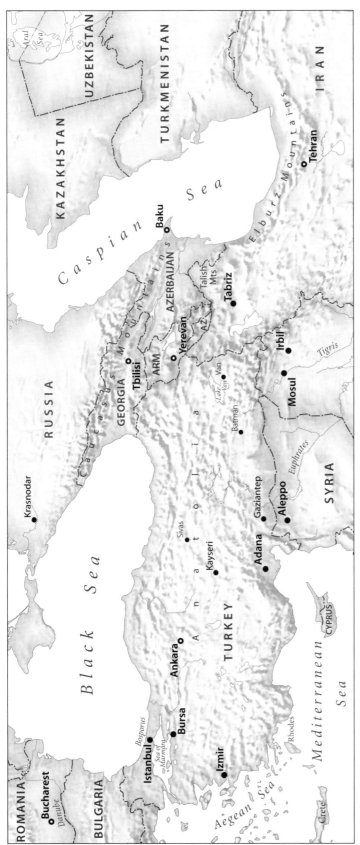

MAP 4: from Turkey to the Elburz Mountains

Britain, when he rejected my offer to join him in Turkey. He once took a bulb grower from the Czech Republic on a trip to the mountains and showed him a few spots where bulbs were growing. On a later trip he found no bulbs there at all. Somebody had repeated their route the next season and dug out everything. After that he swore he would never again bring a nurseryman on his trips.

In such cases I can understand the "green police." The most difficult thing is to know where collecting for scientific purposes ends and gold digging begins. There are occasions in which no bulb can be found in the type locality of a plant because commercial collectors have stripped the area for rarities. This was the case with *Iris pamphylica* (Plate 253), an unusual Reticulata iris from Turkey that is very distinct from other species and very difficult in the garden. Many years ago I bought some bulbs of this iris from a Czech gardener. I still grow them, but I can't say they are very happy with me. This species was only described in 1961. In the garden it is rather tall and very unusually colored—the falls are deep brownish purple with a yellow blotch, and the standards and style branches are a combination of light blue and green. The perianth segments are rather narrow and on the whole the plant is somewhat brownish green. My plants sometimes give me a good seed crop and make small bulbils at the base of the mother bulb; the stock increases and then for some mysterious reason all the larger bulbs die and only those from grains and non-flowering seedlings remain. Then the cycle starts again.

Iris pamphylica can no longer be found at its original locality in Antalya. In Turkey we found it growing in a very restricted area on almost flat mountainsides among shrubs where little other vegetation occurred besides another novelty, *I. stenophylla* subsp. *allisonii*. The latter was discovered by Brian Mathew and described in 1981. It is an early-flowering Juno iris that has very short leaves at flowering time. The flowers are pale violet-blue or lilac-blue with prominent dark purple spotting on very light falls. In general it is a dwarf species, not exceeding 10 cm in height. Gardeners can best distinguish between subspecies *allisonii* and subspecies *stenophylla* by the falls, which are generally concolorous blue in subspecies *stenophylla*.

Subspecies *stenophylla* (Plate 251) is much more widely distributed, growing on rocky slopes where there is little competition from other plants and in the openings between shrubs. It can be found at fairly high altitudes in southern Turkey in the Taurus Mountains. It generally has a single violet-blue or lilac-blue flower on a stem. The ridge is bright yellow and surrounded by a more or less white-striped zone, while the falls are blue, lightening toward the edge and usually ending with a very thin whitish line. The leaves are nicely undulate in the wild but not so distinct in cultivation. Though it is not a very difficult plant in the garden, it requires greenhouse treatment.

We visited a few places where *Iris stenophylla* subsp. *tauri* was known to grow (it was then listed as *I. tauri*, and *I. stenophylla* subsp. *tauri* is now considered a synonym of *I. stenophylla*, but I prefer to keep it as a subspecies). In both of the populations that we encountered the plants grew in plain stony meadows at the very tops of ridges, somewhat like the areas where *I. stenophylla* subsp. *allisonii* grows but without any shrubs. They had finished blooming long ago and seemed rather different from the populations growing on the slopes. Overall the leaves of subspecies *tauri* seemed short and rather blunt-attenuate, while in subspecies *stenophylla* they were rather long and acute-attenuate. They were wavy but not undulate.

We sought another beautiful Juno iris that one of Arnis's friends had seen in a location where the Mediterranean region changes into central Anatolia (Plate 252). When I first saw a photo of it I thought it must be a new species, and when I later visited the place where the photo had been taken, the foliage of the plant and its manner of growth only strengthened this conviction, even though there were no flowers at the time. It increased extremely well vegetatively—we found clumps with more than twenty specimens in each. We knew from having seen earlier photographs that this population was very variable in color, so we searched specifically for large vegetative clumps. We selectively dug these out, divided them between us, and then replanted the rest so as to preserve this wild population. When these plants started to bloom back in Latvia, almost each one was a different color, varying from the purest white to almost blackish blue and all shades of purple. On the whole this iris somewhat resembles *Iris stenophylla*, but all the flower parts are larger, stouter, and more robust. It is most unique for the wings of its style branches, which are extremely frilled, plicate, and larger than those of traditional forms. If there is one Juno worthy of being called "the goddess of Junos," this is it, at least in Turkey. It proved to be a very good grower in my garden, where it also usually sets seed well. Unfortunately, it is very typical for this Juno to develop a small replacement bulb when the seedpod is forming, but in no other species have I seen such well-filled seedpods and such a good seed crop.

Colchicum variegatum (Plate 254) grew in the same district as *Iris pamphylica*. (I'll not bother describing the ubiquitous ornithogalums of the area, which were so variable and so distinctive that a large volume could be written about them.) Many years before this Michael Hoog had told me that a new crocus species could be found in each valley of Turkey, and now I could say the same about colchicums. Even today many Turkish species remain unknown to botanists. *Colchicum variegatum* grows in southwestern Turkey from Izmir to Antalya and is one of the most heavily tessellated *Colchicum* species. The climate in my region is too harsh to grow it outside, but I have seen beautiful specimens in an open garden in the Netherlands. It needs a good hot baking in summer to form flowers, which appear in autumn. I grow it only in a greenhouse, where it flowers marvelously each autumn. Its wide-open, purplish white blooms are adpressed to the soil and marked with a colorful pattern resembling a chessboard.

In all my travels to Turkey only once did we find nothing. Herbarium samples of a white-flowering *Iris persica* had come from the vicinities of the village of Yarpuz, and it was very tempting to find such a form, so we went there. We walked up a slope in the area and spent several hours checking various sites and ecotypes, but the slope was extremely hot and dry and we found nothing more than a pair of wilted cyclamen leaves. We stopped at a few more spots on the way down but with the same success.

A year later I repeated the attempt, this time with a bulb grower from Lithuania.

High in the mountains, after enduring dust storms, strong winds, and fog, we found a small pedestrian bridge leading to the other side of the gorge, and there was *I. persica* in incredible abundance. It grew along a cattle path and most of the plants had been trampled and pressed into the soil. We collected only damaged plants, as they in any case would have been destroyed by the cattle. Alas, later on in my garden no white forms emerged among these plants.

Iris persica is unusually variable in color and remains among my favorites. It doesn't have a good reputation among gardeners, however, and there is very little demand for it in the trade, so from a nurseryman's point of view growing it is a waste of time, space, and money. Even so, I do not know of any other species with such amazing colors, from almost white to almost black through all possible shades of bluish, purplish, grayish, and greenish. I most enjoy the ash gray plants. I have never seen anything so spectacular among other flowers, whether they are pure gray or greenish gray—all forms of this color range are indescribably beautiful. A few years later near Gaziantep, which is in the same district, we found a very light greenish form (Plate 255). This may have been the "white" plant seen earlier by botanists at Yarpuz. Another form, this one ash gray, came from Ulukişla (Plate 256), a pure gray form came from near Aksaray, and some forms that combine yellow and blue shades came from Niğde. A population we encountered along the roadside between Kayseri and Sivas turned out to be extremely variable in color, with forms ranging from purely yellow (Plate 257) to blue through many various smoky shades. We also found brownish forms on a bare, stony slope before the village of Güzelyayla, and in a plain, stony, gravelly meadow before the village of Yavca we encountered a cleanly reddish purple form (Plate 258). At the same time, Arnis and company found a reddish brown form near an old road to the village of Hizan. All forms share one feature: very dark falls with a light edge that can be very narrow, almost invisible, or several millimeters wide and diffused.

In my experience *Iris persica* has not been among the most difficult species. My first stock came from the Netherlands, and I successfully grew it outside for many years until a very bad spring with never-ending rains killed almost all the bulbs. The biggest problem for all of these small Turkish species is *Botrytis*, which occurs when flowers wilt and water gets into the leaf rosettes during watering. Someone once advised me to dust the leaf rosettes with Captan fungicide after each watering to prevent rot. In earlier years I lost some of the stocks I bought from Czech growers to rot because I used overhead watering. When I introduced drip irrigation these problems went away, and my *I. persica* now grows far better, increases extremely well vegetatively, and sometimes also produces seeds. The folks at Gothenburg water using a small pipe, carefully checking that the water does not get on the leaves, and use fans to dry the leaves from any inadvertent drops. They have no losses there, either.

Very similar to *Iris persica* in flower, habit, and overall appearance is *I. galatica*. The sole easily visible difference between both species is in the shape and size of the bracts and bracteoles. In *I. persica* these are markedly unequal—the bract is leaf-like and longer, the bracteole shorter, thinner, and often semi-transparent. In *I. galatica* they are more or less equal in length, similar in texture, and green. *Iris galatica* has a more northern distribution, being a plant of central Anatolia (Plate 259). In the south and east it is replaced by *I. persica*, a plant of southern and southeastern Anatolia, entering northern Syria and northeastern Iraq. In places where these two species meet it is not always easy to tell which is which, and I would be tempted to merge them into one species if the karyotypes were not so different. The flowers of *I. galatica* are more on the purplish side of the spectrum, though among them there are yellowish-shaded plants. Plants with silvery purple flowers are more common in areas where both species meet, and some authors suspect these might be of hybrid origin. *Iris eleonorae* (now considered a synonym of *I. galatica*) was described as coming from the Armenian Highland. Our samples from there have not yet bloomed in the garden, so I cannot express any opinion about their taxonomic status. *Iris galatica* has a reputation as a better grower for the garden, and this is understandable based on its more northern distribution in the wild, but I have noticed no differences between the two species in this regard. When I have had problems with *I. persica* I have had the same problems with *I. galatica*. In my view *I. galatica* is somewhat less spectacular than its southern relative. Among the many plants that I found, the only very eye-catching forms grew within the area where both species met.

On our first trip to Turkey, we encountered the most difficult road conditions on the third day. We had set off in the morning from Beyşehir and after crossing several mountain passes finished late in the evening in Silifke at the seaboard. The road was a narrow stripe of asphalt with endless twists and turns, snaking its way through small villages and deep gorges. I was most deeply impressed by Tashkent, a small city that shares its name with the capital of Uzbekistan. The Turkish Tashkent was pressed flat against an almost vertical rocky cliff with narrow houses one above the other. We only later realized that we had forgotten to stop and take pictures. We covered a total distance of approximately 500 km that day, including several stops to examine various plants. We found *Iris stenophylla* subsp. *tauri* along this difficult stretch of road, but I was most astonished by the Belpinar pass (1850 m), where in a deep ravine there was still plenty of snow and at its edge in full bloom was *Anemone blanda* (Plate 260). It was the first time I had seen it flowering in the wild. It made a brilliant carpet in all shades of blue and white. One form was deep blue with a large white eye in the middle, an alternative to the pink-white Dutch 'Radar'. I later tried growing this form at home (and had even decided to name it for Guna to show her how grateful I was for her patience and to compensate for the horrors of the road), but it did not survive.

Never again during my travels to Turkey did I see anything similar despite many thorough inspections of all the flowering populations found on subsequent trips. At Ziyarettepesi Pass I arrived late in the evening of a cloudy day when all the blooms of *Anemone blanda* were closed. Somehow they seemed different, so at the foot of the rocks where there was still some snow left, I collected three clumps with interesting colors. At home one of them turned out to be uniformly blue, somewhat similar in color to 'Enem' from the Krasnodar region at the northern coast of the Black Sea, but smaller. Another had a lighter eye but was far from the beauty from the Belpinar pass. Near Ermenek in small valleys among limestone rocks I found a few plants that turned out to be very light blue, resembling in color the summer sky when it is covered with almost translucent, thin, white clouds. Plants from the surroundings of Akseki and specimens I received from Czech collectors had pure white flowers but were smaller and only a third as tall as clumps of the Dutch 'White Splendour'. These Turkish stocks produce much smaller tubers than Dutch varieties. I grow all my Turkish samples of *A. blanda* only in a greenhouse, and they have not yet suffered from the plague of anemones (*Dumontinia tuberosa*), which destroys them in the open garden. I suspect they would be able to grow outside, too, but I do not want to risk losing any plants because my stocks are still quite small.

Approaching Silifke we stopped at a small roadside shop to buy vegetables and fruits. It was run by a kind Turk with his wife and daughters. The family was delighted by our quite ample purchase and immediately offered us cups of tea. I wondered how local merchants such as these could make any money selling such huge amounts of produce when there were so many shops and so few customers.

We found a hotel near the main street of Silifke. This was a city full of ancient monuments, and we decided to rest here for a day after our horrible drive through the mountains. While Guna and Indra stayed in town, Arnis and I used the next day to visit nearby Uzuncaburç in search of *Iris stenophylla*. Along the way we stopped to see the unique two-story ancient Roman tombs at Demircili. One was especially distinctive, resembling a small-scale version of the Leaning Tower of Pisa (Plate 261). It had received its sloping walls from an earthquake. The area all around it had been plowed up and was intersected by stone walls that were built during the clean-up of the surrounding fields. We didn't find any of the bulbous plants we were looking for, but we did encounter *Allium* aff. *albotunicatum*. We also later found *Arum dioscoridis* (Plate 262) with a deep purple spathe. The plants were quite variable in terms of the spathe color and overall size.

We had heard reports of a population of *Iris stenophylla* on the roadside outside the village. At the first suitable resting place with a spring, we left our car and tried to find it. On the left side was a clear-cut forest—not a place where this Juno would ever grow. The other side looked more promising, although there, too, all the slopes had been plowed up and terraced by stone walls. Finally, at the very top where a *Juniperus* forest began on slopes too steep for farming, our sought-after Juno came into view. There was plenty of it, too: every clearing among the trees was crowded with this Juno.

The next morning our wives rejoined us as we turned in the direction of Cappadocia. In ancient times two gigantic volcanoes nearby this unique place had covered the surrounding areas with a very thick layer of volcanic ash. Later on this ash compacted into a special kind of tuff that was very easy to cut, and this was used to build cave-like structures. For centuries the local people had used these caves as living quarters, churches, and monasteries. The region became a very famous tourist destination, and hotel rooms usually had to be booked well in advance. Still, at the very heart of Göreme we were lucky enough to find lodging in a beautiful cave with an excellent name: S.O.S. Hotel. Various kinds of apartments were available—cheap ones for students, more expensive ones with all the amenities, including a shower, a comfortable bed, and a nice terraced balcony to sit on in the evening while enjoying an ice-cold beer and a beautiful meal prepared by the hotel owners. It really would be an excellent place to vacation. The only thing that annoyed us were the noisy hot air balloons that carried tourists over the valley early each morning.

Again Guna and Indra had a day off to visit various museums and monuments, which we seemed to come across with every step. Meanwhile Arnis and I drove in the direction of Aksaray to search for *Iris persica*; the form from this area was described as having an unusually silvery gray color. An enormous volcano, Hasan Daği (3268 m), dominated the landscape south of Aksaray, while on the north side we could see Ekecik Daği. We were able to reach the latter by driving along a dirt road traversing small villages and turning from the main road near the remains of Alayhan. A surprise awaited us as the road entered some hills with slopes covered in large, rounded stones. We did not expect to find another Juno species, but here was *I. caucasica* subsp. *turcica* (Plate 263). This form has a smooth leaf margin and so is easy to distinguish from subspecies *caucasica*, whose leaf margin is distinctly ciliated or scabrid. In Turkey subspecies *caucasica* grows only in the very northeast, in Kars Province, whereas subspecies *turcica* is much more widely distributed, growing in inner Anatolia from central to northeastern Turkey and entering northeastern Iraq.

Iris caucasica has a far better reputation than *I. persica* and *I. galatica*. It is a taller plant and much easier in cultivation, setting seeds fairly readily and also increasing by bulb division. I grow it only in a greenhouse. The form from Aksaray turned out to be a slightly greenish-shaded creamy white; others found in locations further east and north were less greenish, having white or yellowish flowers with a prominent yellow blotch on the falls. Plants with dirty bluish green blooms, supposedly hybrids with *I. persica*, have been reported as growing to the south from Lake Van, but I have never seen them.

We found the sought-after *Iris persica* much closer to Aksaray as we drove along a tractor track and entered a side valley between plowed fields. There were plenty of irises along the edges of the cornfields where the ground was too steep for a tractor to till. The plants were quite feeble and we found only a few seedpods. We found another few plants near the city border on terraced slopes that looked to have been partially forested while also being used as a dumpsite by the locals. Regardless of the terrible smell, we stopped to collect *Hyacinthella heldreichii* and a cluster-forming *Allium* species.

The next day led us to Kahramanmaraş—we wanted to visit the Akdağ, where nice alliums were known to grow. As we headed in the direction of Kurdistan we immediately encountered more roadside checkpoints and fortified military posts. The roads were not very good, either. On the roadside we saw a police station, and just near it was a cage made from metal bars with a double-wire fence around it. This was not a cage for zoo animals, however: there were humans inside it.

As we drove through the mountains we were surprised by the beautiful land-scapes. The mountains here resembled those of Central Asia—steep slopes, peaks covered with snow, a narrow valley below us with a stream cutting through it. Near the village of Eikenek we crossed the shallow waters of a river and went deeper into the mountains. Our jeep was an excellent vehicle despite its small size; we were able to cross the same river several times in it and get quite far into the valley. There was a road leading upward, but we decided to stop here and try walking up the steep slopes of the Akdağ.

Like everywhere else on this trip, the first bulbs we found were Juno irises, in this case *Iris persica*. We also found *Hyacinthus orientalis*, the ancestor of garden hyacinths. Two subspecies of *H. orientalis* grow in Turkey: subspecies *orientalis*, with narrow (4–10 mm across), linear leaves and perianth lobes shorter than the tube, and subspecies *chionophyllus*, with wider (12–15 mm across), more elliptic leaves and perianth lobes equal in length to the tube. Judging by the leaves the common form here seemed to be subspecies *chionophyllus*, with light blue, quite large blooms on a nice spike. Back in Latvia it proved to grow very well in my greenhouse, where it even sets seed without additional pollination. All the acquisitions of subspecies *orientalis* in my collection have more violet flowers and the leaves are distinctly narrower.

The next plant I found had a surprise in store for me. I was absolutely convinced it was *Sternbergia colchiciflora*, which has narrow, nicely twisted, markedly spiraled leaves that provide an additional charm when the plant is not in flower. However, when the plant came up the next spring in my garden it had wide, shiny green leaves. It hasn't bloomed for me yet, so I haven't had a chance to find out whether it is a spring-flowering species—*S. fischeriana* is easy to distinguish from another spring-flowering species, *S. candida*, by its yellow blooms. Atypical forms of *S. fischeriana* with shiny green leaves (the leaves are normally dull gray-green) have been reported from the vicinity. Another possibility is the autumn-flowering *S. clusiana*, but it always has dull green leaves.

I collected *Sternbergia clusiana* some 30 km from Tunceli on a very steep, stony clay slope under various shrubs. In my region it flowers nicely every autumn with very large, distinctly greenish-shaded, yellow blooms. It has the largest flowers of any plant in my *Sternbergia* collection. Stocks from northern Syria collected around the town of Bludan and on Mount Cassius have not yet flowered for me; it might be too cold for them in Latvia, or the bulbs might still be too small.

The only *Sternbergia* species with white flowers is the spring-flowering *S. candida*. I have been growing *S. candida* for many years now, and it is an excellent increaser in the garden and sets seed well, too. This species is very rare in the wild (known from just one tiny locality) and strictly protected, and has easily found its way into the garden. I grew it for many years in the open garden with varying degrees of success. My stock increased well, then for some reason only a few bulbs came up in spring. After this I sowed seeds in an open bed and these germinated and developed well, some reaching flowering size, but my plants never did consistently well outdoors. Perhaps our winters were too harsh for this species, or the springs too capricious. When I began to grow it in the greenhouse, everything changed. I now have a stock of beautiful plants, only the demand for it is so big that I cannot offer it each year.

Another *Sternbergia* species that recovered at the last moment just before I would have lost it was the ubiquitous *S. sicula*. It forms leaves in autumn, and before I built my greenhouse, where it now increases much faster than I ever really wanted it to, it seriously suffered every winter from frost damage. The stock I originally received from the Netherlands was partly infected with a virus, and it took some years to clean out the infected plants. Now it blooms in abundance every autumn. It is widespread in Italy and Greece. Alan Edwards collected a beautiful form in Selia Gorge, southern Crete. 'Arcadian Sun' is a Dutch-raised form with softer, deeper yellow flowers.

The most widespread species, *Sternbergia lutea*, can be found from Spain to Turkmenistan, but in Latvia it is the weakest grower. Its leaves, which appear in autumn even in a greenhouse, are usually damaged by frost, and it doesn't flower as well as other species. Plants from Italy have never flowered for me. A specimen of 'Autumn Gold' that I bought in the Netherlands was virus-infected and had to be destroyed. Only the form I received from Britain under the name *S. lutea* var. *angustifolia* turned out to be a good grower and increaser, although I suspect it may in fact be a form of *S. sicula*. The width of the leaves and size of the bulb are the only real differences between these species as far as most gardeners are concerned. *Sternbergia lutea* var. *angustifolia* is the last sternbergia to flower in my greenhouse.

We encountered three different large-leaved *Colchicum* species in the Akdağ. Two had lanceolate leaves (wider in one, narrower in the other), one had rounded leaves, and all were autumn-flowering types. I collected only one of them. It turned out to be the earliest autumn-flowering *Colchicum* in my collection, always blooming before I plant it, while still in the box. Even in the very cold, late summer of 2004 it was in full bloom in my bulb shed on 12 August. I haven't yet confirmed its name.

The *Allium* we were searching for in the Akdağ grew only on mountaintops, so we had to climb very high. It was the same old story: seeing a ridge in front of us we hoped it would be the last, but then as we moved along another opened before our eyes, then another. Where the snow beds started we found plenty of *Anemone blanda* in all possible shades of blue and white, but since I suspected I had already collected the best forms at the Belpinar pass, I did not pay much attention to them. Nor did I give much consideration to the countless ornithogalums we saw of all heights and with endless variations of flower and leaf shape. As often occurred when an expedition drew to an end, we were tired and became somewhat lazy about collecting "common" plants. Later I regretted not having collected any of the colchicums.

As we finally reached the last snowless peak, there it was: a beautiful, dwarf, white-flowering *Allium* with nicely rolled leaves. A strong wind blew the flowers from side to side, making it difficult to take pictures, but it was clearly *A. kharputense*—not the species we were searching for, but nice enough to make the trip worthwhile. It grew among stones on the top of a side ridge, its bulbs lying very shallow in hard clay. I was especially pleased with the curved leaves and large, dense, round inflorescence of pure white blooms on 30 cm stems. In the garden this species sets seed well and is a good grower.

During later expeditions we collected other white-blooming alliums from Turkey, most of them growing high in the mountains, but they have not flowered yet in the garden so there has been no chance to check their names. While the ornamental onions of Central Asia are quite rarely white-flowered, I got the impression that those of Turkey with globular inflorescences held at a distance from the soil are mostly white. In any case many species from Turkey have white blooms. *Allium orientale*, which I bought from Potterton and Martin in Britain, is quite similar to *A. kharputense* but taller and less impressive overall. Only one of the three bulbs I received was true to name.

One of my favorite Turkish white-flowering alliums is *Allium myrianthum* (Plate 264), which we found at Göreme during our first trip to Turkey when it was not in flower. When I first saw it flower on a 1 m stem with an extremely dense, large inflorescence packed with tiny, pure white flowers, I gave it the nickname "white pussy," for it was as fuzzy as a kitten. It was not difficult to find its true name because it was so distinct from other species due to the smaller size of its florets. My experience with it is still too limited to make any assessment about its increasing capacity, but my first impression is quite favorable. My bulbs have increased favorably and the seeds have germinated well.

On the flip side is *Allium cassium* var. *hirtellum*, which has a lax inflorescence on a stem only 30 cm tall, its large, pure white individual blooms appearing in June. It was collected on a rocky limestone slope in the Gülek Boğazi mountain pass on Bulghar Dagh. It thrives in a greenhouse and sets seed well, although it increases so well vegetatively that I stopped collecting the seeds. I like it very much as a cut flower for its airy inflorescences but have yet to try growing it outside.

Guna left me halfway up a ridge of the Akdağ and I reached the top only in spite of myself, asking myself as I went along whether I was still a man or had become an old derelict dodderer. I was very lucky when I reached the top; the few photos I took there were a good reward for such an arduous walk. As we headed back to meet up with Arnis and Indra, we met a Kurdish farmer who had built a small stone house here high in the mountains and passed his days removing stones from the soil, planting fruit trees, and regulating streams for irrigation purposes. It was a pity that we understood so little of each other, so that our conversation resembled sign language more than anything. He showed us how to find food even on these sunbaked slopes where only very spiny perennials grew. One of the extremely horrible thistles around us became a source of refreshment as the man removed the thorns from its stem with a sharp knife (Plate 265). The open core of the stem and flower bud looked a bit like an artichoke. It turned out to be a very edible vegetable—not something I would want to eat every day, but not too bad.

Shortly before Ziyarettepesi Pass we noticed a *Crocus* species growing in abundance on rock openings where a little bit more moisture was available. Its bulb resembled *C. kotschyanus*. Only later did I realize that it was *C. kotschyanus* subsp. *cappadocicus*, a most beautiful and only quite recently described subspecies of this common crocus. The old corms were growing very densely and there were many seeds I could have collected which would have no chance of germinating there. But I did not collect any of these seeds at all. Instead I settled down to collect seeds of *Hyacinthus orientalis* subsp. *chionophyllus*, which also grew here in abundance, only in the cracks and soil pockets of a very steep, rocky slope. Only after this experience did I truly appreciate the value of the work Arnis did at home when planning our routes. Now I understood how important that preliminary study of botanical literature and herbaria was for a successful expedition.

At Eikenek, Arnis was lucky enough to find *Corydalis erdelii*. Its flowers are pale pink to reddish purple with a dark purple spur. It is quite widespread in southern Anatolia but is not among my favorites. It belongs to the *C. oppositifolia* complex. *Corydalis oppositifolia* is distributed more to the east and north and is a much more attractive species, forming compact spikes covered with large flowers. They are clear pink and deepen to red with age. The best species from this group is *C. lydica*, which grows in the mountains of western Anatolia where it is known from just three localities. My stock is of Czech origin and is a very nice, compact plant with plump, ivory white blooms that blush to pink in a most charming way. It retains its compact habit even in a greenhouse. Like other species with perennial tubers, it can be multiplied only by seed, so careful seed collecting is essential. They are all self-incompatible, so at least two tubers are needed to ensure your own seed crop. Self-pollinated seeds can be set, but it happens so rarely that it is not worth waiting for.

There are several bulbs I have never collected in the wild. The first I must mention are orchids and cyclamens. I am not a fan of either type of plant. I grow some cyclamens but all are of seed origin. *Galanthus* species are also somewhat "taboo" for me. I once grew a few of them, mostly from acquisitions made during the Soviet period, but I never collected them in Turkey. I did acquire some of the Turkish rarities from other growers, however, the most unusual being *G. koenenianus*. This seems to be among the rarest snowdrops and was only recently described. For many years I grew it only as "*Galanthus* species from northeastern Turkey," only finally learning the name from Aaron P. Davis's *Genus Galanthus*. It is a unique species due to its distinctly furrowed abaxial leaf surface. It grows surprisingly well for me on leafy soil in light shade and even sets seed here.

I also want to mention *Galanthus krasnovii*, another rarity earlier known only from the Soviet half of the Caucasus Mountains but recently discovered in Turkey. There are only two *Galanthus* species without an apical notch on the inner petals. One is *G. platyphyllus*, which grows in high mountain meadows in Georgia; the other is *G. krasnovii*, which grows at lower altitudes, tending to prefer forest clearings. I acquired *G. krasnovii* from Czech gardeners and do not know the exact origin of my plants, which surprised me with their very wide leaves in which the widest part is from the middle upward. When I received my first bulbs it was just this feature that confirmed the plant's identity. I grow it in very light shade where the soil in spring is very wet regardless of the drainage. *Galanthus platyphyllus* grows in my garden in much lighter, drier conditions (probably even too dry).

While talking of snowdrops I want to mention *Galanthus reginae-olgae*, although it does not grow in Turkey. It is an autumn-flowering species from western Greece, the west coast of Serbia and Montenegro, and Sicily. I failed with it several times before building my greenhouses. It flowered each autumn but became weaker and weaker and inevitably died within two to three years. It usually started forming its leaves during thaws in the middle of winter, and later they were damaged by frost. After I built my greenhouse I decided to try growing it again, and Mary Randall from Britain was kind enough to give me a few bulbs of early- and late-flowering forms from her garden. The earliest form now usually flowers during November and December, while the latest one starts to bloom only in February (it also has well-developed leaves at flowering time, at least with me, so it may actually be subspecies *vernalis*). Despite the very dry conditions in my greenhouse from June until September, the plants grow very well there and flower perfectly every year. Another species, *G. elwesii*, grows in the greenhouse just as well as outside regardless of the dry conditions.

Searching for Garden Pearls

In general each of the expeditions we carry out focuses on a specific group of plants. This does not mean, of course, that other plants will be overlooked, but while planning our routes we always bear in mind our main goal. This particular trip was dedicated to *Muscari* species, including plants with a similar shape of inflorescence, like species of *Bellevalia* and *Hyacinthella*. *Muscari* is divided into *Muscarimia*, *Botryanthus*, *Leopoldia*, and *Pseudomuscari*. In English these plants are commonly known as grape hyacinths, while in Latvian they are called pearl hyacinths, possibly for the small, roundish, pearl-like blooms attached to the stem.

This was the longest trip in my experience as a plant hunter. We spent sixteen days in the mountains of Turkey, covering 5500 km, making more than a hundred stops, and returning with almost five hundred samples of seeds and bulbs. It was a fabulous trip that I shared with Henrik Zetterlund from Gothenburg and Arnis Seisums from Riga. Having learned a few things from our earlier travels, we rented a microbus that was large and comfortable enough to sleep in if necessary and which had plenty of space for our luggage.

We did not find all the plants we were looking for. In some cases we were short on time or energy. But even so, in the end the results of this expedition surpassed our greatest hopes. As the end of the trip approached, we joked that not a day passed without us discovering a new species. We found not only *Muscari* sensu lato but also an unexpectedly large number of *Colchicum* species and many other plants. As I again had some problems with my legs, I assumed the role of driver, financial manager, and record keeper. Henrik became the bookkeeper (Gothenburg Botanical Garden was the main sponsor of the expedition), and Arnis was the tireless climber of mountain-tops, bringing down many of the rarest finds while we two older men scanned the lower altitudes. Arnis was also the map keeper and roadside checker, having the amaz-ing ability to see the smallest of plants through the window of a fast-driving car. Sometimes I nearly jumped at the sound of his sudden calls to "Stop!" Strangely enough, the plants he spotted were usually something we were searching for.

As a matter of fact, the experience we had accumulated over so many years of bulb searching seemed to have given us both a sixth sense about knowing where to stop. I began driving more slowly, watching Arnis and predicting when he was about to sug-gest we pull over. On one such occasion I had already found a place to park before he had even opened his mouth.

This time our route went along the Turkish border with its southern and eastern neighbors—Syria, Iraq, Iran, Armenia, and Georgia—with many unplanned stops and short side trips along the way. On the first side trip we found *Scilla cilicica* and the tiny *Crocus sieheanus*, which is superficially similar to *C. chrysanthus* but with its corm tunic split lengthwise and without basal rings. We found the crocus growing in a sparse pine forest on a very sunbaked slope. Turkey really is a paradise for crocus aficionados—so many species and such unique forms grow here, and there are still many new forms to be found. Confirming their identities is not always easy, especially if you do not know where your plants come from.

The first plant we were looking for was *Colchicum archibaldii*, named in honor of Jim Archibald, the tireless plant hunter who first found it near Gaziantep. At the place noted as the type locality we saw a nearly bare, flat, stony plateau of brick-hard clay where it seemed that nothing could grow. But soon we found a few plants of *Hyacin-thella nervosa* with two beautiful, undulate, twisted leaves. The bulbs lay very shallow, no deeper than 5 cm, and their scales were covered with very thin hairs resembling cotton wool. Only then did I finally understand why I had never had nice flowers of hyacinthellas in my nursery. I had simply planted them too deep and kept them too cool in summer. In the wild the bulbs get a real baking during their summer rest. The wool covering protects them from overheating and moisture loss, but at the same time the high temperature is required for flower inducement. Now during their rest period I always keep the hyacinthellas in my nursery side by side with the bulbs of *Fritillaria persica* and rhizomes of Oncocyclus irises, which need similar treatment.

Hyacinthellas are among Jim Archibald's favorite plants and he always searches for them during his trips. I discovered their beauty in the Gothenburg Botanical Gar-den, where I first saw how large and dense their spikes of flowers could be, but up until my trip to Turkey I had kept them in my nursery only because they were bulbs. I was hopeful that when I changed their growing conditions my Cinderellas would transform into princesses.

Then we found *Colchicum archibaldii*. I had never before come across anything like it—its bulbs lay very deep in extremely hard soil. There were seedpods everywhere packed with seeds just ripe enough to open in a few days, so we collected these.

We made a few more stops on the roadside but could find no more *Colchicum archibaldii*. The soil changed into a very calciferous gritty clay. Fruit trees had been planted here and apparently some kind of herbicide had been used, as there were no weeds or other plants around. On a few very steep slopes we found very large clumps of *Iris persica*. We also found *C. serpentinum*, a species very similar to another small spring-flowering colchicum, *C. falcifolium*, but with fewer leaves. In fact, colchicums can be very difficult to identify, with many species names listed as valid by one author and described as a synonym by others.

During another brief roadside stop we encountered *Muscari longipes* (syn. *Leopoldia longipes*). Its flower spike can reach up to 60 cm long and hold as many as two hundred florets. The fertile flowers are beige or mauvish brown and slightly nodding, the short pedicels elongating after fertilization to form a conical inflorescence. The sterile flowers are bluish violet with spreading pedicels.

The taxonomy of *Muscari* sensu lato is so unclear and has been treated so differently by various authors that we tried to collect samples everywhere we went in order to get a better impression of their variability. We even collected such well-known species as *M. comosum* (syn. *Leopoldia comosum*), which can be extremely variable, reaching anywhere from 15 to 50 cm (sometimes even 80 cm) tall with fifteen to a hundred blooms. The fertile flowers are brownish with beige lobes and are attached by short violet pedicels. Especially nice, though, is the tuft of bright violet sterile flowers at the top of the inflorescence. This species grew everywhere in Turkey—on rocky slopes, near streams, in clearings among trees and shrubs in pine and oak forests, even in cultivated fields. It is not surprising that for a species distributed from southwestern and central Europe to Syria and Iran there are many variants under different names described as *Muscari*, *Bellevalia*, and *Leopoldia*.

We were headed in the direction of Bahçe Köyü, a village in which a large population of *Iris aucheri* was reported to grow along the riverside. This is an extremely variable species in some populations, although only very light blue forms are generally grown in gardens. I have been growing it for many years now, but before I moved it to a greenhouse I almost never saw it flowering. It grew well in the open garden and my stocks increased, but no flowers were formed. In the greenhouse, however, it is among the most floriferous species in my collection. It seems that our summers are simply too short and too cool to induce the flowers. I have two stocks in my collection: one is the traditional form, the other was received from Gothenburg as "a dwarf form collected by Alan McMurtrie." In truth the dwarf form is only slightly shorter than the typical species, but it has a more compact habit, flowers early, and has large, almost white, slightly bluish-shaded blooms with white falls and a slightly greenish-toned crest. It was collected near Lake Leylek. I once received another form through

Václav Jošt from the Czech Republic that was described as "large." It was only slightly larger than normal but had distinctly bluer flowers with narrower petals.

The 1990 KPPZ Expedition from Gothenburg (attended by Michael Kammerlander, Jim Persson, Erich Pasche, and Henrik Zetterlund) came across *Iris aucheri* in full bloom at Leylek Station. They collected some exceptional color forms, including 'Shooting Star' with almost blackish blue flowers with a white crest on the falls, 'Leylek Ice' with ice white flowers and a creamy yellow crest, 'Snowwhite' with pure white flowers, and 'Vigour' with deep blue flowers and very light blue, almost white falls. A dwarf form was collected by Arnis, Jim Archibald, and Norman Stevens at an altitude of 1900 m. It reaches only some 10–12 cm tall and has three gigantic (7–8 cm across) pure white blossoms with a large yellow blotch on the falls. Most likely it is *I. nusairiensis* or even a new, still undescribed species. The population at Bahçe Köyü was reported as another very variable one, dominated by beautiful deep and bright blue forms.

We nearly missed the road sign pointing the way to Bahçe Köyü—since the name of the village was in Kurdish, the sign had been left to rust and was now barely legible. *Iris aucheri* was meant to grow along the small, shallow river here, but we didn't find anything. We drove a little further and noticed some stunning plants of *Arum conophalloides* sending up their beautiful flower spathes along the riversides. Each had a different amount of black coloring on the inside of the spathe and grew among large stones.

A Kurd driving a tractor approached us. He was very interested in what we were doing there. Henrik showed him a picture of *Iris aucheri* and we started to talk, but the only word we knew was *chichek*, which means "flower." The Kurdish man nodded. "No *chichek*," he said, then pointed to the road and said, "Asphalt." Unfortunately we had to leave the place, only allowing ourselves a few minutes to take pictures of a marvelous, very wet meadow covered with long spikes of a purple-flowering orchid and bright white spikes of *Ornithogalum pyramidale*. I had never before seen such a beautiful ornithogalum.

We had covered less than a kilometer when Arnis shouted, "Stop, stop! There it is!" As it turned out, the Kurdish man had told us everything—*Iris aucheri* was growing on either side of the asphalt where he had indicated with his hands, and the blooms were wilted. The flowering season had finished long ago and the seeds were almost ripe. We saw no individual plants, only large clumps growing on very wet clay. Seeing such a moist habitat, I immediately understood why this species was so easy to grow in an open garden in Latvia. It likes moisture, although it prefers drier soil in the second half of summer.

We took the opportunity to collect a lot of seedpods, which ensured long hours of work that evening after we arrived at the hotel. Each seedpod had a small brown spot outside and a fat white worm inside. In some pods only a few seeds were left, so we came away with less than half of the potential crop. The seeds germinated very well, though, and we expect a nice display of the Bahçe Köyü variability.

Iris nusairiensis, described as growing in Syria, is very similar to *I. aucheri* and even looks like a smaller form of it. It may enter Turkey, too. Regardless of its southern distribution it is a good grower in northern conditions. My plants from Syria and from Gothenburg are nearly identical to the dwarf *I. aucheri* except for a couple of minor differences: *I. nusairiensis* has wider wings at the haft and is somewhat frilly in appearance. Both samples have the traditional (most widespread) light bluish shade of *I. aucheri*.

Having spent the night at a hotel in Diyarbakir, we now headed in the direction of Uzuncaseki Daği, stopping for breakfast along the way. While our meal was prepared, our eyes darted around in search of plants. This spot seemed very unpromising; there were no bulbs of interest whatsoever. But then we found two aroids, one a *Biarum* species, the other an *Eminium* species, both forming a mixed group. After checking the *Flora of Turkey* we came to the conclusion that these were *Biarum bovei* and *Eminium rauwolffii*. At that moment neither Henrik nor I (Arnis wasn't collecting aroids) could imagine the rarity we had come across. In September I received a phone call from Gothenburg: "Jānis, did you check our number *036*? It has nothing in common with *B. bovei*. It must be a new species." I hurried to my greenhouse and found that this plant was flowering for me, too. The shape and color of the plant surprised me— I had never seen anything like it before. In color the spathe resembled a flower of *Fritillaria*, marked on both sides with brown-green tessellation (Plate 266). In spring it formed very distinctive foliage, too. Indeed, a beautiful beginning to the list of new species! The next year we decided to name it *B. splendens*, but Peter Boyce cooled us with his opinion that it must be *B. eximium*, unknown in cultivation for more than a century. Well, that wasn't so bad, either. I later found that I had a very similar plant under that name from Iran (collection number *PF-1032*), the correct name of which is *B. carduchorum*. *Biarum eximium* was earlier known only from a restricted area near Adana and Mersin where it grew on low plains at an altitude of 60 m. It was collected only twice during the nineteenth century. We found it in central Anatolia some 500 km east of its type locality at an altitude of 1025 m.

We continued along a road that lay at the foot of extremely steep slopes. It was not far from the border with Syria, and every main intersection seemed to be a military fortification or gendarme post. I cannot say that this boosted our feeling of safety; on the contrary, it made us somewhat nervous, as if danger awaited us.

We decided to stop at a place where a narrow road entered a small side valley. It led to a deserted village of caves; only some steps and open holes in an almost vertical rocky cliff proved that people had once lived there. We found many bulbs growing in this area, including *Gentiana olivieri* and a dwarf, very bright red form of *Ranunculus asiaticus*. I was most pleased with two plants in particular. The first, the miniature *Muscari discolor*, has an inflorescence that is 10 cm tall and covered with blackish purple florets with a wide white rim at the tip. The sterile flowers are pale violet or even whitish. This is a beautiful plant for a pot or rockery and increases well vegetatively in the garden. The second plant, the dwarf *Allium sieheanum*, is only 10 cm tall with a nice umbel formed by arched pinkish violet pedicels of unequal length and bright purplish rose blooms. In flower color it somewhat resembles another favorite of mine, *A. tchihatschewii*, a much taller plant with longer pedicels. I acquired *A. tchihatschewii* from Czech collectors who found it near Gümüşhane, south of Kösedaği Geçidi, growing on hard, rocky slopes. In Latvia both species bloom in the second half of summer, set seed well, and increase vegetatively. I grow both of them only in my greenhouses.

We wanted to move in the direction of Siirt, from where *Hyacinthella siirtensis* had been described, but Henrik insisted we stop in a city named Batman, promising us a surprise. On the way to Batman we tried to solve the riddle of what exactly he might have in store for us. Was it an unusual Turkish sauna he remembered from his first trip? Was it an exclusive restaurant? A local meal? Perhaps it was some extraordinary monument he wanted us to see.

As we neared the entrance to the city, Henrik called out for us to stop, then opened his bag and started pulling out Batman costumes. He had bought these costumes for all of us, knowing we would be passing by here. So now, with all of us dressed like Batman, a lot of photos were taken beside the "Batman" sign at the city border. At Henrik's suggestion the abbreviation for our expedition's gatherings was *BATM* (or *BATMAN* as is noted in the Index Seminum [seed list] of the Gothenburg Botanical Garden).

We made several stops but found nothing other than a *Bellevalia* species. Then as we approached the farthest place where *Hyacinthella siirtensis* was known to grow, we stopped by a very steep rocky slope. Arnis quickly ran up while Henrik and I followed more slowly. And there was *H. siirtensis* (although only after the bulbs had flowered would we be able to identify it with certainty). This species is very similar to the more widely distributed *H. nervosa*, but the two can be distinguished by the length of their anthers—in *H. nervosa* the anthers reach the apex of the perianth lobes, while in *H. siirtensis* they only reach the base of the perianth lobes. The blooms of *H. siirtensis* are also somewhat smaller. To tell the truth, this plant is generally of interest only to professional botanists.

Arnis later returned from the top of the slope with a few alliums and a plant that he named *Scilla autumnalis*. Neither he nor Henrik wanted the scilla, so Arnis gave it to me. It turned out to be another great acquisition! In autumn in my greenhouse the typical *S. autumnalis* starts to flower with tall, loose spikes of tiny blue flowers, its narrow green leaves emerging at the same time. It is a plant only for *Scilla* fans who want to acquire all the species, although it sets seed well and is not a bad grower, providing some variety among the usual autumn-flowering bulbs. *Scilla autumnalis* is distributed from northwestern Africa through Spain and southern Europe as far as southern Russia, the Caucasus, Iran, and Syria, and is widely distributed in Turkey. My stock was found by Czech collectors near Gencek, Turkey, at an altitude of 1200 m. The scilla that Arnis found flowered much later and reached only half the height of my other stock, and what's more, the inflorescence did not elongate but remained very compact and densely covered with bright pink (not blue) blooms. In early spring, when its blue cousin had long leaves, it was still leafless. I even feared that I had lost it, but then the leaves came up when spring was in full swing. The differences between the two forms were so great that Arnis's plant had to be a new species. It was such a beautiful present, too—thanks a lot, Arnis! Together with Henrik we decided to name it *S. seisumsiana*.

Another autumn-flowering species, *Scilla scilloides*, grows near Vladivostok in the Russian Far East. This scilla (named *Barnardia japonica* in the *Flora of China*) flowers in my region in late August and September just before *S. autumnalis*. The stem is 15–20 cm tall and holds a fairly dense raceme of small bluish pink flowers. It is much rarer in cultivation than the better-known *S. autumnalis* but is easier to grow. I have not yet tried growing *S. autumnalis* outside, but *S. scilloides* grows well in the open garden.

Next we headed in the direction of Lake Van, spending the night in Tatvan, a city just near the lake. We were interested in finding a *Fritillaria* species that some tourists in the area had called *F. straussii*, although Lake Van would be quite far from its usual localities. We made several stops and indeed found a very interesting fritillary, but it more closely resembled *F. crassifolia* and had nothing in common with *F. straussii*. At the same time it looked very different from all the forms of *F. crassifolia* we had ever seen, so we registered it in our files as *F.* aff. *crassifolia*. It grew in the shade under shrubs in quite peaty soil. In drier spots we found *Bellevalia longistyla* with very curved leaves. This species has a lax raceme of purplish, white-lobed blooms on short pedicels. At the fruiting stage it becomes conical as the lower pedicels prominently elongate. We also again came across *Iris persica*, which grew everywhere in more open spots.

In this same area we encountered *Colchicum kotschyi*, a very widespread species with large, usually white blooms. Almost all the stocks in cultivation called *C. kotschyi* are in fact a sterile hybrid with large purple blooms, and the true *C. kotschyi* has not even been involved in the parentage. The flowering times of clones from Iran and northeastern Turkey vary, ranging from August to late November. This species is also fairly variable in color, with flowers ranging from deep pink to pure white, occasionally tinged pale purplish in the upper part or even yellowish. It is the only autumn-flowering species with creamy yellowish white blooms in some populations. I had one such plant that was collected by Czechs between Gaziantep and Adiyaman at an altitude of 1050 m, but I eventually lost it. Since then I have been in constant search of bulbs of *C. kotschyi* in any population, hoping to again find a creamy yellowish white form. This species' biggest advantage in the garden is its very thick perianth segments, which ensure excellent bad-weather protection, each flower lasting for three weeks. There is a superb clone from north of Tehran with pure white blooms that appear in early autumn (in Latvia from August through September). Arnis named it 'White Wonder'.

From Lake Van we traveled in the direction of the border with Iran. Our next stop was the Kuskunkiran pass (2235 m). A year before this, when Arnis, Jim Archibald, and Norman Stevens were here, there was a military post with armored cars, but now there was nothing. We left our bus and went to check the slopes. The first plant we found was *Crocus cancellatus* subsp. *damascenus*, a beautiful autumn-flowering crocus easily distinguished from other species by its very coarsely netted corm tunic. The spaces between the tunic fibers of subspecies *damascenus* are larger than in any other crocus. Its flowers are pale to mid lilac-blue, often with lilac or purple feathering at the base of the petals and a white or pale yellowish throat. The style is often exceeded by the anthers. The type subspecies is more commonly grown in gardens, known also under the name *C. cancellatus* var. *cilicicus*. Its petal exteriors are much more prominently feathered, and its bright orange style well exceeds the anthers. With the exception of the type subspecies, all forms of *C. cancellatus* can grow in my region only under covering, and even subspecies *cancellatus* sometimes suffers when grown outside. Subspecies *damascenus* requires even warmer, drier conditions.

Large amounts of *Fritillaria minuta* (syn. *F. carduchorum*) grew beneath shrubs here, easy to recognize by their slightly opened, campanulate, uniformly reddish brown flowers. This species seems to be the most orange-shaded fritillary. The leaves are a bright, shiny green. It forms a great number of small grains at the basal plate and reaches only some 10–15 cm tall. In the garden it is taller, and in Gothenburg I saw samples with much darker brownish flowers. *Fritillaria minuta* is a good grower in the greenhouse and needs dry summer conditions. I grew it once in the open garden but cannot say that it was happy there. It survived but only managed to bloom when I moved it to the greenhouse.

In this same spot I encountered *Ficaria* aff. *kochii* with spectacular, large, shiny, golden yellow flowers. Back in Latvia I don't take the risk of planting it outside, but it survives in my greenhouse, although summer growing conditions are very dry. As it grows side by side with *Fritillaria minuta*, it must be able to endure dry summers.

On the right-hand side of the road we could see the remnants of Çavuştepe Castle, built by King Sardur II of Urartu. We had reached the beginning of the growing area for *Iris paradoxa*, a beautiful and unusual representative of Oncocyclus irises. Forma *choschab* (Plate 267) grew here, its white or pale lilac standards slightly veined with blue, the falls almost reduced, tongue-like and blackish purple with black beards. Choschab was the name of the capital of a bygone Kurdish kingdom, but the Turks had renamed the town Güzelsu. *Iris paradoxa* f. *choschab* and a magnificent castle on a hilltop near the village were now the only reminders of this once-powerful nation. This is a very nice iris that can grow in the garden quite successfully for years and then disappear for mysterious reasons. I lost my first stock, though not for this reason—I destroyed it myself when I found yellow stripes on the foliage that made me think the plants might be virus-infected. The stock was of garden origin, so it was very possible.

Like all Oncocyclus irises, *Iris paradoxa* needs a long, dry summer rest. It is usually recommended that it be planted late and watered only once in autumn. I prefer to grow it for two years without replanting. In the first year the leaf development usually starts in spring and flowering is scarce. In the second year the leaves usually develop in autumn, and this is followed by abundant flowering. Clumps of well-grown plants become too dense, making replanting necessary. The biggest concern with this species is the foliage, which must be checked regularly during winter. The tips of the leaves sometimes freeze, begin to wither, and can easily be infected with *Botrytis* or *Fusarium nivale*. I check the plantings every week, carefully remove all dry leaves, and cut the dry tips with sharp scissors. This is my regular routine with all Oncocyclus and Regelia irises and their hybrids.

Now that I had found *Iris paradoxa* in Turkey, I would have the opportunity to try growing it again. It was very uniform here. I found no real variation in any flowering plants until at our next stop my eyes suddenly fell on a very unique-looking clump. The color was generally the same, but its veins, which on all the other plants were very thin, were much more prominent, thicker, and not so densely distributed. It really was something quite special.

I acquired another form of *Iris paradoxa* from Gothenburg, who had received it from the famous Czech plant collector Milan Prášil. It originated in the surroundings of Sevan Lake in Armenia. Known as forma *paradoxa*, its standards are bluish purple with deeper veining, white only at the midvein on the basal part of the petals; the petals are wavy at the edge. Forma *mirabilis* has been described from Azerbaijan but hasn't yet been introduced in cultivation. It has white standards and a golden yellow beard on the falls.

Allium scabriscapum grew side by side with *Iris paradoxa* near Choschab. As previously mentioned, I had already found this species in the Kopet-Dag in Turkmenistan. The Turkish population was very far from Turkmenistan, and I continue to wait impatiently for its flowers to bloom so that I can compare the two forms. Like *Iris paradoxa*, *A. scabriscapum* grows on fine, gritty clay slopes.

Henrik collected *Colchicum trigynum* here, too. This beautiful spring-flowering species has medium-sized lilac-pink to pure white blooms and increases well vegetatively. The pink form sometimes appears in catalogs. I grow a very abundantly flowering white form that Arnis collected on Bitschenag Pass in Nakhichevan, Azerbaijan (Plate 46).

We had to find a hotel before it got too dark and all the shops closed, so we headed toward Van. On the Kurubas pass (2100 m) we found a beautiful *Bellevalia* species that looked very similar to *B. longistyla* but with longer pedicels. It was growing near a plowed field in very wet clay. It was almost too dark to take photos, but I managed to photograph a stunning plant with two inflorescences. Its most impressive feature was its foliage.

With surprising ease we found a good hotel, and here our papers were carefully checked. This was the core of Kurdistan. Police were everywhere. I later spoke with the owner of a small shop who spoke a little English, and he explained that all the important positions here were held only by Turks. Kurds, who formed 90% of the population, were left the lesser-paying jobs. He had high hopes that this would change when Turkey entered into the European Union. I told him that I was from the Baltics and understood the Kurds' attempts to win their freedom, that we had a similar fate under the Russian occupation and now felt much safer belonging to the EU. I wished him victory in the fight for freedom.

The next morning we drove along the same road in the direction of Güzelsu. Shortly before the castle in the valley there was a police checkpoint. It was the first time our papers were thoroughly checked and our car was registered. The police were kind to us but treated the Kurds very differently, kicking their bags, throwing them out of their buses, and so forth. Seeing such brutality we well understood why the Kurds were so resistant to their oppressors.

On one side of the road just before Güzelsu was a petrol station; on the other was a fortified gendarme barracks surrounded by a barbed-wire fence and gun posts hidden behind sandbags. A gigantic clump of *Iris paradoxa* f. *choschab* grew among bits of garbage on a nearby slope; there were at least a hundred flowers and flower buds on it. On the other side of the stream high on top of an almost vertical hill stood the Kurdish castle of Choschab, above which fluttered a Turkish standard. We stopped in the village to buy some vegetables, and moments later the main street suddenly filled with army cars. When soldiers carrying guns jumped out and started whistling loudly, all the people around us froze as if some magician had turned them into stone. Thus began a form checking of every house and every person in the village. Seeing that we were foreigners, a gendarme told us to get in our car and drive away—they did not like us witnessing their methods.

In a sandy, flooded meadow near a stream at an altitude of 2150 m, we stopped near a bright blue blotch we could see at the waterside. It was *Muscari polyanthum* (Plate 268), a species that many botanists do not recognize and that in the *Flora of Turkey* is included among the synonyms of *M. armeniacum*. For many years I adhered to the *Flora of Turkey* and thought that both names were synonymous. Here, however, and in many other places during the following days, I saw clear differences between them. *Muscari polyanthum* is a plant of sandy soils with broad leaves, and I never found any bulbils around the basal plates as is so characteristic of *M. armeniacum*. Here the bulbs had usually split in two, and many had two large inflorescences from a bulb. The flower spikes were densely covered with bright blue blooms.

Growing in the same meadow was the very widespread *Colchicum soboliferum*, a species with long, stoloniferous corms. Though usually a plant of limestone rocks and stony open areas, here it grew in very sandy river silt. In my nursery it has been a somewhat odd plant. I grew it for years without problems and it seemed to prefer the open garden, but then a less favorable spring arrived and all the corms I harvested were tiny, long, and thin. The same thing once happened in my greenhouse. My stock has since recovered, however, and is increasing very well. I'm still not sure exactly what caused the loss of growing capacity.

Our next stop was the Czug pass, at 2730 m. (I deliberately use the Kurdish name here rather than the name the Turks introduced. On our trips through Turkey it was our policy to use only the original local names whenever possible.) This was the place from where *Bellevalia rixii* (Plate 269) had been described, and indeed we found it growing here. The first plants we saw near the roadside were quite weak and had damaged blooms, but the species appeared in all its beauty somewhat higher up, especially where road construction had loosened the soil. In general the spikes were not very tall, but in the best spots they were twice as long as usual and densely covered with beautiful blooms of a very unusual reddish purple shade. I had never before seen any *Muscari* sensu lato of this particular color. *Bellevalia rixii* has been described as easy to grow in a bulb frame but rather plain-looking. I cannot agree with the second half of this statement. In any case it was very spectacular in the wild.

On the pass grew more *Iris paradoxa*, and some new plants came into view, too, such as *Puschkinia scilloides*. I collected this extremely variable species wherever I found it with the hope that a special form would show up in my garden. We also saw plenty of *Tulipa humilis* (syn. *T. pulchella*), a variable dwarf tulip with generally lilac-purple blooms. A brick red tulip from northeastern Iraq was described by Per Wendelbo as *T. kurdica*, but some botanists regard it as a color variant of *T. humilis*. I prefer to keep them as separate species. The flowers of *T. humilis* vary in shade from mauve and lilac-purple to pink-purple, and the basal blotch can be yellow, blue, or deep purple (in *T. kurdica* it is almost black). It is well established in cultivation and many color variants have cultivar names. In the early 1980s I received seeds that were collected "around Lake Van," and from these I grew plants showing the entire spectrum of variability. I selected a few clones and it soon became clear that they increased vegetatively at different rates—I still have only a few bulbs of some, while my stocks of others have increased to a hundred bulbs or more. The white-flowered 'Alba Coerulea Oculata', selected in the Netherlands, is a beautiful form with a steel blue base. All of these forms are very easy in the garden.

As a safeguard and to make it easier to get seeds when I need them, I divide most of my tulip stocks into two parts, planting half in the garden and half in a greenhouse. Naturally the rarest tulips are planted only in a greenhouse, where they are protected from excessive moisture and early summer rains. It is very important to cut off the seedpods immediately after flowering if you don't need the seeds. This will cause the plant to focus the circulation of water and nutrients on the bulbs. If you do need to collect the seeds you'll have to bear in mind that the bulb crop will be much smaller and the replacement bulbs the following season will be mostly without blooms.

Another miniature tulip species that we encountered on the Czug pass had yellow flowers. In overall appearance it looked like *Tulipa biflora*, but the flowers of *T. biflora* are usually white with yellow only in the center of the flower, whereas the petals of this tulip were pure yellow for their entire length. Since I was not so interested in tulips, only Arnis collected this one.

The first bright blotch that greeted us on the pass was *Iris pseudocaucasica*. We had seen it earlier at lower elevations where it was not in flower, but up here it was at its peak. Unfortunately, most of the blooms were damaged by rain, which fell regularly in this part of Turkey during this season. This was the start of the distribution area for *I. pseudocaucasica*. We saw it almost every day over the following week, and I later found plants with undamaged flowers. This species was very uniformly colored here, a striking difference from the considerably variable forms of the Talish Mountains in southern Azerbaijan. In all the populations we saw during our trip to Turkey, the flowers were creamy white with a larger or slightly smaller bright yellow blotch on the falls and with widely winged hafts, making it easy to distinguish from *I. caucasica*.

Another plant here, *Allium akaka* (Plate 270), further revived memories of the Talish expedition, during which Arnis had searched for this species almost without success. *Allium akaka* is very variable in color, with flowers ranging from dirty white to almost purple. I now have some eight samples of this beautiful Turkish relative of the Central Asian *A. karataviense* (the *Flora of Turkey* even mentions that *A. akaka* is sometimes mistakenly listed as *A. karataviense*). My favorite form, received from Gothenburg, was collected by Per Wendelbo and has bright pink blooms. At the Czug pass these plants were just beginning to flower; the buds were still closed but were clearly bright purple. The leaves were somewhat longitudinally wavy or wrinkled. The inflorescence was very dense and lay at the soil level between two leaves or at the base within a single glaucous leaf. I have never known this plant to increase vegetatively, so in order to raise a stock, seeds have to be collected. It is not a plant for the open garden; all the stocks I planted outside were lost within two or three years.

Several kilometers ahead in the pass we found *Bellevalia pycnantha* with almost blackish blue blooms in a dense, multi-flowered raceme. It was growing in a very wet meadow just near a stream, almost directly in the water. This species was already well known in gardens and was offered by various Dutch companies, but the stocks in the trade were usually virus-infected. Although the bellevalias did not suffer much from the infection, they spread the virus to their neighbors. Now we would have the opportunity to introduce a healthy stock from the wild. Right beside the *B. pycnantha* grew marvelous specimens of *Colchicum szovitsii* with light violet-blue blooms. The flowers in this population looked larger than those of the Turkish form I had grown at home. I noted how extremely wet the soil conditions were in early spring here when the plants were flowering. This was a good lesson for me. Up to this point I had kept many of my dwarf colchicums too dry before and during flowering.

Arnis found *Fritillaria crassifolia* subsp. *kurdica* on rocky outcrops on the opposite side of the road, but the next stop was much more prolific. While I again searched for bulbs on alluvial meadows near a river, Arnis ran up a mountain slope, returning with the most magnificent spring *Colchicum* species: *C. kurdicum*.

He had also gathered *Iris reticulata*. But how could there be anything extraordinary about a plant as common as *I. reticulata*? This was my thought until the following spring when it bloomed. It is a very small form, similar to the white-blackish form from Iran (collection number *GLUZ-98-323*; Plate 271) but of a very different color. Its standards could be described as pink; in any case they are more pinkish than in the well-known *Crocus tommasinianus* 'Roseus'. The falls are deep purple with a yellow ridge, but the haft is almost white, only along the midvein it is dotted and spotted with brownish and purplish. At the same time it is not *I. reticulata* var. *bakeriana* (syn. *I. bakeriana*), which grows in Turkey and adjacent Iran and Iraq and is characterized by whitish claws, and whose flowers are blue and without a yellow ridge on the falls.

The leaves of variety *bakeriana* have eight ribs in a section, but *I. reticulata* typically has four-ribbed leaves, as does the plant we collected. In truth Arnis's finding was intermediate between variety *bakeriana* and the typical form, and I decided to describe it as a new variety. Since it grew in Kurdistan, I named it *I. reticulata* var. *kurdica* (Plate 272). Perhaps collection number *GLUZ-98-323* from Iran belongs to this variety, too.

Another two relatives of *Iris reticulata* grow in Turkey: *I. histrio* and *I. histrioides*. Both can be distinguished by their larger falls and by their bract and bracteole, which in *I. reticulata* are green and rather rigid but in the other two species are thin and papery, white, or only faintly tinged green. *Iris histrio* has falls that gradually merge into the claw, while in *I. histrioides* there is a clearly defined sinus between the falls and claw. I have never had an occasion to collect *I. histrioides* in the wild, and all the forms I grow are of Dutch origin. The most spectacular is 'Lady Beatrix Stanley' with large bright blue flowers and falls covered with white spots. It is so similar to all the samples of *I. histrio* that I have collected from Turkey that without studying the falls and claw it is not easy to tell which species is in front of me. In the case of *I. histrio* I would characterize the falls as white with blue spots in the middle. The forms of *I. histrio* from Syria are more violet in shade, with smaller falls that look more nervate than spotted. In general they more closely resemble *I. histrioides* var. *sophenensis*. None of these forms are difficult in the garden. They all grow well for me on open beds as well as in the greenhouse, where I plant half of my stock as a safety measure.

Iris histrio is split into two subspecies. Subspecies *aintabensis* is much more widely cultivated than subspecies *histrio* but in my view is less spectacular, having smaller blooms with narrower falls and less prominent, darker blue blotches that are concentrated around the pale yellow ridge. Both are easy to grow but tend to split into numerous small bulblets after flowering. This is not so marked as in *I. danfordiae*, however, and can be avoided with a deeper planting and additional feeding during the vegetation season. I have always found *I. histrio* side by side with *I. persica* in the southern part of Turkey, but always growing in the protection of shrubs, while *I. persica* prefers to grow in the openings among them.

The last Reticulata iris is *Iris danfordiae*, an oddity with standards so reduced as to seem thread-like. It is distributed from central Turkey in the north as far as the Taurus Mountains in the south. My attempts to find it in the northern part of its area were fruitless, but in the same year Arnis, Jim Archibald, and Norman Stevens found a new location near Gürün where *I. danfordiae* was growing on a large, flat, very stony plateau at an altitude of 1800 m. It seemed that there were more stones than soil there. When they first collected it no one could imagine that it would turn out to be *I. danfordiae*, and only when the bulbs started to flower at home was it finally identified. It is a deep yellow form with very few greenish spots near the ridge, and the backs of the petaloid style branches are without the green stripes seen in other populations of *I. danfordiae*. Alan McMurtrie found it growing on rocky cliffs in soil pockets with some *Muscari* species and grass. He has succeeded very well in using it in hybridization and has obtained a broad spectrum of variously colored hybrids from almost pure white to dirty blackish green. The last generation of his hybrids have recently begun to bloom with two-toned flowers of various color combinations, but common to all these hybrids are small, thread-like standards or even the absence of them.

Iris danfordiae has an odd habit of splitting into many grains after flowering. We observed this in the wild, where there were many clumps with solitary small leaves formed by grains, although more often there was a large bulb surrounded by small ones. As suggested for *I. histrio*, this feature can be curtailed with a deeper planting and ample doses of fertilizer. I have even planted flowering-sized bulbs 15–20 cm deep, and these have flowered without problems, the old bulb replaced by only two or three new ones.

After some 20 km we turned toward Yüksekova. We made our first stop long before Yüksekova where on a very steep slope a splendid *Leopoldia* species was growing with as many as eleven leaves from a bulb. The lower fertile flowers were whitish and the upper ones had become dirty lilac, while at the top of the 40 cm flower stalk there was a very large, bright violet tuft of sterile blooms. No *Leopoldia* species as leafy as this is mentioned in the *Flora of Turkey*. The bulbs are white (the color of the bulb tunic is quite important in the taxonomy of leopoldias), but I really have no idea how to name this beauty. I hope that it will be a good grower in the garden and will retain its distinct beauty in cultivation.

Only some 100 m further Arnis demanded we stop again—he had spotted an incredibly gigantic *Iris pseudocaucasica*. The stem was some 30 cm tall, much taller than anything we had seen before. In the garden it turned out to be an absolutely ordinary plant, no bigger than other forms, only the flowers were of a much greener shade and actually much less pleasing than others. In the same spot, however, we found *I. iberica* subsp. *lycotis* (Plate 273) at the peak of its bloom. It was completely new to me, both the standards and falls very heavily veined and spotted with brownish purple. There were magnificent clumps with some twenty to thirty blooms and buds in each, but all were very uniform in color. This is the only area in Turkey from where this iris has been described, having been more widely distributed in western Iran and Armenia. The plants are large, reaching a height of 40 cm. It does not have a good reputation in cultivation and is reportedly susceptible to root rot in wet weather, but in my garden it still grows quite well. It goes without saying that I grow it only in the greenhouse, without nursing any hopes of introducing it in the garden.

Clump-forming *Iris reticulata* grew alongside the *I. iberica* subsp. *lycotis*. In the garden the flowers of this form of *I. reticulata* are very similar to those of the "pinkish" form, only the haft is more yellowish, with a narrower white edge, and it is somewhat more purplish-spotted. Otherwise both forms are very similar—they were also growing quite close to each other. In overall appearance they look very different from all the forms of *I. reticulata* I had seen previously. Not only their color but also their size makes them very exceptional, suggesting that thorough studies are needed to clarify the taxonomy of *I. reticulata*.

In Yüksekova we missed a turn and only many kilometers later realized that we were on the wrong road. It was quite late and rainy by this time, and I did not want to drive in the dark in bad weather. So another very special beauty that grows only in this district—*Iris barnumae* f. *urmiensis* with lemon yellow blossoms—had to remain undiscovered. This was a pity because unlike *I. iberica* subsp. *lycotis* this iris had a good reputation in cultivation and was grown quite successfully for many years at the RHS Garden Wisley.

When it became quite dark we headed back to Van at top speed, but regardless of the late hour we were again stopped by a mouthwatering spot. We collected two belle-valias. One of them seemed, in Henrik's opinion, to be very similar to *Bellevalia tristis*, which hadn't been recorded in Turkey and was known from Iran. The other was the well-known *B. pycnantha*. Both grew by a river, with the *B. tristis* type growing higher and in drier spots. I am rather doubtful about the name *B. tristis*—I think these plants were just older flowers of *B. pycnantha*. Arnis again brought us something special from a higher altitude. It was *Allium shatakiense*, 30 cm tall with a dense, multi-flowered, hemispherical umbel of campanulate, rosy pink blooms formed by acute segments. There are still many unknown *Allium* species in cultivation in Turkey, and each newcomer is welcomed before a final decision is made as to which is the most vigorous and spectacular.

We returned to Van in complete darkness and left early the next morning heading in the direction of Ağri. Arnis wanted to show us the place where a year ago he had taken marvelous pictures of another Oncocyclus iris, *Iris barnumae* subsp. *barnumae* (Plate 274), with large, bright purple blooms and a white beard on the falls. When we reached the place where thousands of these irises had grown, we saw only a large ditch from which soil had been taken for road building. A very narrow strip of irises was all that remained, and if we had come just a day or two later these would have been gone too. The bright sun had opened the new blooms, so at least we had a chance to take a few pictures. It was another case in which we could collect bulbs without any reserva-tion—we were saving them from extinction.

At breakfast we broke with the tradition of eating in the open air and instead ate at a roadside restaurant. We were just near the Muradiye Falls where on one side of a shallow gorge the restaurant stood surrounded by flowering wild bulbs, mostly *Muscari* and *Ornithogalum*. The waterfall was only some 20 m high but mesmerizing nonetheless.

A few kilometers after the waterfall we stopped by a dirt side road and found some new plants: a dwarf *Muscari* species, a *Bellevalia* species, and a *Tulipa* species similar to *T. julia* growing on a very steep stony slope. At the very foot of the slope in a wet meadow near a plowed field was a nice form of *Iris iberica* subsp. *elegantissima*. Here its standards were white with narrow purple stripes and dots that made them seem light lilac overall. It was growing in a very wet spot, which is quite atypical for this species, but this was probably just an impression made by the heavy rains that had recently fallen there.

Until this trip the only form of *Iris iberica* subsp. *elegantissima* that I grew had been distributed in previous years by the Van Tubergen nursery. The standards of the Van Tubergen form are so densely striped and flushed with lilac that they create an impression of a violet bloom. The falls are much lighter and have an almost black blotch. It is the only form I have seen that strongly matches the description of this subspecies, which states that the falls are tightly reflexed. The falls of all the other forms of *I. iberica* subsp. *elegantissima* that I grow are less bent down, being somewhat intermediate between subspecies *elegantissima* and subspecies *iberica*, in which the falls are less vertical and usually deflexed at an angle of about sixty degrees. Subspecies *iberica* is distributed in Georgia and is reported as extremely variable, although it is now quite a rare plant due to overcollecting in the 1930s. Local botanists have described some nineteen color forms.

The weather was getting worse. Dark clouds chased us and drops of rain fell from time to time. We wanted to reach Mount Ararat, the symbol of Armenia that was cut off from Armenia by a pact between Russia and Turkey. The terrible genocide against the Armenians in the 1920s, during which 1.5 million Armenians were brutally slaughtered by the Turks, is a black mark in history. Very few Armenians escaped.

We made a stop soon after the Tendürek pass. It seemed that the mountains behind us somehow held back the clouds and rain. Here on a shady slope close to the border with Iran we found copious amounts of *Allium akaka* with beautiful bright purplish lilac flowers, the brightest form we had seen yet. *Iris caucasica* subsp. *turcica* in its typical white-yellow form also covered the slopes around us. Unfortunately the rain had so seriously damaged its flowers, which were very close to the ground, that no flower was good enough for a picture. Some unusual fritillaries were growing on the other side of the road. One was clearly *Fritillaria armena* but the other was more difficult to identify. It looked very odd, somewhat intermediate between *F. crassifolia* and *F. michailovskyi*. It had very deep reddish purple blooms with a small yellow blotch in the middle of the petal tips and was much darker than all forms of *F. crassifolia* and *F. michailovskyi*. It even seemed as though it could be a hybrid with *F. armena*.

Fritillaria michailovskyi is now very well known to gardeners, although it was only rediscovered in 1965 after having not been seen since 1914 when it was first found. It is a beautiful plant and a good grower in the garden but not a quick increaser. As a result of micropropagation it has become readily available at a reasonable price. The traditional commercial form has brown flowers with petals that are wide and deep yellow at the top. There are usually one or two blooms at the top of a stem. The most often distributed form is the dwarf one, which grows to 15 cm tall. It sets seed very well, and wider variation occurs among the seedlings. An excellent dwarf plant with up to seven blooms on the stem was selected in the Netherlands by Wim de Goede and is known under the name 'Multiform'. In my garden I still have never had more than four or five blooms on a stem, but this may be due to the smaller size of the bulbs I received from Wim as pot plants after the Breezand show. An excellent form known as variety *aurea* is grown in the Gothenburg Botanical Garden. It has greenish golden yellow blossoms throughout. I mostly grow *F. michailovskyi* outside, with only a few bulbs planted in the greenhouse; there is no big difference between the growing rates. I usually collect the seeds, but some forms can be easily increased by breaking a bulb in two.

As we approached the border with Georgia and Armenia we saw more and more plants that I knew from the other side of the former Iron Curtain. Just before leaving the mountains and entering a large valley where the city of Doğubayazıt was situated, we were again stopped by Arnis. His hawk eyes had spotted one of the most beautiful plants of the expedition (there were so many "mosts" during this trip that it was not possible to bestow the title of beauty queen to any one of them). It was a superb form of *Iris iberica* subsp. *elegantissima* (Plate 275) with gigantic flowers and creamy-shaded, very large, rounded standards. I collected a plant with more creamy-shaded standards than I had seen on typical forms and immediately thought of a name for it: 'Pearl of Ararat'. Again the rain kept us from taking pictures, but by the time we found a good hotel at the city border the weather improved and even Mount Ararat showed its spectacular silhouette over the clouds. Since the locality of *I. iberica* was not far from the city, we returned and took a few pictures despite the water-damaged petals.

The next day's route first led us through gigantic ancient lava fields. The landscape was surreal, like a planet where only lichens and mosses would find conditions acceptable. The weather was very gray. It was drizzling and a cold wind was blowing. We didn't even want to get out of the car but made a few stops to inspect some Oncocyclus irises that much resembled *Iris sari*. The soil was a gritty clay, and a *Leopoldia* species was growing there, too.

We were on a highland plateau in Kars Province. We stopped by a small river for a brief lunch. The landscape was unusually flat, though surrounded by mountains visible on the horizon. The river cut through plowed fields, taking sharp turns and rounds, everywhere washing out the banks and revealing the bulbs of *Bellevalia sarmatica*, which otherwise would have grown very deep in sticky clay. This species has a multi-flowered, lax raceme with white flower buds that become brownish by the end of flowering. At the beginning of flowering, the pedicels are only 2 cm long and erect, but in fruit they elongate up to 10 cm and become arcuate. It is a widespread and variable species. At the time of our expedition there was much confusion over the naming of this plant, so living material was needed for studies. It was a good addition to our collection.

Leaving the plateau we drove through new villages built for farmers. The houses resembled small, family-sized barracks, all identical and arranged in straight lines, but compared with the conditions in which peasants had lived earlier they probably seemed very comfortable. Later, somewhat higher up on stony outcrops, we found *Fritillaria caucasica*, *Scilla armena*, and the common *Muscari armeniacum* with long, narrow leaves and a deep blue flower spike. It was very cloudy, cold, and wet, and we soon had to leave to reach the nearest hotel. The town of Ardahan was not characterized very complimentarily in the tourist brochure but seemed to be the only place within reach where there might be lodging. The mountains looked very unfriendly. Black clouds hovered above them, lit up by continuous flashes of lightening, with water streaming down the slopes.

As we approached the city center we could see that the river was so swollen with water that it would soon flow over the bridge, so I pressed the accelerator. Ours was the last car to cross the bridge before it was closed to traffic. A hotel stood between the main street and the river. It took some time to explain to the receptionist that we did not need separate rooms with king-sized beds and that all of us could stay in one room with three beds. In the end we were put up in one room but charged as if we each had our own room. Through the window we saw the river overflowing its banks and reaching the roofs of the lowest houses in the valley. A few days later at a petrol station we would see a newspaper with pictures and an article about "the flood in Ardahan."

Only that night did we come to understand why the receptionist had wanted to give each of us a separate room with a large bed. This hotel served as a red-light house. All night long we heard prostitutes talking with each other and with their clients in the hotel's hallways, and at breakfast the next morning a few "night butterflies" at a neighboring table discussed the previous night's affairs. As we left the city we saw that the fields around it were underwater, but our route again led us up into the mountains.

Our first stop was Cam pass. The weather was so cold and rainy that we could only leave the car for a few minutes. Just on top, in full flower, was *Scilla rosenii*, but the strong wind made it impossible to take any pictures. *Crocus kotschyanus* subsp. *suworowianus* grew here, too. I already had white-flowering plants collected from this location by Czech growers, so I collected only a few *S. rosenii* to compare them with the plants from the Soviet Caucasus Mountains.

As we drove somewhat lower than the pass, the sun broke through the clouds and below us unfolded a stunning valley with a long, serpentine road leading downward. This was the district where *Iris galatica* was known to grow, including a form listed as *I. eleonorae*. *Iris eleonorae* is now considered to be a synonym of *I. galatica*, but at the time some botanists believed that it was different from *I. galatica*, even while others declared that the two were identical. We wanted to see some plants for ourselves to compare the two.

We found Juno irises at two stops within the area from where *Iris eleonorae* was known. In both places it was growing on very steep, stony slopes. The third place where it was known to grow was quite deep in the mountains by a village called Sarigor, some 20 km away from the main road. The road to the mountains turned out to be extremely narrow and difficult, and when we reached the center of Sarigor we were surprised to learn that the irises actually grew among the ruins of an old Christian monastery still some 10 km away along an even narrower, more difficult road. Our car wouldn't be able to handle it. In fact the driver of the car behind us had pulled up to let us know that our shock absorbers weren't working properly. After a long phone conversation with our car rental company, it was decided that we would go to Erzurum, where a repair team would fix the car.

All the rivers were brimming with water from yesterday's rainstorm. In some places the water almost reached the asphalt, and gendarmes were ready to halt traffic near the bridges. We were driving though a large gorge between very steep rocks, but even here there were plenty of marvelous plants. We most enjoyed the flowers of *Campanula choruhensis*, which was in full bloom in the cracks of almost vertical rocky cliffs.

Once our car was fixed we headed in the direction of Çat, where *Bellevalia forniculata*, the most attractive species of all bellevalias (and of all *Muscari* sensu lato, I can assure you), was known to grow. Its rather dense racemes of bright sky blue blossoms attract the attention of every visitor to my nursery. Everyone asks, "What is this wonder?" Having seen it in its natural habitat at flowering time, I no longer question why it is so easy in the garden. I grew it much less successfully in a greenhouse where conditions were too dry for it. It likes moisture, at least in the first half of the growing season. I have had no problems keeping the bulbs dry in the bulb shed. In fact this species' only fault is its mode of increasing—it has never given me any offsets, and all the seeds must be collected to build up the stock. This is the main reason why it is so rarely offered and has not found its way to large Dutch nurseries. Every spring many nurserymen from the Netherlands come to visit my garden, and they always ask about *B. forniculata*; as soon as I explain that the seeds must be collected, their interest disappears.

As we approached the mountain pass we could see wide, shallow valleys that seemed to be carpeted in sky blue, with bits of silver blinking here and there. At first we couldn't make out what this was, but we soon saw that it was water blinking in the sunlight and masses of *Bellevalia forniculata* flowers coming right up through it (Plate 276). Henrik and Arnis took off their boots and began to walk barefoot through the shallow water, which covered acres and acres of the flat meadow (my boots were so good that I was able to keep them on without even moistening my socks). I encountered a similar situation in the Eastern Carpathians where *Crocus heuffelianus* flowered through streaming water and at Kugart in Central Asia where *Allium fedtschenkoanum* came up from water even half a meter deep.

There are reports of white-flowering forms of *Bellevalia forniculata*, too. Are they of any garden value? They certainly must be of recessive mutation, which means that very long breeding under careful control must be done in order to obtain a stock that will reproduce from seed, otherwise micropropagation of the original plants would be required, thus raising the bulb price too high. There are plenty of other white muscaris, so another one would be of no special interest. No doubt a white *B. pycnantha* or *B. paradoxa* would be much more interesting. After all, the exceptional beauty of *B. forniculata* is just in its blue color. Nevertheless, something wouldn't allow us to leave the meadow, which we combed again and again. Something white finally shone from a distance—white-flowering plants. We also found a plant whose white petals ended with very light blue lobes.

Another species grew side by side with *Bellevalia forniculata* but in a somewhat drier place, just some 10 cm higher: the blackish blue *B. pycnantha*. This species grows equally well in the garden and unlike its much brighter neighbor increases quickly vegetatively and from seed. It is so similar to *B. paradoxa* that Brian Mathew (1987) thinks they could be one and the same species. *Bellevalia paradoxa* reaches higher altitudes, the perianth lobes are not lighter as in *B. pycnantha*, and the leaves are somewhat different in shape. It is reported from drier places, too. Some plants here looked different from others, and we supposed these could be hybrids between the two bellevalias. The last muscari was collected by Henrik. It was the very common *Muscari armeniacum*, which grew here a little higher than *B. pycnantha*.

We made our next stop on the Yaylasuyun mountain pass (2330 m), where we found a large number of bulbs. This was the first place I saw *Fritillaria alburyana* flowering in the wild. It is a very uniform species, virtually without any variation (although more recently our team found a population [*LST-247*] with purplish lilac blooms, a color previously unknown for this species), and I had a very good stock of it at home, so I was only interested in taking pictures. It was not easy to find good plants after the recent rains, although it grew better in the wild than it did in cultivation. The biggest flaw of this beautiful frit is that in the garden its very large, bright pink blooms open at soil level and actually lie on the ground. Only later does the stem elongate to push the seed capsule upward. In the wild it is taller at flowering time, with stems some 10 cm high holding the large flowers well above the ground. In the garden it is a very easy plant, however, growing nicely both in the field and in a greenhouse. It forms small grains at the basal plate and increases vegetatively, though stock can be built up faster by breaking the bulbs in half. It sets seed well, but the seeds ripen best in a greenhouse, since in the garden they are often attacked by *Botrytis*. I grow half of my stock outside and half in the greenhouse.

Fritillaria armena and *F. caucasica*, both also quite uniform, grew side by side on the pass. A somewhat stony slope was surprisingly rich in bulbs. *Scilla armena* with its bright blue stars had just started to flower, and close by we found *Crocus kotschyanus* subsp. *suworowianus* with ripe seeds. Three different ornithogalums awaited us. A dwarf one grew in a plain meadow together with another one with pyramidal spikes and small bulbs. The third one had pyramidal spikes but was growing in more rocky spots and had much larger bulbs. Identification is so difficult with *Ornithogalum* that in this section of my nursery there are lines of stocks still grown only under their collection numbers, waiting for "better days" when I will have time for them. It is not that I do not try to name my plants. I identify many stocks each spring, but then new ones arrive. So it goes.

Somewhat higher up grew a nice *Allium* species. Its couple of leaves were 1 cm wide and the scape between them was only just emerging. I grow it now in Latvia but it has not yet flowered for me, so I am still unsure of its identity. During this expedition we encountered many plants of this species and all were without flowers.

At Yaylasuyun we also found *Iris reticulata*, which formed very large clumps with 10–20 small bulbs in each. Many of the sheaths were empty; the clumps were too overcrowded to form a new bulb. Two years later they flowered with very deep reddish purple blooms. The blooms were quite uniform in color, with standards the same shade as the style branches and only slightly lighter than the falls—typical *I. reticulata*.

In drier spots higher in the mountains grew an abundance of bright red *Tulipa armena* subsp. *armena*. Arnis collected this species everywhere. At Çat he found an orange form. There are records of yellow- and orange-flowering plants, but they are always noted as very rare. In the garden it is a lovely tulip some 25 cm tall, growing well both outside and in the greenhouse and increasing well vegetatively. Subspecies *lycica*, which grows in southern Anatolia, is easy to distinguish by its very hairy tunics with long twisted hairs. In the garden it is not so vigorous.

Some 40 km from the pass we entered a valley that looked quite unique because of its gritty, unstable slopes. We again stopped at a spot where we saw something blue blooming by a stream. Just by the riverside grew a beautiful population of *Muscari polyanthum*, which only confirmed my conviction that this is a separate species well distinguished from *M. armeniacum* and growing in different ecological conditions. The soil here was sandy and the muscari was broad-leaved. But there were more surprises awaiting me. Here too was a nice group of pure white *M. polyanthum*, and what is more, one of the plants had violet flowers (Plate 268). I had never seen anything similarly colored among grape hyacinths.

A plant with an incredibly pleasant aroma flowered just near the unstable road-side. It was *Neotchihatchewia isatidea* (Plate 277), a monocarpic species with a large spike of lighter and darker violet flowers similar in shape and aroma to the blooms of lilacs. The leaves were extremely hairy. What a shame that after flowering this beauty would die and leave only seeds! It is a very local endemic.

More surprises were in store on the other side of the road. The slope was even more unstable here, but we managed to climb up using stones for footholds and grasping tufts of grass. It was well worth the effort, for at the top we stumbled onto a new species of *Colchicum*. It was so different from any others we had seen that there could be no doubt about its taxonomic status. Confirmation came from Gothenburg the next spring: we were right, it really was a new species, which will soon be published. Nearby we found a very strange-looking *Bellevalia* that also seemed to be a new species. This one hasn't yet flowered for us, however, so we will have to wait a bit longer for a final decision. Both of these finds have one great advantage in the eyes of a gardener: they increase extremely well vegetatively, making clumps in the wild.

It was incredible how rich a short stop in the mountains could be. While Henrik and I enjoyed the flowers of *Neotchihatchewia isatidea* and inspected the *Colchicum* and *Bellevalia* species, Arnis returned from higher altitudes where he had found *Allium balansae*, another very local endemic. This allium flowers late in summer, its hemispherical umbels composed of deep rose-purple blooms with very obtuse segments.

The following stop was on top of the next mountain pass. The growing conditions were very different here—a shallow and extremely stony layer of clay covering disintegrated rocks. The rocks were mainly bordeaux red intersected with white lines of marble; other outcrops were greenish gray—typical serpentines. Three *Fritillaria* species grew here. The first remained unidentified, the second was *F. alburyana*, and the third was *F. pinardii*. It was the first time we had encountered *F. pinardii* during this trip. It is a very widespread and extremely variable, easy-growing species, but I have never tried it in the garden.

The most interesting plants growing here were two *Eremurus* species that looked very different from each other. They were not flowering yet, but in this area only one species had been recognized: *E. spectabilis* (which in spite of its name is not very spectacular). The oddest thing about these plants was the width of their leaves. One form had very narrow leaves, no wider than 2.5 cm, while the other had very broad leaves, some 8 cm wide. Meanwhile the *Flora of Turkey* described the leaf of *E. spectabilis* as "up to 4.5 cm broad." The broad-leaved plant resembled a Central Asian species. Despite its large, heavy rootstock, I collected a specimen to see what it would be. Surprisingly, unlike many eremurus from Central Asia, which probably would have died if collected so early, this one survived and I am looking forward to its first flowering in my greenhouse.

Our road here turned to the city of Bingöl, which only a year before had experienced a severe earthquake. Arnis had been there a month afterward and described how the houses were without chimneys, most of the windowpanes were broken, and the people were still living in tents. Just before we reached the city we were stopped by something unbelievable on the flat slope. It was one of the most superb arums, *Arum conophalloides* var. *caudatum* (Plate 278), which at flowering time reaches 1 m tall. Half of its stem is formed by a petiole, the other half by a gigantic purplish brown spathe. We collected and divided among ourselves several seedlings, and in the autumn I had five small tubers to plant. I do not know if they will reach the same size and beauty as the plants we found. Peter Boyce (1993) considers *A. conophalloides* a synonym of *A. rupicola*, but although I usually adhere to recent taxonomical discoveries, this is a case in which I must respectfully disagree. *Arum conophalloides* simply looks too different from the plants that I grow as *A. rupicola* (especially variety *virescens*), and my heart will not allow me to put them under one hat.

From Bingöl, which showed no traces of the catastrophe it had endured, we approached what many called "the heart of the Kurdish resistance movement," the Munzur Valley, where many beautiful plants had been discovered. A few years before this we would have been stopped before this point and told that we needed some kind of special permission to enter, but Arnis had been here the year before and had only had to endure a long questioning at a checkpoint.

A couple of stops had to be made along the way, the first one for a new *Bellevalia* species, *B. leucantha*. This plant was known to grow here by the millions, covering all the meadows, but it had been lost in cultivation at Gothenburg over the course of time, so a new sample was needed. We spent several hours scouring every meadow and rocky outcrop in the area, searching among every shrub—there were no plants anywhere! We even collected a nice dwarf *Ornithogalum* species that hadn't yet flowered, thinking by the overall shape of its leaves that it must be the bellevalia we were looking for—only Arnis's laugh upon seeing our "bellevalia" let us know what we had found. Nevertheless, for me this stop was very fruitful. While scanning the copious amounts of *Colchicum kotschyi* in the area, I noticed some different-looking leaves coming up from beneath some shrubs. According to the *Flora of Turkey* this strange plant was *C. paschei*, which was only described in 1999. It flowered beautifully its first autumn in my garden and turned out to be much smaller than the related *C. kotschyi*, with pure white, medium-sized blooms and different foliage, which appeared in spring.

An unusual *Ornithogalum* species also grew here. Like *Colchicum paschei*, we only found it growing under shrubs. Its inflorescence was 30–40 cm long with pendulous, campanulate flowers on short pedicels sparsely placed along the stem. The effect was something like a longer, sparser spike of *Scilla hispanica*. Unfortunately, all my attempts to identify this species have been unsuccessful. The beautiful *Paeonia mascula* also grew in the shrubs here. From a distance it looked very impressive pushing its large red flowers through the shrub. In this position it was protected from the armies of hungry sheep.

Surprisingly enough, we could not find *Bellevalia leucantha*. It seemed that years ago the area had become a place for flocking large herds of sheep. The sheep came through here as they moved on to mountain pastures in summer. For a bulb the only place left was inside a strong and spiny shrub.

This was the beginning of the distribution area for *Iris sari*, which was in full flower. It was quite uniform in color, varying a little in the darker or paler yellowish base color, which was more or less veined with reddish brown, reddish purple, or black. Only once did I find a plant with distinctly orange-shaded blooms. There were very dwarf forms as well as taller ones, but I saw no plants exceeding 30 cm. *Iris sari* is one of the easiest Oncocyclus irises in cultivation, growing and increasing very well in a greenhouse. Two different forms are distributed, and we did not come across any mixed populations despite having specifically searched for such. Like everywhere in eastern and southern Turkey, it was the taller form that grew here, its leaves distinctly erect. In the western part of the area this was replaced by the dwarf form with distinctly falcate leaves and somewhat smaller blooms. The dwarf form was once called *I. manissadjianii*, but this name is now considered a synonym of *I. sari*. I cannot agree to such lumping of both forms. They do not form mixed populations and must be at least different subspecies, although in flower color they look similar. They are more dissimilar than *I. iberica* subsp. *iberica* and subspecies *elegantissima*.

When our road turned toward Tunceli we were stopped at a heavily armed checkpoint. Here began the Kurdish territory, where in 1990 Henrik and company had traveled without problems and found the beautiful spring-flowering *Colchicum munzurense* and many other nice bulbs. On this trip, however, we were stopped, our car was searched, and we were invited to "tea," at which our interrogation began. When we told them we were on our way to Erzincan, they wanted to know why we had selected this particular road to get there. Did we know someone living here? Were we planning to stop somewhere in the valley? We were told that this was a rebel region and that we were not allowed to stop anywhere on our way through. We were not allowed to talk with local people, either, and had to be out of the valley before nightfall. This, they stressed, was only for our own safety. I still remembered very well the frequent references to our own "safety" during my last visit to Uzbekistan.

In the end we were cleared to go and our trip through "the most dangerous place in Turkey" began. Just outside of Tunceli we stopped for a rest. While I made coffee, Arnis walked to the nearby knolls, soon returning with *Iris persica*. We were again in the part of Turkey where this iris grew everywhere on slightly open, stony clay slopes.

The valley seemed abandoned. We saw ruins of homes and restaurants but no people. The surroundings were marvelous, however, and our older maps indicated that there had once been some famous tourist spots here, with beautiful landscapes and waterfalls. Our next stop was some 30 km inside the valley where there had once been a parking area. We stopped here for a more substantial lunch, then tried to climb an extremely steep, woody slope nearby. We immediately spotted plants of interest. There were at least two *Muscari* sensu lato—one a *Bellevalia* species, the other a *Leopoldia* species—but for me the most important find was *Sternbergia clusiana*, a very common plant that I still didn't have in my collection. This sternbergia flowered in my greenhouse the same autumn with large, distinctly greenish-shaded blooms. It was without leaves at flowering time. In the same spot we found a dwarf *Colchicum* species making very large clumps with some twenty to twenty-five corms in each. It was *C. munzurense*. This species normally has more or less stoloniferous corms, but the corms of this form are very different in shape, vertical and without the shoot-bearing lobes so characteristic of *C. munzurense*. In the garden *C. munzurense* grows and increases surprisingly well, with small, light violet blooms and blackish purple anthers. The new form looks very similar in flower, having the same swelling at the base of the filaments, which in the basal part of all my samples are bright orange (not yellow to green-yellow, as written in the *Flora of Turkey*). Like everywhere else, in this location we also found a few *Allium* species, *Ornithogalum* species, and a *Gladiolus* species, as well as a *Biarum* species.

The valley became narrower and in many places we drove through anti-avalanche tunnels. Just before the sixth tunnel we noticed a new scilla. It was the light lilac-blue *Scilla leepii*, morphologically similar to *S. armena* but with blooms that are a different shape at the base and leaves that are distinctly shorter than the tallest scape. Like *S. armena* it has only one or two flowers on a stem. It was discovered in 1977 and is still known only from a few spots not very far from this location. At the next tunnel we saw *Iris reticulata*. It was the common deep reddish purple form characterized by purple claws and deep blackish purple, white-spotted falls with a yellow ridge. In flower color and size it was very similar to variety *caucasica*, only with more heavily white-spotted falls. These plants were very similar to the form we found at the Yaylasuyun mountain pass, only the standards were somewhat lighter; they were very different, however, from the plants collected near the border with Iran after the Czug pass and at Yüksekova. This only strengthened my conviction that the plants growing in Iran were another species, or at least a variety, of *I. reticulata* and that I was right to name them variety *kurdica*.

At the end of the valley on a very steep slope we came across our "queen of the day," *Muscari massayanum*, one of the most magnificent leopoldias. From the base of two to four long, thick, strap-like, canaliculate, slightly wavy leaves emerges an inflorescence that is 25–30 cm long and densely covered with violaceous (but later greenish or yellowish brown) fertile blooms on very short pedicels (Plate 279). At the top of the inflorescence is a dense cluster of pink or bright violet sterile blooms. After flowering, the blooms are replaced by very large, deeply trilobed seed capsules densely attached to the flower stalk, and the plant is as attractive at this stage as it is when flowering (Plate 280). In the wild it grows on calcareous screes, in fallow fields, and in clearings among dry pine forests. It grows well in a greenhouse but not in an open garden and needs a hot, dry period of summer rest to induce flowering. After the very cold summer of 2004 I had no flowers the following spring, although earlier this plant flowered quite well and set seed, too. The seeds germinate very well and plants reach flowering size in four to five years. The biggest flaw of this beauty is the absence of vegetative increasing, but as with other *Muscari*-like plants this can be induced by cross-cutting the bulb's basal plate.

We found a similar plant a day later. When in seed *Bellevalia crassa* (Plate 281) resembles a miniature *Muscari massayanum*. Only some 10 cm high, it is a rounder plant with an inflorescence between one to two broad, strap-like leaves, which are shorter in proportion to the size of the plant. The fertile blooms are white, the sterile blooms purplish. It is an extremely rare plant that grows in very specific conditions, thriving on sunbaked slopes without competition from other plants. It was known only from a single locality until 2005, when a team of us found it growing some 10 km northeast from its type locality. If Henrik had not been with us and had not remembered exactly where *B. crassa* grew when he had seen it on a trip in 1990, we might never have found this beauty. It remains almost unknown, even among botanists. A few of the plants that I grow do well in my greenhouse, flower, and even set seed.

Before leaving the valley we went through another checkpoint. Our data already lay on the table in front of the gendarmes, and we were again interrogated about the stops we had made and the conversations that had taken place with the local people. By now we understood that the Turks were most concerned about contact between Kurds and foreigners, worrying that the truth of what life was like here in Turkey would come out in the open.

The landscape changed incredibly after we left the gorge, and we found ourselves driving along a wide, plain valley. It was dark when we reached Erzincan. There were plenty of hotels, so finding a good one was not a problem.

Early the next morning we continued our way into the mountains, making our first stop soon after entering the valley. Here we found something new, *Fritillaria crassifolia* subsp. *crassifolia*, which is quite similar to subspecies *kurdica* in terms of the growing rate but is easy to distinguish by its much wider leaves. Moments later I saw my first snake of the trip. I seemed to have interrupted her breakfast—when I didn't immediately retreat, she spewed out a large green lizard and then hid beneath a shrub. (Needless to say I didn't stick around to see whether she returned to her game.) In this same area we found a *Gladiolus* species growing along a stream in very muddy clay.

On the Sakaltutan mountain pass I found the first undamaged blooms of *Iris caucasica* subsp. *turcica* to photograph. The sun shone brightly and it seemed that at least during the past few days there had been no rain. The flowers were light creamy yellow, slightly greenish-shaded, and scattered all over the plain slope. *Muscari coeleste* was flowering in a very marshy spot near the road. It had small bulbs without any offsets and a rather lax inflorescence of sky blue flowers. This muscari is sometimes mistakenly placed in *Hyacinthella*, with which it shares some similarities.

Just as we passed the highest point of the pass, Arnis and I simultaneously cried, "Stop!" I had shouted because I realized I had failed to collect samples of *Colchicum szovitsii* from here, but Arnis had noticed a very large, bright, deep blue spot on the opposite side of the road. As we approached a wet meadow with a beautiful stream meandering through it, our eyes opened wide at the incredible beauty: it was a muscari of a color we had never seen before (Plate 282). The blooms were an extremely bright, deep purplish blue and held in large, dense spikes. We were spellbound—no cultivated form could vie with this beauty. If in lowland conditions this plant would retain its color, it would be the best newcomer to gardens because it also increased well vegetatively. We were all wary when it came to naming it. It looked somewhat similar to *Muscari armeniacum* but with broader leaves, so it could have been *M. polyanthum*, but the spikes were of an incredible size. Perhaps it was an interspecific hybrid? On the other hand the population was quite large and we found no candidates for parenthood. We recorded it in our notes only as "*Muscari* species."

At the Kizildağ pass (2120 m) we encountered snow. Beautifully flowering *Scilla armena* grew right near the snow, and the slopes were replete with the leaves of *Crocus kotschyanus* subsp. *suworowianus*. I also collected *C. biflorus* subsp. *taurii*, a very easy-growing spring crocus with bright blue blooms and a deep yellow throat. It is one of the best subspecies for the garden, increases well vegetatively, and is quite uniform within its entire area. Its blooms are usually without prominent stripes on the exterior. The best stock (collection number *LP-7260*) was collected on the mountains of Sivas at an altitude of 2350 m, and I have been growing it since 1982. Similar to it in color but less leafy and with narrower leaves is subspecies *pulchricolor* from northwestern Turkey, another good grower and increaser for the garden. My stock of subspecies *pulchricolor* (collection number *BM-8514*) originates from the first seeds Chris Brickell sent me in the 1980s, which were collected in Bursa Province on Uludağ. Both subspecies have thinner corm tunics that are more membranous than coriaceous but are very distinct chromosomally. Although subspecies *taurii* is reportedly paler in color than subspecies *pulchricolor*, I have not noticed any considerable differences in this regard. Plants from the Kizildağ pass, which undoubtedly belong to subspecies *taurii*, have even darker yellow throats and deeper blue perianths than my stock of subspecies *pulchricolor*, although according to Brian Mathew (1982) it must be vice versa.

We stopped some 15 km further where a side stream flowed down the mountains. While Arnis ran up the slope, I inspected a specimen of *Geranium macrostylum* with purple-spotted leaves growing just near the road. I had seen similarly colored leaves only on *G. charlesii* from Sina. Here the marks were not so prominent, just deep purple spots or dots on the leaf blade, but this plant was very unusual nonetheless. Meanwhile Henrik noticed a beautiful *Leopoldia* species with deep blue basal blooms on short pedicels in a long spike. Arnis returned from the tops with another *Allium* species belonging to section *Melanocrommyum*. Unfortunately, it was too windy to take pictures.

We spent the next night in Sivas at a rather unpleasant hotel. We were tired from the precarious roads and never-ending rain. It was easy to see how high the water had reached during the floods by noting the rubbish on the tree branches—plastic bags, papers, textiles, and so forth. The whole area looked quite surreal.

We headed in the direction of Gürün, making many stops along the way, collecting *Iris stenophylla* wherever we found it to check its variability and the distribution of various forms. The straight-leaved form of *I. sari* was replaced in this area by the arched subspecies *manissadjianii*, a distinctly smaller plant that seems slightly more variable in color. It grew on flat spots where there were more stones than soil. I collected a form that seemed especially dwarf, but in cultivation this difference disappeared. At one stop we found a form of *Allium lycaonicum* whose flowers were very deep purple, even shining purple. It was growing together with *Tulipa armena* and an unidentified spring-flowering *Colchicum* species that turned out to be a quick increaser. *Anemone blanda*, a lovely blue-flowered plant, and plenty of *Crocus cancellatus* grew on a spot slightly protected by large stones. Another beauty from here was *Sternbergia colchiciflora*. I never saw it growing in large groups, but we found several bulbs at every stop. In cultivation they all looked identical.

Around Gürün grew a very variable population of *Iris schachtii*, a beautiful, dwarf, rhizomatous iris with flowers ranging from white to yellow and purple. Since I had never grown it before, I restricted it to my greenhouse; its rhizomes survived the first season with me but have not yet flowered. In Gürün we also came across *Hyacinthella acutiloba* with a pale blue perianth, and on the rocks grew a tiny *Muscari* species—most likely *M. discolor*, although it has not been recorded from this location, being a plant of more southern origin.

From Gürün we turned to the southeast, where we encountered a place with very special soil conditions. The soil was white—so unusual-looking that we had to stop and inspect it for ourselves. It had been formed from disintegrated limestone, and every plant in the area was growing in pure lime. Most surprisingly, the same plants grew here as elsewhere: *Iris sari*, *I. stenophylla*, *Colchicum* and *Ornithogalum* species, even a *Leopoldia* species (something resembling the common *Muscari comosum*). Only one plant that we hadn't seen already was growing here. It resembled *Asphodelus fistu-*

losus but the flowers were at least twice as large as stated in that species' description. The only alternative was *Asphodeline tenuior* var. *puberulenta*, which was known to grow near Gürün in dry, open places. When I read in the description of this *Asphodeline* that all the leaves could be basal, I knew we'd found the right name. I had never tried growing any *Asphodeline*, but this plant was so compact, only some 40 cm tall, and so attractive with its pyramidal inflorescence of large, light pink blossoms, that I decided to give it a try. Unfortunately it did not come up in spring. Similar white, limey slopes are very characteristic for *Muscari adilii* (Plate 283), a recently described and very rare species with deep blue flowers and large seedpods. I have only seedlings from this rarity, which is still known from only three localities, and can only imagine how beautiful its deep blue flower spikes must look against a pure white background.

At the following stops we found only one novelty: *Crocus pallasii*, a beautiful autumn-flowering species whose very silky, netted tunic makes it easy to distinguish from other crocuses. Subspecies *pallasii* grew here, with lighter or deeper lilac-blue perianth segments, red or orange style branches, and a weakly developed "neck" of old tunics at the apex of the corm. Subspecies *turcicus* has a long neck and is distributed more to the east and south. Subspecies *dispathaceus* has a reddish purple perianth and pale yellow style branches and is more characteristic of northern Syria, although there are some gatherings from Turkey, too. *Crocus pallasii* is a good grower in the greenhouse and forms very large corms, increasing well vegetatively and setting seed, especially if the grower offers some help with the pollination. By the time it flowers in my region the bees are no longer very active, leaving their hives only if the days are very sunny and warm.

At every stop in this area we found specimens of *Colchicum*, *Ornithogalum*, and *Allium*, and we noticed that *Iris stenophylla* was replaced by *I. persica*. Shortly before Göksun, Henrik noticed a *Sternbergia* with large and very twisted leaves. None of us could remember such a plant, but the *Flora of Turkey* explained that *S. clusiana* could have twisted leaves like this.

After Göksun we planned to head back to Cappadocia. On the way there we wanted to check a few mountain ranges and chose to follow a very narrow red line on our map that would take us away from the main roads. This took us across the district from which *Muscari macbeathianum* had been described. Jim and Jenny Archibald had discovered it there but had failed to find it again once the forest had been chopped down and the land plowed up. We stopped at a very strange-looking place in the area marked by small knolls covered with low pines and with plenty of sunbaked clearings. The day was hot and the pines exuded a strong aroma of resin. I found only a few very typical plants of *M. comosum*, but Arnis was more successful. While running through the forest he had spotted a few seedpods on a minute, narrow-leaved *Muscari* species that in overall shape much resembled the true *M. macbeathianum*.

Muscari macbeathianum is a tiny plant that belongs to *Pseudomuscari*, regarded by some botanists as an independent genus. In color it somewhat resembles *M. pallens* from the North Caucasus, having small spikes of white to ice blue flowers without a constricted mouth, and like *M. pallens* it usually does not produce offsets. It is a plant of much drier growing conditions, however, and is probably suitable only for pots in a greenhouse, even though in the wild the soil is wet at flowering time. It is also similar in flower color to *M. coeleste* but has fewer and much broader leaves and grows much further east. The seedlings of *M. macbeathianum* that I grow are from seeds kindly presented to me by the Archibalds.

At the next stop I stayed near the car while Arnis and Henrik tried to reach the melting snow. While they were away I checked the roadsides and found some washed-out tubers of a *Biarum* species. (Roadsides such as this are often good places to look for bulbs. When the roads are resurfaced by bulldozers each spring, the bulbs roll right out of the ground and are very easy to collect if you can get to them before the sun bakes them dry.) I also noticed some *Scilla* seedpods beneath a very large *Juniperus* in pure peat, and while I tried to reach them a few *Corydalis* tubers rolled out, too. By the time my colleagues returned from higher altitudes I had no doubt about the species names: these were *Scilla ingridae* and *Corydalis tauricola*.

Corydalis tauricola is a delightful plant that grows in southern Anatolia and the eastern Taurus Mountains, usually in hornbeam woods, where it forms pea-sized tubers. In the garden it grows larger but still retains its dwarf habit, with large, broad-lipped blooms in colors ranging from white to pale pinkish purple. It grows equally well for me outside and in the greenhouse and increases both vegetatively and from seed.

Corydalis tauricola is replaced in the southwest (around the Mediterranean) by *C. wendelboi* subsp. *wendelboi* and in the northwest (around the Black Sea) by *C. wendelboi* subsp. *congesta*. The variable subspecies *wendelboi* generally has white or pale to smoky bluish flowers. The most spectacular form, 'Abant Wine', has wine-colored flowers and was found above Lake Abant. (Unfortunately, it is the only Turkish wine I can recommend—the Turkish version of the kind found in bottles is most unpleasant.) Subspecies *congesta* is a more compact plant with denser racemes and broader, light bluish flowers. All forms of *C. wendelboi* are easy to grow in the garden or greenhouse.

Another relative, *Corydalis paschei*, is still known only from two localities within the area of the type subspecies of *C. wendelboi*. In my opinion it is one of the best in this group, with very distinctive foliage of rounded lobes and bracts, and erect, pinkish lilac racemes. The flowers are on long pedicels, giving the inflorescence a very attractive shape, and like *C. wendelboi* it grows easily both outside and in a greenhouse. *Corydalis paschei* was discovered in 1985 by Erich Paschee and Manfred Koenen and was described at Gothenburg, from where my stock originates. Another species, *C. haussknechtii*, grows in Kurdistan. I lost my stock quickly because it started into growth so early in spring.

Just as I began worrying about where my friends had gone off to, they arrived very tired and happy, having found a beautiful, tiny, very deep blue *Muscari* species flowering side by side with *Anemone blanda* and *Scilla ingridae*. In the brightness of its flowers the *Muscari* resembled the mysterious species or hybrid we had seen on the Sakaltutan mountain pass, but this was a very miniature plant. The three of us agreed that it must be a new species and decided that our next expedition to this district would have to include a more detailed scrutiny of the area.

At Cappadocia we again stayed at the S.O.S. Hotel, where we were welcomed and treated like well-known regulars. But before entering the cave district we stopped by some sandstone outcrops of tufa where there was plenty of another dwarf *Muscari* species. Its seeds were almost ripe and it stood only some 7 cm tall with five to ten blooms in a spike. The bulbs were very shallow in the soil, only a few centimeters down, and globular. We had no way of knowing what this species was before seeing it flower, but needless to say we hoped it would be something beautiful. Arnis later found a very tiny *Leopoldia* species on the other side of the city. It too was a size we had never seen before. Had its arid growing conditions reduced its dimensions or was the trait inherited? This was a question that could only be answered in the garden.

I had been here a year before and had seen hundreds of *Iris galatica* plants on each slope, but they were all infested with worms. Now there were almost no Juno irises left. Nature is sometimes very cruel—a serious invasion of a pest or disease can destroy large populations. Yet there are always seeds remaining in the soil from which these populations can rebuild themselves. I well remember how long I searched for just one healthy specimen of *Allium giganteum* at the Kopet-Dag in Turkmenistan. I found none.

On the way back we wanted to see the type locality of *Hyacinthella campanulata*. This is one of the largest and most beautiful Turkish hyacinthellas, featuring pale blue, campanulate blooms with large, spreading lobes in dense spikes. Especially exciting are the deep blue, even blackish anthers in the center of its blooms. It is quite a rare plant and grows on limestone cliffs near Konya. Henrik knew its type locality well, but there were no bulbs there. Only when we were some 10 km away did we see some naturally terraced limestone slopes. Here we found a sea of this beautiful species.

We made another stop near a large limestone factory and found one more *Muscari* species at the edge of a quarry. It was the first *Muscari* with distinctly yellowish-toned bulb tunics. The color of the bulb tunic is often important for identification, but in this case we couldn't find anything like it in the *Flora of Turkey*. Since I haven't yet seen it in flower, this plant remains another nameless number in my collection.

Crocus Paradise

I never searched specifically for crocuses during my trips to Turkey—they simply fell into my hands during my pursuit of other plants. In Turkey they grow almost everywhere. Here I will discuss some of the crocuses I haven't already mentioned.

The most beautiful and common crocuses in the garden are those with annulate corm tunics (those that split into rings at the corm's base), and the most widespread of these are the various subspecies of blue-white *Crocus biflorus* and its yellow cousin, *C. chrysanthus*. For the moment I must return to southern Anatolia, where between

Muğla and Konya grows the beautiful *C. biflorus* subsp. *isauricus* (Plate 288). Several crocuses feature true black in their flowers, whether it is the color of the stigma or the anthers. In the case of subspecies *isauricus* the connective part of the anthers is black or grayish. The flower color of this crocus is quite variable, ranging from lilac-blue to white, and sometimes the petals have a buff exterior. The petal exteriors are also usually strongly feathered or striped. On the way to Ermenek I found an especially beautiful plant with buff-colored outer petals. It was growing side by side with *Colchicum imperatoris-frederici*. The attractiveness of the flowers depends very much on the weather conditions: this buff-toned plant was extremely lovely after a warm summer, but the following year it looked like nothing special, regaining its beauty a year later.

There are several subspecies of *Crocus biflorus* with black anthers. Two of them, subspecies *melantherus* and subspecies *stridii*, come from Greece. The first is autumn-flowering, the second spring-flowering. In gardens subspecies *melantherus* is mostly known under the name *C. crewei*, which grows in southwestern Turkey and is a spring-flowering crocus. My plants of subspecies *melantherus* were collected near Manthira in the Peloponnese, Greece, and have a small but very bright orange-yellow throat in which the black anthers look very striking. I tried growing it several times outside but always lost it. It now grows perfectly in my greenhouse. When I lost subspecies *stridii* in the same way it was no longer possible to buy.

I grow two of the three Turkish subspecies with black anthers: the true subspecies *crewei*, with very few but broad leaves, and subspecies *nubigena* (Plate 289), with more numerous but very narrow leaves. Flower color in both varies from whitish to light blue with prominent stripes along the petal exteriors. Subspecies *crewei* can grow in my region only in a greenhouse, but subspecies *nubigena* is a plant of high altitudes and therefore can withstand outdoor conditions.

An autumn-flowering form of *Crocus biflorus* was also recently found in Turkey. It is named subspecies *wattiorum* and has beautiful, entirely violet blooms. It is a very rare plant and I have never had it, but I received another new form quite accidentally under the name subspecies *isauricus*. For some years I grew it as "false isauricus," but it is extremely beautiful, with a throat of such a bright orange-yellow that it shines through the petals. The outer design of the petals differs a little from the photograph shown in *The Plantsman* (Kerndorff and Pasche 2003), but in all other aspects it perfectly corresponds with the description of *C. biflorus* subsp. *atrospermus* (Plate 290). I would include it among the most colorful spring crocuses. In color brightness it somewhat resembles *C. cyprius*, another annulate crocus. My stock of *C. cyprius* (Plate 291) originates from Hendrik van Bogaert and has deep blue flowers with an almost orange throat and a blackish purple basal "tongue" on the petal exteriors. In general it is somewhat similar to subspecies *atrospermus* but has more rounded petals and the deep yellow throat is usually not visible from the outside. Both are plants of quite arid regions and I grow them only in a greenhouse.

The subspecies of *Crocus biflorus* are not the only crocuses that feature black in their flowers. Some forms of their yellow relative, *C. chrysanthus*, also have black in their blooms. The black tips of *C. chrysanthus* anthers are nothing unusual, but there are reports of forms with entirely black anthers (although I have not seen this for myself). 'Sunspot' (Plate 292), a most unusual form from the Taurus Mountains, even has a black stigma. I don't know of any other crocus with this feature. This black stigma combined with bright orange-yellow petals makes 'Sunspot' a most attractive plant.

Crocus chrysanthus is a very widespread species, growing wild from Bulgaria to Greece and central and southern Turkey. Not surprisingly, different chromosome numbers have been recorded from various populations, with $2n$ ranging from 8 to 20. The form with $2n = 8$ is one of the brightest and most early-flowering; it was collected in Turkey near the village of Uschak and named 'Uschak Orange' by the Van Tubergen nursery. It has orange-toned flowers and is among the first spring crocuses to bloom—only Central Asian crocuses bloom earlier in some years, but quite often they all show their noses through the snow at the same time. The style of 'Uschak Orange' was bright orange in the first stock I received from Van Tubergen. I later received a stock with a yellow style, but in other aspects the plants are identical.

From the seedlings of my *Crocus chrysanthus* stocks I selected 'Goldmine' (Plate 293), a very special form with semi-double flowers. I received another nice form from Czech growers who collected it near Gencek, Turkey (Plate 294). It has not yet been named, but its deep purple or even blackish purple flower tube contrasts well with its deep yellow perianth. It is not as unusual as 'Sunspot' but is very impressive, especially before its blooms have fully opened.

Crocus chrysanthus readily cross-pollinates with *C. biflorus*, and many varieties have been selected. One of the pioneers in their hybridization was E. A. Bowles, who always had a "cook's fork" in his pocket at the flowering time of crocuses. He wrote about *C. chrysanthus* in *My Garden in Spring* (1914):

> So, if there is an extra fine white flower with orange throat, a deeper blue self than ever before, or some specially peacocky chameleon with an inventive genius for external markings, I shall shout and flop on my knees regardless of mud and my best knickers donned for the visitors, and the cook's fork will tenderly extract the prize.

How familiar all of this is to me, too. Many years ago I collected open-pollinated seeds of the so-called *C. chrysanthus* cultivars, and from the seedlings I selected many beautiful forms. In those years I had a very good collection with almost all of the varieties available at that time. When my collection became too large I gave these varieties to other growers, and I'm afraid that very few are still grown in Latvia. However, I still grow some of the forms I selected, and a few have even been named. 'Charmer' has soft creamy yellow blooms with a dark grayish yellow throat and petals with a beautiful light lilac flush over the back. 'Snow Crystal' (Plate 295) has flowers that are pure white inside with a greenish yellow throat, while on the outside they are a slightly creamy-flushed white with a large, deep purple tongue at the base of the petals. Both of these plants have exceptionally large, rounded blooms and to me they are far better growers than the recent Dutch-raised varieties.

I don't think it's exactly appropriate to claim that all of these cultivars belong to *Crocus chrysanthus*. Many of them, especially the white and blue ones, are hybrids with *C. biflorus* sensu lato, and in my view it would be better to apply to them the hybrid name *C.* ×*annulati*, in such a way emphasizing that they all have annulate corm tunics. In the wild *C. chrysanthus* and *C. biflorus* rarely meet—the former is generally a plant of drier places at lower altitudes, while the latter grows near melting snow at higher altitudes. But where they meet, hybrids can occur.

Another very small plant with the same type of tunic is the tiny *Crocus danfordiae*. I collected this species in a very open pine wood on a sunbaked rocky slope. Its seeds were ripe. It is easy to identify by its small corms, which are covered with very hard, coriaceous tunics. The flowers, which seem to be the smallest of the annulate crocuses, are pale yellow or blue, rarely white. It is not an eye-catcher and is best described as a species for crocus aficionados. I grow all forms of it only in a greenhouse. Having seen its wild habitat, I will never try growing it outside.

There are some other *Crocus* species from Turkey that I want to mention here, although I collected only a few of them myself. One form, *C. reticulatus* subsp. *hittiticus*, has black anthers but does not belong to the annulate crocuses. It has more weakly structured petals than the type subspecies and is much more difficult in cultivation. All the stocks I have grown outside have died within a few years. This subspecies is not difficult in the greenhouse, however. Soon after Gülnar I found a very beautiful form near a road to Gökbelen, where it grew on a flat, stony field among small shrubs. This form has more strongly structured petals. The back of the outer petals is slightly creamy in shade, and instead of having solid purple stripes, the petals are only speckled. This plant also seems to be a better grower.

Crocus ancyrensis is another Turkish crocus with a coarsely reticulated tunic and bright yellow flowers. As the name suggests, it grows around Ankara, but it is actually distributed much more widely in central Turkey. I have many acquisitions from Turkey collected by various travelers but have not found any differences between them—all have very bright blooms, are excellent growers outside, and are very floriferous. The flowers of *C. ancyrensis* are uniformly colored and rounded in shape, not starry as in the closely related *C. angustifolius* and the blue *C. reticulatus*. There are records of clones with a purple flower tube, but I have never seen any of them.

Crocus gargaricus (Plate 296) is a very beautiful yellow species from Turkey, and in my garden it grows much better when I do not pay any attention to it. When I received my first corms of *C. gargaricus* subsp. *herbertii* from Michael Hoog, I planted them in a peaty, sandy soil under an old apple tree, and they have been growing there for more than twenty-five years without any problems. Whenever I lose plants in the nursery, I use plants from this spot to rebuild my stock. Two forms are known to gardeners as subspecies, although these names are not accepted by Brian Mathew (1982) or the *Flora of Turkey*. Still, since they are important to ordinary growers, I prefer to keep this division. The form grown under the name subspecies *herbertii* is stoloniferous and usually produces corms that are very minute, sometimes even less than 5 mm in diameter, as well as smaller blooms. The corms are almost impossible to collect; some will always remain in the soil, marking the place where the plants grew in previous years. When planted in a permanent place this form slowly spreads. Another form, subspecies *gargaricus*, usually makes larger corms, up to 10 mm in diameter or more, and forms larger blooms. When I first received this subspecies it was unidentified and the blooms were so large that I initially thought it might be *C. flavus*. In 1629 John Parkinson described the flowers of *C. flavus* as a "deeper gold yellow . . . so that they appear reddish withal" (Bowles 1952), but I have never seen such intensely colored specimens. For me *C. gargaricus* more closely matches this description. Some of my stocks really are orange-toned, especially in the throat, which is an even deeper orange than the petals.

Crocus flavus is one of the most widely grown yellow crocuses, although one plant distributed under this name is actually a sterile hybrid with *C. angustifolius* in which the features of *C. flavus* dominate (in another hybrid, *C. ×stellaris*, the features of *C. angustifolius* dominate). It is sold under many names. I prefer a cultivar named 'Dutch Yellow', which is quite similar to the wild form only larger and sterile. I grew it for many years but finally lost it during a harsh winter. Now I grow only the fertile, truly wild species, which I received from Willem van Eeden in the Netherlands. I have never had the opportunity to grow a form of known wild origin, neither have I searched for such. *Crocus flavus* is easy to distinguish from other species by the presence at the corm apex of a long brown "neck" of the old cataphylls. They are so strongly attached to the corm that they can be cut off only with scissors, especially if the corms are harvested before the leaves have completely desiccated. In the wild it is very widespread from Bulgaria and Romania through northern Greece to northwestern Turkey. Further south and higher in the mountains it is replaced by subspecies *dissectus*, in which the style is distinctly dissected into six or more slender branches (in subspecies *flavus* it is dissected into only three short branches). I grew it from seed that was sent to me by Chris Brickell in the 1970s, but although it did very well, the entire stock was eaten by mice a few years after the first flowering. I collected it again at the edge of a light pine forest north of Antalya, where it was easily recognizable by the very long, persistent neck of old tunics. The corms of subspecies *dissectus* lie some 20 cm deep in the soil.

A smaller relative, *Crocus olivieri*, has a similar wide distribution. There are three subspecies, two of which I grow. The form of subspecies *olivieri* in my collection came from Lake Abant in Bolu Province, northwestern Turkey, and is almost as bright as *C. gargaricus*. I have not yet tried to grow it outside, but it must be hardy. Subspecies *balansae* is more widely distributed in gardens and is offered by Dutch companies, too. The best form has deep orange-yellow blooms with chocolate brown exteriors. Unfortunately, I do not have this form, and the form that I do have is quite an ordinary plant with yellow flowers striped brown on the back of the outer petals. It also flowers later than the similarly colored forms of *C. chrysanthus*. The main difference between this form and the type subspecies is the style, which in subspecies *balansae* is split into twelve to fifteen branches, while in subspecies *olivieri* there are only five to six branches. Subspecies *balansae* is very easy in the garden and I grow it on open beds.

Before turning to the bluish species I want to mention one very special crocus: *Crocus fleischeri* (Plate 297). It is quite a unique crocus and one that you will never confuse with any other species, whether it is in flower or you have nothing but its corm. The corms are bright yellow and covered with a distinctive tunic in which the fibers are interwoven. I once received a complaint from a Russian customer who insisted that the white blooms of *C. fleischeri* that he had been promised had in fact come up blue. I had to explain to him why this wasn't possible. Mistakes occur at any nursery, but the corms of *C. fleischeri* are so unique that they could never be confused with those of another species. Even if a mouse brought the wrong corm to a box of *C. fleischeri*, it would be impossible to overlook the imposter.

Crocus fleischeri is readily obtainable from various nurseries, although I think that for the most part the best forms are not offered. The commercial form is late-flowering and has uniformly white blooms with a multi-branched, bright orange or scarlet stigma in the center. Stocks of wild origin flower earlier. Plants from the Gülek Boğazi mountain pass have a large, deep orange-yellow throat, but I prefer the form collected between Kale and Muğla, which has a small but very dark blackish throat changing to a more greenish shade at the edge. Its corms are usually very small; the small cormlets remain between the sheaths, sometimes creating the impression of a larger corm. Until the black frosts of December 2002 I grew *C. fleischeri* without any problems in the garden, but that winter I lost all my stocks and was left with only the few corms I had planted in the greenhouse. According to Ole Sønderhousen, this species sometimes makes stolons and prefers alkaline soils (Mathew 1982). Despite the small size of its flowers, it is a very valuable plant for its bright colors. When I found it in the wild it was generally growing beneath pines and among small shrubs.

Crocus mathewii, found only recently and named in honor of Brian Mathew, features a deep purple-blue throat below white petals. A bluish throat is not unusual among crocuses—it is common for spring-flowering *C. michelsonii* from the Kopet-Dag and not atypical for autumn-flowering crocuses—but it is rarely combined with pure white petals. The Greek form of *C. cartwrightianus* exhibited at the Sussex show in the autumn of 2003 by Pat Nicholls (who kindly presented me with a few corms) so closely resembled *C. mathewii* in color that only the long, red style branches helped to correctly identify it. *Crocus mathewii* is not a difficult species, although it is somewhat tender. In Latvia I lost the plants that I tried growing outside, but in the greenhouse this species sets seed perfectly, and the seeds germinate well. It is among the most beautiful autumn-flowering crocuses, and I hope it will soon become much more widely available. In the wild it is known only from several localities in the provinces of Muğla and Antalya in southern Turkey.

There are four blue crocus species from Turkey that I want to mention, all non-annulate except one. If someone were to ask which was my favorite, it would be difficult to answer. First is *Crocus adanensis*, significant for its excellent combination of colors. Then there is *C. baytopiorum*, the most unusually colored species, and *C. antalyensis*, a close relative of the yellow-blooming species. Finally there is *C. abantensis*, which in my experience is the best grower. Each species has its own merits. I grow two of them successfully in both the open garden and the greenhouse.

Although *Crocus adanensis* (Plate 298) is included among the annulate crocuses, the basal rings of its tunics are poorly developed. It is most closely related to *C. biflorus*, though its tunic is thin and vertically split. It is a plant of southern Turkey and is known only from one locality. I received my corms from Hendrik van Bogaert in Belgium and another stock from Gothenburg, but both turned out to be identical. The flowers are light lilac without any blue shade and with somewhat pointed petals. The flower exterior is somewhat buff-toned with a grayish-flecked base. In the wild it grows in a district with mild winters and dry summers. I have not tried growing it outside, and I almost lost it to frost once even in a greenhouse, but I like it very much just for the shape of its blooms combined with its large, starry white throat.

Once you have seen the flowers of *Crocus baytopiorum* (Plate 299) you will never mix this species up with any other. It is generally described as having pale blue flowers, but I would add that this color is enhanced by a slightly greenish shade. Like *Bellevalia forniculata* and *Corydalis solida* 'Zwanenburg', it is very eye-catching from afar. In the same way that *Crocus adanensis* has no shade of blue, this species has no shade of violet or lilac, and the blooms are marked with delicate, slightly darker veins. The throat is described as white, but it is not the white of *C. adanensis*; rather, it is a white with a grayish or very pale greenish shade. *Crocus baytopiorum* is a plant from open limestone screes in southwestern Turkey in the Honaz-Dag and has also been found from Denizli to Antalya. For many years I grew it outside, but each spring as I approached the bed where it had been planted, I did so with a trembling heart—had it survived the winter? Even though I have never lost it and it grows in the open in the Netherlands, I now prefer to keep it in a greenhouse. In this way I get seeds from it every season, which didn't occur in the open garden due to its very early flowering.

For me the most problematic of the blue crocuses has been *Crocus antalyensis*. I have lost most of my stocks of this species, presumably because I planted them too shallowly thereby causing them to suffer from winter frosts even in the greenhouse. In the wild the corms lie at a depth of 20 cm, but somehow I always forgot this at planting time. *Crocus antalyensis* is related to *C. flavus* subsp. *dissectus* and has a similar long neck formed by the persistent old sheathing leaves, but it can be easily distinguished by its blue flower color. It is grown outside in the Netherlands by some nurseries and is quite variable in color. I had two strikingly different forms: one with clear blue blooms and a bright yellow throat, the other with heavily striped purple blooms. There are reports of a white form, too. I now have only seedlings of *C. antalyensis* and these have not yet flowered, but I hope to rebuild my stock within a few years.

I have different stocks of *Crocus abantensis* (Plate 300), which undoubtedly is the best-growing crocus of this blue quartet of Turkish species. Some were collected by my Czech friends, some came from the Gothenburg Botanical Garden, and some came from Dutch bulb growers. Superficially *C. abantensis* is quite similar to *C. biflorus* subsp. *pulchricolor*, but it has a reticulate tunic, so it is not surprising that it was overlooked for so long, being quite a common plant at its type locality near Lake Abant, Bolu Province. I even have a stock received from a British gardener that is still labeled "*Crocus* species sub nom *abantensis* but annulate" and not distinguishable by flower from true *C. abantensis*. In color *C. abantensis* varies from mid to deep blue with a yellow throat. It increases well both vegetatively and from seed in the garden or greenhouse. In my garden it is one of the most vigorous species and has even withstood winters when most other outdoor crocuses were severely damaged. This should come as no surprise, since in the wild it grows in mountain meadows near melting snow. Two of my stocks were reportedly collected at altitudes of 1500 m and 1700 m, although Brian Mathew (1982) describes *C. abantensis* as growing between 1100 m and 1350 m.

Crocus abantensis is related to *C. sieberi* from Greece and Crete but is easily distinguished by its much narrower leaves and much bluer flowers (*C. sieberi* is always definitely lilac or violet in tone). Although *C. sieberi* is not from Turkey, I can't finish this book without describing it and its relatives, which form another group of crocuses of special beauty.

Crocus sieberi and all its forms have quite a limited distribution, growing in Crete and throughout Greece. There are four recognized subspecies. The type subspecies, which grows only in Crete, is the most tender of all *C. sieberi* forms and is undoubtedly among the most variable. The first bulb in my collection had the traditional color: deep purple with a white band across the petals near their tips. I received it from Chris Brickell in the 1970s and lost it after two winters in the open garden. I received the next corm from Eduard Hanslik in the Czech Republic who had collected it in Crete, and by then I had my first glasshouse. When this plant flowered it turned out to be a beautiful, pure white form. It was a good increaser and within a few years I had built up a good stock. I decided to name it 'Cretan Snow' (Plate 301). It is a comparatively small but abundantly flowering plant with medium-sized, pure white, rounded blooms, a large golden yellow throat, and a small purplish-shaded blotch at the base of the outer petals. In color it is similar to the famous 'Bowles' White', which E. A. Bowles described as appearing among his seedlings "after thirty years of hopeful expectation" (1952). 'Bowles' White' is a plant of incredible beauty, its large, pure snow white, rounded petals complemented by a yellow throat edged in bright orange. I have never gotten any seed from it, so it is clearly of hybrid origin. It can undoubtedly be listed among the best white spring-flowering crocuses. It is a plant for the open garden, but in some seasons I have lost it in my own garden, so I always plant some corms in the greenhouse.

I recently received another form of *Crocus sieberi* subsp. *sieberi* from Crete that was collected on the plains of Omalos. It has the more typical color, white on the inside but with outer petals so intensely speckled, striped, and spotted with deep purple at the back that they look purple with a white margin. The throat is a typical deep orange. This form also increases quickly vegetatively. The insufficient hardiness of the Cretan forms prevents subspecies *sieberi* from being more widely distributed in gardens, but it makes an excellent pot plant.

The Greek forms of *Crocus sieberi* are much hardier, although in Latvia even these have sometimes suffered from frost damage after very cold winters. They are divided into three subspecies: the lowland subspecies *atticus*, the higher-altitude subspecies *sublimis* with a pubescent throat, and the higher-altitude subspecies *nivalis* with a glabrous throat. In gardens these plants are generally represented by cultivated forms grown by Dutch nurseries. The cultivated form of subspecies *atticus* has attractive, light violet, somewhat more pointed flowers with a deep orange throat. One of the most beautiful crocuses is *C. sieberi* subsp. *sublimis* f. *tricolor*. Its flowers feature three color zones: a deep yellow throat is surrounded by a wide white zone, and the upper halves of the petals are lilac. All of these colors are easily visible when the flower is closed in bud and are even more prominent when the flower opens in full sunshine. Brian Mathew (1982) has mentioned a form with a fourth color zone: deep purple petal tips. I have plants of subspecies *sublimis* with dark petal tips, but they lack the white zone and are less spectacular than the famous forma *tricolor*. I have never had subspecies *nivalis* in my collection.

Hubert Edelsten succeeded in crossing the Cretan subspecies *sieberi* with subspecies *atticus* from the mainland. The resulting hybrid has the color of the best Cretan forms but the larger blooms and hardiness of the Greek forms. The best selection, 'Hubert Edelsten', is an excellent crocus. Its deep purple flowers have a very prominent white cross-band at the tips of the petals and a deep orange throat. The purple on the flower exterior is so deep that when the flower opens the inside color seems somewhat rose-toned even though it is almost white. The inner petals are white with small purple tips on the outside. 'Hubert Edelsten' is much hardier than the Cretan forms but is more susceptible to frost damage than other forms. In one or two seasons I lost all the plants growing in my open garden; only the few corms that had been planted in my greenhouse survived. Dutch nurseryman Willem van Eeden selected a more large-flowered, rounded mutation from 'Hubert Edelsten' and named it 'George' in honor of George Rodionenko. In Latvia it always flowers later.

In the 1970s a new autumn-flowering species, *Crocus robertianus*, was described by Chris Brickell. In the mid-1980s I bought five corms of it, freshly collected from Greece, from Michael Hoog, but they all flowered in spring and turned out to be *C. sieberi*. With its beautiful lilac petals and bright orange throat, this form of *C. sieberi* is very different from all the other forms I have known. Its petals are thinly but densely veined a deep lilac on the back. It is very floriferous, a good increaser, and exceptionally hardy. It has never suffered from winter frosts in my open garden and has flowered even in seasons when other forms of *C. sieberi* only dragged out a miserable existence. I named it 'Michael Hoog's Memory'.

I later acquired the true *Crocus robertianus*, a beautiful plant with generally light lilac flowers with a pale yellow throat. There are white forms, too. Overall it is somewhat similar to *C. sieberi*, and Brian Mathew (1982) thinks it has evolved from *C. sieberi* by mutation. It is among the most beautiful autumn crocuses, but I still haven't tried growing it outside, since my stock is too small. I harvest the bulbs in summer because according to Mathew they can suffer if kept too hot and dry.

Crocus dalmaticus is very similar to *C. sieberi*, and various Dutch nurseries offer a plant under this name that is identical to *C. sieberi* 'Firefly'. The true *C. dalmaticus* is quite variable in the wild but is generally distinguished by its light yellow throat, which is never as intensely orange-yellow as that of *C. sieberi*. Additionally, the petal exteriors of *C. sieberi* are never buff, yellowish, or silvery, and the leaves are broader. Even so, it is not always easy to tell these species apart. Both are cytologically and geographically distinct, so they must be regarded as different taxa regardless of their superficial similarities. I grow a strain collected near Petrovac in Montenegro that is quite variable. The exterior of its large lilac-toned blooms varies from cream to pale or deep lilac-purple marked with fine purple lines. The throat varies too, from lighter to darker yellow. Some of these plants are so similar to *C. sieberi* 'Michael Hoog's Memory' that only the deep yellow throat of the latter confirms that the stocks have not mixed. I grow *C. dalmaticus* in the open garden as well as in the greenhouse.

This is not a monograph on crocuses and so not all the species I have grown are mentioned, although many of them are quite lovely. There is one species, however, that I want to list before I finish. Mostly this is for sentimental reasons, but it is also simply a beautiful plant. When I first started collecting and reading about crocuses, I visited the University of Latvia botanical garden. At that time I had only some thirty crocus varieties in my collection. The curator of the rock garden, Andris Orehovs, removed a small pot from a bulb frame. It held a flowering crocus. "What's its name?" he asked. After looking at it for a moment, I whispered, with a trembling heart, "*Crocus corsicus?*" Dr. Orehovs took out the label and read "*C. corsicus*, spont." I had passed his test, and as a reward I received this pot. I think that because I had so many times read Bowles's *Handbook of Crocus and Colchicum for Gardeners* and George Maw's excellent *Monograph of the Genus Crocus*, my mind had formed an image of many species never seen *in vivo*. I still grow this stock. I nearly lost it a couple of times to frost, but on both occasions the corms recovered from the tiny remnants after the mother corms had been killed. Now I grow it only in a greenhouse, where it flowers beautifully every spring, its bright violet blooms deeply striped outside with purple. It sets seed well, too.

◆ 26
Dream Destinations

T HE BULB WORLD is very large. Bulbs grow almost everywhere. Not all of them would grow in Latvia, however. Most South African bulbs are very difficult in cultivation, and I have never tried them myself despite their beauty. It is simply impossible to grow everything. There are many bulbs in tropical countries that are not hardy at all.

I grow quite a lot of North American bulbs, but I'm afraid I will never go to North America to search for bulbs in the wild. So many people already grow them, and so many seeds are available—even without going there myself I have a very good collection of bulbs from the northern United States, especially *Allium* species. *Fritillaria* and *Erythronium* are less well represented, although I am interested in growing species from both genera. *Calochortus* species are the only bulbs I don't grow at all. I once ordered the "beginner's collection" of seeds from Jim Archibald, but he sent me a collection meant for "experts in *Calochortus*," which included seeds of the most difficult species. I was very surprised by my results—about half of the species flowered—but later I sent all my bulbs to a friend in Belgium.

Bulbs of North America (McGary 2001) is an excellent book that describes bulbous plants in the wild and the secrets to their successful cultivation. No other book covers all the species so completely; it is my reference for North American bulbs. Likewise, *Trillium* species are discussed in *Trilliums* by Frederick and Roberta Case (1997), and I don't know of a better source of information dealing with all aspects of *Trillium* culture. I have learned many secrets from this book, too, although trilliums are not among my favorites.

To me a more interesting destination would be the extreme end of South America, where many *Oxalis* and some dwarf *Alstroemeria* grow. I especially like hardy species of *Oxalis*, the most widely grown of which is *O. adenophylla* . This plant is easy to obtain from Dutch nurseries, although it is mostly propagated in Poland because there is a lot of handwork needed for dividing the clumps. It is not difficult in the garden but prefers sandy soils because it is susceptible to waterlogging. The common Dutch form has large, rosy lilac blooms that are whitish at the base with a deep purple eye in the center. It flowers so abundantly that the open blooms completely cover the beautiful, deeply dissected leaves. In the wild it is extremely variable, ranging from pure white to dark blue and purple. I have two other small-growing clones. One has whitish petals changing at the edges to lilac with a green eye. The other is entirely deep rosy lilac with darker veins, much brighter than the Dutch clone. This last selection is most unique for its foliage: each leaf is deep reddish purple at the center and the lobes are purple-toned at the edge. Though tiny, this plant is ornamental even without blooms. I named it 'Purple Heart' (Plate 302).

Oxalis laciniata and *O. patagonica* have beautiful foliage and large blooms. The leaf lobes are extremely curved and wavy, accompanied by deep blue or purple, darkly veined flowers. *Oxalis ennaephylla*, too, has flowers quite variable in color. All grow in the wild in southern Chile, Patagonia, and the Falkland Islands but are surprisingly hardy in my region. At first I tried growing them in the greenhouse, where they did superbly despite the hot and dry conditions during the summer. When I planted half of my stocks outside, I was extremely surprised to find that they survived even after a terrible black frost that seriously damaged many crocuses. Alas, South America is extremely far away from Latvia and I'm afraid I will never go there. All I can do is hope that someone will collect more beautiful forms of these tiny plants, as Peter Erskine did when he brought so many nice forms to Britain. Unfortunately, photographs are all that remain of many of Peter's plants after a rust killed them off in his garden. This is doubly unfortunate since chemicals such as Tilt are now available that can stop all kinds of rusts after a single spray. From Peter I received a few rhizomes of *O. patagonica* 'Seven Bells' and 'Sweet Sue', which grow perfectly and increase well in my garden. He originally collected 'Sheffield Swan' on the Falkland Islands, and a stock of it was carefully increased by my great friend Kath Dryden. It has large, pure white blooms. Harold McBride in Scotland has also obtained many beautiful hybrids between *O. laciniata* and *O. ennaephylla*. Kirsten Andersen in Denmark has a magnificent collection and sent me many of the unusual forms she collected in Argentina.

Most important is that the aforementioned *Oxalis* species are hardy, unlike the South African and Central American species, which must be overwintered in frost-free conditions. In my collection I also grow a very nice species from the Far East. *Oxalis obtriangularis* has green leaves (in shape resembling the native Latvian *O. triangularis*), which in my region come up in the beginning of May together with creamy white blooms. It is a nice rhizomatous plant for shady locations and is absolutely hardy here, although its leaves can be killed by late-night frosts. In the extreme spring of 2005 the leaves of my plants were killed this way three times; after the third episode, no new leaves emerged and the harvested rhizomes were very tiny.

Alstroemerias also grow in South America and have tuber-like roots. They are not generally considered to be hardy in Latvia, but after considering the altitudes at which some dwarf species grow in the wild, I decided to experiment with them. The first species to reach me from Jim Archibald was *Alstroemeria pygmaea* (Plate 303). I raised it from seed reportedly collected in Argentina, and it turned out to be very dwarf and perfectly hardy (in an unheated greenhouse!), with beautiful, red-spotted, bright yellow blooms emerging among grayish leaves. Reaching only 5 cm tall, this species is marvelous for pots, and it seems that it could be hardy even outside in a well-drained, sunny spot. As far as I can tell its only flaw is its habit of shooting ripened seeds a good distance away from the mother plant, which causes seedlings to appear among other plants, on paths between beds in the greenhouse, or even in seedling boxes of other bulbs. In this way it has become a kind of "weed" for me. I now grow a few other *Alstroemeria* species, but they have not yet flowered. *Alstroemeria pygmaea* starts blooming in its second year after sowing.

Returning to nearer regions, I would like to visit China to see the beautiful *Corydalis*, *Fritillaria*, and *Arisaema* species growing there. Unfortunately the most interesting country, Afghanistan, is off-limits for botanical expeditions. Some Czechs offer seeds claimed to have been collected from the wild in Afghanistan, but I'm afraid that these are probably of garden origin.

Many of the plants that I grow come from Iran. I cannot forget my expedition to Kopet-Dag and would like to see more of it. I would also like to visit the Zagros Mountains—in fact, at some point in the future I will undoubtedly join a "green" tour and travel there armed with nothing but my camera. I must also visit Greece, Serbia and Montenegro, and the Mediterranean islands, where so many bulbs grow that are still unknown to me. Then perhaps a day will come for the Maritime Alps in France, where Alan Edwards found the autumn-flowering *Crocus medius*—its incredibly large blooms surpass even the biggest blooms of the Dutch spring crocuses. I would also like to see the meadows of wild narcissus growing in Spain, even though I don't want to grow them (they're not hardy here and all my greenhouses are occupied by other bulbs). There are wild populations of *Erythronium dens-canis* in Spain, too, as well as *Allium moly* and many crocuses, although I cannot pride myself on much success in growing them.

Trips are quite expensive, so I still like to seize the opportunity when a botanical garden offers to send me on an expedition. This helps me keep my expenses down. My next trip will be to Turkey, and then to Armenia in the Caucasus, where the living conditions have gradually improved. Beyond that, who knows what awaits me?

Now the season has ended, the bulbs are replanted, and "I see the rows of labels sticking up in the frames and seed-beds in August just after replanting. 'Looks rather like a cemetery, doesn't it?' friends mockingly ask. 'I don't mind,' say I, 'so long as it has an annual resurrection" (E. A. Bowles, *My Garden in Spring*).

Descriptiones Plantarum Novarum (Descriptions of New Plants)

Allium karataviense subsp. *henrikii* **Ruksans, subsp. nov.**

Typus: Uzbekistan, western end of the Karzhantau Range, Camel Mount near Tashkent at Tovaksai, stony slopes, Ruksans & Seisums 1996-2-5, *ARJA 9678* (GB, holo, ex culturae in horto Janis Ruksans). Ic.: *Buried Treasures* (Portland, OR, 2007), Plate 95.

A subspecies *typica* scapus valde longius folius bone differt.

Erythronium sibiricum subsp. *altaicum* **Ruksans, subsp. nov.**

Typus: Russia, republic of Tuva, upper course of the river Ka-hem, altitude 2300–2500 m, alpine meadows (GB, holo, ex culturae in horto Janis Ruksans). Ic.: *Buried Treasures* (Portland, OR, 2007), Plate 220.

A subspecies *typica* flores colores (albidus), florescentia praecox et plantes magnus bone differt. Plantes alpinus (subsp. *sibiricum*—plantes subalpinus).

Erythronium sibiricum subsp. *sulevii* **Ruksans, subsp. nov.**

Typus: Russia, Altay region, village of Altayskiy, near the border with the Altay Republic, forest edge (GB, holo, ex culturae in horto Janis Ruksans). Ic.: *Buried Treasures* (Portland, OR, 2007), Plate 221.

A subspecies *typica* antherae colorae anthracinus bone differt.

Iris pseudocapnoides **Ruksans, sp. nov.**

Typus: Uzbekistan, Chimgan, on rocky outcrops, Ruksans 1975, Ruksans & Seisums 1996-28-4, *ARJA 9622* (GB, holo, ex culturae in horto Janis Ruksans). Ic.: *Buried Treasures* (Portland, OR, 2007), Plates 108 and 109.

Subgen. *Scorpiris*. Radices longae, tumidae. Caulis c. 30 cm altus. Folia p.m. falcate sensim angustata, infima 25–30 mm lata, initio approximata, demum distantia. Flores 2–5, albus. Perigonii phylla exteriora ad unguem nervo aureolinus percursa; crista alba crenata; interiora 17–22 mm longa, trilobata.

Iris capnoides et *I. orchioides* affinis. A *I. capnoides* flores colores et radices longioribus bone differt; a *I. orchioides* crista crenata (*I. orchioides*—ciliata) et radices vel tumidae bone differt.

Iris pskemense Ruksans, sp. nov.

Typus: Uzbekistan, Pskem Range, Ihnachsai, stony slopes, altitude 2500–3000 m, Ruksans & Seisums 1998-17-6, *ARJA 9865* (GB, holo, ex culturae in horto Janis Ruksans). Ic.: *Buried Treasures* (Portland, OR, 2007), Plate 138.

Subgen. *Hermodactyloides*. Bulbus tunicis reticulate-fibrosis. Folia 2–4, primum flores non excedentia, demum valde elongate, falcate. Caulis obsolescens. Perigonium colore variabile, pallide coeruleum. Segmenta exteriora cum lamina atroviolacea candido-marginata. Segmenta interiora 3–4 cm longa, erecta, obovata, torsiva, pallide violaceus ad albidus.

Iris kolpakowskiana affinis sed plantes alpinus (*I. kolpakowskiana*—plantes subalpinus); a *I. winkleri* (plantes alpinus) bulbus tunicis reticulate fibrosis bone differt.

Iris reticulata var. *kurdica* Ruksans, var. nov.

Typus: Turkey, 27 km south of Bashkale, 60 km before Hankari, steep serpentine slopes, Ruksans, Seisums, & Zetterlund 2004-27-5, *BATM 04-118* (GB, holo, ex culturae in horto Janis Ruksans), Ic.: Buried Treasures (Portland, OR, 2007), Plates 271 and 272.

Var. nova intermedius var. *typica* et var. *bakeriana*. Folia tetragona (var. *bakeri-ana*—teretia costis 8 distinctus). Flores parvus (var. *typica*—magnus), segmenta exteriora mit ungue sub lamina albidus (var. *typica*—saturate violaceum vel saturate coeruleum); segmenta interiora erecta, 3 cm longa, pallidus purpureus (subroseus) ad albus.

Scilla seisumsiana Ruksans et Zetterlund, sp. nov.

Typus: Turkey, Siirt-Baykan Road, 6 km south from the Silvan-Tatvan junction, altitude 950 m, Ruksans, Seisums, & Zetterlund 2004-25-5, *BATM 04-055* (GB, holo, ex culturae in horto Janis Ruksans).

Ex affinitate *Scilla autumnalis* L. foliis vernalis, scapus non elongatus poste anthesis et flores colores (roseus, non violaceus) bone differt.

Bibliography

Andrusaitis, G., ed. 2003. *Red Data Book of Latvia: Rare and Threatened Plants and Animals.* Vol. 3, Vascular Plants. Riga: Institute of Biology. (In Latvian.)

Artamonov, V. I. 1989. *Rare and Vanishing Plants.* Moscow: Agropromizdat. (In Russian.)

Artjushenko, Z. T. 1970. *Amaryllidaceae of the Soviet Union.* Leningrad: Nauka. (In Russian.)

Avrorin, N. A., ed. 1977. *Ornamental Plants for Open Gardens in the Soviet Union: Monocotyledons.* 2 vols. Leningrad: Nauka. (In Russian.)

Baranova, M. V. 1990. *Lilies.* Leningrad: Agropromizdat. (In Russian.)

Bishop, M., A. Davis, and J. Grimshaw. 2002. *Snowdrops: A Monograph of Cultivated Galanthus.* Maidenhead, United Kingdom: Griffin Press.

Botschantzeva, Z. P. 1982. *Tulips: Taxonomy, Morphology, Cytology, Phytogeography and Physiology.* Ed. H. Q. Varekamp. Rotterdam: A. A. Balkema.

Bowles, E. A. 1914. *My Garden in Spring.* Reprint. Portland, Oregon: Timber Press, 1997.

Bowles, E. A. 1952. *A Handbook of Crocus and Colchicum for Gardeners.* Revised ed. London: Bodley Head.

Bown, D. 2000. *Aroids: Plants of the Arum Family.* 2d ed. Portland, Oregon: Timber Press.

Boyce, P. 1993. *The Genus Arum.* London: Royal Botanic Gardens, Kew.

Bryan, J. E. 2002. *Bulbs.* Revised ed. Portland, Oregon: Timber Press.

Bush, N. 1913. Genus 6: *Corydalis* Vent. In *Flora of Siberia and the Far East*, vol. 1. Saint Petersburg: Academiae Scientiarum. 30–71. (In Russian.)

Case, F. W., Jr., and R. B. Case. 1997. *Trilliums.* Portland, Oregon: Timber Press.

Davies, D. 1992. *Alliums: The Ornamental Onions.* London: Batsford.

Davis, A. P. 1999. *The Genus Galanthus.* Portland, Oregon: Timber Press.

Davis, P. H., ed. 1984. *Flora of Turkey and the East Aegean Islands.* Vol. 8. Edinburgh University Press.

Fedchenko, B. A. 1912. *Flora of Asiatic Russia.* Fasc. 3. Saint Petersburg. (In Russian.)

Fedchenko, B. A., M. G. Popov, B. K. Shishkin, and V. V. Nikitin, eds. 1932. *Flora of Turkmenistan.* Vol. 1. Leningrad: Academiae Scientiarum. (In Russian.)

Fedchenko, O. 1899. *Iris winkleri. Sad i Ogorod* 15 (12): 1. (In Russian.)

Fedorov, A. A., ed. 1979. *Flora Partis Europaeae URSS.* Vol. 4. Leningrad: Nauka. (In Russian.)

Flora Europaea Editorial Committee. 1980. *Flora Europaea*. 5 vols. Cambridge University Press.

Galenieks, P., ed. 1953. *Flora of Latvia*. Vol. 1. Riga: Latvian State Press. (In Latvian.)

Galenieks, P., ed. 1955. *Flora of Latvia*. Vol. 2. Riga: Latvian State Press. (In Latvian.)

Galushko, A. 1978. *Flora of the Northern Caucasus*. Vol. 1. Rostov-na-Donu, Russia: Rostov University Press. (In Russian.)

Gorchakovski, P. L., and E. A. Shurova. 1982. *Rare and Disappearing Plants of the Urals and Surrounding Areas*. Moscow: Nauka. (In Russian.)

Grey-Wilson, C. 1997. *Cyclamen: A Guide for Gardeners, Horticulturists, and Botanists*. Portland, Oregon: Timber Press.

Grey-Wilson, C., and B. Mathew. 1981. *Bulbs: The Bulbous Plants of Europe and Their Allies*. London: Collins.

Grossheim, A. A. 1940. *Flora Caucasica*. Vol. 2. 2d ed. Baku, Azerbaijan. (In Russian.)

Grossheim, A. A. 1950. *Flora Caucasica*. Vol. 4. Moscow, Leningrad: Editio Academiae Scientiarum URSS. (In Russian.)

Güner, A., N. Özhatay, T. Ekim, and K. Hüsnü Baser, eds. 2000. *Flora of Turkey and the East Aegean Islands*. Vol. 11. Edinburgh University Press.

Gusman, G., and L. Gusman. 2002. *The Genus Arisaema: A Monograph for Botanists and Nature Lovers*. Ruggell, Lichtenstein: A.R.G. Gantner Verlag KG.

Hall, T. 1998. The cultivation of Juno irises. *Quarterly Bulletin of the Alpine Garden Society* 66 (3): 282–295.

Halliwell, B. 1992. *The Propagation of Alpine Plants and Dwarf Bulbs*. London: Batsford.

Hohrjakov, A. P. 1965. *Eremurus: Morphology, Biology, Evolution and Systematics*. Moscow: Nauka. (In Russian.)

Ischenko, L. E., M. B. Atayeva, L. E. Soboleva, and S. N. Abramova. 1972. *Wild Ornamental Perennials of Turkmenistan*. Ashkhabad, Turkmenistan: Ilim. (In Russian.)

Jefferson-Brown, M., and K. Pratt. 1997. *The Gardener's Guide to Growing Fritillaries*. Newton Abbot, Devon: David and Charles. Portland, Oregon: Timber Press.

Kamelin, R. V. 1988. *Keybook to the Plants of Turkmenistan*. Leningrad: Nauka. (In Russian.)

Kerndorff, K., and E. Pasche. 2003. *Crocus biflorus* in Anatolia. Part 1. *The New Plantsman* 2: 77–89.

Kerndorff, K., and E. Pasche. 2004. *Crocus biflorus* in Anatolia. Part 2. *The New Plantsman* 3: 201–215.

Kharkevych, S. S., ed. 1987. *Vascular Plants of the Soviet Far East*. Vol. 2. Leningrad: Nauka. (In Russian.)

Kharkevych, S. S., and N. N. Kachura. 1981. *Rare Plants of the Soviet Far East and Their Protection*. Moscow: Nauka. (In Russian.)

Kharkevych, S. S., and S. K. Cherepanov, eds. 1981. *Keybook to the Vascular Plants of Kamtschatka*. Moscow: Nauka. (In Russian.)

Komarov, V., ed. 1935. *Flora of the Soviet Union*. Vol. 4. Leningrad: Editio Academiae Scientiarum URSS. (In Russian.)

Komarov, V., ed. 1937. *Flora of the Soviet Union*. Vol. 7. Leningrad: Editio Academiae Scientiarum URSS. (In Russian.)

Krasnoborov, I. M. 1984. *Keybook to the Plants of the Republic of Tuva*. Novosibirsk, Russia: Nauka. (In Russian.)

Kudrjaschev, S. N., ed. 1941. *Flora Uzbekistanica*. Vol. 1. Tashkent, Uzbekistan: Editio Sectionis Uzbekistanicae Academiae Scientiarum URSS. (In Russian.)

Kurbanov, D. 1998. A new species of the genus *Iridodictyum* (Iridaceae) from Turkmenistan. *Botanicheskii Zhurnal* 83 (6): 110–111. (In Russian.)

Lapin, P. I., ed. 1983. *Rare and Vanishing Plants of the Flora of the Soviet Union Cultivated in Botanical Gardens and Other Introduction Centers of State*. Moscow: Nauka. (In Russian.)

Leeds, R. 2000. *The Plantfinder's Guide to Early Bulbs*. Newton Abbot, Devon: David and Charles. Portland, Oregon: Timber Press.

Lidén, M., and H. Zetterlund. 1988. Notes on the genus *Corydalis*. *Quarterly Bulletin of the Alpine Garden Society* 56 (2): 146–169.

Lidén, M., and H. Zetterlund. 1997. *Corydalis: A Gardener's Guide and a Monograph of the Tuberous Species*. Pershore, United Kingdom: Alpine Garden Society.

Malyshev, L. I., and K. A. Sobolevskaya, eds. 1980. *Rare and Vanishing Plants of Siberia*. Novosibirsk, Russia: Nauka. (In Russian.)

Mathew, B. 1973. *Dwarf Bulbs*. London: Batsford.

Mathew, B. 1978. *The Larger Bulbs*. London: Batsford.

Mathew, B. 1981. *The Iris*. New York: Universe Books.

Mathew, B. 1982. *The Crocus: A Revision of the Genus Crocus (Iridaceae)*. London: Batsford.

Mathew, B. 1987. *The Smaller Bulbs*. London: Batsford.

Mathew, B. 1998. The genus *Erythronium*. *Quarterly Bulletin of the Alpine Garden Society* 66 (3): 308–322.

Mathew, B. 1999. Reticulate irises. *Quarterly Bulletin of the Alpine Garden Society* 67: 299–306.

Maw, G. 1886. *A Monograph of the Genus Crocus*. London: Dulau.

McGary, J., ed. 2001. *Bulbs of North America*. Portland, Oregon: Timber Press.

Ministry of Agriculture, Fisheries and Food. 1984. *Bulb and Corm Production*. Reference book 62. London: Her Majesty's Stationery Office.

Ovcinnikov, P. N., ed. 1963. *Flora of Tajikistan*. Vol. 2. Moscow, Leningrad: Editio Academiae Scientiarum URSS. (In Russian.)

Phillips, R., and M. Rix. 1989. *Bulbs*. Revised ed. London: Pan Books.

Rees, A. R. 1992. *Ornamental Bulbs, Corms and Tubers*. Wallingford, United
    Kingdom: C. A. B. International.

Riedl, H. 1963. Araceae. In *Flora Iranica*, vol. 3. Ed. K. H. Rechinger. Graz,
    Austria: Akademische Druck und Verlagsanstalt. 1–7. (In Latin and German.)

Riedl, H. 1985. Araceae. In *Flora of Iraq*, vol. 8. Eds. C. C. Townsend and E.
    Guest. Baghdad: Ministry of Agriculture. 187–203.

Rix, M. 1982. The herbaceous Berberidaceae. *The Plantsman* 4: 1–15.

Rix, M. 1983. *Growing Bulbs*. London: Christopher Helm.

Rix, M. 2005. Northwestern Chinese fritillaries. *The Alpine Gardener* 73: 179–188.

Rodionenko, G. I. 1961. *Genus Iris—Iris L*. Leningrad: Nauka. (In Russian.)

Rodionenko, G. I. 1999. Genus *Alatavia*. *Botanicheskii Zhurnal* 84 (7): 103–109.
    (In Russian.)

Rukšāns, J. 1981. *Crocuses*. Riga: Avots. (In Latvian.)

Rukšāns, J. 1998. The hunt for *Iris winkleri*. *Quarterly Bulletin of the Alpine Garden*
    Society 66: 366–376.

Shipovskaya, E. I., V. I. Kolokolnikova, and G. V. Matrosova. 1972. *Lilies: Species,*
    Forms and Hybrids. Moscow University Press. (In Russian.)

Skakunov, G. V. 1977. Variability of *Erythronium sibiricum* in nature. In *Ornamen-*
    tal Plants and Their Introduction in Western Siberia. Ed. K. A. Sobolevskaya.
    Novosibirsk, Russia: Nauka. 76–87. (In Russian.)

Species Group of the British Iris Society, ed. 1997. *A Guide to Species Irises: Their*
    Identification and Cultivation. Cambridge, United Kingdom: Cambridge
    University Press.

Synge, P. M. 1980. *Lilies: A Revision of Elwes' Monograph of the Genus Lilium and Its*
    Supplements. London: Batsford.

Takhtajan, A. L. 1975. *Red Book: Native Plant Species to Be Protected in the Soviet*
    Union. Leningrad: Nauka. (In Russian.)

Takhtajan, A. L. 1981. *Rare and Vanishing Plants of the Soviet Union to Be Protected*.
    Leningrad: Nauka. (In Russian.)

Tsitsin, N. V., ed. 1979. *Introduction of Plants from the Native Flora of the Soviet*
    Union. Moscow: Nauka. (In Russian.)

Van Scheepen, J. 1991. *International Checklist for Hyacinths and Miscellaneous Bulbs*.
    Hillegom, Netherlands: Royal General Bulbgrowers Association (KAVB).

Vorobiev, D. P. 1982. *Keybook to the Vascular Plants of the Surroundings of Vladivos-*
    tok. Leningrad: Nauka. (In Russian.)

Vorobiev, D. P., V. N. Woroschilov, N. N. Gurzenkov, and J. A. Doronina. 1974.
    Keybook to the Vascular Plants of Sakhalin and the Kuril Islands. Leningrad:
    Nauka. (In Russian.)

Voronin, V. V. 1987. *Tulips from Steppe and Mountains*. Alma-Ata, Kazakhstan:
    Kainar Press. (In Russian.)

Vvedenskyi, A. I., ed. 1971. *Conspectus Florae Asiae Mediae*. Vol. 2. Tashkent,
    Uzbekistan: FAN. (In Russian.)

Vvedenskyi, A. I., ed. 1974. *Conspectus Florae Asiae Mediae*. Vol. 4. Tashkent, Uzbekistan: FAN. (In Russian.)

Wendelbo, P. 1971. Alliaceae. In *Flora Iranica*, vol. 76. Ed. K. H. Rechinger. Graz, Austria: Akademische Druck und Verlagsanstalt. (In Latin and English.)

Wendelbo, P. 1974. Fumariaceae. In *Flora Iranica*, vol. 110. Ed. K. H. Rechinger. Graz, Austria: Akademische Druck und Verlagsanstalt. (In Latin and English.)

Wendelbo, P., and B. Mathew. 1975. Iridaceae. In *Flora Iranica*, vol. 112. Ed. K. H. Rechinger. Graz, Austria: Akademische Druck und Verlagsanstalt. (In Latin and English.)

Wulff, E. W. 1929. *Flora Taurica*. Vol. 1. Fasc. 2. Yalta, Ukraine: Nikitsky Botanical Garden. (In Russian.)

Yegorova, E. M. 1977. *Wild Ornamental Plants of Sakhalin and the Kuril Islands*. Moscow: Nauka. (In Russian.)

Yeo, P. F. 2002. *Hardy Geraniums*. Portland, Oregon: Timber Press.

Zhengyi, W., and P. H. Raven, eds. 2000. *Flora of China*. Vol. 24. Beijing: Science Press. Saint Louis: Missouri Botanical Garden.

Conversion Tables

INCHES	CENTIMETERS		FEET	METERS
¼	0.6		1	0.3
½	1.25		5	1.5
1	2.5		10	3.0
2	5.0		15	4.5
3	7.5		20	6.0
4	10		25	7.5
5	12.5		30	9.0
6	15		50	15
7	18		100	30
8	20		1000	300
9	23		2500	750
10	25		5000	1500
15	37		7500	2250
20	51		10,000	3000
			13,000	4000

TEMPERATURES

$°C = \frac{5}{9} \times (°F{-}32)$

$°F = (\frac{9}{5} \times °C) + 32$

Plant Names Index

370